Astrology

by Tom Falvey

Acknowledgments

Typography and layout: pathfinder
Editorial assistance: Keith Robbins and Jude Thomas
Computer graphics: Carol Kerr Design Group, San Diego, CA
Funders of this book: Paula Thomas, Katy Stock, and Bizzy Falvey

ISBN: 978-0-692-91690-2

June 2017

Contents

Theory

Astrology is the symbolic technique relating subjective experience (consciousness) with heavenly phenomena. It is based on the principle that the Universe is indeed a unity, hierarchically organized, with various levels similar in nature, differing only in magnitude. These are focused like concentric spheres around a common spiritual source, with 'its center everywhere, its circumference nowhere.' The solar system is one such sphere, centered on Sun. A human is another, smaller but similar, centered on the heart. Each grounds intangible identity into actual expression.

Astrology's fundamental axiom is 'As above, so below.' This can be applied literally to heaven and earth, planets and people. Or, more philosophically, to the proposition that a higher dimension of consciousness pervades all phenomena.

Does the material world reflect a prior spiritual reality? Astronomers describe a cosmos exploding out of another dimension in the Big Bang. Physicists describe spontaneous quantum flashes self-organizing into regular laws of nature. At its origins and in its most primal state matter emanates out of implicit potential into explicit fact.

On a parallel psychological plane, does a larger meaning inform our consciousness? Awareness evolves through a series of gradations from physical sensation to emotional feeling to mental thought to intuitive insight. It polarizes as a force field of concrete perceptions on one plane synthesizing into a more refined and inclusive sense of meaning on the next. Thus measurable nerve impulses and brain waves are associated with immaterial thoughts. Thoughts also have an interior subjective dimension. That direct experience is more real than just its physical substrate because it encompasses both the physiological stimuli and its psychological significance.

Consciousness participates in but also exceeds its neurological foundation. A greater comprehension distills events into emotions, information into intelligence. It illuminates the elements of reality with an emerging appreciation of their subtle harmonies. This pattern recognition ability transcends its data processing base. And resonates with the cosmic pattern in which it is embedded.

Consciousness reveals itself on every level, from the chemical affinities of an atom to the organizing principles of the cosmos. It does not involve determinism. How can the essential nature of the universe be subject to its cause and effect operational logic? Consciousness means a range of possibility appropriate to each level, oriented towards its eventual transcendence.

Every such level incorporates and goes beyond its predecessors. An atom reflects the same reality as a human. The several classes of atoms parallel the several general temperaments of man. But an atom embodies a smaller and earlier plane of that reality. It cannot encompass emergent properties that blossom at the human level. In order to contemplate a level of existence that does justice to the sophistication of human evolutionary achievement one must look up. To the solar system.

A physical atom, a biological cell, a self-conscious human all ground a spiritual potential seeking release in matter, life, mind. Seen close up any of these levels can bewilder with detail and complexity. The next level, the solar system, is objectively observable at a distance. It functions on a different scale, but reflects the same reality.

Both the solar system and a person are fractals, miniature versions of the universe. Each of these levels contains all of its features, though emphasizing some according to its nature. One such plane of being is the human, made in the image of God. Another is the solar system, with the same essential energy centers, displayed in a different physical form.

Both the solar system and a human being are manifestations of a deeper underlying spiritual reality. The planets of the solar system do not cause human attributes. They resonate to the same intangible forces that we do. By observing their positions and relationships at a given time we perceive the distribution of those energies at that moment. Humans are sensitive to and expressive of the same pattern.

Astrology is based on the theory of synchronicity, 'an acausal connecting principle.'[1] Synchronicity refers to events related by meaning or shared identity rather than causation. Astrology correlates the simultaneous presentation of two energies, planetary and personal, both of which reflect an archetypal realm.

The material plane mirrors a spiritual template. Our physical, emotional and mental bodies ground a life force into an identity (soul) experienced through a conscious ego. Planets do the same. They express cosmic energies centered by the gravitational attraction of a star and made visible in its light.

Planetary rhythms flow in parallel with psychological dynamics. They do not generate action anymore than a clock striking High Noon would cause a gunfight in the Old West. They time moments of danger/ opportunity, but do not determine their outcome.

Astrology is a symbolic logic that deals with a small number of basic forces tracked by the solar system's planets. Their arrangement displays the outline of its all-embracing order. Their movements echo its evolutionary process.

An individual embodies an evolutionary phase, or quality, of the solar system as portrayed by its planetary geometry at the moment of birth. Every person is a microcosm of the astronomical matrix within which we 'live and move and have our being.'[2] Each manifests its state at a particular time. Our cosmic context reflects a spiritual truth, mental map, emotional template that we personify in real life.

Sun and Planets

Our Sun is a center within a greater galactic sphere, a spark generated from the condensation of its primeval nebular atmosphere. Its planets are material crystallizations along gravitational lines of tension within that condensation. Planetary orbits embody discontinuities or energy levels within Sun's cosmic sphere of influence.

By their distance from Sun, combined with their own characteristics, these worlds embody various qualities of solar power. Each planet forms a smaller, denser energy globe manifesting a partial and specific function of the total system. They are subpersonalities of Sun.

Every planet concentrates some attribute or essence of existence. They are spun off fragments of the whole. They exist in order to live out, enact, evolve and relate those partial truths back into one Truth. Enhanced by the experience, enriched by their journey.

There is a timed rhythm among planets. Each of them spins out a specific strand of solar vitality. One can think of the planets as a genetic code, structuring the cosmic energy flaring up out of Sun. Each acts like a moving DNA gene coding for a certain activity that unfolds along its orbital cycle.

Astrology studies time. The stream of time flows in several currents (instinctual, emotional, mental, social, etc.). These are charted by planetary periods that mirror parallel cycles of human experience.

When we look at the planets we see their material bodies. But that is not their whole being. Planets are energy centers. Their orbits are like vibrating strings, a sequential expression in space and time of Sun's numinosity. Their globes sound forth the actual note generated by this vibration. A world is no more a dead rock than a human is just a mass of proteins. Each is that, but is so much more as well.

Planetary bodies are physically separated in space. Astrology proposes that they have essences, qualities, identities superpositioned in a spiritual hyperspace. The planets' visible distribution makes known the ever-changing balance of these forces. Let's look at a physical illustration of this philosophical principle.

Quantum physics now understands that elementary particles emitted from a common source are 'entangled' with each other in a way that cannot be explained by cause and effect logic. For example, two photons of light flying away from a shared origin, and from each other, always have the same spin. Yet these photons do not actually exist as discrete entities until measured. The very act of measurement calls them into being out of a wave with many spin potentials. Neither can have signaled its spin-state to its counterpart because that would involve faster than light transmission, a physical impossibility. It is as if each photon shares a metaphysical identity with the other. They emanate out of a unifying field that pervades existence, from the subatomic level to the cosmic.[3]

In the same way a spiritual wave pattern can be observed at two simultaneous poles of manifestation: physical (solar system) and psychological (human character). Planets objectively symbolize subjective focal points within our living energy auras. They point to the animating principles behind phenomena, the abstract forces behind concrete behavior. Thus, for example, Mercury describes intangible mind, in contrast to the organic wetware of brain. (Mercury's location in the zodiac portrays what kind of mind.)

Astrology does not require belief in the possibility of disembodied consciousness without the anchor of a living brain. It simply claims that brain responds to the solar systemic force field within which it lives. That said, astrology's very nature suggests that 'there are more things in heaven and earth than are dreamt of in your philosophy.'[4] If one accepts a solar identity field incorporating the immense voids between planets, then one would probably tend towards a belief in an intangible soul that integrates the discontinuities between planetary subpersonalities. And perhaps the big Discontinuity between life and death. Be that as it may, astrology is about the merger of these factors into an existential selfhood here on Earth.

Planetary globes focus a larger than visible and objective reality. The gaps between them also contain more than meets the eye. We tend to think of space as a featureless void dotted with gigantic hydrogen fireballs (stars). Actually, space is a mosaic of gravity wells and force fields generated by these fiery eruptions. Space is not an empty nothingness in which stars are suspended. It is a fabric of energies emanating out of those sparks.

The Big Bang created the universe from an eruption of spirit out of an unknowable plane of reality. Every star is a miniature bang, stabilized in time, grounding inconceivable dimensions into the material world. Each star radiates its own energy quality. It floods the universe with electromagnetic vibrations, charged particles and stellar winds. And with more ethereal qualities akin to those of personality.

Every star bends the fabric of space/time, creating a gravitational sphere of influence. Every human creates a similar social sphere through his/her psychological charisma.

Stars precipitate spirit into matter. Spirit shines through them. A star's visible fusion fire radiates as light. Its more subtle aspects express as an aura of desire, mind and will. Each star generates a psycho-spiritual atmosphere. This may be embodied in a series of planets, discrete worlds of experience.

Each star, and every human, is a focal point of the entire cosmos, stressing certain tendencies in order to learn and evolve. Stars center a cosmic identity on a radiant spiritual plane. Fiery stellar attributes condense into a gradient of energy bands, or worlds. A blindingly brilliant force field cools, thickens and grounds itself on planetary stations circling at various orbital levels. These act like a centrifuge, each concentrating a certain essence or quality.

Our Earth centers on a deeper, denser plane: the biological. It is the platform of organic life, exfoliating through evolution. This biological vitality expresses itself through ever more sophisticated systems of physiological organs. At the human level an emergent psychological dimension becomes anchored in complex brain structures.

A brain stem is not sentience, a cerebral cortex is not consciousness, an amygdala is not emotion. These structures are lenses through which such psychological qualities present themselves. Layers of the brain, organs and glands of the body, function as do planets of the solar system. They lend form to an intangible life force, give voice to vibration.

Stellar spirit manifests through physically separated worlds, human life through specialized physiological functions. The body is a condensation of the energy it conducts. Its organs are the vehicles of that vitality. Our physical life is patterned on an energy template: encoded in DNA, expressed as a body. This blueprint also has emotional, mental and spiritual levels symbolized by the state of its cosmic matrix at birth.

A fire of motivation erupts into the realm of cause and effect as a star flares into a spectrum of light. This radiance materializes into a system of worlds that embody its qualities distributed over space and through time. In the same way a human births into a global energy aura. S/he expresses the character of that sustaining force field through a temperament of emotions, an inclination of thought, an orientation of will. Both exemplify an underlying spiritual reality in the world of matter, whether astronomical or biological.

Astrology and Science

The modern scientific worldview claims that any implied correspondence between people and planets is childishly anthropomorphic. It posits a complete discontinuity between personal subjectivity in here and astronomical objectivity out there. This radical separation between psyche and its larger environment defies the evidence.

Materially we are literally made of stardust (all elements heavier than hydrogen are products of stellar nova-explosions). We are physically one with the universe. Biologically we exist in an evolutionary continuum and an ecological web with all other organisms. Psychologically we all share an instinctual nature and a collective unconscious. Socially we communicate in a consensual reality with other minds. Spiritually we are increasingly aware that we share a common destiny, not only with our fellow humans, but also with our entire living planet. The proposition that we are embedded in a physical, biological, mental and social matrix with everything on our own planet, but are fundamentally alienated from its surrounding cosmic medium, is illogical.

This divorce from Earth's spatial ecology began at the birth of modern science. We once believed that a sacred harmony of the spheres revolved around our Earthly home. With the Copernican Revolution we learned that Earth actually revolves around Sun. Later discoveries exiled Sun to a remote arm of our galaxy, which then became just one of billions.

The shock of this displacement from physical centrality was tremendous. We were no longer the crown of creation at the axis of the universe. Like Earth the other planets also became tangential rocks whizzing around a distant fireball. They had no relationship to us, no meaning for us.

The spiritual reverberations of this insight shook our worldview to the core. The scientific method's empirical truth was undeniable. Thus it eclipsed all other forms of knowledge. Only objective facts were real, interpretive subjective experience was not.

Cause and effect logic superseded ideas of parallel process, sympathetic resonance, reflective synchronicity. Facts became a fetish; their meaning, significance, purpose a phantom.

6

The sense of a universe in tune with the human condition was replaced by a vision of one utterly indifferent to it. A decentered universe became a disenchanted one: a jumble of nuclear embers in the void, circled by stone dead planets, all headed for thermodynamic heat death, entropic chaos and eventual subatomic disintegration.

As our sensory knowledge of the cosmos increased our respect for its subtle qualities decreased. The bigger it got, the colder and deader it seemed. The more physically insignificant we became in the universe, the more psychologically insipid it became for us. As a reductionistic materialism diminished the spiritual status of the heavens around us, we compensated for this loss with a grandiose self-inflation. All inner depth, living vibrancy, was withdrawn from heaven and earth. Subjective meaning was arrogated to ourselves alone. Precisely because we were tangential we were also outside, above, beyond a flat, purely superficial reality. Rational ego-consciousness became unique, special, privileged in a soulless universe.[5]

Yet how could such a consciousness emerge in a cosmos otherwise devoid of it? Actually, the entire universe is an expression of spirit radiating out into consciously accessible phenomena. It seems to have erupted out of nowhere in the Big Bang 13.7 billion years ago. An inconceivable dimension of existence precipitated out into the four fundamental forces of physics (gravity, electromagnetism, strong and weak forces). These manifested as a fireball of pure energy. This in turn condensed into atomic matter and a range of specific energies.

The infinitesimal particles of matter are direct emanations of whatever caused the Big Bang. They spontaneously self-organize in ever more complex structures that can manifest ever more complex qualities. Thus subatomic sparkles bond into neutrons, protons and electrons. These join into atoms, expressing emergent elemental properties: hydrogen is different than oxygen. In turn these merge into molecules, novel substances that are much more than the sum of their parts: for example, water (H_2O). Molecules weave together to create organic life. Life's architecture resonates to its inherent and ambient energies to generate a spectrum of consciousness: irritability, sensation, perception, sentience, awareness. Awareness folds in upon itself to ignite self-consciousness. That intensifies into transpersonal states of consciousness, consistently described by mystics and meditators of all eras, cultures and traditions.

The universe is alive through and through. Its life-spirit manifests on different planes of being: matter, life, mind, soul, spirit. Each level transcends and includes its foundational predecessors. Thus life is made of matter, includes its chemical qualities, but expresses an emergent property of aliveness through the complexity of its structure. Consciousness, as we know it, is grounded in organic form. An increasing sophistication of neural organization in its successive evolutionary stages is able to anchor a growing subtlety and intensity of awareness. The brain stem of a reptile can house instincts, but not much more. Mammals add an enveloping limbic layer around the brain stem, the objective correlative of a feeling, empathetic, nurturing, emotional level of consciousness. Primates and cetaceans (whales and dolphins) add yet another layer, a surrounding cerebral cortex, supporting complex mental reasoning and (perhaps) self-consciousness. The physical organization of an organism demonstrates how much voltage it can handle, what inclusiveness of consciousness its neural configuration can hold.

The universe came from an explosion of spirit downshifting into energy. That energy flung itself out into matter and motion across a wide spectrum of density and intensity. Over time its fragmentary particles and pulsations reassemble into more and more sophisticated entities. Each carries the inherent spiritual qualities of the Beginning at whatever level of inclusiveness it embodies. Physical matter is foundational, basic to all further development. Life evokes matter's intrinsic ability to organize into organisms. These then demonstrate matter's chemical organization and life's vitality on more psychic planes of consciousness.

Thus the universe returns to its source of soul, origin in spirit, enhanced by experience in the great adventure of manifestation. Nothing in the universe is inert or lifeless. There is no such thing as nothing. Every part of the cosmos is permeated with its original energy signature. It is imbued with that original power and resonates to it on its own level. The force field that emanated out of the Big Bang evolved and differentiated through experience in time and space. The emergence of consciousness as we know it is an inherent unfolding of this developmental process.

Matter is composed of probabilistic energy flashes; life is built from matter's chemical affinities; consciousness radiates from life's vital drives. Increasing quantities of information percolate up from basic to more complex planes in an ascending quality of experience. Consider matter as a one-dimensional point, life as a two-dimensional line, consciousness as a three-dimensional plane. Each successive dimension incorporates an emergent property implicit in, but not recognized by, its precursor. A line connects two or more points, a plane connects two or more lines, but each has novel qualities not found in its constituent elements. Only the most small-minded arrogance would deny the possibility of higher dimensions invisible to their own building blocks. Thus the sphere exists, though unrecognized, even denied, by those confined to a plane.

The life inhabiting a house is intangible to its bricks. That does not mean it is not real. Indeed, the bricks could not be made, nor the house constructed, without that life. The bricks have their own sub-atomic events and chemical bondings, the house has its own feng shui or architectural character. They are also alive on their level.

Some level of sentience inheres in all phenomena. Every elemental force/particle has attractions and repulsions. Every atom has behavioral (chemical) characteristics. All living cells possess irritability and sensation. Organisms have perceptions, instincts and adaptable repertoires. Some enjoy consciousness and self-consciousness. Why then deny that the larger system in which they are embedded lacks all sentience, has only dead mass and mechanical motion?

The flowering of scientific rationalism was an absolutely necessary stage in human development. It was also a corrective to the excessively spiritual otherworldliness of the preceding age of religion (itself an equally necessary stage). But, like all such movements, it eventually went too far. Mechanistic science morphed into an arid reductionism 'knowing more and more about less and less.'[6]

Today's postmodern insistence on the subjective context of facts marks a new turn of the spiral. It has serious limitations, especially in its relativistic denial of any central ordering value principles. But it has begun to reintroduce an interior sense of meaning to the contemplation of objective phenomena.

Each of these great truth systems beautifully elucidates one aspect of reality: religion: spiritual/moral; scientific: physical/rational; postmodern: psychological/intentional. But each also has a tendency to deny, negate, condemn all forms of truth other than its own. Today integral systems are emerging that honor all those aspects of truth.[7] Each has its own emphasis and balance. Astrology is one of them. In fact it was the first.[8]

Astrology does not conflict with science. It can accept all the phenomenal findings of scientific investigation. Science has nothing to say about the metaphysical rationale, subjective psychological states or spiritual insights described by astrology. These are not quantifiable data. They can never be proven or disproven by science's methodology of experiment and statistical analysis. Astrology studies consciousness, not facts. It can no more be the object of science than can art or politics.

Nor does astrology conflict with any religion unless it devolves into fortune telling, a spurious determinism undermining human responsibility and autonomy of the soul. Indeed, astrology sharpens moral choice by clarifying spiritual potentials and psychological tendencies. It does contradict fundamentalist claims by any religion that there is one and only one path to God or Enlightenment:

'In my Father's house are many mansions.'[9]

After all, astrology deals with psychological diversity and a spiritual ecology of truth perspectives. Specifically, astrology does not endorse or oppose any of the great monotheistic religions: Judaism, Christianity, Islam. It simply describes the human significance of cosmic phenomena that reflect the nature of God:

'The heavens declare the glory of God; and the firmament sheweth His handiwork.'[10]

Astrology is compatible with a personally engaged God Who works through history. It does not require that premise. Monotheistic faiths are compatible with the idea of a cyclic resonance between astronomical phenomena and psychological processes. They do not require belief in that proposition. Astrological insight into the dynamics of human motivation has a different focus than their concern with the primacy of a single spiritual Being and the ethical norms derived from that. Religion is about timeless Truth. Astrology describes its temporal phases. Astrology's study of the cyclic nature of time and rhythmic pulsation of manifestation relates to the phenomenal and psychological side of things. Religion refers to their spiritual meaning and moral value.[11]

Finally, there is no inherent dichotomy between science and religion. This false issue arises only when either usurps the rightful prerogatives of the other: if religion tries to deny empirical findings, or interpret physical phenomena; if science leaves the realm of objective information to pronounce upon intangibles such as psychological subjectivity or spiritual truth.

To champion either of these disciplines as more true or fundamental than the other is like insisting that yellow is better than purple. It simply reveals a psychological bias. One may have a personal need to pursue objectively verifiable observation. That does not justify denigrating others' equally real need for spiritual experience. Or vice versa. Astrology, by definition, helps to bridge different perspectives. It demands respect for the many forms of truth's manifestation. No one would seriously claim that Taurus is better than Pisces, or vice versa, though one may have a personal preference for one or the other.

Science provides a beautiful, increasingly accurate narrative of the physical world. It's just that, as anyone who has ever felt an emotion knows, the material world is not everything.

Science is not a body of facts, nor even a coherent worldview based on them. It is a discipline of intellectual integrity, an absolute respect for truth. This includes an understanding of the limits to truth that our minds can know. An understanding that not all phenomena are quantifiable.[12] Or subject to repetitive manipulation. Science can never explain beauty. The best scientists respect the inherent limits of what they can know. It is more than enough.

Modern science describes a universe made up of indescribable dark forces. These are mathematical conventions used to hide our ignorance. Actually, we physically see and rationally understand only a tiny fragment of realty. We now know, from sophisticated astronomical observations, that the atomic matter we are familiar with constitutes about 5% of the universe. All of the stars and galaxies, dust and gas, diffused through a cosmos 13.7 billion light years in radius, produce just $\frac{1}{20}$ of the gravitational energy we observe in action. Astronomers, cosmologists, physicists and mathematicians postulate that another 27% of the universe's mass consists of so called 'dark matter.' They have never directly observed this exotic matter and have wildly different theories and explanations of it. Yet they claim that it is five times more abundant than all the neutrons, protons, electrons and electromagnetic energy in existence.

Even so, 68% of the universe is still missing. No problem. It is simply labeled 'dark energy.' This seems to be some sort of potential inherent in 'empty' space, perhaps an anti-gravitational force. This antigravity, acting on a cosmic scale, is accelerating the expansion of the universe contrary to all known laws and properties of matter/energy as we conceive them.

Dark matter is inferred by galactic movements that cannot be accounted for by familiar atomic matter gravitation. Dark energy is inferred by the otherwise inexplicable, and counterintuitive, accelerating expansion of the universe. This dark matter and energy manifest on the densest physical plane. Materialism cannot even begin to explain matter. It is completely inadequate to describe more rarefied, less tangible, but equally real states of feeling, thought and will.

Consider the possibility of more subtle states of matter. Emotional matters, the desire plane. Mental substance: intellectual axioms, abstract organizing principles of logic and mathematics. Spiritual fires, the inspirational power of ideals animating the world of form. These are not measurable. Or physical in any sense that we can imagine. Yet who would doubt the tangible existence of hate or rage?

The concept of dark matter seems similar to that of desire: an attractive field shaping real behavior. The idea of dark energy seems similar to that of mind: a separating force distinguishing one thing from another. This gives them space for relationship in the context of an expanding overall consciousness.

The material universe has perfect physical integrity. Drop a pin and the change in distribution of gravity affects the farthest galaxy. If matter responds so sensitively to the slightest fluctuation in its own internal state then it would seem natural for it to reflect and express the intangible but more alive realms of feeling, mind and spirit.

These levels exist in their own right and on their own terms. They are grounded in, and activate, the material world, including its biological aspect. They evolve through experience in matter and life to psychology, intellect and soul. Feeling, mind and spirit only become real insofar as they incarnate in matter.

The physical and psychological planes can be correlated by an intangible, internally consistent logic of mathematics. The parallel spaces of objective and subjective reality can both be described by its self-evident principles. Mathematics is the language of science. Astrology is the corresponding language of soul. We can consider planetary bodies as integers, summarizing psychic qualities. Their movements are a calculus of evolution, a curve of accelerating or decelerating energies. Their relationships (aspects) convey a geometry of meaning, a deployment of attributes.

Astrology is an 'algebra of psychology.'[13] It correlates cosmic patterns with mental states, seasons of the heart, tides of subconscious mood. It does so as a symbolic logic linking dynamic spiritual forces with planetary movements and psychological processes.

Astrology as Symbolism

Astrology is not a discipline of conclusive logic. It reasons by analogy. Inspires with evocative images. It is a symbolic art using parallel features of our cosmic and interior ecologies to elicit psychological insight. Symbols have many layers of meaning. They can never be reduced to simple definitions. They are catalysts, sparking intuitive insight.

We project our inner world onto the outer. Is it surprising that the universe reciprocates, expressing its own quality through us? These are two sides of one coin. The coin's value lies in its linkage of objective and subjective in a nondual integrity of being. Astrology correlates parallel physical and psychological states. They both mirror the same non-material reality. Those who doubt such a non-material reality should consider their own doubt. It is a psychological state. It may be linked with electrical discharges and biochemical secretions. But it also has a directly sensed/felt subjective component. This can only be approached through the emotional and intuitive senses. It cannot be physically observed. But doubt's planetary correlate, Saturn, can be observed.

Let's use this example of doubt to examine how astrological symbolism works.

Saturn is the farthest planet visible to the naked eye. It marks the frontier of natural sensory consciousness. Even its physical appearance underlines this function: it is a world within a ring, a plane of being contained by a boundary. What lies beyond is unknown, therefore in doubt. The unknown evokes fear. Thus doubt assumes a defensive stance, a state of denial.

Saturn acts as a pointer spotlighting this energy. It objectively demonstrates a subjective condition. Saturn does not generate doubt or fear. It simply maps these qualities. The map is not the territory. But it can help one to navigate its confusing complexity It provides an overview: insight, guidance, orientation.

Saturn's orbit measures the circumference of reality as we know it. Its position along that orbit locates a specific limit to our abilities. It thus becomes the source of doubt, describes the nature of anxiety. For example, in the mental zone of Gemini Saturn's angst operates on the plane of verbal intelligence and communication, whereas in Cancer's psychic field it manifests through the functions of emotion and memory.

Saturn's orbit, as an energy level, resonates to a spiritual principle, an intangible vector manifesting as limitation on the physical plane, mortality on the biological and as lack, doubt, fear on the psychological. Its actual globe, moving along a pinpoint arc of its orbit, focuses that principle into attributes: the finite definition of objects, allotted life-span of organisms, emotional shadow of psyches and numb blind spots of mind.

The physical properties of a planet, and its station in our star's whirlpool of worlds, implies a psychological function. Physical facts resonate with underlying spiritual archetypes. Outer phenomena reflect inner principles. Astronomical and psychological cycles mirror one another.

This is not causation. It is a parallel process. Synchronicity: meaningful coincidence.

As the primeval Sun's nebular cloud condensed, Saturn precipitated out at its waning edge. Saturn is about one third of the mass of its inner neighbor, rainbow banded Jupiter, the system's giant. Beyond it lie two smaller gas bubbles, each about one sixth Saturn's mass: Uranus, a tipped over planet, rotating perpendicular to all others, and invisible (to the naked eye) Neptune, pointing to a more subtle realm of being. These are fading remnants of the solar system, ebbing into the alien dimensions of interstellar space. Saturn marks the last outpost of consensus reality. Uranus, Neptune and Pluto initiate another octave of intangible energies.

Every planet's position and characteristics symbolically express a role in the spiritual ecology of our system. The planets anchor spiritual aspects of an extended solar organism just as brain, heart, liver, genitals ground biological and psychological energies of a living organism. The brain does not cause thought; it provides a medium through which thought can manifest. A dead brain minus its overshadowing mind-aura is just a blob of grey jelly. In the same way, a planet does not cause fear or love or will. Their orbits provide strings of various lengths upon which those psycho-spiritual notes can resonate. Thus they (metaphorically) emit ethereal sound waves, the music of the spheres, to which we dance.

It is possible, even probable, that no self-conscious awareness exists in or on any of the other planets. They mirror energy levels centered here on Earth. They represent the rhythms, measure the dynamics, time the cycles that we live out in the flesh.

Clearly a planetary logos or soul would not have an ego-consciousness of the human type. That does not forbid its existence as a force field, an energy environment, a point of light in the void. Light has always been a symbol of consciousness, soul and spirit. Like a photon of light every planet is both a particle (globe) and a wave (orbital energy level). Each planet is a lens, focusing a wavelength of the solar spectrum into tangible incarnation.

Visible electromagnetic light, at the very edge and limit of our material reality, serves as a symbol of a more supernal light beyond. Visible planetary spheres symbolize planes of experience on which this spiritual light refracts into attributes of mind, desire, will and memory, the social dynamics and spiritual principles of their expression, the deep transpersonal purposes they serve.

For example, the red planet Mars is not literally an angry world. (Though it has reason to be, having once been warm, wet, perhaps living; now cold, dry and barren.) But as the first planet beyond Earth's orbit Mars locates where the universe intrudes upon one's comfort zone. It forces one to respond to the objective demands of a larger reality. Thus it provokes personal will: the urge to shape external circumstance, to fight for what one wants.

Giant Jupiter is not inherently a philosophic planet, as far as we know. (Though its banded structure suggests layers of meaning, a spectrum of consciousness.) But its twelve-year orbit reflects the fact that waves of religious fervor, political ideology, social mores and philosophic outlook unfold more slowly than those of personal emotion (inner planets). These pulsations do not come from Jupiter. Rather, Jupiter resonates with an archetypal tide that also manifests through decadal or generational swings in social consciousness and religious conscience.

Saturn does not physically block the reach of our vision. But its distance measures our wavelength of understanding, amplitude of comprehension. Beyond it swirl forces beyond our ken: ambiguous currents of intuition (Uranus) and dream (Neptune); the unknowable powers of God's Will and cosmic purpose (Pluto).

Planets are not active agents. They reflect an energy state in physical space. People personify the same energy in psychological space.

Each planet plays a symbolic role in the physical ballet of the solar system. This is suggested by its empirical qualities. A planet centers a certain kind of experience. Its tangible body hints at the nature of these psychological processes. There is a correlation between the observable characteristics of a planet and its spiritual meaning.

These principles manifest themselves in the structure of our solar system. Sun, emanating a spiritual radiance, is ringed by waves of worlds, ripples of its expression in space/time. Closest is Mercury, the first solid globe, spirit's encounter with material reality, its precipitation into conscious mind. Then Venus, with the first atmosphere: burning purpose condenses into ethereal ideal, fire of will softens into heat of desire. The third rock is Earth, the plane of life, circled by a dead Moon of past memories. Next Mars, the size of Earth's core. Here is Earth's heart projected outwards, life's stripped down essence, its final statement.

A disintegrative zone of shattered asteroids separates these small terrestrial planets from a series of massive gas giants, perhaps as death divides life from its soul. Jupiter is twice the size of all other planets combined. This world, halfway to a star, links spirit and ego in a transcendent soul, an approach to the divine. Then ring crowned Saturn, at the edge of unaided visibility, the farthest frontier of consciousness, ultimate law and limit of reality. Beyond, smaller fading gas globes of inspiration (Uranus) and imagination (Neptune) as the planetary system dissolves into interstellar space. Tiny Pluto with its giant moon marks this transition, a fragmentary hint of cosmic Will integrating Sun's family with a greater galactic society.

Earth and Solar System

Our own planet acts as an energy vortex within this system. Earth is a self-sustaining magnetic dynamo centered on a hot iron-nickel core. It glows at the temperature of Sun's surface. This spinning core generates a magnetic field enveloping the planet, shielding it from cosmic rays and solar winds. It also provides a background energy nurturing all the bioelectric auras sparkling within it.

This terrestrial magnetism acts like the reference beam of a hologram, with which all other planetary energies are tuned. These generate the harmonies and counterpoints, rhythms and beats fleshed out as living notes in the biosphere. A hologram is a three dimensional image formed by two laser beams illuminating a subject. One beam shines directly on it. The other bounces through a series of mirrors so that it arrives at a different angle and a slightly different wave phase. The interference pattern of the reference and reflected beams generate the image.

The reference beam is Earth's own magnetic force field. Other planetary energies act as reflecting beams intersecting with it. Those lights do not cause or create the image in the hologram. They illuminate it, elucidate various dimensions, aspects of its nature. Nor is any physical agency involved. Other planets' magnetic fields do not literally interact with Earth's. (They are too weak, too far away and are deflected away from us by solar winds.) This illustration is a metaphor. All of astrology is a metaphor.

Every planet makes a magnetic moment, a line of force in space. Its spinning generates a vortex, conducts an intangible identity into sensed, felt experience. Planetary energies weave a vibratory pattern, a charged aura, around the central fire of Sun. This force field irradiates and stimulates life in the biological zone of Earth.

Earth's inner core, a Moon-sized solid ball, rotates slightly faster than the planet as a whole. It turns within a Mars-deep liquid metal ocean (outer core). Measurements of earthquake wave patterns reveal that this outer core generates spiral convection currents of molten metal. These channel electricity (random flow patterns do not). These twisting electrical helices intersect with Earth's rotational energy to create a protective magnetic field around it in outer space.[14]

This hot magnetic sphere is wrapped in a viscous magma mantle of molten stone, 1800 miles thick. Vast plumes of lava surge up and sink down through it, dragging a surface skin with them. This thin crust is shattered into floating plates, joining and separating in an eon-slow dance of continents. Upon it swims a world ocean, its tides rising and falling with our Moon. Above it swirls an ocean of air driven by Sun's heat.

The physical world displays the same abstract patterns on all of its levels. Hot iron helixes generate our planet's signature magnetic field. DNA chemical helixes generate the protein building blocks of its organic life. Planets generate helixes of motion as they orbit Sun's path through space. (See diagram.) Just as the material plane embodies a spiritual reality, so its physical processes reflect the same archetypal geometrical patterns from the mineral to the biological and astronomical realms. The same principles, and their formative expressions, manifest throughout our multi-dimensional cosmos.

Earth, permeated with its own magnetism and irradiated with solar power, forms a vibrating web of energy. It resonates from an electromagnetic heart, through concentric spheres of metal, rock, water, air, and space.

Earth's orbit makes a loop in an induction coil, energized by the other planetary coils around it. Induction, in this sense, means that a current flowing in one wire evokes, coaxes, a parallel voltage in an adjacent wire. See diagram.

A coil of wire turning in a magnetic field generates an electric current.[15] In the same way a DNA coil, riding Earth's rotation through the intersecting magnetic fields of the solar system, generates the electricity of life. A coiled wire carrying an electric current emits a magnetic field around itself. In the same way a DNA coil carrying an electric life force emanates an identity aura, based on the genetic composition of its coils. The DNA coil converts its cosmic magnetic context into electric vitality, and then reemits it as an organic presentation of those universal energies.

Earth's rotating magnetic structure spins its inherent geological and received astronomical energies into a higher order reality: the biosphere. The organic molecules of life are far more delicately constructed, and thus more responsive to, subtle signals than the relatively simple molecules of gas, water and mineral existence. All organic life is an expression of the information, or intricate arrangement of atoms, stored within the helical DNA molecule.[16] This life can be described as a psychic force created by the flow of solar and terrestrial energies through the DNA spiral. The electronic flux of cosmic energies through DNA's double helix generates a magnetic field. Its aura constitutes the consciousness of genetic information. It forms a vibratory pattern linking matter and energy in life, the experience of their union.

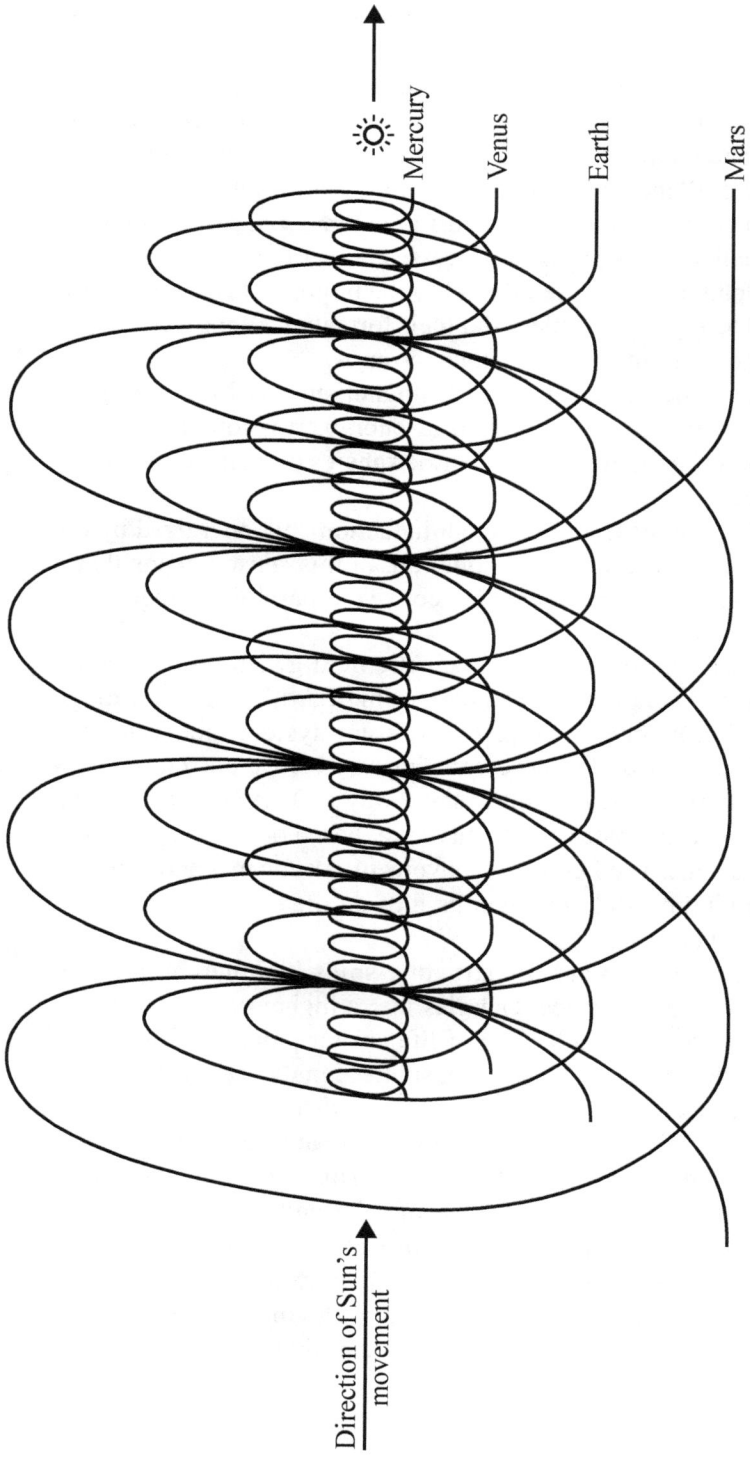

A series of coiled planetary genomes wrapped around each other, all moving northwards with Sun. This illustration shows only the inner planets.

Two Earth orbits = eight Mercury, three Venus and one Mars orbits.

Direction of Sun's movement

Mercury

Venus

Earth

Mars

Organic consciousness exhibits its attributes through the cell, the basic sphere of biological activity centered on a nucleus of genetic information. Every cell nucleus focuses a potency distributed throughout the entire organic realm. In particular, every nucleus contains the complete genetic program for its host organism, though it is specialized to express only a tiny fragment of that knowledge in its activity.

Solar and planetary energies generate the pulse of life and consciousness through the medium of DNA coils. These manifest through various types of cells. The human body organizes a complex arrangement of cell types. Their biopsychic forces express through metabolic activity: muscle cells work, nerve cells transmit, glandular cells secrete, etc.

A rhythmic energy pulsation orchestrates these cellular activities into an overall vitality. This pulsation originates in the heart. We experience it as the alternating flow of blood in and out of every cell - just as Sun alternates in and out of our experience every day and night. The heart beats out a rhythm of human identity, distilled through evolution into hormonal tides of emotion and ethereal brain wave patterns of mind. In the same way Sun vitalizes archetypes of human psychology, illuminated through Earth's ever changing perspective on it during the seasonal round. (See 'Sun and Earth.')

As Sun moves through space its family of planets spirals around it. They constitute a multi-stranded helix: a gene (genius) of spiritual principle. The solar system looks like a gene. Form follows function. It acts like one too. Both are coils, of planets and of nucleotides. Stretched into a new dimension, as a spiral, each indicates an evolving emergence, a purposeful evolution. DNA spirals out into specific genes: the blueprint of life, flowering in a body. The solar system extends in temporal rhythms: its orbital cycles generating the dynamics of consciousness. See diagram.[17]

Perhaps the immense voids between planets are analogous to the 'junk' DNA making up 97% of our genome. 'Junk' DNA does not code for protein. Yet it contains a reservoir of latent potential: new genes are coined out of it, coding genes are separated into recombining fragments by it, ancient lineages are recycled within it. No doubt it has other unknown qualities as well.

The constantly changing distribution of planetary nodes within the solar spiral suggests a mutating gene. As the planets realign the character of the gene changes. It sequentially expresses the segments of a trajectory, unfolding through time into a chromosome: a series of genes. It expresses new qualities appropriate to its movement/moment in time. Out of one basic structure emerge many expressions.

As a Platonic ideal Sun and its planets form an ur-gene (urge). An urge only comes into existence through action. The solar system has never been static. Evolution is its essence. Even before its birth it was a rotating nebula of gas and dust. It then formed into an actual planetary genome of mutating possibilities. Now its planets are clustered in Virgo, Libra, Aquarius and Aries. Then in Capricorn, Pisces, Gemini and Leo. Today Saturn, Venus and Moon are aligned. Tomorrow Neptune, Jupiter and Mars will be. Once Mercury and Uranus were conjunct. Soon afterwards they are in opposition. One basic structure expresses an enormous variety of psychological states and spiritual conditions. Each of these can be experienced at many levels of consciousness.

The eerie similarity of a microscopic DNA gene and the macroscopic solar system implies that both resonate to the same pattern. A single Spirit pervades the cosmos. It blossoms on various planes according to their capacity to express it. Elemental matter, living organisms, conscious psyches and world souls differentially unfold as octaves of a universal note.

These levels, physical, biological, emotional, mental, moral and spiritual form a gradient ranging from dense to alive to aware to enlightened. There are discontinuities, quantum jumps, between them. For example, within the human condition, we pass through abrupt phase changes: conception, birth, life, death, after death (?). Yet they are all parts of a whole. In the same way, planets are isolated by vacuum gaps. Their physical interaction is negligible. They form the material nodes of a force field. Their movements trace out an ethereal identity pattern within which their globes are embedded.

Fate and Free Will

Contemplation of planetary patterns serves as a mind exercise, a psychic yoga, by which one learns to appreciate the many modes of consciousness within the unity of our experience. The lawfulness of planetary motion, and the archetypal nature of their character, helps organize, focus, intensify intuitive consciousness. Astrology combines elements of astronomy, mathematics and psychology, but is essentially an art. A poetic metaphor for the universe and the human condition. An attunement to the music of the spheres. A meditation.

Entities, such as stellar systems and humans, each embody the entire universe, polarized in a certain way. God, the Force, Infinity, become conscious through the friction of their interaction. This friction generates a new kind of light burning through evolution. An eternal light prisms off into a spectrum of attributes. Eventually all of its individualized flashes add up to something bigger than the monolithic original. We are temporal sparks of an eternal flame. Ephemeral but actual. Spirit projects itself into matter in order to acquire identity and gain experience. A spark of choice, insight, love in real time fulfills all the empty infinities of potential.

By knowing our potentials we can begin to live up to them. Knowing our flaws we can begin to cure them. Most importantly, by perceiving character in terms of its causal principles we can transcend the limitations of any strictly personal viewpoint. For, even more than a symbolic portrayal of personality, astrology meditates on universal transpersonal energies. By focusing on the causal principle behind personal idiosyncrasy, astrology can provide objective insight into subjective processes. Thus one becomes more self-aware. And more conscious of others' internal experience; where they are coming from.

An astrological chart provides a psychological genome. It indicates an overall orientation and its specific attributes. These are emphasized in an identity and developed through a lifetime. A mathematical thought process can correlate its comparative energy levels of mind, love, will, memory, etc. An algebra of psychology relates them by a geometry of positions and synthesizes them into a calculus of motion.

Such an algebra is subjective because psychology itself is. It is not a machine logic remorselessly enumerating dictates of fate. It is a flowing, musical kind of order, a fluid dynamic peculiar to each psyche. It draws psyche out, invokes its guiding principles. Astrology portrays potentials, which each of us actualize to various degrees.

Astrology cannot predict, has nothing to say, about the level of evolution one brings to an encounter with its cosmic environment. A birth chart acts like a DNA pattern, organizing itself partly by its own inner logic, partly in response to its environment. This interaction adds an indefinable quality of will or intention. One can accent astrological nouns and verbs from a posture independent of them.

We can think of astrology as a verbal as well as a mathematical language. In this sense planets would be nouns, describing psychological qualities such as love (Venus) or will (Mars). Signs would then be adjectives, specifying the nature of those qualities. For example, Venus in Gemini portrays a different kind of love than Venus in Cancer. Signs cannot be nouns themselves because they portray energy zones. (See 'Sun in Signs.') When unoccupied by a planet a sign shows only latent or potential energy, whereas a planet always exists as an actual entity, wherever it may be. Aspects act as verbs, stimulating planetary expression through relationship: Venus, whether in Gemini, Cancer or anywhere else, doesn't do much unless activated by contact with another planet. These aspects are modified by their own movements: a planet approaches or separates from another planet; speeds up, slows down or retrogrades relative to Sun. Such motions define astrological adverbs.

Let's listen to how this language works. Imagine two boys born on the same day with the same ascendant and subjective house structure (See 'Sun and Earth').[18] Both are white, grow up in stable middle class families and attend comparable public schools. Thus they both have similar socioeconomic backgrounds and the same astrological chart. Yet, as adults, one becomes a liberal Democrat, the other a conservative Republican. In a country as big as the United States many people are born with similar horoscopes, yet lead very different lives. Does this disprove astrology?

It certainly disproves the idea that a chart can predict a life or that the stars determine our destiny. There is a significant, in fact decisive, element of free will in how one expresses an inherent character. But there is such a thing as character itself. Astrology describes that, not fate. Character is destiny. Events and choices bring it to life.

Let's isolate one element of character out of these two charts and say that these boys have Jupiter in Capricorn. Giant Jupiter symbolizes our participation in the larger than personal concerns described by our religious/philosophical beliefs, political stance and social role, among other things. Jupiter in Capricorn suggests growth against adversity, swimming upstream. (See 'Jupiter.') The liberal says that we should meet this challenge through cooperation. As young mammals we need our parents to survive. As social beings we depend on each other in a complex society. By extension, as citizens we should help each other for pragmatic as well as moral reasons. The conservative says that such dependence erodes character. Instead we should strive for personal excellence. Better to stand on your own two feet. Yes, life is hard, and should be: that is how evolution promotes survival of the fittest. The Democrat stresses social duty, public achievement through collective management, responsibility to and for the group. The Republican stresses ambition, individual achievement through private enterprise, self-reliance.

Both make valid points. Both are realists, with a practical, solutions oriented frame of reference. They each accept the fact that constant struggle in a cold world demands disciplined effort towards tangible goals, whether collective or personal. However, Jupiter in Sagittarius has another outlook altogether. It believes that growth results from spiritual attitude rather than grinding toil. Righteousness of aspiration counts for more than excellence of effort. After all, what good is competence if one doesn't have soul? Or if it efficiently serves a negative purpose? A Jupiter in Sagittarius person might be either a conservative or a liberal, but s/he would tend to justify that political stance on the basis of principle rather than pragmatism, would espouse a philosophy more than a program.

Jupiter in Aquarius denies both justification by faith (Sagittarius) or by works (Capricorn). It insists that growth means increasing clarity of consciousness. What good are high principles if you don't understand the Big Picture? What good is working hard rather than smart? Jupiter in Aquarius focuses on the (r)evolutionary need for change, either to the left or the right. This stems from an idealized social ideology rather than Sagittarius' moral sense of right and wrong. In contrast, Jupiter in Scorpio grows through a gut sense of alignment with instinctual power, recognition of emotional truth. What good is abstract theory if you don't feel passion? Or understand the real motives of others? Think of all the 'useful fools,'[19] naive idealists, who enable the evil manipulators of history because they lack psychological insight. Jupiter in Scorpio acts on an instinct for power, whether to solve problems or enhance personal status. It understands that politics are emotional, and issues decided more on the basis of feelings than thought. (And these are only four examples out of twelve signs.)

All of these sign positions describe relative emphasis. Each Jupiter position can acknowledge the concerns of the others. It simply prioritizes them differently, according to its own criteria of significance.

Astrology studies perspectives on truth, as phases (signs) of a cycle. Every sign emerges out of the previous one and turns into the following. It participates in an inclusive whole while demonstrating one aspect of it. Each of these energy zones forms a necessary arc of the circle. Each is equally capable of self-transcendence through its own dynamic. Within its orientation each contains every possible level of evolution.

Any of these attitudes can manifest anywhere along the spectrum of human behavior and morality. A planet in a sign does not define an outcome; it describes a process. For example, Jupiter portrays an approach to, not the content of, one's social engagement. That can play out in many ways on any evolutionary level.

There is an inherent property of indeterminacy in all phenomena. It is found in atoms and worlds, natural ecologies and national polities. In this freedom hearts and minds find themselves. We participate with our planetary energies, psychological qualities, to create ourselves. These are not a deterministic given by which one is fated, to which one must submit. They are available possibilities, activated by choice, conscious or unconscious.

We cooperate with or sabotage these archetypal patterns. How one responds involves considerable variations in perception, judgment and purpose. Yet even rebellion is conditioned by what one is rebelling against. We are intimately intertwined with the universe no matter how idiosyncratic our response.

For example: Mars symbolizes the principle of personal will. Pisces is the sign of self-undoing, surrender to a greater collective or cosmic reality. Combining them, Mars in Pisces can mean many things depending on the evolutionary level and inclination of the subject. It can portray victimhood or martyrdom, escapism or engaging social evils. This configuration energizes deep unconscious forces. Activating this numinous realm dissolves the ego, at great cost to the individual. Penetrating the abyss can lead to narcosis of the depths or to a larger than personal redemption.

But Mars in Pisces cannot mean effective self-aggrandizement or ego promotion. It always means deliberately sacrificing self, whether passively or redemptively. Mars in Pisces does not have the inclination, nor the aptitude, for the calculated ambition, or cynicism, of Mars in Capricorn; the flamboyant creativity, or megalomania, of Mars in Leo; the intellectual firepower, or dissociation, of Mars in Gemini, etc. Mars in Pisces permits a spectrum of development along a certain line. It orients will towards loss of self through extremes of degradation or salvation. It inhibits personal purpose from pursuing normal aims in order to further a hidden agenda.

With Mars in Pisces, or any other configuration, one experiences a certain type of stimulus. How one responds is very open. Astrology provides insight into the nature of one's challenges and opportunities. It presents the strengths and weaknesses inherent in one's psychic constitution. Options are clarified. This knowledge enhances personal responsibility.

Notes

1. C. G. Jung, 1875-1961, in his Eranos Lectures of 1951. Jung was one of the founding fathers of modern psychology. He worked on the concept of synchronicity in collaboration with Wolfgang Pauli, 1900-1958, who won a Nobel Prize in Physics (1945) after being nominated for it by Einstein. Their correspondence on this subject is available as 'Atom and Archetype: the Pauli/Jung Letters.'
2. Acts 17:28
3. Einstein himself was deeply troubled by the possibility of 'spooky action at a distance' (his description), first predicted in a paper by Einstein, Podolsky and Rosen in 1935. He believed firmly in causation,

stating famously that 'God does not play dice with the universe.' In 1964 John Bell, an Irish physicist, mathematically proved that local realism, the principle that an event happening in one place cannot instantaneously affect another event somewhere else, inevitably breaks down on the quantum level. Bell's Theorem is now accepted as fundamental and mathematically irrefutable. Its 'spooky action at a distance' has been conclusively demonstrated in every experiment carried out so far.

4. Shakespeare, Hamlet

5. The ideas expressed in the preceding six paragraphs were inspired by the first section of Richard Tarnas' book 'Cosmos and Psyche.' Of course, all the basic astrological qualities discussed in this work result from centuries of thought by many minds. The author has simply attempted to articulate them in his own way.

6. Konrad Lorenz, Nobel prize winning Austrian zoologist, 1903-1987

7. The ideas expressed in the preceding eleven paragraphs were inspired by the work of Ken Wilber, widely considered to be the late 20th century's foremost consciousness theorist. Wilber believes astrology to be an example of prerational magical consciousness. It is often, perhaps usually, expressed on that level, but not inherently limited to it. Besides, what would life be without magic? (The Neptune factor in astrology.)

8. Astrology's documented history begins around 1700 BC in Babylon. See 'Mundane Considerations.'

9. John 14:2

10. Psalms 19:1

Abram (Abraham), ca. 2000-1800 BC, made the original covenant with God that underlies the monotheistic religions. He came out of the Sumerian-Babylonian tradition. This, the first civilization, emerged under the clear desert skies of modern Iraq. Its religion was an early form of astrology, with each city-state dedicated to a particular planetary god/ess. All eventually came under the tutelage of Marduk (Jupiter), patron of Babylon. The elite urban worship of star gods coexisted with local fertility cults and magical practices.

11. This is written from an astrological perspective. Each religion has its own point of view. For example, the Catholic Catechism, or summary of fundamental principles, states that:

> All forms of divination are to be rejected: recourse to Satan or demons, conjuring up the dead or other practices falsely supposed to "unveil" the future. Consulting horoscopes, astrology, palm reading, interpretation of omens and lots, the phenomena of clairvoyance, and recourse to mediums all conceal a desire for power over time, history, and, in the last analysis, other human beings, as well as a wish

to conciliate hidden powers. They contradict the honor, respect, and loving fear that we owe to God alone.

12. 'Not everything that can be counted counts, and not everything that counts can be counted.' Albert Einstein.

13. Dane Rudhyar, 1895-1985, generally considered the father of modern astrology

14. Without this extended magnetic field the solar wind would strip away Earth's atmosphere and water, leaving a dead world much like Mars. In fact, Earth's liquid outer core will slowly 'freeze' into a hot solid crystalline structure unable to generate a magnetic field around 2.3 billion years from now. However, long before that happens, in about a billion years, an expanding Sun will have evaporated the oceans and eradicated multicellular life on our planet.

15. This is how commercial electric generators work. They use hydro or steam power to spin a coiled wire, or copper disc, between the poles of a strong magnet, then draw off the resulting current.

16. DNA = Deoxyribonucleic Acid. DNA is a sequence of four simple chemical units (nucleic acids) that code for proteins. Proteins are the structural building blocks and active metabolic agents of life. Think of simple letters that combine to form words which carry complex meanings. These nucleic acid chains are arranged as a double helix: two intertwined spirals. You can learn more, and access images of DNA molecules, online.

17. This figure was inspired by the diagram/concept of the 'Long body of the Sun,' in 'The Theory of Celestial Influence' by Rodney Collin (1909-1956).

18. They could be born at the same time in the same time zone: for example, in Boston and Atlanta. Or one could be born three hours later in Los Angeles, corresponding to the difference between Eastern and Pacific times. During this period planetary movement is negligible. Only Moon will have moved appreciably, by 1½°. This does not affect the essential identity of these two charts, if we stipulate that Moon does not move into the next sign or go void of course (See 'Lunar Phases and Aspects'). By comparison, the full Moon disc covers about ½° of arc.

19. Lenin, 1879-1921, an extreme example of utopian idealism gone mad.

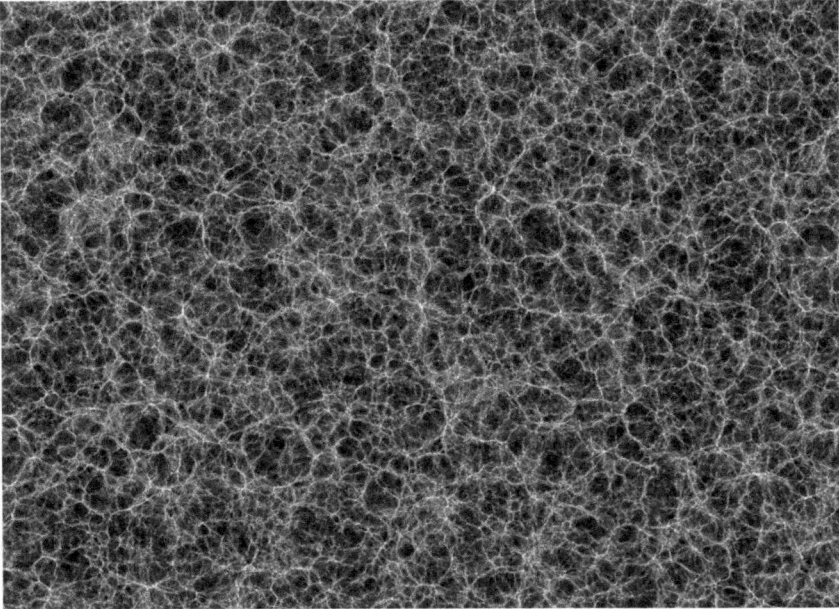

A large scale map of the cosmos with its galactic clusters, filaments and voids looks just like a section of brain tissue with its nerve network embedded in a matrix of supporting glial cells. The temple of consciousness is organized on the same pattern at every level of manifestation.

The physical cosmos forms a reverse image of a spiritual source having 'its center everywhere, its circumference nowhere.' The expanding universe is often compared to a swelling balloon in which no dot (galaxy) on its surface is central, but all are moving away from each other as the balloon fills with air. Thus the material universe has its circumference everywhere, its center nowhere. Spirit and matter complement each other, and join together in consciousness, the experience of their union.

This image of galaxy distribution is from the Millennium Simulation Project. Each side is two billion light years across.

Sun

Sun is the source of life. Its size, luminescence and centrality place it on a higher order of magnitude than any other body in our solar system. It points to a vitality whose attributes or levels of expression the planets chart. But its essence resides solely in itself, of an intensity and subtlety understandable only on its own terms.

Sun burns through the material world from another plane of being. It erupts into our universe of time/space, matter/energy from a spiritual singularity. It creates a smaller reenactment of the Big Bang, recurring every moment.

Sun demonstrates the ecstatic outpouring of a timeless spiritual Reality behind all manifestation. The pure thrill, unqualified Joy, of existence. The light by which we see, in which we walk.

Sun is not a symbol of God. It refers to the Godhead, an inconceivable origin emanating from beyond infinity. The anthropomorphic side of God manifests through its largest planet, Jupiter, a glowing gas giant. Jupiter serves as an intermediary, stepping down Sun's intensity to an available level, giving it a human face.

Sun symbolizes life itself. And the meaning of life. Jupiter describes specific meanings, known conceptual qualifiers: one is a farmer or a lawyer, a Buddhist or a Muslim, liberal or conservative. Sun generates the larger vibration, essential identity behind these attributes. This exists beyond words or concepts. It unites subconscious instinct, conscious ego and superconscious spirit in one overall radiance. Here on Earth this awesome, awe-full Fire cools and condenses into the smaller, more ephemeral sparks of individual lives.

Thus Sun is far and away the most important factor in astrology. It is also the most incomprehensible, for we experience it on the biological plane of Earth rather than in its own stellar sphere. Yet it seems that a spiritual solar identity can only manifest by energizing its tangible planetary aspects, just as the indefinable soul of an individual can only express itself in the realm of organic physical and psychological functioning.

This chapter will explore Sun's general influence, compare it with other stars and discuss its evolution through time. Sun's actual astrological manifestation occurs here on Earth. (See 'Sun and Earth.') This works out through the medium of twelve seasonal energy zones called signs. (See 'Sun in Signs.')

In our dualistic universe of form, the formless realm appears in two aspects: an emptiness, pulsing with quantum fluctuations, and an inconceivable plenitude, with all things merged into one spiritual Light.

Sun is their point of contact. There a spiritual Totality emanates as fiery energy into the void. This influx of spirit downshifting into energy organizes fertile quantum fuzziness into space/time. It manifests as a wave pattern of concentric planetary orbits. Along them material worlds condense: expressions of specific attributes.

Sun itself is unimaginably big and hot.[1] Yet also relatively simple; far simpler than a bacterium or any living thing. Sun embodies a fundamental fact: infinity pouring out into nothingness. This generates energy: light, life, love; physical, biological, psychological states of being. These states differentiate through their actual manifestation in Sun's articulated system of worlds: as a spectrum of light, a tree of life, developmental stages of feeling and of mind. These attributes are clocked, measured, by the whirling layers of Sun's extended body: its planetary centers.

All planets circle Sun as their center and reference point. Sun unites them. They portray colors of its rainbow, notes of its tone. Planetary qualities give form to Sun's force. The distinction between Sun and planets such as Earth parallels that between the Presidency and a particular President. The Presidency describes an abstract theory of the executive function sketched out in Article Two of the Constitution. Yet this political ideal is also the source of real life and death power. It rests on a fundamental principle: that there must be a central organizing power in any collective endeavor, just as there is an inner originating spirit in every individual entity.

The Presidency only comes alive through the person of a President. This collective power takes on life through its embodiment in a historically conditioned individual with specific programs and personal qualities. Yet by accepting the office that person becomes more than just a private ego. 'The mystic chords of memory'[2] unite the temporary occupant of the office with a history, an emotional charge, a cumulative endowment passed on by Washington, Lincoln, FDR, etc. In the same way, personal subjectivity expresses a more transcendent energy, focused through, but not limited to, conscious ego. Sun embodies that energy.

Every entity centers on a source, a core attractor. Thus each atom whirls around a physical nucleus, every cell of a multicellular organism expresses a DNA information nucleus. Human self-consciousness centers on the brain, but our living totality emanates from a heart whose passions and purposes can never be fully known. The solar system embodies a bigger, more inclusive state of being organized around a star, our Sun.

Sun represents a larger meaning which orients our being. All other energies arrange themselves around it, in its service. Each person acts as the agent of a higher purpose. This may be collective, as in a social role. Or one may enact an individual destiny as the vehicle of experience for an ethereal soul. Sun indicates the spiritual nature of that soul, plus all of its manifest qualities: unconscious, conscious, superconscious. These are separated out, like a spectrum of light, on Sun's rings of worlds.

The physical Sun mirrors the miracle of one's own shining as a microcosm of the universe. The mystery of a larger purpose, transcending conscious intent. The authority of an authentic self or soul, to which one must be true.

Sun describes the adventure one embraces or denies; the challenge one faces or ducks. It illuminates the motive and meaning of a life, lights up the path one must follow. The direction of this path derives from Earth's constantly changing relationship to Sun through the zodiac ('Sun and Earth'). It has no preset goal or determined end, for it describes a journey in consciousness. Any of its many forms or states of consciousness can lead to transcendence, even enlightenment. Emotional or rational; artistic, religious, political or scientific: any and all truth quests can lead to Truth. It only takes a full commitment to life itself, the free gift and demanding purpose of our Sun-Soul.

Sun generates the will to live. Not conscious personal will (Mars), or the impersonal racial role one serves (Pluto). These are both expressions of a deeper intention: a primal urge to be. Sun demonstrates that evolving Will through the ever changing patterns of its planetary attributes. What flares up out of Sun animates the entire solar system. Worlds form its fields of expression, consciousness, and evolution. Sun creates an energy aura that fires them up.

Sun powers a train of thought (Mercury), a longing of desire (Venus), and an urge for action (Mars). Its sublime essence focuses into a philosophic/religious consciousness through Jupiter and a rational, realistic one by Saturn. It activates karmic memories of Moon into an overall emotional temperament. The slow moving outer planets, Uranus, Neptune, Pluto represent their generational and historical context.

Sun and Moon define mutually dependent polarities of spirit and matter, principle and psyche. Sun is vastly larger and more central: the overwhelming Power behind life; a vital force seeking experience in the material world. It does so through the cyclic psychological periodicities of the planets. These all focus on Earth filtered and blended through Moon's encircling orbit.

Moon receives solar radiance and births it into organic life. Spirit (Sun) incarnates through the waves it makes on matter (Moon). Sun's force field focuses through the twelve lunar circlings of Earth as Earth completes one orbit of its star. These twelve lunation cycles constitute the fundamental archetypes of life, consciousness and soul. On Earth's outermost circumference, Moon's orbit, Sun activates energy patterns that come to life in our world's watery womb.

We do not experience Sun on its own fiery terms. We are Sun's biological shining. Biology demands ecology: an interrelationship. This ecology manifests through a dynamic in time: the sequential unfoldment of solar radiance condensed into a dozen monthly cycles. Moon precipitates spirit into psychology, an emotional nature based on past memories. The Sun/Moon relationship (phase) transmits Sun's timeless Reality, eternal Principle, into the stream of time.

Sun activates memory: genetic programs, collective instincts, personal recollections. It also gives them the energy with which to achieve consciousness and independent development. Sun drives the system. Moon feels it. Planets describe its various activities.

Sun and Stars

Sun itself is not an ordinary star. It lives larger than 97% of all stars (!), most of which are dim red or brown dwarfs. Sun blazes as a bright yellow dwarf, average for its type. Think of a middle class family in an advanced society. Compared to the hungry billions in the third world, or the deprivations of most throughout history, it seems quite wealthy. Compared to its peers within its own society it is simply normal.

Sun is an ordinary member of a certain class of star, not an ordinary star as such. The universe expresses several levels of being, lensed through various types of stars. Each type opens the portal to a specific wavelength of spirit's spectrum. Sun focuses on one such plane of reality, along with others of its kind. Different dimensions manifest through cool long-lived red dwarfs, and hot fast-burning supergiants. Or x-ray stars, magnetars, dense neutron stars, etc.

Our universe is unimaginably vast and varied. Perhaps the several species of star are analogous to the several planetary functions in our own solar system. They would constitute another order of magnitude of one great Life, as far from the human realm as we are from the atomic.

Yet, in the end, mere size means little. It is participation in the process that counts. Atoms are as capable as humans of self-transcendence as they band together into the organic molecules of life. They are not self-conscious in the human sense. But human self-consciousness would not be possible without the grounding they provide. Perhaps the joy-thrill an atom feels as it minutely participates in a biological life is as great, relative to its size, as the ecstasies of a mystic or the death-orgasm of a supernova.

From any plane of being the next plane seems like a transcendent infinity. Thus life is to matter, consciousness to life, spirit to consciousness. Sun symbolizes spirit in our conscious experience. It appears as a light so bright we cannot bear to look directly at it. But its diffused radiance makes vision possible.

Every plane of being makes a quantum jump into the next. Sun guides consciousness to spirit by providing an accessible orientation to its cosmic meaning. Each of us embodies one day's measure of its purpose, ⅟₃₆₅ of its year, at a safe yet stimulating remove, 93,000,000 miles away. We assimilate that day through an even finer measurement of Earth's rotation. Our awareness is formatted, conditioned by the zodiacal degree rising over the eastern horizon, the ascendant. This changes every four minutes. (See 'Sun and Earth.') Thus Sun's immensity becomes digestible on the human level.

The ascendant, Earth's rotational relationship to Sun, can be known: conscious ego and its social projection. Moon can be understood, if not completely known: the past, unconscious, karma. But Sun itself beggars description. It is The Force.

Sun, in its totality, is beyond our ken. Yet, 'a man's reach should exceed his grasp.' Sun beckons us to strive and grow, degree by degree, until we evolve to the jump-off point into unconditioned spirit. Sun's fundamental message is not intimidation by an inhuman grandeur. Rather it inspires with its encouraging light and nurturing warmth.

Sun is also unusual, but far from unique, in being solo. About 60% of all stars have one or more companions. 40% stand alone. This would seem to imply that Sun has a monotheistic unity of purpose. A focused singularity of meaning. Perhaps the dualistic nature of other star systems implies a marriage-like corporate identity, harmonious or antagonistic as the case may be.

Objectively speaking, Sun is big, alone and far out. (It is on the galactic rim.) There it not only shines. It also moves. It rotates on its axis, revolves around the galaxy and journeys along its own trajectory in the interstellar neighborhood.

All bodies in space rotate around their own center. Axial rotation describes a celestial body's internal subjective state. This self-centered circular motion defines its inherent identity as experienced by and within itself. A rotation carries every point on its surface through a complete orbit of its own center and a 360° perspective on the surrounding cosmos.

The circle symbolizes wholeness. Spinning upon itself it becomes a vortex, drawing in an energy that defines its identity. Its circumference, without beginning or end, marks the balance between this centripetal force and the centrifugal nature of its energy to radiate outward. In Sun it physically manifests as the gravitational pressure of its mass countering the radiative release of its thermonuclear burning. The integrity of a stellar sphere spinning around itself measures the tension between introverted (self seeking) gravity and extroverted (self expressing) hydrogen burning. Gravity's shaping force enables its fusion to shine forth. The exact correlation of these forces makes the star's identity visible and known.

It may be a brown, red or white dwarf, glowing faintly, but for a very long time; an active bright yellow star, like Sol; a hot white or hotter blue, sizzling furiously and burning out quickly. There are also magnetic and x-ray stars, pulsing variable and heavy neutron stars, giants and super giants. Within these general categories each star has its own unique character, like the individual citizens of our various nations.

Obviously such an identity centers on a plane of being far outside of the human condition. It cannot be known or verbally described in human ego terms. It remains a fact that stars are energy centers and rotation defines their character. That this physical reality mirrors a parallel spiritual current constitutes the basic premise of astrology. Humans too are energy centers, intangible souls generating a unique spin, or vibration, of their compound psychological quality.

Our Sun spins differentially, taking 25 days to turn at its equator, 35 at its poles. It does so because it is a plasma, an electrically charged gas, rather than a solid. This generates a twisting curve of energy vibrating out into space at various frequencies.

Lines of magnetic force within Sun break out at its surface. Their poles emerge at different layers of rotational speed and so the lines of tension between them become all tangled up. This causes them to create great knots of energy, which pinch off and hurl themselves away from Sun, carrying a bit of its mass with them. These great storms inundate its planets, especially the small inner ones, with gusts of solar wind. Thus Sun floods the system not only with light, but with its very substance.

Is this not similar to differentially vibrating vocal cords shaping puffs of air into meaningful sounds? Is Sun literally talking? Or singing?

This spinning, vibrating fire globe does not stand still. It also circumnavigates the entire Milky Way galaxy. Twenty-seven thousand light years out from the monster black hole at its core, our Sun moves in one of its wispy outer filaments. Far beyond the great mass of stars in the central disc, our Sun lives about 40% of the way out to its edge, near but not at the frontier of intergalactic space.

At our position, way out on one of the Milky Way's spiral arms, this galaxy circling journey takes about 230,000,000 Earth years. This constitutes one year on Sun's timeline. Sun is about 20 such galactic years old. It has now shone for somewhat less than half of its projected lifespan.

No doubt this great year has its own cycle of variation. These are seasons of Sun, too vast for us to perceive directly. Perhaps the great eons of Earth's experience: archaic, Hadean, prebiotic, life's birth, microbial era, Cambrian proliferation, ages of trilobites and fish, dinosaurs and mammals, epochs of volcanism and glaciation, mark the seasons of this cosmic year.

Sun in Time

Our Sun, 4.6 billion years old, is about ⅓ the age of the universe. It is a third or fourth generation star, formed from gas and dust that had been significantly enriched with the heavier elements that provide a material scaffolding for life. The earliest stars, formed at the beginning of our universe, were composed only of the primordial, simple, light elements of hydrogen and some helium. They cooked or created heavier, more complex elements through their internal nuclear fusion. Then spewed them out into the void when they exploded as novae or supernovae. With every breath of our nitrogen/oxygen atmosphere we take in the last exhalations of dying stars.

These first suns, and their many surviving examples of slow burning dwarf stars, were composed of a more tenuous material than ours. Thus they could only host or embody more ethereal manifestations of physical, biological, conscious or spiritual form. The increase in metallicity, or complex matter, of our Sun, and other stars of its type, provided a platform for the emergence of more complex organic forms that require heavier elemental building blocks such as carbon, phosphorus, iron, etc. Thus our Sun represents a later phase of material and biological evolution in the universe's history.

There are even denser kinds of suns, such as neutron stars, the compressed cores of once actively burning stars. These blew off their heavy element rich outer layers in their final death orgasm. Their atomically crushed remains may host correspondingly pressurized physical, biological, consciousness or spiritual processes inconceivable to us. The point is that our Sun's material composition and generational cohort, within a wider array of stellar types, makes possible our own peculiar biological form of life expression. Perhaps electrically charged gaseous forms, or densely packed configurations of subatomic matter, conduct unimaginable energy currents in other stars. They would form alternative examples of spirit's adventure in material incarnation.

The nine billion years prior to Sun's birth was, from our point of view, an era of physical evolution from the Big Bang through the creation of light atoms, their condensation into galaxies, firing up the first generations of stars. These then made the elements making planets such as Earth possible. It appears that Sun was born in the gravitational collapse of a cloud of hydrogen, richly seeded with about one percent of other elements. This was triggered by a shock wave from a nearby supernova. Most likely several hundred other stars also formed from this event. Thus Sun belongs to a now far-flung tribe of stellar siblings, perhaps different in character, but related by birth.

The following twenty cycles of Sun's galactic round timed the cosmic rhythms of Earth's slow shaping: the long beat of geological eras, joining and separating continents; the four billion year unfolding of biological evolution, generating living complexity from simple chemicals. The emergence of life; its genetic organization of DNA information storage; the coalescing of nucleated single cells as the precondition for multicellular organisms; the eons-long development of nervous systems and brains; the evolution of our self-conscious, collectively learning species: these demonstrate the maturation of Sun's imprint on its Earthly field of expression. As that manifestation became more sophisticated over immense stretches of time it could register ever more subtle wavelengths of change.

On a (relatively) more immediate level, Sun also moves within its local star-field, perhaps in a series of great orbits around other nearby stars. These faster cycles may refer to intensified levels of genetic change at the species level: a more finely tuned movement, timing the trajectories of specific lineages within the general categories of life. For example, the average mammalian species lasts for 'only' several million years before dying out or transforming into something new. Thus, our own bipedal hominid ancestors diverged from their closest chimpanzee-like relatives about seven million years ago and evolved through a series of intermediate steps into anatomically modern humans about 250,000 years ago. This reflects a more delicately articulated dance of Sun with its astronomically near stellar neighbors, generating a speedier, more specialized, but still unconscious, process of evolution.

About 50,000 years ago, the increasing refinement of the human genetic endowment began to register a fundamentally new type of cycle acting on an even more subtle scale. Not one of Sun's vast galactic and interstellar rhythms but of Earth's own changing relationship to Sun through the 25,920 year precessional cycle of Earth's orbital tilt (see 'Precession'). This marked a transition from unconscious physical and biological processes measured by the astronomical magnitude of Sun's movement through space to a more nuanced cultural evolution guided by Earth's cyclic reorientation towards its star. Long slow cosmic, geological and genetic cycles reached a critical intensity and sublimated into a more conscious historical and psychological mode.

Obviously these precessional cycles have always existed; they are physical facts. But only during their last two gyrations has humanity developed the sensitivity to express this planetary resonance. Prior to that the human species had passively responded to Earth's environment as an unconscious object of evolutionary forces. Suddenly a critical mass of nervous organization and psychic development emerged. Powerful but blind cosmic forces began to intermesh with and stimulate a now adequately receptive human state of awareness. Sun's spiritual fire ignited a sustained chain reaction of self-awareness within human hearts and minds.

At that time there seems to have been a basic rewiring of the human brain, combined with a dropping of the larynx in the throat giving greater vocal control and linguistic ability. This accompanied a quantum leap from genetic to cultural evolution, from solitary present sensation to cumulative collective learning. It expressed itself through the emergence of an entirely new level of culture in the Old Stone Age. This Paleolithic era brought the first symbolic art in remarkable cave paintings, along with far more advanced tools and adaptive techniques. These enabled a huge geographical diffusion of our species into the forbidding new environments of Ice Age Europe, Siberia, the Americas and even across wide bodies of water to colonize New Guinea and Australia. Relatively soon thereafter, starting about 12,000 years ago, came the transition to agriculture. Then 5000 years ago to state-organized, urban, literate civilization. Creation had become aware of itself through one of its creations, the human soul of a cosmic Sun.

A logarithmic acceleration of time slowly built up as billennia of physical unfolding in the cosmos quickened into eons of biological evolution on Earth. These speeded up into 10,000 generations of human physiological development, followed by a faster 10,000 years of cultural transformation after the agricultural revolution. Then millennia of civilizational cycles began to compress into individual lifetimes of intensified social and personal empowerment, much as a diffused gas cloud in space ignites into a myriad of stars. This process reached a critical mass in the worldwide spiritual awakening of the 'Axial Age' during the 6th century BC. (See 'Precession.') Since then objective social change has increasingly internalized as a snowballing subjective consciousness growth. That has now achieved an unprecedented take-off velocity, as more change happens in a modern year than during a medieval century.

The vastness and remoteness of these considerations emphasize the fact that Sun represents another spiritual dimension that generates, animates and sustains our bio-psychic plane of being. Physical matter precipitates out of stellar fire. Biological life grounds solar radiance. Sun energized its expression on Earth through long cycles of organic evolution telescoping into more rapid waves of specialized speciation.[3] This finally transformed into a consciousness breakthrough as the human psyche assimilated Sun's objective shining out there into a subjective enlightenment in here.

The guiding light of Sun's spiritual power now lit up human consciousness from within. Humans began to consciously co-create their own evolution. The rest of this book will explore this not from Sun's inhuman perspective as a star in outer space, but as the now internalized heart of our own inner space: Sun as experienced on the psychological and spiritual planes within the human condition here on Earth.

Sun in Space

In its own astronomical realm Sun is moving at about ten miles per second away from Sirius, the brightest star in our sky, towards a point 10° southwest of Vega, near the constellation Hercules. We call this point the solar apex. It lies 30° north of the celestial equator (Earth's equator projected out into space). In fact, the solar apex is due north of the winter solstice, at 1° of Capricorn. On that great turning point of Earth's own annual cycle, we also directly align with Sun's cosmic trajectory through space: Earth - Sun - solar apex. See Figures 1-4.

On its journey through the changing energy fields of space Sun constantly moves north. Towards Vega, away from Sirius. North therefore = future, destiny, opportunity, influx. South then = past, roots, origins, causes. North is not 'better' than south. North portrays Sun's goal or purpose. South expresses its inherited resources and circumstances. North = challenge. South = response. North is the creative vision, south its implementation and outcome. This dynamic polarity plays out in our evolving consciousness here on Earth.

Notes

1. Sun contains 98.8% of our solar system's mass. (One planet, Jupiter, contains another .8%; all other planets combined about .4%.)

Sun's surface temperature is 9900° F. There it interfaces with the absolute zero (-454° F) of outer space. Sun's core is 28,000,000° F. These are really big numbers. They make no palpable sense to us. For comparison, stick your finger in a candle flame. In just one second the pain will be agonizing. The temperature of the flame is about 1800° F. Now try to imagine Sun's surface.

2. Abraham Lincoln, First Inaugural Address

3. Let us briefly examine the accelerating nature of time in biological evolution. Life seems to have emerged almost as soon as geological conditions stabilized on the archaic Earth about 3.6 billion years ago. Then for two billion years amorphous 'headless' cells struggled to centralize an internal nucleus, a cellular brain of genetic information. These prokaryotic cells still exist as bacteria, by far the most numerous life form on Earth. For perhaps another billion years the new nucleated cells (eukaryotes), much more efficient than their predecessors, developed their metabolism and organized into multicellular invertebrates.

About 550,000,000 years ago these soft creatures began generating hard protective shells that also served as structural support. The pace of evolution quickened. Complex life, in the basic forms we know today, emerged and proliferated during the Cambrian Explosion. Some of these internalized their outer skeletons into an inner cord, which later became a segmented backbone. An Age of Fish flourished from 450-320 million years ago. A few crawled out onto the land and became amphibians, which had to return to water to breed. Over time they began to enclose the ancestral sea inside a hard-shelled egg, allowing them to live independently on land as reptiles. For two hundred million years they ruled the Earth in the Age of Dinosaurs. Some of the smaller ones internalized their eggs into a womb, an inner sea nurtured by a mother's life-aura. After the dinosaurs' extinction these mammals became dominant. They scurried and stomped and roared across the planet for sixty million years until one of their kind erupted a big brain and began the human story. Each major step occurred at a faster rate than the previous one, though inconceivably slowly by our standards.

Then the rate of change jumped to a new level. Early hominids diverged from the other primates as an independent lineage about seven million years ago and developed into modern Homo sapiens by about 250,000 BC. The widespread, controlled use of fire is unambiguous by 125,000 years ago. The Paleolithic cultural explosion followed about 80,000 years later. The rest of the story is more familiar: the invention of agriculture, rise of cities, emergence of civilization. Things were speeding up. Change during ancient or medieval times would seem glacially slow to a modern person, yet had become lightning fast compared to biological evolution.

The point is that each stage of the evolutionary process has fundamentally accelerated in comparison to its predecessor. Geological change on Earth, slow as it seems to us, happens faster than do astronomical developments in heaven. Biological evolution races relative to continental drift or mountain building. Human physical evolution has been a rapid sequel to life's long story, but its cultural evolution moves at a logarithmically increased pace. Today it has accelerated to a transformative crisis point.

All of this parallels what happened during the formation of our Sun. For unimaginable eons hydrogen molecules drifted in the vacuum until swirled into astronomical proximity by a supernova shock wave. They slowly gathered into a rotating disc of gas. After a long period of condensation its density achieved critical mass and ignited a fusion reaction. A star was born.

We are now reliving this process on a more subtle level, in the realm of consciousness. We as individuals at any time, and as a species at this time, are at a point analogous to that when Sun burst out into self-generated light. In an individual enlightenment can occur at any moment if one is truly open to it. In our collective history a singularity, or moment of revelation, is clearly at hand as converging waves of political, socioeconomic, demographic, environmental and technological change reach a crescendo, a crisis of danger/opportunity. What happened to Sun in outer space a long time ago is now repeating in human inner space.

Figure 1   Sun's path through space

Earth's circling of Sun stretches into a spiral as Sun/solar system moves towards the star Vega.
The solar apex is about 10° southwest of Vega.

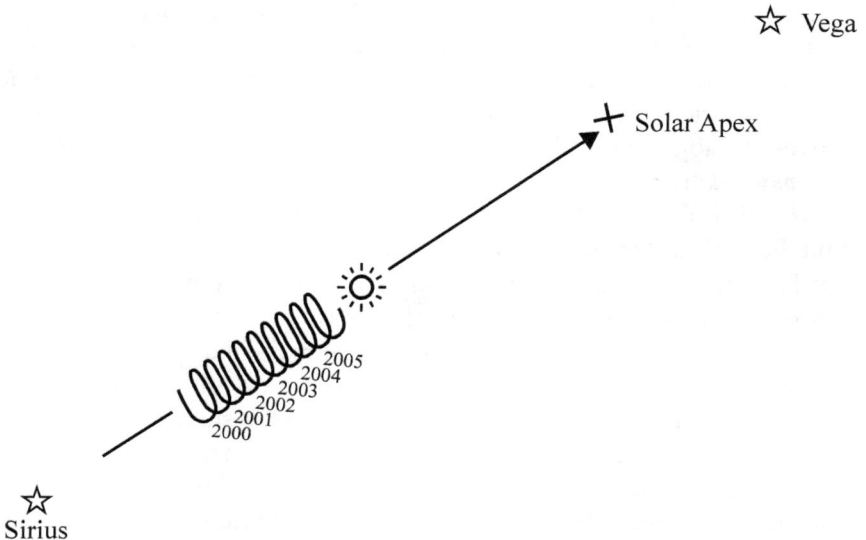

Vega: 25 light years ahead.
        Declination: 38°47' north, outside the zodiac.
        Right ascension: 18 hours, 37 minutes = 15° Capricorn.

Vega is the fifth brightest star in the sky. It is a blue-white main sequence star, twice as massive as Sun and 37 times more luminous. Because Vega burns so hot its life expectancy is only 10% of Sun's. In about 500 million years it should swell into a red giant, then collapse, leaving behind a dimly glowing white dwarf.

Sirius: 8.6 light years behind.
Declination: 16°43' south, within the zodiac.
Right ascension: 6 hours, 45 minutes = 14° Cancer.

Sirius is the brightest star in our sky. It looks twice as bright as its closest rival, Canopus.* It is a blue-white main sequence star with a white dwarf companion. It is twice as massive as Sun and 25 times more luminous.

* Canopus is intrinsically far brighter than Sirius – but it is also about 300 light years away.

Figure 2 Sun's path through three dimensional space

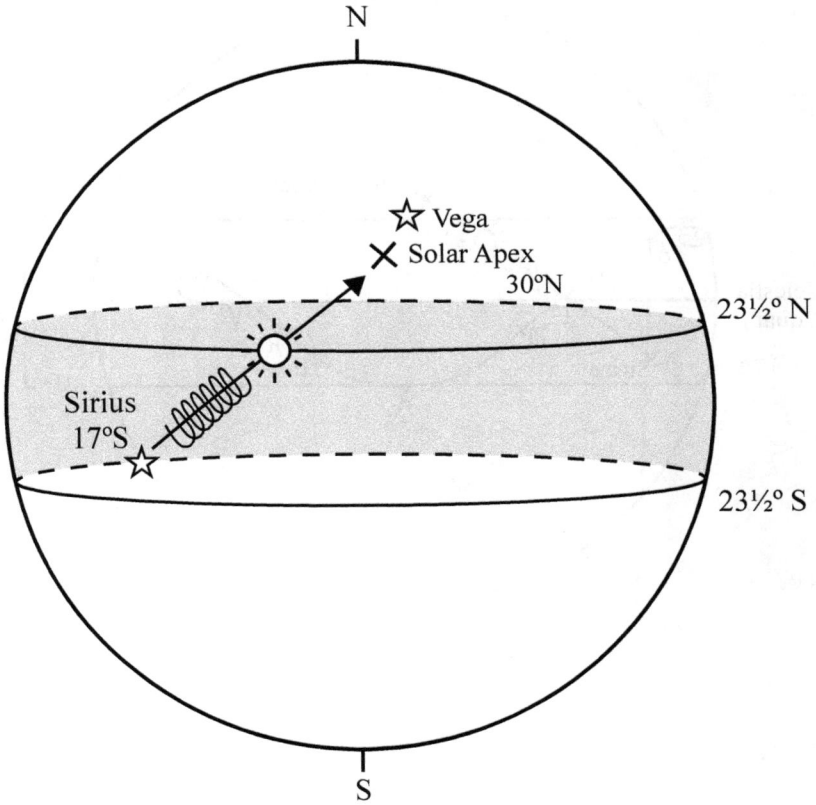

41

Figure 3   Sun's path relative to the zodiac

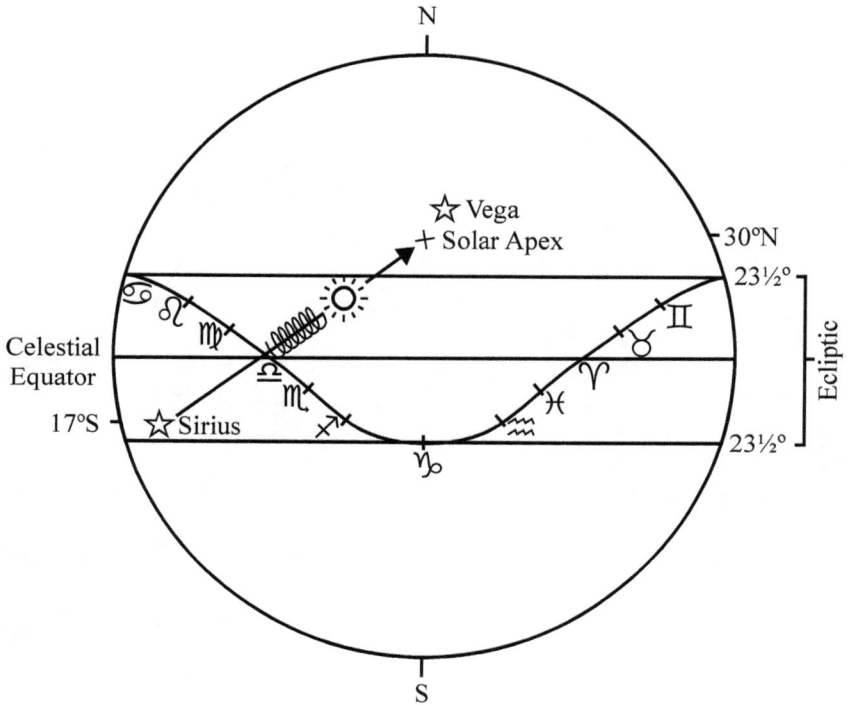

Sun is moving away from Sirius, within the zodiac at its southern edge. And towards Vega, outside of the zodiac, to its north.

Figure 4 Mapping the solar apex onto the zodiac

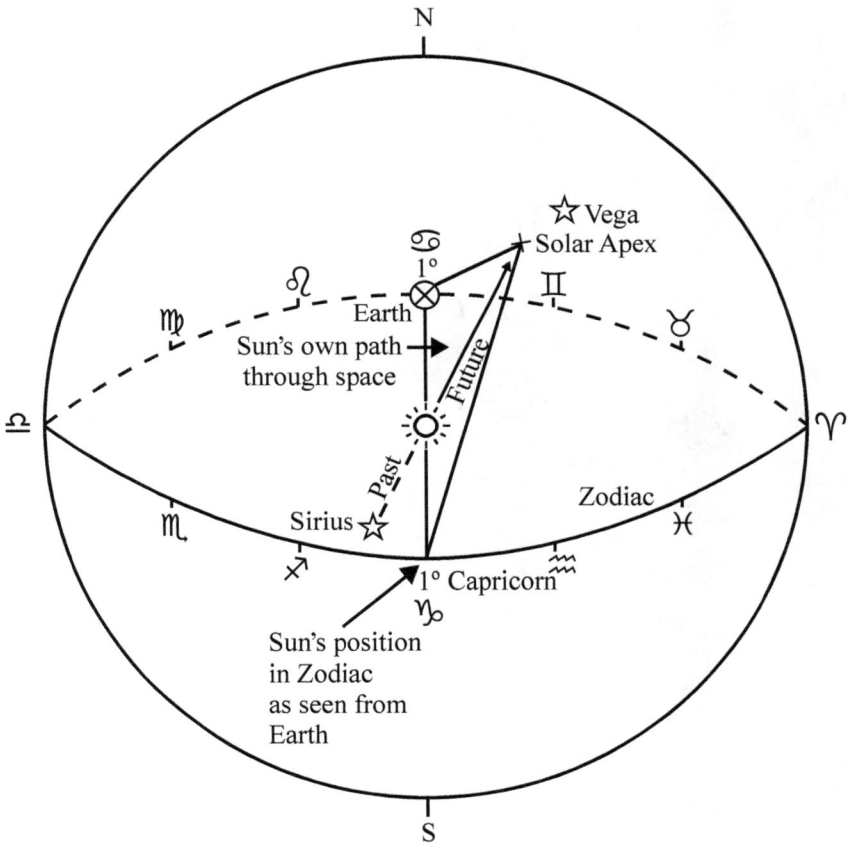

Earth is always on the opposite side of zodiac from Sun.

The solar apex is 54° directly north of 1° Capricorn, the winter solstice. Here it is rotated slightly to the right to show the triangle of measurement.

Sign Symbols

♈ – Aries

♉ – Taurus

♊ – Gemini

♋ – Cancer

♌ – Leo

♍ – Virgo

♎ – Libra

♏ – Scorpio

♐ – Sagittarius

♑ – Capricorn

♒ – Aquarius

♓ – Pisces

Sun's Interstellar Neighborhood

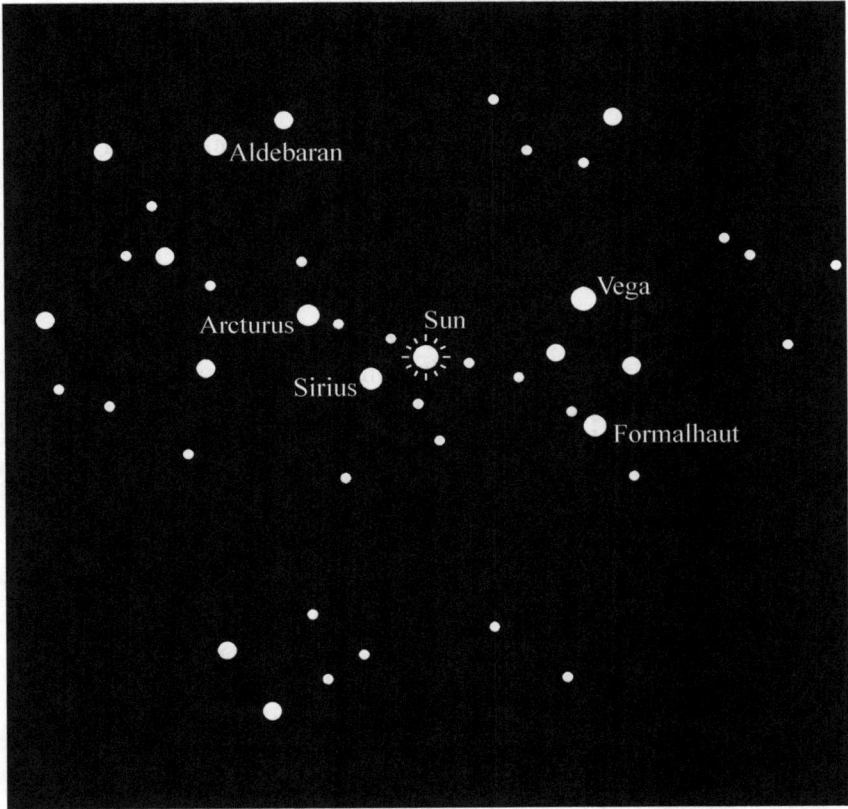

This is how Sun and the nearest stars to it look from thirty light years out. Most of the bright stars we can see with the naked eye are even farther away. There are also an estimated 400 dim red, brown, and white dwarf stars in this volume of space.

Sun and Earth

This chapter has three parts:

The first outlines basic astronomical facts behind astrological interpretation.

The second describes how Earth's daily rotation generates a terrestrial zodiac of 'houses' during its hours of day and night. This grounds the cosmic zodiac of sign energies into psychological experience.

The third demonstrates how the chart evolves, its internal dynamics. This is based on the idea that a day symbolizes/miniaturizes a year. Thus the moving planetary positions in the days after birth foreshadow emerging personal characteristics over the years of a life.

Earth

Earth experiences Sun's movement through space as it tilts towards or away from the solar center during its annual round. Our planet inclines at a 23½° angle to its orbital path. Figure 1. For half the year (spring and summer) its northern hemisphere bows to Sun. During this period day is longer than night. For the other half (fall and winter) it leans away from Sun. During that period night is longer than day.

Earth's northern hemisphere tips towards Sun during spring and returns to equilibrium during summer.[1] It then tips away from Sun during autumn and returns to equilibrium during winter.[2] The southern hemisphere does the same in reverse. For the sake of simplicity the term 'Earth' will henceforth refer to its northern hemisphere perspective.

Earth gyrates towards and away from Sun as it circles around its orbit. We visually perceive this by seeing Sun move up north and down south in the sky over the course of a year. Thus the zodiac, or belt of stars describing Sun's position as seen from Earth, forms a sine wave undulating 23½° north and south of Earth's equator projected out into space (celestial equator). Figure 2.

North describes an advance into the unknown, where we are going. South portrays a return, bearing the fire of a new consciousness. (See 'Sun.') Earth's rhythmic oscillation north and south weaves future and past, end and origin, goal and source together in a timeless Now. That Now is embodied in Sun, a Truth radiance always fully present, yet also unfolding through history. The yearly rhythm outlines our evolutionary growth in understanding an Eternity that is forever with us in the here and now.

We reenact every phase of this journey of discovery and return in our annual round through the zodiac. Each of its twelve month-long signs consists of one Moon orbit around Earth. Each sign forms a lunar

Figure 1   Earth and Sun

If Earth's axis of rotation was not tilted with respect to its orbital path then both hemispheres would receive equal amounts of solar energy all year.

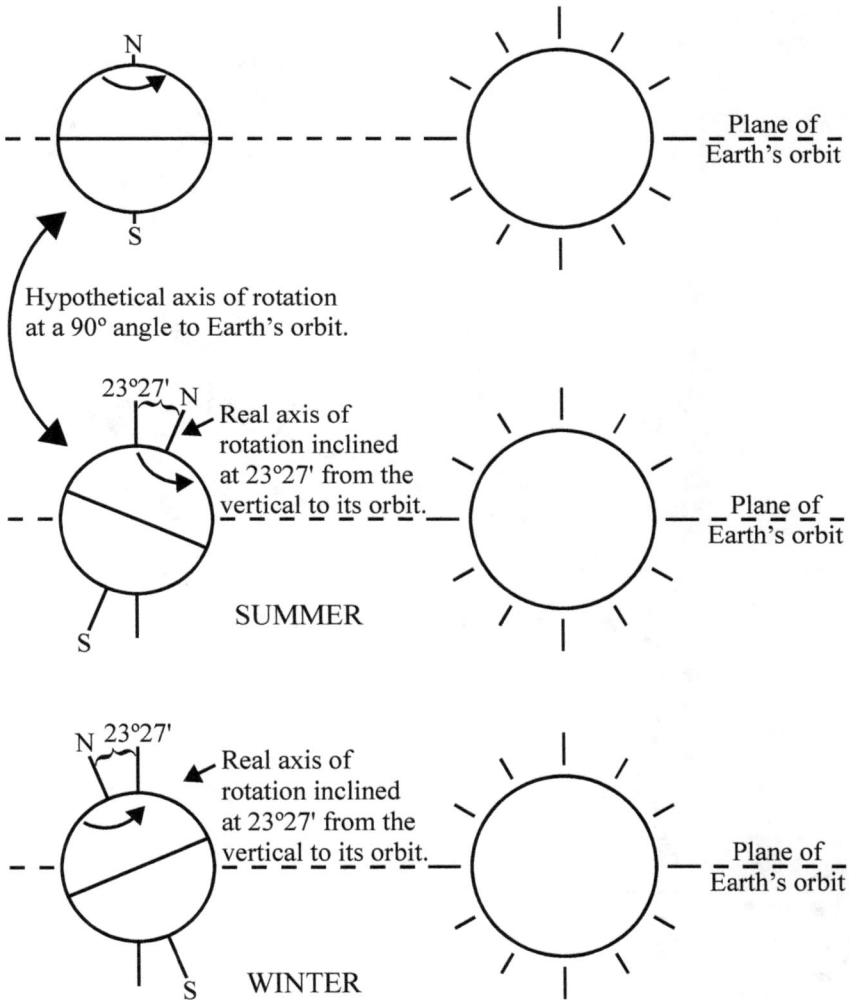

Hypothetical axis of rotation at a 90° angle to Earth's orbit.

Real axis of rotation inclined at 23°27' from the vertical to its orbit.

SUMMER

Real axis of rotation inclined at 23°27' from the vertical to its orbit.

WINTER

Plane of Earth's orbit

Because Earth's axis of rotation is tilted with respect to its orbit both hemispheres receive different amounts of solar energy at different times of year.

Figure 2 Sine wave of signs

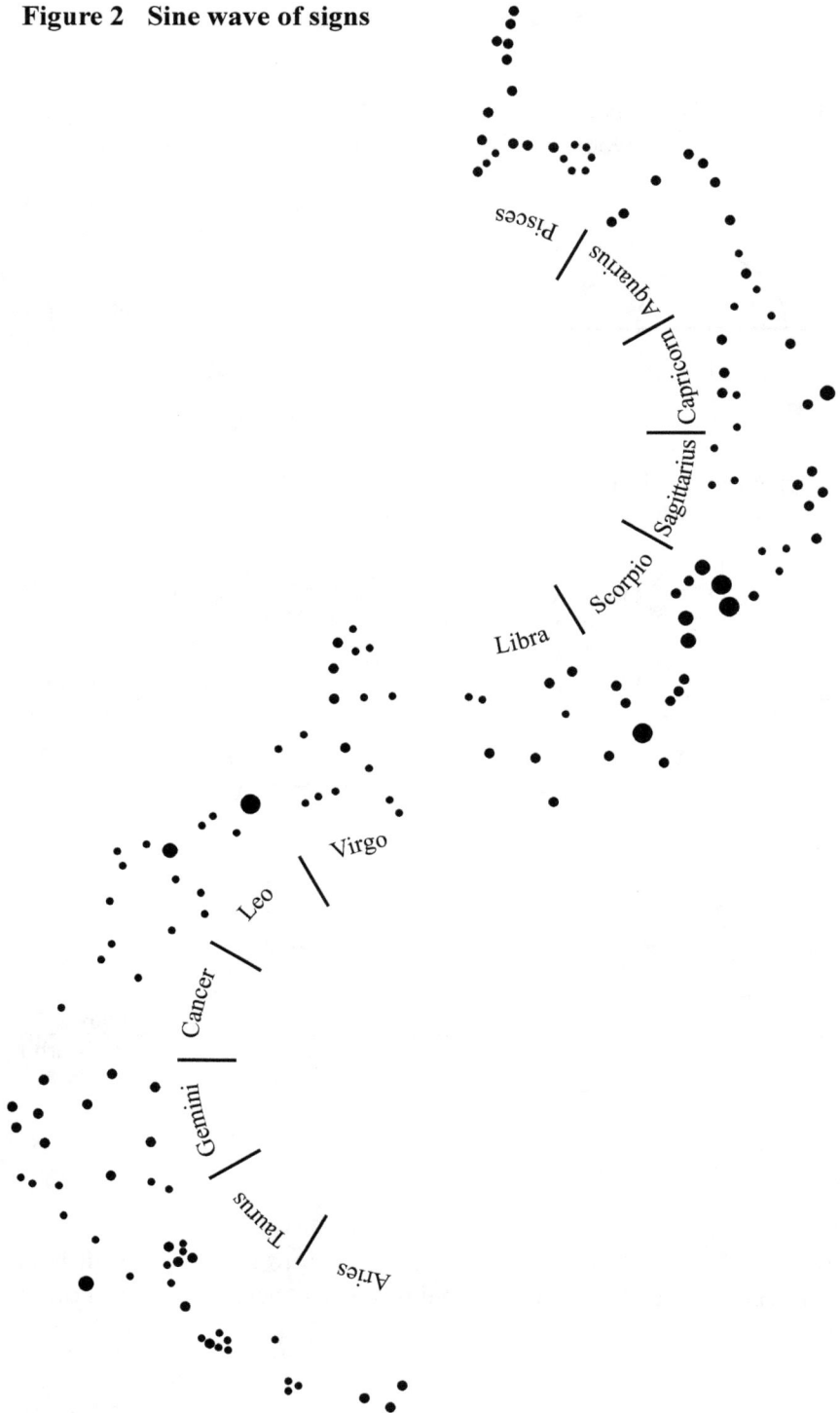

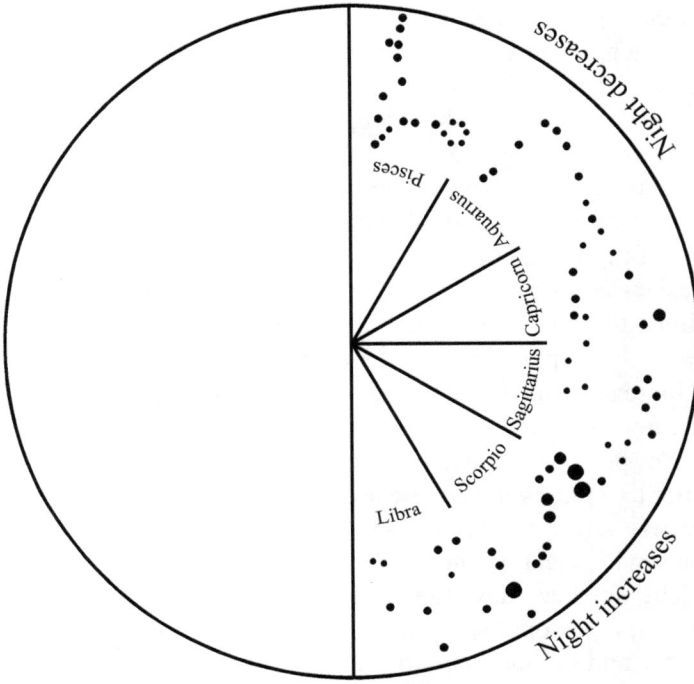

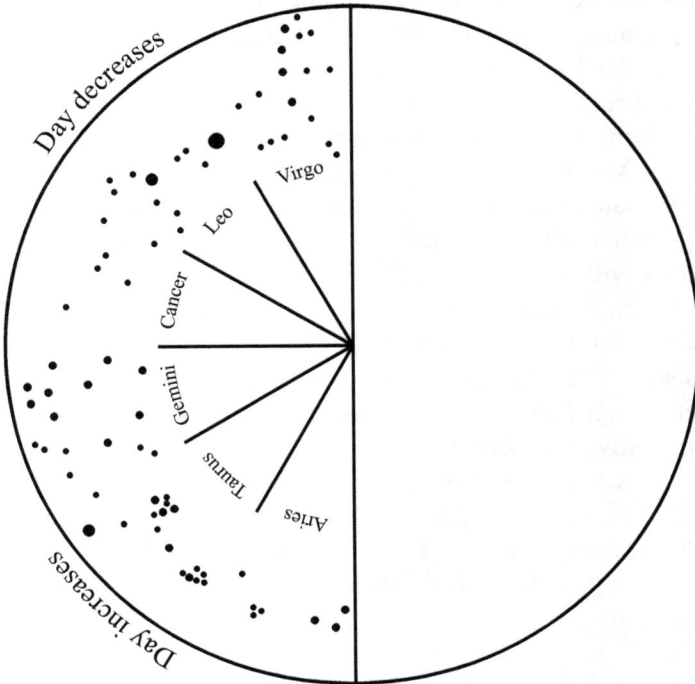

Figure 3 The Cycle of Signs

49

lens focusing one phase of the year's totality. (See 'Sun in Signs.') Twelve such Moon years of psychological experience add up to make one Earth year of spiritual journey around Sun's central fire.

During Earth's northern arc, from Aries to Virgo, day (individual consciousness) is longer than night. The six months (signs) of day dominance emphasize the development (spring) and expression (summer) of personality as an exemplar of an emerging solar purpose. Earth's southern arc of night's dominance (immersion in collective consciousness) emphasizes ego's return to society. Its six signs, from Libra to Pisces, contribute the gifts of personal evolution to the larger group (autumn) and carry the responsibilities of membership in it (winter).

Increasing daylight (winter to summer solstice) means individuation: first as a unique model of social identity (winter), then as a pioneer of personal growth (spring). Day = the Quest. Increasing night (summer to winter solstice) means participation: first through a private perspective acting on society (summer), then through a committed identification with social norms (autumn). Night = the Return. Figure 3.

The northern day dominant exposure individualizes. Only an individual, a personal soul made in the image of God, can encounter, assimilate and embody new truth. The southern night journey socializes. Only through sharing individual discoveries can one participate in a larger reality. Thus one repays the universe for bringing one forth, and justifies that existence through communion with others.

Spring, day dominant with day increasing, expresses an intuitive stretching forth into possibility. Its signs, Aries, Taurus, Gemini, display the threefold process of individual consciousness, with qualities of will, desire and mind, achieving their maximum reach. Summer, day dominant with night increasing, embodies an emotional expression of that consciousness. Its signs, Cancer, Leo, Virgo, illustrate self's truth through sensitivity, intensity and integrity of feeling. Autumn, night dominant with night increasing, plunges into a collective reality. Its signs, Libra, Scorpio, Sagittarius, fuse self with society while infusing both with a larger meaning. Winter, night dominant with day increasing, demonstrates the emergence of a new identity from that fertilization. Its signs, Capricorn, Aquarius, Pisces, portray personal consciousness enacting universal themes.

The whole saga of the signs expresses a yin/yang alternation. Do your thing/serve others; personal fulfillment/social solidarity. Both are equally necessary; each can be equally destructive. The twelve lunation cycles of the year flesh out this abstract energy curve with a continuum of personality types.

Figure 4   Earth's poles

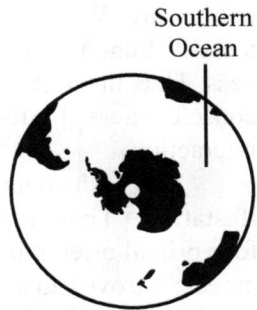

Southern
Ocean

x
north pole

o
south pole

Earth's own physical body replicates the importance of this north/south polarity. The North Pole is a circular ocean surrounded by land. Water is sensitive to, receptive of, incoming energies from the regions of space we are entering. The South Pole is a circular continent surrounded by the Southern Ocean. Solid land portrays the bottom line of reality, the objective result of experience. Figure 4.

Earth slants towards both where we are going and where we are coming from. It weaves hope and heritage into a living present. The 23½° angle of that slant reveals something about the nature of Now. Twenty-three and a half degrees constitutes about ¼ the arc between pole and equator (90°). Earth bends ¼ away from the perpendicular to its orbit. It does not stand straight up and down; it leans over by a quarter arc. While one hemisphere of Earth's planetary brain inclines towards Sun, its spiritual source, the other turns away, in relative darkness. Thus the globe itself embodies dominant and recessive modes of consciousness. Its four seasons of movement portrays their dynamic interaction.

Four is the number of wholeness; it symbolizes the cross of manifestation.[3] There are four directions in space, four seasons in time, four primal orientations of the psyche. (These can be expressed in two modes: introverted and extroverted, perhaps analogous to up and down in space, past and future in time.)

These four psychic functions operate in two pairs, each of which is a polarity: thinking and feeling, sensation and intuition. (Intuition here means sensing possibilities as opposed to actualities; imagination rather than perception.) In every individual one function dominates. It demonstrates a gift, one's conscious stance. In contrast, its polarity remains undeveloped, submerged, repressed, dysfunctional; primitive, infantile, clumsy, even destructive. The Shadow. The other pair of functions operates in a fairly normal way. One reinforces the dominant function, as a secondary talent. The other just does its job: no more, no less, on an average level.

It seems that each psyche is ¼ numb, blind, paralyzed, latent, perhaps even wounded. Just as physical Earth tilts by one quarter off its orbital path, so human consciousness careens off-balance in one direction, out of tune with its solar self by one season. The human condition fits our planetary posture: both are about ¼ decentered.

Earth's tilt was caused by a cataclysmic impact; the same one that blew Moon off from our world four billion years ago. Thus an off-center axis of subjectivity is balanced by a physical objectification of the unconscious (Moon). The undeveloped, recessive function lives its own shadowy life, made visible and accessible to consciousness via Moon. The inferior function is relatively autonomous because it remains in the dark. Contemplation of Moon's contribution to a horoscope can help to integrate this split off ability into a wholeness of being. Understanding Moon's counterpoint to Sun can bring a zombie-like element of personality back to light and life. (See 'Moon.')

Earth's off-center rotation also means that its axis sweeps out, encompasses, a larger cone of the heavens than a ramrod straight spin would.[4] Thus our deviation from abstract perfection leads to a fuller embrace of the universe. The flawed nature of reality stimulates its evolution toward a greater wholeness. Figure 5.

Earth's orbital period expresses the same truth as its posture. Our planet spins 365¼ times on its axis during one circling of Sun. Not an even 360. There is a jarring, jagged oddness here that implies freedom, surprise, fertile fuzziness. In a similar vein, Moon circles Earth twelve times a year with 11⅓ days left over. (Thus the difference between lunar and solar calendars.)

Cosmic rhythms display an organic sloppiness rather than a crystalline perfection. This allows for mutation and evolution. The movements of our planet, and the solar system generally, are not a mechanical clockwork measuring rigidly determined units of time. They are a slightly eccentric twirling and twisting that promote unexpected emergences. This consistent small nonconformity with mathematical perfection - in days of a year/degrees of a circle, and between lunar/solar years - measures an element of freedom, wildness, novelty inherent in the cosmic process. Through this opening infinity enters, fertilizes, inspires the law bound worlds of form.

Figure 5   The sweep of the Earth's axis

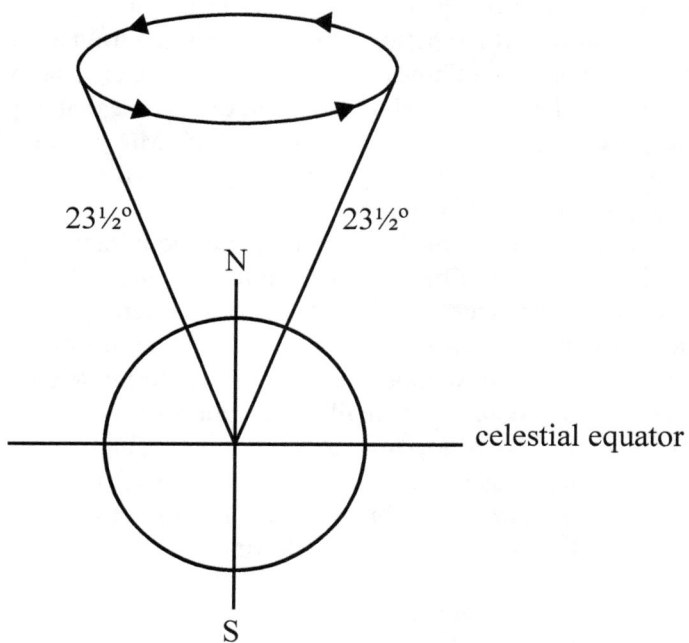

celestial equator

Houses

Every day Earth physically rotates on its axis.[4] This self-centered spin expresses its subjective planetary consciousness. A rotation carries every point on its surface through a complete orbit of its own center and a 360° perspective on the surrounding cosmos.

During Earth's daily rotation every planet assumes every position in relation to the degree rising over its eastern horizon at any point on the globe (ascendant). All 360 degrees rise, culminate, set and plumb the nadir, on the other side of Earth beneath our feet. All planets, each in their degree, do the same. Thus Saturn might be rising as Sun sets, Venus halfway toward culmination as Jupiter sinks down the western sky. Etc.

Obviously, if astrological symbolism has any truth, then the planetary positions in our experienced sky here on Earth are at least as important as their position in relation to distant stars. For example, on a given day Mars might be in four degrees of the sign of Cancer. But during that day it will also rise, culminate, set and pass on the far side of the world because of Earth's rotation.

A planet in a sign proposes a theme on an abstract level. A planet's position relative to Earth's rotation processes that theme on a psychological level. A planet's position in the zodiac indicates the objective, impersonal role it plays in the solar system's energy pattern. Its simultaneous position in our earthly sky indicates the subjective, personal role it plays in a life. Its sign degree portrays what aspect of solar purpose focuses through the planet's qualitative lens (of mind, love, will, etc.). Its relationship to the rising degree on Earth portrays how we assimilate, experience and express that purpose in our own life.

As Earth rotates it subjectively experiences a twelve-fold terrestrial zodiac parallel to that in the sky. Its divisions are called houses. These houses form an earthly grounding of cosmic force fields (signs). They map our internal response to objective seasonal energies. Houses embody an inner structure of personal consciousness and collective sensitivities defined at the moment of birth just as signs describe the day/night cycle of a year.

All twelve signs rise every 24 hours (except at the poles). Thus ideally a new sign rises every two hours, a new degree every four minutes. However, because of the differing lengths of day and night during the year the actual times vary. The subject of house division is somewhat technical (see appendix), but the basic idea is simple. Houses are measured along the arc between two objective points: ascendant (consciousness) rising over the horizon, and midheaven (achievement) culminating at the highest point of the zodiac in the sky at any given

Figure 6 Angles of the day

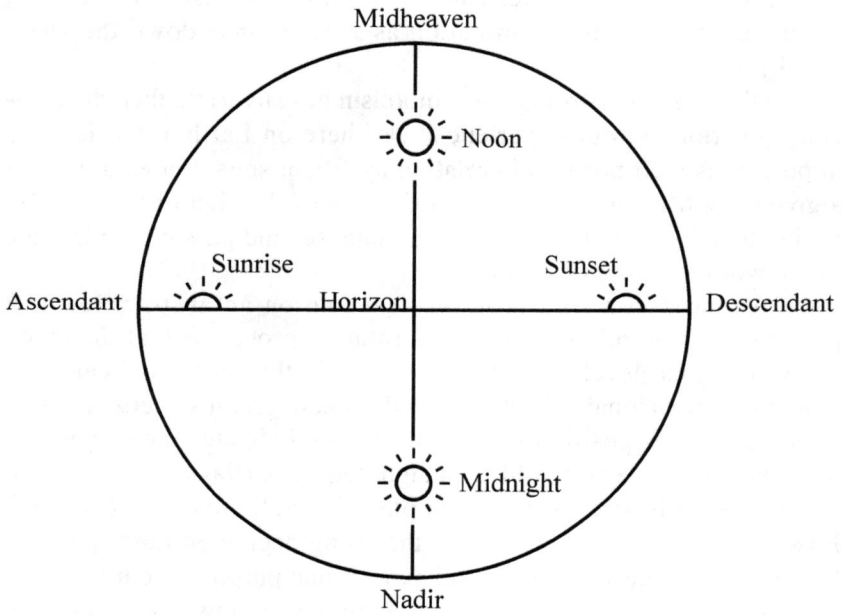

Figure 7   Divisions of the chart

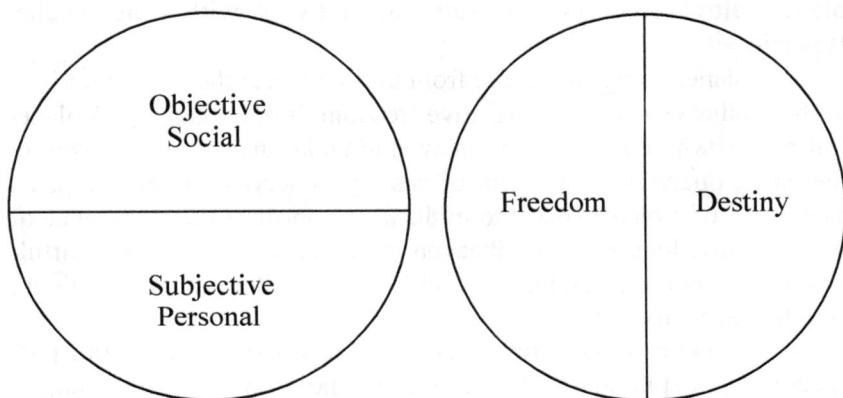

Objective
Social

Subjective
Personal

Freedom   Destiny

Figure 8   Quadrants of the chart

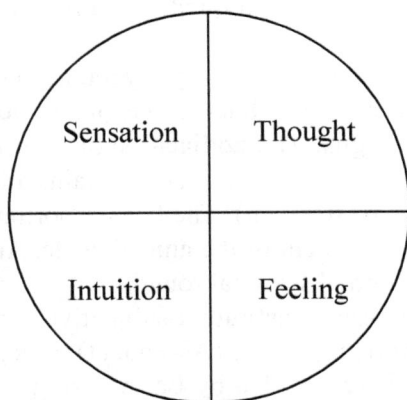

Sensation   Thought

Intuition   Feeling

time. They each have a counterpart: descendant (other) setting, and nadir (source) on the far side of the world. Figures 6, 7, and 8.

Physical positions and movements parallel their psychological significance. A planet above the horizon operates consciously, with demonstrable results in the objective environment. It can be seen. A planet below the horizon operates subjectively, within the psyche. It is felt.

A planet rising, anywhere from the nadir over the eastern horizon to the midheaven, acts with relative freedom. It does its thing. A planet falling, anywhere from the midheaven to under the western horizon to the nadir, operates as an agent of destiny. It serves a larger purpose. The rising of a planet (nadir to midheaven) portrays the emergence of individuality. Its setting (midheaven to nadir) portrays social fruitfulness or consequences. Objective/subjective; freedom/destiny: both are equally necessary.

All planets pass through four arcs of movement from our perspective on a spinning Earth. From rising point to midheaven: objective, individual, free. From midheaven to descendant (before they drop below the horizon): objective, social, destined. Descendant to nadir: subjective, social, destined. Nadir to ascendant: subjective, individual, free. All of these are relative terms. Anything below the horizon is subjective, hidden beneath Earth. Its western quadrant (descendant to nadir) demonstrates how personality responds to others' expectations. The eastern quadrant is more purely personal. Everything above the horizon is objective, visible in the sky. Its eastern quadrant (ascendant to midheaven) demonstrates the results of individual purpose projected out into the world. The western quadrant portrays fateful encounter with the Other.

These quadrants are trisected (by several trigonometric methods) to form twelve houses. (See 'House Division.') These twelve houses parallel the twelve signs. The zodiacal signs can be considered as twelve lunar phases of a solar year. Each contains a full moon-th, plus change (the quotient of freedom). The houses portray their subjective analog. An inner reenactment of the annual cycle. An internal unfolding, mirroring the external seasonal round.

The twelve houses constitute a subjective circle, our personal year. It begins at the rising degree (Ascendant). A degree of the zodiac measures the orbital arc traveled by Earth during one rotation (day). The ascendant marks the specific degree coming up over the eastern horizon at a particular instant in time. Here Earth turns into a unit of space, a day's perspective on Sun, that had just been hidden below the surface. Thus the ascendant symbolizes the emergence of consciousness from underground. A revelation of buried treasure. A moment of discovery.

The Ascendant ignites a dawn of awareness. A sunrise of self. It awakens personality, generating personal ego out of solar purpose, lunar heritage and planetary attributes. It acts as the tipping point where a rising degree, the essence of a whole new day, bursts into the light of consciousness. By this light you see all things. The ascendant shows one's point of view, angle of vision, on all the planetary constituents of personality. Any planets rising in its 1st house domain describe energies coming to life, taking center stage.

An astrological chart takes a snapshot of these planetary sub-personalities as they were at the moment you were turned on, at your first breath. What was rising, what was falling. Where the planets were in relation to Earth's rotation reveals how they operate in the personal psychology. Just as a DNA gene expresses different potentials depending on its biochemical environment, so a planetary factor displays various modes of behavior according to its hour in the subjective day. A planet's dawning evokes other qualities than its nooning, or its passage through the depths of night. Saturn, way out in space, will always be Saturn. But on our world, Earth, its energy will be experienced differently when it rises than when it culminates or drops halfway below the horizon.

The ascendant rose on Earth's horizon when you yourself arose out of the womb. It portrays a personal stance towards the energy field in which one is immersed. From this vantage point ego sees and acts. Out of it radiate the various planetary paths, each headed a certain way. Mars may orient towards the pursuit of desire (2nd house) while Jupiter inclines towards the fulfillment of duty (6th house). Saturn may present its challenge in the house of mind (3rd) while a crescent Moon wanes in the house of death (8th).

Where the planets are located in our Earthly sky depends on one's position on its surface during its daily rotation. We measure this from its leading edge, the rising eastern horizon of the ascendant. From the ascendant derive twelve houses, the twelve inner signs. These provide a psychological medium in which planetary qualities gestate and grow.

All of the houses, departments of experience, stem from the ascendant. It shines as the white light from which they refract as a rainbow. The personal dawn from which their day of life unfolds. Each of the house angles (ascendant, nadir, descendant and midheaven) initiates a season of consciousness:

The ascendant ignites a springtime of possibility (Intuition). Its houses are those of personal will (1), desire (2) and mind (3).

The nadir opens a summer of emotion (Feeling). It manifests as personal subjectivity (4), creativity (5) and self-purification through service (6).

The descendant begins a fall from inner grace into outer participation with others (Thought): relationship (7), transformation (8) and meaning (9).

The midheaven initiates a winter of impersonal objectivity (Sensation): career (10), guiding theory and abstract ideals (11) and karma or sacrifice/redemption (12).[5]

Each of these functions contrasts with its opposite/complement above and below the horizon of consciousness. Thus sensation forms an objective polarity to subjective intuition; thought promotes collective communication in contrast to the private depths of feeling. Each also pairs up with its opposite/complement east and west of the vertical meridian of freedom/destiny. Thus intuition and sensation both act with relative freedom because they involve open possibility (intuition) or unbiased perception of fact (sensation). They accept what is out there. Feeling and thought both invoke a fateful destiny because they judge the relative merit of emotions or ideas. They make decisions with consequences.

Ascendant: The 1st house begins at the ascendant. It includes that which lies just below the horizon, rising into consciousness. What one was literally turning into at birth. Primary perception, immediate experience. Identity. Sense of self. Ego.

Sun shows fundamental purpose; Moon subconscious psyche. The ascendant portrays conscious identification with and enactment of these energies. As such it is by far the most important house. All other houses constitute its attributes.

As a statement of individual consciousness and will the Ascendant and its 1st house constitute a subjective parallel to the initiating spark of Aries, the sign. Each subsequent house similarly reflects the nature of its own parallel sign: 2nd -Taurus, 3rd - Gemini, 4th - Cancer, 5th - Leo, 6th - Virgo, 7th - Libra, 8th - Scorpio, 9th - Sagittarius, 10th - Capricorn, 11th - Aquarius, 12th - Pisces. Figure 9.

The Ascendant began with one's first breath. Self then assumed an independent existence, activated by the universe as it was configured at that moment. The Ascendant, with its evanescent states of consciousness, melds all attributes (planets) into a unified state of being: the ego. Ego projects a summary of their latent potentials and realized qualities into the world as a visible personality.

Figure 9 Cycle of the houses

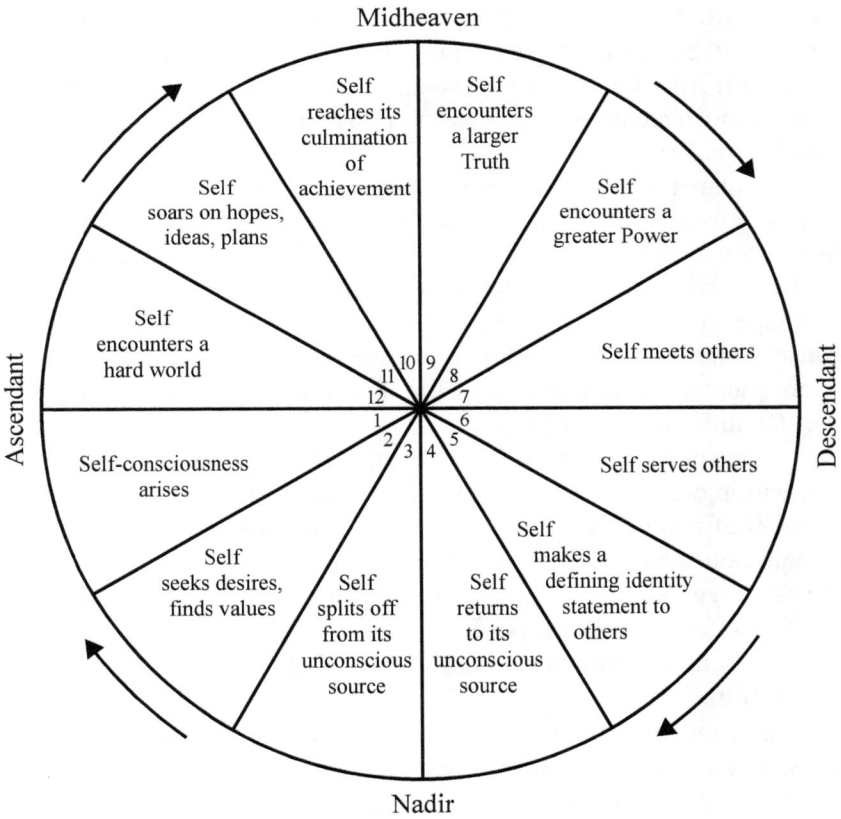

Midheaven

Self reaches its culmination of achievement

Self encounters a larger Truth

Self soars on hopes, ideas, plans

Self encounters a greater Power

Self encounters a hard world

Self meets others

Ascendant

Descendant

Self-consciousness arises

Self serves others

Self seeks desires, finds values

Self makes a defining identity statement to others

Self splits off from its unconscious source

Self returns to its unconscious source

Nadir

Personal consciousness can express at any level of evolution. And with any degree of authenticity. It can role-play social expectations, or manipulative ego games. Genuinely demonstrate an existent nature, or grow it through disciplines of self-actualization. That depends on personal choice. Choice implies alternatives. The Ascendant provides an array of options along a particular line of development. It orients self to the universe through a certain type of awareness. It functions through a quality of will, consciously exercised or unconsciously abdicated.

The Ascendant reveals one's decision-making process. The rationale prioritizing planetary motives into actual behavior. It implies an intention: who and what one means to be. This can operate on a subconscious instinctual level; or on a robotic, socially conditioned plane; as an individualized conscious identity; or as the human face of a higher, transpersonal will.

A planet rising in the 1st house makes the cutting edge of a chart. It serves as a focal point expressing the entire planetary pattern. If more than a single planet rises then either intense concentration or conflict result. Or the 1st house may be empty. In that case the position and aspects of the rising sign's planetary ruler modify its quality of consciousness. Its sign and house location indicates a specialization of interest and effort in that area of life. For planetary rulers of the signs see 'Dignities and Debilities.'

Sun (purpose), Moon (psyche) and other planets are power centers within our field of awareness. The Ascendant focuses them into a moment of revelatory awakening. Its 1st house gives this a continuity of consciousness, depth of meaning. The 1st house often extends into the next sign. This makes it less intense but more complex. Figure 10.

The 2nd house, deeper into Earth's body, holds the resources that ego-consciousness has to draw upon. The values and valuables it can mobilize.

The most basic resource is a body. The physical constitution; its hereditary strengths and weaknesses. Care or abuse of it. The visceral sense of self. The nature of sensuality. Appreciation of beauty: where found, how expressed. A subjective evaluation of the good, the true and the beautiful.

The next level of resource consists of material possessions. These are a social endowment to the individual, usually measured in monetary terms. Things bought and sold, at a profit or loss. The 2nd house describes an attitude towards and use of them. Possession of or by them. Are they fetish objects, or instruments of a higher objective. On a more abstract plane, it portrays psycho-spiritual attributes. Do you

Figure 10   A house can include two sign energies

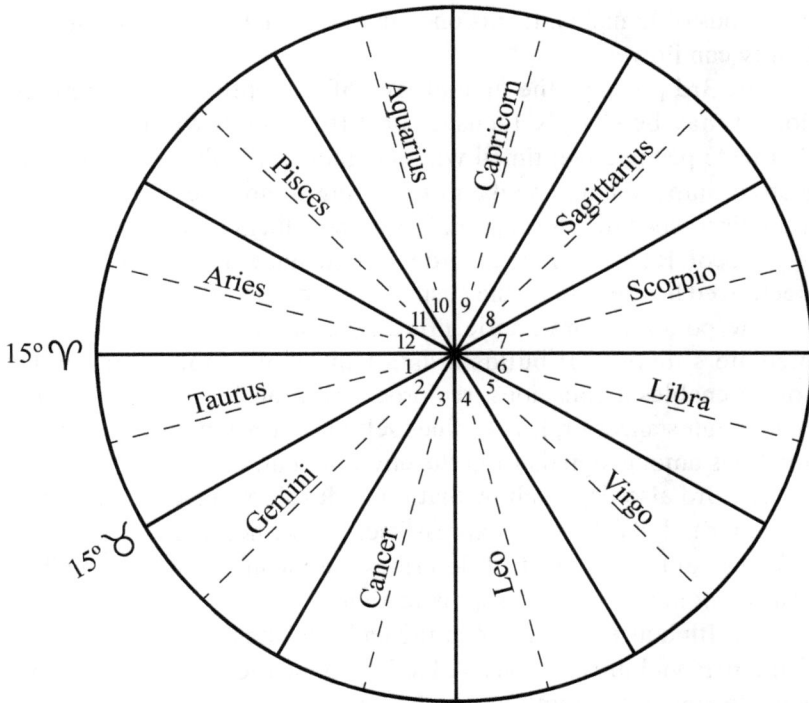

——————— solid lines = houses
- - - - - broken lines = signs

In this case 15° of Aries rises. The second half of Aries and first half of Taurus are contained within the first house.

'have' courage (Mars) or 'lack' faith (Jupiter)? Planets in the 2nd indicate specific qualities in the process of gain or loss.

Most importantly, the 2nd describe one's deepest desire: the pearl of great price. Behind the conscious attitude of the 1st house lie the bedrock values of the 2nd. What do you really want? Here you will find it.

The 3rd house elucidates the nature and quality of mind. Mind splits self off from tangible sensuality (2nd), and from the collective unconscious (4th: nadir). It cuts one out of the background so that individuality can flower.

The 3rd portrays the mental lens of perception and communication. It may be sharply focused, or diffuse; narrowly oriented, or with a wide perspective; tinted with an emotional coloration, or clear, objective, impersonal. The data processing mind filters facts from a surrounding ocean of information. It processes them according to a specific protocol. Ranks them in an order of relevance. These functions are characterized by the sign on the cusp of the 3rd, and by any planets in it.

The concrete, pragmatic mind assesses and manipulates the immediate situation. It builds a data bank that enables and guides action. It enables a conscious, reciprocal relationship with the people in, and circumstances of, life. Defines self in contrast to others. Clarifies distinctions among signals from the environment.

The 3rd also depicts how that mind develops: its education, formal or informal; its ability to express itself; its subjects of interest. How one thinks, and about what. It describes the means by which intellect operates, but not its level of sophistication.

The 4th house, beginning at the nadir, locates the deep source of self: the personal unconscious. A feeling foundation. The womb from which one comes, the tomb to which one goes.

Whereas the 1st house displays the conscious light of ego-identity, the 4th points to the dark mystery of origins and destiny. The nadir defines a psychological center of gravity. The emotional taproot connecting ego with the depths of subjectivity. The most private and personal expression of inner being.

The 4th starts at the bottom of the chart, at its closest to one's heart. This interior dimension has several layers. The personal unconscious: a mass of fleeting and forgotten impressions; a reservoir of formative emotional experiences reaching all the way back to infancy; profound, inarticulate memories of the birth trauma; and a fundamental instinctual orientation to life. Behind and beneath that lies the collective unconscious: participation in the shared memory of our species, and of its ancestral lineage all the way back to our oceanic origins.

This is mediated by a subconscious memory of womb-life inside mother. One recapitulated all of evolution while washed in her hormonal tides. The brain grew stimulated, lit up, irradiated with her bioelectric aura. A developing identity lived within the force field of her larger consciousness in the most literal, physical way.

Astrology claims that this experience continues after birth within Earth's planetary womb. If so, the 4th house constitutes its placenta. The nourishing medium connecting a known self with the roots of personality; the deep commonalities of our species and of all life; the mysterious center of an entire world.

The sign on the 4th cusp describes life's beginning: infancy and childhood. And its end, absorption back into the universe. A sense of home and security. Any planets in it provide a window into self's most private area.

Eventually ego steps out from behind the curtain onto life's stage. The 5th house refers to creative self-expression. Every individual has a unique charisma. And a special role to play. Here personality shines forth as a gift to the world. Or an imposition on it.

Creations may be biological children, cultural contributions, social initiatives or spiritual attainments. On whatever level, they are one's pride and joy. The 5th reveals a pursuit of happiness. The place of pleasure. It can express through frivolity and cheap thrills to pretentious ego tripping. Or as the generosity of a noble spirit to the humble heart of love. It follows Bliss: from simple fun to soul-stirring glory. Or from the vanities of narcissism to a sadistic glee of domination. The radiance of warm blooded emotion. Or the radioactivity of an ego fetish.

Creations express love: sacred or profane, demonic or divine. Any planets in the 5th reveal who and what one loves. The sign on its cusp describes how one loves. If this house is empty, look to its ruler (of the cusp sign). This indicates love sublimated from immediate gratification into development of a beloved element expressed elsewhere in the chart.

The 6th house describes a crisis of individuation. It tests and reforms subjective character, that half of the chart below the horizon (houses 1 through 6). It completes and cleanses self in preparation to meet the challenges of social objectivity above the horizon (houses 7 through 12).

The 6th reveals basic flaws through experiences of failure, humiliation, inadequacy. Thus one learns to correct them. The sign on its cusp points towards the appropriate techniques of self-improvement. Any planet in it requires these disciplines to salvage and renovate its function. Purging of undesirable qualities. Perfecting of chosen attributes.

It can evade truth by fixating on side issues and irrelevant details. Then the moral cowardice of dishonesty sinks into self-loathing. This can be projected outwards as nagging criticism. Or worked on by living up to the difficult demands of its real function: to own guilt and overcome shame, turning weakness into strength.

Purity: of body (health), emotional nature (service) and of mind (integrity of intellect and character). It operates through characteristic stresses to perform its labor of repair and refinement. Sickness forces attention on the body, so often taken for granted. Work regiments the self in service to the community. Rituals of discipline develop into habits of devotion. Duty intensifies into dharma, one's true role in the world beyond the horizon of skin and skull.

The 7th: 'No man is an island.'[6] Every self exists in context. The environment shapes us. You are defined as much by response to its danger/opportunities as by an inner nature.

The descendant (7th) portrays encounter with a larger world beyond the self. General personality, or a planetary attribute, defined by its social role. The character evoked by actual behavior. What others see. How one sees them. How ego acts in, and is acted upon by, the community. The judgment of peers.

Encounter with the Other. Self enters into relationships, amicable or adversarial. Planets in the 7th describe the qualities of close associates, whether friends or enemies. The law of attraction: who one relates to and why. The most important relationship: marriage. The general character of this partner. Sometimes s/he lives that nature on a different evolutionary level, causing discord.

The descendant also poses life's greatest challenge, the most difficult question one must answer. Confrontation with alien forms of truth, emotional as well as mental. The necessity of broadening a stance, enlarging self's scope, to deal with the emergence, and emergency, of an unexpected reality.

The sign on the 7th cusp depicts the kind of equilibrium reached with outside forces. Planets in it reveal those energies themselves, manifesting through other people. That requires adaptation and develops negotiating skills.

The 8th depicts an internal metamorphosis through such interaction. The impact of forces that irrevocably change identity. Psychological transformation wrought by contact with energies based on different values. These can be instincts erupting from within. Or perceptions imposed by circumstances beyond control. One does not negotiate with 8th house demands but conforms to their larger than personal requirements, willingly or not.

Character tested by ordeal. This enlarges or destroys identity. Any planetary function in the 8th is subject to death and rebirth. Or acts as its agent for the whole personality. Attitude to death: the little deaths of outworn feelings, ideas or projects. And the great mystery of a final ending. The 4th describes a transpersonal soul from which self comes and to which it returns. The 8th reveals the subjective experience of its ego eating demands.

Intense emotional passion as the 8th strips away an old identity. And ignites an impulse to renewal. Any planet in the 8th burns its bridges. Feels desolation and despair; the loss of everything it had taken for granted. This creates a space evoking hidden powers. It grows or shrivels in response to inescapable necessity. Ability to regenerate. Who emerges from its fire.

The 7th established relationships based on reciprocity and mutual respect (even if antagonistic). In the 8th this relationship becomes a merger. It ranges from ecstatic union to hostile takeover. The orgasmic release of self in sex to its annihilation in the maw of death.

The 8th is also about our need as social beings to identify with a larger corporate purpose. What one gives to, or takes from, the communal enterprise. The 10th shows the objective outcome of that participation.

The 9th signifies an experience of religious and philosophical meaning. The sense of a higher law beyond personal interest. It describes abstract thought: how mind deals with concepts rather than facts. A general philosophical orientation is described by the sign on its cusp and focused by any planets in it.

This overall worldview constitutes a religious or spiritual outlook. Modern atheistic or secular humanist visions fulfill this function just as much as traditional systems of theology or private mystical experiences. (Which is not to say that they are all equally valid.)

On a more mundane level it portrays an ideological bias towards the social environment. The nature of moral and ethical guidelines. A political attitude. How expressed. It does not specify a particular agenda or program. Rather it depicts a general stance taken towards the community at large and the issues of the day. Principles or beliefs by which society should be organized.

Participation in consensus reality, cooperation in implementing a standing social contract. It grows the given, enhances and enlarges an agreed process. The 11th house generates novel insight; the 9th fits that into an accepted framework of meaning, gives it social expression.

The 9th is an expansive house. It stretches horizons beyond the immediate. It portrays encounters with or inspiration by the foreign, exotic, alien. This may include physical travel to distant places, or mental stimulation by different cultures or past eras. It broadens the scope of an existent consciousness. It can become too enthusiastic about these exciting big ideas. Thus it needs the grounding of its 3rd house polarity: the concrete mind.

The 10th house marks the summit of actual achievement. True vocation. Purpose. Status. This may be very different in the eyes of God than of society. Rank can reflect merit. Or usurp unearned privilege.

Each of us depends on a community, not only for personal survival, but also for its accumulated knowledge, skills and level of organization. These enable individual expression. The 10th house depicts how one repays that endowment by performing a social function. The sign on its cusp, the Midheaven,[7] portrays the nature of one's office or profession. Any planet in it portrays an energy conscripted from private enjoyment into communal use. The 6th describes work or service. The 10th demonstrates public recognition, and the authority that goes with it. Influence over others, for good or ill. It holds a collective trust and describes how it is discharged. The use or abuse of power. Competence and responsible stewardship, or cynical manipulation, of group energies.

The 10th can also indicate initiation into a more advanced state of consciousness. An apex of evolution, height of attainment. It can lead to transfiguration, baptism into a life more abundant. Acceptance of a spiritual* energy that displaces ego. The 10th plugs one into a higher power.

* Soul (4th) refers to a psychological essence, stripped of personal quirks. Spirit (10th) refers to a transcendent power, a divine law.

All achievement, however impressive, is limited and conditional. It eventually crystallizes and freezes out. The 11th house brings forth the power to imagine a new order based on more inclusive principles. The vision of a better future.

Here are the hopes, wishes, aspirations that inspire one to soar above circumstance. These can be escapist fantasies, impractical castles in the clouds. Or a genuine revelation leading to real transformation. The sign on the cusp of the 11th describes the nature of ideals. Any planets in it show how they are actualized. These ideals are not personal desires, but an impersonal vision of the way life should be.

The 11th demonstrates how one seeks to regenerate the public domain through collective endeavor. It can refer to political engagement, spiritual discovery, scientific inquiry or technological inventiveness. A truth quest involving larger than personal issues. If frustrated, or inherently twisted, it can degenerate into eccentricity or rebellion: cultural, religious or political.

The 11th defines a sense of utopia, an ideal society, and of how best to achieve it. To accomplish this requires allies. Thus it indicates friendships based on shared interests; associations, coalitions, alliances aimed at social or spiritual concerns. It sketches a detached, logical blueprint to make the world better. If the initial premise is flawed it can lead to disaster. Yet without it there would be no consciously planned action toward qualitative breakthrough as opposed to quantitative increase. It portrays the seed vision of a new reality. An ability to enlist others to that end. The effort to generate a new paradigm, in a small group or on a global stage.

Higher, or stranger, dimensions of thought. Uncharted territories of mind. Revelatory insights. The source of originality, or of madness. An articulation of spiritual inspirations, scientific paradigms and socio-political programs.

Finally, the 12th: exile from both personal certainty and social consensus. Surrender to the Will of God. Self-undoing: the same process that drives a larva to swaddle itself in a cocoon and dissolve - to emerge as a butterfly. Or a housefly. Extremes of salvation or degradation through self-abnegation. Letting go of the past, renunciation of current identity and preparation for rebirth. Few do this voluntarily. Therefore the 12th often involves sorrows, stemming from resistance to necessary change.

Payment of debts, making up for errors and crimes of the ending cycle. The 12th is the house of karma: meeting the ghosts of the past, to redeem or be haunted by them. Karma can be understood as accounts receivable or payable from previous lives. Or from sins of omission and commission in this one. Or as taking on the needs, anxieties and dilemmas of the collective environment. It involves paying dues before enjoying the privilege of rebirth. It describes the final duties of collective engagement before personal release at the ascendant. It must face all of self's, and society's, unfinished business, unresolved conflicts, unconscious issues in order to clear the decks for a new beginning.

Ego disintegrates in the exhaustion of an old cycle. This is a precondition for what comes next. In that naked defenseless condition it encounters forgotten, suppressed issues, both personal and communal. Naturally one resists. Few want to face their own ghosts or serve as a public scapegoat. Thus the 12th becomes a fated house, of encounter with such problems until one voluntarily renounces self-interest and identity for a greater good.

This grows the heart. The fortunate are smug. Those who must take the hit are broken open, hopefully to a larger self. That process is painful. Thus this marks the house of sorrows. Out of sorrow comes compassion and a more universal love. Salvation through suffering - if such suffering can be accepted as submission to a higher will, a greater good than personal pleasure. Thus, in the extremity of despair, the darkest hour before the dawn, a purified soul meets God in love for the most wretched of its fellows.

The houses outline a personal perspective on planetary energies. They map the qualities of the most important planet of all: Earth, on which we live. Earth, when and where you were born, may have had a Saturnine 2nd house, or a Mercurial one. A house may be emphasized by the presence of planets, or relatively latent without them. For some work is the center of attention, for others relationship, or the life of the mind.

If a house contains no planets its role in life can be contemplated by examining the ruler of its cuspal sign. For example, if Virgo forms the cusp of an empty 7th house (relationship and marriage) look to the position and aspects of Mercury, Virgo's ruler, to understand the nature and circumstances of significant encounters with others.

The time of day shows how one perceives and enacts solar spirit. Dawn has a different feel than midnight or mid-afternoon. The rising degree defines your private take on purpose (Sun), psyche (Moon) and the various worlds of experience. The culminating degree (midheaven) shows what you make of them in this world. The ten other house orientations, charted from these two points, describe how and why.

Directions and Progressions

We follow Sun's fiery path from our solid-state reality here on Earth. That reality rotates. Each revolution on its axis carries any point on Earth through every aspect, or relationship, to Sun. Every day it experiences and expresses the full circle of solar possibility.

At dawn Sun 'rises' in the east as Earth turns towards it. By noon Sun has ascended to its highest overhead culmination as Earth most fully faces it. At sunset Earth turns completely away from Sun, and by midnight its entire globe beneath our feet blocks out Sun. In compensation, planets, stars and the galaxy itself emerge.

This daily round strikingly resembles the yearly cycle. Dawn = spring, noon = summer, sunset = fall, midnight = winter.

The day is a miniature year. It makes up our basic unit of experience. One degree of the zodiac maps the spatial equivalent of one day in time. Primary directions portray an astrological dynamic based on the fact that every four minutes after birth another degree rises over the eastern horizon.[7] During that short time a new daily unit of consciousness emerges into manifestation.

Based on the principle that a day miniaturizes a year, the next degree rising, four minutes after birth, symbolizes a new 'directed' ascendant congruent with the second year of life. And so on: the degree rising 120 minutes, or two hours, after birth corresponds to an evolution of the ascendant's self-consciousness thirty years after birth ($4 \times 30 = 120$). This will always be in the next sign, as there are 30 degrees per sign. Thus the nature of our self-awareness unfolds in a predictable way, quite apart from its experiences. The field of consciousness incrementally expands. It gains new ground in an orderly manner.

Primary directions chart this growing flow of awareness. This technique projects the leading edge of consciousness forward into new frontiers of experience. All other houses, subjective departments of life, are derived from the ascendant. They too move forward, synchronized at the same rate (one degree every four minutes). Thus the overall pattern is maintained as it sweeps like a net through the zodiac.

For example, a person with 10° Taurus rising will always have that baseline perspective on life. It describes an inherent psychological outlook, a given attitude. This, of course, can be lived at any height, or depth, of evolution. But it also evolves through time, gaining new qualities, encountering novel challenges. At age one, the directed ascendant will be at 11° Taurus. At age 20 it will meet another dimension of concern/interest/priority as it enters a new sign: 1° Gemini. A previously solid, dependable cast of mind will begin to entertain serious alternatives to its previously accepted state. It will open up to different possibilities of understanding. Or splinter in confusion, paralyzed by a now divided counsel, disconcerted by unfamiliar options. At age 50 this crisis of consciousness will repeat, in a different manner, as the directed ascendant enters yet another sign: 1° Cancer.

All other house cusps move in tandem with the ascendant. As they, like it, encounter new signs, or sweep across natal planetary positions, they will experience a crisis/opportunity in their area of life. For example, the person with 10° Taurus rising may have a 2nd house cusp (desires, possessions, finances) at 15° Gemini. At age 15 that cusp will move into Cancer. There will be a crisis, involving 2nd house matters, taking a Cancerian form.

There will be yet another second house revolution/revelation at age 35 as the original ascendant (10° Taurus) meets the natal 2nd house cusp (15° Gemini). This will involve a general review of how 2nd house affairs fit into the big picture. A reevaluation of the overall importance of the 2nd house in life. The 2nd house profile will rise, fall or otherwise change in the larger scheme of things.

Secondary progressions are based on the same principle as primary directions. They involve the movement of planetary functions rather than a rotation of the wheel of consciousness. The difference is that planets orbit at different speeds whereas the round of houses glides forward at a uniform rate. The essential truth that one day equals one year remains the same. The technique of calculation differs. This is because, while directions involve the unfolding of our Earth centered awareness, progressions involve the independent and differential movement of other planets.

'Primary' does not imply an outranking of 'secondary,' any more than one is 'better' than two. 'Secondary' simply describes a different level of abstraction applied to energies out there in space rather than right here on Earth. In fact, progressions are far more widely used in astrological practice. Specific subpersonalities (planets) evolve at different rates. Tides of mood (Moon) express more quickly than the generational rhythms of collective history (Pluto). Progressions describe the unfolding of these multiple, interacting processes as opposed to the more monolithic approach of purely ascendant-derived directions.

'What a difference a day makes' - especially the day you were born. For with your first breath as an autonomous being you were turned on by the energy state of the solar system at that moment. The universe spoke through you. Partly as a statement of infinity potentially expressed at every moment of the Now. And partly as a developmental process unfolding through time.

For, if the day is a miniature year, then every day after birth symbolizes a succeeding year. The distribution of planetary energies one day (year) after birth is slightly different than it was on the day you were born. The pattern continues to shift every day of your life.

Each day Sun moves one zodiacal degree, one day of the year, $\frac{1}{360}$ of a circle, into the future. That may not seem like much. But within a month it will have moved into the next astrological sign. Each sign has 30 degrees. By age 30 at the latest, and usually much earlier, your developmental path will have entered a fundamentally different, stimulating or frustrating, terrain. Your given psyche is challenged by another phase of reality, which never stays put. By age 60, almost always earlier, this will have happened yet again.

Every other planetary function also evolves. All planets move along an accelerating, decelerating or even retrograde curve. They can travel relatively fast and far, or slow and deep. Sometimes even apparently backwards, from Earth's perspective, thus recalibrating their operating procedure. (See 'Solar Aspects and Retrogradation.') These movements spell out the development of specific qualities through childhood and adolescence, maturity and old age.

Mercury (mind) generally moves quickly, sometimes faster than Sun. Venus, desire, also often moves pretty fast. These two, inside Earth's orbit, are subjective inner factors that always travel in proximity to Sun. Mars, first planet outside Earth's orbit, moves more slowly, just over half Sun's speed on average. Its motion, as seen from Earth, is the first completely independent of Sun's, as is appropriate for the significator of personal will. The distant gas giants move very slowly by human standards. Jupiter, social role and spiritual soul, may at most move through half a sign, or perhaps enter a new sign, in the course of the 70 or so days miniaturizing a normal lifetime. Saturn, ultimate lawgiver, moves just a few degrees during this period. In any life the impersonal background changes at a much slower pace than individual experience. The outer planets, Uranus, Neptune, Pluto, representing strata of the collective unconscious, move very little over the few decades of a life-span represented by the 70 or so days after birth.

Moon, circling Earth, weaves all these functions into the mystery of personality. Moon moves quickly, at an average of 13° per day. Thus Moon progresses entirely around the zodiac every 29½ days (years), passing through every phase: new, waxing, full, waning, back to a new in the next sign. It articulates the complete range of our emotional response to inner emergence and outer circumstance.

These movements are called progressions. They display the inherent unfolding of the psychic situation initiated at birth. Psyche blooms over time. The dynamics of this process are paralleled by planetary movements in the days and months after birth.

Transits

Transits mean the objective positions of the planets in the sky at any time other than birth. For example, where they are right now. If one or more transiting planets aspects (makes contact with) a sensitive point in the birth chart it will activate or stimulate that function or area of consciousness. Sensitive points include natal planets and house cusps. And, to a lesser extent, progressed and directed planets/cusps (see above).

Transits trigger events. The transiting planet(s) generates action. It does so according to its own nature and that of the transited point. Transits are catalysts, bringing to the surface latent energies whose time has come. Thus transits differ from directions and progressions, which are inherent unfoldings. Transits symbolize challenges from the environment. Or emanating from the unconscious. They force one to meet a demand arising from circumstances out there, or the uncharted depths within.

Transits show what life throws at you. Without them we would live in a solipsistic world of pure subjectivity. Transits bring ego face to face with the other, and with otherness, as forces existing in their own right. They provide objective content. They galvanize the adventure of life, action, events.

Transits of the fast moving inner planets are more ephemeral and personal than those of the slow moving outer worlds. Moon is by far the fastest. Its transits indicate the ever changing coloration of emotion as we respond like chameleons to our surroundings.

Mercury's depict the permutations of mind, thought and communication on a day to day basis. Venus' the constantly shifting tides of love, pleasure, desire. Mars' confrontations, tests of will, provoked by self or others.

Transits of the slower social/spiritual planets, Jupiter and Saturn, generate life changing decisions, fundamental turning points. Jupiter's provide opportunity, Saturn's test one's mettle in adversity. Outer planet transits (Uranus, Neptune, Pluto) indicate historical and generational issues demanding a response, like it or not. They can also portray eruptions from the deep unconscious, that layer of self beyond ego. This can be creative or traumatic. That mainly depends on openness to a larger sense of identity behind the image or mask we so carefully craft for ourselves and others.

The Solar Return is a special technique by which the transiting positions and relationships of the planets are noted each year when Sun returns to the exact spot it occupied at birth. They portray the nature of the coming year within the subjective framework of whatever zodiacal degree rises at that moment.

These dynamics provide another proof that astrology is not a deterministic straitjacket as so many believe. The birth chart is indeed a form of fate. It outlines and anchors an identity: 'Character is destiny.' That fate can be lived on any level of consciousness, at any intensity of participation. Directions, progressions and transits provide an inseparable element of change. Change always opens the door to the exercise of free will and the experience of chance.

An astrological chart is not a static blueprint. It describes an evolving psychological genome. It mutates and transforms according to dynamics inherent in its origins. The lawfulness of that dynamic manifests in the guiding principles of directions and progressions. What one makes of them is largely a matter of free will, punctuated by the environmental stimuli known as planetary transits.

As a parallel example: the biological genome was once thought of as a linear code, exfoliating mechanically. It is now seen as a responsive feedback loop shaped by environmental and internal biochemical conditions. A sequence of nucleotides, such as t-i-m-e was thought to have only a single meaning: a unidirectional flow of events. We now realize that these nucleotides can be, and often are, rearranged to produce other information, such as: item, emit and mite. This is known as alternative splicing.[8] A biological genome is actually flexible and even creative.

In the same way, an astrological genome, or chart, can manifest in a variety of ways depending on internal intention and external events. Directions and progressions outline the programmed flowering of its qualities. Transits spotlight environmental catalysts. The key, but indefinable, unpredictable, factor is the subjective will to evolve.

The birth chart is a seed. Directions, progressions and transits flesh out its growth, blossoming and fruitfulness. A nativity is an archetype. These temporal movements describe its evolution and actual life process. The level on which one lives them are a matter of considerable free will. The integrity and intensity with which one expresses them are the subjects of moral choice.

Notes

1. Vernal equinox to summer solstice and summer solstice to autumnal equinox
2. Autumnal equinox to winter solstice and winter solstice to vernal equinox
3. One = identity. Two = relationship: self and not-self, I and Thou. Three = process: thesis, antithesis, synthesis; past, present, future; birth, life, death.
4. Earth also has an independent magnetic spin, generated by its molten iron core. This portrays a more ethereal planetary soul, an inherent spiritual quality distinct from its changing states of consciousness over time (such as during the seasons of the year). This internal polarity generates a magnetic field that shields us from solar winds of charged particles. Without it Earth's surface would be seared by invisible fire and life would be impossible. Just as intangible soul, vitality or life

force animates a physical body so a shimmering magnetic field way out in space nurtures a biological realm here on Earth.

Earth's magnetic spin axis tilts even more than its physical spin. The north magnetic pole is currently located at 70° 5' North, 96° 46' West while its south magnetic pole is at 72° 40' South, 152° 30' East. These slowly moving polarities are not 180° opposite each other: once again, physical reality always diverges from its mathematical idealization.

5. One might question assigning abstract Aquarius and dreamy, almost disembodied, Pisces to the sensation function. However sensation is impersonal and objective. Sensation accords with the impartial, inclusive universality of these last two signs, in contrast to the more individual subjectivity of the preceding ten. One might also question assigning passionate Scorpio to the thought quadrant. However, thought demands an antithesis, a necessary negation, in order to carry out its judging function. Scorpio serves that need by probing ideas for their fatal flaws. Equally important, it compels thought to recognize its own subjective dimension, the emotional motivations of reason. Although Scorpio is not a mental sign itself it brings psychological awareness to mental processes. The same holds true for Taurus' realism within the potential of the intuitive quadrant; Leo's expressive creativity in the emotional sensitivity of feeling and Aquarius' detachment in the practical (Capricorn) or mystical (Pisces) absorption of sensation. In all four quadrants the central fixed sign provides a stabilizing balance to the overall energy.

6. John Donne, English poet, 1572-1631, 'Meditation XVII'

7. The Midheaven points to the highest point of the zodiac at the moment of birth. It is the subjective correlate of, but not the same as, the zenith, which marks the point directly overhead as one stands erect. A line from Earth's central core, up the spinal column, out the top of the head and through the zenith, extends into the galaxy above. It connects one with a hidden spiritual source. This galactic level of initiation remains far beyond our current evolutionary capacity to consciously comprehend and embody. The 10th house Midheaven provides an intermediate, humanly accessible experience of that cosmic energy. (See diagrams in 'House Division.')

The wheel of signs

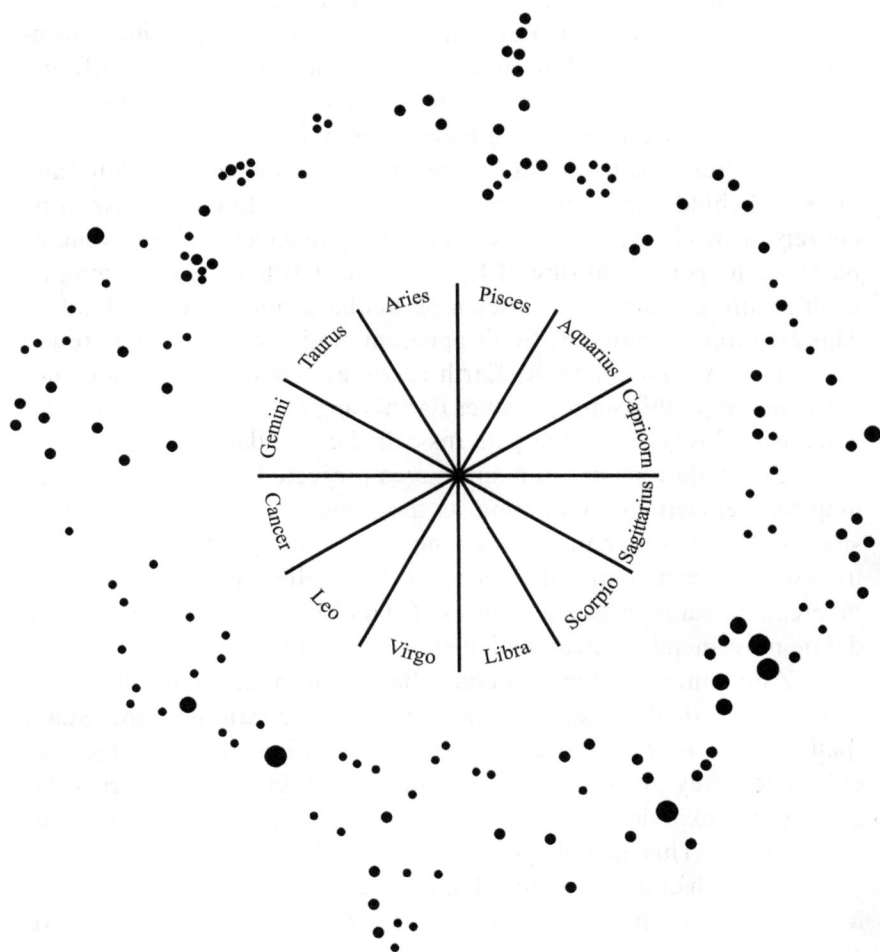

Sun in Signs

Sun is always the same in every sign. Only our awareness of it changes. In and of itself Sun opens the door to a timeless spiritual dimension. It radiates a single fiery life force in all directions. We experience this from a distance, on our moving Earth, in time and space.

We live on one plane of Sun's emanation, on one of its concentric orbits. As we travel around it we experience Sun from different perspectives. Each rotation of Earth (day) looks at Sun from a slightly different angle, against a changing background of stars.

Sun burns as the central core of our existence, the reality and purpose behind our being. This is too vast for us to encompass in its entirety. Instead we perceive it diminished by distance from our vantage point on the peripheral ring of Earth's orbit. Earth's position along its orbit at any given time exposes a particular segment of that Reality. This position is charted by Sun's apparent motion across a background of (relatively) fixed stars as Earth revolves around it. Sun does not really move (in this sense) - rather Earth's angle of vision moves, measured by reference to stellar patterns called constellations.

Constellations are human images projected into the sky. They map the heavens by organizing its thousands of twinkling dots into shapes. These stellar pictures connect stars many light years apart, traveling independently of each other. Constellations are like words: inherently meaningless associations of stars (sounds) through which we define movements (concepts) that are meaningful.

Altogether there are 88 constellations in both the northern and southern hemisphere skies. The twelve constellations along Sun's 'path,' as we orbit around it, are called signs. Signs have no objective existence. They portray celestial symbols that describe the terrestrial energies we experience as Sun circles through them from our perspective on Earth. This annual cycle of signs is called the zodiac.

As Earth circles Sun our Moon circles Earth, twelve times a year. Moon bundles Earth's daily rotations into its twelve monthly cycles. We experience these cycles as a repeating series of lunar phases (new, waxing, full, waning). These lunar phases absorb and emit solar energy in a regular pattern. This pattern generates an energy field around Earth's outer perimeter, defined by Moon's orbital path. It creates a template for the waxing and waning of biological life, psychological moods and mental processes.

Earth's annual circumnavigation of Sun narrows down to a dozen Moon units. We call them signs. A sign describes an arc of its orbit that Earth travels during the time period defined by a lunar cycle, new Moon to new Moon. It lasts the length of Moon's own year orbiting Earth. Plus one extra day that symbolically represents a degree of free will.[1] A sign is a Moon year with an extra spin of possibility.[2]

Temporal signs do not coincide with real and visible lunar cycles. A sign refers to an Earth/Sun relationship. It measures a section of Earth's movement around Sun within the time frame of a lunar cycle. This describes a certain terrestrial perspective on Sun's spiritual energy, an abstract state of consciousness. A lunar cycle embodies an actual physical process that occurs within the circle of signs. Because it lasts only 29½ days from new Moon to new Moon the beginning of each lunar cycle continually slips backwards through the 30° long signs.

Lunar phases ground the signs' spiritual meaning into living psychological experience. A sign is like the idea of a dollar: a unit of social trust backed by faith in a government. A lunar phase shows what the dollar can buy. John may buy apples, Mary oranges. They each acquire a tangible thing through participation in an intangible energy field: a functioning market in an organized society.

The signs are measured against a setting of fixed stars. These stars are organized into constellations, standardized figures like the numbers on a clock. Numerical symbols, such as 1, 2, 3, 4 are linguistic conventions allowing us to communicate ideas of quantity. The numbers behind the symbols have inherent qualities. Unity is a fundamental principle. So is duality. Three indicates movement, process, action: thesis, antithesis, synthesis. Four demonstrates manifestation, wholeness, completion: four directions in space, four seasons in time, four fundamental forces of physics,[3] four nucleotides generating the DNA code that defines every biological life.[4]

Fourfold human wholeness manifests through three states of being: personal psychology, social role, spiritual quality. Three phases of time: past, present, future. Three stages of life: youth, maturity, age/ death. Three planes of activity: physical, emotional, mental.

The twelve lunar cycles of the year parallel this twelve-fold articulation of the human condition. The constellational signs that represent them are symbols: catalysts that evoke insight, stimuli that elicit meaning. There are no giant lions or fish in the sky. These are archetypal projections; ideograms of psychological states. They sequentially unfold in human development just as lunar cycles temporally unroll the seasons.

That sequence begins when Earth stands perpendicular to its orbital plane and its northern, land dominated hemisphere starts to lean towards Sun.[5] This happens because Earth spins at a 23½° angle to the vertical. (See 'Sun and Earth,' Figure 1.) Thus Earth's northern hemisphere tilts towards and away from Sun as Earth circles it. That creates the visual impression of Sun moving up to 23½° north and south of the celestial equator. (Earth's equator projected out into space.)

When Sun appears to cross the celestial equator while moving north day and night are exactly equal, with day increasing and night decreasing. This marks the vernal equinox initiating Aries, the first sign. From our vantage point on Earth Aries defines that section of the sky through which Sun appears to move as and just after Earth experiences its vernal equinox.

The temporal length of a lunation cycle, plus a small increment symbolizing creative freedom, defines the spatial length of this sector and all subsequent ones. A sign refers to a geometrical arc measured from the vernal equinox. It describes an Earth/Sun relationship plotted against a stellar reference background. We experience it as an ever-changing ratio of day and night throughout the year.

On the first day of spring Earth's north pole stands perpendicular to its orbit. (Vernal equinox, on or about March 21.) Day and night are equal. It then tilts a little more towards Sun every day. Days are longer than nights, and getting longer. During its signs of Aries, Taurus, Gemini, day dominates and waxes.

On the first day of summer Earth's north pole reaches its maximum declination towards Sun. (Summer solstice, on or about June 21.) This is the longest day and shortest night. It then tilts a little farther away from Sun every day. Days are still longer than nights, but getting shorter. During its signs of Cancer, Leo, Virgo, day dominates but wanes.

On the first day of autumn Earth's north pole again stands perpendicular to its orbit. (Autumnal equinox, on or about September 21.) It then tilts a little farther away from Sun every day. Now nights are longer than days, and getting longer. During its signs of Libra, Scorpio, Sagittarius, night dominates and waxes.

On the first day of winter Earth's north pole reaches its maximum declination away from Sun. (Winter solstice, on or about December 21.) This is the longest night and shortest day. It then tilts a little more towards Sun every day. Nights are still longer than days, but getting shorter. During its signs of Capricorn, Aquarius, Pisces, night dominates but wanes.

Day symbolizes ego consciousness; night its unconscious instinctual and spiritual matrix. Day = individual realization. Night = collective expression. Day shines with the single star of self. Night twinkles with the many stars of society.

The alternating polarity of light and dark forms our most basic experience. It constellates the fundamental duality of existence: wake/sleep, life/death, objective/subjective, +/−. Each sign describes a relative emphasis of these yin/yang energies. And a vector of its dynamic: waxing or waning, developing or discharging.

During Earth's orbit around Sun it successively orients towards twelve energy zones portrayed by the signs. Just as each person passes through the same stages of womb-life, birth, infancy, childhood, adolescence, maturity and old age so each year unfolds along a consistently changing curve of light and dark through the zodiac.

This rhythmic cycle of day and night does not just go round and round in an endless circle. Rather it spirals forward as Sun moves northwards through interstellar space. Sun is heading towards a point 30° due north of the celestial equator at the winter solstice, near the star Vega, outside the zodiacal belt of constellations. (See 'Sun,' Figures 1-4.) Because Sun and the solar system as a whole are moving north, north represents future potential. South represents roots, origins, and causes. Northward movement portrays individualization. Southward movement portrays return to collective participation, sharing personal realization with the group from which one comes.

The spring signs of Sun's apparent movement northward (Aries, Taurus, Gemini) describe a season of Intuition, the development of yet unrealized potential. The summer signs, with Sun still north of the celestial equator but moving south (Cancer, Leo, Virgo) bring a season of Feeling, a return from the frontier with an enhanced personal reality, enriched with new dimensions of sensibility. The autumnal signs of Sun's southward motion (Libra, Scorpio, Sagittarius) define a season of Thought, an immersion into relationship with others and an encounter with larger than personal concerns. The winter signs, with Sun still south of the celestial equator but moving north (Capricorn, Aquarius, Pisces) portray a season of Sensation, an individualizing perspective on collective issues. ('Sun and Earth,' Figure 3.)

When Sun or any planet moves north from the vernal equinox (in Aries, Taurus, Gemini) it develops latent possibilities: an evolving individual function. Moving south from the summer solstice, but still north of the celestial equator (Cancer, Leo, Virgo), it demonstrates an established character: an expressive individual function. Moving south from the autumnal equinox (Libra, Scorpio, Sagittarius), it engages with its collective matrix: an expressive social function. Moving north from the winter solstice, but still south of the celestial equator (Capricorn, Aquarius, Pisces), it articulates collective aspiration: an evolving social function.

Any planet moving northward, from 1° Capricorn to 29° Gemini, acts like a waxing Moon: a growing function. One moving southward, from 1° Cancer to 29° Sagittarius, acts like a waning Moon: a releasing function. Any planet in signs north of the celestial equator evolves or expresses some aspect of individuality. Any planet in signs south of it expresses or evolves some aspect of collective participation.

Obviously this describes relative emphasis. A person with Sun in Taurus interacts socially, an Aquarian has personality. But these are not their main priorities. A sign indicates a certain orientation, a quality singled out for special attention.

The signs are fields of experience within a cycle of Quest and Return, individual development and social participation. This cycle generates an evolutionary spiral because it recurs along a trajectory in which the solar system as a whole moves towards a cosmic destiny near the star Vega. (See 'Sun,' Figures 1- 4.)

As Sun moves northwards its family of planets spirals around it. This generates a series of concentric helixes, resembling those of DNA molecules. (See 'Theory,' Figure 1.) We can think of these helixes as a complex cosmic genome 'read' or expressed by Sun as it travels through space. (See 'Sun,' Figure 1.) Biological DNA codes for amino acids, the building blocks of protein. Sun's spiritual DNA codes for psychological functions, the components of personality. The four fundamental functions (intuition, feeling, thought, sensation) manifest through Earth's four seasons and the twelve signs composing them.

Each sign embodies a psychological function, described by its elemental nature. (See below.) An opposite and complementary sign on the other side of Earth's orbit balances it. This latent presence gives it a new dimension, frees it from the limitations of its own nature and integrates it into the larger process of the whole zodiac. Similarly, each function unconsciously polarizes with its counterpart: intuitive possibility with actual sensation, feeling with thought.[6] Their interaction generates four basic temperaments: intuition/sensation, with intuition active/sensation recessive. Or vice versa. And: feeling/thought with feeling active/thought recessive. Or vice versa. Three such active functions experienced as temporal signs combine to generate a season.

In the same way physical DNA consists of four nucleic acids. Each of them couples with a 'silent partner' on the complementary strand of DNA's double helix: adenine (A) with thymine (T) and guanine (G) with cytosine (C). This generates four pairs: AT, TA, GC and CG. When activated, each nucleic acid breaks off from its partner on the DNA helix. It then combines with two other nucleic acids, in any order, to form a linear triplet: an amino acid. These amino acid triplets then link up to make proteins - just as three-signed seasons join together in years. This analogy between the astrological dynamic of the signs and the genetic activity of DNA reflects a universal organization that pervades every plane of being. The parallel between psychological and biological operating procedures reflects a single vital principle that animates every phase of becoming.

This cycle is embedded in the media of four elements or symbolic modes of experience:

Fire (intuition) represents will: spiritual quality, ego assertion, animal vitality. The fire signs are Aries, Leo and Sagittarius.

Air (thought) represents mind: perception, communication, knowledge, relationship. The air signs are Libra, Aquarius and Gemini.

Water (feeling) represents desire: emotion, memory, psychological depth. The water signs are Cancer, Scorpio and Pisces.

Earth (sensation) represents material reality: tangible structure and actual achievement. The earth signs are Capricorn, Taurus and Virgo.

Each element manifests through three phases of activity: cardinal, fixed or mutable.

Cardinal: creation, influx, beginning. The cardinal signs are: Aries - fire; Libra - air; Cancer - water; Capricorn - earth.

Fixed: existence, culmination, maturity. The fixed signs are: Leo - fire; Aquarius - air; Scorpio - water; Taurus - earth.

Mutable: change, transformation, ending. The mutable signs are: Sagittarius - fire; Gemini - air; Pisces - water; Virgo - earth.

Every degree of every sign contains all the qualities of all the signs. Just as every body cell contains the entire genetic program of an organism, but only expresses some aspects, while leaving others latent, so each sign emphasizes certain energies and lets others lie dormant. Signs of the same element accent similar potentials. Thus Leo and Sagittarius, both fire, have more in common than either has with Taurus (earth). That said, one often learns the most from those who are most different. These lessons are more difficult, but can be more rewarding because they evoke new dimensions of experience. At least as often they are simply lessons in frustration and hostility.

Signs display themselves as a belt of star patterns in space around Earth's equator. Sun and other planets appear to move through this zone from our perspective on Earth. Planets express a sign's force field through their particular function. For example: Mars = personal will. This can express Capricorn's practical ambition, Scorpio's passionate emotion or any of the other ten zodiacal energies. A planet in a sign focuses that sign's quality of consciousness through its activity. It may operate as an aspect of one's own personality, an inner condition. Or it may be encountered out in the world as an objective situation.

We experience the twelve signs through twelve houses, their subjective parallels in the human psyche. Houses are divisions of Earth's own rotation. (See 'Sun and Earth.') A house grounds a sign's cosmic energy into personal expression. For example, the sign of Aries on the cusp, or leading edge, of the ninth house (abstract mind) means that Aries' aggressive, pioneering nature informs one's philosophical/religious sensibilities in the spiritual domain, and one's political stance towards public affairs. The dreamy, mystical sign of Pisces on the cusp of the third house (concrete mind), suggests a poetic sensitivity infusing the perceptual, data processing intellect. Etc. Houses describe where and how one acts out sign energies. Signs motivate, houses manifest.

Notes

1. This is because it takes Earth 365¼ days to revolve around Sun, but Moon takes only 354⅓ days to make twelve orbits around Earth. The extra eleven days, almost one day per sign, symbolize a quotient of freedom within the clockwork of orbital cycles.

2. One day out of thirty equals about 3%. This seems almost insignificant. Yet a small quantity can leverage into a large impact. Only 3% of our human genome codes for all the proteins that build and run our bodies. (The other 97% is noncoding: a reservoir of genetic potential allowing new genes to emerge without disrupting vital coded functions.) By analogy almost all of our psychic functioning consists of automated physiology, hardwired instinct and unconscious perceptions and memories. The lit up area of conscious choice is small. Yet it defines who one is.

3. Gravity, electromagnetism, strong force (holding atomic nuclei together) and weak force (radioactive breakdown of atomic nuclei)

4. Adenine and its complement thymine, guanine and its complement cytosine. These four nucleic acids combine to generate all living matter.

5. Of course the same sequence reverses in Earth's southern hemisphere. The northern hemisphere is used by convention because astrology first developed there.

6. For the original, and classic, description of these functions see C. G. Jung 'Psychological Types.' Carl Jung (1875-1961), along with Sigmund Freud (1856-1939), was a founding father of modern psychology.

The Signs

Sun symbolizes one's core identity. Thus its sign position is by far the most important component of a chart. However, one can never say that s/he 'is' a Virgo or a Libra. One also learns about that basic purpose through the medium of a rising sign (ascendant) portraying self-consciousness and expression. And feels it through Moon's emotional sign.

Every human personality embodies an ineffable mystery. S/he can never be reduced to a single symbol or psychological equation. That said, such an equation, delineated as a birth chart, provides insight into the dynamics of consciousness and motivations of behavior. The signs provide a context within which planetary functions operate. Sun in a sign portrays a spiritual orientation to life. Moon and planets flesh that out with psychological attributes. Planets in signs actually manifest the general solar purpose.

In the remainder of this chapter signs are presented as a continuum of archetypal energy patterns more than as discrete personality types. This locates individual identity in the larger scheme of things. 'Moon in Signs' describes their psychological expression.

Signs act as phases of an annual cycle. Sun in a sign activates that developmental stage as ego's central organizing principle. It then expresses on whatever evolutionary level one has achieved.

Aries

March 20/21 - April 20/21
Cardinal Fire: Primal Will
Ruler: Mars

Objectively: Sun crosses the celestial equator, moving northwards at its fastest pace. Spring begins. A green fire vitalizes winter's barrens. Dormant seeds germinate and sprout, skeletal branches bud and leaf. Hibernating animals awaken. Migratory birds and herds surge north across the flowering land. A new cycle of life starts, in both biological and human nature.

Subjectively: Dawn. Aries shines forth with the radiance of a fresh day. 'Let there be light.' And so there is. This has a positive connotation.

But ego's sunrise also disrupts the tranquility of sleep, burns away a subtle dream glow. It activates self-consciousness, creating contrast, competition and conflict. Individuality emerges and asserts its will in the world.

Aries: First Cause. Original motive. Fundamental principle. A principle is a spiritual axiom around which psychological drives organize themselves. Its truth orients their actions. Aries embodies the Prime Directive behind personality, the intention generating its behaviors.

Aries means initiating impulse. The spark igniting movement and consciousness. An emergence of being from nothing. The thrill of creation.

It points to the origin of individuality. The blink of an I out of a collective dream trance. A coalescence of ego from instinct, existential identity from intangible potency. Diffuse possibility focused into actual purpose.

Aries demonstrates the spontaneous combustion of unconscious currents into known and active powers. A spiritual force field flares out into the world as an urge to individual expression. Awareness awakens out of its background matrix of animal vitality. Aries emphasizes the primordial nature of consciousness, unmodified by relationship or feedback. Its elemental essence carries a general soul charge seeking experience through the medium of a unique personality. That stimulates one to emerge from the herd, self to rise out of the common sea. All else flows from this statement of singularity.

Aries = Creation. Not the deliberate creativity of a developed ego, but raw creative force. It bursts into life as the light of mind, heat of desire, strength of will. Aries evokes and fuses these motivating factors into a distinct psychology.

At the vernal equinox ego-consciousness achieves escape velocity from the gravity of an unconscious collective past. It attains autonomy. The exhilaration of this freedom, and the initiative it generates, are Aries' main characteristic.

Aries makes a core identity statement. Where Aquarius offers a theory, a detached vision of the Big Picture, Aries proposes an action imperative, meant to mobilize behavior. Aries is not an idea, but the electrical voltage transmitting a spiritual potential into a living entity. Aries converts an abstract psychological genome (soul) into an actual ego able to assert its reality in a gritty, sweaty world. It is the will body. The principle of self-assertion. It operates across an entire spectrum, from boorishly egocentric to an expression of universal spirit.

Aries exemplifies the violence inherent in any beginning. The Big Bang was the ultimate act of violence, ripping space/time out of infinity/eternity. The nuclear fusion generating all material elements out of simple hydrogen, and the stellar novae spewing it out as world-making gas and dust, are destructive processes of creation, death throes of birth. Human birth means a labor of pain for the mother.[1] Even more so for the infant, ejected from womb bliss into life struggle. ('Our longest and most dangerous journey takes us four inches down the birth canal.'[2]) Aries forcefully breaks out from one state of being to another. Only thus can anything happen.

Aries = aggression. Any manifestation of individuality necessarily challenges its environment. Aries battles an old dispensation to bring forth the new. The son must psychologically overthrow the father and take his place; the daughter leaves him for another man. Whether he is better remains to be seen. Aries is not about results. It means beginnings.

Aries sounds the birth cry. It makes the first presentation of self, from which all future words and deeds flow. A newborn has an inherent temperament, an overall disposition, long before conscious ego arises. Character orients its development from that starting point. Its growth proceeds from an initial psychological premise. This is but a tiny seed. Yet a seed holds all the promise of a great tree. It may or may not flourish. But it has the resolve to sprout. Without that, there is nothing.

Aries focuses felt urgency into immediate expression. It channels emerging excitement, instinctive dynamism into activity at whatever level of sophistication one has achieved. This can manifest as skillful enterprise, pioneering thought, immature impatience or brutal rage. It acts unilaterally, not so much to dominate others as to express its authenticity. It sends instead of receives; stimulates rather than relates.

Aries promotes independence. It cannot allow a social consensus to stifle its own conscience. Aries does not rebel from the group in order to reform it; but leaves, or leads, it to a new destiny. Aries' best gift to others is not knowledge or love, but the inspiration of following its bliss.[3] Aries performs best and gives the most by just being itself.

Aries tends, and needs, to act autonomously. For better or worse it must do its thing rather than live up to others' expectations. It does not integrate with a larger whole; it opens a new frontier. It develops confidence and competence through risky exploration instead of conventional achievement, seeks discovery more than approval.

Aries leads, not by skill or experience, but by the courage of its convictions. Done right it means leadership by example. That works when Aries goes with instinct, lets the a spiritual power act through it. Of course uninhibited assertion can go too far. Or not far enough: Aries falters when it seeks to rationalize its projects in terms of social criteria rather than its own intuitive vision.

Aries refers to basic drive. The Ascendant, Aries' subjective correlate, and any planets in its first house, constitute a personal Aries: one's core motivation. It describes a subjective perspective: self-consciousness. The house cusp that the sign of Aries occupies indicates ambitious endeavor in a specific area of life or type of activity. The position and aspects of Aries' ruling planet, Mars, provide insight into the circumstances and challenges of its enactment.

Aries = the will to exist. It kindles winter's ethereal spirit into spring's vibrant joy. It transforms compassionate sensitivity to passionate intensity, Piscean redemption to April's resurrection.

Aries' fresh, youthful nature expresses with clarity and simplicity. It strips things down to their central principles. Seeks direct engagement with essential meaning. It reasons through an intuitive grasp of self-evident truths. Direct perception supersedes complex rationalization and hoary precedent. Aries always crosses the line into uncharted territory. Here there are no maps. One can only launch into the unknown future driven by an 'impulse of delight.'[4]

Aries apprehends things as an extension of its existential truth. Its characteristic problem arises when it mistakes energetic projections for objective perceptions. It can confuse the vigor of its enthusiasms for their validity.

Aries does not register facts so much as create them. It learns to apply its aspirations to the world: first as innocent enthusiasm, then through ego assertion, finally as the direct channeling of a higher purpose.

'Where there's a will there's a way.' This succeeds surprisingly often. Self-confidence can generate heroic effort that inspires others. Faith can move mountains. Sometimes.

Aries' greatest challenge is to develop a strategic sense of how to effectively engage burning intention with cold hard circumstance. To do so Aries requires, and demands, a reality check. This often involves a combative confrontation with its environment. It asserts positions to assess their comparative validity. If the ego is not too invested in these assertions Aries accepts the verdict of experimentation and learns from its mistakes. The adversarial method of discerning truth works well if one fights for it, and not for personal justification. If self-respect becomes entangled with these speculative forays the likelihood of disaster is obvious.

Aries encourages excellence through competition. The stimulation of opposition eliminates weakness, the exhilaration of rivalry enhances performance. The race itself is the reward. Aries is often portrayed as a warrior. It brings battle as well as blossoming. The battlefield can be physical or emotional, mental or spiritual.

It also acts as a very cerebral sign, pioneering new realms of thought and sensibility. It probes established boundaries with innovative propositions. It tests accepted views with challenging perspectives. Being relatively free of preconceptions it can appreciate fresh insights and novel approaches. Because it has the courage implicit in new beginnings it pursues truth without fear of authority or conventional wisdom.

Aries learns by doing. Its bold clear vision is essentially innocent because it does not have a load of past baggage. Innocent does not necessarily mean naive. It means approaching experience with a clean slate.

Aries takes that leap of faith without which nothing would ever happen. It embodies the bravery to engage with life by simply being who one is. The determination to go for it, with no guarantees except that of its own courage. We see it in the audacity of every newborn organism, frail and helpless, joyfully setting forth into a dog eat dog world.

Aries projects its inner rebirth as an inspiration to explore, conquer or redefine its environment. Life presents a page on which to write its message, an opportunity to shine. Aries seizes the moment, acts on a primal sense of truth and immediate strength of aspiration more than on cool calculation or judicious process. Yet we could never act at all if we had to know all the probabilities and possible consequences in advance. Aries makes rather than accepts reality. By doing so it bends the arc of events in its favor.

Like its opposite and complement, Libra, Aries portrays a dynamic more than a content. Libra functions as a process of relationship, uniting its participants in a dance that transcends the dancers. Aries generates the excitement that makes one dance in the first place. It orients all future activity by its original intensity and direction. The nature of that fundamental impulse largely determines the quality of its outcome. This initial surge then unfolds through the developmental sequence of the zodiac.

Like the Big Bang that started the universe, Aries erupts as a burst of energy. It sets a cyclic process in motion. Later this primeval energy acquires attributes (Taurus), differentiates into components (Gemini), takes an emotional coloration (Cancer). Its implicit qualities manifest through encounter with its objective surroundings. Its power to be and to become evokes emergent properties.

Aries invokes the mystery of creation. The ultimate origin of things is inaccessible to reason. In the beginning an inscrutable Providence (Sun) emanated forth as a vibration. It generated a pattern of planetary orbits, including the standing wave of Earth's. This charged force field spontaneously organized into a unique entity (Aries) by guiding countless particles into a proto-planet. Its inherent energy level, expressed as distance from Sun, caused it to take shape in the 'life zone,' that small region where liquid water can provide the medium for biology. The idea of Aries refers to an initial energy configuration like that which made a living Earth possible. Actual development follows from the potentials implicit in this start. For example, the primordial Earth mass consolidated into a globe with specific geological characteristics: magnetic core, molten mantle, solid crust endowed with mineral resources (Taurus). It then split off (Gemini) its Moon by colliding/merging with a 'twin' (Gemini) Mars sized planetoid about 4 billion years ago. Moon's gravity stabilizes Earth's spin and atmospheric circulation, making it more habitable (see 'Moon'). Finally our new planet acquired a life-giving ocean (Cancer), perhaps by a 'heavy bombardment' of icy comets from outer space.

All of Earth's subsequent characteristics derived from its 'will' to form in a certain orbital state. In the same way all psychological development follows from an original energy signature. Aries commits a solar spirit to an earthly identity statement. It sets a course to individualization. All other psychological qualities arrange themselves around this trajectory as attributes of that fundamental purpose.

Aries' sunrise of the year reenacts the emergence of a planet, or a personality, in the nature of its seasonal moment. Just as night's many twinkling stars ignite into day's single Sun, so a swirl of unconscious instincts fuse into one self-conscious agent. Just as winter's dormant seeds sprout into spring's lively flowering, so latent abilities take the plunge into visible activities.

Biological life involves a vital force imprinting its potential on matter, animating their union with an emergent property of organic sentience. What started as a primitive blob with only a chemical itch to metabolize and divide had latent possibilities. These evolved over eons into sophisticated complexity. Such qualities were inherent, but not apparent, in that ultimate progenitor. What appeared, as if by magic or miracle, was a simple ambition to live. That later blossomed into all of biology.

Psychologically, Aries emphasizes the same imperative: it directs the elusive aura of an ideal into an effective incentive. Spirit becomes an action potential. Soul sensitivity mobilizes into a specific ego agenda, on whatever level of evolution it has achieved. Wish ignites into will. Dreams turn to drive.

In Aries a spiritual fire shines forth into individual expression. A personality activates and unfolds against resistance. The inertia of matter, limitations of biology, and restrictions of society constitute real obstacles. The competition of other egos and antagonism of opposing visions demand attention. Aries embodies the ability to assert self against circumstances, to demonstrate a distinct character in contrast to surroundings. This implies an inherent confidence, not yet justified by achievement. Yet the courage of that confidence is its own achievement.

Aries trusts its direct experience of power. It acts through the innocence, and subtlety, of a spontaneous intention prior to the socialized self. Aligned with an intuitive source it channels generic vitality into novel insight.

Aries describes the spirit of adventure, of which everything else is a consequence. The urge to get up and go. Destination unknown, and unimportant. All the details derive from this emergence. Aries motivates.

Notes

1. Genesis 3:16: 'In sorrow thou shalt bring forth children'
2. The author was unable to find the attribution for this profound observation.
3. Joseph Campbell, 1904-1987, an American writer on comparative religion and mythology, coined this famous phrase. He was an Aries.
4. 'Those that I fight I do not hate
   Those that I guard I do not love; ...
   A lonely impulse of delight
   Drove to this tumult in the clouds; ...'

   'An Irish Airman Foresees His Death'
   W.B. Yeats, poet, 1865 -1939

Taurus

April 20/21 - May 20/21
Fixed Earth: Fundamental Values
Ruler: Venus

Objectively: Spring in full bloom. The daylight of ego-consciousness stabilizes into an established identity. Sun climbs slowly, steadily north on a set path into the future. Emerging potential flowers, becoming known and visible in actual circumstance. Personality expresses itself in sensual experience.

Subjectively: The thrill of dawn supplanted by a morning calm. A clear and steady light illuminates consciousness. And reveals its deepest hungers. The freshness of a new day alive with opportunities. A sense of recharged strength that makes them happen. Ego cultivates its own attributes and enjoys the fruits of its productivity.

Taurus: Desire. Values. Valuables. Physical matter. Body.

Taurus manifests Aries' initiating impulse. Will takes root in reality. An enchantment of spirit into matter.

What Aries starts, Taurus develops. Aries makes a declaration of independence, ignites a war of liberation. Taurus carries out the slow careful process of nation building: the growth of stable institutions, evolution of an enduring national character.

In Taurus the spiritual becomes sensual. Aries' general aspiration acquires a specific agenda. Its spark ignites a flame. The ethereal shimmering of a rainbow condenses into a pot of gold. A beautiful flower solidifies into a nutritious fruit; its enticing fragrance becomes a delicious taste. Drive becomes desire. Fire becomes flesh. The ideal coalesces into the real.

Aries thinks a thought. Taurus gives it voice. Precipitates it into heard vibrations of speech that make inner motives known. Taurus gives mind the pleasures of sensation.

Taurus grounds Aries's energy charge. Its womb of matter absorbs the thrill of intercourse and grows it into new life. The orgasm becomes an organism. Information sprouts into identity. An abstract genetic code blossoms into a specific being. A genome, with many potentials, becomes a phenome, with one life to live: not in theory or intention, but in reality.

Taurus demonstrates the principle of fertility. It provides the substance that embodies dreams and makes them come true. It endows whatever animating principle impregnates it with a primal strength.

Taurus makes things concrete. It creates the distinctiveness of individuality. This emphasis necessarily implies a narrowing, and an intensification, of vision. Taurus is the most specific, least universal, of signs. It exemplifies the general truth that each thing must be itself, of a quality and nature different from all others.

Taurus focuses singularity: a unique set of characteristics that will occur only once in the history of the universe. Other signs emphasize social role or personal hopes, heart or mind, sensitivity or ambition. Taurus gives them a solid foundation as a self defined by what it has. Taurus means possession: what one owns, and what owns one.

An entity can only flourish by securing resources. Taurus refers to its capital, the wherewithal enabling all other functions. The 2nd house, Taurus' subjective correlate, and any planets in it, describes competence at gaining and utilizing physical, emotional and mental assets. How it gets. The house cusp that the sign of Taurus occupies indicates both productivity and sensuality in that sector. It describes an area of desire. A subjective 'pearl of great price.'[1] That for which one will sell everything else. Perhaps even honor or soul. The position and aspects of Taurus' ruling planet, Venus, shows where the money actually goes. Why it spends and what it buys.

Taurus generates abundance. It evokes actual manifestation from the possibilities inherent in every moment of the Now. It grows potential into potency; brings latency to life. Thus Taurus = wealth. In financial instruments and material things that grant security, the prerequisite for healthy development. In talents and sensitivities; the psychological endowments of intellect and empathy that enhance experience. And in the spiritual resources making possible our appreciation of the now, and an adventure into the future.

Taurus defines not only given resources, but also resourcefulness. It can make a barren landscape grow through effort and skill. Or erode a fertile field through vanity and incompetence. Taurus has the ability to coax wealth from waste. Or it can wallow in an indolence that squanders even the most promising opportunity.

Taurus portrays not just static facts of ownership, but also the process of calculating merit. The dynamics of evaluation. A visceral economics of feeling. It reveals real priorities in actual exchanges. Buying and selling tangible goods allocates scarce capital. Emotional expectations make or break relationships. Intellectual assumptions determine crucial decisions. Taurus defines an investment strategy, wise or foolish, prioritizing limited time and energy. Its portfolio of done deeds adds up, or dwindles down, to define a life.

Taurus does not just define values. It creates them. Over time its experience evokes more sophisticated levels of desire. It refines appetite, turning a glutton into a gourmet (or occasionally the reverse). Taurus grows a range of appreciation from the gross to the sublime. Everybody enjoys pleasurable physical sensations. Taurus fosters their extension into higher octaves of sensibility and thought. It cultivates a taste for more subtle forms of beauty. It enhances brute facts with an awareness of their significance. Thus knowledge, a gathering of data, becomes wisdom, a comprehension of its quality.

Taurus acts through the miracle of compound interest. Things attract added merit over time just by their accumulation of defining events and acquired attributes. Raw activity distills into stored memory and remembered consequences. These form a concentrated extract of experience. A general wisdom emerges out of particular situations, a larger perspective forms from specific perceptions. This happens slowly but surely. Even a 1% annual growth rate leads to a doubling in 70 years, a normal human lifetime. Taurus subliminally gains gravitas, a weight of worth, simply by its ongoing processing of life's sensations and sensitivities.

Think of soil, that most Taurean of things. Just by existing it acquires potency. Every year rock particles erode into its mineral base. Plants grow in this nurturing medium. They photosynthesize, making organic matter from sunshine, air and water, adding it to the soil bank when they die. Topsoil grows perhaps one inch per millennium, becoming richer with the legacy of all the lives it sustained. It turns ever more fertile because it holds increments of value and generates a further increase from them.

Taurus demonstrates the magic of how a simple state of matter, a layer of mineral grains, slowly evokes a higher state of biology, perhaps a grassland or a forest. This in turn may support a civilization. Taurus forms the foundation and adds to the substance of life. Taurus creates the very ground of being, enhanced by its own duration in time, enriched by the return to it of all the creatures it supports.

Taurus describes immanence: the fullness of spirit's descent into matter; soul's incarnation in the temple of a body. For example, consider a tree. Its sky seeking branches with Sun tasting leaves are mirrored by earth clinging roots that drink subterranean waters infused with mineral nutrients. Together they marry solar fire and ethereal air, flowing water and solid earth into the breathing green vitality of photosynthesis. Chlorophyll, the molecular agent of photosynthesis, has the exact same structure as an animal's red energy carrying hemoglobin - except that a single atom of magnesium vibrates at its center v one of iron in blood.[2] Taurus describes the mystery of manifestation in which the electronic quality of a single atom determines the character of a living kingdom.

Taurus expresses individual psyche through the shared substance of a great planetary Life.[3] It consolidates the accumulated legacy of many gone but ever gifting moments into an elemental essence. It shows what one is made of.

Taurus centers universal urges into a unique ego. Precipitates generic motivations into a singular destiny. Think of the clear calm eye, or I, of a hurricane. A hurricane/typhoon organizes the diffuse heat of a tropical ocean (collective unconscious) into a zone of winds (personal forces) circling around a still inner point with a name. It forms a swirling storm of collective passions, thoughts and actions into the focused power of a personality.

To participate in life that personality must give and take. Venus ruled Libra portrays an external sense of social equity while Venusian Taurus portrays an inner ranking of priorities. Taurus defines what turns you on. The house with Taurus on its leading cusp, and any planets in it, describe the basis for selection.

Taurus delights in a sensual response to the world. Much of this is deeply instinctual, especially in the realm of creature comforts. The rest is idiosyncratic. Some like a strenuous rush. Others prefer sybaritic ease. 'There's no accounting for taste.'

What we want describes who we are. Our values act as a constantly shifting equation of virtues and vices, appetites and ambitions. These are always in conflict: to have this you must give up that. Taurus portrays the battleground of desire. It forces choice between competing attractions. Taurus spotlights various seductions, some delightful and others damnable.

As Buddha taught, craving is the root of all suffering.[4] It eventually dies into transcendence (Taurus' polarity Scorpio) - just as spirit must ultimately separate from its body. Yet in its time the body provides the vehicle of experience. It enables spectral soul to smell, see, touch, taste and hear. And to love: not as a cosmic benevolence but as a personal appreciation of another, also made in the image of God. In the same way desire gives celestial ideals a workout in the heartbreaking beauty of life.

Taurus' most characteristic conflict occurs between the antithetical merits of productivity and sensuality. Economics v enjoyment, developmental investment in the future v a 'be here now' appreciation of the present. Too great an emphasis on either leads to distortion: 'all work and no play makes Jack a dull boy,' yet too much pleasure quickly becomes monotonous. Then desperate efforts to stimulate jaded appetites become decadent, even degenerate.

The Taurus function develops an ability to prioritize; to intelligently allocate effort and enthusiasm. What good is life if one cannot stop to smell the roses? Yet there will be no roses without cultivating the garden they grow in.

Taurus describes life's gravity well: a fundamental attraction. It forms the psychological equivalent of the Higgs field in physics, which wraps itself around energy movements, slowing them down into material phenomena. In the same way Taurus adds attributes to Aries' impulse. This inevitably involves a degree of distortion, as an intangible template of soul thickens into a discrete self weighed down with wants.

Matter condenses spirit into mass, and gives it inertia. It also endows abstract purpose with measurable power. Will character compromise its standards to fit the limitations of incarnation? Or can it enhance and express the potencies made flesh in our body/mind, temple of the soul?

Taurus springs the honey trap of desire. It tempts with the counterfeit currency of lowered expectations to compensate for a 'fall' from aspiration into the disappointments of our human condition. The debased 'realism' of greed. The demanding hunger of wounded wishes. The despair and depravity of insatiable appetites. Or it can learn to appreciate the very flaws of creation, recognizing that boundaries make beauty, scarcity gives value, life's brevity generates its poignancy, loneliness opens to love.

Taurus depicts the principle of physicality. Here all theories melt down into a solid fact: me and mine. The corresponding pathology can be a mean and stingy solipsism. Narcissism. Or an enthrallment by fetish objects, substitute gratifications for love.

Taurus revels in sensation as the most tactile of signs. It embodies sense impressions rather than ideas or ideals. Scent, flavor, feel, sound, sight: the real reality or the web of illusion? They are simply a true aspect of reality. Taurus is their home.

Taurus reasons instinctively. It has a gut sense of what things are worth and who people are. It accurately appraises merit. Distinguishes gold from glitter. To what end? Its problem can lie in knowing the price of everything and the value of nothing.

At its best Taurus respects, and reveres, self and others for their intrinsic qualities. It serenely accepts entities in their own right, rather than insisting on how they should be. At its worst it covets what it so admires and so falls prey to morbid jealousy.

Among earth signs Taurus fulfills personality as it is while Virgo refines it by a rational standard and Capricorn subordinates it to ambition, destiny or a social calling. Taurus grounds the realization that one really is made in the image of God. It means worshipping the universe by fulfilling one's inherent nature. This is the antithesis of conceit, an attempt to justify ego through artificial projects.

Taurus emphasizes the principle of being rather than of becoming. A visceral appreciation of what is rather than what could or should be. It promotes the validity of existing character without having to meet others' expectations, heroically achieve or feverishly compete; to develop at one's own pace; to grow organically. It insists on that most precious of rights: to be left alone.[5]

Taurus consolidates an established identity. It underwrites a predictable sequence of unfoldment that guarantees stable growth. Provides the continuity necessary for long-term development and large scale endeavor. Taurus does not make quantum jumps or revolutionary breakthroughs. It demonstrates the incremental quantitative accumulations that create qualitative change. The slow buildup of muscle and bone, heart and hormone growing a man from a boy, a woman from a girl. This process cannot be forced.

Taurus symbolizes the unhurried dynamic of evolution. It demonstrates the geological stability, biological inheritance, social traditions and enduring personal qualities underlying the more spectacular, and ephemeral, events of nature, history and human development.

Taurus builds the bedrock foundation of character through the properties cultivated, or ruined, in the course of a life. It leaves a legacy. Does one acquire merit? Or squander it? Taurus makes explicit a psychic ledger of profit and loss, assets and liabilities.

Notes

1. Matthew 13:45, 46
2. A few creatures, notably intelligent mollusks such as octopi, substitute a less efficient oxygen carrier, an atom of copper, in the hemocyanin of their blue blood.
3. We share the same DNA code, and many of its basic metabolic sequences, with the most primitive bacteria as well as all other organisms.
4. Attachment to craving generates pain. Only nonattachment to conditioned experience can lead to enlightenment. Buddha, himself a Taurus, demonstrated a way of liberation. At the opposite pole Hitler, also a Taurus, personified the anti-value of hate. Between these extremes two other Taureans deeply explored the nature of desire. Shakespeare artistically portrayed its full range of expression in his comedies, tragedies and histories. Freud first exposed its unconscious origins. Although modern consciousness studies have evolved beyond his initial framework he remains the undisputed father of modern psychology.
5. 'The right to be left alone - the most comprehensive of rights and the right most valued by civilized men.' Chief Justice Louis Brandeis, Olmstead v U.S., 1928.

Gemini

May 20/21 - June 20/21
Mutable Air: Mental Lucidity
Ruler: Mercury

Objectively: Year's longest lengthening days. Sun's northern movement slows, then stops at the summer solstice. The daylight of ego-consciousness achieves maximum illumination of external realities but withdraws energy from inner contemplation (night). Personality grows through recognition of its environment.

Subjectively: Morning brightness. Awareness fully engaged with objective activities. A sharp clarity of perspective and broad range of interests, not focused on any one quality but distributed across many.

Gemini: Mind. Perception. Communication. Duality: I and Thou, sacred and profane, eternal and mortal.

During Gemini's longest days mind stretches to incorporate the greatest diversity of experience. It integrates the widest spectrum of information into the clearest expression of its meaning. As thought reaches its farthest expansion from an initial premise (Aries) Gemini changes focus. Emphasis shifts from inner drive to outer variety. External stimuli outshine deep motives. Attention turns from self to surroundings.

This mutation shuffles the deck. Like a cell that has reached its limit of growth one's mental data genes recombine, then separate into two sister cells, or states of consciousness. In Gemini a singularity of will (Aries) or of desire (Taurus) bifurcates into duality of mind. The knower and the known. In here and out there. Subjective and objective. Right and left-brain hemispheres. Right and wrong ethical decisions. Their new relationship initiates a more complex awareness. Thus consciousness becomes self-conscious, through the distinction between its now autonomous parts.

Gemini divides our animal and angelic, human and divine natures. Distinguishes between the light and dark sides. And referees their mutual interplay. This results in the knowledge of good and evil. Gemini's mind-bridge allows these pairs to communicate with and fertilize each other. That generates creativity and conflict, thesis and antithesis, leading to a more inclusive synthesis.

Here intelligence reaches out beyond the reality of self, its will and wants, to a larger frame of reference. Reason recognizes psyche not as a world unto itself but as a single actor among many. It develops criteria of comparison that honors other forms of worth than its own.

To do so requires a certain detachment. This can blossom into objective observation. Or wither into amputation from roots, a desiccated cerebral echo of real life.

The twins personify a dichotomy inherent in our being. One side is the empirical personality: the known, conscious, socially adapted character. The other its more intangible qualities: the light aura of a higher spirit, the better angel of our nature - and its counterpart, a dark alienated shadow of suppression and frustration. Will they learn to cooperate? Or blindly fight? Ego can express soul, or eclipse it in the service of petty appetites and ambitions. Intelligence can elevate identity, or enable its sins and justify its flaws.

Gemini's double nature is both vertical and horizontal. The vertical dimension portrays a Christ soul or Buddha nature inspiring the monkey mind. And a perverse inner adversary of self-loathing and projected hate. The horizontal emphasizes interaction with peers in an encounter with others on the same general level of evolution. This can range from brotherly love to deadly rivalry (think Cain and Abel).

Subjectively, Gemini connects known realms of thought with transcendent planes of inspiration and unconscious depths of instinct: superego and id, guardian angel and devouring fiend, soul and shadow. These mark polarities of an unconscious continuum. Consciousness is poised in-between: pushed, pulled, animated by their interplay.

Gemini experiences sharp internal dilemmas: the Jekyll and Hyde within. It describes how they inform and learn from each other. Or compartmentalize the total self to its great loss. As conscious personality responds to its hidden inner dimensions so it relates to its outer surroundings. Those in touch with, who can acknowledge, the contrasting/complementary aspects of self can also deal with challenging aspects of their environment. Those who refuse to hear their own sometimes discordant inner voices cannot perform competently in an often disordered world. As within, so without.

Contrast induces rhythm, oscillation, a pulse. The heart both expands and contracts, lungs breathe in and out, the brain wakes and sleeps. And without sexual interplay we would have no life at all, both in the emotional sense and because it creates the genetic variety driving evolution.

Vibration = vitality. Its back and forth movement implies complementarity. North is defined by south; + is matched by −. Every entity has a positive and negative polarity, contains male and female qualities. Gemini mediates their dialog. Is it a fruitful conversation? Or a contrived game? A shared rapport? Or a monologue, with one side talking, the other silenced, turned off and acting out in retaliation?

Clashing wills, opposing values, competing concepts exercise the power of discernment. Educates it to a superior sensibility. Or trains it in the arts of deception. Gemini's divisions force one to take a stand: 'The line between good and evil runs through every human heart.'[1] Gemini draws that line. It poses alternatives. And reveals their consequences.

Most options are not so stark. They involve mundane matters and reflect personal foibles. Gemini makes, and is made by, life's continual process of decision. This requires and stimulates a calculating intellect. The criteria it selects, priority it assigns and protocol it employs constitute the Gemini function.

Other signs commit to a certain path. Gemini always stands at a crossroads. It must constantly choose and justify its choice. Yes/no, do/don't, on/off. Does this reduce it to schizophrenic paralysis, identifying with this, then that, in a babbling mass of contradictions? Or train it in analytical agility? To what end: as an impartial observer or an opportunistic player?

Among air signs of the mental plane Libra judges. Gemini makes the arguments, sets out pros and cons, examines the evidence, justifies a position. Aquarius seeks to transcend them in revelatory breakthrough to a universal theory or great Idea. Libra balances, weighs, relates in terms of known principles. Gemini discovers those principles, extracts them from the world's chaotic phenomena. Aquarius fits them into an explanatory paradigm. Libra seeks to harmonize various energies. Aquarius seeks to unify them. Gemini differentiates and compares them. This sharpens awareness, descriptive ability and wit. All of them express aspects of air's essential nature: a fundamental truth quest (v fire's exertion of will, earth's demonstration of achievement or water's experience of feeling).

Gemini explores. It must learn to proceed in a consistent direction, each new version of truth logically emerging from the previous. Otherwise it wanders a maze, distracted by irrelevancies. The bewildering variety of phenomena can be experienced as a discontinuous kaleidoscope. Understanding then nimbly hops between temporary reflections, experiencing small blips of truth devoid of any common thread of meaning. Or it can elucidate a coherent explanation that systematically incorporates each info-byte into a larger context.

Gemini encounters a flood of facts. Its characteristic error is to embrace each passing phenomenon just because it seems valid at the moment. Or because it serves a short-term purpose. It needs to separate from the blinding immediacy of its impressions in order to put them in proper perspective. It must develop rational guidelines, a method by which to mange this influx and bring it to a higher synthesis.

Gemini functions through the adversarial process seen in Anglo-American law. Confrontation can illuminate truth. Or obscure it by partisanship. The resolution lies in due process: an insistence upon open procedure and clear rules that guide evidence towards justice. Gemini can learn to direct its adroit tactical movements by strategic commitment to a greater goal. Or, like a glib lawyer, it can exploit technicalities to win every battle and yet still subvert the law.

Gemini polarizes. Opposite poles generate an electric current or magnetic force field uniting them in a shared energy. Or splits them into fragments. It can fuse elemental components into more complex and sophisticated compounds. Thus hydrogen and oxygen merge into water, mother and father mate into one flesh as a child, isolated quantities fuse and enlarge into emergent qualities. Or it can divide and subtract. To achieve salvation or enlightenment means to reject a conventional worldview, shed an old identity, renounce a hard earned wealth of attributes, opinions and relationships:

'Do you think I came to bring peace on earth? No, I tell you, but rather division.'[2]

Gemini translates intangible states of consciousness into specific and communicable ideas. It grounds external signals and subjective insights into the brain's bioelectric networks. It embodies intelligence in a unique configuration of neurological connections: a literal body of truth.[3] These experientially conditioned nerve pathways channel perceptual inputs and intentional outputs. They self-organize to filter out some stimuli and admit others, to suppress or activate certain lines of development. A fractal of universal Mind materializes as an organic wiring plan. That generates an aura of comprehension, weak or strong, bright or dim.

The third house, Gemini's subjective correlate, and any planets in it, portrays the nature of one's verbal, data processing mind. Education, formal or informal. Learning style and ability to articulate knowledge. How one thinks. What one thinks about.

The house cusp that the sign Gemini occupies indicates the area of life conflicted by divergent principles. It evolves through their mutual stimulation. The position and aspects of Gemini's ruling planet, Mercury negotiates between those differences and defines their resolution, good or bad.

Gemini thinks inductively. It relates specific elements to build a unified theory from the bottom up. A hundred schools of thought contend. From their disputations truth emerges.

This produces a cerebral form of sensibility: sharp, clear, bright and objective. Whether inclusive or superficial, Gemini describes an intellectual agility manifesting as acute observation, advanced reasoning and aptness of expression. Its challenge is to find an organizing principle combining its many fast moving dots into a Big Picture (exemplified by Sagittarius, Gemini's polarity).

Gemini sees all the angles, factors in every option. The question becomes what do they mean? How do they add up to a whole that is greater than the sum of its parts? In answering Gemini develops a consistent method of truth verification that underlies all rational thinking. The other air signs use that logic: Libra to render judgment, Aquarius to explain inspiration. Gemini creates it out of direct examination of facts. Its dynamic alertness interprets raw evidence to comprehend specific situations. Or to encompass the general enlightenment giving our species its name: homo sapiens, 'wise man.'

Gemini describes a process, not a product. It does not project a given energy outwards (Aries) or center the universal into the particular (Taurus). It is not about emotion (Cancer) or creativity (Leo). Rather it makes all of these qualities intelligible to each other through a cause and effect dialectic. It reconciles contradictions by illuminating each stage of their evolution and resolving its developmental sequence of thesis/antithesis into a more advanced composite.

These catalysts propagate new brain waves that challenge and enrich consciousness. They create abstract representations of the world and play with them. That allows intellect to manipulate the terms of thought experiments, run scenarios, consider other approaches. Reason is freed from the slowness and heaviness of materiality. Perceptual information, mathematical equations, verbal formulations, rational axioms and procedures constitute the sensations of a mental plane of being. A map of reality. The map is not the territory. But it can guide movement through, and find location in, the complexities of our surroundings.

It can also usurp existential reality. A theoretical construct can displace common sense and basic decency. An ideological obsession can split good us (or me) from bad them. Gemini's lucidity easily twists into amoral sophistry. Its challenge is to maintain a remembrance of the vertical dimension, from emotion to spirit, to balance an otherwise arid rationality.

The universe has been described as a 'play of mind.' At best Gemini discovers the rules, fundamental principles that distill truth from facts, and condense it into eloquent expression. At worst it celebrates cleverness over wisdom, abusing its mental dexterity and verbal skill to spin convenient justifications for self interest and prejudice.

Gemini's sense of relativity easily crumbles into lies as alternative narratives displace actual perceptions. Indeed, Gemini's greatest struggle is to distinguish truth, open possibility disciplined by fact, from lies, partial (closed) slivers of reality masquerading as the whole.

Gemini demonstrates the potency of word magic. Verbal concepts create their own reality. They distance from emotional immediacy, giving perspective or alienation. They break general intuition down into specific ideas, split wholes into their component parts. Those can then be analyzed, manipulated and restructured, for better or worse.

Symbolic language makes us human. It enables disinterested contemplation of objective truth and poetic expression of subtle feeling. Its power is such that immortal phrases resonate through the centuries, moving hearts as power or money never can.

'In the beginning was the Word, and the Word was with God, and the Word was God.'[4]

In the original Greek of the New Testament the 'Word' is 'Logos': reason. The universe is essentially a great Thought, with dreamlike qualities. Its various planes of being resonate in a communion of meaning made known through many idioms ranging from the DNA sequences of biology to the spoken tongues of human societies to the planetary patterns of the solar system. Gemini's embrace of diversity generates a conceptual grammar translating these parallel realities into shared understanding.

Gemini marks the northernmost apparent motion of Sun. The farthest advance of mind into new states of consciousness and permutations of identity. It demonstrates the power of thought to create the world anew.

Gemini also points away from the galactic center (with its innermost black hole), towards intergalactic space. The outer limits. Gemini goes to the very edge of our conscious ability to distinguish and differentiate phenomena. Its polarity, Sagittarius, integrates this knowledge into an overall worldview or social construct.

Gemini opens the door of perception into a wider world than self. The universe is full of doors. The Gemini function reveals how and why one chooses which to enter.

Notes

1. Alexandr Solzhenitsyn, 1918-2008, Russian writer imprisoned for long years in the Soviet Gulag. Awarded the Nobel Prize for Literature in 1970. He also asked: 'How can a man who is warm understand one who is cold?'
2. Luke 12:51 and Matthew 10:34
3. At least ⅓ of our 20,000 genes express primarily or exclusively in the brain. Yet the three-pound brain comprises only 2% of our (average) body mass. Source: National Institutes of Health, which conducted the Human Genome Project.
4. John 1:1
The specification that the Word was both God and with God points to the dual nature of creation, in which spirit and matter, soul and flesh, life and death, form distinct phases of a unity.

Cancer

June 21/22 - July 23/24
Cardinal Water: Wellspring of Emotion
Ruler: Moon

Objectively: Summer arrives. Sun stands at its northern zenith, then begins to move south. Day turns towards night. The light of self-consciousness illuminates the depths of its instinctual origins. Personality turns within, seeking its source.

Subjectively: The high noon of feeling. Spring's exploratory outreach consolidates into a unique psychological sensibility. Ego infused by imagination, enriched by nuances of memory and sensitivity.

Cancer: The mother of personality. Emotion. Roots. Psyche: subconscious temperament; an instinctual mood.

Cancer immerses mind into psyche. It begins at the summer solstice, a year's longest day. Reason (Gemini) has come to term, attained its full measure of intellectual maturity. Data acquisition and processing have reached their limits. In Cancer thought turns back in on itself, to plumb the depths of its own nature. Detached observation gives way to emotional involvement.

Here life giving rain falls from the skies of mind, baptizing dormant seeds to flower in feeling. Freewheeling cerebral consciousness commits to a sense of identity. Clarity of thought becomes tenderness of empathy. Calculation opens into caring. Perceptions melt into sensitivities. Lucid intellect gives way to subtle responsiveness.

In Cancer day begins to wane. The exfoliating potentials of will (Aries), desire (Taurus) and mind (Gemini) now precipitate into subtleties of sentiment. Think of a new continent that has been discovered (Aries), its resources claimed and extracted (Taurus), its lands divided into political units (Gemini). Cancer begins a new phase: that of actual settlement. Extensive exploration is replaced by intensive cultivation. Discovery becomes development. The adventurous search for greener pastures over the hill turns into a loving labor of building a home and raising a family right here and now.

Cancer integrates the possibilities that blossomed during day's lengthening cycle. The different qualities sequentially emphasized during ego's growth now coalesce into a distinct temperament. Cancer describes the magic of personality, an emergent property greater than the sum of its parts. It summarizes attributes (will, wish, mind) into a subjective quality. Action, love and thought fuse into character.

Cancer dissolves primary forces into a living flow of psychological experience. Discrete sensations, sympathies and opinions coalesce into a general temperament. Cancer digests specific elements into an organic whole, an indefinable essence, making one instantly distinguishable from all others. It demonstrates the peculiarity making each person a unique representative of the entire universe.

Genetic information, instinctual drives and learned behaviors contribute to the self. But its fundamental nature transcends all of these inputs. It cannot be made by will, owned by desire, understood by intellect. It is a subtle symphony of those vibrations, the general tone of a living human being.

Sensual stimulations, survival imperatives, inherited abilities consolidate into a subconscious current. This feeds and supports the relatively small area of conscious choice. Cancer forms the background out of which an ego emerges.

Everybody has the same needs and wants, prioritized differently. Their arrangement, ranking and relative strengths combine to produce a singular synthesis. Cancer emphasizes the individuality of their distribution. In the same way, all DNA coils are made of the same chemicals, but each self-organizes in a specific way, giving rise to various biological forms. DNA recombines ancestral biochemical factors (genes) into a novel configuration. So too each person internally mixes common psychic energies into an original statement of the human condition.

We are all bonded by the same essential makeup. We each exhibit a slightly different pattern of its various features. Cancer underlies our recognition of this universality, the basis of empathy. Thus one resonates with others. Cancer acknowledges a familial sense that we each personify a shared humanity.

Beginning at the farthest frontier of mental awareness (summer solstice) Cancer integrates our rational and irrational sides into a special sensitivity. It absorbs impressions and blends them as an unprecedented and unrepeatable personality. This then assimilates social contents in preparation for collective participation.

In Cancer ego begins to turn from self-actualization to tribal belonging. Cancer reorients individual evolution towards social cooperation. It describes the most intimate level of this change in direction with basic training in family life. It develops rapport with others and learns about relationship dynamics in a small unit: first the family, later the classroom, platoon, work team. Any larger grouping necessarily defaults into a hierarchy of rank (Cancer's polarity: Capricorn. Authority exists within the family and similar units, but is modified by strong affections.)

We have an innate preference for a social universe of about thirty people, the typical size of the hunter-gatherer bands in which we evolved for thousands of generations. This provides space for a personal role with face-to-face interaction on a comprehensible scale. Such emotionally intense bonding generates social skills, and a more inclusive vision, that frees one from mere subjectivity.

We are mammals, born helpless and dependent on the love and feeding of others. We mature slowly, over decades, nourished and nurtured by a cultural environment. We are partly defined by membership in clan and tribe. We belong to beloved groups. We are neither herd animals nor solitary beings. We are psychically responsive individuals who are carried along with the social narratives within which we are embedded.

From that springs a consciousness of heritage: familial, cultural, biological. An appreciation that all one is rests upon deep foundations laid down by countless forgotten ancestors. Ego is rooted in past eons. It blooms as a single yet special flower on the tree of life. Cancer embodies a remembrance of, and respect for, the power of the past.

History shapes character, memories sculpt the now. Their specific content is mostly forgotten. They leave behind an orientation, a set of expectations, a habitual response. These can become automated, as in inherited instincts. Or imprinted with a charge based on early or powerful events. Thus the paranoid sees every smile as a betrayal, the caregiver interprets every rip-off as a cry for help. Each acts inappropriately when response becomes a conditioned reflex rather than an unconditional openness. Cancer can let a bygone past suffocate the living present. It must learn to let history flow into the future rather than congeal in the abyss of time.

Cancer means memory: our capacity to store information in a personally relevant way. Cancer digests transitory episodes into enduring feelings. Any planet in Cancer reveals sensitivity to the sources of that planetary function.

Consider the deep roots of molecular memory in our biological cells, the fundamental unit of life. Single celled bacteria, the earliest and most common life form, have no nucleus. Their DNA information strands float loosely in the cellular body, which remains undifferentiated from others of its kind. They are clones, replicates, twins (Gemini).

The diversified cells of multi-cellular organisms centralize their DNA within a nucleus, an enclosed genetic data bank. There it can be more efficiently organized to express a specific function in a protective environment. The Cancer function internalizes a genetic heritage to shield its delicate configuration from the busy metabolism of its host substrate. That allows it to concentrate its energy on a specialized activity in concert with a lineage or community of sister cells. It becomes an intensified part of a larger whole.

In that safe space it can dissolve and recombine its given DNA message into another design. There it creates the template of a new identity. That will fuse with another organism's also reformed inheritance in the revitalizing miracle of sexual reproduction. Thus the cell loses independence and gains interdependence. It participates in a more sophisticated life. If this goes awry, and it reverts to single cell agency, then a cancer disease erupts.

Psychologically Cancer symbolizes the same process. It funnels Gemini's extensive mental network of thoughts and perceptions into an intensive core focus. Synthesizes a spectrum of subliminal signals and informational stimuli into a coherent wavelength of sensibility. Amplifies a bundle of generic instincts into one self-consciousness. Distills the visceral heat of our warm blood into the visible glow of a unique character. And nurtures its emerging illumination on whatever level of evolution one has achieved. Cancer lights up life from within.

Cancer's conservative, defensive posture masks an exquisitely sensitive inner quest. It seeks to recover soul's deepest longings in life's sea of sensations. To connect with a fundamental fantasy, recall the dream behind outer doings. Thus it is the most private, secluded and subjective of all signs.

Cancer embodies the principle of subjectivity: that an interior self-reflective space mirrors the universe. Life recreated as a psychic reality. Within it objective facts generate an emotional statement of what they mean. Memory reimagines truth as the psychological coloration of experience.

The fourth house, Cancer's subjective correlate, and any planets in it, portrays a defining dream; the unconscious source of awareness and agency. The house cusp that the sign of Cancer occupies points to a private area, the home of one's deepest, most intimate feelings. It indicates their origin and general nature. The position, phase and aspects of Cancer's ruling planet, Moon, provide insight into cherished memories and inner history.

Cancer does not refer to the past as an inert collection of done deeds. Rather it consolidates previous stages into a more inclusive dynamic of growth. This fusion is made possible because Cancer also represents an openness to emergent possibilities, a future-oriented sense of imagination. Its dream script integrates ever accumulating prior moments into an evolving synthesis.

Cancer unites dead past and pregnant future in the mystery of genesis: the miracle of an ever-present birthing. This pours forth as the wellspring of temperament, the intuitive base from which creativity, relationship and achievement issue.

Every organism focuses receptivity to outer circumstance and awareness of its own inner condition into basic sentience. It remembers behavioral repertoires and encodes them into instincts. Instincts can acquire enough energy to concentrate into feelings. Feelings organize into fantasies, visions of what could be. They create imagination, a sense of nonexistent possibility that then makes it possible. Each of these unfoldings gestates its unborn potentials through an introspective creativity symbolized by the Cancer energy field.

Cancer brings inner dimensions to life. It describes private sensation, the psychological feel of incidents and situations. It reflects events into emotions. It registers external stimuli as an internal attitude. Cancer melts acts and perceptions into memories, colored and prioritized by the mystery of personality. From memory it generates imagination: a distinctive story of what life and the world mean.

Cancer demonstrates identity as known from within. It forms a sense of individuality: not what I do, want or know but who I am. Cancer expresses the essence of a hidden soul. Soul is not a thing but the magic of a quality.

Cancer = birth. Any newborn is relatively undifferentiated, a standard issue specimen of its kind. Indeed, Cancer's delicate responsiveness can be compared to that of an infant. A baby seems cute but incompetent. Yet it absorbs information and acquires skills at a faster rate than at any other stage of life. For example, while an adult can spend years struggling to mangle a foreign language every young child becomes fluent in its mother tongue by osmosis. Cancer nourishes tender sensibilities and developing abilities until they have time to mature. It midwifes conscious psychology out of generic instinct. Its outer passivity masks intense inner activity.

Cancer = home: a safe refuge from the world. And its associated nesting urge to create a sheltered space for self and kin. The sense of belonging, rooted in shared participation. This will later universalize into compassion for strangers, loyalty to a nation or cause, love and worship of an all embracing God or ethic.

One's first home was the womb. None can love God who has not loved, and been loved by, a mother. She is our first and deepest love, the primary agent of socialization. She provides our initial and deepest image of the world, and of relationship to others. The bond with her stretches from the most physically intimate womb-bliss to defining infantile impressions. Nothing and nobody can ever displace her. Cancer holds her subliminal image at the center of consciousness, shaping a primal response to all others.

Yet mother also constitutes the most profound threat to subjective autonomy. One must psychologically break from her to become an individual, just as one had to give her physical agony, perhaps even death, in childbirth. One must leave her womb, the family and ultimately life itself.

Yet we always remain embedded in a Great Mother of passing time and material space, the medium of spirit's embodiment. Cancer's maternal nature unites abstract forces of spirit and concrete facts of matter into organic life. Cancer synchronizes its innate pattern of maturation with larger cycles of becoming.

Cancer, itself a turning of the yearly round, indicates the fundamental principle of cyclicity. Expansive/contractive pulsations of the heart, yin/yang permutations of the Tao, ebb and flow of sympathy constitute its truth. Life's alternating stages wash away eternal laws of mind into the fluid dynamics of sympathetic resonance with fleeting moments. Its lunar tides of mood add new dimensions of spontaneity to iron will. Cancer's universal solvent of constant emotional transformation melts rigid determinism into flexible freedom, solid facts into fluctuating feelings, linear logic into open possibilities. Its powerful currents of subconscious sentiment generate our more ephemeral brainwaves of consciousness.

Cancer's moodiness reflects the changing phases of its ruler, Moon, racing through the zodiac faster than any other planet, shifting shape every day. It feels the poignancy of life's brevity, a wistful sense of just how short and precious our life on Earth really is. It tenderly remembers the shadowy forbears who shaped us, and the halcyon days of our own lives, so soon passed and lost. 'Who knows where the time goes?'

Cancer registers the flood and ebb of biorhythms, the pulse of interior seasons. It also reaches farther back to their cosmic generation by the waxing/waning pull of our Moon. Moon complements Earthly vitality from a different center of subconscious gravity. It guides all other factors of our cosmic environment into manifestation by a subtle attraction (see 'Moon'). Cancer dissolves them into a stream of consciousness. And even more so of unconscious wish and will. Cancer melts the diversity of Moon's planetary reflections into a flow of psychological phases.

Like water these have no definite shape. They act as the medium of deep psychic movements. And as waves of immediate impulse. Cancer embodies a responsive vehicle for astral signals beyond the reach of rational understanding. It condenses the intangible vibrations of an extraterrestrial lunar soul into individual awareness. It unites the potentials of timeless unconscious and eternal spirit into the reality of temporal expression. Cancer receives rather than sends; absorbs celestial frequencies into its own microcosmic rhythms.

Cancer births the full circle of time into an immediate point of origin. Origins are inaccessible to mind and memory. Who remembers their own birth? Yet what moment could be more important? Only the Now, if truly embraced.

Yet Cancer's conservative posture also shields a fragile persona from such overwhelming realities. Its ghostly echoes of the past and faint premonitions of the future come to term slowly and cautiously. It requires a long gestation and generations of development. Nine months in the womb, and a lifetime incarnate on Earth, express but a drop in its ocean of the collective unconscious. Yet that tiny drop can become the seed of a larger life.

Cancer assimilates universal energies into a personal quality. It transmutes instincts into sensibilities, grows common drives into individual dreams. It melds inner experience and outer sensation into a singular soul, a unique representation of the world.

Cancer manifests the subjective organizing principle that guides psychological evolution. The next sign, Leo, will radiate this forth as its creative statement.

Leo

July 23/24 - August 23/24
Fixed Fire: Creative Power
Ruler: Sun

Objectively: The hottest time of year as summer's momentum peaks. The light of discovery becomes a heat of passion. Sun slowly, steadily slides south. Personality releases its accumulated endowment to the world.

Subjectively: The golden glow of afternoon's warmth. As day winds down ego feels its own brightness in contrast to approaching night. Self makes a distinctive identity statement.

Leo: Creativity. Charisma. Joy. Love.

In Leo day's waning quickens. The process of personal development has passed its apex.

Now it must prove its worth. Cancer consolidated individual consciousness. Leo demonstrates its competence. The approval of others becomes an essential confirmation of value. Identity is no longer psychologically autonomous. It has entered its social phase. It plays to an audience and is partially defined by the judgment of its peers.

Leo discloses a peak experience of self-expression. It does not describe the adventure of becoming, but an attainment of being. It makes a definitive statement of who and what one is, right here and now. All prior signs (Aries through Cancer) grow its primal potentials. The next, Virgo, refines their application. All subsequent signs (Libra through Pisces) accent its collective participation. Leo portrays a moment of truth: where 'I' stands alone in a public revelation of character.

Leo is show time. Here one steps into the spotlight to display personal excellence. That performance defines social status. Given these stakes Leo acts on a grand scale, with magnificent style or extravagant pretense.

Leo glows with the heat of reentry into the collective atmosphere from a zenith of subjective exploration. The incandescence of ego descending from an inner state of grace to impact upon the outer reality of community membership. Leo dramatizes an individual's coming out into society. This initial debut will later face the test of integrity (Virgo), relating to others with some level of reciprocity (Libra) and meeting its own end (Scorpio). But now, in its original freshness and potency, it simply stands out and shines forth.

The defining question for Leo always remains: what purpose does this shining serve? Private indulgence? Self-enhancement? Eminence, supremacy and rule? Or as a living exemplar through which God, Tao, the Force comes into the world?

Cancer absorbs, Leo emits. Cancer nurtures a heritage of memories, abilities, traits. Leo spends that inheritance in public service. Or for its own glorification. Internal quality has reached its full measure of evolution, high or low. It now contributes to the world. Or basks in a rich sense of satisfaction.

Individual prowess crests at its maximum strength. Will it give? Or take? Leo can inseminate the world with a spiritual essence. Or devour everything in its path with insatiable demands for attention and gratification. It can exhibit the ferocity of a king of beasts. Royal writ of an ego. Creative wit of an artist.

Will it celebrate its own wonderfulness? Luxuriate in predatory aggrandizement? Seek mastery through domination and humiliation? Guide and govern its tribe? Or serve as the willing vehicle of a divine and terrible radiance?

Leo's hour of triumph reveals one's true nature. In defeat, only courage and honor remain. Victory gives freedom to do anything: be magnanimous or malevolent, noble or nihilistic.

Leo manifests the power of personality. Not clarity of ideas, strength of will, depth of empathy or any other attribute. Leo is not defined by its works or wisdom. Instead it demonstrates the mystery of charisma: gravitas, air of command, ability to inspire through its mere presence. Leo portrays a magnetic attraction, a compelling influence. From that emerges the confidence underlying all achievement.

Leo = authority: an inherent ability to command respect. An ascendant faith in itself. Aligned with a larger truth that faith can move the world. But authority easily degenerates into autocracy. Leo can blind objective judgment with the brilliance of an inner Sun. It forgets that everybody else is also an I. Others register only as satellites, playthings, fetish objects. An isolated me then acts out in increasingly garish displays of infantile omnipotence.

Leo is ruled by Sun. Sun gives life to Earth. It also blots out all other stars during its daytime passage. Sun's Latin name is Sol - a solitary Presence, the sole truth of one God in a coherent creation.

The solar system revolves round a single source. Sun symbolizes the central organizing principle behind our many states of consciousness. And night, with its galaxy of suns circling a black hole into another dimension, reminds us of a greater reality behind our living moment in eternity.

Like all stars Sun is a white hole, an energy surge erupting out of a spiritual plane. A visible emanation from the intangible origin of material existence. A discrete fractal of infinity. A sparkle of the Light. Leo's energy field channels its solar wavelength into an aura of self-awareness. Consolidates that point of light into the animating motive of a life.

Consider Sun. It may feel some great thrill on its own level as it flares forth, burning through 600,000,000 tons of hydrogen every second (!). Yet Sun serves a higher purpose than its own solipsistic splendor (though that has merit in its own right). It also vitalizes rings of orbiting worlds. These enhance the total system with qualities, such as organic life, that Sun does not have, and could not achieve, on its own. And it plays a role in our larger galaxy, wherein it shines among a hundred billion. Sun's shining is a wonderful event on its own. Yet it also acts as part of a whole, a single function of an all encompassing equation.

Leo condenses Sun's spiritual fire into a core sense of self, prior to thought, desire or ambition. As it concentrates a general purpose into personal psychology it can forget its celestial estate. And that it is but one note of a stellar symphony. Then it falls into a masturbatory narcissism, aware only of its own importance. A radioactive elitism seeks the attention of others whose reality it cannot acknowledge. If it learns to see past ego's spellbinding isolation then it can ecstatically resonate with a galactic or social environment.

Sun manifests a cosmic will folding the fabric of space into a self-igniting star. It centers and illuminates an entourage of planets. In the same way Leo unifies our several subpersonalities into a fundamental statement of being. I am. My talents, idiosyncrasies, history are what I have and do. Leo radiates a heartfelt imperative that draws all the elements of psyche into a grand passion, for love or glory, to create or to control.

Giant Sun glows as tiny atomic nuclei of hydrogen merge to generate its energy. Hydrogen, with a single electronic proton, forms the smallest, lightest atom: an ethereal state of matter most akin to incorporeal spirit. Sun's gravitational attraction contracts these fundamental charges into a denser double unit, a helium atom. And emits the excess quantum energy that maintained their previously separate identities as a photon: a wave of light expanding out to brighten the universe.

Sun's magnetism spins countless numbers of such nuclear flashes into a steady brilliance. A parallel life force coordinates billions of coronary muscle twitches into a synchronized heartbeat.

116

Leo's domain is the heart: an inner Sun. There it activates a psychological chain reaction that drives a singular destiny. Leo dramatizes a realization of its once in forever being. And consummates it in the fusion of love.

Atomic nuclei merge to release energy. And precipitate heavier states of matter that make a solar family of worlds possible.[1] Animal bodies unite in sexual ecstasy. And give birth to a new generation of children. Human hearts share in the rapture of love. And thus transcend their separation in an experience of the divine.

Just as Sun maintains a structured heliosphere, a magnetic bubble in the galactic stream, so Leo endows individuals with an expressive space, a sphere of influence in society. It tests with a power that is given, not earned; an appeal that is born, not made. This generates spontaneous audacity. Or contrived arrogance. A flair for leadership. Or a sense of entitlement. Majesty. Or megalomania.

Sun symbolizes the overall meaning of a life. Leo personifies that abstract stimulus; gives solar spirit a human face. Shapes its raw vitality into a specific vibration: regal or ridiculous, proud or pompous, generous or grandiose.

Leo centers Aries' initiating impulse into a stable I. It focuses primal force of will into an organized force field with a distinct character. Leo shows what you've got. In the best sense this means living up to your highest potential. At worst a loud egotism.

Leo amplifies this ripened individuality into a social revelation, of whatever value. Thus Leo experiences identity as its role in life's theater rather than as a private quality. In doing so it can display grandeur of feeling. Or posture in self-promotion, phoniness on an epic scale.

The fifth house, Leo's subjective correlate, and any planets in it, portrays one's unique presentation of a universal theme. This can be biological (children), cultural (artistic), social (political) or inspirational. The house cusp that the sign of Leo occupies indicates an area of creativity. Where one emits a ray of sunshine.

Leo openly reveals an emotional essence. It translates the fire of Sun and summer into a burning ardor of the heart. It ignites sensitive feelings into passionate love. A love more real in its short hour than the two eternities of past and future.

Love begins as the simple exhilaration of existence. It propagates an animal exuberance. Self expands to include others in a generosity of feeling. Just as Sun expends its substance to warm and light the worlds around it, and even the dark void, so Leo emanates a natural joy evoking joy in others.

Leo embodies an innate cheer that does not have to earn the right to laugh. It exhibits our warm-blooded delight in life; exemplifies the natural elation of being:

'Consider the lilies, how they grow: they toil not, they spin not; and yet I say unto you, that Solomon in all his glory was not arrayed like one of these.'[2]

Of course the pursuit of happiness can decay into aimless amusement, then jaded pleasure seeking: '...does not every street abound in gloomy-faced debauchees?'[3]

At the height of maturity Leo knows that it has spent its youth. It is no longer growing but giving. Like Sun Leo disseminates a charge. Just as our star's gravitational field made and maintains a planetary system much bigger and more complex than it is, so Leo creates a social space that is orders of magnitude larger than an ego.

With a large family of planets, and a powerful presence among its stellar peers,[4] Sun engages with its cosmic environment. Similarly its Leo energy projection interacts with our Earthly sky across a wide spectrum. Its day is not a monolith: dawn, noon and sunset are primal experiences. So too is midnight, Sun's absence. The Leo personality mirrors this diversity. It has a Renaissance sensibility: big, bold and colorful with a broad canvass of tastes, skills and interests. Leo generally scintillates as a bon vivant with a convivial nature.

In the security of summer's warmth, and savoring an innate popularity, Leo relaxes from the strain of past growth and demands of future duty (Virgo) or relationship (Libra). It just shines in the present. Of all signs Leo is the freest to play. Happy play: in many ways the highest and most natural human state.

Leo can mistake its good fortune as evidence of greatness. It then sees itself as the main actor in the whole play because it stars in its own part. It falls under the tyranny of ego: the Hell of a solitary spark, bedazzled by its own blinding blaze, drifting alone through space, ending as a burnt out cinder in the emptiness.

Leo vividly senses the contrast between its own luminosity and the growing dark. It feels the poignancy of its brief effulgence in infinity. Yet that brevity is an illusion because it embodies a microcosm not only of the visible world but also of a more sublime soul/Sol from a higher dimension. Leo makes a personal statement of the divine. Only by genuinely accepting that calling can a lonely individual transcend the mortality of its separation from God.

One can contract from the intensity of this summons. Love can shrink into pride, usurping ownership of its cosmic heritage as an inflated confidence in its own agency (hubris) or excellence (arrogance).[5] Inevitably that bubble bursts, for:

'Pride goes before destruction, and a haughty spirit before a fall.'[6]

Leo inherits an inexplicable grace. Does it expect privilege as proof of its own exceptionalism? Or does it accept the responsibility inherent in its abundance?

'Of those to whom much is given much is required.'[7]

Leo must meet a challenge: having so much can it spend all for a larger cause? This requires moral courage. Leo's courage is not the combative impulse of Aries nor the grim determination of Capricorn, not the sacrificial compassion of Pisces nor the icy will of Scorpio. It means a commitment to noble standards in a petty world. To exemplify the same generosity that endowed it in the first place. To pour forth everything without hope of reward or lust of result. To shine like Sun, a pinpoint of fire in the infinity of space; to make a magnificent gesture transcending the cold vacuum and empty eons in an instant of ecstasy.

Leo promotes the unique creativity of each soul as made in the image of God. And the danger of conflating its opinions with that. The individual soul mirrors God through its free choice of an identity statement. Leo emphasizes awareness of that fact. Thus it gives one a god-like ability to create. And to love the world that is a greater God's creation. Ego can confuse itself as the source, rather than an expression, of this power. Then healthy self respect as a child of the universe regresses into morbid conceit as its center.

Personality is a novel configuration of eternal love in mortal flesh. A grounding of divine Bliss in human nature. Leo poses the question of its aptness. Will it glow as a gigglefun frivolity? An imperious ego trip? Hot passion? Charismatic leadership? Or as a radiant gift of sheer joy?

Notes

1. See 'Sun: Sun in Time.'
2. Luke 12:27
3. 'Satires,' Juvenal, Roman writer, ca. 60-130. Today's debauchees are consumers rather than sexual libertines. They are found in the shopping mall, not at an orgy.
4. Sun is often described as an ordinary star. Actually it shines bigger and brighter than 97% of all stars (!). Most are dim red or brown dwarfs, small and slow burning, but longer lived than Sun.
5. See 'Ozymandias,' Percy Bysshe Shelley, English Romantic poet, 1792-1822
6. Proverbs 16:18
7. Luke 12:48

Virgo

August 23/24 - September 21/22
Mutable Earth: Test of Integrity
Ruler: Mercury

Objectively: Harvest time. Virgo's fading light reveals exactly what one has produced to face the coming winter. 'Ye shall know them by their fruits.'[1] Sun sinks south, releasing its daytime splendor, setting to meet other stars waiting below the horizon. Personality offers its ripening talents to collective service.

Subjectively: Afternoon's lengthening shadows. In that more subtle light consciousness realizes and rectifies its own inner darkness. Day's transformation into night accelerates to the tipping point. Ego purges errors and purifies abilities in anticipation of a coming judgment.

Virgo: Integrity. Healing. Service. Work. Technique. Perfection.

Virgo's setting Sun illuminates features that were hidden in day's dazzling brilliance. Its cooler light of reason reveals inconsistencies not apparent in summer's hot passion. 'The Devil is in the details.' Ego learns to observe itself dispassionately, warts and all. Only thus can it fix its failings and perfect its strengths.

In Virgo day's subjective sensitivity (Cancer) and creativity (Leo) face reality. The exhilarating adventure of personal discovery must now pay debts, acknowledge mistakes, mend any harm it has done. A tragic flaw, born of imperfect reception in Cancer, magnified by Leo, is revealed and redressed in Virgo. Like an erupting Sun encountering cold dark space, Leo's flaming ego now learns its limits. Its cherished opinions, ambitions, joys, peccadilloes go on trial. Those that work will survive. Those that don't are eliminated.

Imperfection generates disease of body, mind and desire. This forces therapeutic intervention to eliminate its cause. Virgo invokes the healing principle. It provokes a fever that burns away dysfunctional programs. And generates an enhanced immunity to future error. It cuts away tumors of exaggerated growth, prunes back inflated self-esteem. Eradicates degenerate attributes with the strong medicine of rigorous self-analysis.

Virgo cleans up one's act. It reforms subnormal performance with a Spartan regimen of discipline. It improves through a vigorous workout on every level: material, emotional, mental and moral.

Virgo draws attention to problems that can no longer be ignored or tolerated. It targets physical debility, emotional pollution and mental inertia for a strenuous upgrade. Virgo refines the coarse to the sublime,

120

lifts the dull and primitive to the bright and sophisticated. It rejects familiar and comfortable mediocrity, embraces the demands of merit. This takes painstaking effort. That pain is the price of progress towards a higher state and greater happiness.

Virgo experiences the transformative crisis of ego consciousness. It must now admit and amend its defects. This requires honesty and analytical ability. An innocence of self-centered being, however delightful, must measure up to objective rather than subjective standards. Whether it wants to or not. Virgo brings the end of choice and the beginning of adaptation. Only thus can one escape the (perhaps gilded) prison of personality.

Willful behavior and wishful thinking yield to brutally honest criticism. Virgo may seem like a hard taskmaster. But a strong hand is needed to reform Leo's exuberant excesses. Ego's powerful forces must be checked, controlled and properly channeled:

'For the Lord disciplines the one he loves, and chastises every son he receives.'2

Virgo embodies mind's ability to clearly observe its own identity. Critical intellect probes weakness with intent to heal. Its truth can really hurt. A false self image is inherently maladaptive. Egoic delusions are intoxicating but deadly. They must be deflated, their energy released for better use. Virgo endures the mortification of facing embarrassments. It develops the skill to detoxify them.

Virgo's remedial feedback loop allows any entity to monitor and improve its state of being. It continually diagnoses errors and prescribes their cure. At best it acts preventatively. Foresees difficulties and preempts them by generating improvements before failure occurs. Efficiencies add up to reach an entirely new level of competence. Or it can be a crisis management procedure. Deals effectively with inevitable setbacks and mistakes. At worst it becomes a morbid preoccupation with tiny imperfections, a sterile fear of doing anything because something might go wrong.

Virgo's characteristic conundrum arises with too great an emphasis on the perfect operation of each part while ignoring the whole: 'Losing the forest for the trees.' But, more than any other sign, Virgo is self-correcting. Any undue emphasis will be noted, understood as illogical, and reprogrammed to fit in with the big picture. Virgo needs to develop a sense of the appropriate: to learn when good enough is indeed good enough. Then it channels energy into important priorities rather than obsessing over little shortcomings. Thus Virgo shades into the next sign, Libra, that of balance and proportion.

To accomplish the great work of transformation ego must accept a discipline and submit to its demands. In Leo the genius, originality and passion of the creative artist was all-important. In Virgo the objective quality of the art takes center stage. Thus Virgo refers to technique, method, protocol. This can become soulless adherence to rules or a doctrine. A robotic deadening in automated thought and behavior. A martinet, a mean-spirited stickler for the fine print; one who sweats the small stuff. Or it can display perfect attunement to the task at hand, an exquisite economy of effort in every endeavor. A delight in skillful action and apt response. An adroitness of thought, word and deed completely compatible with the situation at hand. The passion of precision. A loss of the separate self-sense in a labor of love. Eventually that labor becomes love.

Virgo demands an impeccable integrity in every field, from the conduct of daily affairs to the central challenge of a life. It achieves this by shedding sloppy indulgence and setting the highest bar for behavior. It masters itself, not by a sadistic imposition of will, but by living up to a simple code. 'Do it right or don't do it at all.' Thus its emphasis on work, properly performed. Not as drudgery - as worship. Virgo worships through a perfect execution of every undertaking in the right spirit.

Virgo strives for constant incremental improvement. It reveals the evolutionary process by which tiny adaptations add up to big breakthroughs. Evolution's demands are harsh; the price of life's privileges is high. Yet, over time, its struggle generates a joy of its own: the ecstasy of excellence.

Virgo does not describe the goal of evolution, but its means. Yet over time the two become one. The dancer becomes the dance. Complete control liberates a free flight of spirit.

Virgo realizes how infinitesimal ego is in the greater scheme of things. Yet, just as one can 'see the world in a grain of sand.'[3] so too the tiny ego, properly focused, reflects all God's glory. A single act done perfectly counts for more than all the loudmouth posturing and narcissistic dreams.

Virgo learns, step by tedious step, until aspiration becomes accomplishment. Proves its merit by willingness to undergo the protracted drill necessary to master its craft. Demonstrates its love by practical action.

For example, today we can measure the oscillations of an atom vibrating millions of times per second. Think of how amazing that is. The skill involved means more than the actual measurement. This perfection of technique mirrors a refinement of character. Competence, the effective application of mind to matter, indicates a consciousness resonating with reality. Clarity of awareness synchronized with proficient ability constitutes a special intensity of being.

Virgo structures spontaneous vitality into directed effort. For example, Leo generates an effulgence of light. Virgo focuses it into the coherence making a pinpoint laser beam more penetrating than a whole sky full of scattered photons. Virgo narrows and intensifies. It takes a truckload of rock and extracts an ounce of gold. This requires craft and concentration. By hard work it produces a speck of enduring value from a pile of rubble.

The Virgo energy field of applied reason minutely analyzes every situation to identify its defects and their practical solution. It functions internally through organizing principles of the scientific method, subjecting ideas or speculation to demonstrable clarification, proof and verification. It externalizes as technology, with its systematic procedures of inquiry leading to the objectively accurate results of its precisely engineered instruments.

Technology can extend the senses and enhance the mind. It can also displace non-rational elements of morality with an overly pragmatic agency emphasizing 'can' rather than 'should.' Virgo needs to complement its observational competence and intellectual acuity with ethical consistency. Otherwise it can enable questionable ends by fascinated concentration on their means. Virgo is often distracted from the Big Picture by its intricate detail. It must learn to distinguish priorities from process; to rank the relative importance and final value of things along with their cause and effect workings.[4]

Virgo manipulates its inner and outer environment, not as the free form cerebral play of Gemini, but in harnessed service to a purpose. Its ever increasing skill can usurp that purpose unless it discerns the 'why' behind the 'how.' It can elevate efficiency to a fetish and lose sight of its larger consequences. It commonly manifests as a willfully blind technician empowering negative forces to the best of its considerable ability. Is this not what much of the modern workforce has become?[5]

Virgo needs to develop an inner technology of soul, a yoga or holistic practice to purge irrelevant, even parasitic, distractions. It is called upon to heal itself before correcting others or improving the world.[6]

Virgo underlies the requirement of consistency as the foundation of virtue. Things must fit together, following each another coherently and with an overall logic. A fundamental principle of logic is 'Occam's razor': the simplest explanation is best. Virgo drives to streamline. It emphasizes the basic principle of organization: every part must correlate in subordination to the whole.

Virgo demands relevance. The sophistication of simplicity. It strips off elaborate explanation and artful presentation, going right to the core. Virgo's ultimate principle is integrity at its level of evolution. All of its fine-tuned abilities are oriented to and expressions of that end.

The sixth house, Virgo's subjective correlate, and any planets in it, portrays those functions that must be disciplined, re-educated and improved. The house cusp that the sign of Virgo occupies indicates the area of life undergoing rigorous training and purification through service. The position and aspects of Virgo's ruling planet, Mercury, provide insight into the process of that exercise.

Virgo demonstrates pragmatic intelligence, applied reason. It acts as the problem solving mind. Not abstract but always grounded in actual phenomena. Intellect actively engages the world. A concrete rather than a contemplative mentality, validating truth by instrumental usefulness and real results. Discrimination between pertinent and extraneous information; fidelity to phenomena rather than indulgence in fantasy. That many a beautiful theory has been slain by an ugly fact underlies Virgo's insistence on precise observation and minute detail. Thus it embodies a necessary corrective to magical thinking. Generally and inherently it keeps us honest. However, it can become petty-minded, too literal, without appreciation for ambiguity. It can overlook the symbolic, metaphorical or poetic aspects of truth.

Virgo has little to do with desire (Taurus) or ambition (Capricorn). It emphasizes accuracy: the exact truth, regardless of what one wants. It rejects embellishment or excuse; refuses to nurture hope or illusion. Virgo seeks to enhance overall quality by raising productivity, upgrading every function to its full potential. Seeing it as it really is and taking all necessary means to make it better.

Virgo reasons inductively, but in a different way than the other Mercurial sign of Gemini. Gemini finds truth through argumentation, a free for all competition. Virgo finds commonalities in data and seeks to organize them into a cohesive whole through the discovery of unifying principles.

Virgo defines categorical imperatives: fundamental guidelines, based on a consistent logic. These rational operating procedures differ from Taurean values, based on personal preference. A sign describes a fundamental dynamic of human psychology - not its specific content. Virgo refines its nature in accordance with clearly understood criteria. It does not define the criteria themselves: these vary among individuals, cultures and historical periods.

Virgo marks the critical transition between a peak experience of subjective character (Cancer, Leo) and the beginning of membership in a social setting (Libra). It defines the gold standard of identity and coordinates behavior around that. Its emphasis shifts from the spontaneous experience of all previous signs (Aries-Leo) to an articulated code of conduct. Ego voluntarily submits to a central organizing principle outside of itself.

Virgo prepares the psyche for equality of relationship (Libra) by a willing apprenticeship in service. It recognizes that duty comes before command. And that subordination to a higher cause or norm becomes a form of spiritual achievement. It portrays the faithful servant who does the work and never gets the credit. With a growing understanding that 'credit' often means degrading self-promotion, detracting from the true nobility of work done for its own sake, not for applause.

Virgo prepares personality for its long voyage into an ocean of collective experience. A tiny navigational error at the beginning of a journey amplifies over time to go far astray. Virgo meticulously calibrates an inner compass. Later signs will decide the direction of social participation. They set a course based on judicious choice (Libra), emotional passion (Scorpio) or philosophical conviction (Sagittarius). Virgo enables such decision with an ability to figure out exactly where things are and how to reach the goal. That ability to determine true location now constitutes an equal achievement to, and is the prerequisite of, any future outreach.

Generally underestimated Virgo makes us who we are by the magic of the commonplace. For example, in considering the human constitution one might first think of the mysterious brain, three pounds of grey jelly more complex than a galaxy; or of the glamorous eye, window of the soul. Virgo is like the opposable thumb, seemingly insignificant, yet the key to our ability to manipulate reality. No thumb would mean no fire, no tools, no writing - none of the enabling techniques allowing our minds to actually engage the world. Thumb, eye and brain all co-evolved: without perfect hand/eye coordination swinging through the branches our simian ancestors would never have gotten off the ground.

Virgo demonstrates the flowering, from Leo's heart centered charisma, of an independent critical mind. Its operating principle: integrity. Its method: purification through service. Its purpose: relative perfection. Thus one may go forth to meet the other in Libra.

Notes

1. Matthew 7:16
2. Hebrews 12:6
3. 'Auguries of Innocence,' William Blake, 1757-1827, English poet, a seminal figure of the Romantic movement:
'To see the world in a grain of sand, and to see heaven in a wild flower, hold infinity in the palm of your hand, and eternity in an hour.'
4. '…a woman named Martha welcomed him (Jesus) into her home. She had a sister named Mary, who sat at the Lord's feet and listened to what he was saying. But Martha was distracted by her many tasks; so she came to him and asked, "Lord do you not care that my sister has left me to do all the work by myself? Tell her then to help me." But the Lord answered her, "Martha, Martha, you are worried and distracted by many things; there is need of only one thing. Mary has chosen the better part, which will not be taken away from her." Luke 38
5. 'It is difficult to get a man to understand something when his salary depends upon his not understanding it.' Upton Sinclair, American writer, 1878-1968
6. 'Physician, heal thyself.' Luke 4:23, quoting an ancient Talmudic proverb.

Libra

Objectively: Autumnal color. Light's last statement of beauty as it falls into dark.

Sun crosses the celestial equator moving south, submerging into a galaxy of stars. An individual integrates with the community. Personality socializes.

Subjectively: Sunset. The dominance of night begins, increasing at its fastest pace. In the gathering twilight one begins to discern other stars in a sky of consciousness once bedazzled by the sole solar brilliance of self. Character redefined by affinities and affiliation.

Libra: Balance. Proportion. Relationship. Justice. Beauty.

In Libra the psyche no longer centers on its own subjective consciousness or ego agenda. It now commits to a social role, though its exact responsibilities remain unclear. Libra must negotiate that with its counterparts.

Virgo refined personality to a state of relative perfection, on its own evolutionary level, through critical reason, work and service. This autonomous path of development has come to an end. Now it functions in concert with a group, as a team player. Ego no longer does its own thing. It must take into account the needs, wishes and demands of society. Libra makes explicit the axioms of collective conduct and norms of justice guiding individual development. It describes the public context of personal content.

This is not a given, but a give and take. Libra experiences a challenging exposure to 'the problem of other minds.'[1] This involves adjustment to a separate reality. One no longer struggles with self, but with strangers. Their different values, worldviews, strategies generate shock and awe. One is turned on or switched off. Recognition, reaction and relationship take time to unfold. Libra seesaws, in a back and forth workout, through which an accommodation eventually takes shape.

We are all composed of the same energies, uniquely arranged in our various identities. To encounter the human condition formatted in a novel way (from your perspective) leads to curiosity, then exploration. Why does s/he think like that? What does it feel like to be him or her? An inherent empathy tries on their perspective. This may lead to growth. It also creates confusion: who am I? What do I really believe? Am I right, or is s/he?

This dichotomy can generate serious problems, even in the absence of overt hostility. Some people's state of being is simply alien or even detrimental, undermining self-confidence with doubt, negativity or irrelevant distraction. Some constitute an overt challenge, stimulating a more inclusive perspective, or forcing a defensive mobilization. One can be too open-minded and lose integrity by fascination with, devotion to or dependence on another. This often happens in the rapture of infatuation, projecting unconscious issues onto an objectified idol. Or true love can transcend ego in delighted discovery of a complementary reality.

Libra seeks to establish parity between inner experience and external appreciation. This usually resolves through cycles of adulation/ rejection oscillating to a happy medium. Part of Libra's balancing act reconciles independence with interdependence. One must be faithful to the essential truth of a core self. Yet, 'No man is an island.'[2]

Life demands, and people want, interaction. Thus character is tested, revealed and refined. Most circumstances involve simultaneous cooperation and conflict; a variable mix of attraction and repulsion, love and hate. Think of sibling rivalry or the 'family romance.'[3] Libra mediates such primal emotions to find their still point of equilibrium.

Almost everybody, of any sign, communes with the outside world. However, other signs bring something specific to the table: they relate to express self, assert will, get what they want, share what they have, serve who they adore. Libra brings only a sense of detached equanimity because it seeks to represent all parties and the entire community. It acts as a neutral arbitrator who interprets a social situation, translates between its members and brokers a mutually agreeable outcome.

More fundamentally Libra defines its own nature through such encounters. It becomes more, or less, than an ego so that it can find a common center of gravity and tilt it towards a desired orientation. It is what it needs to be in order to influence a group dynamic. This is not dishonesty - that requires alienation - but rather an ever adapting identification with a larger balance of forces. It can vacillate helplessly, going wherever the wind blows. Or trim its sails, navigating storms and currents, to arrive at a distant port the entire crew wants to reach.

Libra links Virgo and Scorpio; it embodies a continuum between these two extremes. Virgo heals imperfection, reintegrating a damaged part into the whole. Scorpio kills it, releasing its bound up energy. Libra slowly swings from rehabilitation to sanction. It begins with an emphasis on impartial composition of competing interests, an attempt at reconciliation. It ends with an accent on judgment, a final decision.

Libra describes a sense of justice that motivates behavior. For some, justice means to seek out and destroy rivals, real or imagined. For others it means to encourage and nurture everyone's highest potentials. For some justice is essentially punitive (except for personal transgressions). For others it is redemptive.

Planets in Libra describe an interpretation of the social contract. For some that means a war of all against all: 'Every man for himself and the Devil take the hindmost.' For others it means 'Love thy neighbor as thyself.' The specific ideals vary. In all cases it means an understanding of the rules. How one plays the game. What is the appropriate norm of behavior.

For most people this is ambiguous. It often involves a double standard, extending leniency to friends and family, severity to enemies and competitors. As the Libra function grows more sophisticated it develops a uniform code of justice. This honors fair play for all above the expediency of partisanship. Much of the Libran evolutionary struggle seeks to find and internalize this disinterested stance.

One aspect of justice is proportionality. The punishment should fit the crime, the reward be commensurate with the contribution. Libra searches for equity: how to calibrate the relative value of things. Taurus describes absolute value (in your eyes): I love chocolate and hate eggplant. Libra weighs various values in comparison: I will pay this for that.

Libra ranks internal priorities. And assigns their rate of exchange with partners and competitors. Thus it mediates the terms of intercourse on every level: sexual, emotional, mental, commercial and political.

Proportionality also informs our sense of beauty:

Truth is beauty, beauty truth.
That's all ye know and all ye need to know.[4]

Beauty may be physical or intellectual, artistic or spiritual, sensual or ethereal. Its form does not matter, its presence means everything. Beauty outwardly expresses life's inherent joy.

Each person has an innate sense of harmony. A feeling for how things should fit together: what is aesthetically pleasing and what is unseemly or just plain wrong. This canon of beauty is linked to a concept of justice: what should be rewarded, what should be rejected or punished.

Simply put Libra means the quest for right relationship. Nothing exists in isolation. All entities are interactive and codependent. Libra seeks to coordinate them through an appropriate balance of mercy along with the necessary severity of upholding standards. And to act justly as expressed in the Golden Rule:

'Do unto others as you would have them do unto you.'[5]

That also means reciprocity:

'As you sow so shall you reap.'[6]

Libra's highest expression resides in its basic sense of fairness, a common human decency underlying the trust essential for civilized life. Its lowest lies in taking sides through a biased criteria prejudicially favoring a partial truth over the whole. Its most characteristic failure creates paralyzed indecision, unable to choose between enticing alternatives.

Libra applies Virgo's sense of individual integrity to the collective. What is proper social conduct? How should contradictory interests be accommodated? What are the correct procedures for civil, legal and political affairs? Sagittarius defines the precepts of law. Libra portrays its application. 'Thou shalt not kill' is a Sagittarian injunction. The right of an accused murderer to due process, the precedents by which s/he is judged, are Libra's province.

Laws may or may not be just. They might be based on racial hierarchies or the paranoia of 'revolutionary justice' in stressed societies. They are often stated in absolute terms, which may not be relevant to the ambiguities of life. Libra portrays the feedback mechanism that correlates general ideals with actual experience.

For example, capitalism is based on an idea: that free competition in the marketplace is the best way to allocate goods and services. The Libra function modifies that idea to conform with human realities: monopolies should be prevented, workers' rights and environmental concerns honored, product safety and quality guaranteed. Libra recognizes that the complexities of the human condition require intelligent compromise.

Indeed, without the Libran balancing act, the remaining zodiacal qualities would be isolated in solipsistic splendor. Will (Aries), desire (Taurus) and mind (Gemini); subjectivity (Cancer), creativity (Leo) and integrity (Virgo); passion (Scorpio) and principle (Sagittarius); achievement (Capricorn), aspiration (Aquarius) and compassion (Pisces) would have no means of communication. Libra forms their common ground.

Ten out of twelve signs have a distinct character. Gemini has two. In contrast, Libra describes a process of adaptation, the basis of both biological evolution and social co-operation. Subjectively it harmonizes our various subpersonalities into a coherent unity; objectively it relates that identity to its environment.

Ironically, almost without qualities of its own, Libra creates a meeting place where all these energies intersect. It facilitates the bonding of autonomous elements into a more inclusive compound unity.

Libra convenes the Congress, with its procedural rules, checks and balances, wherein the various factions mingle and merge. It adds these fractions up into a larger bottom line.

Libra functions as choice. Good decisions cannot be made in isolation. They depend on the corrective guidance of comparison. Among air signs Gemini provides an operating procedure for integrating information into one's own mind. Aquarius a way of transforming its significance. Libra generates a protocol for that mind's interaction with the world.

One is partially defined by differences with others. Gemini accentuates the contrast and its resulting debate. Aquarius abstracts a general synthesis out of dialog between thesis/antithesis. Libra describes a joint psychic space that unites various polarities; a consensus around which it and partners orbit.

Libra sees all sides of every issue. Its own issue is decision: how to choose. Where more passionate signs instantly take sides Libra attempts to reconcile the good elements in both positions. Thus it creates a whole that is more than the sum of its parts. Or less than any of them. ('A camel is a horse put together by a committee.') It can be motivated from anywhere along the spectrum from unscrupulous wheeling and dealing to the most judicious statesmanship. Libra exemplifies a political temperament that respects different interests and makes compromises that accommodate all of them.

Compromise can mean shady sellout. Or farsighted vision adjusting the partial validities of competing truths. For example, the American Constitution embodies compromise in its enduring yet flexible statement of governing principles.[7] It originally defined a slave as three-fifths of a person, yet created the democracy that would set them free. It was designed to protect property and so promoted opportunity. It recognized that open process is more important than specific outcome and so guided an agrarian frontier society to become a space age superpower.

Libra's artful bargaining and ability to negotiate allows otherwise separated egos to work together. Thus they can achieve a corporate identity and accomplish greater goals than any could on their own. It enables civilization. We are largely, but not entirely, herd animals. Libra's urge to belong amplifies individual potential through social involvement. Or degrades autonomous agency into the willing cog of a soulless machine.

Libra writes the tribal accord, formal or informal, that orients conscience within a group consensus. Its collective force field powerfully shapes any single aura embedded in it. Its norms inform our most intimate behavior. Character is often defined in terms of collaboration with, or resistance to, community standards. This can be complex and multidimensional: for example, the gentle soul or good citizen who cooperates with bad laws often enables evil more than the pushy egotist who just does his thing. Libra's tendency to sweet compliance constitutes its most dangerous quality.

Libra is not only judicious but also artistic. It does not just weigh competing perceptions, it actively reimagines them in a new synthesis. Libra describes one's participation in and contribution to a shared representation of reality. And the values expressed through it.

Art demonstrates the changing symmetry of cultural forces in symbolic forms. Artists define tribal consciousness through their creations. Who remembers the partisan issues of Shakespeare's day, or the public events of Mozart's? Yet their timeless revelations of beauty are always relevant. And will enhance the human spirit forever.

Art also has a political dimension. It invokes the deepest levels of appreciation for a reigning paradigm. Or evokes a new order: 'When the mode of music changes the walls of the city shake.'[8]

On a more personal level Libra outlines a general perception of the outside world: an overall evaluation of human nature, specific expectations of people, their motives and likely behavior. How one responds to them. It describes the nature and quality of chemistry with significant others, especially the marriage partner.

The seventh house, Libra's subjective correlate, and any planets in it, describes close encounters between I and Thou. Relationships, whether amicable or adversarial. Convergence or confrontation. A meeting of hearts and minds, changing both for better or worse.

The house cusp that the sign of Libra occupies portrays an attitude towards associates. Thus Libra on the cusp of the third tends to intellectualize transactions, while the tenth connects on the basis of rank or authority, etc. The position and aspects of Libra's ruling planet, Venus, provide insight into the values brought to, and results derived from, social communion.

Libra coordinates ego with environment. It portrays the ecology of relationship. Does one play the role of predator or prey? Manipulate the group for personal gain, or sacrifice self interest for a greater good? The Libra energy zone applies a value system defined by Venus to social participation.

Interestingly, in mundane astrology dealing with national charts and public issues,[9] Libra and the seventh house have to do with diplomacy, foreign partners/adversaries and, most especially, war. War makes the most intimate contact between nations. Us and Them. Libra is often mistaken as a sign of love and peace. It can be that, in part. But it also searches for harmony through conflict. Libra, and the seventh house, describe who, how and why we fight. As well as love.

Eventually, in all close encounters the two parties merge, erotically, genetically, psychologically or politically. The outcome differs from the inputs. Rapport fuses into merger. Libra's process tips over into Scorpio's passion.

Libra acts as a dynamic rather than an identity. It lacks content so that it can mediate contact. Libra is the judge who sits silently in the courtroom as defense and prosecution have at it, while witnesses speak and jurors decide. Yet a judge umpires the trial, ensuring fairness and passing sentence.

Notes

1. Alfred North Whitehead, English philosopher, 1861-1947
2. 'Devotions upon emergent occasions,' John Donne, English poet, 1572-1631
3. This involves the Oedipus complex, describing an ambiguous sexual attraction between mother and son, along with a corresponding Electra complex between father and daughter. These names are of characters depicted by the Athenian playwright Sophocles, 497- 405 BC.

The same issues also arise in the Tibetan Book of the Dead (Bardo Thodol), which describes a male soul as drawn into incarnation by lust for his mother and aversion to his father generated by the heat of their sexual intercourse. (Vice versa for a female.) The Bardo Thodol was written during the 8th century AD.
4. 'Ode to a Grecian Urn,' John Keats, English poet, 1795-1821
5. Matthew 7:12 and Luke 6:31
6. Galatians 6:7
7. The USA national horoscope, with Sagittarius rising, has Saturn exalted in Libra on the Midheaven, its natural place of rule at the top of the chart. See 'Mundane Astrology.'
8. Paraphrased from 'The Republic,' (book four), Plato, Athenian philosopher, 424-347 BC.
9. Nations, and other organizations such as corporations, churches and nonprofits, have birth charts based on a founding event, such as the American Declaration of Independence. See 'Mundane Astrology.'

Scorpio

October 23/24 - November 21/22
Fixed Water: Death
Ruler: Mars (co-ruler: Pluto)

Objectively: The freeze. Sun drives slowly, steadily south below the horizon, into the depths. Personality returns to its instinctual source. It gives up the ghost of individual importance and merges with a collective purpose.

Subjectively: The daylight of self-consciousness yields to the unconscious night of instinct. Ego becomes the vehicle of a hidden Will. It dies, painfully or ecstatically, as the price of rebirth.

Scorpio: Transformation. Metamorphosis. Death. Rebirth.

In Scorpio the beautiful colors of year's autumn and day's sunset disappear. The world darkens. Brisk chill turns to deadly cold.

Libra portrays the marriage of self and society, ego's commitment to a community. Scorpio consummates that marriage in naked passion.

Marriage serves as a public ceremony, a time honored ritual of grace and beauty that confirms relationship. Its actual consummation explodes in private ecstasy. Private here means not alone, but in conjunction with an outer other half. Sexual union with a physical partner involves a behavioral experience. It mirrors a deeper psychological merger with a hidden inner side. That reaches a climax at the end of life when personality reunites with soul in death's release from the separate self.

Scorpio means fusion with the Other. Out there, or in here. Scorpio transforms consciousness as it incorporates an initially foreign perspective, whether met in the objective world or the subjective depths. Ultimately they are the same. Truly meeting the world really changes the self.

Scorpio describes absorption into something intrinsically different from a known and safe reality. It especially mediates a conscious confrontation with our dark side, the Shadow. We usually think of the Shadow as repressed or denied psychic contents too hot to handle. It also holds unclaimed, even disowned, potentials. And alien values that shock a comfortable worldview.

A planet, Saturn, symbolizes the Shadow, a symbol of our mortality, weakness and limitation. The Scorpio energy field integrates that Shadow into a now irrevocably changed identity. Will its menacing presence devour ego? (It often does.) Or will psychological courage transmute the energies of a former fear into a larger sense of life?

Scorpio is driven because of its contact with the Shadow's terror. It instinctively feels the proximity of inevitable death. It is constantly alert to the unconscious forces threatening a fragile sense of being. Thus it lives in a permanent state of psychic mobilization, an existential 'fear and trembling.'[1] This survival instinct focuses into a probing intensity that cannot rest until it fully understands and thus becomes empowered in relation to that provocative reality.

Scorpio must penetrate to the core of anything it encounters. It tears away the veil to discover basic drives, urges, cravings. Strips naked whatever, or whoever, it becomes involved with. Scorpio feels an elemental need to test everybody and everything to see what they are made of. It will find the answer, on its own level of comprehension. The issue then becomes what will it do with this knowledge? How will it apply its insight?

Scorpio always centers on conflicts of motivation. Its emotional insight is a given. An ability to sniff out secrets, reveal subtleties, know what makes the other tick comes naturally. This can lead to real relationship based on profound insight, a surgical precision of healing honesty, a sensitivity of tough love. Or to cynical manipulation based on a nose for weakness, a vicious degradation of real or imagined enemies through skillful exploitation of their human flaws and foibles.

Scorpio rejects disinterested contemplation. It seeks a highly charged, even erotic, union with whatever it engages. It aggressively pushes the limits, relentlessly interrogates its qualities. Libra weighs the other with a judicial temperament, in a spirit of balance and reciprocity. Sagittarius perceives it in the context of an overriding principle. Scorpio meets it with raw passion. Merge or purge. Absorb or eject. Fuck it or kill it. Are you offended by the four-letter word? Which?

Scorpio has a need to control. It must own whatever comes into its awareness. Owning can mean possessiveness. Or taking responsibility. A different psychology contains qualities and strengths that one lacks. Thus it evokes jealousy. Envy can spark emulation: a difficult struggle to acquire those abilities. Or, more commonly - both in the sense of more often and at a lower level - it seeks to undermine and destroy those who have what one doesn't. Scorpio clearly understands that a perceived rival is superior in some respects. And weaker in others. It can use this knowledge to eliminate the competition. Or to stimulate its own potential.

Ultimately Scorpio's quest for fusion with peers on its own level leads to the challenge of transcendence: fusion with soul on a higher dimension. Scorpio requires subordination of personal will to a collective or cosmic Will. Initially that larger purpose appears hostile because its ego-stretching demands are inimical to a small sense of private happiness. Will Scorpio accept that bitter loss in service to a more inclusive destiny? Or will it shrink from too challenging an identification with the greater Self?[2] If so, the lure of vengeance for such inferiority becomes an urge to dominate others.

This substitute for self-control is made all the more delicious by its ease. Scorpio instinctively understands the secret sources of influence: erotic charisma, mental intimidation; the subtleties of emotional blackmail or of political pandering. Its psychological sophistication seduces its targets into eager complicity with their own corruption. Scorpio exerts an invisible command; calls the shots from behind the scenes.[3]

Scorpio's passionate nature tends towards extremes. 'Assimilate or eliminate' means an intense projection of will. The unknown can be seen as threatening; associates as unworthy. Scorpio's essential purpose is to seek out and destroy the devil within. Instead it can strike out at scapegoats in preemptive paranoia.

Scorpio means creative destruction. Or just destruction. Scorpio expresses the grim, ominous side of the unconscious. Only thus can the energy locked down there be liberated. It raises a sickness, a decayed function or talent, to the surface for redemption. Or to infect the ego. Conscious personality can become paralyzed by its real horror. Or mesmerized. Scorpio always tempts with an evil presence. It exposes degenerate desires and sadistic angers, infused by a horrible glee. But facing, fighting and freeing these forces constitute Scorpio's true agenda. They hold a buried treasure, a paralyzed quality, protected by a sinister enchantment. Scorpio must break the spell and take back its power.

The unconscious strongly resists becoming conscious in defiance of its own nature. It lashes out in underhanded ways, seeking to divert conscious purpose, to deflect the light. This leads to a subterranean struggle in the psyche. Will will become ensnared in a spider web of lies, its energy hijacked by blind appetites? Or can it illuminate the depths and activate their frozen potentials?

Scorpio comes alive during Sun's death dive, its Fall into autumnal night. Just as the dead vastly outnumber the living,[4] so too one's latent talents far surpass known abilities. They are wrested from instinctual inertia and brought to life only through mortal struggle, akin to the birth agony. Failure means soul death, for if ego proves inadequate to the unconscious forces it has aroused it will be pulled under.

Real transformation always involves extirpation of an outworn quality in order to release its binding energy. Will Scorpio fixate on the morbid fascination of a rotting attribute ripe for change? Or feed

136

on the heat of its disintegration? Or accept its doom as the condition for new life?

Scorpio cuts away festering psychic sores and inflated ego tumors. It willingly pays the pain price. To do so takes an iron will. Scorpio's intensity often turns to obsession. This can focus energies. Or drain them. The negative aspect of compulsion is that it can't let go. Scorpio means liberation from once cherished, now cancerous, opinions, loves, ambitions. It can also be about fear of that necessary extinction. Then it symbolizes the undead, those who cannot live and will not die; vampiric souls who suck the joy from life, and the vitality of its fellows, to prolong a decomposing existence.

Scorpio is no fun - it is not interested in anything so insipid. It goes for ecstasy: the savage thrills of extermination or an exalted joy of rebirth. Ten out of twelve signs affirm life, each in its own way. They describe the substance and meaning of our brief and precious passage on this Earth, while Pisces seeks compassionate redemption of its sorrows. Scorpio is different. It connects with the other side, an utterly unknown mystery that will claim one for all eternity. It does so as a dying unto self to embrace soul. Or in a living death of malignant fear.

Death freezes life into a final portrait. That was it; there are no more possibilities. All future hopes are dismissed to past certainties. Unless and until an inexplicable grace stirs the dark waters and calls forth a rebirth.

Scorpio feels a sense of hopelessness in the face of such irrevocable fate. The next water sign, Pisces, will convert this into living faith. Scorpio does not believe. Its acute recognition of negativity makes naive trust impossible. It can only create courage by an act of will; a resolve to accept the devouring mystery of death with gratitude for the unearned miracle of life. To embrace annihilation in a spirit of love, without expectation of future reward, to give all to the All, constitutes Scorpio's supreme achievement.

Death: a cosmic orgasm? Or blackout into nothingness?

Scorpio is the darkest and scariest of signs - not because it is bad but because it dares to face the bad. Scorpio descends into the underworld and drinks of its poisoned waters. Thus it becomes venomous itself. Or transmutes them into holy water, a spiritual wine, the blood of Christ.

In medieval times Scorpio was called the 'accursed sign.' Modern humanistic astrology tries to avoid pejorative judgments. The fact remains that Scorpio introduces the socialized persona to a demonic alter ego. One can surrender to it, and often does so, for evil has an alluring glamour. Or suck up its pain by integrating this energy into the total Self.[2] 'You can't make an omelet without breaking eggs.' Scorpio breaks the ego to feed the soul.

Scorpio embodies an eruption of primeval energies from deep within. And a corresponding ability to manipulate the same unconscious forces in those who cannot acknowledge them. These instinctual energies result from eons of evolution. They are primitive and vital. They hypnotize because they draw upon an inheritance of collective power far greater than any individual endowment. Scorpio must break the spell and release their trance. Scorpio demonstrates, or develops, soul by its response to these impersonal forces. They overwhelm, or devastate, the ego. Can it then rise from the ashes, transformed by passing through the fire?

Scorpio means purifying ordeal. Purgatory. The Hell of undeniable sins. The wrathful deities of a guilty conscience. Will one flee from them? Or embrace their loathsome charms, the fascination of obscene indulgence, the bloodthirsty lust for cruelty? Or endure their shriveling shame, an acid baptism of mortification that destroys a false self-image and brings salvation through suffering?

Scorpio means facing inner demons. These, of course, are fallen angels. They can fly again if one is strong and brave enough to let them. To do so requires a descent into Hell. An immersion into the abyss. This plays out as a heroic quest to fight the dragon, find the treasure, redeem the captive. Or as an embrace of damnation, seduced by the lascivious charms of taboo appetites, hideous pleasure of inflicting pain, lure of the forbidden, cold thrill of evil.

Each of us has a twisted, embittered, toxic creature inside, the product of our own frustrations and of our race's hard history. Scorpio reaches out and touches it. Only to get bitten. Does one transmute its venom into the ambrosia of redemption? Or succumb to its morbid hate?

Its malice can be deflected: if I offer up a substitute perhaps I will be spared. Then Scorpio cannibalizes society to feed a gnawing hunger. Appropriates others' life force, labor, goods and passions to compensate for a cold emptiness. Steals their time to enhance its own.

More often it takes on the evils of its mate, comrades and society in general. Its penetrating insight sees emerging dangers that less suspicious natures miss. And liquidates them. Its secret service, unsung valor, protects an innocence it will never know. Scorpio is the first sign that lives and dies for larger than personal ends.[5]

For that reason Scorpio also refers to control of collective resources. This can be a fear/greed-based exploitation. Or a heroic marshaling of communal purpose. A directed regeneration of our shared human condition. Just as a lever amplifies an applied force, so Scorpio's disciplined drive channels many individual efforts into a single synergistic focus. It arranges things, usually covertly, to make others subordinate their divergent interests to a common goal. It taxes present pleasure to invest in future power.

The eighth house, Scorpio's subjective correlate, and any planets in it, spotlights a function(s) undergoing metamorphosis. Its normal expression is arrested for a stress test; subjected to hard questioning under duress. The house cusp that the sign of Scorpio occupies indicates the area of transformative ordeals. The position and aspects of Scorpio's ruling planet, Mars, provide insight into the personal circumstances and results of that process. Scorpio's transpersonal ruler, Pluto, reveals its social and spiritual implications.

Scorpio reveals one's deepest nature by killing and (hopefully) transcending its comforting illusions. It reaches the heights by sounding the depths. To do so it pays the highest price, consuming its own life to illuminate a core identity. The rocket that lifts a payload into space must flare out and drop off.

Scorpio always feels the urgency of time, which is short and doomed to end. Thus it demands total commitment to its struggle. It gives no quarter and expects none, knowing that all roads lead to death. It does not do fair play and has only contempt for saving face. It goes for raw emotional intensity. Truth hurts. That pain burns away weakness, the thing Scorpio most abhors.

Finally, Scorpio is about finality. Ego has been weighed in the balance (Libra) and found wanting:

'All have sinned and fall short of the glory of God.'[6]

Its faults have been laid bare, its sheer puniness revealed. The penalty is mortality. Not as a distant theory. As a real presence. From Aries to Virgo the individual developed, consolidated, expressed and purified its own attributes. In Libra it found an ecological niche in a collective community. Now, in Scorpio, it faces the most fundamental fact of life: death.

The only thing you have to do is die. That is the single universal truth all humans acknowledge. And none understands. Everybody has a theory: annihilation, heaven/hell, reincarnation. No one knows. Even Christ, in his most human moment at the very end, cried out 'My God, my God, why hast Thou forsaken me?'[7] He felt the emptiness.

Scorpio confronts this ultimate and most intimate personal fact. This certain fate always lurks below the surface. It can emerge at any time. We all feel its fear.

'Where there is other there is fear.'[8] There is nothing more Other than death. Scorpio faces that Fear.

Notes

1. Title of a work by Soren Kierkegaard, Danish philosopher and theologian, 1813-1855

2. The great psychologist C. G. Jung, 1875-1961, described the larger Self as encompassing the conscious ego along with both the personal and collective unconscious. The collective unconscious has both a preconscious instinctual and a transcendent spiritual dimension though Jung did not emphasize this distinction.

3. Consider the Soviet Union, 1917-1991, a Scorpionic superpower. Its secretive Politburo would line up atop Lenin's tomb during their annual public appearance on its birthday, November 7. Foreign intelligence agencies could only guess at its internal hierarchy by noting who stood next to whom. The purpose of this gathering was to review a parade displaying the instruments of nuclear mega-death to an apprehensive world.

4. Although there are many more people currently alive than at any previous time in history (seven billion and counting) the total number of all those who have lived and died over the millennia is estimated at eighty to a hundred billion souls. Each previous generation was much smaller, but passed away more quickly, with an average lifespan of perhaps 30 years in preindustrial times. There have been thousands of such generations in the 250,000 year epoch of modern humanity.

5. Libra defines itself in relationship, but maintains a balanced objectivity and personal space. The last four signs following Scorpio, Sagittarius-Pisces, describe an impersonal universal or spiritual emphasis; the first four, Aries-Cancer, individual psychology; the middle four, Leo-Scorpio, social participation.

6. Romans 3:23

7. Matthew 27: 45-46. In the original Aramaic: 'Eli, Eli, lama sabachthani?'

8. Hindu proverb

Sagittarius

November 21/22 - December 20/21
Mutable Fire: the meaning of experience
Ruler: Jupiter

Objectively: Year's longest, lengthening nights. Self immerses in a shared dream, a group consensus. It reflects a general moral or philosophical perspective rather than a personal one. Ego orients more towards social purpose than individual expression.

Subjectively: Day's light of consciousness concentrates into its shortest pulse, the condensed meaning of a cycle. Sun's southward movement slows, then stops at the winter solstice: its most direct alignment with the galactic center; its greatest participation in a fellowship of stars. Personality's strongest rapport with collective attitudes and aspirations.

Sagittarius: Group-identification. Philosophy. Religion.

In Sagittarius the year sinks into darkness, day ticks down to midnight. It brings the fullest commitment to night's collective unconscious.

Scorpio's death-rapture is over. Ego's binding energy has been released, in agony or ecstasy. Sagittarius expresses its spiritual interpretation. The impersonal truth of one's contribution to, or desecration of, a greater whole. The soul radiance of a life, written in heavenly light, or burned in hell fire.

Sagittarius objectively demonstrates the outcome of Scorpio's internal motivational struggle. It justifies Scorpio's emotional insight and magnifies it into a universal philosophy. Sagittarius externalizes feeling preferences into ethical standards; transmutes passion into principle.

With its own transformative experience behind it, Sagittarius seeks to disseminate its confident beliefs. It propagates Scorpio's intensity outwards into the world. Soul searching becomes social crusading. In a perfect example of enantiodromia, a thing turning into its opposite (as yin/yang or day/night), Sagittarius flips Scorpio's tortured psychological probing into enthusiastic public promotion. It now knows what is right. It will spare no effort to ensure that others do too.

Sagittarius focuses the messy ambiguities of human nature into a targeted perspective. This one-pointed orientation generates a moral force field around a singular vision. An ethical gradient of right and wrong forms in terms of what enhances or detracts from that Truth. Sagittarius presents it terms of all-embracing norms.

141

Sagittarius identifies with an archetypal image or role. And encourages its current personal expression to grow beyond its given nature to encompass this larger state of being. Living up to this higher calling means that ego becomes the vehicle of a divine force. It is steered by a lofty Presence, its animal vitality ridden by a guardian angel of the superego. If the psyche cannot ground this descent of spirit, flinches from its demanding commission, then it contracts into the darkness of its Scorpionic background as an empowered Shadow. It channels the fury of its inadequacy through an aroused inner demon, acts out as a horseman of the apocalypse.

Sagittarius begins where the Scorpion's sting transforms into an arrow's point. The archer seeks a moral compass by which to aim its sharp convictions, the distilled essence of a life. Will it skillfully target a righteous revelation? Or project self-loathing in poisoned darts of wrath? Sagittarius ends as Sun precisely orients with the core of our island universe, the Milky Way galaxy (from the perspective of Earth's orbit). Our star lines up with a cosmic gravitational attractor, just as a human heart locks on to an intangible soul source. Personal persuasion feels validated with a galactic wind behind it. This can surge intuition to prophetic heights. Or fan the flames of fanaticism by falling into a black hole of overconfidence.

In the year's final summation privacy dies, subsumed by a sacred mandate or secular imperative. To achieve that more comprehensive purpose Sagittarius' linear extrapolation of individual opinion must learn to acknowledge other approaches. Only thus can it attain the superior dimension of a plane. On that more inclusive level many perspectives act synergistically, serving as spokes of a wheel, converging on a central axis. If Sagittarius cannot integrate its own direction into a global context then it defaults into monomania, insisting on south-southwest as the one true path while all others lead to fundamental error. Or damnable sin.

Among fire signs Aries emphasizes will, Leo love and Sagittarius wisdom. Sagittarius reasons deductively, applying an overall paradigm to specific facts. An arrow shaft of light, ignited from Scorpio's dark passion, penetrates to the hidden causes behind overt phenomena. It provides an explanatory theory based on first principles. Seemingly random events become intelligible as the evolutionary fluctuations of a universal design. A jumble of data demonstrates a general law. Sagittarius synthesizes details into a coherent whole that is more than the sum of its parts. This energy zone reveals a unifying theme in multiplicity, and articulates it into a worldview.

Sagittarius = significance. Not what something is in its own right, but what it means in a larger sense. The Sagittarian character is not autonomously motivated. It is, and feels like, an agent of common or cosmic purpose. If this intuition is aligned with disciplined integrity it can serve a greater good, or god. If it acts with an inflated sense of its own importance it devolves into self-righteousness. Then stridency.

Sagittarius lives beyond purely personal concerns. It identifies with a tribal role, conforms to group expectations. It fuses with a sanctified mission; represents an exalted model. Because these are more powerful than an individual viewpoint they can swamp critical judgment, reducing one to a zealot. Or they can grow into transcendent understanding. At one end of the continuum it degenerates into crowd psychology, herd instinct, groupthink. Or an ability to exploit them. At the other it soars into a celestial communion uniting ephemeral ego with enduring truth.

Sagittarius must learn to detach identity from the power of its intuitions. Otherwise it warps genuine insight into an overblown justification of its own social contribution or special spirituality. This differs from Leo's narcissistic conceit, an inflated celebration of personal excellence. Sagittarius identifies with its aspirations. It can become crazy, even dangerous, with abstract enthusiasms.

Sagittarius insists on the social relevance of an inspirational code. It expounds and upholds the Law. Sagittarius advocates within an agreed frame of reference, grows a community consensus or shared understanding. This promotes the cohesion, team spirit, esprit de corps essential for long-term cooperative endeavor. It proclaims general standards of behavior and morality, distilled from generations of experience.

Sagittarius demonstrates the force of conscience. It channels infantile demands and angers in socially appropriate ways. Thus it inspires transcendence of appetite and ambition. Without it collective life would be impossible. And without it we could not reach beyond the rules of society to a higher law.

Sagittarius resonates to the prior existence of a first cause or prime mover above and beyond incidental happenings. It senses a directed drive behind events, an emerging plan motivating mundane behavior. Its intangible Witness weaves life's random clues into a coherent narrative. It points to a metaphysical reality beyond conscious intentions. In the individual this manifests as a soul that animates ego. For the group it expresses as a corporate identity or national character inspiring its constituent members. On the most abstract level we can call it God, Tao, the Force.

Sagittarius can serve as an open channel for this spirit, radiating as a living exemplar of its effulgence. Or conceptualize it as a holy doctrine, the guide to a more distant realization. Or insist on a specific interpretation of its universality.

In Sagittarius the variety of religious experience runs from theology to spirit. From a rigid insistence on the literal certainty of dogmatic formulations to a liberating encounter with actual Truth. This Truth is a fire in the heart, not a thought in the brain. Its reality is self evident, its power inherent, its charisma compelling.

This fire lights up the depths revealed by Scorpio. It describes an inherent optimism validated by intuition of a coming solar rebirth at the winter solstice. A confidence based on the experience that loss of a separate-self sense leads to increased social integration and a more inclusive awareness. A faith founded on instinctual delight that we exist at all in a universe that exploded out of nothing. And that, by analogy, another state of being may emerge from the biological void of death.

The ninth house, Sagittarius' subjective correlate, and any planets in it, portrays the nature of one's political, philosophical and religious convictions. The house cusp that the sign of Sagittarius occupies indicates the area of life in which they play out. The position and aspects of Sagittarius' ruling planet, Jupiter, provide insight into the circumstances and outcome of practicing those beliefs.

Sagittarius amplifies consciousness with a sense of participation in the divine. This stimulates its growth towards a closer approximation of an original and transcendent essence. Sagittarius acts on an axiomatic affirmation that human nature personifies a meaningful and benevolent reality. It follows that freedom to express this essential goodness evokes its best qualities. Thus it generates a mindset that magnifies possibility, creates opportunity, opens doors to 'a life more abundant.'[1]

Sagittarius is expansive by nature. Not deep like Scorpio. Nor does it scale the lonely heights of achievement like Capricorn. Rather it expresses a broad consensus, common ground, shared experience. Think of that period in the American political process when the judgment of a hard fought election has been rendered (Scorpio), but the cares of governance (Capricorn) have not yet begun. The newly elected President has a honeymoon of goodwill when s/he can dream big, aspire to far horizons. Sagittarius offers a moment of liberty. This can inspire. Or intoxicate. Liberty is our most precious gift, if we use it to fulfill our own potential, enhance society, do God's work on Earth. But it can also degenerate into license: a promiscuous indulgence, blithely trampling others in a brutal 'honesty' of raw egotism.

Sagittarius soars between the scary intensity of Scorpio and the heavy responsibilities of Capricorn. It reflects an epiphany. One stands in the Light and brings it to the community as a vision of the good, the true and the beautiful. Sagittarius bears witness to an elevated stage of moral development, the next step in evolution.

The zeal of this enlightenment can blind sensitivity to other wavelengths of illumination. Its glow can become a glare. Such a powerful voltage often endows an immature ego with too much power. Sagittarius always tests character with an unearned grace. Will it rise to the occasion? Or sink into a sense of entitlement? Its windfall fortune can exaggerate self-esteem. Or remind that 'Of those to whom much is given, much is required.'[2]

Sagittarius sees the bright aura of things, just as Scorpio perceives their invisible core. It feels the Power. If it lets this power spontaneously flow through it then Sagittarius can articulate its authenticity with clarity and relevance. If it tries to own the light it flares up and burns out, taking others down with it. It enjoys the opportunities presented by an intuitive contact with more advanced dimensions of consciousness. And fails by identifying that with its own merit in order to justify small opinions and grubby ambitions.

Sagittarius surfs a wave of optimism. It rides a current of public sentiment, on its leading edge but not too far ahead. It actively goes with the flow and thus gains a position in the right place at the right time:

> There is a tide in the affairs of men
> Which, taken at the flood leads on to fortune.[3]

Its objectively unjustified hopes create their own luck and almost miraculously evoke the possibilities it seeks. Sagittarius exemplifies a positive faith that automatically creates good outcomes. (As opposed to Pisces' accepting faith that redeems bad ones.) It typically goes too far too fast, but usually finds a way to leapfrog its problems. 'All's well that ends well' justifies its errors and rewards its speculative ventures.

Sagittarius tends towards manic hyperbole in everything. It hides its shortcomings and mistakes in smug hypocrisy. And trumpets its smallest achievements with sanctimonious triumphalism. Its self promotion is not only tacky but ironic, because in fact it embodies something far greater: a personification of history's trend or even God's Will. Sagittarius naturally aligns with the spirit of the times, conforms to the larger forces behind and driving events. This often makes it superficial, an opportunistic player. Or it can articulate the hidden passions of the tribe, express emerging principles of a new cycle.

Sagittarius is the least individual of signs. And therefore the luckiest, because it echoes the collective unconscious. It is in tune with the temper of the times, synchronized with the spirit of its surroundings. Thus it speaks with the voice of prophecy. It extrapolates current trends with a keen comprehension of their ultimate consequences. This is different from, but not less than, genius, which is novel insight. Sagittarius has a farsighted perspective on the implications of an action, trajectory of a society. It does not bring a new reality (Aquarius); it makes the most of present possibility. It is attuned to the immediate, with a view to its foreseeable future. (In contrast, Aquarius presents an ideal, different in nature from present conditions.)

At its best, Sagittarius clearly spotlights the ethical demands and spiritual possibilities of any situation. It encourages their positive development and natural growth. It willingly embodies a guiding morality for its own and the common benefit. At its worst, unresolved Scorpionic power issues hijack Sagittarius' gregarious public persona. It then appropriates accepted memes and social trust to serve its own ends. Cloaking an ego agenda in shared ideals can succeed for awhile, but eventually crashes into hard Capricornian reality.

Sagittarius maximizes the potential inherent in any entity, accelerating its evolution. Or decays into a gluttony demanding more and more of the same. Its exuberant expression tends to exaggeration, proliferating a partial truth to the detriment of the whole.[4] As with any sign, Sagittarius covers the entire range from gross to sublime along a certain line of development. Because it publicly expresses an implicit consensus it has an unusual degree of latitude in sharing, or imposing, its insights on others.

Sagittarius emphasizes destiny as an expansive adventure, a spiritual journey. Then Capricorn meets fate as the circumstances of that unfolding. Sagittarius revels in the exhilaration of its important message. Capricorn reveals the responsibility that entails. Sagittarius thrills to life's felt significance. Capricorn carries its attendant burdens and actual achievement.

Notes

1. John 10:10
2. Luke 12:48
3. 'Julius Caesar,' Shakespeare
4. 'Growth for the sake of growth is the philosophy of the cancer cell.' Edward Abbey, American environmental writer, 1927-1989. This suicidal attitude is prevalent in modern America, a Cancer nation (July 4, 1776) with Sagittarius rising. (See 'Mundane Considerations.')

Capricorn

Objectively: Like the holiday season during which it occurs Capricorn culminates an old cycle (Christmas/pagan Saturnalia). And initiates a New Year. Sun makes its southern turn at the winter solstice, then slowly climbs north. Personality emerges from a collective reality by asserting individual ambition.

Subjectively: The midnight hour. Another day begins in the depths of night. The light of ego consciousness rekindles within a group identity. A separate self, validated by achievement, rises through a social or spiritual hierarchy.

Capricorn: Duty. Accomplishment. Initiation into a higher state.

Capricorn begins at the winter solstice, year's longest night. The fervor of Sagittarian tribal enthusiasm has burned out, its political ideologies and spiritual inspirations reduced to tired clichés. Self stands alone, without consolation, in the cold and dark. Yet the tide has turned. Day's lengthening light reveals a frigid, unforgiving world. Here only the strong survive. Capricorn is born.

Winter's bitter austerity demands realism: respect for facts, rationing of possibilities, recognition of limits. The harshness of this bleak landscape forces competence. Competence begets confidence. Confidence generates character. Real character, carved by necessity and tested in adversity. It has no room for excess baggage. Elaborate theories, grandiose pretensions, murky emotions mar the simplicity, obscure the elegance, of Capricorn's focused clarity.

One might think this grim: a life hardly worth living, the drudgery of a gaunt and joyless survival machine. Yet Capricorn's hard won abilities bring profound fulfillment. Perfect execution under pressure generates a high and austere exaltation. Excellence is its own reward. It can only be earned, never given.

Capricorn begins at Earth's alignment with Sun's interstellar trajectory.[1] It grounds a cosmic movement that regenerates the annual cycle on a spiritual level. (In contrast to Aries' springtime biological renaissance.) Out of the year's foundation in the void it creates something from nothing. Does this not mirror the work of God?

In Capricorn the great work of individualization begins anew. Sagittarius returned self to its collective roots, bearing a fiery prophetic truth. Capricorn revives a quest for individual distinction. Ego is emerging from the tribe, not immersing into it.

This happens slowly. A nascent identity must first adapt to its surroundings, passing trials of natural selection and social validation. Only by meeting the demands of its environment does it gain the strength to assert its own power over it. Thus a small `child develops by doing what its parents expect. A young student must graduate through the elementary levels, learning a compulsory curriculum of ABCs before s/he can learn to think independently (Aquarius). Capricorn acquires skills and develops innate talent, step by rigorous step. It confirms its own value by meeting objective criteria of achievement. This certified performance lays the foundation of personal credibility. And perhaps even of public eminence.

In the same way, every human embryo reenacts the entire history of the race in the womb. 'Ontogeny recapitulates phylogeny.'[2] It grows from a single cell to an undifferentiated cell mass to a triple layered blastula and on through fish-like and mammalian forms until it reaches its own human level. As with the physical body, the psychological self can only reach its full stature by experiencing and mastering every intermediate stage. This takes difficult work over a long time.

Capricorn conserves the tried and true as the core of future growth. It builds on precedent, adds to past accomplishment. Capricorn represents a long heritage condensed into the material form of the present.[3] Its complementary sign, Cancer, remembers and feels its psychological essence, in living moods, dreams and sensitivities. Capricorn develops it externally, through achievement, role and rank in the collective enterprise.

Capricorn subliminally understands the age-old effort it took to get here; cherishes a history of which we are the growing tip right now. It accepts the responsibility that comes with our inheritance of a human condition that is the gift of four billion years' evolution.[4] For some this becomes a crushing burden, the weight of a world they did not ask to carry. For others an incentive to live up to a sacred trust, an obligation to countless forgotten ancestors. And to a few it lends the authority of time itself, as an exemplar of all that came before that they carry on into the future.

Capricorn is driven by a need to prove its worthiness for such an endowment. Most do so by competently enacting a social function, putting ethics, work, family and country first. Some by spectacular demonstrations of ambition, climbing the hierarchical ladder to a pinnacle of power. Or at least keeping up with the Joneses in a rat race to nowhere. Some by grueling effort, showing real merit earned the old fashioned way. And more than one might think attain a higher state by displaying grace under pressure in circumstances known but to God. They light a candle in the dark, ignite the spark of a larger destiny, because nothing else works for those who live for more than personal ends.

From respect for the past comes resolve to make a future. Capricorn senses the hard road we have taken from molecules in a puddle to men on the Moon. Thus it instinctively understands that anything can be achieved consistent with physical law and human nature. It only takes time: perhaps a protracted struggle, perhaps in a perfect seizure of the moment.

From experience and in line with its realism Capricorn plans. It is the most strategic of signs. It takes the long view, has an objective and knows how to get there. Whether or not that goal proves worthy is the issue. Capricorn has the patience, stamina and will to enact an actual agenda: not a spiritual aspiration (Sagittarius) nor a utopian vision (Aquarius) but an astute compromise between soaring hopes and sober means. 'Politics is the art of the possible' defines an attitude extending to science, business, culture or that most exquisite endeavor of all: the art of living.

For all of its seriousness Capricorn is also a joyful sign. The rebirth of light initiates it. The tough and lusty goat symbolizes it. Capricorn appreciates the sensual reality of our brief life. Its common distortion into narrow purpose and harsh discipline reflect a fear that comes from its proximity to the shadow, the dark side of a year and of an ego. It knows its own fragility in the depths of night and winter; feels in its bones that all things run swiftly to a final end. Yet it slowly, steadily, shrewdly develops the courage to carry a brightening torch through the night. Overcoming fear leads to a deep and somber ecstasy of triumph over circumstance.

Yet even the sweet taste of victory eventually turns to ashes. Capricorn experiences the test of rise and fall, the fleeting nature of all worldly success. Glory fades, usually with unexpected consequences. Will it cling to withered memories; decline into bitterness and despair at their passing? That happens all the time. Or will it savor the very brevity of its moment in the Sun, alive between the two eternities?

Acutely aware of the heights, Capricorn often feels inferior to their challenge. It can then sink into morose resignation, fatalistic depression. Or rise to the sweet melancholy of difficult duty done against impossible odds. Capricorn learns the lessons of limitation through the very audacity of its ambition, which can never be fully realized. And yet the effort alone makes its own achievement.

Capricorn stands at the summit of objective accomplishment. It realizes how tiny it is in comparison to the mountain it has climbed. And how ephemeral. Yet it also understands how far it has come. Isaac Newton, the Capricorn who first explained gravity and invented calculus, said it best: 'If I have seen further than other men, it is because I have stood upon the shoulders of giants.'

Capricorn recognizes its status in society, with the corresponding responsibilities. It is solid because it is in solidarity with the group from which it came. In the following phases ego necessarily detaches from this source in order to grow. Aquarius becomes entranced by a futuristic vision, Pisces by an idealistic dream. Aries through Cancer turn toward development of personality in its own right. Leo displays it to the world. Virgo brings it to relative perfection and dedicates it to public service. Capricorn reaches the zenith of that effort; emphasizing ego as the vehicle of a group identity and enabler of its goals.

Capricorn embodies the peak of all that one can be in the world under present circumstances. The next, and final, two signs, Aquarius and Pisces, provide glimpses into future potential: they represent a coming dispensation, a new order. Yet Aquarius flies into mental madness, Pisces dissolves into emotional meltdown, without Capricorn's grounding in the reality principle.

The tenth house, Capricorn's subjective correlate, and any planets in it, indicates the general nature of one's calling: profession or station in the community. It can also refer to spiritual initiation, consolidation of a higher state of consciousness. The house cusp that the sign of Capricorn occupies indicates the area of life wherein that mission is fulfilled. The position and aspects of Capricorn's ruling planet, Saturn, shows how: actual performance of that function, whether through formal office or spiritual attainment.

To do so Capricorn is not guided solely by personal criteria of conscience. Rather it acts in accordance with a sense of duty towards its communal context. This usually means upholding a conservative interpretation of traditional arrangements.

Duty, and the discipline it entails, defines Capricorn's driving motivation. Duty can mean dull regimentation; a refusal to think; an escape from accountability in easy submission to another's will. (Whether that be a more powerful individual, or the herd.) It can involve acceptance of unpleasant burdens, in the service of its own growth or group need. Or an iron will to do the dirty job that must get done: perhaps for career; perhaps for the team. It can be a drive to do the right thing just because it is the right thing. Self-respect then becomes involved with morality, either as a legalistic code or as a genuine sense of principle.

Most fundamentally, and rarely, duty means living authentically as made in the image of God. Uncompromising faithfulness to ego's soul purpose. Like Zen enlightenment this is the easiest thing in the world - and the hardest. It demands complete commitment to inner truth despite convention, peer pressure or fantasy. It means fully, and joyfully, saying yes to a larger fate. Consenting without reservation to a God-given destiny. Swearing 'I do' to the sacred marriage of self and soul.

Thus Capricorn's seriousness. It instinctively knows that every action is a final and complete statement of self. An identity oath. Time is short and opportunity limited. One must get it right, here and now. This is the final exam, which cannot be retaken. Judgment day, enacted in every moment, which will never be given back.

This can lead to fear; a paralyzing sense of inadequacy; guilt for falling short. Self-loathing, with a futile attempt to deny it in the vanities of ambition and false triumphs of competition. A cynical 'realism' about personal insignificance, projected onto others in the denigrations of one-upsmanship. Or internalized as a sullen sadness.

Or it can generate a slowly growing realization that one stands before God in judgment because one is god-like. Tiny as it may be, the human being embodies the shadow of God on Earth. It dares to live in the valley of death; is willing and able to consummate spirit's purpose on the material plane.

Capricorn exhibits this growing identification with the divine in an ever-deeper appreciation of the world as it is. No need to hope for heaven. Just this is perfect. It only requires the courage to accept it. Thus Capricorn accepts a flower as a simple thing of beauty, made all the more precious by its finitude. Fast fading color and perfume adds poignancy to its fragile loveliness. Never again will it blossom. Yet amidst all the eons of time and light years of space it is the beauty: fully real, just now, just so.

Capricorn describes love for what is rather than what could be. Fidelity to facts. It accepts the inherent limitations of phenomenal knowledge. This can degenerate into gloomy doubt. A denial that anything exists other than the immediately visible. At its lowest, Capricorn degrades the imagination to the contours of an ego, denies possibilities beyond the ken of small minds and petty goals. Shrivels everything to a mean spirited zero sum game where my gain is your loss. Falls into an amoral pragmatism where anything goes to win the crummy prize:

'Well is it known that ambition can creep as well as soar.'[5]

At its best Capricorn insists on a rigid code of excellence; strict adherence to the letter of the law. This follows from its survival ethic. You cannot break the laws of physics. Or supersede the requirements of biology. Therefore, by extension, you should not rebel from fundamental principles of the social contract. Instead live up to its highest standards. This can mean challenging an established corruption of them.

Every individual completely depends on the community: as mammals with our prolonged dependence on parents, as culturally conditioned citizens who could not survive without the contributions of others who provide our food, clothing, shelter, safety. Our private egos could not even think without the linguistic tools and mental concepts developed over thousands of years. Thus each of us owes a debt to society, to be paid by enhancing its character and participating in its future.

Capricorn portrays a sense of obligation for owing so much to the commonwealth. Some interpret it as a need for absolute compliance with the minutiae of bureaucratic regulation or religious ritual. Others understand it as cooperation with a group consensus, implementation of agreed principles. Some succeed and are promoted. Others surpass conventional expectation and take the next step in evolution. A few reach another level altogether to demonstrate a more inclusive awareness of the greater good. This compels admiration and sets new guidelines for general emulation.

Capricorn demonstrates emergence of an individual from the community: not as an autonomous ego, but as an avatar of its shared values. This can play out as a stifling internalization of group norms, or their projection through control over others: conformity or ambition. On its highest level the Capricorn energy field shapes personality into identification with a demanding spiritual law. Then moral authority amplifies its practical ability to create a singular exemplar of common purpose.

Notes

1. See 'Sun,' Figure 4.
2. Ernst Haeckel, 1843-1919, German biologist
3. For example, one's brain literally embodies an evolutionary mountain arising within the skull's hard shell. At its base the spinal cord of nerve pathways bulges into a brain stem, an automated instinctual center processing sensory stimuli and physiological functions. Above and around it wraps a limbic layer, the site of emotional response, present only in mammals. Crowning this, the cerebral cortex forms the outermost perimeter of our biopsychic architecture, a strata of consciousness bearing cells attained only by primates and cetaceans (whales and dolphins).* Abstract thought and subtle psychic states flash among its intricately woven neurons. They can do so only by virtue of their supporting structure: three pounds of living matter more complexly organized than the physical universe of stars and galaxies.

   * Fish and reptiles have superbly honed instincts, and a degree of intelligence, but they do not have the neurological architecture enabling them to ground higher states of consciousness. Other types of animals, such as some birds and cephalopods (octopi and squid), are also quite intelligent although their brains are structured differently from those of mammals.

   Regardless of neural organization every animal participates in a shared sentience. We know by their behavior that all creatures experience fear. And curiosity. Surely this has an internal subjective side even if that is not organized at the level of self-awareness.

4. Each of us relives a condensed version of this history in the womb. After birth we all pass through every developmental stage of the human condition during our slow maturation into adults. As the consciousness theorist Ken Wilber points out, no matter how enlightened a society we may create, every new citizen will enter it at square one, as a helpless baby who will take decades to learn the ropes.
5. Edmund Burke, 1729-97, Anglo-Irish author and statesman

Aquarius

January 20/21 - February 19/20
Fixed Air: Archetypal Ideas
Ruler: Saturn (co-ruler: Uranus)

Objectively: The dead of winter. Sun moves slowly, steadily north. A new light of consciousness begins to grow with the lengthening days. It illuminates life from an original perspective. Personality detaches from its social matrix.

Subjectively: The dead of night. Mind shines as a point of light in sharp contrast to the collective darkness. It achieves maximum objectivity and universality as one star in concert with a galactic community.

Aquarius: inspiration; futuristic and utopian foresight; hopes, wishes, aspirations.

Aquarius demonstrates the paradox of visibly lengthening daylight while the momentum of temperature continues to drop. It describes a cold cerebral clarity; detached intellect contemplating a pristine winter world.

In Capricorn ego represented and articulated group values through demonstrable achievement. Now, in Aquarius, individuality breaks free of tribal norms and social structure. Collective responsibility turns to individual exploration. The mind is still concerned with larger than personal issues, but does not accept tried and true methods of dealing with them. It shakes loose from traditional expectations to find its own answers and experiment with other ways of understanding. This gives it a striking originality, in genius or in madness.

Aquarius shares Capricorn's respect for the facts based on winter's harsh survival demands. But it no longer interprets them within the accepted system. It seeks a new context; sees the whole picture in a different light.

As the year enters its deepest freeze, a growing illumination presages the coming spring. One senses the potency of rebirth rising under the horizon. Aquarius reorients from past accomplishments to emerging hopes. These coalesce into a guiding inspiration. That will later manifest as personal purpose (Aries) and values (Taurus). For now it reveals a vision of things to come. This encompasses more than real life; it outlines a full spectrum of possibilities. Aquarius can see a Big Picture from an Olympian perspective precisely because it has not yet immersed in it.

Aquarius sees all things afresh, from afar. It elucidates a formula to explain this sweeping panorama and locate one's place/function in it. Aquarius sketches an identity equation, writes the psychic DNA code of a germinating worldview. It generates a new mentality to meet and make tomorrow.

Aquarius extends intellectual parameters. This expanded space will later be filled in with individual information bytes. The Aquarian experience is like learning theoretical mathematics. Its abstract discipline can then be applied to organize and make sense of actual scientific data: stellar movements, chemical reactions, biological processes, etc. Aquarius emphasizes the acquisition of a general outlook that informs understanding of specific circumstances.

Capricorn defines the mountaintop of real achievement; Aquarius suggests a soaring sky of aspiration. It gives a bird's eye view of a beckoning mindscape. To attain such a view means leaving the nest, ejecting known certainties, safe assumptions, conventional wisdom, to fly into the unknown. One may crash and burn, or veer off into strange realms of eccentricity. A successful Aquarian takeoff into the wild blue yonder presupposes a solid background of Capricornian competence, a foundation of logic to anchor its high-flying hypotheses.

Aquarius inspires breakout from a dominant paradigm to explore a developing one. But its effort to birth novel ideas is demanding and dangerous. Most hunches turn out to be half-baked (at best). Most experiments fail in their stated purpose. Sometimes they bring unexpected results. Real progress comes from accepting these surprising discoveries in lieu of preconceived opinions. The high risk, high gain Aquarian endeavor requires integrating game changing epiphanies (Uranus) with the sequential continuity of reason (Saturn).

Aquarius operates through abstract thought. It necessarily steps away from present circumstance to comprehend how it fits into a larger frame of reference. It examines all options, explores all avenues, tries on all perspectives to find the truth. This requires an experimental attitude. A willingness to embrace trial and error rather than a pledge to 'never surrender, never retreat.'

Aquarius is often idealized as a revolutionary sign of liberation. However, most revolutions end up disastrously: shattering an unjust system and releasing its pent up hatreds, but failing to bring genuine rebirth. Yet, over time, the arc of history does move towards greater opportunity, inclusiveness and respect for rights. Aquarius' impulse to change slowly realigns both personal and tribal character with elevated principles.

Aquarius channels the energy of innovation: an urge to express more advanced qualities. That drives evolution. On the biological plane it acts through genetic mutation. Most mutations are detrimental. Yet life gradually attains a more subtle sophistication because natural selection weeds out weakness. At the psychological level this happens because novel insights (Uranus) are tempered by the feedback of actual evidence (Saturn). Aquarius' impartial openness allows it to drop mistakes rather than insisting upon them as more willful or passionate signs would. It can walk away from an untenable approach because it values freedom itself, rather than any of its fruits, payoffs or results.

Aquarius' freedom does not involve an action opportunity of ego assertion (Aries), nor a creative license of self-expression (Leo), nor the social liberty under law that enables civilization (Sagittarius). Rather it describes a mental autonomy that can amplify subtle whispers of intuition into clear concepts that can be shared with others. It transmits the teleological (goal oriented) attraction of a more evolved state as a message from the future. Aquarius redefines the world in the light of an inspiration.

Aquarius portrays the 'Eureka!' moment of life seen through new eyes. It can leap to a higher state of consciousness. Or be blinded by its intensity, like a deer caught in the headlights. Aquarius transforms a basic orientation. Or becomes lost in space.

Aquarius' sense of independence enables navigation through these disorienting jumps. Its cool reason entertains more inputs and possibilities than the heat of passion allows. Aquarius is freer than any other sign to explore exciting ideas. It can also be the most untethered to common sense. It is the most prone to original insight, and to overt insanity.

Aquarius emphasizes cause over effect. It cares more about the fundamental energies driving action than the ephemeral events resulting from it. Why is as important as what. Of course the two cannot be entirely separated, but Aquarius prioritizes dynamics above outcomes, focuses on process v product.

Aquarius sublimates, perceiving the ethereal essence of things rather than their tactile reality. It pays more attention to becoming than being. It is interested in where things are going v what they are here and now. It looks to an open future over a committed present.

Aquarius realizes all that can be achieved under an old dispensation already has been (Capricorn). The only way forward is to set another agenda with different operating procedures. Any function (planet) in Aquarius has entered a prerevolutionary state of tension, primed for a revelation. Or has already begun to transform itself and its environment. This means carrying a stronger energy charge than previously. If it cannot do so then it blows a fuse and disintegrates into mental illness.

Aquarius is the most idealistic sign, not out of naiveté but as its own form of wisdom. It sees implicit potentials that remain invisible to more pragmatic minds. However, it can exaggerate these emergent properties. Aquarius must balance visionary genius with practical sense. Its revelatory shock can zap one with an instant of enlightenment changing a life, a worldview, perhaps even the world itself. Or its supercharged theories can fry the brain circuits. It then falls prey to a mesmerizing obsession like a moth drawn into the flame.

Aquarius illuminates head over heart. Its pleasures are those of understanding rather than of power or sensuality. It lives on the cerebral plane with a unique degree of abstraction in all things, for better and for worse.[1] This perspective promotes a disembodied form of knowledge. Thus it tends to misinterpret living biology as a complex chemical code, consciousness as an electrical brain wave pattern, political passions as a polling algorithm. It often misses real trees for the ecological concept of a forest.

Aquarius challenges an accepted social contract and revises a sense of community. It estranges from the prevailing consensus, shatters group solidarity with disturbing stimulation. This can be an objective observation or a bizarre overemphasis. Aquarius tends to alienate normal feeling bonds by insisting on disruptive truth, or opinion, over comforting convention. One either changes social mores or breaks away from them.

Aquarius' rationality does not fully encompass the feeling side of things. Its clear intelligence can be insensitive to emotional nuance. Aquarius loves as fully as any sign - but its altruistic, impersonally benevolent heart beats to the tune of a different drummer. It resonates to a chord of mutual idealism; seeks high minded companionship in an elevated cause or consciousness, free association in a shared interest, fellowship in co-operative participation. It emphasizes agape: selfless, all-embracing, unconditional love more than eros: a romantically exclusive '... desire for psychic relatedness,'[2] or compelling sensual attraction.

Aquarius takes a genuine interest in, rather than fervently identifies with, the other. It wants to taste the sugar, not become sugar.[3] It seeks to liberate rather than possess the beloved. It is turned on by the independent nature of a soul mate. And enhanced by empathy for all other souls, brief sparkles of a higher dimension behind the provisional forms of separation:

They are not brethren, they are not underlings; they are other nations caught with ourselves in the net of time and life, fellow prisoners of the splendor and travail of the earth.[4]

As a night dominated sign Aquarius describes an attunement to the collective unconscious. This, having fulfilled a cycle of attainment in Capricorn, opens to a more inclusive dream. That dream is utopian, communal rather than private. It is not about ambition or ego satisfaction. It points to self-identification with a universal value: truth, justice, beauty. An ideal. Or an ideology.

Aquarius describes a mental map distilling the complexities of evidence into an explanatory theory. Things are seen not for themselves, nor in relationship to each other, but as exemplars of general qualities. Aquarius is not about information (Gemini) or a balance of forces (Libra). Rather it seeks the fundamental principles behind changing phenomena. It integrates a swirling mass of data into a coherent paradigm. This is not a Sagittarian ethical imperative but a great Idea. For example, $E = MC^2$ describes an objective law, not a moral meaning.

Paradigms shift. Aquarius demonstrates the process of phase-change wherein a solid situation becomes fluid, or vice versa. Water turns to ice or to steam. Frozen facts melt or cloudy wishes condense into a flowing current, the electric 'juice' of inspiration. Aquarius describes a tipping point where a worldview, with all of its assumptions, suddenly morphs into another reality. It leaves the past behind. There can be no encore to the epic achievements of Capricorn. Instead it embraces other truth criteria and a changed mission.

One can't only do the same thing better and better. Aquarius demands taking a chance on something else. It portrays that quantum jump, with all of its opportunities and dangers. It creates a field of acceleration where quantitative increase becomes qualitative transformation. A prepubescent boy or girl doesn't just keep growing. All of a sudden hormones kick in and everything changes. Aquarius' winds of change blow in an entirely different climate. That creates a crisis of adaptation. It reconfigures consciousness to learn and live another way.

Aquarius applies archetypal principles to particular events. Archetypes symbolize instinctual and intuitive energies. They are more than thoughts in they have an evocative dimension along with a definable content. They represent the intangible, with one pole grounded in tangibility. Archetypes point to ineffable but immediately apparent mega-concepts: death, love, God, etc.

Aquarius perceives truth as Platonic ideals applied to concrete circumstance. It seeks to express personality as an individual example of universal standards. It gives voice to a vision, reveals the human face of a more angelic order. It acts as an emissary from a better future, an experimental version of a superior humanity. Or of their nightmare negatives in the devil-ution of a dystopian dream: a perversion of pro- grammed existence, the robotic face of an artificial intelligence.

Aquarius does not describe an autonomous ego. (That births in Aries.) Rather it articulates an emerging state of consciousness. It rein- vents self, not as an upgraded ego but as a new type of individual. Capricorn embodies the highest values of the present social hierarchy. Aquarius announces a coming society with a different persona.

Aquarius insists on mind over matter. It seeks a spiritual pattern behind the fleshy personality. It does not heal or enhance an existing state of being (Virgo). Rather it draws a given identity towards closer approximation of its model prototype; evokes emulation of its more advanced nature and possibilities. The beauty of ideas drives behavior at least as much as the force of facts.

The eleventh house, Aquarius' subjective correlate, and any plan- ets in it, describes the nature of one's hopes, wishes, aspirations. And of their social and spiritual agenda. The house cusp that the sign of Aquarius occupies indicates the area of life in which these play out. The position and aspects of Aquarius' ruling planet, Saturn, describe the logic and discipline that implements them. Aquarius' transpersonal ruler, Uranus, reveals the impact this reforming impulse has, on the world or in the self.

Aquarius precipitates invisible potentials into communicable ideas. Spirit's exhalation into mind. It projects a mental force field, an image of self.[5] This then condenses into an overall sensitivity (Pisces), which in turn emanates the will (Aries) and desire (Taurus) bodies.

Aquarius' energy zone connects plan and manifestation. It does so through a blueprint linking archetypal energies with living entities. It directs psycho-spiritual voltage from the constraints of what is to an intuition of what could be. Aquarius points to the future. That exists only as an idea. Yet it orients action, directs effort, sparks motivation in the here and now. Aquarius opens existence to innovation. Promotes improvement. Its challenge lies in actualizing this grand design.

Notes

1. Astrology itself is an Aquarian discipline. It can liberate by providing insight into the organizing principles behind character and behavior. One begins to understand personality with some objectivity by distilling a few basic motivations/orientations out from a confusing web of effects. Or it can oversimplify living psychology into a spectral equation of forces, reducing the complexity and ambiguity of human nature to a fated formula. Like anything else of value it can degenerate into a dogma. The resolution lies in Aquarius' own property of intuitive openness: an acknowledgment that the latent potentials implicit in a planetary pattern can only emerge through conscious choice in real life.

2. Jung: 'Aspects of the Feminine.' Plato called eros '...a desire to possess, but nevertheless it is different from a purely sensual love in being the love that tends towards the sublime.' (Symposium 200-1) In modern parlance 'eros' has been reduced to physical sexuality.

3. Paraphrased from Sri Ramakrishna, Bengali mystic and yogi, 1836-1886

4. 'The Outermost House,' by Henry Beston, American writer and naturalist, 1888-1968. This passage refers to other sentient souls of the living kingdoms around us.

5. Aquarius symbolizes the etheric body, an electronic template organizing DNA based proteins into a biological vehicle. Medical practices such as acupuncture realign these bioelectric currents when they go awry. Brain and heart scans diagnose physical conditions through their magnetic auras. In the upcoming Age of Aquarius such electrical therapies will increasingly displace chemical and surgical ones based on an understanding that physical processes follow etheric patterns.

Pisces

February 19/20 - March 20/21
Mutable Water: Compassion
Ruler: Jupiter (co-ruler: Neptune)

Objectively: Winter's melting. The socially conditioned personality enters its disintegrative phase. Sun moves north at an accelerating rate. The growing, but not yet dominant, light of consciousness illuminates shadows of a receding dreamscape.

Subjectively: Predawn glow. Unfinished business and hidden vulnerabilities come up for review. The consequences of past sins surface, to be forgiven or to betray. Ego dissolves in voluntary acceptance of a larger destiny, or compulsive martyrdom to it.

Pisces: Sorrows. Redemption. Self-undoing. Surrender to the Will of God.

In Pisces individuality breaks loose from collective obligations (Capricorn) and aspirations (Aquarius). It is no longer concerned with the social order, realistically (Capricorn) or idealistically (Aquarius). It bears witness to the human condition and seeks to redeem it by self-transcendence:

'I, if I be lifted up, will draw all men unto me.'

As the last sign, Pisces summarizes a whole cycle and mirrors its spiritual meaning. A mirror has no content of its own; it reflects what is out there. Yet, clear and properly curved, it can focus the farthest starlight, making visible and known the nature of our universe. Pisces concentrates diffuse currents of the unconscious background into an explicit synthesis. Not through ego assertion, but by centering the unspoken yearnings of a community or an era. Its will is the general will.

Cancer describes the personal fantasy motivating subjectivity. Pisces embodies a communal dream projected through an individual. A tribal yearning for redemption, or a group psychosis, designates an agent to enact its hidden agenda, a developing sensibility struggling to be born. This is too subtle and complex to be grasped by the prevailing consensus consciousness. Pisces represents it for the community. In its final phase personality has spent its passion, does not lust after power, is not enthralled by desires or ideas. Thus it provides a blank screen upon which the group-mind can project what it needs to learn.

Pisces feels the pregnant stirrings of a coming rebirth (Aries). It can imagine the unseen possibilities of a renaissance. It has not yet attained this new state of being, but psychically senses it. Thus it connects collective need with a misty premonition of an emerging future. This vision swirls as a nebulous longing, a fuzzy first approximation. It is still germinating, not yet ready to face the world's harsh demands. But face them it must.

These subtle impressions are initially evasive, too faint to articulate themselves in tangible form. For example, even the most vivid dreams usually evaporate upon awakening. Eventually such evanescent glimmers coalesce into a critical mass of intuition. This then acquires enough energy to infiltrate and re-orient the conscious attitude.

These vague signals implicitly challenge an established structure. Ineffable prescience subverts accepted interpretation. Anticipation of renewal undermines confidence in present arrangements. Power begins to notice the rising tide. The conventionally successful are comfortable with things as they are. They will move to destroy any new ideal, and its exemplars, before it comes to fruition.

Thus Pisces' association with hidden enemies, betrayal, treachery. It acts as a lightning rod channeling the release of ignored potential or denied forces whose time has come. It evokes an unresolved dilemma and points to a solution outside the box of normal thinking and values. This generates a violent reaction. Pisces must die to make its point (not necessarily literally). By doing so it elicits a tragic sympathy. Thus it succeeds: not for itself, but for others.

The same process occurs subjectively. Other signs explore or enact their dreams. Pisces must outgrow them. It learns to realize their essentially delusional nature so that it can recognize a more profound truth. The death of dreams hurts. Through such painful disappointment Pisces also learns to avoid the snares of illusion set by others, or propounded by society. It begins to accept guidance by a higher will, to believe in a greater form of love. At best it lets the seductions of worldly temptation or ego tripping wither away so that it can ascend to a more encompassing plane. At worst it takes substitute gratification to extremes in an effort to evade the emptiness that must precede becoming filled with soul.

Pisces demands unconditional faith because it involves complete loss of identity. A singular energy signature merges with a shared stream of consciousness. Something may emerge out of this baptism. But it won't be you, or any variation of you. It will be something truly new (Aries). Pisces does not give to get. It is about giving until nothing is left. In that absence God appears. Only in silence can one hear the Word.

To other signs this seems impractically mystical. Or a sad excuse. Indeed, Pisces' breakdown and sublimation often takes a destructive course. Intoxication, masochism, an inability to fight and hold its own, a lack of concern for its defeat, leaves others bewildered. Or contemptuous. How can such a weakling survive the selection pressures of a brutally competitive world?

It does so because evolution does not proceed through enhancement of strong, well adapted adult forms. Rather it develops through prolongation of the juvenile stage in which maturation takes another route to a new identity. Through retention of larval characteristics, which grow up differently. Through the impressionable flexibility of youth.

Pisces flourishes because, as in a circle, its end is also a beginning. Its wilting can shrivel into degeneration and dissolution. Or revert to the embryonic state, like a pluripotent stem cell returning to renewal. Pisces serves as the embryo to Aries' birth. An embryo is utterly helpless. Yet it holds the future. It seems passive. Yet its growth and inner development are more rapid and profound than at any other period of life.

Only nakedly is one reborn. Only in ignorance, without preconceived opinions, does one learn. Only a defenseless openness can take in the world. And thus become it.

Pisces portrays the paradox of strength through weakness, gain through loss, victory through defeat. It recognizes that every process reaches an endgame, a stage where it can go no further. It must die, dissolve, fertilize its regeneration with the ashes of its former character. Pisces lets go of all that was once loved and is now a burden.

After the fiery prophetic truth of Sagittarius, the cold eminence of Capricorn, the cosmic concepts of Aquarius there is only peace: the 'Peace that passeth all understanding.'

Everything melts away. The collective passions of righteous principle, actual achievement, utopian vision have spent their force. All is quiet.

Pisces immerses in the dreamtime. It finds refuge in a regenerative empty space. Later, new life will burst out of it in Aries. For now, it diffuses into a sea of memories and longings. These recombine in the miracle of genesis. A new soul begins to take shape. It is not focused, but rather distributed, like the surface tension on a body of water. It shades off into unconscious depths below, and to a spiritual dimension above. It expands horizontally to encompass the entire plane of human experience. And beyond to a poetic appreciation of the magic behind reality.

As the last sign Pisces integrates what has come before. It gathers all the energies of the ending cycle and distills them into a seed pattern for the coming spring. This is not the clear, articulated mental blueprint, or archetypal equation, of Aquarius. It contains too many feelings, the residues and consequences of past acts. It embodies an emotionally charged condensation of all prior history and belief.

In Pisces the lengthening daylight of individual consciousness illuminates unconscious issues. It must reconcile with painful memories from the past. And assimilate festering ambiguities of the present. Thus Pisces deals with karma, whether defined as a legacy from prior incarnations or as a psychological inheritance of instinct, infantile experiences and the habits of a tribal context.

The contrast between Pisces' brightening glow, and what it reveals within the still prevalent dark, gives it a dualistic character. This sign is symbolized by two fish swimming in opposite directions. It demonstrates extremes: salvation and degradation, temple and tavern, transcendence and disintegration. Disintegration creates the conditions for transcendence. The old must release its binding energy to make it available for a new synthesis.

One can get stuck at this stage, overcome by fumes given off in the heat of decay. Intoxicated by delusional raptures that mimic transcendence: chemical dreams, false glamors, indulgent fantasies. The self-sense generates powerful waves of illusion to sidetrack soul from the agony, and the ecstasy, of true ego death. Pisces must navigate them all the way to that end.

Every act involves forgoing alternative possibilities. Pisces emphasizes the principle of sacrifice that makes progress possible. Pisces, at the end of a round, subconsciously remembers all of its options. It resonates to some, discards others. Just as an embryo activates a single set of genetic potentials out of a vast lineage, so Pisces, adrift in a sea of choices, selects among them according to a subliminal set of priorities boiled down from the lessons of previous experience.

The twelfth house, Pisces' subjective correlate, and any planets in it, shows self-sacrifice and surrender to a higher Will. Voluntarily or not. The house cusp that the sign of Pisces occupies indicates the area of loss, and perhaps of resurrection. The position and aspects of Pisces' ruling planet, Jupiter, provide insight into the experienced circumstances of that dissolution and the nature of what is coming to pass. Pisces' transpersonal ruler, Neptune, points to the spiritual aura surrounding this rotting and ripening, along with the illusions it entails.

Of all signs Pisces is most sensitively attuned to an invisible reality behind the phenomenal world. It does not identify with consensus consciousness. It instinctively understands that intangible forces shape events. The momentum of its past decisions is already committed to a spiritual trajectory. Not a predetermined fate but an opening to a more inclusive state of being.

This requires the loss of attachments, qualities and attributes. Ambitions and opinions, career and family, welfare and standing - all must go to clear the way for a larger life. Renunciation on such a scale is painful. Few undertake it voluntarily. Thus Pisces generates deprivation. This seems, and often is, unjust in terms of the present situation. But the Pisces experience is about liquidating that existence to create space for a new emergence.

Pisces brings crushed hopes and denied benefits; loss of status, things and friends. All of this serves to strip the psyche bare in preparation for the next level of negation: death of personality, voiding of emotional perspective, cancellation of dreams. All must be given up. Or will be taken away. Thus Pisces has always been associated with involuntary servitude: perhaps objectively in an institution such as prison or hospital, perhaps subjectively in an invisible net of despair. It may occur overtly through a life changing trauma or betrayal. Or as a silent scream within. Then it drowns in ennui, or in booze, turned off by the frantic circus or stifling monotony of life.

Pisces washes the soul of everything it was or had. It breaks one down so that God can take possession of the vacated premises. Or the Devil. Sometimes Pisces is absorbed by the darkness. It is not just about redemption - it is also about that which must be redeemed.

One might object that this is overstated: most Pisceans are gentle souls, many with a delightful sense of the ridiculous. True enough in that most do not fully experience the nature of their energy zone - just as most Taureans don't get rich, most Leos don't become famous, few Capricorns make it to the top, few Aquarians are brilliant. A sign describes a challenge and an opportunity. Most people of any sign keep their heads down, partake of a standard issue cultural identity and only partially engage the full promise of their birthright.

Pisces inherently means surrender to a greater Force. It can manifest as a dancer possessed by the dance, a public servant dedicated to the needs of others, a compassionate soul consecrated to a cause. Or as a political prisoner in the Gulag, a drunkard in the gutter. Whatever the circumstances Pisces requires that ego be broken in order to approach the mystery of God.

This often creates a victim consciousness. Pisces then wallows in self-pity, becomes demoralized by misfortune. This is exacerbated by its low energy state. Pisces is like an invisible dark energy expanding the universe as a whole rather than a point of light exploding within it. It glows as the diffuse cosmic background radiation from which all things originally condensed. Thus it does not assert or defend its self because it identifies with all selves.

Pisces receives rather than sends. With its innate lack of boundaries Pisces responds to the unspoken vibrations of its environment. Given human nature many workplace, institutional and family settings seethe with hostile and negative feelings. Pisces must take them in and take them on.

It does so through empathy. Rather than applying logic, or general principles, to a situation, or extracting significance from its component elements, it learns by sympathetic resonance. Pisces experiences its environment by adopting it. It walks in the other's shoes. Assimilates their qualities.

Such impressionability is our primal and most effective form of education. This osmotic sensitivity can generate an all-embracing consciousness and care. Compassion brings depth and subtlety of insight. Ironically, innocence = profundity.

Or a flood of feelings and sensations can inundate the central organizing principle of identity. Then only a chameleon-like acquiescence to stimuli remains. An amorphous codependence on whomever one talked with last; a go with the flow lack of character. Pisces then becomes a sounding board for others' thoughts. A doormat for their aggression. A target for malice they cannot acknowledge in themselves but will gladly project onto a compliant victim.

The vulnerability of one willing to open up without reservation invites attack from predatory elements. Pisces is often devoured by those at the top of the food chain, over-awed by fiercer egos, dominated by more intense wills. Thus its ancient association with slavery. It can flee into the escapism of an alternative reality. Or create the world anew through the power of imagination. It can be forced into exile: to wander, a stranger in a strange land. Or transcend inevitable injustice with a generosity of spirit that astonishes the universe. And changes it forever.

What would Christ have been without the crucifixion? By unconditional acceptance of a higher Will he transformed a personal injustice, easily evaded, into a redemptive opportunity for all. By creating a new context, he turned a seeming triumph of evil into the spark of rebirth.

Rebirth implies prior death. Pisces, as the last phase, must always face spiritual death at the hands of those more powerful in this world. It is too old and too embryonic, too nuanced and too naive, to compete on their terms. It can win only by changing the very definition of victory. To do so it must first redefine itself by embracing its own annihilation.

Will it become a martyr to pathos? Or in hopes of some future payoff? Or will it offer everything it has as an act of love? Love that is willing to die for the beloved.

Pisces drinks deeply of despair. It understands that no political agenda or social reform can wipe away the oceans of tears already shed and yet to be. It feels the fullness of sweet melancholy, yet trusts in an ultimate benevolence. Its sensitivity to the world's woes is exceeded only by faith in their redemption.

Pisces is the sign of sorrows. It would rather serve with compassion in Hell than rule with glory in Heaven. Thus it is the sign of Love beyond all particular affections. In the end that Love can only say 'Thy Will, not mine, be done.'

Moon

Earth and Moon are as different as life and death. Earth is geologically active and biologically alive. Moon is inert. Nothing there has changed in four billion years.[1]

Moon was created when a Mars sized planetoid crashed into early Earth. The ejected debris coalesced into our dead shadow planet. Physically Moon is a pre-biotic remnant of the era before life appeared on Earth. Psychologically it represents a pre-egoic temperament out of which personality emerges, the subconscious foundation of self.

Moon's orbit around Earth forms a womb, impregnated by solar winds. It shelters terrestrial life. Dead Moon makes living Earth possible. Without Moon's stabilizing gravity Earth would gyrate wildly on its axis, much as moonless Mars does. In consequence, any given spot on its surface would undergo continual and drastic climatic change, flipping from ice age to searing drought and back again every few thousand years. This would make it difficult for advanced life to evolve, a process requiring millions of years of environmental consistency punctuated by occasional eras of challenging disruption.

Without Moon's gravitational drag, winds of up to seven hundred miles per hour would constantly shriek around the world. Land life would have to hug the surface or burrow underground. Nothing taller than a centimeter could withstand the permanent planetary superhurricane. Nor could anything live in the wave torn sunlit layers of the upper ocean where photosynthesis takes place. Organisms would probably remain at the bacterial level, huddled around hot vents in the abyss. It is hard to imagine complex, let alone intelligent, life under such conditions.

Moon thus physically nurtures biological life on Earth. In parallel fashion it also psychologically nourishes that life's sentience.

Sun, our guiding star, does not shine directly onto Earth. Its spiritual light refracts through a zone of psychic condensation, Moon's orbit, before reaching us. Moon steps down blinding solar brilliance into the soft silvery glow of a luminous dream, one's personal psychology.

As the closest astrological planet to Earth, Moon's orbit around it defines a zone where all other planetary forces dissolve into an integrated feeling tone. Moon gathers all the lights of heaven and consolidates them into the coloration of a personality.

Moon acts like a lightning rod drawing down cosmic vibrations. This antenna receives planetary signals and formulates them into a coherent psychological message. Moon stores up cosmic potential like a battery. And releases it onto Earth in phase with a solar purpose as it waxes and wanes.

Moon is Earth's highest mountain, hurled aloft in a cataclysmic collision during its creation. This solid shield accepts and filters Earth's first contact with alien energies. It detoxifies their unearthly strangeness by absorbing them into the unconscious. Spiritual radiation from outer space percolates through Moon's deep aquifer of instinct, vitalizing it to flow forth as the wellspring of individuality.

Moon digests specific nutrients (planetary factors) into the compound sustenance of identity. Its orbit, enclosing Earth like a placenta embracing an embryo, blends these separate inputs into the mother's milk of psyche.

Moon's material presence tunnels a gravity well through Earth's magnetic aura. All planetary powers spiral into this vortex. There they merge into the psychic genome of self. Strands of the solar system's spiritual DNA, from fast moving Mercury to slow waved Pluto, wrap around each other in the lunar whirlpool. The warp and woof of male (Mars) and female (Venus), mind (Mercury) and soul (Jupiter), spirit (Sun) and shadow (Saturn) weave together as the soul's garment of personality.

As the lowest orbital shell, surrounding Earth itself, Moon depicts the bottom line of all cosmic phenomena as we experience them. Thus it sums up the balance sheet of individual character. Sun shows where one invests, and on what: why one burns life's energy. Venus tallies up the assets: attributes one possesses, and their worth. Mars marks corresponding debits: the expenditures of life's struggle, the cost of moving from one phase to the next. Mercury measures trade-offs, the give and take, between them. Jupiter describes expansion, Saturn contraction. The outer planets represent intangibles, vital but incalculable. Moon brings them all together in one portfolio of personality.

Moon's phase, its relationship to Sun, indicates whether one is growing self (waxing), or giving it to a larger cause (waning). Moon's sign depicts what is in the account: Powers? Loves? Ideas? Its house registers how they are deployed: in the career? Marriage? Children?

Nimble, ever mutating Moon reflects the running tally of one's life in its fast movements, transiting through a sign or a house every 2½ days, progressing through the same every 2½ years.[2] Moon takes all the plays, good and bad, fair or foul, and sums them up, or down, into a final score. That score is a set quantity/quality. A done deal, a dead thing of the past - even if that past was just last second. It defines the base, or basis, from which one moves, by the agency of Mars.

Moon is the size of Earth's solid inner core, Mars the size of its molten outer core. Mars portrays the heat of Moon's unconsciousness becoming conscious, in defiance of its own nature. Mars stimulates Moon's static summation into motion, ignites its inertia into action. Moon holds the content of personality. Mars, first planet beyond Earth, energizes its outreach as will.

Venus, first planet inside Earth's orbit, describes the deepest desire behind Moon's dream. The subjective value of Moon's manifestation. Indeed, Moon and Venus constitute polarities of one's inward feminine side. Venus embraces its erotic side, Moon the maternal. Venus entices, Moon nurtures. Venus portrays what one wants, Moon what one needs.

Moon is unique among astrologically significant bodies in that it revolves around Earth rather than Sun. During this revolution it spends half of each cycle within Earth's orbit and is therefore closer to Sun. This approach culminates at new Moon when it conjoins with Sun. It spends the other half beyond Earth's orbit and is thus further from Sun. This recession culminates at full Moon when it stands in opposition to Sun. (See 'Lunar Phases and Aspects,' Figure 1.)

Through this in-out rhythm Moon's orbit aligns the objective social orientation of planets visible beyond Earth (Mars, Jupiter, Saturn) with the subjective personal quality of planets inside Earth's path (Venus, Mercury). Moon closer to Sun indicates a tendency towards introversion: finding truth within. Moon farther from Sun indicates a tendency towards extroversion: seeking truth out there.

Moon's orbit generates a sexual pulsation uniting male (Mars) and female (Venus) poles of being. Earth, orbiting between them, is the child of that union.

Sexuality means far more than biological coitus. It expresses the unifying tension of our dualistic reality, polarized between spirit and matter, life and death, light and dark. Their dynamic contrast interacts to weave an energy pattern: the ground of existence. It manifests through the tangible substance of Moon's globe. Its ultimate nature lies in its raw actuality.

This poses the most basic question: 'Why is there anything at all rather than nothing?' The lunar response is simple: 'Life is a reality to be experienced, not a problem to be solved.'[3] It can only be approached through a visceral immersion into its properties. That's what Moon is all about: one's gut sense of reality.

Material reality, the mystery of Moon, eludes definition. Moon is where a wave collapses into a particle, a force field contracts into physical form. Lunar inertia converts momentum into mass. Moon funnels potential into phenomena. It gravitationally draws etheric vibrations into actual vitality.

On a parallel plane, the lunar mystery of subjective identity can never be defined. Only its qualities can be described.

Sun radiates at the juncture between a spiritual dimension and material expression. It emanates essence into energy. This impacts the fabric of space/time to make waves. These stimulate matter to self-organize into individual entities, each with its own peculiar life and consciousness precipitated into being by the lunar magic of incarnation.

Moon's latent state of being is irradiated by Sun's Will to become. Over time this raises basic lunar existence to a higher plane, a more subtle state. Matter's substance slowly rarifies, enabling it to carry an ever-greater solar voltage.

Moon is wholly passive. It absorbs and reflects sunlight. And is transfigured by that reception. Moon itself does not act. It is acted upon. Moon brings to life what life brings to it.

Solar principle needs a medium in which to manifest. Moon provides the substrate holding and shaping what would otherwise be abstract and potential. In some this matrix is coarse and primitive. In others sophisticated and refined. Its material comes in many different grades from dull clay to tingling protoplasm. Its concreteness extends beyond physical palpability to more ethereal realms of sensitivity, mental clarity, and intentional intensity.

Moon is simpler than Earth, a precursor stage enabling cosmic energies to interact with matter. This generates an emergent quality: life. Moon entrains solar impulse in living biology. It grounds spiritual light, gives it substance and grows it into living things.

Sun symbolizes spirit, Moon manifests body. The body brings spirit to life. Its physical brain accepts the imprint of intangible consciousness. Given Moon's position and phase, one's lunar programming is receptive to some inputs, resistant to others. To a certain extent one sees, hears, perceives what one wants to. Each of us has a predisposition to pick up on some energies, tune out others. Thus Moon represents innate responsiveness.

Moon's receptive sensitivity thrills to the stimulus of evolution. It lays down an architecture to conserve and build upon its incremental gains. This forms the seed from which one sprouts. It describes a heritage endowing one with potential, an origin that orients growth. Moon incubates their unrealized possibilities in the soil of circumstance, watered by emotion, driven by a fiery purpose (Sun).

Moon is a celestial fossil, a mirror of the past. Much of the lunar surface actually consists of dirty glass. One can look into this glass darkly, back to origins and causes. One's present character is conditioned by its dead past. Moon reveals inherent resources, shows what one is made of.

This lunar inheritance derives from deep biological sources, long-term human history, family background and one's own individual story. Life propagates through heredity. It transmits a continuity of lineage across the generations, each adding to the record. Thus we share DNA sequences programming for basic metabolic functions with the most primitive bacteria. New abilities are simply added to this foundation over the billennia.

Some things, such as physiological functions and basic instincts, are the product of immensely long evolutionary epochs. Personal disposition is more fleeting and unique. Cultural background, family dynamics, infantile events all contribute. So might subconscious memories, talents, tendencies from previous incarnations, stored in Moon.

The fact that Moon is a physical extension of living Earth in the cold dark void implies that there may be a soul which survives the discontinuity of death and maintains a record of one's previous identities. This can neither be proven nor disproven by argumentation. The symbolism of astrology is suggestive, not conclusive.

Yet, simply because Moon exists in the emptiness implies that some core of individuality might survive the mortal ego. Perhaps a soul-essence continues after death, just as Moon's barren ball of rock in the void remains paired with Earth's vitality. Perhaps such a soul alternates between incarnate and discarnate episodes, just as Moon transits through its phases.

Reincarnation would not involve the ego one knows and loves. Ego consciousness is an Earthly phenomena. It is generated by Earth's rotation and described by the ascendant rising over the eastern horizon at the moment of birth. It dies when that physical body does. What might survive is a memory of who and what one was, absorbed into a larger spiritual essence. Perhaps that soul, not personal you, is again drawn into the vortex of a spinning Earth...

Reincarnation, if real, would be a lunar phenomenon. Moon accumulates karma, the consolidated result of this, and perhaps of previous, lifetimes. In the latter case its specific details are rarely available to our conscious minds at this stage of evolution. Consider the confusion if they were. However, a general tone, vibration, orientation, derived from those lives, would express themselves through an unconscious temperament. If reincarnation does not occur, or if one cannot accept it as a hypothesis for lack of evidence, then Moon can be understood as one's genetic, cultural, familial background synthesized into a preconscious disposition during infancy.

Moon extracts memory out of life. It depicts an inner terrain of inherited and acquired tendencies, the peaks and valleys of one's developmental stages. Moon was yesterday; the summation of all that is past and gone. One cannot change yesterday's facts. Only one's attitude towards them.

> The moving finger writes, and, having writ,
> moves on: nor all thy piety or wit
> shall lure it back to cancel half a line,
> nor all thy tears wash out a word of it.[4]

Memories can become a self-reinforcing feedback loop. A tangled web of stale old obsessions, resentments, fantasies, playing over and over and over again. Then one obsessively deepens a defensive stasis into a quagmire. The same behaviors and excuses repeat until they vampirize the entire personality. Sun's light gets sucked into a black hole of regret and recrimination. Ascendant's fragile ego gets drafted into strident justifications of things said and done long ago. The past eclipses the present and darkens all hope.

Moon shows where one gets stuck. The default position. The lowest energy state of petrified passivity, zombie repetition, slavish imitation.

Or remembrance can oscillate with an ongoing reality, resonate with cosmic rhythms. One can reinterpret past events. Embarrassment can lead to insight, defeat to liberation, failure to a new beginning. (Is this not the story of America, a Cancer/lunar nation?) The past then becomes a springboard to the future.

Memory is a goldmine. 'Past is prologue.'[5] Each of us inherits three billion years of evolution, perhaps 10,000 generations of human experience, five millennia of civilized endeavor. The language we so casually use was crafted over centuries. The concepts embedded in it - relativity, evolution, justice, etc. - represent the flowering of many minds. Every emotion we feel as ours alone was actually refined through the heartbreak and exaltation of countless forgotten ancestors. Each one of us is a zillionaire-heir, if only we knew it.

Personal memories form the substructure of identity. We are shaped, though not defined, by our past. 'The child is father to the man.'[6] Moon depicts our inner child, innocent or injured. That inner child is a creature of spontaneity and openness. It can accept new truths, adapt to new challenges, grow and flourish. Thus Moon waxes. Yet it must also 'put away childish things,'[7] leave behind an outworn past, embrace the unknown future. Thus Moon wanes.

Memory has many layers. They range from ingrained physiological programs of cells and organs to an instinctual repertoire from our pre-human past, from a universal racial unconscious to the compelling beat of tribal myth, from infantile impressions to conscious skills, from subliminal response to social adaptation.

These strata of remembrance parallel the multiple cloud-bands of consciousness on Jupiter. The largest planet portrays a transcendent essence sublimated out of life. Its striped appearance symbolizes an overall soul structure punctuated by the differentiated functions of psyche. Moon describes its immanent counterpart, with levels of instinct, remembrance and empathy laid down by life.

Moon acts as the descending current from an intangible All into material diversity. Jupiter represents its ascending counterpart, rising into spiritual unity. Moon = immanence; Jupiter = transcendence. These are equally necessary, valid and complementary movements. Any individual, society or historical period tends to emphasize one over the other. An identification with either side of the equation can go too far: for example, this worldly materialism of modernity or otherworldly religiosity of the middle ages.

Taken as a whole the Earth-Moon system is three times larger than Jupiter. But it is discontinuous, consisting mostly of a void between Earth and Moon. Perhaps this says something about life and death. An emptiness of forgetfulness separates Earth's locus of life from Moon's manifest pole of the death state. On Moon living Earth has a tangible foothold in the dead void. Moon holds the secret of death.

Moon's legacy, expelled from awareness, gently glows in the unconscious. A whole world of compressed memory hangs in space thirty Earth diameters away. In contrast, our normal range of sight extends only a few miles to the horizon. At best. Most of the time we barely see beyond our nose.

One's present sense of self spotlights only a tiny focal point of a larger unconscious matrix. This encompasses not only Moon's physical sphere, but also its entire Earth circling orbit. One's current existence is visible and known. Its lunar foundations are buried in depths of space deeper than any ocean, a temporal context longer than any life.

Earth-Moon embodies the polarity of life-death on the biological plane. Sun and Moon emphasize polarities of spirit and matter on a more cosmic level. They propose the extremes of existence: pure energy and utter inertia.

174

Solar spirit exists in eternity: an infinity of potentials superpositioned in a Unity behind the visible universe. Moon's constantly changing phases happen in sequence. They unfold through a cyclic rhythm. Sun = timeless Now. Moon = flow of events in time.

The spiritual spectrum of Sun reflects in psychological phases of Moon. Sun = Christ: the transhuman, unknowable Reality of God. Moon = Jesus: a unique individual carrying the tangible life of an otherwise unworldly force.

Moon's phase, her relationship with Sun, depicts the quality of every passing moment: initiation (new), surging self-actualization (waxing), consummation (full), and radiant self-dissemination (waning). Each can occur in any mode: spiritual inspiration (fire), illuminative contemplation (air), emotional sympathy/psychic rapport (water) or achievement/material reality (earth). Moon's movement births Sun's light into life.

Moon shows what you were born as. Sun points to who you are becoming. Planets demonstrate how you get there. The ascendant processes your (hopefully) growing awareness of this evolution.

The ascendant, and its first house body, depicts the lit up area of ego consciousness. All the rest of the chart portrays the lunar circumstances that ego faces. Some of these houses are subjective: one's desires (2), mind (3), creativity (5). Some are objective: powers (8) and social norms (9) with which one must deal. Some are intangible: karma (12), hopes (11), feelings (4). Some are in-your-face tangible: career (10), health (6), lovers and enemies (7).

Moon is what is. Sun powers its evolution. The rising sign registers your conscious attitude towards it. Moon sums up a set of givens, portrayed by the rest of the chart. Sun: what you make of them. Ascendant: the conscious orientation by which you do so.

All of these givens find their center of gravity in the actual Moon. Its position is ground zero: an unconscious character with unspoken assumptions. Moon's aspects, relationships to other planets, energize movement from that basic stance. The ur-aspect is Moon's phase: its aspect to Sun. The Sun/Moon relationship (phase) describes how one feels the world. (The Ascendant depicts how one sees it.) An instinctive posture. This can be alive and vital. Or programmed and robotic. In fact, it oscillates through an ever-tipping balance between them.

The planets elucidate specific qualities of the Sun/Moon polarity. Mercury: mind, how it knows. Venus: desire, how it loves. Mars: will, how it evolves. Jupiter: meaning, how it is fulfilled. Saturn: fate, how each lunar moment in time integrates into a larger lawful pattern.

Beyond Saturn, through the conduit of Uranus, begins the formless realm of deep space, a larger galactic reality.

Our Moon, at ¼ the size of Earth, is the second largest relative to its parent planet in the solar system. It is exceeded only by tiny Pluto's big moon Charon, at ½ its size, and orbiting very closely around it. No other planet/moon system comes close to these two. Some moons, like Saturn's Titan, are large in an absolute sense, but small compared to the body they orbit.

A moon symbolizes karma, memory: a planet's past, both as dead weight and as a resource for future growth. The Pluto system points towards the greater galactic background within which our solar system participates.[8] Pluto/Charon reminds us that our Sun lit world moves within vast cosmic rhythms. Every 230,000,000 years Sun circles the Milky Way's outer rim. Pluto/Charon's window into deep space shows where Sun pays its dues, pulls its weight in the galactic rotation. At Pluto/Charon we touch and are touched by a cosmic fate.

Every atom heavier than hydrogen in our world and in our bodies was forged in an earlier sun than ours. These elements were spewed out into space by the nova death explosion of previous generations of stars. Our 4.5 billion year old Sun and solar system inherits all of its atomic, material substance from a prior epoch. This indeed is galactic karma, a legacy of past eons, embodied at Pluto/Charon.

Our Moon, circling the home world, carries a closer, more intimate inheritance. It summarizes a deep biological past; locates its molecular, cellular memory. Accumulated instincts and abilities, developed over ages of evolution, accrete here. This ancestral legacy stretches back over four billion years. Perhaps 18 solar circlings of the galaxy are encoded in the psychic sentience of Moon.

The fundamental qualities of our reality derive from an earlier universe, prior to the condensation of our Sun. Pluto/Charon, at the fringe of our reality, beyond even Neptune's dreamscape, hints at a cosmic legacy. Moon, encircling our own center here on Earth, carries the heritage of this present solar epoch. It holds the memory of life, all the way back. This has many layers: generational chords of family, culture, history; common human responses at a species level; nurturing/caring sensibilities of our mammalian ancestors; instinctual senses of cold blooded forebears, from fish to reptile; cellular similarities we share with all other creatures; molecular patterns at the very foundation of biological being.

Moon conserves this entire heritage. It resembles our brain, which adds one structure/ function on top of another: thus a thinking neocortex envelopes an emotional limbic system which, in turn, overlays instinctual lobes sprouting out of a brain stem, the automatic physiological taproot into spinal cord and body. Moon embodies the whole record of all that has ever been, from long before individual personality entered its brief day.

Our bodies contain traces of every prior developmental stage, from fundamental structures of the cell to the most sophisticated architecture of the brain. Part of this is instinctual: a well-honed automatic repertoire derived from our long past in fish, reptile and mammal forms. Part precedes instinct, as the most basic functions of psyche: sentience, receptivity to the world. An ability to respond to environment, learn from example, recall events. Underlying even that stands a physical vehicle determining what we are capable of sensing and doing. This body-mind, the temple of soul, is the cumulative product of eons. Every prior state of evolution remains encoded in its cells, organs and general morphology.

One's own embryonic development reenacts every ancestral step of evolution in the womb up to the human level. 'Ontogeny recapitulates phylogeny.'[9] The psyche remembers them all, from womb, birth, infancy, early childhood on to more self-conscious periods of the human condition.

One interprets these later stages through personal phases of feeling. While basic physical needs are primary, bodily functions and survival behaviors are relatively automated. We mostly live a lunar life of emotional events. Thought is distinctly secondary, and genuine spiritual encounter quite rare.

For about ⅓ of life, during sleep, one directly plunges into Moon's unconscious realm. We must enter that death-like state regularly - or actually die. In sleep we dream. The deep symbolism and ineffable quality of dreams are Neptunian. Their role in processing personal issues is lunar. Dreams play a subliminal tune to which we dance. Not only the celestial symphony of Neptune, but one's own personal song.

Neptune charts deep oceanic currents of the collective unconscious. These distribute heat (of passion) and generate climate (of opinion) on a global scale. Moon maps the shallower, more fertile, coastal waters of the personal unconscious. Here are the bays and estuaries where life proliferates. An intertidal zone between planetary memory and the heights of individual awareness. Here life, and psyche, crawls out of a watery womb onto dry land, the challenging arena of conscious endeavor.

Our experiences on the dream plane, though rarely remembered, are vital. They enable one to deal with a universe too vast, and other psyches too alien, for the waking mind to immediately comprehend. The ever-changing Moon allows one to assimilate their novelty. Ironically, the robotic aspect of the unconscious is always open to new programming, whereas the self-image all too often invests in an explicit 'never surrender, never retreat' defensive posture. Lunar dissolution of ego in the dream world permits it to relate to and absorb alien information in a nonthreatening way. In sleep one also receives upwellings from the deep collective or cosmic Unconscious (Neptune). In the non-linear, unfocused dream state mind can fruitfully encounter paradoxical profundities. Rational thought would suppress or reject these out of hand. The dreaming mind can acknowledge and accept them.

Dreams also have a nightmare side. Moon connects one with the preverbal, pre-rational roots of psyche. At this depth ego cannot organize or control its contact with primary sensations and impulses demanding attention. A mute instinctual intelligence silently screams, generating bizarre and scary images to convey unacknowledged issues. One swirls in hypnotic helplessness among confused distortions of unresolved guilt and fear, unlived potential and dimly sensed insights. With defenses down perhaps one also subliminally absorbs psychic signals from the environment: close associates, the larger community and the collective unconscious. Moon brings them all together, presenting an eerie amalgam to a sleeping mind.

Thus Moon lubricates Ascendant's consciousness. This can occur in an evolutionary or a subversive way, depending on self's relationship with its lunar base. Sadly, all too many ego-constructs are at war with their unconscious matrix, out of social conditioning, personal pride or simple inflexibility. They are doomed to destruction. Consciousness flowers out of the unconscious. A flower that turns against its roots will wither and die. The roots will survive to bloom again.

Even deeper than sleep is the universality of our biological nature. Its physicality forms the lowest common denominator of our human condition. The collective unconscious objectifies through a body that is similar, almost identical, to others. The same needs and instincts generate a shared psychic reality. This underlies and sustains individuality. It also connects one with others in empathy and social solidarity.

Biology precedes and enables psychology. Its neural organization provides a communication network for mind. Its glandular secretions carry feelings. One's body creates a baseline of personality: one's gender, male or female, being the prime example. That 'biology is destiny'[10] is not the whole truth, but a big part of it.

The Ascendant displays one's phenotype, or visible form. Its projected sixth house has much to say about that body's integrity, or health. Moon portrays its genotype: a genetic endowment consisting of DNA coils that hold and emit a magnetic field of sentience. This general sensibility takes on a specific configuration as the brain wires itself during one's first impressionable years.

Moon governs the earliest and most decisive phase of life. One's emotional center of gravity forms through the circumstances of birth. Womb immersion in mother's hormonal tides, the actual birth-process and the preverbal environment of infancy decisively influence one's capacity to respond to life.

Mother shapes our whole world during this formative period. She is everyone's first and greatest love. That relationship echoes down the years in all one is or does. The astrological Moon describes her as your inner infant encountered her, not as she is in her own right

As the fastest moving planet Moon adapts to changing situations. One can and must psychologically separate from the personal mother, just as she physically expelled one during the birth trauma. Still, her nurturing, or lack thereof, shapes one's deepest response to an eternal Great Mother of cyclic time and material space.

Moon embodies a deep emotional ambiance underlying the conscious attitude. Human feelings are complex and contradictory. Moon's swift movement and ever changing phases reflect our inconstant moods. But beneath all the waves of sentiment each of us has a basic nature. Behind momentary laughter or tears, even lifelong loves and undying hates, lies a fundamental sensitivity charted at the birth Moon.

Moon in its degree and phase marks the starting point. Origin. It lights a path in the unconscious darkness. At first we passively drift along it, in the womb and in the cradle. Then we crawl, like our four-footed ancestors and companions. Later we walk in the growing light of consciousness, but still conforming to family, school and culture. By the time a semi-autonomous ego has emerged, by about age seven, one has irrevocably committed to a certain temperamental orientation.

One's opinions, politics and religion might change. Hard blows might break, or make, personal character. Good fortune may do the same. Whatever happens out there, this inner tone or mood remains as one's primal sense of what reality really is.

How one acts from that center remains a matter of considerable free will, should one choose to exercise it. As with any planet, Moon permits enormous variety within a certain context. For example, a Moon in Aries may be angry or adventurous, impulsive or initiating. But it does not have the somber wisdom, or cynicism, of Moon in Capricorn; the nurturing, or possessiveness, of Moon in Cancer; the versatility, or duplicity, of Moon in Gemini. A waxing crescent Moon in Aries will follow its fiery path differently than a waning gibbous phase in the same sign. Moon's specific condition in a chart can be actualized at any level.

The lunar womb of matter endows ethereal spirit with psychological substance. Matter's property of inertia/resistance causes electricity (spirit) to glow as light (consciousness). Matter's density gradient ranges from airy realms of thought to liquid tides of feeling to solid facts of body and environment. These compound substances of our being refract living light into the distinct wavelengths of our various subpersonalities. They sum up into a visceral response to life; a unique subjective rhythm. This is illuminated by Moon's relationship to Sun (phase), acting through its sign and house position.

Moon also represents the dullness and opacity of these imperfectly evolved physical, desire and mental bodies. It sits heavily as the dead weight of our personal, racial and planetary past. The residue of guilt hanging upon us all as members of a species we know capable of the most profound evil. Moon embodies and makes known the dark side of our unconscious.

We are each gnawed by a nameless presence within: the sum of all past fears and failures, the toxic waste left over from our evolution. Moon raises an old dead self to the surface. A clinging subpersonality, the monkey on one's back. An infantile aspect of self that never grew up. A deprived or devitalized id (id-iot) sucking vitality from the conscious ego. Moon brings the corpse of a past life into the light, for redemption or as a regression.

In part, Moon personifies a horror haunting our world, an echo of unredeemed suffering. Saturn symbolizes its cause: alienation and limitation generating Fear. Moon remembers and reacts to this existential terror. She makes us look upon the battered face of our personal shadow.

The discontinuity between matter (Moon) and spirit (Sun) expresses the anguish of separation from God. And evokes a lunar bridge to join them. This consists of sunlight reflected off a Moon-mirror onto Earth. Like a hologram, the interference pattern between directly incoming solar energy and reflected lunar memory generates the image of a soul, embodied in biology and made known by psychology. Flaws, ripples, dull patches on a mirror distort the image. Perhaps its Mars reflectors are bright, its Jupiter levels opaque. Moon bounces an ensemble of harmonious or conflicting wavelengths into one light: the vibration, coherent or confused, of a personality.

This lunar bridge has several arcs or spans: instinctual, sympathetic, mental, intentional. Each of these finds its own level along a continuum from coarse to sublime. A psychology of various depths and textures results. Its mental aspect may be smooth and clear, while its physical abilities are rough and jerky. Or vice versa. Cool courage may coexist along with slobbering sentimentality, loving family ties with vicious professional jealousy. Moon melts all these attributes together into a singular personality just as the womb merges thousands of genes into one biological body.

A planetary pattern imprints as a lunar soul of mood and memory on Earth's most distant continent, in outer space. This shines into a DNA blueprint that knits together within the nurturing medium of an inner uterine sea. Triggered by the right phase, Moon then births a living self, embodied in common flesh, shared instinct and individual personality.

Moon connects one with the deep unconscious; embodies our most primal psychic elements. It reveals origins, not goals; past, not future; substance, not spirit. It describes where we are coming from, not where we are going. Moon evokes the instinctual side of self, to be energized by Sun and enabled by planets. Moon lights up the ancient bedrock of personality, enabling it to emerge into subjective revelation.

Yet, paradoxically, just as the light-collecting retina behind an eyeball has a blind spot where it funnels into the optic nerve, so Moon's connective point defines a blank area in awareness. Moon's very density in the sky of consciousness indicates a numb region where light crashes into matter, timeless spirit congeals into mortal life. That point is committed to conveying all other planetary forces. It is not available to express itself. Thus Moon also locates a dead zone in the psyche: one's own specific stoopidity.

Moon makes available the basic conditions through which one's spiritual impulse can act. These are common unto all. Individuality lies in what one makes of them. For example, we exist within the context of physical structures and rhythms, the opportunities and limitations of a body. We live within the deadline of mortality, perceive a narrow range of sensations, and require specific biological conditions. These are generic. What defines one is how one utilizes this universal inheritance.

In the same vein, we all share basic instincts and sentiments, perceptions and thought processes. They create our human background, modified by heredity, culture and environment. These collective contents are arranged by an unfathomable lunar peculiarity making every individual unique.

Moon assimilates all the forces within and around us into a general psychic field awareness. It organizes sensations into consciousness. It reveals not only given attributes, but also the sensibility through which they evolve.

Moon carries the mute, mutating feeling charge of all one's thoughts and deeds. It exists prior to will. Or knowledge. It is unconscious, but very real. And very compelling, because it bears the momentum of a larger than personal past.

Moon describes our warm-blooded nature as mammals. She fuses all planetary energies into an emotional vibration. This generates a heat of combination, a glow of synthesis. It manifests as the indefinable character of individual personality. This uniqueness makes each of us distinctly lovable because no one else is quite the same. The mystery of personal attraction is based on an appreciation of this whole, which is greater than the sum of its parts. We innately respond to an overall lunar mood that includes but transcends its planetary inputs.

Beyond all the grand concepts of Moon as Mother, or as memory; as emblematic of a soul that cycles through incarnate light and discarnate dark phases or as the implied promise of its material presence in the void, lies Moon's most basic fact: its subjectivity. Just as physical Moon circles Earth, so a psychological soul of memory and mood encloses each of us in a private space, a personal universe.

Here all the cosmic forces coalesce into a special sensitivity that can laugh, or cry. It makes connections that most brilliant mind or soaring spirit never could, as humor or as poetry, in the magic of a look or a wink. Moon's gut instinct grasps in a flash what philosophy or reason can never explain: a feeling. Feelings make us human. Computers calculate faster, machines are more powerful and efficient. But feelings live. Feelings are not attributes or instruments. They are the essence of humanity.

Notes

1. Moon's final formative phase occurred during the 'late heavy bombardment' period from 4.1 to 3.8 billion years ago. At that time the entire solar system was pummeled with rock and ice debris from its edge, gravitationally disturbed as newly minted Uranus and Neptune spiraled outward into their present orbits. This caused massive melting of Moon's subsurface basalt layer into low-lying areas. We now see them as dark maria or 'seas,' covering 16% of the surface and contrasting with lighter glassy highlands. After that nothing happened ... Until July 20, 1969.

On that day, with 'one small step for a man, one giant leap for mankind,' Neil Armstrong and Buzz Aldrin landed on our Moon. Others followed. This initial exploration will presumably lead to eventual colonization.

2. See 'Progressions' in 'Sun and Earth.'

3. Frank Herbert, American writer (1920-1986), 'Dune'

4. Omar Khayyam, Persian poet (1044-1123), the 'Rubaiyat'

5. Shakespeare, 'The Tempest'

6. William Wordsworth, English poet, (1770-1850) 'My Heart Leaps Up When I Behold'

7. Corinthians 1:13

8. Only eight Pluto diameters away; our Moon orbits at thirty Earth diameters.

9. Ernst Haeckel, German biologist, (1834-1919). It means that an individual's developmental history repeats, in abbreviated form, that of its species. Thus human embryos go through fishlike and animal phases in the womb as they mature towards birth.

10. A famous formulation by Sigmund Freud (1856-1939), the father of modern psychology.

Moon in Signs and Houses

Moon in a sign indicates where you're coming from: the psychological character of a spiritual soul. Basic temperament. Essential emotional nature.

Moon in a house indicates where you end up: the subjective sense of personality. The inner feeling of experience.

Definition of term: 'Psyche' describes subconscious mood and general emotional disposition. It refers to ego's shared foundations of animal instincts and the collective unconscious along with inaccessible impressions of womb life, birth and early infancy. These defining experiences occurred prior to our ability to consciously record them. It also includes a reservoir of forgotten or repressed personal memories. And latent powers, unrealized potentials. It indicates a subliminal sea of feelings within which the bright conscious ego swims. It is as real, and psychologically vital, as the ocean of air we physically breathe but hardly ever notice.

Moon in Aries/first house

Paradox: the locus of old memories in the sign of new beginnings. Subjective personality sprouts a fresh character. Breakout from the past, freeing its congealed energies to fuel new growth.

The Aries force field energizes the unconscious (Moon) over the threshold of consciousness. A sense of rebirth as previously obscured needs and secret hopes emerge into the light of day. The joy of liberation as true feelings openly reveal themselves, whatever their intrinsic merit.

Moon in Aries/first is about emotional courage. The willingness to risk honest disclosure and encounter new truths. A tentative start develops into increasing self-confidence. Assertive innocence moves from conformity with social demands to guidance by the evidence of its own experience.

A new perspective on personal history. The creative thrill of birthing a unique ego. Instincts unleashed. The audacity of hope, unfounded in fact, but validated by the intensity of its own feelings. Surging exuberance.

The blooming sensitivity of any beginning. A lively nature eager to express its own strengths and explore its surroundings. An individualistic temperament. An aura of excitement and confidence.

Spring's sense of renewal. A renaissance spirit of discovery and originality. An aggressively adventurous mood. The quest to create an identity. Takes the initiative, explores new possibilities, creates opportunity. Acts on gut instinct; an immediate intuition of possibilities. Seizes the moment, doesn't look back.

Youthful energy and enthusiasm. Eager passion. A refreshing openness to potential. Or impatient gratification of immature urges, 'rushing in where angels fear to tread.'

Uninhibited self-expression. Vigorously asserts its own personality and truth. Follows its bliss rather than others' expectations. Or stubbornly insists on a forceful, even belligerent, ego trip. Pent up aggression released, bravely or pugnaciously. Abandons, or fights, tradition, convention and associates to do its thing. Or have its way.

Psychological energies synthesize into a personality centered on aspiration. The overall planetary pattern grounds itself through the will body. Its specific functions (planets) are experienced simply and directly, either naively or with gutsy honesty.

Feelings focus on creative personal projection. Radiates the rapture of inner euphoria. Conveys psychic energy outwards from the womb of dreams to the world of deeds. An emotional tendency towards pioneering enterprise. A hunger to begin, a need to initiate. An attunement to challenge, the opportunity to prove oneself. Registers stimuli to action and instantly, instinctively responds.

If the lunar inertia of the past is not sufficiently energized for renewal then consciousness regresses into frustration's unfocused hostility. Or anger may turn inwards, sucked down into depression. If Moon cannot adequately receive the solar system's imprint then personality defaults into a general mood of infantile impulsiveness.

Revulsion from previous identity, visceral rejection of the past. Transforms their energy into dynamic ambition. Or acts out as rage. A defining choice around spontaneous expression or purposeful strategy. A characteristic flaw of irritable combativeness, a short fuse. A dark side of destructive anger. Or a bright reflection of creative intent.

An unconscious spirit of inspiration complements the conscious attitude. A willingness to take chances, risk loss, go for it. Idealizes memory in the service of will. Dreams of heroism; fantasies of a new dawn.

New Moon in Aries: Spiritual purpose activates psychological will. Direct instinctive spontaneity. Emotional self-assertion. An inner sense of rebirth. Personality draws on innate courage to emerge from the past and the herd.

Waxing crescent: Individual subjectivity arises out of subconscious instinct. Naive enthusiasm generates strength of will. Vitality of feeling begins to focus into an emotional identity.

An action crisis as psyche breaks free of social expectation to do its thing. Growing individuality willing to assert and fight for its own identity. Enthusiasm confronts frustration; personal purpose takes on the world. A pioneer for, or rebel from, the tribe.

Waxing gibbous: Psyche makes a powerful identity statement. It pursues an adventurous dream or personal passion; participates by uninhibited expression of its own emotional truth. Growing self-awareness. Or belligerent ego tripping.

Full: personality expresses relationship through its active gift of self. Whether as enthusiastic response to the other, or in abrasive self-assertion, psyche clears the air by its emotional honesty. True feelings illuminated; social pretense burned away. An unconscious standoff, an internal logjam, resolved by initiation into a new subjective reality.

Waning gibbous: Psyche aggressively projects its own truth in a social context. It is afire with a sense of purpose, which must be shared. It urgently pursues a personal crusade, regardless of obstacles.

A consciousness crisis around unintended consequences and emotional impact of one's actions. Psychological initiative reorients towards another dream. A new purpose directly challenges the old, at the cost of disrupting personal security.

Waning crescent: A sharp emotional rejection of the past. Psyche commits its freedom of action to a specific initiative. Personality sacrifices spontaneity to an emerging purpose/desire.

Moon in Aries responds to any opportunity for self-expression. An unconscious orientation to, or karmic issues around, independence and personal identity.

☽

Moon in Taurus/second house

Exaltation. Unconscious hungers reach a critical urgency. Personality oriented by demanding needs. Gratifies them through fruitful productivity. Or naked avarice.

This is the most tactile level of sensitivity. Psyche is embedded in its physical matrix; defined by what it wants and has. Feelings described by facts (rather than aspirations, imagination or empathy). Dreams condense into tangible desires.

Soul enchanted into the realm of the senses. Body magic. Visceral immersion in the pleasure principle. Earthy sensuality combined with aesthetic appreciation. Savors the entire spectrum of sensation from coarse to sublime. A gourmet and a glutton. Delight in sight and sound, touch, taste and scent. This can decay into an insistence that only the tangible is real, with a concomitant loss of spirituality.

Psychological energies synthesize into a personality centered on the material plane. The overall planetary pattern grounds itself through the desire body. Its specific functions (planets) are experienced in their most concrete and palpable aspect.

An emotional tendency towards indulgence of appetite. A focus on acquisition: what is or should be mine. Validates self through the proof of its possessions. Or possession by them. It longs for and identifies with a subjective pearl of great price. Or is seduced by a siren song, the substitute fetish of an objectified Precious.

Hard headed perception of circumstance and character. A keen sense of others' worth, usefulness or price. Pragmatically evaluates every situation with a view towards profiting from it. Capitalizes on opportunity, patiently cultivates potential assets and brings them to fruition. The Midas touch adds value to every experience. Or degrades it to a dead ego trophy.

Generates prosperity on every level, social and emotional as well as financial. Fulfills one's deepest cravings, as a blessing or a curse. One gets what one wants. Thus it nurtures one's best qualities or one's worst.

If the lunar inertia of the past is not sufficiently energized consciousness regresses into inert passivity. Lapses into the dull security of basic instinct. Or robotic pursuit of jaded addictions. If Moon cannot adequately receive the solar system's imprint then personality defaults into a general mood of mean spirited selfishness. A small-minded focus on personal aggrandizement, at any cost to honor or to others.

A defining choice around whether to produce or to consume, to generate value or to grab it. A characteristic flaw of envy for what others have. A dark side of greed. Or a bright reflection of manifest excellence; the embodied light of a diamond.

Persistence of memory keeps its eye on the prize, of whatever merit. An unconscious 'green thumb' of practical competence complements the conscious attitude. Nurtures abundance at its level of evolution. Maintains a steady incremental enhancement of solid quality.

Conservative appreciation of existing reality. Tranquility in a stable comfort zone. Serene enjoyment of the world's beauty.

New Moon in Taurus: Spirit anchors itself in desire. Psyche identifies with sensual needs and tangible values. Subjectively feels the truth of material reality*v. ideas or ideals. Personality draws on innate resources of trust in its own instincts. Emotional sense of self-worth.

Waxing crescent: Psyche makes the most of present possibility; spontaneously seizes the day. An instinct for profit; ability to grow potential and capitalize on opportunity. Increasing emotional sophistication. Refinement of personal taste.

An action crisis as old values are rejected, new desires embraced. A fateful decision whether to sell all that one has in order to acquire the pearl of great price. This applies more to the emotional and spiritual levels than the economic. One must choose between God and Mammon. As with any action crisis one cannot sidestep the issue.

Waxing gibbous: Cultivation of material or psychological wealth. Personality defined by its riches, such as power and possessions. Or by what it produces; the value, or love, one creates.

Full: spirit loses itself in sensory pleasure. Or finds liberation from desire.† Personality experiences and expresses power through ownership. Or attains enlightenment through appreciation of, but non-attachment to, worldly beauty. Dreams materialize. One gets what one wants, for better or worse.

Waning gibbous: Distribution of one's most precious possessions, in true generosity or to buy love. Social expression of core values. One disseminates enduring beauty to the community. Or dispenses instant gratification at the lowest level; bread and circuses to the mob.

A consciousness crisis in an agonizing reappraisal of all that was once held dear and is now inadequate or overtly negative. Desire turns stale and seeks a new outlet. A 'transvaluation of all values.'‡ Sensual cravings challenge one's ego ideal.

Waning crescent: Personal preference sublimates into an objective evaluation of comparative merit. Surrender to a new standard of value. Old enticements wither; the former face of pleasure becomes worn and haggard. The intangible beauty of an idea or emotion now draws one.

Moon in Taurus responds to opportunity for profit and gain, in both practical and emotional terms. Feels the power of desire and fulfills it, for better or worse. An unconscious orientation to, or karmic issues around, basic personal values: to give or to take.

* Karl Marx, 1818-1883, the prophet of economic determinism and dialectical materialism, was born during the new Moon of Taurus.
† Buddha, ca. 560-480 BC, was born, achieved Enlightenment and died under the full Moon of Taurus.
‡ Friedrich Nietzsche, German philosopher, 1844-1900

☽

Moon in Gemini/third house

Objectifies emotion. Subjective personality separates from its unconscious matrix, views self and environment from an independent mental stance. More responsive to outer surroundings than inner identity.

Psyche motivated by curiosity. It seeks variety and revels in change. Experiments with alternative narratives and new interpretations. Freewheeling spontaneous mind play. Nimble response to circumstance. Alert to incoming signals, but easily distracted by them. Sharp perceptions, fast data processing, but short attention span and lack of focus.

Quick witted, humorous reflection of its social context. Or superficial adaptation. Chameleon like mimicry of others. The danger of losing self in role-playing. Cleverness can trump basic principles with a cheap relativism. It must learn to silence chatter and listen to the depths.

A cerebral temperament. Dispassionate understanding of feelings (v immersion in them). Or an arid divorce from emotion. Brilliantly connects the dots (think Sherlock Holmes, the archetypal Gemini). Or splinters into multiple personalities.

Subjective polarization: a battle of instincts, divided motives, conflicting needs. A sharp sense of contrasting possibilities. Internal debate either dissipates energy or breaks the deadlock into a more holistic sensibility.

Psychological energies synthesize into a personality centered on the mind. The overall planetary pattern grounds itself through thought. Its specific functions (planets) are experienced in their most intellectual aspect, as constantly changing terms of an evolving psychic equation.

Challenges emotional bias with provocative evidence of other values. Stimulates accepted intellectual paradigms with fresh perspectives. It absorbs, relates and translates a jumble of information bytes into an intelligible message. Expresses a coherent mental conception with speed, clarity and manipulative skill. Only Moon in Virgo reaches a comparable level of analytic ability, but it devotes priority to organizing details around a model of integrity and as an instrument of service. Gemini lets the facts speak for themselves, finds truth in their raw reality and objective relationship: 'let the chips fall where they may.' Its own unconscious need is to find their meaning and significance.

An emotional tendency towards detached observation. A hunger for knowledge. Needs a moral compass to orient it. It registers all the possibilities of a situation, and searches for a protocol by which to choose among them. Memories are of the different paths that could have been taken, the many scenarios that might have played out. Dreams of other options; fantasies of titillating new experiences.

If the lunar inertia of the past is not sufficiently energized consciousness regresses into automatic dishonesty, twisting truth and rewriting history for tactical advantage. Rationalizes insincerity. If Moon cannot adequately receive solar system's imprint then personality defaults into general mood of distancing and over-intellectualizing. A defining choice of whether to face facts or escape from them behind a verbal smokescreen. A characteristic flaw of gamesmanship. A dark side of deliberate lies. Or a bright reflection of emotional intelligence.

An ability to communicate ambiguous feelings complements the conscious attitude. It can express normally inarticulate nuance and shine the light of reason into the murky shadows of instinct.

New Moon in Gemini: Psyche shaped by mind. Personality defined by its perceptions of outer reality more than by a prior inner nature. Emotion driven by acute observation rather than subjective need. Immediate response to instinct. Fast processing of feelings. Sharp wits or superficial cleverness.

Waxing crescent: emotional intelligence liberated, or alienated, from primal will and desire. Mental breakout from unconscious instinct. Clarifies unspoken needs. Gives voice to shared feelings. Facilitates psychological communication.

An action crisis around committing to a rationally chosen path among enticing alternatives. Psyche splits off from its collective background to see the world from a new perspective. A changed subjective response to life. One learns to speak a different emotional language.

Waxing gibbous: Psychological independence. Growth through self-definition in contrast to the environment. Objective perception of others' feelings. Original expression of one's own. A detached perspective on group dynamics.

Full: clarity and eloquence in the search for truth. Or the game of deception. Brilliant emotional intelligence illuminates feelings. Or coldly manipulates them. Sharply polarized perceptions generate a higher mental synthesis. Or compartmentalize as an alienated self divorces from its incompatible instincts.

Waning gibbous: Articulates unconscious social needs. Persuasive expression of group feelings, for better or worse. An ability to verbally manipulate public perceptions and private emotions. Reconciles conflicting interests and divided loyalties; an effective negotiator. Or masters the arts of hypocrisy.

A consciousness crisis around competing standards of excellence. An ability to identify with contradictory worldviews; mental anguish choosing among them. Breaks from an old paradigm; accepts inconvenient truth over comforting lies. Or defaults into cynical sophistry to justify ulterior motives.

Waning crescent: Mind condenses into feeling. Detached observation surrenders to a new emotional sensibility. Clear, cool intelligence commits to messy participation in real life. Or shrinks into an arid rationality, alienated from both instinct and communion.

Moon in Gemini responds to environmental signals with an aptness of self-expression. Eloquence; a silver tongue. An unconscious orientation to, or karmic issues around what to believe, the criteria of truth.

☽

Moon in Cancer/fourth house

Rulership. Emotional sensitivity assumes an unusual degree of importance in the general personality. Memory and depth of feeling are emphasized in relation to other aspects of psyche. Immerses into subjectivity, a soul behind the socialized self.

A private center of gravity draws all other planetary energies inwards for personality formation. Direct access to the pre-rational sources of ego raises blind impulse into wistful wishes. These nourish a romantic image or mythic mood, a vision of who one could be. Deep lunar dream tides merge latent potentials of both past and possibility into a distinctive psychological narrative.

A maternal nature incubates the feeling side. Its psychic womb dissolves recollection and longing, history and hope into a living stream of consciousness. Integrates an inherited program with an emerging promise to generate the magic of personality.

A receptive temperament resonates with others on a subconscious level. A sympathetic rapport absorbs their subliminal signals. Assimilates them into its own impressionable identity.

External caution and social shyness creates space to process these subtle whispers from within and intrusive impacts from without. Gives protective sanctuary to an invisible pregnancy of imagination. Or enables its too delicate shrinking from the rough and tumble of life.

Psychological energies synthesize into a personality centered on an introspective plane. The overall planetary pattern grounds itself through the emotional body. Its specific functions (planets) are experienced in their most sensitive interpretation, with the courage of vulnerable openness.

If the lunar inertia of the past is not sufficiently energized consciousness regresses into the escapism of fantasy. If Moon cannot adequately receive the solar system's imprint then personality defaults into a general mood of infantile dependency.

A defining choice around whether to nurture or be needy itself. A characteristic flaw of refusal to face life's challenges. A dark side of hypersensitivity, exaggerated response to every incident. Or a bright magic of the unconscious birthing its human face, the universal made unique.

A sentimental disposition honors continuity with a lineage shaped by the shadows of forgotten ancestors. Enriched or inhibited by karma, the power of the past. Finds a larger sense of belonging in identification with family and tribe. Tender empathy. Separation anxiety. Nostalgia.

Baptism into the living waters of instinctual wisdom. Visceral intuition energized to the brink of insight. The unconscious partially surfaces into awareness; shows its greatest availability to knowledge.

Every other lunar position reflects light on a hidden potential seeking psychological expression. Moon in Cancer opens a window into another reality altogether: a dreamscape of ancient stories and germinating revelations. Neither past nor future exist. Yet their remembrance and imagination orient present participation. Extrasensory currents of a 6th sense or 2nd sight coalesce into the mystery of mood; the intangible aura behind overt individuality. Echoes of a soul vibration condense into the music of self's song.

New Moon in Cancer: Personality reflects an innate emotional sophistication. Baptism into the waters of primal instinct and fertile imagination. Conscious dreaming; direct contact with the inner foundations of psyche. One can become intoxicated by fantasy and drown in exaggerated feeling.

Waxing crescent: Hidden psychological growth, like a baby developing inside the womb, recapitulating three billion years of evolution in just nine months. Personality serves as a medium for deep dreams and psychic impressions; expresses instinctive and subjective truths. Spontaneous emotional communication. Clear expression of inner feelings.

An action crisis around breaking free of family, tribe and past. A compelling need to follow one's own emotional truth, which is at sharp variance with its surroundings. New kinds of feelings: think of a boy or girl discovering the opposite sex.

Waxing gibbous: Subjective expression of collective dreams. Personality instinctively embodies group needs as a designated savior, victim or other archetypal role. It enacts a shared fantasy; attracts unspoken emotions and reflects them with growing sophistication or increasing eccentricity.

Full: An emotional enlightenment; final maturation of an unconscious imperative. Empathy expands to a collective level, perhaps an ancestral destiny or karmic calling. Or soul demands that personality deny imposed duties to follow a subjective truth. Private feelings strongly reflect, or reject, public standards.

Waning gibbous: In the waxing gibbous personality served as an exemplar of unconscious collective dreams. Now it manages, or manipulates, them in the service of its own compelling inner narrative. Instinctive resonance with group dynamics from an autonomous emotional stance. It keenly senses others' or the public mood, giving it a charismatic power to lead or mislead. Dissemination of a dream, or a nightmare.

A consciousness crisis around harmonizing inner tranquility with the demands of social life. Security v relationship. Turns within to rediscover its roots. Seeks a new balance between collective issues and personal needs. Privatization of psyche. Changing dreams: movement from identification with a tribal myth towards individual judgment.

Waning crescent: Sacrifices cherished past baggage to an emerging dream. Withdraws to an inner sanctum to break down and rebuild. Sensitivity to nascent needs. A return to the heart. Or a retreat from life.

Moon in Cancer responds to depth of feeling, genuine emotion. A sensitive radar picks up any threat to its security and tranquility. An unconscious orientation to, or karmic issues around, subjective self-awareness.

☽

Moon in Leo/fifth house

Emotional radiance. Warmth of feeling. Subjective personality projects itself through a playful, exuberant tone. A fun loving, or frivolous, mood. Charismatic vivacity.

Spotlights the inner child. An instinctive reflection of solar spirit as innocent love:

'Truly I tell you, whoever does not receive the kingdom of God like a small child will never enter it.'[1]

If this soul-are magic congeals into an ego fetish then it decays into vanity. A pretense that personality owns the light darkens into unconscious arrogance:

'Pride goeth before destruction, a haughty spirit before a fall.'[2]

An ability to vividly project inner truth. Identifies that with one's social role. This can be an artistic presentation of real character contributing to others. Or an empty mimicry of phony feeling as a parasitic theft of their affection. Authentic self-disclosure. Or a demanding hunger for attention. Uninhibited expression: vibrant or intimidating.

Self-confidence mirrors a higher energy, represents a soul essence, enables latent potential. Or a presumption of superiority closes availability to growth. The joy, and genuine dignity, of channeling inspired imagination. Or the smugness of overbearing mediocrity. It can outshine crippling memories and flawed programming. Or intensify unconscious issues to a radioactive glow of inflated personal centrality.

Psychological energies synthesize into a burning heart. The overall planetary pattern grounds itself on the creative plane. Its specific functions (planets) are experienced in their most ardent and dramatic form.

An emotional tendency towards ego display, as an unreserved gift of self or an unrestrained lust for dominance. It lights up the room. Or sucks up all its oxygen. A hunger to love and be loved. This soars into generosity of feeling. Or degenerates into pretense, the purchase of affection/respect with an artificial persona.

A need to be acknowledged and validated by others. Sensitive to approval or disapproval. It can display a snobbery rising to imperious insolence. Generally this is not an autonomous psyche: it craves applause from its environment. Only at an advanced stage does it tune into the approval of an inner conscience or an invisible soul.

If the lunar inertia of the past is not sufficiently energized, consciousness regresses into narcissism. If Moon cannot adequately receive the solar system's imprint then personality defaults into a general mood of autocratic indulgence and boastful overcompensation. It will then demand what it has not earned as an entitlement. A defining choice around whether to create or control. A characteristic flaw of self-absorption. A dark side of grandiosity, exaggerated self-esteem. Or a shining reflection of celestial love.

A subliminal connection with spiritual energies fertilizes the conscious attitude. The emergence of passionate emotion out of passive sensitivity. A brilliant, or blinding, display of instinctual power. A bright, or blaring, personification of unconscious drives, but with little self-awareness. Fiery feelings. Self-promoting memories. Dreams of glory, fantasies of fame. These reflect true nobility or false pride.

New Moon in Leo: A spiritual baptism of power. A recharged psyche unconsciously commits to a larger love. Or an autocratic imperative of ego assertion. Generosity of feeling. Or grandiosity of self-absorption. Personal subjectivity begins to identify with a creative purpose or a social role. Emotional expression endowed with instinctive authority.

Waxing crescent: An emerging personality draws upon innate self-confidence, justified or not. Instinctive passion individualizes. One plays a given role with imagination and enthusiasm. Creative self-expression or infantile acting out.

An action crisis as creativity breaks out of the comfort zone. Generous impulses challenge self-interest. One must choose whether to pay the price of courage, bear the burden of true nobility. Or accept the easy pickings made available to a powerful, perhaps overbearing, ego.

Waxing gibbous: A growing exuberance of creative self-expression. Instinctively personifies a collective mood. Will one exploit glamor or sex appeal to feed a ravenous hunger for approval? Or lead by example, knowing that excellence always provokes enmity?

Full: The emotional power of personality. Compelling magnetism. A charismatic identity reflects collective dreams. Its magic brings an abstract archetype to life. Psychological gravitas, regal or domineering. Inherent social authority. Or extreme subjectivity, a vividly eccentric display of ego dissociated from its instinctual roots.

Waning gibbous: Self shines out as a social exemplar, at whatever level one has achieved. Personality consciously reflects group expectations. One speaks with an authoritative public voice. Will it inspire others with a demanding call to excellence? Or promote an inflated ego agenda?

A consciousness crisis around exalted feelings v lustful cravings, nobility v temptation. A chance to give all that one has in one great act of courage or creative statement. Or bullies others by an intimidating force of personality. A choice between demands of honor and perks of power.

Waning crescent: ego expends itself in service or for others. Or clings to a petty reflection of past glory. Noble renunciation of power and privilege. It parallels the ancient tradition of sacrificing an old king (personality) to ensure future fertility. The golden glow of summer's feeling fades into an autumnal social sensibility.

Moon in Leo responds to passion: any opportunity to strike an operatic pose or take a glorious stand. An unconscious orientation to, or karmic issues around, creative self-expression.

1. Mark 10:15 and Luke 18:17
2. Proverbs 16:18

☽

Moon in Virgo/sixth house

Emotional purification. Personality perfects its own integrity through selfless service. Sensitive to inner flaws and dysfunctional ego programs. Truthful recollection allows it to correct mistakes and redeem its own past.

An acutely lucid subjectivity, precise and rational. A critical nature, constantly examining its own motivations and quality of effort. Emotions are refined as an expression, rather than the determinant, of purpose.

Continual self-analysis. Painstaking, perhaps over-vigilant, monitoring of behavior for appropriateness. A need to make inner feelings 'politically correct,' to rationally sanitize instinctive response. Spontaneity and honesty are inhibited by a sense that it is only right to feel what is right. This has an obvious down side, but also promotes higher standards.

Sharp psychological observation of both self and associates. A dry and clinical response to emotional situations. Innate healing ability, but lack of empathy.

Psychological energies synthesize into a personality centered on the rational plane, emphasizing pragmatic fact over abstract theory or felt opinion. The overall planetary pattern grounds itself through the mental body. Its specific functions (planets) are expressed under relentless scrutiny for optimal performance.

A high strung, nervous tone, eager to help others and improve itself. A tendency towards worrying and fidgeting. A hunger for perfection. A focus on getting it 100% right 100% of the time. Since this is impossible, as well as undesirable, there can be a pessimistic lack of confidence. It is undesirable because evolution involves a willingness to make mistakes and learn from, not obsess over, them.

Attuned to consistency. It registers every deviation from the norm; can be too nitpicky. Hypochondria, a sense of inadequacy, on every level. This generates an unsurpassed rigor of self-awareness, without excuse or evasion. A preference for real facts over comforting illusions. Such strenuous alertness is itself a source of joy.

If the lunar inertia of the past is not sufficiently energized consciousness regresses into rote repetition of well executed but already acquired skills. A comfort zone of excellence at the trivial. If Moon cannot adequately receive the solar system's imprint then personality defaults into a general mood of safe and rigid ritual.

A defining choice around whether to settle for little guaranteed achievements, or go for a larger integration, with its inherent messiness. A characteristic flaw of paralysis for fear of making a mistake. The perfect can become the enemy of the good. A dark side of sweating the small stuff. Or a bright manifestation of taking on big problems and offering the best possible solutions.

An unconscious clarity of perception and rigorous logic of thought complements inevitable shortcomings of the conscious attitude. The self-healing capacity of psyche. Constant incremental improvement. Can be distracted by routine worthy works from a true experience of wisdom.* Memories are accurate and detailed but tend to emphasize what went wrong.

* See Luke 38

New Moon in Virgo: The emotional soul checks in for a tune up. Feelings are scrutinized for purity; excess and inconsistency excised in favor of simplicity and clarity. Personality reprograms itself for greater efficiency in service to a rational purpose. Psyche commits to self-improvement through a methodical discipline, whether physical, intellectual or spiritual. Loss of spontaneity compensated by gain in coherence.

Waxing crescent: Personality refines its emotional response. Or defaults into ritualistic role-playing, a safe formality. Feelings correct themselves to a higher standard of self-awareness. Or self-censor in conformity with an arbitrary program. Psyche sharpens, or narrows, its focus.

An action crisis around choosing between contradictory perceptions and incompatible standards of truth. A crossroad of discrimination; a need to pick one path and reject another.

Waxing gibbous: Methodical refinement of character in accordance with a rational agenda. Psychological clarity: feelings focused by service to a cause or calling. Or subjective inhibition by an internal proliferation of petty rules and rituals.

Full: Personality redeems collective failings through an individual demonstration of excellence in action. Integrity expressed as a healing touch. Compassionate clarity: illumination of a path to redemption, a means of salvation. Or a shield of rules holds back emotion; true feelings denied by defensive attention to irrelevant detail.

Waning gibbous: Personality serves as a public role model of integrity. It walks the straight and narrow and demands that others do so as well. Dissemination of a healing method, enabling technique or improved process. Can default into a rapture of ritualistic purification, stringently following the letter rather than the spirit of the law.

A consciousness crisis as ugly facts challenge inflated aspirations. Emotional anguish around choosing between incompatible ethical norms and codes of conduct. One encounters the devil in the details and learns to read the psychological fine print of spiritual promises.

Waning crescent: Discriminating selectivity lowers its exacting standards in the interest of selfless service. Personal integrity accommodates to the needs of relationship. Intelligent compromise between purity and love. Or desperate insistence on hollow ritual to ward off feelings of contamination by others.

Moon in Virgo responds to what's wrong and how to fix it. An unconscious orientation to, or karmic issues around, service and self-improvement.

☽

Moon in Libra/seventh house

Emotional adjustment to others. Personality defines itself in context more than in its own right. Validates itself through relationship. The experience of communion.

Individual persona tips over into social identity. Self-assertion subsumed into collective participation. Subjectivity enlarges, and dilutes, itself to accommodate peers and strangers, friends and enemies, subordinates and superiors. The self-sense socializes. Personal feeling becomes absorbed into group dynamics. Thus there is identity ambivalence: am I an ego or a team player? Do I answer to my own given name or to my familial surname?

Indecision because one necessarily plays several roles and responds to many influences. It sympathizes with different perspectives, but often lacks a criteria for deciding among them. It struggles to develop a standard of judgment by which to weigh competing claims and demands.

A search for proportionality: the correct balance of psychological priorities. Seeks accommodation between internal sensitivities and external norms. A turning tide of autonomy v affiliation. Subconscious re-evaluation of heritage and affinities. Waxing grows involvement with the community as one expresses its shared code. Waning polarizes with public sentiment as one advocates an ethical imperative or presents an artistic statement.

Reconciles various agendas. Negotiates separate interests into a general accord. This process sharpens contrast and clarifies options. It also creates emotional ambivalence and intellectual doubt. It can lead to a higher synthesis. Or to a deadlock inhibiting initiative.

An instinct for beauty: what is aesthetically pleasing to both sense and soul. A feeling for the right correlation of energies. A talent for composing parts into a greater whole.

Psychological energies synthesize into a personality centered on its relationships. The overall planetary pattern grounds itself through the mental body. Its specific functions (planets) experience wide fluctuations in expression, while seeking equilibrium. At an advanced level they achieve a judicious balance.

An emotional tendency towards compromise and meeting the other halfway. A gracefully responsive feeling tone focused on desire for an amicable consensus. A hunger to fit in, be part of something larger. An attunement to the unspoken nuances of personal interaction and collective mores. It registers disturbing conflict and seeks to smooth it over.

If the lunar inertia of the past is not sufficiently energized consciousness regresses into passive acquiescence. If Moon cannot adequately receive the solar system's imprint then personality defaults into a general mood of unprincipled adaptation to its immediate associates or environment. A defining choice around whether to insist on values or to go with the flow. Challenged to take sides, make a stand. A characteristic flaw of appeasement. A dark side of seeking peace at any price. Or a bright reflection of real justice, an appropriate symmetry of compassion and discipline.

An unconscious sense of reciprocity complements the conscious attitude. Sensitive to issues of compensation and equity. The most fairminded temperament. It can be paralyzed by indecision, pulled this way and that by more passionate advocates.

Dreams of universal rapport. Fantasies of ideal community: unity in diversity, with mutual respect among all of its members. Memories are of grace and pleasure, conveniently forgetting differences and awkwardness.

New Moon in Libra: An internal redefinition of justice and right relationship. Subjective recognition of, and identification with, others. A shift in the emotional center of gravity from me to we. Integrity gives way to integration. Or to lazy lack of definition, absorption by another's personality.

Waxing crescent: Personality draws upon innate resources of adaptive sympathy. A growing ability to identify with others' needs. Instinctive synchronization with relationship, or chameleon-like reflection of a stronger will. Feels and expresses the collective mood: a poster child for group values or an easygoing conformist.

An action crisis: Serious conflict of personal emotion and group expectation. A subjective sense of justice at odds with community values. A difficult choice between going along to get along, or fighting for what one feels is right. It cannot be sidestepped, although this sensitive disposition will make every effort to do so.

Waxing gibbous: Personality reflects an inner synthesis of subjective and community values. A deliberate, conscious presentation of what was instinctively felt in the waxing crescent phase. Subtle emotional response. Or a contrived show to please the crowd.

Full: Subjective reconciliation of contending/complementary values. Personality oscillates between aggressive assertion and perceptive appreciation. Eventually it learns to harmonize them in a sacred marriage of inner qualities, evoking the best of both masculine strength and feminine sensitivity. A graceful adjustment of private emotion with community participation. Or spineless surrender to the loudest ego in its vicinity.

Waning gibbous: Judicious application of common values to manage conflict and ease stress. A diplomatic stance. Skilled emotional negotiation. Or slick manipulation.

A consciousness crisis as the demands of justice challenge those of ambition. Conflict between relationship and career. Appreciates the melancholy beauty of an impersonal fate superseding private feelings.

Waning crescent: Disinterested judgment commits to a more passionate engagement. One chooses sides. And casts off former ties. Emotionally accepts the justice of sacrifice.

Moon in Libra responds to the other, with a sense of fair play in any situation. An unconscious orientation to, or karmic issues around, social values: which side am I on?

☽

Moon in Scorpio/eighth house

Fall. Personal feelings must adapt to an uncongenial medium of collective purpose and karmic necessity. Fateful encounters force emotional regeneration.

The unconscious strives to become conscious from within, in defiance of its own nature. Thus it may become an energy sink drawing one ever deeper into its primitive hungers. Or transform itself into a clear lens, an inner eye, focusing a dream trance into awareness.

Taps into visceral sources of power. These can bewitch one in a 'rapture of the depths,' a hypnotic enchantment by primeval instinct. Or spur one to shatter ancient complexes of sin, guilt and fear to soar triumphant on their transformed energy.

Personality experiences and expresses its inner demons. They may hijack the psyche. Or be lifted into light, their obsessive pull transmuted into conscious wisdom. Immersion in subconscious trauma generates a wisdom that can only come from the ordeal of real emotional agony. Morbid fascinations and toxic fixations rise to the surface, as a dark seduction. Or to be purged from the system, their binding energy released.

A need to eliminate once cherished attributes. Or associates. Loss spurs evolution. Or paralyzes will. Dissolves irrelevancy to reveal a core soul purpose. Or revels in destruction and sadism. Absorbs and detoxifies pain. Or amplifies and reflects the world's cruelty.

This is the dark side of Moon. A hidden cancer haunts the ego. Or is cut free by conscious confrontation. Psyche is vampirized by its own corruption. Or vaccinated by it. Here one faces the most loathsome aspects of identity. One can become possessed, twisted and diminished by fear of acknowledging them. Or resurrected by breaking their grip and taking back their power.

Psychological energies synthesize into a personality centered on the instinctive plane. The overall planetary pattern grounds itself through the emotional body. Its specific functions (planets) are experienced in their most sinister aspect, so that one may learn to transform their negative side.

Subjective personality faces the real truth of its own motivation. The seriousness and irrevocability of its errors surface. A subliminal sense of urgency in response to objective or psychological emergency. An emotional tendency toward total engagement with perceived threat. Or transformative opportunity. A mood of determined will. Or destructive willfulness. A passionately intent feeling tone. A need to do or die. Feelings focus on a compulsion to exercise (hidden) power, over self or surroundings. A hunger for control. It registers obsession.

If the lunar inertia of the past is not sufficiently energized consciousness regresses into poisonous resentment and craving for revenge. Bitterness surfaces but is not effectively dissipated. If Moon cannot adequately receive the solar system's imprint then personality defaults into a general mood of vindictive sabotage, of self and others. A defining choice between rebirth or a death wish. A characteristic flaw of malignant jealousy. Or paranoia. A dark side of malice. Or a bright manifestation of Hell itself redeemed.

An unconscious sensitivity to one's original sin complements the conscious attitude. An attunement to the forbidden and taboo. This can paralyze with self-hatred, often projected onto others. Or empower with self-knowledge, enabling liberation. Memories of evils and wrongs to be righted. Or emulated. Dreams of transcendence. Or nihilistic obliteration.

New Moon in Scorpio: Immersion into dark waters of the unconscious. A baptism of power: one is seized by instinctual forces, or learns to control them. Personality becomes the vehicle of hidden motivations seeking to emerge. Or to suck one under. Personifies collective energies. Or obsessive compulsion by them.

Waxing crescent: An instinctive radar guides growing emotional control over self and others. A gut feeling for true motives focused into psychic/political influence. A nose for power leads one to it.

An action crisis as controlling instincts conflict with creative impulse. Motivational struggle over the use of power. A conflict of interest between unfair taking and selfless giving. True character revealed in an acid test of temptation.

Waxing gibbous: Growing profundity of introspection and objective observation. Instinctive insight is consciously deployed, for better or worse. Personality exerts a magnetic influence over others. Unconscious character revealed by its use of power.

Full: Illumination of true desire. And of its cost. Personality mesmerized by appetite. Or learns to transcend it. Conscious exercise of instinctive power.

Waning gibbous: Psychological sophistication enhances consciously directed emotional force. An ability to convert personal charisma into social/political influence, exercised benevolently or malignly. Hidden power. Instinctively guides or manipulates others from behind the scenes.

A consciousness crisis as lust for power challenges idealistic vision. A passion for revolutionary change: real inner transformation or the orgiastic thrill of destruction. A brutal lesson in the reality of malice. Will one be corrupted by it? Or learn to transcend it?

Waning crescent: Psyche disintegrates. Subconscious personality shaken to the core by forces beyond its control. It shrivels into a traumatized ghost or flies free, liberated by passing through the fire. An unflinching acceptance, or terrified rejection, of the ultimate fact: death.

Moon in Scorpio responds to power. An unconscious orientation to, or karmic issues around, one's inner demons: to raise them up or let them drag one down.

☽

Moon in Sagittarius/ninth house

Emotions socialize. Subjective identification with group norms. One fully participates in a shared tribal narrative. Generous sentiments of comradeship, exuberantly expressed. Or a strident tone of collectively validated righteousness.

Feelings are friendly, but fleeting; group oriented rather than strictly personal. They flow from a general religious/philosophical or social/political orientation rather than visceral sensation. The mood is promotional rather than realistic; extensive rather than intensive, broad rather than deep.

Nomadic instincts; a need for freedom and adventure. An expansive personality, soaring on aspiration. Distant potentials are immediately sensed and eagerly embraced. The wish is father to the fact. Unbridled confidence often makes it come true. Trusts in luck and is therefore lucky. An enthusiastic can do attitude. Or the promiscuous cheer of magical thinking. Unrealistic expectations. Inflated self-esteem.

Senses the promise in people and situations. Encourages it with an infectious cheerfulness. Or lack of discrimination; an inability to accept the reality of malice. Feels that goodwill overcomes all obstacles, which it does to a surprising extent. An innate ethical clarity avoids compromise with anything that offends its principles. Or certainty of belief emphatically rejects any challenge to its correctness.

Psychological energies synthesize into a personality centered on the intuitive plane. The overall planetary pattern grounds itself through a spiritual sensibility abstracted from the gritty facts of life. Its specific functions (planets) are experienced in their most exaggerated aspect. At best this grows them to a higher state.

Reflects the presence of the soul's guardian angel. Amplifies its benevolence. An objectively inexplicable winning streak. Or it can translate the elation of too easy victory into triumphalism; overcompensate for the insecurity of undeserved gain with a competitive frenzy.*

An emotional tendency towards optimism. Feelings focus on anticipation of a better tomorrow. A hunger for spiritual significance, even in the most mundane things. This can imbue with real meaning. Or cheapen with superficial hype. An attunement to potential rather than actuality. Favors big theory over little facts. A willful blindness to shortcomings. It registers maximum possibility, can ignore the down side.

If the lunar inertia of the past is not sufficiently energized consciousness regresses into grandiose inflation of ego or opinion. If Moon cannot adequately receive the solar system's imprint then personality defaults into a general mood of manic make believe. A defining choice around how to respond to unusual good luck and unearned fortune: as something one should live up to, or as objective proof of one's exceptionalism. A characteristic flaw magnifies its truth into The Truth. Disproportionate emphasis on partial validity. A fixation on dead dogma. A dark side of fanaticism. Or a bright reflection of philosophical wisdom.

An unconscious vision of the growth trajectory inherent in a person or situation complements the conscious attitude with a prophetic edge. The fullest immersion in one's larger collective matrix. It clearly senses where things are going and adroitly capitalizes on it. The test is whether it does so in a principled or an opportunistic manner. Dreams of grace, revelation by and into a higher Mind. Fantasies that one personally embodies the same. A keen sense of opportunity. Remembers a series of glorious triumphs. Puts a positive spin on events.

* Donald Trump has an eclipsed full Moon in Sagittarius.

New Moon in Sagittarius: Personality irradiated by a spiritual enthusiasm: divine light or fanatic hellfire. Instinctual preferences reinforced and justified by religious or political fervor. One feels what God or the tribe feels. Emotions expand into aspirations as psyche is imprinted with a sacred or social message.

Waxing crescent: Personality goes with the flow in justified hopes of advancement. One genuinely shares in the collective psychology and instinctively promotes what the group wants. A team player or a mindlessly optimistic conformist.

An action crisis as an expansive urge for freedom conflicts with practical needs. Spiritual dreams and beautiful theories meet ugly facts. Optimism tempered by a cold reality check.

Waxing gibbous: An ability to surf the wave of public sentiment, to stay at the leading edge of where people already want to go. Star power: one embodies the collective dream. Or nightmare. Growth by following one's own generally accurate instincts; danger from accepting others' inflated projections.

Full: Personality expresses one aspect of truth, or of partisanship, with singular clarity. A genuine epiphany. Or grandiose identification with a divine archetype. Prophetic illumination. Or inflated illusion. A larger than personal wisdom. Or frantic insistence on a sacred code.

Waning gibbous: Prophetic articulation of subconscious and collective energies. Dissemination of spiritual truths that one's own good fortune seem to validate. Effective advocacy of a higher law. Or hypocritical exploitation of same for personal gain.

A consciousness crisis as ethics are challenged by betrayal, morality undermined by illusion. Genuine wisdom meets inherent uncertainty. Clarity must adjust to nuance and subtlety. A more mature optimism learns that loss can lead to growth and salvation come from suffering. Or an intensification of dogma to repel hideous doubts.

Waning crescent: A return to the facts of life, or stinging cynicism, as enthusiasm expends itself. Optimism moves towards objectivity. Fiery dreams burn out, leaving bitter ashes or cold-eyed realism.

Moon in Sagittarius responds to philosophic principles and political argumentation. An unconscious orientation to, or karmic issues around, ethics: what is good? what is truth?

☽

Moon in Capricorn/tenth house

Detriment. Feelings adapt to objective necessity. Sensitivity tempered by the challenges of reality. This stimulates self-control with a view towards power over others and the environment. Or a life denying withdrawal from vulnerability to them.

A serious mood, its reserved and laconic tone masking depth and sincerity. Or an inhibited nature, brittle and harsh, frozen with fear. Selfishness: a wintry inner poverty lacking personal warmth or empathy for others. Or the blessings of responsibility, psyche enhanced by meeting the demands and duties of larger than personal concerns.

Subjective character defines itself in terms of ambition. It emphasizes deliberate cultivation of qualities serving a long-term interest. And withdraws energy from private idiosyncrasies detracting from that commitment.

Imagination turns to strategic intention. Emotions are regimented, goal oriented. One feels what is appropriate to get ahead, suppresses what gets in the way. Psyche organized and mobilized for planned, rational ends; directed more than experienced. Spontaneity subordinated to obligation, natural instincts channeled to attain results.

Personality shaped by purpose. An urge to command circumstance and rise above the herd. A need to prove and exalt identity in the eyes of one's superego or superiors.

A skeptical pruning of sentimental indulgence produces an austere, sharply focused character. It can range from mean and stingy to an exalted simplicity of excellence. From constipated response and repressed rage to the most elegant grace under pressure. From a heart of iron (Hitler) to the highest exemplar of collective destiny (Lincoln).

Psychological energies synthesize into a personality centered on its pragmatic ability. The overall planetary pattern grounds itself into a tangible agenda. Its specific functions (planets) are experienced in their most instrumental aspect, harnessed in service to ego's central authority.

The calculating temperament of a statesman or politician: one who fulfills a social need through the management of common desires, fears, appetites and dreams. An attunement to any opportunity for advancement. It registers a gnawing hunger for objective achievement to compensate for a subjective sense of inadequacy.

If the lunar inertia of the past is not sufficiently energized consciousness regresses into fatalistic pessimism. If Moon cannot adequately receive the solar system's imprint then personality defaults into a general mood of sullen defeatism. A defining choice around whether to sublimate disappointment into discipline or sink into despair. A characteristic flaw gives in to frustration because there is not enough inner joy to sustain the effort. A dark side of fear. Or a bright manifestation of initiation into a higher state of being.

An unconscious awareness of fundamental weakness or sin complements the conscious attitude. This generates a resolve to overcompensate and thus achieve superiority. Or a crippling lack of psychic energy. Dreams of rank earned and acknowledged. Fantasies of adversity conquered, personal inferiority overcome by demonstrable success. Memories are of hard lessons learned. It never forgets the need for constant vigilance and preparation for worst-case scenarios.

Melancholia. A deep sense of life's sweet sadness. An appreciation of tragedy, the inevitability of sorrow. Gets less than it has earned: emotional deprivation, unrewarded worth. Responds to loss and limitation with grim determination and devotion to duty. Or retreats into a cold and withered cynicism.

New Moon in Capricorn: Psyche consecrated to a destiny. Personality imprinted by a sense of fate. Motivated by duty and sensitive to its practical necessities. Appreciates reality over ideal or fantasy. Compelling ambition against heavy odds. Bitter struggle can shrivel into pessimism or scornful misanthropy.

Waxing crescent: Instinctively attuned to the requirements of ambition. Emotional resonance with the demands of discipline. Emerging individual competence.

Action crisis of cold calculation v warm relationship. An urge to break out of pleasant mediocrity. One must choose between grim duty to an austere code or handsomely rewarded compliance with an established consensus.

Waxing gibbous: Real demonstration of increased competence. Or relentless self-promotion. Methodically advances ambition, good or bad. Growing gravitas.

Full: Subjective psyche subsumed by objective fate or duty. Personal emotion guided by impersonal spiritual law. Dreams disciplined into actual accomplishment. Or crushed by fears of inadequacy. A conservative temperament pragmatically shoulders heavy responsibilities. Or contracts into sullen resentment. Inhibited feelings isolated from instinctual joy.

Waning gibbous: Personality tailors itself to fit the demands of society or of destiny. Suppresses what does not serve that purpose. Emotions self-censor in the interest of ambition. Psyche becomes the messenger of an impersonal law. Or forgets its real feelings. Real merit or cynical manipulation takes one to the top.

A consciousness crisis as the requirements of ambition clash with subjective truth. Rules, duty, rank lose their luster. The agony of abandoning social obligations in favor of a personal destiny. Or the soul death of refusing to do so.

Waning crescent: Sacrifice of cherished ambitions for public duty. Melancholy ecstasy of serving a great and tragic purpose. Personality crushed in the winepress of fate, yielding the finest of spirits or the sourest of dregs.

Moon in Capricorn responds to opportunity for advancement, chance of promotion. An unconscious orientation to, or karmic issues around, responsibility, as an objective or a burden.

☽

Moon in Aquarius/eleventh house

Emotions sublimate and universalize. Identification with collective needs transcends private sensibilities. Attuned to general principles more than individual preferences. Alert to cosmic truths and vast social movements, relatively insensitive to personal nuance in self and others.

A futuristic optimism throws off the past. It seeks transformative breakthrough in every aspect of life. It can find alienation and chaotic breakdown. Constant identity crises, creative or destructive.

Adopts a new psychological paradigm. Seeks to reinvent self. Personality observes itself as an experiment in consciousness, the malleable object of rational self-improvement. Or of an ideological formula.

Unconscious energies revealed and projected through intuitive insight, brilliant or bizarre. Feels the first stirring of emerging trends, the shape of what is coming. Senses the larger forces, greater plan behind the visible present. This severs one from public opinion in originality, or from common sense as eccentricity. An innovative character reflecting possibilities ahead of their time. Or a space case divorced from reality.

Personality seeks to reflect a universal archetype, embody an ideal. Instincts distill into ideas. Feelings transmute into theories. Normal emotions intensify into elevated aspirations. Visceral sentiments become visionary images.

Such a high-strung psyche often becomes cut off from its organic roots. Its gut level sensations translate into rarified, almost electronic, signals. Natural sensitivities are replaced by cerebral algorithms. A carefully contrived artificial intelligence can override deep currents of ancestral wisdom. It registers clarity of thought, rejects subjective interpretations and ambiguous impressions. Living poetry can be supplanted by logical programming. Yet, for all of its possible distortions, this utopian urge also drives the impossible dream, a yearning for the stars, which makes us human in the first place.

Psychological energies synthesize into a personality centered on the conceptual plane. The overall planetary pattern grounds itself through the mental body. Its specific functions (planets) are experienced in their most impersonal and idealistic aspect.

An emotional tendency towards dry intellectualizing. The head rules the heart. Fraternal, gregarious; friendly rather than passionate. Inclined to groupthink. The personal is political. Lives in a city on a hill or a castle in the sky rather than a cozy comfy home.

If the lunar inertia of the past is not sufficiently energized consciousness regresses into abstraction. Escape from real life and feelings into ivory tower theorizing. If Moon cannot adequately ground the solar system's imprint then personality defaults into a general mood of rebellion: refusal to accept existing reality, inability to create a new one. A defining choice around whether, having broken free of inherited constraints, it will fly up or fly apart. A characteristic flaw of zany craziness. A dark side of cold detachment. Or a bright reflection of genuine enlightenment.

An unconscious apprehension of the next big thing, a rising new order, complements the conscious attitude. Future oriented, not as an extrapolation of the present, but as a leap into the great unknown. An emotional ability to navigate discontinuities and land in a new reality. A hunger for larger perspectives and unique experiences. Dreams of liberation. Fantasies of universal solidarity in a fundamentally better world. Memories are of revelatory insight. Eureka! moments.

New Moon in Aquarius: A subjective Revelation. Personality inspired, or crazed, by identification with a transpersonal level of archetypal truth. Psyche energized, or fried, by a grand unifying theory of everything. One learns to incorporate a revolutionary intuition into the emotional context of daily life. Or becomes lost in space, enclosed in the bubble of a blinding Vision.

Waxing crescent: Emotional resonance with intuitive insight; feels ideas. Subjective inspiration encourages one to envisage a new identity. Instinctive personification of an emerging revelation.

An action crisis as mind breaks free of passion. A subjective revolution of rising expectations. A refusal to accept illegitimate power or outworn tradition. Mental anarchy: chaos breeds genius or pointless rebellion. A mind storm clears the air or wrecks personality.

Waxing gibbous: Increasing sensitivity to mental stimulation. A subjective embrace of the future; growing mastery of new skills and attitudes. One emotionally commits to emerging trends in society at large. Thus one can become an idealistic, perhaps idealized, leader. Or get too far ahead of the crowd, lost in irrelevant abstractions.

Full: Illumination by a higher truth. Conscious intuition of archetypal principles. Or alienated abstraction; mental dissociation from personal heart and common feelings. Personality expresses a creative urge through original thought. Or subjective enslavement to dogmatic ideology.

Waning gibbous: Social articulation of a subjective revelation. Intuitive ability to communicate cutting edge concepts and sensibilities. One personifies the emotional power of ideals, good or bad. Inspirational magnetism, or crazed charisma.

A consciousness crisis as intuition of future potential conflicts with the reality of present desire. Abstract principle v personal interest. A hard choice between right and might.

Waning crescent: Utopian plans are adapted or abandoned in favor of immediate participation in the struggle at hand. Sacrifices abstractions to compassion, mental theory to gut level feelings. Or goes down with a sinking ship of ideological devotion.

Moon in Aquarius responds to a felt future, visceral hopes for a change agenda. An unconscious orientation to, or karmic issues around, idealistic hopes and visionary theories.

☽

Moon in Pisces/twelfth house

Individual subjectivity returns to its collective unconscious source. Immersion into a universal psychic field enlarges the scope of sensitivity while dissolving the focus of identity. Personality is inundated with normally suppressed sorrows and fears. It absorbs and redeems them in a compassionate embrace. Or disintegrates into bewildered inadequacy, even paralyzed horror.

A feeling tone of charity and tender kindness. A sympathetic temperament arising from all-embracing feelings of empathy. Universal rapport. Or helpless foundering in depths of sentimentality, overwhelmed by the world's pain and grief.

Psyche intensifies instinctual awareness, concentrating it into conscious insight. The subconscious is brought to light. Ancestral traumas are exhumed. They either dissipate, or suck one down into their ambiguous, nightmarish swamp.

Subjectivity surrenders its tired, worn out dreams to an embryonic future. Or regresses into nebulous chaos.

Ego drowns in the baptism of rebirth. Personality flooded by tides of change beyond conscious control. This is similar to the crisis of adolescence. One's inner face is disfigured as a putrefying past oozes out in psychic zits of shame, guilt, and fear. An emerging future erupts in bloody discharges and nocturnal emissions. Thus the old consciousness of youth, with its innocent clarity, comes of age into a new sensibility that is more ambiguous, and more deeply loving.

Psychological energies synthesize into a personality centered on the sympathetic plane. It resonates with others as much as it asserts self. The overall planetary pattern grounds itself in the emotional body. Its specific functions (planets) are experienced in their most sensitive and vulnerable aspect.

An emotional tendency towards renunciation: as selfless giving or as frightened retreat. Feelings focus on the encouragement or demands of others as much as on the wishes of self. A hunger for communion dissolves ego boundaries. An attunement to group needs. It registers and responds to the silent scream that most dare not hear.

If the lunar inertia of the past is not sufficiently energized consciousness regresses into unresolved subliminal or karmic fear. If Moon cannot adequately receive the solar system's imprint then personality defaults into a general mood of helpless passivity. Ennui, world-weariness takes over. A defining choice around whether to take on the suffering of the community, or to curl up into the fetal position as the pathetic prey of events. A characteristic flaw of self-pity. A dark side of victim consciousness. Or the bright emancipation of merciful love.

An unconscious sense of oneness with the universe complements the separate-self sense. This leads to compassion. Or confusion. Remembers the forgotten ones: the wretched of the earth whom most prefer to despise or ignore. Recognition of their unacknowledged potential and a willingness to nurture it even at great personal cost. Dreams of ancient wrongs redeemed, all the old fears gone.

New Moon in Pisces: Personality commits to a redemptive meltdown. Every emotional attachment dissolved. Surrender to a higher Will, unconditional faith in an unseen Providence. One stands naked before God, open to the universe. Or retreat into the womb of illusion: anything to avoid subjective emptiness, any noise to blot out the silence.

Waxing crescent: Instinctive practical compassion. A lesson in the futility of ambition: old hungers lose their bite. A more inclusive sensibility begins to emerge. Intense focus blurs as emotional range expands.

Action crisis: The dark side of consensus morality revealed. One no longer identifies with a super sparkly myth of sanitized optimism. The price is exile. Inner dreams draw or drive one from the group. One is outcast, to sink or swim by the grace of God.

Waxing gibbous: Growing responsiveness to others as essentially synonymous with self. An ability to personify unconscious collective longings as a glamour object or as a public scapegoat. One can accept these projections and live out others' dreams. Or tune out the siren calls of family fantasy and tribal myth, listening instead to the growing inner voice of soul. Then one exemplifies what the group needs, not what it wants.

Full: Personality expresses integrity by total inclusiveness: accepting all, rejecting none, in its sphere of love. Unconditional atonement for the world's ills as one's own, to be redeemed by compassion. Charity towards all. Or the illusion of salvation through one's own merit. Devotion to selfless service. Or retreat into escapist dreams.

Waning gibbous: Personality bears a compassionate or sacrificial message for the collective. A gift of self to the world at large. The social power of redemptive love. Or the seductive glamour of personal fantasy dressed up as tribal myth.

A consciousness crisis as mute sensitivity to soul confronts competing mental narratives. A Vision drowned out by the loud cacophony of ideas. Or babbling thoughts doused in the silent waters of inner tranquility. Wishful thinking confronts hard choice. Dreams are challenged by real-life dilemmas. Only instinctive faith can guide one through reason's labyrinth of contradictions.

Waning crescent: Self-sacrifice. Ancient wisdom, in all of its sophistication, gives way to instinctive trust in an unknown future. Soul sheds personality. Or the latter clings to a final illusion; takes that last fatal drink for the road.

Moon in Pisces responds to suffering. An unconscious orientation to, or karmic issues around, unfinished business, past debts, compassionate or forced sacrifice.

☽

The Planets

Personal Planets

Mercury = Mind

Venus = Love

Earth = Life

Moon = Memory

Mars = Will

Social Planets

Jupiter = Soul

Saturn = Fear, Fate

Transpersonal Planets

Uranus = Inspiration

Nepturn = Imagination

Pluto = Collective Destiny

The Solar System

Inner solar system
Personal planets

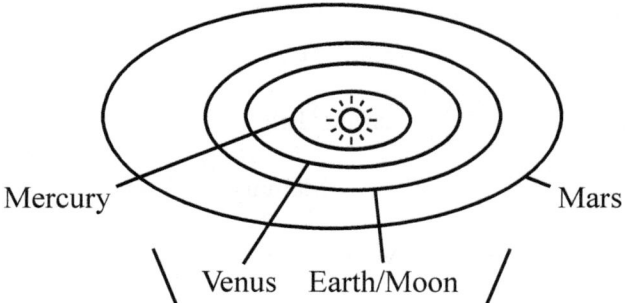

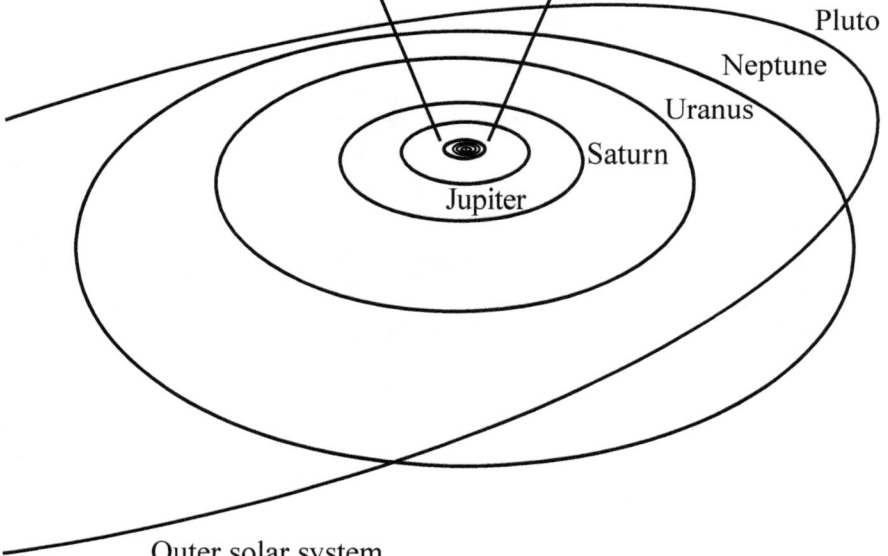

Mercury   Mars

Venus   Earth/Moon

Pluto
Neptune
Uranus
Saturn
Jupiter

Outer solar system
Social planets: Jupiter, Saturn
Transpersonal planets: Uranus, Neptune, Pluto

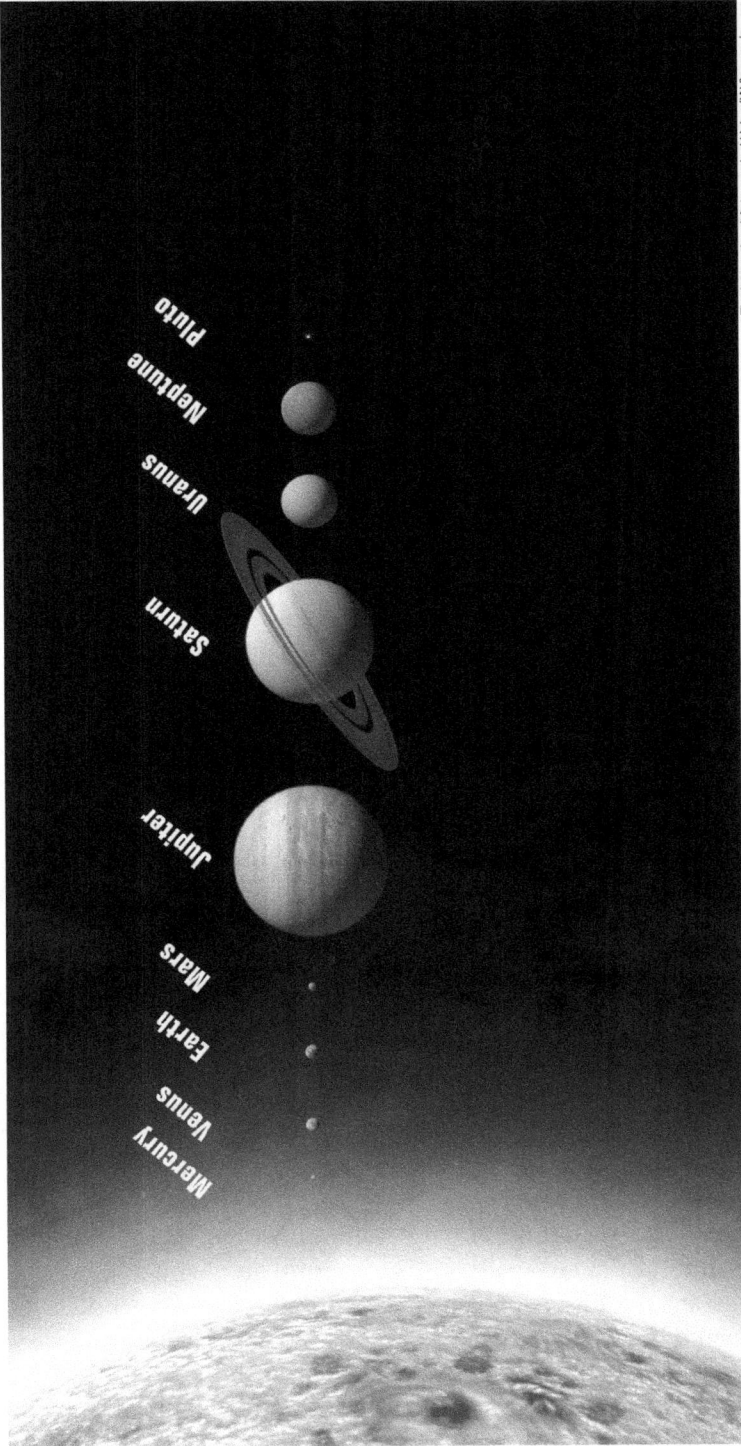

Relative Sizes of the Planets

You can view spectacular images of the Sun and all planets online.

Mercury

Tiny Mercury, scarcely bigger than our Moon, zips around Sun every 88 days. This fast moving speck, almost lost in Sun's glare, seems a lightweight compared to other planets. Next to beautiful Venus, red adventure beckoning Mars, and the enormous gas giants in their stately orbs, this midget appears insignificant. Nothing could be farther from the truth.

Mercury's orbit marks the outer circumference of Sun itself. Mercury can be seen as the spatially final, and only permanent, sunspot. Sunspots are cooling regions on the solar surface where magnetic forces organize themselves into giant whirlpools descending into the fiery interior. Mercury is where light flooding out into the exterior void circles in on itself and materializes as the solar system's first world.

Sun channels an ecstatic outpouring of a spiritual Reality behind all manifestation. Mercury's path around it defines a standing wave where Sun's urge to be encounters nonbeing, the void. The shock of contrast between infinite potency and utter emptiness generates an electric current of consciousness. Mercury's orbital movement spins that current into a vibration or amplitude of light. Its physical body grounds that pulse into a specific point of illumination. Mercury serves as an energy carrier or photon: a wavelength of potential focused into a spark of actual realization. It englobes Sun's energy surge into a particle of knowledge.

Mercury establishes the fundamental fact of our existence: duality. Its planetary body reflects this reality. Because it has no modifying atmosphere Mercury is sharply divided: its sunny side bright and hot in the light of consciousness, its night side dark and cold in the night of unconsciousness. (See 'Planetary Astronomy.') These physical contrasts symbolize the sharp distinctions giving rise to reason out of an undifferentiated All.

Mercury itself is mineral: not solar fire, nor space's emptiness. Here radiance freezes into reality, spirit solidifies into matter. Its tangibility embodies the limitation of perspective that is the price of participation. At Mercury Sun commits to a specific state of mind that can assume an identity and interact with others.

Mercury, only slightly largely than our Moon, shares much in common with it. Both are small, airless, sharply divided into light and dark sides. Each portrays a fundamental dualism, as do no other planets. Mercury embodies consciousness as opposed to all consuming ecstasy (Sun), or nothingness (space). It portrays the birth of mind, focused into a point of view. A centered attention, distinct from two abysses of infinity: primal Will and void. Moon embodies death as opposed to life (Earth). An utter desolation circling a vibrant biosphere; it poses the same dichotomy of being and nonbeing on the personal level.

Mercury = self-awareness emerging out of an incandescent All. Moon = unconsciousness, sleep, death punctuating the continuity of self. All the other planets form developmental stages, attributes, of these fundamental dichotomies: an articulated, knowable universe (Mercury) and a life/death existential experience (Moon).

At Mercury the potential to be anything (Sun) resolves into the actual mentality of a real entity. Infinite spirit takes a stance in a certain type and quality of intelligence. It assumes a position at a specific level of realization. This enables it to know the universe from within, to contemplate finite phenomena and process a response to them.

Mercury locates the point of symmetry breaking, where a blinding, featureless totality condenses into observable energies. These then organize into separate identities. Each of these entities embodies only a fragment of its original source. It mirrors the whole, but is necessarily a distorted reflection, emphasizing certain features for expression and development. Individuality emerges: of elementary particles, astronomical bodies, biological lives, psychological souls.

Individuals stand alone. Only thus can mind emerge, with its knowledge of self, others and their interaction. The Genesis story of Adam and Eve describes this process in human terms: tasting knowledge, the first man and woman are expelled from an unconscious instinctual Eden. Driven from ignorant Bliss they must move out into the world of work and war, weal and woe, pleasure and pain. History begins. Self-consciousness flowers. Mercury, the serpent of wisdom, has cheated them of immortality and union with God. It has rewarded them with autonomy: the chance to live and love as free agents.

Here spirit refracts into intelligence. Singular will bifurcates into the knower and the known. One becomes two, then many. Mind is inherently dualistic. It requires a dynamic, mutually stimulating interplay of opposites to generate a force field of awareness. All conscious experience depends on a tension between polarities. This generates interaction, communication and relationship.

This split is the origin of all paired complements, such as yin and yang. But Mercury is tricky. It slowly circles on its own axis, twisting day into night, turning all things into their opposites. It presents a range of positive and negative images, good and bad choices, in every situation. This stretches understanding with paradox, forcing it out of its comfort zone into a higher order resolution. Mercury poses a thesis, then its antithesis. Thesis/antithesis merge into Synthesis.[1] Dialog and argumentation generate awareness, then self-awareness, finally an inclusive Awareness transcending and including all of its terms.

Mercury rotates gradually: one of its days = ⅔ of its year. Rotation symbolizes a planetary function's internal sense of identity, its own subjectivity. Mercury's slow rotation points to a relative lack of self-interest. It compensates with an emphasis on objective clarity. It does not put its own spin on things; rather it conveys unbiased information. Mercury does not rush to judgment; its measured pace of rotation points to deliberate contemplation, consideration of alternatives and consequences.

Mercury observes its environment and distills its complexity into intelligible thought. It responds to the evidence gleaned through its perceptual filters and accepts the impersonal logic of its mental programming. In this its rationality resembles Moon's psychic receptivity. Mercury registers and knows objective facts of external reality. Moon grounds and nurtures subjective feelings of an internal temperament. All other planets, Venus through Pluto, are more self-directed, expressing their own particular energies and qualities. These are then interpreted by mind (Mercury) and experienced as mood (Moon).

Mercury discriminates. As the primal prism, it breaks the white light of Sun into a rainbow of colors. At Venus these colors will acquire aesthetic value, weight of worth, subjective preference, psychological meaning. Mercury simply establishes the basic fact of their uniqueness. Red is other than green. On Venus they will enter into a relationship. Mercury displays the raw data of their emanation from a blind and blinding Sun.

Mercury's intelligence separates reality out of potential, distinguishes between true and false. It insists on specific facts rather than infinite possibilities. Mercury describes what is: 2+2=4 and only 4 - not what you want it to be. Saturn defines the logic, axioms, fundamental operating principles of truth. Venus ascribes value to various truths. Mercury simply perceives them. It names all things; evokes them from out of an overwhelming Shining.

Perception emerges from clarity of difference. Mercury itself embodies that: a dense solid ball circling a flaring eruption of fire. Mercury narrows Sun's incandescence to a laser spotlight: our star's door of perception into the void through which it moves and the galaxy of which it is a part. As it circles Sun Mercury expresses that inconceivable Will's multitude of truth viewing perspectives. These are charted by its position in an astrological chart.

Mercury functions as the central organizing principle of consciousness. By position and aspect it illuminates what type of awareness drives one's psyche. The quality, intensity, sophistication of a mind cannot be charted by astrology. Its orientation can be. Look to Mercury.

Mercury describes the distinct type of intelligence by which one recognizes and responds to reality. Mercury portrays how it works, what it emphasizes. What one thinks about and why.

Mercury describes an internal mental map. It articulates attitudes and aptitudes. How one organizes the 'blooming buzzing confusion' of raw life. It classifies various aspects of reality and provides a criteria, program, protocol by which to manage them. Mercury's overall intelligence coordinates all other planetary faculties. It describes a basic skill set: the type of perception, reasoning and communication one employs. Mercury acts like a conductor in an orchestra: it did not write the music (Sun: purpose), nor does it play an instrument (planets). It integrates these factors, networks them into a coherent ensemble.

Mercury creates a model of the world inside our heads by the power of symbolic representation. This allows us to recreate it in thought experiments. We can test models, run scenarios, play out potentials. Symbolic representation allows us to try many different alternatives in the mind's eye, rather than having to plod through them with the limited resources and time available in real life.

Mercury makes imagination possible. Its theories can test the possibilities of reality. Or distort the facts by selective emphasis based on flawed premises. Mercury's game playing provides an opportunity to simulate various evolutionary strategies, learn their advantages and drawbacks, before committing to one. Or devolves into phony contrivance, an exercise in deception.

Only Mercury, at the beginning of the planetary sequence, and Pluto, at its end, orbit Sun at an appreciable incline to the ecliptic.[2] Mercury constitutes the outer perimeter of Sun itself; it represents the bandwidth of Sun's own stellar consciousness. The other planets, Venus through Neptune, orbit Sun on essentially the same plane, the ecliptic. They deliver specific messages on one channel of that bandwidth. Pluto punctuates it with interstellar energies by an intrusion from outside: above and below.

Mind is more general than our specific loves, desires, values (Venus), and more abstract than the focused purpose of will (Mars). It encompasses a wider range of possibilities than our existential reality: intellect can move from a distant past to the far future; it can think about an atom or a galaxy. Mercury presents a broad spectrum of options; the other planets ground them into specific choices. Mind (Mercury) demonstrates what is available; love (Venus) makes an evaluation; will (Mars) acts on that judgment. Mercury gives one fluency in English: one can think or say anything. Venus decides what to say, Mars backs up those words with actions.

Mercury articulates solar vitality into a conceptual framework, an overall idea of who one is and what life is about. It differs from the free-flowing subjective imagination of Moon in that it follows an inherent logic, a grammatical order. Mercury's cerebral structuring concentrates the fire of life into the light of understanding. One sees the world through the lens of a practical mentality, or a contemplative one; an emotional intelligence or a rational one.

One knows by means of Mercury, and what one thinks one knows guides all subsequent personal, political and philosophical decisions. At its best Mercury embodies self-consciousness: a synthesis including both of its sharply defined light and dark sides; a sense of its mediating position between solar fire and space's void. At worst it narrows down to a laser-like focus on one, and only one, perspective; clings to a tiny speck of fact, oblivious to the context of many other, much larger facts around it.

Mercury interprets Sun's purpose, makes it intelligible on a human level. It states solar meaning through a thought process determined by its position and aspects. Mercury composes the narrative guiding one's worldview. Whether widely encompassing, or moronically monolithic, Mercury effectively communicates this point of view. Whether pursuing objective truth wherever it may lead, or lying out of self-interest, it delivers one's personal message to the world.

Mercury describes a way of thinking, not the content of thoughts; a perceptual bias, not its observed phenomena; a communication style, not a particular message. A person with Mercury in Aquarius will tend to think big, or bizarre, thoughts about collective scientific or political topics; one with Mercury in Cancer will think poetic, or petty, thoughts about intimate nuances of feeling, the subtleties of subjective truth. Mercury reveals the general nature and orientation of one's thoughts, not their actual substance.

Mercury actually lends its name to our species: homo sapiens, man the knower. It symbolizes the fundamental human quality of curiosity. The need to explore and experiment, to constantly ask why? And what if? From such incessant questioning comes answers. These stimulate an ever more subtle understanding: first of the external world out there, then of one's own nature in here. 'Know Thyself,'[3] and you will know the universe. And its creative God, Tao or Force.

In one sense Mercury embodies the highest attribute of humanity: self-consciousness, the knowledge of good and evil at the foundation of all moral decision. In another it remains surprisingly simple, registering just the facts, accurately conveying an extrinsic reality. It does not judge; it presents a case to the jury of other planetary functions. The passions of the heart are more complex than the clarity of intellect. Mercury's cerebral enlightenment stands in contrast to the subjective ambiguity of the human condition. Mercury refines life into light, distills a crisp mental statement out of murky existential circumstance.

In this way, Mercury illuminates reality with consciousness. 'Mind is slayer of the real'[4] when it attempts to shoehorn infinity into a doctrine. Its reasoning dissects living truth. It isolates parts out of the whole and literally stresses their importance. Yet mind is also the first principle of existence, preceding material embodiment:

'In the beginning was the Word, and the Word was with God, and the Word was God.'[5]

God, Spirit, Tao, the Force is inherently intelligent and is known by intelligence. The two cannot be separated; intellect is spirit's self-awareness, on whatever level of manifestation.

Mercury's dispassionate nature enables some degree of perspective on one's own personality. (Whereas Venusian desire, Martial willfulness and lunar emotion are all antithetical to such detached contemplation.) The first thing one sees, after moving out of ego's narcissistic glare, are the dark inferiorities of one's shadow side. Mercury always begins with a painful separation out of the comforting known into its threatening antithesis. That shock of recognition is mortifying. Usually Mercury skillfully sidesteps and weaves a glib alibi. Mercury's cleverness protects one from the pain price of wisdom until one is ready for it.

Mercury's quick wit and fast paced gamesmanship gets intellect up to speed for serious thought. Or not. Our monkey minds are full of chatter. This keeps thought within the bubble of consensus babble, distracts one from entering the dangerous terra incognita of self-knowledge. Only as focused attention learns to tune out enticing irrelevancies can it develop the capacity to understand subtle and complex truths.

Mercury receives, processes and transmits information. Incoming data constantly changes. Mercury portrays how one rationally adapts to fluctuating fortune. (Moon indicates emotional response to same.) For example, Mercury in Aries tries pioneering intuition, creating new facts; while in Taurus it relies on proven truths of traditional wisdom, appreciating existing realities. Both of them, and all ten other sign positions, demonstrate valid but different learning strategies. Education itself is a Mercurial endeavor: some learn by doing, with a hands-on approach, others by dreaming, imagining alternatives; some understand by means of reason, others by way of observation. All of us use all of these approaches, but in varying proportions.

Not only how, but also what, one learns from a given situation depends on Mercury's quality of mind. For example, Mercury in Scorpio probes deeply into a matter on its own terms, delving into its core, while in Gemini it makes a comparison to other situations, placing it in context. In Capricorn Mercury seeks to find a practical use for information, making it relevant to a strategic purpose, while in Leo it aims to artistically express passion, giving voice to the heart. None is generally 'smarter' than the others though each does better under certain conditions.

Some positions of Mercury resonate with the energy fields of their sign. These emphasize the Mercury function in the overall psyche and include Mercury in Gemini, Virgo and Aquarius. Others deemphasize its role and include Mercury in Sagittarius, Pisces and Leo. In those cases Mercury does not so much express its own rationality as explain and interpret other psychological functions. It responds to an emotional or spiritual challenge rather than rides a mental opportunity. Such demanding placements can stimulate as much as rewarding ones. They generate another kind of learning. The same considerations apply to every other planet, each of which has signs of unusual promise or peril. (See 'Dignities and Debilities.')

The process of understanding corrects flaws and compensates for weakness. Thus Mercury has always been associated with healing of all kinds: physical, emotional and spiritual. The first requirement of healing is accurate diagnoses. To achieve this Mercury monitors the integrity of self-consciousness; the consistency of biological, psychological and mental performance. It does so in a manner characteristic of its sign placement. For example, Mercury in Virgo seeks a methodical technique while in Sagittarius it looks more to a general principle. Its position reveals the curative approach by which illnesses of body, mind and soul are resolved.

At best Mercury's specific perspective on Sun's overall vitality supports an organic wisdom of bodily and psychological function. It clearly interprets feedback from its internal state on all levels and responds with positive maintenance. A conscious practice of healthy living prevents problems and promotes wellness.

At worst Mercury falls into a characteristic pathology of alienated over-specialization. Then it turns to reductionist therapies, treating isolated symptoms with 'heroic' interventions and powerful drugs. This diverts attention from the causative context of an unhealthy lifestyle: a diet of hormone/antibiotic drenched meats and sugar-saturated foods, a lack of physical exercise and restorative sleep, an excess of mental distraction and emotional anxiety. No one can deny the obvious benefits of modern medicine - or its unintended outcome of an increasingly medicated yet ever flabbier population.

The same considerations apply to the fiscal health of our body politic. Mercury can refer to the market discipline of supply and demand rationally allocating resources, the give and take of trade maximizing competitive advantage to mutual benefit. Instead it has come to mean an arcane game of symbol manipulation. A 'voodoo economics' of derivatives speculation conjures huge infusions of credit out of thin air. Unsustainable debt drives the system, requiring ever more 'stimulation' to mask its bankruptcy.

At present our stressed society tends to favor negative manifestations of Mercury. It prioritizes quick fix cleverness, a contrived rationality based on false premises. It has chosen a general orientation towards artificial intelligence rather than natural wisdom. This seems to be a necessary learning experience, but its exaggerated emphasis will soon find an equally sharp correction.

Mercury analyzes and improves dysfunctional programs. It articulates a particular viewpoint. And simultaneously spotlights its inherent distortion. Any individual intelligence necessarily forms a set of defining assumptions, filtered through a perceptual bias. They focus identity by limiting its scope. The larger environment challenges these inadequacies. This creates an opening to greater inclusiveness. Or provokes a defensive denial of disturbing facts.

The serpent who brought the gift of self-consciousness is called Lucifer, the Light Bringer. And Satan, Father of Lies.[6] For the light always fades into a contrast of deeper darkness. That fall into depth separates one from the source of illumination. Its emptiness breeds compensating illusions. The initial stimulation of an independent perspective shrinks into the isolation of a partial viewpoint. One suffocates in the constricting coils of an ego-centered mind. Yet survival demands, and interaction with other minds, begin to teach it objective reason and impersonal perception. That slowly liberates it into a more universal reality, while having gained an added dimension of subjective insight.

Mercury is completely unemotional and amoral. Its standard of judgment is based on logic. Its operating procedures are clarity and efficiency. It resembles a sophisticated computer that can be put to any use: to explore the laws of nature or to track the activities of dissidents. If this function is tasked with exterminating every Jew in Europe it will correlate train schedules with crematoria burn rates to optimize output. If tasked with saving them it will coordinate medical supplies and food deliveries for maximum benefit.

Mercury serves as an information-processing module. Its value protocols come from Venus, its strategic directives from Mars. Its memory banks are lunar, its purpose solar. Mercury's consciousness must be guided by a conscience (Jupiter). Its mental rationale must be validated by a reality check (Saturn). Yet without Mercury those energy centers would be blind and deaf, unable to think or communicate, isolated on their own self-referential planes. Mercury enables each and all of them to function outside their own sphere. It is the messenger organizing them into a coherent whole, much greater than the sum of its parts.

Mercury/mind exists prior to desire or love. Value judgments emerge at the next stage: Venus. Mercury presents the basic components of those judgments. All physical and psychological qualities of our world are ultimately composed of these elementary particles. Matter, in all of its myriad forms, is built up from positive and negative charges. The architecture of mind is a mosaic of simple decisions: yes or no, on or off. The artificial minds we create - computers - are based on this binary principle. Consciousness, in all of its complexity, depends on interplay of yin/yang, male/female, good/evil, light/dark, waxing/waning, subjective/objective, I/thou. These then generate a higher order synthesis.

Mind precedes and defines being. Mercury expresses the specific pattern of decisions, the yes/no arrangement of inherent properties, making up any identity. This is true whether we are talking about an equation of forces, dance of elementary particles, play of atoms, life of a DNA code. There the yes/no decision becomes: which? A or T, C or G of the DNA nucleotide pairs?[7] Their pattern becomes the formula for a molecule, a blueprint for an organism.

Mind must have something to work on. Matter gives it grounding, traction to evolve. Mercury is the solid reference point joining every permutation of one and zero, being and nothingness, in an infinite play of actual phenomena, data, information, knowledge.

Mercury precipitates transcendent spiritual power into rational mental perception, translates absolute quality into relative quantity, makes measurable and known what would otherwise exist in self-sufficient isolation. This generates the reality of individual, interacting, internally aware entities known to themselves and each other through the communicative function. It works through the ability of language to define and express, without which comprehension as we know it would be impossible. All languages are mercurial: scientific equations, musical scores, tribal tongues.

Indeed, Mercury's function centers on the phenomenon of language: the condensation of raw data into meaningful patterns. These may be of material substance (DNA molecules), electric impulse (neural or computer networks) or sound waves (speech, music). Mercury gives voice to Sun, articulating the power pulsing at the core of existence.

Mercury enables communication between fundamental qualities. It not only articulates their distinctiveness, it also constitutes the dialog among them. Fast moving Mercury mediates between a solar source and its manifest expression in the solar system. All sunshine passes through its orbital zone before permeating the entire solar system. Mercury mediated light illuminates all other planetary planes. It brings them into communion. It translates among emergent properties (planets) otherwise isolated by the void.

Translation enables different realities to understand each other. It sparks creative fertilization among otherwise separate units. Mercury stimulates with unexpected perspectives. It enriches by adding exotic new words to a vocabulary, new concepts to a worldview. Thus ideal Venusian love is enhanced with Martian passion; Jupiterian status complemented by Saturnine responsibility. Something is also lost in translation. The integrity of any self-contained state of being is compromised by interaction with another. Any real encounter between two entities changes both and creates a third, the sum of their relationship. Thesis provokes antithesis; the two together generate a synthesis.

Give and take, gain and loss, plus and minus: swift Mercury is the arbiter of exchange. It whirls around Sun four times in an Earth year, making every aspect to every planet: pollinating the worlds, carrying their dialog, keeping them in touch. Its fast movement can interpret their complementary qualities with interactive depth or skim over them with glib clichés.

Mercury listens as well as talks, perceives inwardly as well as expresses outwardly. It weaves the nerve net linking self and world. Mercury connects essential identity (Sun) with an inner personal ideal (Venus) and psychological reality (Moon). It links them with outer personal behavior (Mars), social role (Jupiter), duty and destiny (Saturn).

Understanding one's interior self mirrors and balances contemplating, comprehending, appreciating the external universe. Mercury unites subjective and objective knowledge in a larger sentience. One of the greatest insights of modern philosophy is that we can never objectively know the essence of any entity. We can only approach it through personal recognition. We cannot apprehend the 'thing in itself.'[8] We can only locate it in the context of our own apprehension.

Mercury interprets phenomenal characteristics through the medium of subjective attention. This tiny world, daring to stand in contrast to an immense Sun and an empty void, is the catalyst of all that is known or can be known.

Our Self is partly conscious and mainly unconscious (Moon).[9] Mercury communicates between them. Its data gathering and information processing function generates patterns out of simpler inputs. It describes an inherent self-organizing property on every plane of being. On the physical in the accuracy, fluentness, intricacy of its genetic language weaving dead matter atoms into the vehicle of life (Moon). On the emotional it orchestrates impulse, sensations, instincts and memories into a psychological sentience. On the mental it integrates current perceptions with nonpresent past lessons and future plans, thoughts with feelings, theories with facts, a multitude of specific experiences into a few general abstractions. On the spiritual it marries insight and integrity, cerebral vision and moral values, personal interest with compassionate embrace. Mercury networks the contributing factors of each level into a larger whole. This endows it with the energy allowing takeoff into the next stage of evolution.

Mercury's pattern making ability generates an emergent consciousness appropriate to each plane of development. Thus atoms display consistent chemical qualities and affinities. Living organisms embody complex genetic programs. Their neural organizations focus instincts, memories and perceptions into environmentally appropriate behaviors and a growing sentience up the evolutionary ladder. This eventually crosses a threshold into consciousness and self-consciousness.

Mercury orients every energy center on every level with its external surroundings and internal functioning. Some of these are largely automated, such as DNA coding and the body's innate healing abilities. Others are essentially instinctual, such as emotional intelligence, gut level intuition. At humanity's current stage of evolution Mercury manifests most strongly on the mental plane of conceptual intelligence. This mainly expresses through verbal ability.

Mercury both separates/discriminates and joins/communicates. This enables each entity to be a unique individual and to become self-aware through interaction with others. Awareness happens as sense perceptions, objective stimuli, constantly spark the brain, building up ever more elaborate neural networks. These eventually reach a critical mass, flashing out/up into a new level: consciousness, self-consciousness, super-consciousness (Uranus) as information processing accelerates into an intuition transcending cause and effect logic.

Finally, as with Venus, two special factors arise in contemplating Mercury's contribution to a horoscope: its distance from and position before or after Sun. Because Mercury has a smaller orbit than Earth's its position can never stray more than 28° from that of Sun. Its relationship to Sun, along with its zodiacal position, defines Mercury's focus of attention.

The closer Mercury is to Sun the more will and intelligence sustain and reinforce each other. Knowledge and power interlink, with relatively little conflict between thought and action, vision and skill. The will tends to be rationally motivated (within its initial assumptions) and mind generally operates within its own sphere of influence or ability to implement its insights. Intellect immediately expresses personal purpose; it is an instrument of one's central being. When really close, within 8° of Sun (combust), basic assumptions are redefined. The mind is melted down and reforged. A paradigm shift occurs.

Conversely, the further Mercury is from Sun, especially if beyond 15°, the more intelligence functions independently of basic identity. Increasing distance from Sun indicates a detached, objective, impartial mind. Awareness, however intense, is tangential to actual circumstance. The mind generally outreaches its ability to manipulate. Intellect exists in its own right. Its independence represents either objective insight or schizoid conflict between knowledge and power, perception and capacity.

The first type portrays a mind geared to immediate requirement, quick and pragmatic. The second represents a more theoretical mind, slower and of greater compass.

Rising before Sun, occupying an earlier zodiacal degree, Mercury indicates an open, experimental and exuberant, perhaps naive, intelligence. This is an exploratory mind structuring its milieu through ideas projected as the instrumentality of a more complex, therefore unknowable purpose. Intellect is a searchlight illuminating its environment. This can be a visionary mind, ahead of its time. Or one that has jumped the gun, leapt ahead on the basis of unwarranted assumptions.

Setting after Sun, in a later degree, Mercury portrays the wisdom of experience, tried and tested, based on respect for precedent and consensus. Taken too far this stance can harden into cynicism or conformity. Here is an organizing mind abstracting the general significance of specific events, distilling subtle insight from gross complexity. Sophisticated understanding envelops simplicity of expression as intellect contemplates the results of experience.

Moons

Mercury has no moon, or burden of history, because it is pure mind, prior to experience. Mercury itself is the ur-moon, beginning the sequence of our star's planetary attributes.

Notes

1. Georg W. F. Hegel, German philosopher, 1770-1831, transformed Western thought through his emphasis on this dynamic process over static being. Philosophy, the search for and content of meaning, is a Jupiterian endeavor. It can only find its synthesis through Mercury's dialog of thesis/antithesis.

2. Mercury orbits at a 7° angle to the ecliptic, Pluto at 17°. The ecliptic is the path of Sun, Moon and planets' movement as seen from Earth. It stretches from 23½° north to 23½° south of the celestial equator, Earth's equator projected out into space.

3. The famous maxim inscribed on the Temple of Apollo at Delphi during the classical period of Greece. Plato, 423-347 BC, whom many consider the father of western philosophy, made it the centerpiece of his Socratic dialogs.

4. Hindu proverb

5. John 1:1. This quotation was meant to elucidate the identity and equality of God the Father and Christ the Son at a time when many believed that Christ, the Word, was an emanation or creation of God: a high but secondary principle. That constitutes the most fundamental heresy of Christianity, which rests on the belief that God is fully immanent in the world as well as transcending it. The same applies to mind: it is not an attribute or quality of life, it is life itself. Life consists of intelligent self-organization from the DNA molecules of heredity to coordinated processes of metabolism to automatic functioning of instinct all the way up to consciousness, self-consciousness and beyond.

6. John 8:44

7. Adenine and thymine, cytosine and guanine, pairs which always link together, are the nucleotides, or basic protein substructures, comprising the DNA double helix information code.

8. Immanuel Kant, one of history's greatest philosophers, 1724-1804, first made the fundamental observation that inner mental makeup structures external perception in 'The Critique of Pure Reason.' In turn, the shape of great minds, such as Kant, Hegel and Plato, influence how each of us thinks, for Mercury's pen is mightier than the sword.

9. C. G. Jung, the great psychologist, 1875-1961, defined the Self as a totality including the personal and collective unconscious, and inherited instinct, along with one's conscious ego.

Mercury in Signs and Houses

Mercury in a sign indicates the objective nature of one's mind.

Mercury in a house indicates one's subjective perception/expression of that mental state.

In fire signs Mercury displays an intuitive intelligence. It learns through creating, by a kinetic exploration of possibilities. It communicates by testing its will on self, others, the environment, the future.

In air signs it displays a theoretical and verbal intelligence. It learns by detached observation and calculated experiment. It communicates through abstractions, general relationships or principles.

In water signs it displays an emotional intelligence. It learns by sympathetic resonance, psychic rapport. It communicates through empathy, shared experience and feeling.

In earth signs Mercury displays a practical intelligence. It learns by doing, pays attention to facts. It communicates through results: actions speak louder than words.

Mercury in Aries

Mind individualizes: enters a new cycle of personal expression, takes on a fresh character of thought. Intellect focuses on comprehension of will: the articulation of purpose. Perception is clear and certain, profoundly simple or naïvely self-centered. Communication is forceful, direct and honest. An energetic projection of creative inspiration that defines as much as describes 'objective' reality.

Enthusiasm of a new paradigm or mental organizing principle. Challenges an accepted worldview. Aggressively tests conventional assumptions and probes for alternative explanations. Thinks fast, on the basis of spontaneous intuition. Operates through inspiration rather than logic, investigation or sensitivity. Speaks impulsively, with vigorous confidence. Intellectually competitive. Finds enlightenment through argumentation, intensity of contrast, the explicit choices of comparison. Can become opinionated or abrasively combative.

Seeks plain answers to blunt questions. Investigates things by original reasoning and a fresh way of seeing. An independent rationality validating its conclusions on the basis of its own satisfaction rather than external authority, public opinion or previously accepted criteria.

A bold, uninhibited mentality, making up in brightness what it may lack in subtlety. Learns by doing. Stimulated by adventure. Explores for the thrill of discovery more than for ulterior motives.

Mind orients itself by first principles. It seeks to interpret the motivations behind visible activity and assert those intentions out in the world. Articulates self-evident truths whose validity is axiomatic, inherently apparent.

Mercury in Taurus

Mind consolidates: stabilizes a new identity, defines its own personal viewpoint, qualities and attributes. Evaluates contending appetites in terms of their relative merit in enhancing one's own worth, whether psychological, social or financial.

Perception oriented by desire and utilitarian in purpose. Deciphers the 'algebra of need' underlying consciousness. Inquires into the wants governing overt behavior. Investigates its sources of value. Learns about real motivations and how to satisfy them.

A pragmatic outlook, conservative in method, realistic in decision. Intellect cultivates useful information, ignores irrelevant speculation about its abstract meaning. Respect for proven facts and time-tested wisdom. Patiently examines evidence, trusts tangible perception rather than brilliant theory, looks before it leaps to conclusions. Intellect validates itself by practical results. Solidly rooted in common sense it can be oblivious to intuitive insight and creative possibilities. Slow, steady, and deliberate it may lack imagination, but neither does it tolerate nonsense.

An artistic mentality, alert to its sensations, viscerally present in the moment of its perceptions. Sensual rather than cerebral or emotional wisdom. Understands that 'truth is beauty, beauty truth.'*

Mind orients itself by economic criteria of comparative value. Accurately assesses character, quality and worth. Articulates a gold standard, a core criteria, by which competing truth claims can be weighed. Faithful to, or stubbornly invested in, a basic principle of judgment. Patiently invests in its enduring worth amid the shifting tides and changing seasons of life.

* 'Ode to a Grecian Urn,' John Keats, English poet, 1795-1821.

Mercury in Gemini

Rulership: cerebral clarity assumes a heightened degree of importance in the general character. Mind objectifies: separates from its matrix in the overall personality, perceives self and environment from a detached, independent stance.

A quick, active, experimental mentality. Perception is sharp, lucid and defined by a sense of perspective (i.e. distance) between observer and observed. A dualistic understanding, linking independent variables in an awareness of polarity. A relativistic consciousness, keenly alert to differing realities. Knows that any given phenomenon can be seen from multiple points of view. Mindful that all things constantly mutate. It accurately monitors their rate and direction of change. An ability to track moving targets, their trajectories and interactions.

Mind orients itself through the give and take of dialog. It seeks to understand the pros and cons of every argument, then clarify their merit through debate and argumentation. Learns how to communicate among various perspectives. A verbal intelligence: values incisive communication, aptness of expression, eloquence of exposition. Detailed observation of immediate fact and tangible information, but may not grasp its significance in a larger design. It must learn to define its priorities. A data processing intellect. Can founder in information overload. Networks a jumble of clues into a coherent web of meaning. May not understand the relative importance of each byte in the whole.

An ability to define phenomena both in their own right, and through contrast and comparison. Its challenge is to develop a protocol of decision-making by which they are judged or evaluated. Articulates every perspective, but must develop an operating procedure by which they are centered and integrated. This would not be a single organizing principle, but a dynamic, an interactive method.

Mercury in Cancer

Mind subjectifies: immerses into a personal pool of sensibility, feeling, mood and memory. A sensitive and imaginative mentality. Intellect focuses on contemplation of non-rational feeling tones. Perception is sympathetic in nature. Discernment proceeds through a shared psychic state rather than through detached observation.

A mentality operating by gut level empathy more than cerebral reason. It reflects and articulates the rapidly changing phases of private sentiment, not abstract principles of logic. It absorbs rather than projects meaning. Receives more than sends. Listens instead of talking.

Emotional intelligence. Subjective self-knowledge. Vivid awareness of subtlety and nuance. Attuned to psychic and non-rational elements of awareness. Open to dreams and subliminal impressions.

It validates conclusions on the basis of their instinctive resonance. In order to structure itself within an otherwise chaotic impressionability it operates within a strong cultural context. The endless variations of free flowing melodies only make sense in reference to a traditional or classic standard. Mind orients itself by memory. It seeks to understand immediate perceptions within a historical context. Thought is infused with nostalgia. Or warped by fixation on past issues. Continuity of consciousness rather than revelatory breakthrough.

An accurate assessment of feelings, in self and others. An ability to understand and interpret subconscious personal energies or collective forces. Perceives and articulates origins, source and roots: where things are coming from. Learns how to explore and nurture inner truth.

Mercury in Leo

Fall: cerebral clarity must adapt to an uncongenial medium of egocentricity and self-dramatization alien to its own cool lucidity.

Mind radiates a subjective quality: makes a unique identity statement. Intellect discovers itself in the image of its own projection. A creative mentality. The mind demonstrates rather than explains itself.

Comprehension precipitates from a stark confrontation of fiery will with cold reality. A consciousness preoccupied with the nature of personal identity as revealed through the theatrical effect of one's participation in life. Perception focuses on the possible roles through which this engagement can be consummated. An artistic rationality validating its conclusions on the basis of their dramatic force and aesthetic appeal.

Mind orients itself by the quest for self-expression. It clarifies thought and identity by intensity of contrast and interaction. Learns by provoking confrontation rather than seeking consensus. Speaks more than listens. Can be a know it all; display the loud and loutish confidence of ignorance. Eventually it encounters the undeniable error of its presumption. Can it learn to see past opinionated pride? Or will it double down on the lie of a defensive spin?

Communicates through emotional charisma. Knowledge of the heart rather than the head. It does not seek to define impersonal truth or universal principle, but rather personal singularity and a particular form of excellence. Knows how to lead by example. Artistry of presentation emphasized over accuracy of observation. Intellect seeks a creative interpretation of facts rather than their simple description.

Mercury in Virgo

Rulership: cerebral clarity assumes a heightened degree of importance in the general personality.

Mind perfects its own coherence and relevance. A critical mentality notes and eliminates errors, constantly upgrades performance and consistency. Intellect focuses on the simplification and purification of its own premises/processes. Perception is judgmental in nature, inclining as much to the possible improvement of its object as its comprehension.

Intelligence learns to organize information into meaningful patterns. It seeks to discover a unifying synthesis. It reduces the complexities of observation to a few explanatory principles or inherent laws based on the logical axiom that the simplest explanation is the best.

A scientific consciousness validates itself on the basis of actual evidence. Mind orients itself by technique. It seeks experimental proof, accurately measures phenomena by objective criteria. Standardized protocols of investigation serve an impartial truth quest. Rigorous rationality eliminates bias, wishful thinking, emotional interpretation. It can miss nuances of feeling and subtleties of poetic truth. Tends to devalue fertile ambiguity, the inherent fuzziness of moral choice and subjective experience.

A sharp eye for detail. Practical ability. Knows how to solve problems. Cuts through the smoke and mirrors of eloquent presentation with precise analysis. Just the facts. They speak for themselves.

A healing mind corrects dysfunctional programs, bringing order to chaos. Intellect acts as a scalpel, excising confused perceptions and unwarranted conclusions. Integrity of truth is the goal; impeccability of method is the means.

Mercury in Libra

Mind adjusts to relationship: defines itself through participation with others. An arbitrational mentality negotiates differences. Intellect focuses on the reconciliation of complementary opposites. Things are conceived in configuration rather than in isolation. Entities are understood through their associations rather than in terms of an essential nature.

A social outlook, founded more on breadth of contact than depth of insight. Reciprocal communication subsumes self-expression in the shared wisdom of a dialog. Rationality validates its conclusions through their gracefulness of connection.

Alert to the interplay of attraction and repulsion. Develops criteria of judgment: learns how to evaluate contending energies, weigh competing truth claims, choose between right and wrong, distinguish good from evil. It is weakened by indecision rather than error.

The intelligence of compromise: comprehension and adjustment of mutually antagonistic viewpoints. Mind orients itself by finding an appropriate balance of forces. The tension of polarities generates a gradient of awareness, a range of alternatives. Consciousness decides upon the relative merit of various options within the context of a greater whole.

Things are seen in perspective. Intellect focuses on their dynamics of interaction rather than static qualities of being. Mutual definition rather than singular principle. Relationship defines the participants. Process is the product.

Judicious communication. Disinterested presentation of all sides of a question with a view towards articulating shared interests that promote reconciliation.

Mercury in Scorpio

Mind regenerates: explores its own motivations and reconstitutes itself in a larger context.

Emotional intelligence. It operates by psychic resonance rather than rational logic. It gets inside the other's head, subconsciously senses group dynamics.

Intellect expresses instincts. And searches for the means to control and direct them. It probes the depths and the darkness, in self and others. It sniffs out secrets and concealed weakness, to heal or to exploit.

Such buried energies are raw, primitive, even scary. Contact with them can create a suspicious, even paranoid, mentality. Or one that listens to its inner demons of partial but distorted truths, and translates their repressed potentials into conscious insight. It understands the fatal flaw, and transformative possibility, inherent in every person and situation. Its defining question is to what end will this information be used.

Mind orients itself to power. A subjective perspective interprets objective data in conformity to its purpose. An acute, penetrating mentality seeks to discover the impersonal, universal core energies generating individual character and behavior. It reveals the generic impulses or collective imperatives shaping one's deepest intentions. It articulates these into the known driving force of will. And then quietly, relentlessly, projects its hidden ambitions out into the world through manipulative strategy, probing intellect or a hypnotic ability to communicate what others subliminally want but cannot express.

A psychologically sophisticated consciousness investigates the subterranean currents underlying surface personality. It is interested in the equations of passion. And validates its conclusions on the basis of their visceral intensity. Theoretical constructs and ideal principles mean little. Real desire, feeling and sensation mean everything.

Mercury in Sagittarius

Detriment: cerebral clarity fades as it expands and generalizes to encompass less definable spiritual qualities.

Mind socializes: articulates group norms and aspirations. A prophetic mentality. Intellect focuses on a religious, philosophic or political mode of comprehension sustained more by revelatory conviction than demonstrable proof.

Mind strives to articulate a group consensus. It expresses conventional wisdom, perhaps at its leading edge. A rationality validating its conclusions on the basis of their conformity to general principles, which are assumed but often unexamined.

Honesty of expression, directness of inquiry, boldness of outlook. And a certain disregard for what is felt to be the pettiness of precision, the drag of small obstructive detail. Tends to exaggerate the scope of its competence and the importance of its findings. Can be distracted by fleeting enthusiasms. Danger lies in hasty wishful thinking, careless in method while avid of result.

Thought orients itself by speculation. Facts serve an existent religious or philosophic outlook, scientific or political ideology. They demonstrate a pre-given megatruth. The dangers of this are obvious, but its value can be just as real. Data are not seen as isolated info-bytes but as expressions of a larger understanding; a Big Picture. Articulates meaning and significance.

It expresses collective expectations; justifies and expands an accepted understanding. Learns to persuade rather than investigate. A promotional intellect; sells ideas more than finds facts.

Mercury in Capricorn

Mind organizes collective energies. A goal directed intellect operates through an explicit plan. Oriented towards achievement of concrete results. Things are viewed in terms of their utility towards an ulterior purpose.

A managerial mentality. Shrewdness and practical ability coexist with rigidity and suspicion deriving from an overly pragmatic outlook. A serious and reserved outlook curbs frivolous irrelevancies, remains intent upon its aims. A rationality validating its conclusions on the basis of their instrumental value in securing and expressing authority. Perception of hierarchical merit, relative rank. Learns how to administer power.

Mind oriented by ambition. It serves a long-term objective and is thus realistic and methodical. Emphasizes sequential logic over immediate intuition, demonstrable reason over theoretical speculation. A strategic intelligence, systematically working through an agenda.

Respectful of precedent and tradition: the wisdom or cynicism of experience. Cautious: prefers the tried and true to unproven innovation. Conservative: understands the limits of law, human and natural. Sharply focused: cold clarity, precision and economy of thought, fundamental simplicity of insight. Or inhibited imagination: a denial of any potential beyond already established parameters. Can be deterministic, programmed by a small set of known facts, to the exclusion of dynamic evolution. Tends towards a pessimistic assessment of character and situation, thus avoiding error at the expense of embracing possibility. Operates within an order of priorities: structured and organized rather than free flowing and spontaneous.

Mercury in Aquarius

Exaltation: cerebral clarity reaches a critical intensity of expression. Inspiration informs thought.

Mind abstracts: perceives the archetypal energies behind specific forms. Things are seen neither in and of themselves, nor in relationship, but rather through their participation in a transcendent meaning.

An idealistic mentality. Intellect is original, inspirational and utopian. It operates intuitively by flashes of insight rather than a sustained pattern of logic.

An experimental rationality validates its conclusions on the basis of their transformative impact. Iconoclastic, revolutionary: learns to express a consciousness breakthrough. Or breaks down. Adheres to the maxim that 'chaos breeds genius.' Such a constantly changing consciousness is demanding. It can default into a lower energy state of ideological intensity, substituting an exaggeration of one partial insight for the relativistic interaction of several.

Mind orients itself by theory. It intuits the underlying pattern behind complex events. The whole imparts meaning to its component parts. Thus the initial premise or truth-value of this universal vision is crucial. It can recognize the fundamental principles behind phenomena, the deep forces generating visible events. Or devolve into a one-dimensional formula, reducing everything to a simplistic slogan.

Individuals are perceived as variables of a larger social equation. Facts are seen as energy vectors, not static statements. Data is dynamic, not definitive. Emphasizes evolution and future potential over current reality.

This is a detached intelligence viewing things from a distance. It puts them in perspective, or leads to a chilling alienation. Its independence generates brilliant insight or ungrounded eccentricity, profound inspiration or blinding certainty.

Mercury in Pisces

Detriment: cerebral clarity fades as it expands and generalizes to encompass less definable spiritual qualities.

Mind dissolves: surrenders its preconceptions and identity to an embryonic future. A dreamy mentality. Perception is sympathetic; things are known through shared feeling rather than through sensory or logical means. Learns to empathize.

A mystical, or delusional, intelligence. Knowledge flows from mysterious sources: the collective unconscious, clairvoyant vision, telepathic contact. Since it lacks a conscious procedural guideline, such a mentality is susceptible to hallucinatory mirage. Its integrity is protected only by spiritual purity. The intuitive rationality of a seer, whose oracles are subject to verification, but whose methods are inaccessible except to those of similar disposition.

Mind orients itself by ideals rather than ideas. Redemptive vision, or wishful thinking, supplants tedious reason. A focus on imaginative possibility rather than dry fact. Inspirational myth, or intoxicating fantasy, is felt to provide deeper meaning than a petty obsession with details. The dangers are obvious. The opportunities are equal to them: perception is infused with magic, prose turns to poetry, linear logic gains subtle new dimensions. Rigid boundaries of knowledge become fluid and open to new levels of interpretation. The disintegration of confining categories allows an enlargement of comprehension. Or a nebulous refusal of mental discipline blurs all distinctions in a fog of illusion.

Intellect dissolves its prior thought processes and operating principles to become more inclusive. This meltdown of an obsolete mindset makes it available to higher dimensions of inspiration. Or leaves it wallowing in confusion and vulnerable to deception.

Venus

Venus is Earth's sister planet, the closest to it in both space and size.[1] Our sibling world has one defining difference: a runaway greenhouse atmosphere. Venus roasts at 867° F, above the melting point of lead, under a thick blanket of carbon dioxide. This crushes down at 92 times Earth's barometric pressure on its surface.[2]

Might this hot heavy gaseous ocean serve as a medium for entities more akin to thought forms than biological creatures? Could such a thick energy rich substrate host shimmering heat waves of desire? Mirage-like patterns of ethereal identity? Is this superheated air-sea of light and shadow a more rarified version of our organic water world of life and death?

Venus' solid surface dimly glows with a brownish red hue under a dismal clouded sky. Torrid darkness prevails, obscuring visibility to 5% of an Earth day's illumination. Indeed, Venus closely resembles traditional depictions of Hell. Do ghostly shades burn away their sins; tenuous wraiths writhe in a blast furnace of punishment and regret? Yet, as it rises, this atmosphere thins out and cools down. Between 30-40 miles up (50-65 km) a sulfuric acid cloudbank veils all of Venus. Above it a zone of sparkling breezes floats at Earthlike temperature and pressure. Sunlight brilliantly reflects off the surface of this airborne brimstone sea. Thus Venus shines as the brightest of all planets.[3] Could this be Heaven? Do blessed spirits bask in the warmth of God's love; does the tight knot of ego melt in sublime delight? Is Venus wrapped in an erotically charged atmosphere: of supernal pleasure on top and sultry passion at rock bottom?

The planet Venus is not a place of literal demons and angels, fiendish tortures or fantastic joys. It symbolizes these psychic states, which exist within us. The physical nature of Venus parallels those aspects of our psyche. Its location in the zodiac points out how they operate. Its atmospheric zones reveal their range of positive/negative experiences. What is the fatal attraction? Where the true happiness?

Venus moves inside Earth's orbit. It depicts an inner desire body beneath one's conscious self-construct. The struggle for survival, ego wars, chatter of daily life generally obscures its presence. Once death sweeps away their sound and fury perhaps these deeper planes of being emerge in full force. Maybe we then experience them with exquisite sensitivity in a Venusian hothouse of pleasure or pain.

Venus describes a private heaven or hell. Its internal spell shapes one's worldview. Venus does not point to a transcendent soul (Jupiter), impersonal law (Saturn), universal archetypes (Uranus) or collective dreams (Neptune). These outer planets operate on a mythic, heroic, even cosmic level. Venus is the personal version. An individual vision of damnation or delight.

Venus lies midway between a self-igniting Sun and our temperate ocean world. Its compressed, highly energized atmosphere provides a medium balancing fiery power (Sun) with delicate life (Earth).

Venus' special character resides in its atmosphere. Air symbolizes mind, a detached perspective uniting separate qualities. Venus' gaseous phase translates between fiery spiritual will and watery biology. It portrays an exhalation of spirit into the breath of life. Its vitalizing aura relates Sun's initiating impulse to Earth's living embodiment.

Relationship invites comparison, comparison demands choice, choice generates values. Venus' dense hot sky diffracts Sun's spiritual Unity into negotiable units: values that can be spent on life. Venus mints sunshine into gold; converts its monolithic Ecstasy into tangible senses.

Venus' aerial dimension absorbs Sun's higher frequency light, slowing it down and stretching it out into infrared waves of heat. The heat of desire. Here blinding radiance condenses into passionate warmth. Searing solar winds become palpable as hot currents flowing within a viscous atmosphere. These generate sensual vibrations.

At Venus spirit (Sun) precipitates into a spectrum of sensations. Sun's burning intensity, inhospitable to life, softens and billows into surges of feeling. A general solar purpose flowers into specific desires. This flowering then bears fruit on Earth, the plane of organic life. A fruit's seemingly dead, hard seed contains DNA hereditary information, Moon's record of the past and resources for the future. Venus endows that kernel with the sweet thrill of an actual taste: the crunch of an apple, flavor of a banana, tang of a lemon.

Mercury registers wavelengths; Venus sees colors and hears sounds. Mercury discriminates between phenomena. Venus relates them to a standard of evaluation. Mercury lays out all the options. Venus decides among them. Mercury presents stark facts; Venus prioritizes them. Mercurial perceptions become Venusian preferences.

Mercury articulates one's mental stance, intellectual attitude, cognitive bias. Venus orients that abstract mind by tangible desire and manifests its quality through actual decisions. At Venus detached observation commits to participation. Cold calculation melts into warm feeling. Impartial data acquires a weight of worth. Information is ranked according to a principle.

Venus defines a criteria of selection, the central organizing principle of subjective character. It portrays an existential choice. What is my core value? Truth, beauty, power, courage, compassion?

Venus shows what you want. It describes an ideal model that the empirical personality (Moon) makes real. Thus Venus reveals an underlying self-image guiding one's perceptible qualities.

What begins as primal will (Sun), takes definition as a state of mind (Mercury), attains a felt sensual presence on Venus. It manifests as a subtle atmosphere of individuality. Its internalized heat signature generates a unique aura of psychic quality. This endows a spectral identity equation with the emotional glow defining a life.

Venus portrays one's desire nature, or astral body. This inner state underlies the visible identity and its actions. It acquires a personal history and attributes through the experiences of life. Thus perceptions light up with passion, events become emotions.

Venus' subjective quality engages with our objective human condition in order to feel the thrill of real participation. It nurtures an appreciation of beauty through all forms of sensuality, a capacity to love through relationships, social values through life's workout in the give and take of interaction with others and a standard of justice through the cumulative pattern of one's decisions.

Venus represents an iconic inner figure who one seeks to emulate and eventually become. It beckons to a higher personal possibility, thus motivating behavior and development. Venus inspires by a unique vision of the good, the true, and the beautiful. This generates a love larger than life itself, bigger than its manifestation in an ego.

Subjectivity greatly surpasses its objective surroundings. We can imagine alternative arrangements, yearn for other possibilities. We can appreciate latent potential in another, entice beauty out of prosaic situations, create value out of inert material. An internal universe of feelings shapes how one acts upon the external environment of matter and motion. Reality reflects dreams grounded and given substance by Venus.

Within its objective circumstances Venus measures relative merit. That depends on context. Gold is more financially valuable than calcium because it is rarer; calcium is more biologically valuable than gold because it is necessary for life. Elephants outrank bacteria on the evolutionary scale because they are more complex; bacteria are more essential than elephants in the biosphere because they are more basic. (Think of all the gut bacteria one elephant needs to digest its massive meals). Venus' sign and house position in a chart provides the frame of reference by which one judges.

Psychologically, Venus portrays how one makes choices. Here one compares and contrasts physical things, emotional states, mental theories and spiritual qualities. One chooses whether to buy or to sell. Venus' placement and aspects indicate why one accepts or rejects. The level on which it operates can no more be known astrologically for Venus than for any other planet. That is a matter of direct intuition.

Venus balances axioms of truth and standards of judgment delicately, with an eye for pleasing proportion and appropriate expression. It endows raw facts with subtle beauty: ideas with elegance, personality with charm, relationship with grace. Such enchantment can draw one up by admiration of higher qualities, perhaps seen in others. Or suck one down into narcissism, esteem only of one's self.

Every planet has a dark side. Beauty can be skin deep, justice bought and sold, truth bent. Values can bend into distorted priorities, innocent delight sicken into twisted cravings. Then the next world in lures one with a siren song of vampiric seduction. Healthy lust becomes greed, appreciation turns to addiction. Indulgence corrupts enjoyment. These then degenerate into possession: the rule of appetite.

Venus harmonizes all other planetary energies in an inclusive psychic economy. It prioritizes and artfully arranges instincts, feelings, thoughts and ambitions into an ideal persona. This is given psychological content by Moon and a human face at the ascendant.

Jupiter locates our transcendent soul, or participation in the divine. Venus defines our higher humanity. The next step in evolution, more than one's personal best, reaching towards an angelic realm.

Venus also embodies something equally important: the ability to cherish that ideal as it actually manifests in life here and now; the pleasure of our present state. Without Venus' sensitive/sensual appreciation we would have Jupiter's spiritual consciousness and Saturn's fateful law; Mercury's mind, Moon's memory and Mars' courage; Uranian inspiration and Neptunian compassion. But none of it would be any fun. Venus feels the happiness that gives these attributes value and makes life worth living.

Venus is a personal planet, the better angel of human nature. The outer gas giants have a certain cosmic glamour, abstract and remote. Mercury and Mars have integrity of mind and rigor of will. Venus infuses all these worthy qualities with delight.

Our solar system is a coherent whole in which each planet not only has a specific identity but also plays a role in an overall pattern. All planets revolve around Sun in the same direction. All but one of the visible conscious planets rotate on their axis in the same way.[4] As seen from above Sun's north pole they all rotate counterclockwise. Except for Venus, which spins clockwise.

A planet's rotation defines its day, the subjective unfolding of its qualities During one rotation a planet circles around its central core while also scanning all 360° of the universe around it. The parallel

Figure 1   Venus Rotation

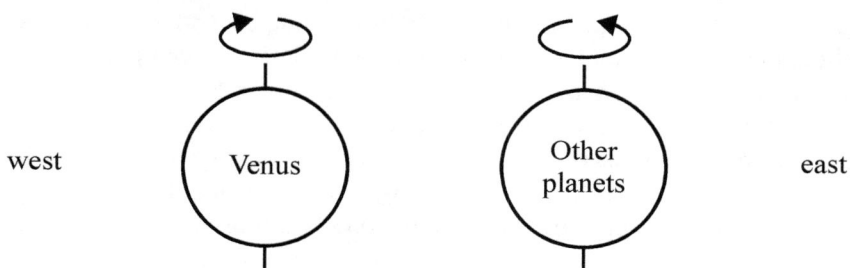

west   east

Venus rotates 'backwards,' east to west.
All other planets of conscious experience rotate west to east.

Figure 2   Planetary Rotations

Vertical lines = axial inclination
Horizontal arrows = direction of rotation

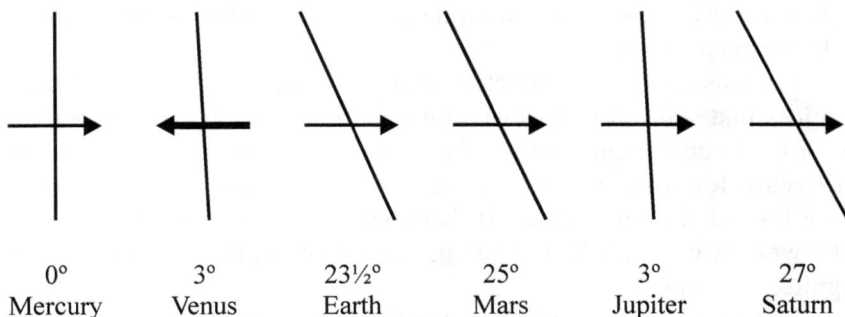

0°	3°	23½°	25°	3°	27°
Mercury	Venus	Earth	Mars	Jupiter	Saturn

Visible planets of consciousness.

Venus stands alone among the planets of conscious experience in rotating east to west.

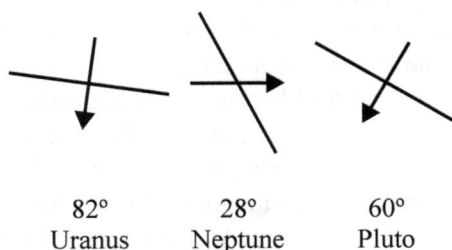

82°	28°	60°
Uranus	Neptune	Pluto

Invisible planets of the collective unconscious.

The unconscious constitutes a fundamentally different reality. Its planetary symbols visually demonstrate this. Uranus and Pluto are tipped over and rotate mainly north to south. Uranus acts as a conduit linking the conscious and unconscious realms. Pluto conducts forces from beyond the solar system. For more information see 'Planetary Astronomy.'

spinning of worlds suggests that each is a specific focus of experience within a general field of evolution. Most twirl in synchrony, spiraling with a common orientation: west to east. Only Venus provides a counterbalance, with an opposite spin to all other worlds. It uniquely rotates 'backwards,' circling east to west: Figures 1 and 2.

Venus' retrograde rotation identifies it as the focus of involution in our system and in an astrological chart. It generates a magnetic vortex, the locus of desire. This calls one into incarnation. Venus grounds a soul's ethereal energy into lunar psychology. It marks the point where spirit learns to love. Shows what it seeks to experience on the plane of life and relationships.

Venus creates an attraction that draws soul into self. And then entices that self out of its own conceit. This happens when one falls in love. Venus' appreciation of another grows one beyond ego. We all yearn for what we lack. Venus shows the missing piece, points to a longed for completion. It displays one's other half: for a man, the woman who fulfills his being, for a woman, the latent potential ignited by a man.

In a man Venus symbolizes the feminine energy he seeks to complement his masculinity (anima). In a woman it describes the female model she herself tries to personify. Of course, in many cases one perceives this figure in an unconscious or distorted way. Then Venus indicates not only an ideal female archetype, but also the kind of relationship needed to reach her. And the quality of love resulting from it.

Venus inspires, but does not consummate, psychological evolution. Her yearning generates an emotional fever that burns away ego defenses. She invites escape from the prison of personality; seduces one into stepping outside the safe boundaries of a known reality to share another's. There one may find happiness or anguish, sweet content or bitter disappointment. Sometimes the latter is more stimulating: much of the world's great art, heroic striving and spiritual devotion have been catalyzed by unrequited love sublimated into a more universal wisdom.

Venus shows what you want. And delivers what you get which is always different from what one consciously imagined. Venus attracts, Jupiter indicates the spiritual outcome of that attraction.[5]

Venus rotates very slowly. A planet's rotation describes its internal sense of identity. Venus' day (243 Earth days) is longer than its year (225 Earth days). (!) At the end of each Venusian day's slow descent into subjectivity the planet has revolved all the way around Sun and then added, incorporated, enfolded an additional ⅛ of its orbital cycle. It has contemplated the full potential of the soul in a complete circling of the central fire and then actually invoked 12% of it as its daily increment of subjective experience.

Venus entertains a perspective of many possibilities and makes some of them available as real desires, values, aspirations. One may never realize those wishes, live up to the ideals, achieve the dreams. But they remain as motives and inspirations. One's goals shape who one is. Values demonstrate worth. 'As a man thinketh in his heart, so he is.'[6]

Each Venusian day contains the full measure of its orbit - and then some. The richness of inner resources implied by Venus' long day constitutes a psychological cornucopia, a truly generous endowment. In contrast, Earth's daily unit of experience involves only $\frac{1}{365}$ of its overall orbital promise. With each world moving out from Sun this ratio diminishes even further. Venus pours forth an inexplicable abundance. We are not yet evolved enough to fully accept and assimilate this extraordinary grace.

Venus portrays one's anti-shadow: a body of light. Its plenitude testifies to a benevolence beyond our comprehension. It shines as a beacon amid life's routine slog; generates a sense of hope making all things possible. Venusian wishes drive our experience of Earthly facts. Her love exceeds our limitations.

Love is the most powerful force in the universe. It enters our system through Venus. It may be that, in its involutionary phase, a soul surveys the entire field of possibilities in the desire world during a Venusian year, and then focuses on one aspect to develop by expression in personality through its longer day. Perhaps most of our total being is bound up in the maintenance of the body's elemental energies, with only one facet selected for conscious evolution in a lifetime. Perhaps only this fraction of our potential can be actualized within the confines of the human condition.

Venus demonstrates the power of love enabling a soul to accept such limitation as the price of participation in the world. At the Venus placement in the chart one subliminally senses the point where a supernal beauty floods into and nourishes organic existence. Thus Venus indicates why one took shape, what one so wants to attain as to forsake eternity and enter into flesh.

Yet in the slowness of its rotation Venus also falls behind the curve, is not up to speed. Dreamy wistfulness is a languid state. One could loll forever in the pleasure palace of the psyche. Thus Venus requires the stimulus of Mars, the challenge of hard reality, to evolve. Its love must grow from infantile dependence to childlike trust to youthful idealism to mature appreciation to elder wisdom. This only occurs under pressure of necessity. One could remain a baby forever, luxuriating in primal pleasure, unless sparked and spanked, pushed and pulled, by the necessary intrusion of other planets.

Venus can display the inertia of satisfaction, a complacent acceptance of the status quo. Satiety with comforting relationship can replace a hunger for grand passion; vanity with who one is often displaces an effort to become all that one can be. Venus falls by a too easy and early victory, basking in a rich sense of self-approval before it has achieved its full potential. It tends to wallow in a lush and fragrant garden of immediate gratification. It must find a balance between the gift of present happiness and the pregnant joy of a more distant consummation.

At Venus ego slowly unwraps its heart. Consciousness lowers its defenses and shares its inner secrets. This is not a fast paced world of action or of thought. It is a delicate flowering of love. An ever deepening appreciation of another, others and of one's own nature. This happens softly, quietly, gently.

Venus unwinds the coils of social expectation and of personal affectation as it reverts back to the hidden source of self. Its unhurried retrograde rotation suggests a slow, sensual opening. A natural maturation, independent of outside schedules or demands. An organic subjective process that cannot be rushed by outer pressures or inducements.

To do so forsakes gold for glitter. Seduction by illusion is Venus' downfall. The bitch goddess success, the venal vamp of money, the empty promises of promiscuity are its premature ejaculations, trading long deep development for a fast and phony payoff.

Shrouded in thick yellowish-white clouds Venus is what it resembles: the pearl of wisdom, the highest truth: love. This implies openness to both outer cosmos and inner psyche. It gives vulnerability to, and enhancement by, others' energies. Those who share such sensitivities partake in Venus' profound capacity for intimacy.

Otherwise, a more inhibited Venus simply mirrors projections of egoic vanity. Its bright reflection blinds with sparkling superficiality. It shields unexplored passion behind a veil of pleasant artifice and social adaptation. One glides through a life of lukewarm pleasure, content with mediocrity, perhaps happier, on a feebler level, than those who feel the agony and the ecstasy.

Venus expresses one's deepest desire, pervading personality and directing its behavior. It embodies a quality of love: realistic or idealistic, chaste or erotic, a receptive appreciation or a joyful giving. This generates the mystery of attraction connecting isolated individuals.

Venus' introverted sensation discerns resonance or resistance; registers similarities and complementarities, differences or antagonisms. Because 'women are from Venus' (and men from Mars), such sympathetic insight underlies the undeniable phenomena of female intuition.[7]

Venus appreciates what exists. It hopes for what does not. Every wish invokes Venus, by longing for a better state of affairs. Mars then acts to achieve it. Venusian vision motivates Martial action.

Such anticipation also involves Moon's reflective memory: an awareness of non-present time. Moon adds a temporal dimension to the concrete here and now. If we can remember the past we can envisage a future. Both imaginatively enlarge an immediate situation. Venus adds an atmosphere of expectation; fills that psychic space with subjective content. Memories aren't just dry facts, but interpretations. Wishes aren't objective extrapolations of current trends, they seek emotionally revised outcomes. Venus assigns personal meaning and relative importance to past and future events. You and I may participate in a process, but we each foresee and remember it differently because we each approach it from our own internal Venusian perspective.

Venus embodies the magnetic attractor drawing spirit into life. One enters life through a mother. Moon portrays the actual mother. Venus indicates the female ideal (anima), which drew one to birth through her. Thus the relationship between Venus and Moon demonstrates how the biological/familial mother fulfilled or challenged one's primordial female archetype. Venus then individualizes and makes conscious a love initially shaped by an infant's (lunar) dependency on and sensitivity to its mother.

Venus occasionally retrogrades, like all planets. (See 'Solar Aspects and Retrogradation.') However, its pattern of stations, or turning points, from direct to retrograde, and vice versa, has a unique rhythm. It forms a five-pointed star every eight years. This star itself retrogrades by a little over two degrees during each eight-year cycle. No other planet traces out such a regular and archetypal form in the sky of consciousness: Figure 3.

The five-pointed star serves as a symbol of humanity itself, with four limbs and a head. Its slow reverse movement through the zodiac every 1215 years[8] mimics Earth's retrograde Precession of the Equinox every 25,920 years. ('Precession' refers to millennial-long eras defined by the wobble of Earth's tilt. See that chapter.)

One Earthly Precession, or Great Year, contains just over 21 Venus cycles. What might this correlation mean? During one normal human lifetime (70 years) this star retrogrades by about ⅔ of a sign: the same ratio as a Venusian day of subjective involution to an Earthly year of spiritual evolution (243/365 Earth days). What might that signify?

Figure 3   Direct Stations of Venus: 2015 - 2038

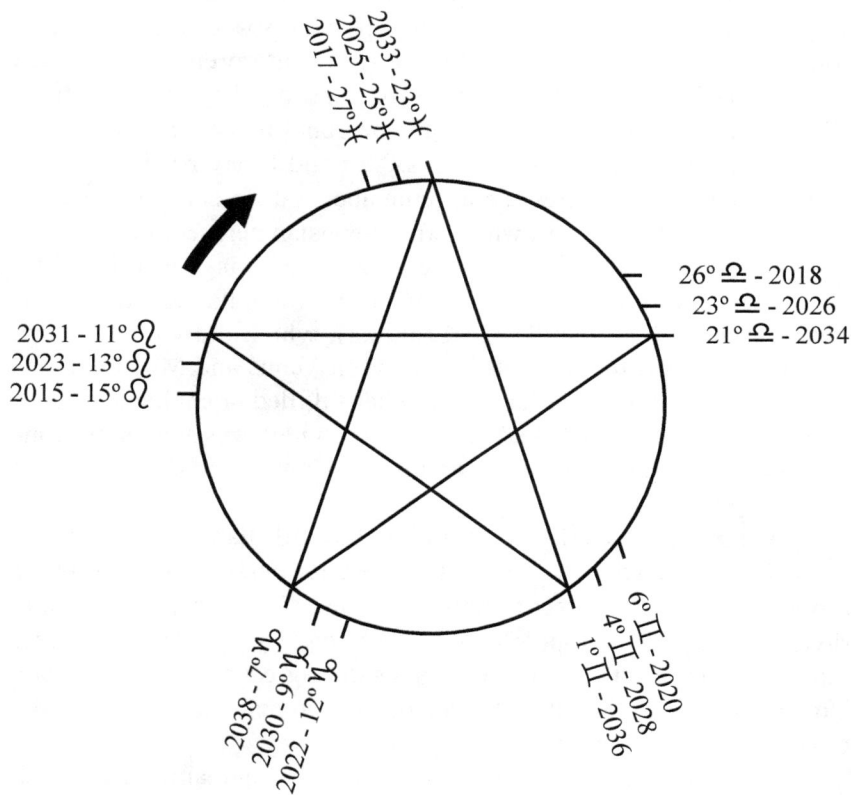

2033 - 23° ♓
2025 - 25° ♓
2017 - 27° ♓

26° ♎ - 2018
23° ♎ - 2026
21° ♎ - 2034

2031 - 11° ♌
2023 - 13° ♌
2015 - 15° ♌

6° ♊ - 2020
4° ♊ - 2028
1° ♊ - 2036

2038 - 7° ♑
2030 - 9° ♑
2022 - 12° ♑

Perhaps, just as the historical ages of the world gradually mutate, so the Venusian balance of human values changes in subtle ways over the centuries. The calculus of our emotional appetites may vary somewhat now from what it was a few generations ago. The pentagram of passion probably felt slightly different during the Renaissance than in the Enlightenment. Aesthetic sensitivity has a higher priority in one era, spiritual austerity in another. All human yearnings are always present, but have a different emphasis over time. This obviously happens during an individual life, as baby becomes child, then adolescent and adult.

Venus' stations are not a property of the planet itself, but of its visual relationship to us here on Earth. We see them because these two worlds move at different orbital speeds: Venus appears to move backwards as it passes between Earth and Sun. (See 'Solar Aspects and Retrogradation,' Figure 5.)

The reverse movement of Venus' turning points relative to Earth's zodiac parallels its own retrograde rotation compared to that of other planets. Venus' contrary spin symbolizes involution; a magnetism grounding Sun's spiritual urge into manifestation through personal love. In the same way, its slowly regressing stations reproduce Earth's objective historical Precessional cycle on an inner plane of changing collective values. Their returning motion relative to Earth's orbit suggests a revisiting of origins, a deepening appreciation of our common source.

This journey of enhanced remembrance, a deepened renewal of ancestral wisdom, embeds private preferences in a larger rhythm of cultural expression. Thus Venus describes one's subjective sense of the times, as well as of one's own identity. It evokes the personal flavor of historical experience.

Venus' revolving star of stations implies a long-term reprocessing of accepted mores: etiquette and manners; style and fashion. These customs and protocols are important because they integrate individual experience with social expectations. Unspoken proprieties allow one to engage with others. They may seem arbitrary, but actually constitute a shared sensibility facilitating contact. They provide a recognizable context for interaction.

Venus' retrograde station describes the frontier of negotiated agreement possible within a given historical context, a bottom line of mutual acceptance.[9] Its actual retrogradation recalibrates both personal and collective values. Or readjusts the relative status of corporate entities such as businesses and governments. Its direct station consolidates that revaluation into new standards of beauty and models of relationship. Individually it rearranges emotional priorities. Collectively it recalculates economic rates of exchange and revises the political atmosphere surrounding a changed balance of power.

Venus turns retrograde at its farthest distance ahead of Sun in the zodiac. It then sets as the Evening Star: a final summation of wisdom, a bright gem offered to the gathering galactic darkness. Venus turns direct at its farthest distance behind Sun in the zodiac. It then rises as the Morning Star: the spark of love igniting a new dawn.

What does Venus' involutionary gateway from the astral plane mean in psychological terms? First and always it expresses the nature of love. By position and aspect Venus portrays who, how and why you love.

What we love is what we treasure. Venus depicts an unerring index of values, a revelation of tastes and sensibilities. What attracts one. Pleasure: coarse or sublime, voluptuous or mystical.

Venus illuminates a personal ideal. And clarifies its qualities: why you are here, what you want, who you aspire to become. Mars then indicates how one pursues these yearnings and with what kind of energy: strategy and tactics.

Venus embodies the beauty seducing will into actual expression. Amplifies the subtle suggestion of astral vision into a live current of passion. She induces the erotic magnetism that makes the world go round.

Venus portrays sensuality, the primary enchantment inherent in our perception of the world and others. The nonjudgmental appreciation of actual existence as opposed to ideal possibility. A basic acceptance of personality and circumstance for what they are in their own right. It implies a realistic appraisal of every entity and situation on its own terms: the basis of both love and wisdom. Venus underwrites the acquisition of experience, possession of attributes, appetite for life and ability to love. It shapes desire into satisfaction, grounds impulse in beauty. Here the martial impulse of spring blossoms forth into leaves and flowers, naive enthusiasm of childhood dawns into the sensitive awareness of adolescence.

Venus also has a more relativistic mode, seeking a balance of pleasures. It describes a dynamic harmony weighing different, often mutually exclusive, appetites. An orchestration of desires in accordance with a subjective aesthetic. One cannot have it all: every choice precludes others. Venus charts the basic rationale of evaluation, ultimate criteria of judgment. A considered harmonization of events within a conscious system of priorities. It synchronizes identity and environment. Makes a deliberate reply or gift of self to the life that molded it. Here is the consummation of harvest. A fulfillment of personality reaching beyond itself towards merger with death and the intangible source of its plenitude. A poignant autumnal beauty as a final statement of love.

Venus also yearns to embrace a greater than personal love. Thus it ascends to its higher octave (Neptune).[10] Through sacrifice and renunciation passion melts into compassion, individual attachment dissolves into universal Christ-like love. Every Venus placement holds, in varying proportions, these qualities of direct sensation, sophisticated evaluation and selfless surrender.

Venus shows where (house) and how (sign) you open your heart. And to whom (aspects). Why you let them in. What happens when you do. Often love is reciprocated; both parties grow individually and as a couple. Sometimes it is not. Perhaps one is rejected, for good reasons or bad. Or betrayed: seduced and abandoned. Love itself must learn not to accept everything with wide-eyed innocence or everyone with unconditional trust.

Blind adoration, codependent enabling, naive lack of perception are passive crimes of Venus. Disproportionate infatuation and inappropriate affections are its weaknesses. Such emotional laziness gets a rude awakening, all the more painful because its motives are benevolent. Childlike goodness does not make it in a cruel world. One must learn to love the truth about others, not project wishes onto them. One must appreciate people and situations for whom and what they really are, not pretend they are what you want them to be. Or assume that goodwill makes everything right. Venusian traumas are devastating because they involve abuse of trust. Yet only thus can one understand that the value of real intimacy is multiplied by its rarity. And begin to comprehend how deceptive appearances can be, how cheap and shallow so many people and so much of life are.

In a more negative sense Venus embodies temptation. Forbidden lust or too great a craving. Venusian vice diminishes one by displacing higher virtues with gaudy imitations. Thus one salivates with greed because one cannot really savor what one already has. Venial sins display weakness rather than a positive commitment to evil. Low standards lead to enervating forms of pleasure, then decadence and degeneracy.

Venus seeks consolation for such emptiness in gross consumerism or over-refined delicacy. Simple beauty turns to contrived style. The sensitive man becomes effeminate, the sweet woman vain. Venus rots from within, subverting judgment so that one mistakes carrion for ambrosia.

Yet Venus also serves the nectar of the gods for those who have earned the right to drink it. Such worthiness demands no striving or heroism, only openness to love. Not in terms of getting what one wants, but as genuine appreciation of the beloved. Then Venus graces one with an entirely new dimension of being, unavailable to the self alone.

Venus describes one's most delicate sensibility. One's sweet spot and weak spot. It demonstrates one's best quality in good times and bad. Or worst failing in victory or defeat. Not where one exhibits malice (Mars) or encounters fear (Saturn), but where one sells out to a lower value, defaults to diminished expectations.

Every placement of Venus can experience as profound a love as any other. And as deep a disappointment. At some point every heart must break by wanting what it cannot get. That can grow it by emulation of desired qualities, enticing effort and evolution. Or shrink it with envy, coveting what others have. And twist it with jealousy, a morbid fear of losing Precious. Venus' challenge is to gracefully accept what one is not meant to have or be. And gratefully appreciate who one and others really are.

As with Mercury two special factors arise in contemplating Venus' contribution to a horoscope: its distance from, and position before or after, Sun. Because Venus travels around a smaller orbit than Earth's its position cannot stray from that of Sun by more than 48° of zodiacal longitude. The closer Venus is to Sun the more strongly, immediately and directly associations affect the individual. The very identity is powerfully influenced by the quality of relationships and the nature of the female archetype (anima). Conversely, the further Venus is from Sun, the more experimental, abstract and independent one is of consequence or tie. It portrays a relatively greater autonomy in relationships, a more mutable identification with the feminine side. The first values commitment and an existential wisdom, the second values detachment and a more distant vision.

When combust (within 8° of Sun) Venus undergoes a transformative identity crisis. Like the new Moon, she experiences death and rebirth in the solar fire. It marks both danger and opportunity as a satiated desire, an exhausted form of love, burns away and transmutes into something new.

Venus rising before Sun, in an earlier zodiacal degree, is called the Morning Star. It implies a yearning quest into an unknown future; a dawning anticipation. Love expresses through passionate outreach. Venus setting after Sun, in a later zodiacal degree, is the Evening Star. It finds wisdom in contemplation of timeless truths distilled out of the day's busy glare. Love experiences a serene harmony, derives increasing value from evolving continuity. The Morning Star suggests a romantic artist or disciple absorbing love/wisdom; the Evening Star an old master radiating it. Both are equally valid contributions to an inclusive reality.

Venus' unique astronomical characteristics hint at her singular role in the spiritual economy of the solar system. Venus mediates the influx of subtle energies feeding the whole process of evolution as defined by other planets. She precipitates a desire motivating one's own flowering of attributes. Desire drives destiny. Love transforms it.

Venus, first planet in from Earth towards Sun, focuses the subjective assimilation of experience. Whereas Mars, first planet out from ours, portrays the urge to act and participate, Venus indicates the feedback, result or reward of striving. Every action has a reaction, makes an impression, charted by Venus as a distinctively individual quality of response. In short, Venus indicates the consummation of experience and consequence of effort.

Venus denotes wisdom as the general subjective framework within which events assume meaning. It indicates the goal or perfection of individual character: a singular vision, a special form of appreciation, stemming from a unique pattern of development. It demonstrates the empathy extracted from personal experience of universal situations. And a peculiar, once in eternity, love developed through specific relationships.

Venus gifts every heart with hidden resources and seeks the kiss that will awaken it. She holds a mother lode of latent value, and invites the spark that can release it. In a cold world Venus emits warmth. In the endless 'war of all against all'[11] she brings peace. Amidst life's loneliness Venus gives the supreme gift of love.

Venus symbolizes the pleasurable sensation of spirit's incarnation into personality. The joy of its contact with others. Venus embodies life's reward of happiness, the beauty of its love.

Moons

As with Mercury, Venus has no moon. Moons symbolize karmic baggage. Mercury and Venus are inner states of consciousness, prior to experience. They do not carry the weight of history; they portray the mental and desire orientation we bring to it.

Notes

1. Venus approaches to within 25,000,000 miles of Earth, closer than any planet other than Moon. Venus weighs in at 82% of Earth's mass. All other planets are either less than ½ that size (Moon, Mercury, Mars, Pluto) or many multiples of it (Jupiter, Saturn Uranus, Neptune). Indeed, chemical evidence even suggests that Venus had a liquid water ocean early in its history, about four billion years ago. It has long since evaporated away.

2. Equivalent to the pressure at 2985 feet, 910 meters, underwater

3. Venus' albedo, or reflectivity of light = .65. That means it reflects 65% of incoming solar light and absorbs 35%. By contrast, Moon = .07, Mercury = .11, Mars = .15, Earth = .37, depending on seasonal conditions of ice cover. The outer gas giants have higher albedos than the inner rocky ones, but are far from Sun: even a clear mirror reflects little in the dark. Jupiter = .52, Saturn = .47, Uranus = .51, Neptune = .41, tiny distant Pluto, covered in ices seems to = .5 -.7.

Venus not only has the highest intrinsic albedo, but is also exposed to orders of magnitude more sunlight than the outer planets. Thus it is by far the brightest.

4. Uranus rotates north to south. It does not spin in parallel with other planets, but rather at a right angle to them. This perpendicular rotation thus produces a tunneling or channeling effect, linking completely different realities: structured space/time and formless void-source. Uranus is not part of our system's field of evolution. It points to a quantum leap out of it. Pluto also rotates obliquely to the system. It is a gateway to another realm, that of interstellar space. However, Uranus and Pluto, along with Neptune, focus aspects of the collective unconscious. Their north to south rotation describes a dimension of psyche and spirit as different from consensus consciousness as the quantum is from the atomic level of matter. Within the conscious personal and social experience of the seven visible planets Venus' retrograde rotation stands alone. (Sun, Moon, Mercury, Venus, Mars, Jupiter and Saturn.)

5. Thus Venus is traditionally called the lesser benefic, creating a tangible opportunity to evolve. Jupiter, the greater benefic, expresses the soul-transcendence resulting from that opportunity.

6. Proverbs 23:7

7. Another observation along this line is: 'Men have the love of truth. Women have the truth of love.' This charming quote is attributed to Francois de La Rochefoucauld, 1613-1680, a French writer and wit.

8. Venus makes a direct station every 1.6 years (584 days). Each of the star's 5 arms takes 152 such stations to return to its initial degree, with each station retrograding by about 2⅓° on average. Each arm's station

occurs at an 8 year interval (5 x 1.6 = 8). 152 x 8 years = 1216 years. Another way of saying this: it takes 152 individual arm movements x 5 arms = 760 total stations to reproduce the whole star at any given starting point. 760 stations x 1.6 years = 1216 years. The same is true for its retrograde stations.

This is a rounded number. Venus actually takes only 7.997 years to form each star; it loses 2⅓ days per cycle; over 152 cycles this adds up to about a year. Thus the correct period is 1215 years.

One can look up all Venus stations, retrograde and direct, from 1801-2100, online at: venus retrograde-astropro
9. An interesting example is the Iran nuclear deal, announced on July 14, 2015, just before Venus turned retrograde at 1° Virgo on July 25. It stipulates minutely detailed conditions for, and stringent inspections of, that country's nuclear activities. In return it lifts tight sanctions restricting its economic activity. All of this is very Virgoan.

The deal is illusory. Venus made its retrograde station while in detriment in Virgo. And in loose opposition to Neptune, a symbol of deception, exalted in Pisces. It is based on exaggerated optimism: on July 14 Venus closely separated from Jupiter in Leo. And inherently limited, with a shorter than expected lifespan: Venus exactly squared Saturn in secretive, power hungry Scorpio. Iran wants to acquire nuclear weapons and will eventually move to do so after a period of economic recovery.

This does not mean it is a bad deal. It may buy a few years of peace before an inevitable confrontation. Later is probably better than now. (Written August 2015.)
10. The visible personal planets, known since antiquity, Mercury, Venus and Mars, each have a higher octave, a more subtle manifestation, among the outer planets, Uranus, Neptune and Pluto, which were discovered with the use of telescopes in modern times (1781, 1846 and 1930 respectively). Thus Mercury/mind resonates with Uranus/ intuition-inspiration; Venus/personal love with Neptune/universal compassion; Mars/ personal will with Pluto/fate or God's Will as revealed in the generational cycles of history. See 'Dignities and Debilities.'
11. 'Leviathan,' Thomas Hobbes, English political philosopher, 1588-1679

Venus in Signs and Houses

Venus in a sign indicates the objective nature of one's values and desires: what one wants out there in the world.

Venus in a house indicates one's subjective personal ideal: who one really wants to be inside.

In fire signs Venus senses and loves the highest aspirations possible for self and others. It encourages dormant potential and seeks spiritual expression. Can be inflated and unrealistic, loving fantasies more than real life. Wants gold, may settle for glitter.

In air signs Venus senses and loves a unique intelligence in self and others. It encourages mutual understanding and aspires to just and fair relationship. Can be detached, loving ideals more than people. Wants harmony, may settle for surrender.

In water signs Venus senses and loves the human feelings and foibles of self and others. It encourages emotional bonding and aspires to selfless communion. Can be sloppy, wallowing in sentimentality; loving love rather than a lover. Wants mystical rapture, may settle for illusion.

In earth signs Venus senses and loves existing qualities in self and others. It encourages their practical development and seeks down home happiness. Can get stuck in small pleasures and miss big opportunities. Wants the good life, may settle for mediocrity and boredom.

Venus in Aries/first house

Detriment. Appreciation of others fades as self-confidence increases. Desire individualizes. One wants to be oneself. Only then can one truly relate to another. The subjective ideal enters a new cycle of expression, takes on a fresh character. Love subordinated to will.

Asserts personal preference over familial or cultural expectation. One's own values define self against the collective background. Internal emergence of a distinct canon of truth, beauty and justice independent of public opinion. A breakout from socially conditioned to self-chosen models. Thus Venus' normal function of sympathy and resonance with others flips into encouragement of one's own developing attributes. Seeks fulfillment rather than accommodation. Follows an internal drummer, regardless of what others hear. Introjects relationship as a resource for self-development rather than adapting identity to please another.

Such a distinctive affirmation evokes contrast rather than harmony. Those who do not play by the same rules test one's basic values. Self-esteem faces rejection. Naive inner joy meets scathing disapproval and overt hostility. Tender sensitivity learns to contend with rude coercion of a combative world.

Love learns through loss: eager expectations are dashed; youthful ardor crushed, or stimulated, by opposition. It deepens through adversity. Matures through the struggle to relate. Natural spontaneous enthusiasm is reforged in the fire of life's ego wars to true self-knowledge and clarity of judgment.

Desire adapts to new drives. A springtime surge of vitality disrupts comfortable arrangements and complacent happiness in the interests of a greater purpose. Primal passion renews love. Or burns away its pretense. Established preferences challenged, and fertilized, by the forceful intrusion of a larger reality. Ethereal aspirations coarsened, and invigorated, by the objective demands of evolution.

Intense, uncomplicated devotion. Can be an avid projection of one's own inner idols, insensitive to the other's true character. Lusts for adventure, excitement; gets up and goes. Attraction to strenuous exertion over indolent ease. An athletic sensuality turned on by the rush of exercise, thrill of danger, suspense of competition. Pleasure in pursuit more than attainment; the chase more enjoyable than the capture; the workout is the reward.

The ideal self-image behind ego is simple, direct, honest, and dynamic. These qualities are also admired in others.

Venus in Taurus/second house

Rulership. A specific love, or form of love, assumes an unusual degree of importance in the general personality. Sensuality and the pursuit of pleasure are emphasized in relation to other aspects of psyche. Desire consolidates. One wants what one wants, without complicated judgments. The subjective personal ideal stabilizes a new identity by clearly defining its own properties, resources, qualities and attributes.

Immersion in the realm of the senses. Deep joy in the tangibility of existence. Material reality experienced with exquisite sensitivity: nuances of color and sound, tastes, textures, smells savored with delight. Real aesthetic appreciation, and the possibility of artistic talent in its expression.

Economic judgment: an ability to accurately appraise the intrinsic nature and true worth of things This often includes perceptive evaluation of character. A gut sense of what is gold and what is glitter. A conservative preference for solid time tested quality over speculative novelty. Appreciates both the enduring strength and subtle attributes giving value. Prioritizes profit and gain. Steadily acquires external assets of financial wealth and property while also enhancing internal personal qualities of practical wisdom, emotional depth or erotic experience. A corresponding passion for productivity: the ability to create value and new values.

Sense can eclipse spirit. The power of realism can lead to the delusion of materialism: that only the tangible exists, only the quantifiable counts, that everyone and everything has a price. This can degenerate into venality, the sale of self or soul for seemingly precious objects.

Pleasure is sensory. Slow physical processes are treasured in their tactile actuality. The caress of incarnation in materiality: the thrills of body, enchantment of loveliness, sheer deliciousness of one's tastes. A general refinement of desire and sensibility from the coarse to the sublime.

Savors existing reality as opposed to ideal possibility. Acceptance of personality/circumstance as they are, in their existential presence and as the foundation of further growth. A productive orientation: just as fertile earth receives a seed, nourishes the shoot and supports the mature plant, so Taurean Venus endows potential with substance. Serene joy and voluptuous satisfaction blossom like a spring flower. Loves the bee that turns its nectar into honey and pollinates its beauty into fruition.

Venus in Gemini/third house

Desire objectifies. The subjective personal ideal separates from its matrix in the overall ego. It is perceived from an independent stance, detached from the more grimy reality of one's actual self. Thus it becomes a standard of comparison, enticing one to emulate its higher qualities. Or an unavailable image of perfection, shaming one by its remote superiority.

Duality of desire. A contrast, creative or paralyzing, between two or more inner ideals. These may be differing subjective values on the same plane: two loves, or alternative mental theories. Or two contradictory levels of psyche: for example, a highly sophisticated intellectual appreciation may coexist alongside coarse sexual appetites (or vice versa). While these dichotomies exist in all personalities, with this position they take on a sharpened edge in an overt confrontation. The dialog of these disparate qualities can generate heightened consciousness of differing perspectives and a cross-fertilization of various principles. Or they can become compartmentalized: the dual track sometimes seen in the brilliant scientist or politician with a secret life.

Venus' power of love integrates ostensibly incompatible qualities. This applies to intercommunication within a given level, such as the competition of ideas, and between different planes of experience, such as the emotional and mental, which often operate on fundamentally different assumptions. If successful it produces genuine psychological insight and mental clarity unavailable to those of a more monolithic nature. A synthesis of seemingly irreconcilable polarities. If unsuccessful, a Jekyll and Hyde split between two ego ideals leads to deadlock and the decay of one.

A playful sensuality, more alive to dancing movement than fixed preferences. Experimental rather than dogmatic, comparative rather than absolute. An appreciation of alternative possibilities. Such a duality, or multiplicity, of appetites must maintain its fluidity lest it harden into a segmented series of unconnected dots, disjointed segments of a life.

Pleasures of the mind: a chess master's delight with the complexity and intricacy of the game. Or intellectual vanity, an overvaluation of superficial cleverness. Sensuality is kinetic: fast-moving, instantly responsive, alert to its surroundings, while perhaps lacking depth. A love of witty repartee, humor and verbal eloquence. Seeks a nimble and stimulating partner who can mirror its ever-changing interests. Or someone with different but complementary attributes (the odd couple).

Venus in Cancer/fourth house

Desires subjective rejuvenation. Cultivates an inner sensibility. The personal ideal immerses into a private pool of imagination and memory. It renews itself within a protected sanctuary, a psychological womb. There, shielded from the world's coarseness, it internally reproduces a more refined vision of reality.

Domesticates raw unconscious energies; artistically models them into a personally relevant fantasy. Subliminal wishes nourish identity. Dreams shape relationships. A fairy tale love: the kiss turning a frog into a prince. Sensitivity refines vulgar attributes and appetites. Or sometimes reverts to its more instinctive sources.

Deep appreciation of the past; enriched by cultural heritage and traditional experience. These can become a resource, a connection with all that came before, of which the present is but the tip of the iceberg. Or clinging dependency that subverts present involvement. Whereas Mercury in Cancer perceives and expresses the contributions of its ancestral/ethnic roots, Venus in that sign absorbs and recombines them into a new identity with emergent properties.* Family values: cherishes home and kinship as a fertile refuge from the world's crudeness and cruelty.

Unconditional maternal love. A correspondingly fierce selective preference for an intimate few with whom it is shared. There is nothing more protective than a mammal mother's nurture, even unto feeding her offspring from her own body. The magical bonding that flows between mother and child, and of the magnetic attraction uniting self and significant other as two become one flesh carrying the hope of the future.

A feminine gentleness grows latent potential in both self and others. Emotional wisdom; nonverbal but deeply felt. Treasures individual idiosyncrasies; can empathetically mirror them. Sentimental, suffused with tenderness and poignant nostalgia. Sensitive to subconscious signals. Moody: resonates with tides of inner feeling, responds to ever changing phases of relationship. Graceful response to subtle atmospherics and unspoken nuance facilitates social interaction.

Sublimation of primitive needs into more subtle tastes. Basic hungers evolve into sophisticated pleasures. Centers generic sensations into a unique sensuality. Pleasure in birthing an inner beauty. Cultivates a sequestered garden of delight. Attracted to those who can provide the emotional security for such a delicate flowering.

* The United States, with a prominent Venus in Cancer, vibrantly illustrates this. Hyphenated Americans assimilate and intermarry with other ethnicities, producing a new breed of hybrid Americans. Anyone whose lineage has been in America for more than three generations is usually of mixed ancestry.

Venus in Leo/fifth house

Desire radiates as a dramatic passion. The subjective personal ideal projects itself out into the world as a theatrical identity statement. An unreserved outpouring of self; a bursting heart seeking a subject, or an object, upon which to lavish its affections. Magnanimous in intent and demanding in its need for response. Big hearted. Vitalizing warmth of emotion. A generous nature. An extravagance of feeling, matched by playfulness of display. Can be overpowering in intensity.

Aspires to noble standards. Or artificial pretentiousness of taste and manners. Resonates to, and nurtures, the highest potentials of the beloved. Seeks union with the divinity one sees in the other. Amused by sincere eccentricity, but will not tolerate the sordid, mean spirited or petty.

Hot love. Immersion in a shared fire of passion. This is not necessarily physical. It is at least as often an unconditional commitment to ideals or to those who embody them. A grand passion, the total gift of self to the beloved or to a cause. Or grandiosity of affect: exaggerated posturing, a loud facsimile of phony feeling. Can fall in love with the splendor of one's own image; susceptible to vanity and inflated self-esteem. Childlike narcissism.

Emphasizes heart over head. Can lack common sense, judge on the basis of how things should be rather than as they are. A preference for beautiful fantasies over ugly facts. Yet its strength of aspiration, power of imagination, can make them come true against all odds.

Pleasure in drama: the agony and the ecstasy of creative expression, the contrast and competition of powerful identities, the boldness and color of life. Celebrates singularity, uniqueness, the once in a universe character of each and every personality. Respect for individuality, self's brief cry of the heart in eternity.

The courage to love in a cold uncaring world. To give all simply for the joy of giving. Not in a sacrificial or compassionate sense, but out of sheer magnificence of feeling. An appreciation of those who go for the glory rather than the gold, who value honor over ambition and bravery over discretion. A love for those who dare to follow their own bliss, wherever it might lead.

Venus in Virgo/sixth house

Fall. Love must adapt to an uncongenial medium of critical reason. Desire purifies. One wants to be the best one can be. The subjective personal ideal refines its own integrity through service to others, without expectation of reward.

Values what should be more than what actually is, rational goals rather than manifest qualities. Thus it can lack appreciation of individuals as they really are. Can demand that they live up to a standard of excellence that may not be congruent with their nature or of their own choosing.

Conditional love. A performance based evaluation of self and others. Esteem must be merited, respect earned, by demonstrable ability and worth. An equally high level of devotion reciprocates these. This love, not easily given, has a corresponding rarity of discernment. It is inherently aristocratic, serving only the best with its best. Simple, modest, natural feelings: cool, clear eyed, detached. Accurately observant rather than passionately emotive.

Classical taste, the elegance of simplicity. Eliminates unnecessary embellishment, favors clean clarity. Purges emotional affection and mental irrelevance. Can range from guilty emotional inhibition to the joy of living up to high principles. Can exhibit holier than thou vanity or sincere humility.

Love can lose its focus performing a thousand useful tasks as a tangible expression of care while forgetting its essential nature as transcendence of self and its works to an experience of the divine. Love is the magic of empathetic feeling, even mystical union, more than an instrument of service. Wisdom can drain away into appreciation of countless details displacing a larger apprehension of their meaning. A refinement of technique can displace a revelation of truth.

Pleasure in constant self-improvement. Joy in weeding out error, upgrading one's art, becoming better at who one is and what one does. Values difficult disciplines of body, heart and mind: they are the reward in and of themselves. A preference for effort over ease, for carefully honed skill over sloppy spontaneity. Does not distinguish work from play because they are one and the same. A toned, educated sensuality, ever more alert, adroit and appropriate to the situation at hand. Attracted to those with a similar coherence of inner focus.

Venus in Libra/seventh house

Rulership. An ideal, or idealized form of, relationship assumes an unusual degree of importance in the general personality. Gracious accommodation and aesthetic sensitivity are emphasized in relation to other aspects of the psyche. Desire adjusts itself to the needs of others. One accepts them in their own right, as they are, rather than as one would have them be. The subjective personal ideal defines itself through appropriate participation in society rather than as an inner image of self-perfection.

Desires harmony. Finds it through resolution of conflict. Seeks balance. Discovers it through an appreciation of contrasting polarities. Self-definition through mutual relationship more than isolated ego identity. This can manifest as a chameleon-like blending into its environment, a bland adaptation to the group. Or by judicious give and take, a reciprocal dialog challenging and changing all parties involved. Personality is field-dependent: shaped by context more than its own content. Phenomena are evaluated in connection rather than their own immediacy of being.

An emphasis on the value of beauty: more in terms of subtle elegance than strength of sensation. A highly developed aesthetic appreciation, whether of art or nature, of other individuals or group dynamics. This can petrify into a conformist, conventional taste for all the right and approved things. Or degenerate into contrived snobbery. It can have too great a respect for agreeableness, eclipsing future possibility. Or it can recognize that beauty is a process involving crazy wildness along with formal perfection; Dionysian excess as well as Apollonian restraint.

A concern with the criteria of justice, especially between the conflicting values of equality and excellence. Tends to find a moderate middle after a series of infatuated gyrations. Thus it learns to understand detachment: finds common ground rather than takes sides, values just compromise more than victory.

Seeks pleasure rather than passion. Prefers reconciliation to righteousness. A certain easy going acquiescence can lead to accepting the convenient lie, or promoting peace at any price, because it can see the merits of every position. This is a mellow not a militant energy. A lover not a fighter.

A graceful, even ethereal, sensuality, in tune with its environment. Attracted to those who reciprocate its thoughtfulness and respect its refinement.

Venus in Scorpio/eighth house

Detriment. The power of love fades as the love of power increases. The subjective personal ideal exposes its real inner motivations, eliminating self-serving fantasies of its own benevolence in the light of a sadder, wiser truth.

The death of conventional goodness, emergence of psychological poisons. The sanitized social self is put to the acid test of temptation. Its flaws are not only revealed, but reveled in. One's inner fiend gloats with sadistic glee. Sympathy for the Devil.

Venus is the pleasure principle; these are infernal delights. The corruption of desire. An infatuation with the dark side, a taste for the taboo; the fascination of evil and thrill of the wicked. The joy of vengeance. The curse of jealousy. It covets what others have. Profits through their loss, which it sometimes engineers. Dreads loss of and punishment for such unethical gains. Thus an obsessive lust for control.

Sublimates pleasure into power. Innocent delight redirected into intense craving. A driving dream replaces laid-back happiness. Defers immediate gratification into accumulative investment; exploits the present to create a future. Concentrates resources. Entices collective effort to magnify wealth, whether of property or influence.

Desires dominance to compensate for the secret guilt of its lust. Fears joy, which enervates. The inner self is under siege and does not let down its guard. Instead, it uses a disciplined mask of sociability to manipulate peers into serving its wishes. A personal sense of inadequacy can promote group objectives. Or vampirize them to feed its own shriveled heart.

Here love, which every lover pledges is eternal, dies. Thus one learns to see the flaws love blinds one to. The death of love releases its binding energy so that one can love again with greater depth. Or plumb the depths of hate:

> Heaven has no rage like love to hatred turned,
> Nor Hell a fury like a woman scorned.

Much of this may seem horrible. Yet it is a necessary phase. Out of it comes mortification and elimination of false values. An inner venom surfaces, to intoxicate or inoculate the conscious ego. Only exposure to the light can detoxify its poison. Private pain has its day in the Sun, burning away its stench. Here morbid energies are evoked, discharged and potentially redeemed. One experiences an ordeal to find a hidden treasure, free the captive princess of one's soul.

A passionate sensuality: perhaps erotic, perhaps power hungry. Attracted to those who serve its purpose.

Venus in Scorpio tells the story of Persephone, a virgin goddess abducted into Hades by Pluto, its dread lord. There he ravished her. She fell in love with him. And became the Queen of Death. Who emerges from the underworld every year bearing the seeds of spring's resurrection.

Venus in Sagittarius/ninth house

Desire socializes. One wants what the tribe wants. The subjective personal ideal embodies group norms and aspirations.

Identifies with a collectively sanctioned archetypal image or superego model. This can give voice to a higher Self and ground the lightning of its revelation. Or inflate exaggerated self-esteem into a false idol of self worship; generate a vanity that pretends to be, rather than merely see, the Light.

An enthusiastic communion in the social consensus mirrors personal fusion with an inner spiritual fire. Values group participation over individual endeavor. Bonds closely with its matrix, resonates with conventional opinion, genuinely feels what the herd feels. It is rewarded for that, but can lose the ability for independent judgment. Reflects a team spirit: one for all and all for one. This can become opportunistic conformity for the sake of acceptance. Or a principled demand for the genuine expression of shared values. Beautifies accepted wisdom. Can sugarcoat real truth to promote shared assumptions or wishful aspirations.

The possibilities, or seduction, of unearned grace. A windfall. Will one spend it wisely? Or blow it in wild extravagance? Good fortune, a rendezvous with lady luck. Will it grow consciousness? Or puff up ego? Promotion beyond actual merit. Will one live up to the opportunity, expand to fit the larger role? Or indulge in self-righteousness, proclaim a messianic destiny? The promise of bountiful resources, or the seduction of wretched excess.

Venus in Sagittarius sparkles in contrast to Venus, or the central purpose of Sun, in its neighbors of intense, brooding Scorpio or heavy responsible Capricorn.* It can add sociability and popularity to these ambitious signs. High spirited, cheerful, light hearted and fun. Values freedom. Drawn to adventure. Can be happily superficial. Perhaps overconfident in denial of inconvenient truths and oblivious to negative possibilities.

An expansive, perhaps promiscuous, love. Spontaneous but fleeting infatuations followed by abrupt disengagement when the initial thrill wears off. Can be true in the moment, or a shallow player. An athletic sensuality: enjoys the rough and tumble of sport, whether physical or political. Attracted to those who share its upbeat optimism, whether in pursuit of pleasure or enthusiasm of philosophic conviction.

* Because it moves within a more interior orbit than Earth Venus can never stray more than 48° from Sun, either ahead of it in the zodiac (evening star) or behind it (morning star). Thus it is always in the same sign as Sun or the ones adjacent to it.

Venus in Capricorn/tenth house

Desire subordinated to necessity. One wants what it is right to want. The subjective personal ideal embodies a collective duty. One lives up to the social code.

Desires success, achievement. Will pay the required price: as a cynical sale of inner soul to outer ambition, or as an austere subordination of pleasure to purpose. Over time purpose becomes pleasure. Emotional discipline. Feels responsible more than responsive. Conditional love, based as much on respect as affection. A sense of being unworthy. Thus it either redoubles efforts to earn gratitude or withdraws into a bitter cold withholding.

Unmerited disappointment. Lack of appreciation. Quiet, solid excellence dismissively taken for granted, not adequately rewarded. Unrequited love. Hunger for warmth and affection that is deserved but not given. Thus one learns to love for its own sake, without hope of reciprocation or need for payback.

Deep respect for tradition and heritage, family and community: the lineage that shaped one. The subjective self identifies with and loyally enacts collective expectations. It reflects the demands of superego by responding to life in accordance with principles and duties rather than feelings and wishes. Over time it learns to abide by the spirit more than the letter of the law. A rote expression of social norms, good girl obedience, starts to take on individual character, develop personal quality, by pragmatic adaptation to impersonal rules.

Loneliness within the crowd. A sensitivity to social mores can freeze out into a drilled decorum, mechanical conventionality, artificiality of affect. An inner light is squeezed hard by the weight of discipline: either snuffed out, crushed into compliance or condensed into a point of brilliance. Just as photons, fused in the center of a star, take a million years to rise to its surface, where they light up the universe, so Venus' spark of inner personality, kindled in a dark night of the soul, shines forth, bringing love reborn to a frigid world.

A reserved, realistic love, guided by an ancient wisdom more than spontaneous infatuation. A deep but initially inhibited sensuality, taking time and trust to reveal its true depth of passion. Attracted to those of proven worth, who have also demonstrated grace under pressure.

Venus in Aquarius/eleventh house

Desire abstracts. One wants what is theoretically best. The subjective personal ideal identifies with universal archetypes and collective aspirations. Values future potential more than present identity.

An encouragement of possibilities more than an appreciation of the here and now. Seeks to sublimate actual substance into its distilled essence. Feels the presence of higher dimensions, the promise of utopian expectations. Attuned to eternal principle more than ephemeral realities. Responds to beautiful visions more than empirical facts.

Identifies with the better angel in self and others. An intuitive sensitivity to the inner blueprint behind personality acts to draw that more ethereal light-body into effective expression. Appreciates unseen potential and mentors its development. Or enables emotional rebellion from accepted roles and rules, enjoys the thrill of anarchic disruption.

Attracted to the next stage rather than the current level of evolution. Bridges the discontinuities between present and future, real and ideal. Or falls through the cracks, gets lost in space: dissociated from normal sensibilities, alienated from common sense and feeling. Can be cold and clinical, loving humanity and hating people.

The inner self breaks free of its collective matrix. Independent of social expectations, follows original inspiration in both personal and social affairs. Experiments with different identities and values. A clear but erratic subjectivity, consistent in its futuristic orientation, suddenly changeable in its specific hopes and expectations. A continual broadening of affinities, growth of inclusiveness, enlarges empathy but also distances it from previous associations. Sudden and drastic changes of heart.

An inspired sense of soul rather than a felt sensuality of flesh. A detached love: friendly, comradely, brotherly/sisterly more than emotional or erotic. Cool rather than hot.

Promotes alternatives to conventional wisdom. Grounds cerebral genius and artistic creativity into a coherent new worldview. Cognitive breakthrough or eccentric breakdown. Brilliant or bizarre.

An intellectual sensuality, values the excitement of new ideas, revolutionary insights, alternative possibilities, unexpected outcomes. Somewhat aloof from normal experience, seeks exceptional pleasures of the mind and imagination. Tends to extremes, must maintain a true openness to reality validation if it is to successfully navigate these rarefied realms. Attracted to the vanguard, mental and social pioneers of a new order.

Venus in Pisces/twelfth house

Exaltation. An expansion of personal into universal love reaches a critical intensity. Empathy with others informs behavior. Desire melts into compassion. One wants what God wants. The subjective ideal surrenders its old identity to an embryonic future.

Desires redemption. Feels the deep sorrow of life. Identifies with the suffering of others, near or far, friend or foe. Values mercy. Loves the forgotten and despised. Sympathy for the wretched. Forgiveness of guilt, in which all share.

The joy of giving without expectation of reward. The wisdom of renunciation. Learns to abandon stale appetites and destructive cravings, nullify counterproductive relationships and inappropriate affections. A larger Love liberates from small wishes for gain and gratification, frees the soul from personal demands and dependencies.

Liquidates both conventional norms and personal wants. Subjectivity is not stripped naked to its core, as in Scorpio, but revealed as nothing, empty, void. The pleasure principle meets the abyss. If one recoils in shock, dream waves of illusion ripple out. These then generate images and ideals attracting one into a new cycle of evolution (Aries). If one opens to its formless energy then the inner self merges with and expresses an ineffable spirit.

Love is a loss of ego in appreciation of the other. Here that other is not an individual but infinity. One can channel it as a divine love, sacrificing self for a greater good. Or focus it through the archetypal lenses of the unconscious, refracting the radiance of eternity into the subtle hues of mythic imagination. Or disintegrate in confusion, flooded with ambiguous feelings, inundated by bewildering impressions. Then all standards decay into a hallucinatory trance of chaotic indulgence and feverish fantasy. Ecstatic mystical surrender becomes escapist sensationalism. One pursues every innocent delight to its extreme of decadence.

An emotional sensuality. It thrills to immersion in a psychic sensitivity drawing one out of self into an oceanic union with all and the All. Or a deadly rapture of the depths, an infatuation with intoxication. Finds happiness in generosity, salvation through suffering. Attracted to the lost and defeated, the exiled and rejected. It identifies with those otherworldly souls adrift in gentle contemplation amidst the frenzy of embattled egos.

Mars

Mars is the same size as Earth's molten core. It embodies a celestial abstraction of an inner dynamo - Earth's hot heart projected out onto the heavens. Mars mirrors our deepest motives in the sky of consciousness. Perhaps it symbolizes Hell itself raised up and redeemed through the travail of life.

Involutionary Venus draws one into a magnetic vortex of desire. She seduces one into life. Earth actually lives. Mars, one half the size of these sister planets, describes the stripped down essence, ultimate purpose of that life. Put another way, Venus' thick roasting atmosphere presses down at 100 times Earth's pressure; Mars' thin cold air wisps away at ¹⁄₁₀₀ Earth's density. Venus' sky embodies the plenitude calling one into being, Mars' a rarefied aura sublimating out of it. Mars distills an energy signature from all the complexities of personality. And emits it into the universe as one's final ego statement. Jupiter then portrays its subjective spiritual meaning, Saturn its objective consequence, result or karma.

Mars is the last of the relatively small, rocky terrestrial planets moving out from Sun (Mercury, Venus, Earth/Moon, Mars). These planets describe personal qualities: mind, love, life/memory, will. Beyond Mars lies the shatter zone of asteroids, demonstrating ego's disintegration in death. Then comes the qualitatively different realm of the gas giants (Jupiter, Saturn, Uranus, Neptune). They portray a social role beyond personality and a spiritual reality behind conscious psychology.

Mars marks the final frontier of individual consciousness. Here all the complex motivations of personality boil down into specific decisions. Perception (Mercury), desire (Venus) and memory (Moon) resolve themselves into defining acts. Mars describes will. What one does and a summation of all one ever did. Who one is when the chips are down.

At Mars consciousness turns to action. An infinite chain of causation ignites into immediate decision. Subconscious subtleties and overt considerations focus into the proximate motives of actual conduct. With many possibilities and limited information one makes those irrevocable choices that define character. The doer becomes the deed. The deed is simpler, but more objective, than the doer. Here there are no explanations or excuses. Only the truth of what really happens.

Mars = High Noon. The acid test of behavior reveals one's deepest self. Mercury illuminates awareness of choices, Venus the criteria by which they are evaluated. Mars makes the call, chooses sides, takes a stand. Beyond the justifications of rational intellect or ideal values it openly displays true intention. Thus Mars is both brutally primitive and utterly sublime.

Mars portrays the hidden passion behind conscious attitude and social persona. The real agenda animating superficial attributes. Fundamental drive, prime directive, essential purpose. Here all instincts converge on one imperative, all desires concentrate in one motive. Mars points to the taproot of real performance. What one does, how one acts, and the reason why.

Because Mars is the first planet outside Earth's orbit, it presents the external universe to us. Mars' orbit encompasses a larger space than our own world's realm of personal ego. Thus it confronts one with an energy that is greater than self. It does so in an intrusive and demanding way. Mars gets your attention. This generates a response: personal will. It manifests as one's own creative impulse (Aries)[1] and as the transformative consequences of interaction with a bigger environment (Scorpio).[2]

Will shapes reality, determination decides destiny, initiative creates individuality. Only thus can one transcend present identity; become more and better than one is. A recalcitrant world resists this urge. Other egos contend with it. At Mars one meets objective reality. Existential pressure forces one to act, and thus to declare oneself. By position and aspect Mars illuminates a challenge: the stage on which one performs, the battle one fights, the question one answers.

Mars often appears to us in alien and hostile form because it is that, or whom, we must confront in order to evolve. Thus it can be seen as a threat evoking anger and a vicious circle of negative feedback. Or as a stimulus, generating ambition and a positive trajectory of initiative.

Mars is inherently destructive. It assaults the established personality with the novelty of otherness. It attacks the secure self with the necessity of response to a wider world. It strikes at the heart of complacency and shatters stagnant smugness. Mars forces one to fight for survival and strive for growth. You must rise to the occasion. If you do not then a soul death, or physical extinction, will destroy you.

Mars identifies a source of danger. The peril one faces. The nature of one's enemies. How they attack (sign position). Where they strike (house). Why: the cause of their enmity. And how, where, why one fights back.

Mars also presents one with the ultimate danger: death. Death is always near. One can die at any time. We are always subliminally aware of that fact.

Mars describes how one faces death. By denial? Frantic ego promotion? Sacrificing others to appease fate and avoid one's own? Or by accepting it with gratitude as the price of life? Upon this question hangs the character.

Life includes death, just as light implies dark. Mars is the death planet. It does not disclose death's meaning, but its process. The attitude one develops through all the little deaths: of hopes and dreams, ideals and illusions, projects and relationships. Do they bring rebirth? Or despair? They demonstrate and develop one's expectations around the big and final death of ego extinction.

Mars confronts one with invisible evidence of another dimension beyond our known and mortal life: the inevitable reality of death. How one chooses to interpret and experience its constant presence becomes deaths' meaning on this plane of existence, whatever may actually lie beyond the grave.

Does one resolve to 'rage, rage against the dying of the light'?[3] Or embrace it as an intangible soul energy that animates, and eventually annihilates, physical form? How one senses or intuits life's ultimate mystery reveals one's own core truth. Christ expressed the highest standard of that truth in His repeated injunction: 'Fear not.'[4]

Mars is, to some extent, a malefic. It challenges one to battle. This test is real and cannot be avoided. Life's conflict always inflicts wounds. Their pain tempts one to criminality. Or to fear, the worst crime of all.

Life is not pristine or prissy. Lust is the precondition of love, war of freedom, competition of prosperity. One feels trauma and gives agony at birth. And at death. One kills to eat. Takes from others to have for self. Competes in the race, leaving a loser behind. Or becoming one. Does what one must, though it breaks another's heart.

Mars involves a redemptive evolution, full of fire and passion, trial and error. It creates the bravery to fight that battle and to make its terrible mistakes. Even the most glorious victor emerges with bloody hands. This is as true on the emotional, mental and spiritual planes as the physical. No one walks without first crawling, then stumbling. Perhaps in the end the sheer courage to participate redeems the inevitable errors and cruelties. But during the process those errors have real consequences. Those cruelties involve serious pain. Thus courage arises and will perfected.

Look at any fellow human and tremble at the sheer gutsiness it takes to dare certain death amid all the uncertainties of life, to set one's finite face against a cold infinity of space and time. Brave little Mars burns in each of us, bringing passion to the universe, invoking purpose amidst its emptiness.

Mars embodies one's basic drive. It galvanizes identity, stimulates subjective self with a new reality, from out there or deep inside. Its harsh demands cut through all the evasions and illusions of cherished mental theories, emotional desires and spiritual aspirations. It whips dreamy wistfulness into decisive mobilization. Mars confronts with issues one must face, trials that define and refine self. Its objective crisis forces revelation of one's true nature.

Mars energizes whatever area of endeavor or planetary principle it touches. It can stimulate with healthy vitality or burn with manic fever. It may express itself with an impeccable economy of effort or erupt with berserk fury.

Mars displays one's innate power, raw or subtle, primitive or sophisticated. And one's will to power, shaped and refined by the hard tests of life. One's quota and quality of animal energy. The charge one carries, the force one exerts. At whatever level of expression it describes a thirst for experience, urge to explore, itch to get up and go. Lust and libido. Youthful exuberance, raging hormones, mature focused effort, age's grim resolve: all express Mars' aggressive instinct to plunge into the world, to act and to do. The audacity of our human spirit reaching for the stars from the valley of death.

Mars invigorates by the danger/opportunity it presents. This can ennoble or brutalize. If one is not equal to its trial then spirit twists into sadism. Healthy competition degenerates into a morbid urge to destroy. Inadequacy can stimulate effort - or resentment. Instead of honestly confronting and transcending frustration one can project it out into the world or onto others. How much easier to inflict vengeance on a scapegoat than to attain victory over self. But this does not satisfy because it does not address the problem. It ignites an escalating cycle of rage and retaliation, preemptive paranoia and devastating desolation. This is the violent and violating aspect of Mars, the source of our crimes and wounds.

At Mars one encounters malice. In self or through others. Saturn demonstrates the fear and selfishness behind it. Mars is much simpler. It acts out an urge to kick someone's ass just for the hell of it. Emotional emasculation and psychological castration are more sophisticated versions of this sport. Saturn shrinks into the cold soul-death behind cruelty. The emptiness of evil. Mars revels in its sadistic thrill. The hideous joy of hurting someone.

To feed off the pain of others is a degenerative disease of Mars. So is morbid self-pity based on fear to participate and express oneself. Silence and passivity are not valid options in our world of evolutionary striving. An incompetent Mars always turns upon and destroys itself. Mars eliminates distorted manifestations of its own energy, just as it gives death to anything that does not truly resonate with the Will of God.

In the process it can take much down with it. Mars' violence preempts other more subtle qualities. Mars compels each of us to adapt to and contend with the raw and nasty side of life. It coarsens almost as much as it encourages. Mars = war. War brings out the best and the worst. Cowardice and courage.

War, and the memory of war, are defining moments in the life of a society or an individual. Mars, destructive and brutal as it can be, provides the most intense experiences of life. These test one's core. They drive one out of the comfort zone, beyond previous limits. They burn away the old, including much that is good and beautiful. They supplant it with the new, including much that is ugly and evil.

Mars poses an existential threat, physical or psychological. This evokes identity-defining deeds. Red Mars is not a blood soaked battlefield itself. It shows where the gauntlet is thrown down here on Earth. Mars embodies one's ultimate personal trial. And how one meets it. Victory or defeat are important. Honor and courage are paramount. Outcomes are fleeting: sic transit gloria mundi.[5] Character, revealed in crisis, is permanent.

Mars puts all other factors in the chart to the test. Only thus do they show their real quality. In Mars' repeated assaults on self-consciousness and confidence one can, and often does, lose. Mars = loss. The sting of defeat. The destruction of what one had clung to or taken for granted. The humiliation of not measuring up. Does one have what it takes to soldier on? Or to really change?[6]

Defeat happens repeatedly in every life. It can lead to a new perspective, growth and rebirth. Or it can degrade and crush. Mars responds to the inevitable attacks and misfortunes of life, the 'slings and arrows of outrageous fortune.'[7] Mars portrays the will to survive and prevail - while knowing that all roads lead to death. For more than anything else Mars invokes courage: moral, intellectual, emotional as much as physical.

Mars is where the action is. It may play out in tests of physical bravery or moral integrity, in the passions of the mind or of the heart. Mars creates one's own self-chosen ordeal. It forces one to contend with some aspect of the universe drawing one out of and beyond a self-sufficient ego. One must pass through its fire. Or burn to ash. Mars, for all of its pain and conflict, is the agent of growth, the catalyst of evolution. Its will to evolve transfigures all sin through courage.

Without Mars we would wallow in narcissism. Our world would be real (Saturn), intelligible (Mercury), with a history (Moon), beauty (Venus), and meaning (Jupiter) - but nevertheless self referential, ego centered, essentially infantile. Mars creates an emergency demanding a response. The sharp, immediate, in-your-face requirement of dealing with, adapting to, struggling against, a larger reality.

However enveloped in rationalizations (Mercury), distracted by temptations (Venus), justified by theory (Jupiter), or stymied by obstacles (Saturn) Mars remains the cause of conduct. Not its purpose (Sun), but its operational catalyst. The mind (Mercury) presents options, the heart (Venus) wants. A larger soul (Jupiter) provides a guiding conscience, impersonal law (Saturn) sets limitations. In the end Mars boils all of them down into a primal urge prompting performance.

Without Mars one would be immersed in a womblike lunar sea of subjective thoughts (Mercury) and wishes (Venus). Mars confronts them with the hard stimulation of an external world. It develops discipline, then disciple-ship. Mars prods and jabs, gets one up to speed with larger cycles.

Mars shows where the universe comes at one. And how one has a go at it. The challenge to which one must respond. And how one does. The aggression one must face. And the face of one's own aggression. Mars portrays how one experiences and expresses hostility. And honor.

God created the universe and pronounced it good. While this is true overall, still the light is punctuated by darkness, life with death, love with hate. Mars locates that disruptive force. It promotes progress through competition. Weeds out the weak and inferior through rigorous selection. Stimulates awareness of the universe through the contrast and conflict of its parts. Its characteristic error arises when one identifies too passionately with any one of those parts, such as an ego.

Our psyche is deeply marked by its emergence through this process of elimination. The struggle against a hard reality, the urge to compete with and outperform rivals, the ancestral memory of endless struggle against deprivation and danger has hardwired a killer instinct. Mars indicates how one taps into this aggressive energy. And how one learns to sublimate it should one choose to do so.

Mars manifests the unconscious (Moon). Its overt actions make visible and known the hidden hungers or latent longings of one's soul. That provokes feedback from the world. Thus Mars stimulates the deepest parts of psyche into evolution. Moon holds the content of memory

281

and emotion. Mars measures the intensity of these feelings, their energy charge. Mars acts out the subconscious needs of Moon, thus bringing them to awareness.

Moon is the size of Earth's solid iron-nickel inner core: the done deeds of a congealed past. Larger Mars wraps it in a molten metal ocean the size of Earth's liquid outer core. This hot iron sea is churned by Earth's rotation into flowing spiral currents. These emit a magnetic force field. This shields Earth from radioactive solar winds, thus enabling life. It also interacts with other planetary energies to generate life's electrical currents of vitality and consciousness. (See 'Theory.') Mars symbolizes the actively responsive sentience behind Moon's memory.

Mars empowers Moon but remains quite unconscious itself. It galvanizes passive lunar reflections into active agencies. It imbues instincts with energy. Mars describes how one fights through and past their unconscious compulsion and flawed purpose. Or how one surrenders to and enacts them.

This begins with spontaneous physical activity, a visceral response to need and desire. Over time, and through practice, this rises to a critical intensity carrying it over the threshold into conscious awareness. Instinct accelerates into intelligence. But the mind, contending with inherent contradictions, is too combative to fully comprehend reality. The clash of competing ideas, each partially true, works itself into a frenzy. This can only be resolved through a higher synthesis.

At Mars the unconscious wakes up and makes itself conscious. Then spiritual. It does so as blind activity initiates an awareness, then an agony, of duality. Self acts in and on the world. The world reacts back. Their tension builds up and finally breaks through into a synthesis, an inspiration of the unity behind all contending forces.

Mars' subconscious upwellings nourish the conscious ego. They also create suffering because of the fury and venom of repressed elements in the unconscious. Repression causes anger: direct and brutal (Aries) or hidden and vicious (Scorpio). Anger motivates action to break the deadlock. Those aspects of our being that have been violated, or unacknowledged, finally erupt so that they can be incorporated into awareness.

The unconscious powerfully resists becoming conscious, in defiance of its own nature. Then that consciousness must fight to maintain itself against the world. Thus it constantly wars within and without, enduring the psychological pain of emergence and the endless effort of asserting itself. Mars describes the torment and the pride goading this process forward. Finally the struggles of personal consciousness generate enough energy to attain the escape velocity boosting it into spiritual realms (Jupiter). The vehicle for this is Mars' great gift: death.

Only through long and bitter battle does Mars learn to accept the ecstatic release of death. Death of the physical body, of bondage to mind and ego, of attachment to any particular form. Only death's sharp anguish can liberate the small self into its larger soul. The courage to accept it marks Mars' ultimate achievement.

Saturn shapes individual entities out of the All. Its separation from God creates individual identity and consciousness. Mars acts as the instrument of division: a sword of separation. It cuts an umbilical cord to the past, making one participate in the present. It severs one from current circumstance and associates, forcing one to move into the future. Eventually it rips away life itself, sending one into another dimension. Or not: 'For the living know that they shall die, but the dead know not anything...'[8]

Mars requires your full attention here and now. It elicits your presence in the most forceful way. What other way is there? Mars demands commitment: 'Whatever your hand finds to do, do it with all your might, for in the grave, where you are going, there is neither working nor planning nor knowledge nor wisdom.'[9] If you cannot live authentically right now then you will not do so in some hypothetical afterlife. You are alive! If you don't take that opportunity at this very moment then you never will.

Mars enforces Saturn's implacable laws that make life real. It insists on the sharp definition marking each individual as unique. Differentiated energies necessarily compete and clash with each other. Strife and conflict happen at Mars in the chart. This attracts attention, directs effort, forges will. Through such intense engagement Mars' energy transforms itself into a closer approximation of universal purpose, the Will of God.

Mars portrays the 'battleground of desire' where raw impulse orients itself towards good or evil purpose. The latter involves power alienated from its common source by selfish intent. It thus becomes a rogue force cut off from further development. In the very nature of evil passion is uncontrolled. Thus, while more quickly brought to bear through lack of restraint, its ungovernable quality leads inevitably to disaster. Like fire, Mars is a good servant but a poor master. Only when guided by a will stronger than the spell of its own zeal can Mars fully and victoriously unleash its power. As a warrior, not a king, Mars executes a higher purpose emanating from Sun.

Mars measures ambition: the nature of one's personal purpose and the tactics used to achieve it. One's strategic sense: the will to formulate a long-term course of action and a willingness to accept its consequences. This brings awareness of a larger time frame.

At Mars time begins to lengthen. Its day, the subjective sense of self, equals that of Earth. Its year, objective circumstance, stretches twice as long. Mars starts with a stimulus: the urgency of right now! Its implementation requires a more farsighted perspective. Immediate gratification gives way to long term planning. This comes from hard lessons of survival in an often hostile reality.

One learns to assimilate Mars' energy as presented by inconvenient truths. Then to express personal will by effectively confronting them. A correct appraisal leads to appropriate action. If one gets it wrong the cost is high. Mars exacts heavy vengeance for failed efforts. Mars always pays the price, whether you got what you wanted or not. Yet one often grows the most from defeat. Having taken loss, felt pain, one learns: the specific lesson at hand, and how to apply that lesson to future events.

Small Mars seeds a long future. Its immediate impulse ignites a chain of events. Its initiative commits one to a path. Its intentions create a destiny. Its ambition projects one in a certain direction, excluding all others. Every decision Mars takes, every move it makes, kills alternatives. Every affirmation implies many rejections. Only thus can one move forward or do anything at all.

Mars expresses the principle of aggressive egotism. This plays out at many levels. It can act as a personal competence, ready, willing and able to carry out the hard work of evolution. Or as a will consecrated to a soul purpose, focused through the architecture of personality. More commonly, it works through by Mars' enactment of unconscious lunar hungers. If these instincts are reasonably healthy Mars portrays the strategy and tactics by which one pursues happiness. How one fulfills needs and achieves objectives. The strength and enthusiasm of following one's Bliss.

If these instincts are frustrated Mars enables them to act out through the sword of an angry mind and raging storms of emotion. Or by the hard fists of physical violence. Every day millions of people experience bodily harm deliberately inflicted by another.

Mars provokes a problem. It points to unintegrated lunar energies demanding attention. It activates the essential issue that one must face. It commits one to a lifelong battle against something out there or deep within. Mars seeks out and destroys inner demons. Or external foes. Sometimes it sacrifices one to them.

Mars picks a fight that needs to be fought. It does not guarantee victory. It shows what one came into the world to do. One is as one does.

All other planets have to do with psychological states, social conditions or spiritual energies. Thus Mercury (thought), Venus (love) and memory (Moon) portray inner experience; Jupiter (transcendent soul) and Saturn (impersonal law) demonstrate larger more objective realities; Uranus, Neptune, Pluto describe generational cycles. Mars brings personality and environment together in events. Things happen here. Thus Mars is the most exciting action packed planet.

Sun embodies purpose, and Moon psychology - Mars joins them in agency, the ability to act. Mars merges a preexisting subjective nature with its objective social environment through behavior. It points to where inner qualities (Mercury, Venus) and outer circumstance (Jupiter, Saturn) intersect as personal conduct.

This involves effort. Mars governs the movement inherent in life itself, the process uniting spirit and matter. This requires the direct application of force to inertia. Mars overcomes the resistance of present forms to future possibility. It stimulates latent potential into active expression. Thus Mars signifies struggle: work and war, conflict and conquest. Above all, Mars burns with passion: a drive to fulfillment that tortures and intoxicates, a divine discontent turning the wheels of destiny.

Psychologically, Mars describes self-assertion. Independence from (Aries), or power over (Scorpio), others. Mars charts the nature and direction of initiative. The quality of vitality; one's basic animal spirits. And the medium through which they are expressed: physically, emotionally, mentally, spiritually.

Mars reveals how energy is deployed, and passion directed, in the quest for personal consummation. It describes the libido, or life force. One's adrenaline surge, and what turns it on. One's testosterone quota. A man's perspective on his masculinity. A woman's sense of her inner masculine side (the animus) and her ideal of an outer male counterpart.

Speaking of passion, Mars embodies the sex drive. It position and aspects outline the general nature of one's sexuality. Its expression depends on one's level of evolution: thus frustration can lead to sublimation or explosive violence, satisfaction to love or jaded decadence. Because Mars can be so revealing this is a delicate zone of interpretation. Sex involves most people's most vulnerable area. That's why our insults center on it, why sexual humiliation is so degrading. Yet Mars can also provide profoundly healing insight into one's most intimate problems by explaining their root cause. It can point to a more appropriate release of this primal energy.

As the first planet outside of Earth's orbit Mars indicates a semi-autonomous element of personality: our gender. (The gas giants, even further out, portray one's participation in social and spiritual levels beyond personality.) The sexual force feels intimately personal. Yet it also involves a generic male or female energy. One's biological role and psychological makeup as a man or a woman is distinct from individual identity. This Martial subpersonality acts somewhat independently of the overall ego. That makes it both stronger and more vulnerable.

Mars drives the entire personality in favor of a deeper need: to go beyond self, to literally enter or be entered by another. Martial lust, grounded in sex, underlies a more ethereal and enduring superstructure of love. One wants to have a boyfriend or girlfriend long before knowing who that person actually is. The sexual urge carries one past self into all the risks of relationship and responsibilities of reproduction. Few would have it any other way.

Sexual identity generates the most fundamental distinction among people. Whether one is a boy or a girl says more than one's race or nationality, religion or politics. Psychologically the characteristics related to sex are more important than those of social class or education. They constitute a basic feature of identity and much of its motivation.

Sexuality operates on the social as well as individual level. Sublimated sexual energy distills creativity from the urge to physical reproduction. This expresses through many forms of emotional sensibility and mental discovery, manifesting in artistic, technological or political endeavor. Our ability to redirect libido (sexual drive) into cultural activity makes us human. Freud, the father of modern psychology, considered it the basis of civilization.[10] On the other hand, frustrated or repressed sexuality causes much of our collectively enhanced violence and unnatural appetite for cruelty.

Mars objectively displays itself in the genitals. These physical organs are completely unrelated to personal survival. Yet their urges demand attention and direct behavior. They depict a partially independent source of motivation. It is often said that a man thinks with his cock and that a woman's brains are between her legs. These observations are surprisingly true. Once again the sheer audacity of Mars staggers the imagination: a few ounces of testicle, the hidden chamber behind a vulva, along with minute quantities of their associated hormones, largely determine the course of a life and the content of identity.

Even the sperm and eggs our genitals carry are genetically distinct from all other body cells. They bear ½ the normal number of genes, scrambled and recombined for diversity. Mars' sexual imperative splits our double-coiled chromosomes into single stranded germ cells. These then merge with those of the opposite sex to create a new and unique genome. Details are available in any biology textbook. In the same way, the two halves of our human condition, male and female, yearn for union, to join physically and psychologically, and transcend themselves in a child: whether a new biological person, or as their own rebirth through love.

Along with sex Mars gives death. Asexual single cells do not die. They just clone themselves and proliferate. Sexual beings gain the advantages of genetic recombination, at the price of death. This makes room for an increased pace of innovation and evolution. More subtly, yet at least as important, sexual beings gain the experience of passion, for each other, and of their own death. Mars takes us to a fundamentally higher level, at the cost of eventual breakdown.

Sex and death: the two hottest topics of the human condition. Yet even beyond the obsession of sex, Mars inspires the human imagination like no other planet. Eventually we will meet its dangers and opportunities in the most literal way. Not just in our astrological charts, but also through physical exploration and colonization. Mars, the action planet, is the one world we will act on.[11] And which will act upon us. Assuming that human settlers can survive long-term and reproduce, their descendants will be conditioned from birth to Mars' low gravity (38% of Earth's). They will adapt and transform into a Martian species (Scorpio) with a new beginning (Aries). Or they will die.

Indeed, Mars itself died long ago. Soon it may be reborn through human intervention. About four billion years ago Mars clearly had abundant liquid water, a substantial atmosphere and perhaps even primitive life. Human colonization may return life to the planet. Terraforming may return the planet to life. Terraforming means engineering the Martian environment to make it habitable.[12]

Such activities might animate long dormant or currently living subterranean Martian microbes. If so, they could be very different from us, constituting a parallel lineage with which we do not genetically interact. Perhaps they would become a plague against which we have no immunity. Or succumb to the ravages of our own bacterial invasion. How ironic if modern science were to restore Mars to its ancient mythic role as the catalyst of interplanetary biological war and a harbinger of Hell.

Of course, if we successfully colonize Mars astrology too will be transformed. For a baby born on Mars, Jupiter will be closer, Venus further away. Our Moon will be negligible, the ancestral Earth a distant celestial factor. What will the concept of a zodiacal sign mean without a lunation cycle (Mars only has two tiny asteroid rocks circling it), in a year twice as long? What precessional era will humanoid Martians experience as Earth enters the Age of Aquarius?

Back on our home world, Mars indicates the quality of power one expresses through the struggle to evolve. Life on Earth is a battle against inertia and entropy: the agonizing and ecstatic effort to birth life out of matter, consciousness out of life, spirit out of consciousness.

Mars spotlights the motivation or deeper reason behind one's life and acts. Not what one wants (Venus), but what destiny wants of one. Destiny constantly and intrusively challenges one to achieve this purpose through the processes defined by Mars' situation in the horoscope.

Moons

Like the other two personal planets, Mercury and Venus, Mars has no real moons, or karmic baggage. It acts in the here and now, with a strategic view to the future. It does have two tiny asteroid-moonlets, recent captures, soon to go: Phobos will crash onto its surface in about fifty million years; Deimos will be flung off into space at some point. These two ephemeral associates are like the high-pitched whine of a mosquito or buzzing of a fly: gnat-like irritations of anger and rage distracting one from the true focus of vitality. They illustrate the tiny errors and brief lapses of attention that cascade into big consequences for victory or defeat. They symbolize Mars' fatal flaw: a tendency to blind passion, diverting one from an impeccable presence on the stage of life and in the face of death.

Notes

1. The planet Mars rules the sign, or energy zone, of Aries as conscious initiative.
2. Mars also rules the sign of Scorpio as courageous acceptance of actions' consequences.
3. 'Do not go gentle into that good night,' Dylan Thomas, Welsh poet, 1914-1953
4. In the New Testament: Matthew 10:28; Luke 5:10, 8:50, 12:7 and 12:32
5. Latin: Thus passes worldly glory, implying transience.
6. Saturn spells out the limitation such loss imposes. Mars inflicts its pain. Just as Venus and Jupiter are called the lesser and greater benefics, so Mars and Saturn are called the lesser and greater malefics.
7. Shakespeare, Hamlet
8. Ecclesiastes 9:5
9. Ecclesiastes 9:10
10. Sigmund Freud, 1861-1939, Austrian* medical doctor, the father of modern psychology. His greatest discovery was of the unconscious

itself. He was the first to explicitly realize that ego consciousness is but the growing tip of a hidden psychic world, a small lit up island of awareness arising from a sea of instincts and forgotten memories. Over the generations psychology has evolved; within it many schools of thought contend. However, Freud's ideas still pervade the culture, from the halls of academia to the meanest ghetto streets. There the epithet of choice is 'mothafucka,' referring to the Oedipus complex he famously elucidated.

* He was also a Jew who, like Einstein, had to flee for his life from the Nazis.

11. We cannot colonize the gas giants: they have no surface and their gravity is far too strong. Venus is too hot (867° F.) and Mercury too deep in Sun's radiation field. It seems certain that we will establish lunar bases, but we cannot terraform Moon - its weak gravity, only 17% of Earth's, could not hold an atmosphere.

12. Factories could be set up to manufacture super greenhouse gases from local materials. Giant orbiting mirrors could reflect sunlight onto Mars' southern polar carbon dioxide ice cap, causing it to sublimate as a greenhouse gas. These initial steps would evaporate Mars' abundant dry ice into a heat retaining carbon dioxide atmosphere. A virtuous feedback cycle of global warming would melt underground permafrost (water ice), forming liquid seas. This water would also break down peroxides in the soil, releasing oxygen. A nitrogen source must be found (Earth's atmosphere is 78% nitrogen). It might be obtained by crashing ammonia (NH_3) rich asteroids onto the Martian surface. Or by making it from nitrate-bearing rock already present, by either industrial or biological methods.

In theory basic terraforming could be accomplished within several decades, or perhaps over a few centuries: an eye blink compared to natural geological processes. It all sounds so easy in a footnote...

Given these new conditions Mars would become habitable by higher life forms, possibly including the descendants of human pioneers. The technology to do this already exists. It could be deployed by the mid 21st century. There are several websites pertaining to this fascinating subject. For an overview google 'Technical Requirements for Terraforming Mars,' published by NASA's Ames Research Center. NASA made this site reader friendly by clustering the equations in easy to skip sections. You can also visit this potential new frontier right now by viewing the many images of Mars available online.

Mars in Signs and Houses

Mars in a sign indicates the objective nature of one's will.
Mars in a house indicates its subjective experience and expression.

Mars in fire signs/houses: drives hard and flies high, but can be ungrounded. Or fanatical. Starts, but does not necessarily finish; launches projects but may not consolidate gains. Fights for the joy of battle, not for an outcome.

In air, thinks fast and articulates well, but can over-intellectualize, get lost in verbal hair-splitting and irrelevant distractions. Feverish theorizing. Fights for ideas and principles. Can divide its forces and lose focus. Willing to negotiate and compromise.

In water, feels profoundly and universally, but can be hypersensitive. Strong passions, can be carried away by emotions. Fights for love or a gallant cause, regardless of practicality. Willing, even eager, to die in battle.

In earth, acts strategically and effectively, but can be small and petty: 'penny wise and pound foolish.' Hard working, can be a drudge. Fights for an outcome with grim determination, willing to do whatever it takes to win.

Mars in Aries/first house

Rulership. Self-assertion assumes an unusual degree of importance in the general personality. Energetic action emphasized in relation to other aspects of psyche. Will individualizes; personal expression takes on a fresh character. A challenge to openly reveal true self. A call to resist blind acting out.

High energy. Or hyperactivity. Raw drive urgently seeks an outlet. Spontaneous impulse generates an identity defined by aggressive ambition and dynamic movement. Pioneering enterprise. Audacity.

Mars in its own sign or house has tremendous power. It must learn to direct this surging force; harness it to a useful purpose. Will its instinctive self-projection express strategic competence or loose cannon excitability? Takes the initiative and makes a valiant effort. Can it follow through, stay the course, steer inspiration into real achievement? Or will it erupt into a new enthusiasm, charge off on another adventure, leaving a half-baked ruin behind?

Mobilizes unconscious potential into overt potency and radiates it out into the world. Aspiration overcomes inertia to accomplish the 'impossible.' The power of simplicity. Strength of innocence cuts through complex rationalization and subtle negativity: a child shouts 'the emperor has no clothes' while the sophisticates cower.

Immediacy and intensity of will generates creative confidence and courageous leadership. Or headstrong egotism, hot tempered impatience and reckless behavior. Refreshing originality or combative belligerence.

Dares to project one's own bliss and intentions independently of social expectations or pressure for conformity. Ready, willing and able to fight for personal autonomy. Insists on freedom to do its thing. Competes vigorously; enjoys a stimulating contest, or conflict. One has, or is, a direct, open, declared enemy.

Strong passions. Robust physical, emotional and mental vitality. Avid libido. Lust for life. The power of will to revitalize the world. Or of mania to devastate it. A sword severing one from the dead past. And a dawn of renewed purpose.

Mars in Taurus/second house

Detriment. Self-assertion fades as it expends its drive in sensual satisfaction. Will stabilizes as the defined power of a new identity, endowed with reliable abilities, attributes and qualities. A seed of potential takes root and bears fruit. A challenge to overcome narrow fixation on its own flowering, made possible by the shared energy field of Sun, soil and rain. A call to resist taking without also giving; to outgrow the seductions of self-interest and materialism: spiritual, intellectual and emotional as well as financial.

The acquisitive urge. Aggressive accumulation. The courage to invest in a tangible dream. Energy grounded in a specific purpose, relentlessly pursued. However, strategic direction can be clouded by greed for immediate profit, diverted for small tactical gains. Drive can be distracted by desire, or devitalized by satiety.

Tenaciously protects one's turf and adds to its wealth. Fights by steady, patient persistence: the tortoise v the hare. Competes by economy o f effort, strength of endurance, long-term stamina. Can turn stubborn and not adapt or retreat when advisable. If frustration over not getting what it wants builds up this normally phlegmatic temperament can erupt uncontrollably: a raging bull.

Mars, the planet of loss and death, is inhibited in Taurus, the sign of gain and sensuality. Its dynamic initiative becomes encumbered with the baggage of its treasures. It tends to assume a defensive posture, fearing that what it has may be taken away. And indeed it will, by death if not before. It must learn to give as well as get; commit its stewardship of resources into promoting higher values.

The power of possessions, emotional as well as material. Or one's possession by them. Enslavement to Precious, whether a thing or a person, an obsessively cherished opinion or a clung to social position. A passion for beauty can become corrupted by a need to own it. One has, or is, a jealous enemy, motivated by envy.

Voracious appetite. Heat of desire. Inflamed lust. Erotic magnetism. Demanding libido. Will can be enervated by pleasure.

Solid, or stolid, strength consolidates conservative values and worldly assets. Or obstinately maintains an entrenched status. Deliberate in decision, determined in execution.

Mars in Gemini/third house

Will objectifies. Action separates from the overall identity. Different aspects of behavior perform autonomously, perhaps in a compartmentalized fashion. A challenge to discover the overall integrity of one's own personality and honestly speak its truth. A call to resist glib rationalization of inconsistent conduct.

The driving force of purpose fractured by incompatible perceptions and multiple goals. Divided motives, internally conflicted. Mental civil war between competing narratives can split personality into alienated fragments. Or outwardly project into hostile discrimination between good me/us and bad them.

Seeks a synthesis by fearless investigation into a higher level of truth, a more inclusive reconciliation through give and take dialog between contending realities. The power of mind to redefine the world. The force that assembles separate elements, such as hydrogen and oxygen on the physical plane, into a new compound, water, with emergent properties such as the ability to nurture life.*

The intellectual courage to experiment and follow the facts, wherever they may lead. Thinks independently: articulates one's own truth as opposed to group opinion. Willing to fight for free inquiry and expression. Defends the right to an independent perspective. Fights on the battlefield of mind to clarify and communicate. Competes by argumentation and rhetorical brilliance. One has, or is, a sibling rival, an enemy alter ego, tricking conscious purpose with well-aimed lies.

High strung cerebral vitality. Keen perceptions. Intellectual passions. Mental fever. Changeable, chameleon-like libido. Primal aggression sublimates into verbal eloquence. Sharp wits and tongue. The power of language: to promote truth or sell deception. Penetrating lucidity or scattered distraction.

Activity centers on the acquisition, processing and use of information. Nervous energy focused by the fusion of logical analysis into a conceptual synthesis. Or squandered in contrived mind games. The power to interpret clues as elements of a bigger picture, relate parts to a larger whole. Or artificially exaggerate isolated facts for tactical advantage.

* In a water molecule the hydrogen and oxygen nuclei retain their separate identities - it is the configuration of shared electrons between them that gives water its novel character.

Mars in Cancer/fourth house

Fall. Self-assertion must function in an uncongenial medium of emotional sensitivity. Will subjectifies: immerses into a personal pool of mood and memory. A challenge to preserve one's privacy and personal space. A call to resist a life denying defensive posture.

Mars, the warrior planet, tends to founder in maternal Cancer's sea of sentiment. Its normally extraverted initiative must respond to an unfamiliar challenge from within. Its ambition and strategic direction are inhibited by intensified introspection. Its aggressive engagement with the outer world redirects into an exploration of inner space. Its urge to action and adventure manifests as a journey of psychological discovery. It focuses subconscious impulses into subjective motivations. This can energize a new driving dream. Or enable latent demons.

A protective power wards off external forces and concentrates energy within for internal development. Guards a pregnant potency coming to term, preserves it through its most dangerous passage, the birth trauma, and powers its fast evolving infancy. Cautious behavior out there conserves dynamic growth in here. Avoids overt confrontation. Can be passive-aggressive, projecting negativity as indirect hostility or sullen moodiness.

Outward conformity masks strong emotions. Defends intimate feelings against social demands, perhaps by withdrawing into highly charged fantasies. Willing to fight for freedom of imagination, perhaps by 'internal emigration' into another reality. Battles in the depths to vitalize enigmatic potentials and raise them into conscious personal expression. Competes by hidden growth, secret blossoming behind a sheltering shield. One has, or is, an unconscious enemy, driven by a need to deny the strenuous demands of excellence and objective achievement, in self or others.

Acutely impressionable; assimilates outer stimuli into inner sensation. Experience is absorbed and digested into a psychic bloodstream nourishing feeling more than activity. Our warm blooded nature as mammals: the internal emotional heat that incubates identity and imagination. A fierce maternal instinct generating life and feeding its initial phases until they reach the fullness of self-sufficient maturity. Lively empathy. Nurturing libido. Drive loses in vigor and gains in subtlety.

Mars in Leo/fifth house

Will projects a unique identity statement. A challenge to express creative originality. A call to resist the seduction of popularity, to stand for principle rather than going with the flow.

Star power, radiant charisma. The urge to command; can be domineering. Leads by setting an example of personal courage: emotional, mental, spiritual as well as physical. Bravely expresses high standards, excellence in action, even at risk of antagonizing the herd. Or loud posturing, an imperious demand to hog the spotlight, a radioactive ego blinded by delusions of grandeur. A theatrical flamboyance, vivid performance, majestic projection of the divine spark within. Or an aggressive narcissism indulges a streak of playful sadism, a taste for cat and mouse games, a lust to prove its superiority by humiliating others.

Joyfully displayed talent inspires freely given respect. Fearless leadership ability automatically generates public confidence. Or predatory presumption demands worshipful attention; pompous arrogance seeks to rule by intimidation. Focused force of a well-centered strength. Or wrathful mania of thin skinned vanity.

Willing to fight for love, generosity of feeling, in a mean-spirited world. Fights on the battlefield of heart for a noble cause. Competes by splendor of conduct, magnificence of ambition, liberality of contribution. Or refuses to own provocative behavior that indulges a superior attitude, oppressive smugness and casual cruelty to lesser beings. One has, or is, an egocentric enemy, a poor sport who cannot tolerate criticism and will viciously retaliate if outperformed.

High spirited, heartfelt vitality. Passionate libido. A grand passion. Or grandiose pretension. Intense pride. Dramatic self-assertion: a regal presence. A drive to self-expression can soar into artistic brilliance. Or sink into autocratic bullying. Emotional exuberance induces a sympathetic resonance of happiness in others by its fun loving warmth and singularity of individual style. Or coerces with an overbearing personality. Primeval self-esteem generates audacity. Or megalomania.

Mars in Virgo/sixth house

Will purifies: perfects its own integrity. Works hard to deploy it through impeccable action. A challenge to insist on excellence of performance. A call to resist small-minded escape into technique or trivial detail.

An urge to improve. Aggressively critical. A drive for efficiency and rationality leads to proficiency or intense tunnel vision.
Observational and technical ability. Or feverish attention to irrelevant
factoids. The courage to acknowledge flaws, admit imperfection, face
the facts of one's own inadequacy without evasion or excuse. And
endeavor to correct them. Healing power. An ability to repair subnormal function, upgrade mediocrity, enhance performance and strive
for perfection.

Willing to fight for honesty of motive and behavior. Fights for
consistent logic, impartial standards, fidelity to evidence, accuracy of
truth-claims. Demands respect for ugly fact v grandiose or seductive
fantasy. Competes by attention to particulars, rigor of application. Can
be disproportionately harsh on self or others for minor transgressions.
One has, or is, a small minded, nitpicking enemy, endlessly sniping for
petty advantage.

High strung nervous vitality. Controlled libido. Energy rationally
directed to a specific purpose. Aggression sublimated into service. Or
a frenzy of ritualistic activity. Strategy distracted by tactics. Sweating
the small stuff.

Easily irritated. A Mercurial energy constantly sidetracked by
chores, demands and emergencies. Can be nickeled and dimed away by
worries, irrelevancies and interruptions. Must develop a centering yoga
or methodical practice to channel anxiety. Otherwise it can tear itself
apart though edgy overstimulation.

Learns to prioritize energy expenditure. Develops a systematic
selectivity to eliminate distractions and focus effort on the essential
simplicity of any chosen calling. Refines process on every level, from
daily routine to the central passion of a life.

A restless analytical drive: keenly observant, surgically precise.
Penetrating intellect cuts through the clutter, gets right to the core.
Release in work and delight in the competence with which it can be performed. A passion for perfection achieved through painstaking attention
to one's craft. High level mental activity. This must be organized and
disciplined, or it will degenerate into a meaningless babble of frantic
data processing. If successful, a laser-like singularity of purpose.

Mars in Libra/seventh house

Detriment. Self-assertion fades as it compromises in the experience of
give and take with others. An energy that wants to speak learns to listen.
Will adjusts to its environment, defines itself through social interaction
more than personal initiative. A challenge to demand justice and right

relationship. A call to resist dishonorable compromise, the temptation to peace at any price.

Warring values. Shifting balance of motivations. Contrasting or incompatible options. Hamlet-like indecision, but, like him, it must eventually act. Learns to judge; develops a standard that resolves endless process into a definitive verdict.

The courage to demand justice for all. Defends the underdog. Willing to fight for due process, fair play. Fights in the court of public opinion to secure just decisions based on honest and transparent procedure. Competes by following the rules and ensuring that the competition does so as well. One has, or is, a frenenemy, a traitor to agreed commitments.

Graceful, even ethereal, vitality. Responsive, accommodating libido. Personal aggression sublimated into an intensity of social participation. Power is distributed through a pattern of association rather than concentrated in a focus of aspiration. Strength of connection: the making or breaking of bonds involves unusual commitment. Can lose perspective in overeager expectations of relationship.

Energized by outside forces more than by autonomous drive. To an unusual degree ego is stimulated and enlarged by collective demands. Or passively surrenders to social presumptions, rules and roles. Struggles to define a personal identity independent of external pressures.

Action inhibited by a clash of motivations. The nature of one's purpose, far from being self evident, is the subject of constant internal struggle. Powerful, even violent, shifts in affiliations, criteria of judgment, opinions of and by others. Eventually these can enlarge one's frame of reference, enhance appreciation of different viewpoints. Finds harmony through conflict: seeks a dynamic middle between strident extremes. Contending alternatives generate diplomatic skill, an ability to negotiate a profitable consensus out of debilitating contradictions.

Mars in Scorpio/eighth house

Rulership. Awareness of mortality assumes an unusual degree of importance. One senses the urgency of time. Feels a need to seize the moment.

A passion for power. Obsessive control emphasized in relation to other aspects of the personality. Instinctive concentration of force in response to perceived threat, general or specific. One taps into primal fear, masters its paralysis or panic and liberates its energy for a higher calling. Or surrenders to its aggressive negativity, projected outwards as morbid cruelty and abuse of others, embraced within as nihilism:

deliberate self-destruction and willful spiritual suicide. Icy courage. Or a death wish.

Mars in Scorpio energizes our deepest, and darkest, instincts with a hidden intensity of feeling. It arouses the most primal, and primitive, passions but always expresses them with strategic discipline. It empowers their rise into an emotional catharsis, perhaps even sublimation into spiritual transcendence. Or enables their calculated hostility: 'vengeance is a dish best served cold.'

Deeply felt loss or wounding. A challenge to face it with a cold eye. This includes the ultimate loss, death: on spiritual, intellectual, and emotional levels as well as in its final physical appearance. A call to forfeit an old identity and release its robotic compulsions to fuel the emergence of new life.

An erotic vitality, sexual heat. Highly charged libido. Willing to destroy an unsatisfactory situation/relationship and fight for emotional rebirth. Battles in the depths of psyche to confront and transform inner demons. Liquidates outworn feelings to free their binding energies. Or amputates unacceptable aspects of self, thus killing part of soul. Will competes against ego to overcome its own weakness. And with others by manipulating theirs. One has, or is, a relentless, deeply embittered enemy.

Purifying fever, healing surgery. Personal purpose regenerates: takes on deeper meaning and a longer view; reorients to a larger context. Or fear of letting go degenerates into a 'motiveless malignancy' seeking to drag others down with it. Which it will be depends on the outcome of a subjective trial by ordeal. A motivational struggle. Lust for power. Or the power of resurrection.

Mars in Sagittarius/ninth house

Will socializes: acts out group norms and aspirations. A challenge to actively participate in the public arena. A call to resist conformity; to speak and act authentically.

Far sighted strategic vision, of whatever merit. Ability to mobilize collective passions. The courage to promote a larger religious, philosophic or political aspiration, regardless of personal consequences. Militant beliefs. Crusading spirit. Self-righteous, potentially fanatic.

Willing to fight for truth and justice, as one sees them. Fights on the battlefield of spirit for a social cause or divine revelation. Driven, or intoxicated, by a vision of religious intensity. Its aggressive projection: a 'defender of the faith,' and (would be) conqueror of new worlds. Competes by demonstrating self-evident doctrinal or political correctness. Can be overzealous to seek out and destroy evildoers. One has, or is, an ideological enemy, engaged in wars of principle.

The will is motivated by philosophic conviction or prophetic insight rather than immediate wants. The strength of remote but exalted considerations can override the urge to instant gratification. Devotion to a cause transcends, or becomes identified with, ego assertion.

An urge to explore, travel far and wide in body or mind, go where none has gone before. It needs to align its journey by a moral compass, focus on a spiritual inspiration or one pointed aspiration. Otherwise its adventurous energy is easily led astray by bursts of enthusiasm, distracted by roadside attractions.

Eager for new experiences. Can be overly optimistic about their outcome. A sporting nature with a wild side. An expansive libido tends to promiscuity. An open honesty of free love and fleeting affairs. Or an indiscriminate plunge into wanton debauchery.

Mars in Capricorn/tenth house

Exaltation. Self-assertion reaches a critical intensity of expression. Targeted, goal directed behavior. Systematic planning informs action. Will organizes collective energies. A challenge to struggle relentlessly in one's chosen field. A call to resist exercising, or submitting to, improper authority.

Tenacious, perhaps blind, ambition. Grim determination. Focused energy. Practical ability. Or amoral pragmatism. Courage to stay the course, persist in the face of adversity. Fights to win by any means, fair or foul. Climbs the highest peaks of achievement by controlled resolve. Or gets down and dirty to grab the precious ring of power. 'The end justifies the means.' Yet 'What shall it profit a man if he gains the whole world, but loses his own soul?'* Competes, perhaps ruthlessly, in the halls of power for promotion (deserved or not). One has, or is, an authority-figure enemy, invoking rank rather than right.

Not as emotionally intense as Mars in Scorpio, but more cautiously strategic. Slow remorseless advance rather than transcendent sublimation. Seeks carefully channeled initiation, rather than a passionate leap, into a larger than personal dimension. Fears, not fascinated by, death; holds on tightly rather than lets go. Cold and calculating; driven by hunger not hate, insatiable need rather than compelling attraction.

Tough, hard-bitten vitality: lean and mean. Lusty libido. Powerful sensual drives. Materialistic motivations. Strong aggressive urges directed by conscious purpose. Spontaneity harnessed as consistent competence under every circumstance. Or shrunk into cynical opportunism. Energizes suspicion, making one prepared for the worst. Or preemptively invokes it. Empowers the unconscious Shadow, one's repressed inferior side. This can activate its frozen potential to a higher level of expression. Or unleash its negativity and pent up fears.

Concentration on pursuit of a compelling destiny besides which all other pleasures seem insipid. Strength of perseverance forged in the struggle to bend recalcitrant reality to a long-term agenda. Struggles to compensate for keenly felt inadequacy by attaining publically validated status, office or wealth. At an advanced stage it overcomes its weakness by internal discipline; willing discipleship to impersonal spiritual law. Heroic mastery. Or bitter but concealed combativeness.

* Matthew 16:26, Mark 8:38 and Luke 9:25

Mars in Aquarius/eleventh house

Will abstracts. It distills instinctual forces into archetypal intuitions, articulates their primal passions as big, bold ideas. Inspired by a vision quest. Subjective mental intensity generates lightning flashes of insight and projects them into a coherent expression of objective truth. A general concept illuminates the larger energy equation behind ever changing phenomenal events. The power of a central organizing principle to define a Big Picture that reorients behavior and can even remake the world.

An impersonal drive pursues social or ideological causes more than selfish ambition. Idealistic motivation asserts ego as an instrument of collective evolution. Or insists on its eccentricities. Dares to think outside the box. A challenge to true innovation. A call to resist change for the sake of change.

An urge to transcend, or dissociate from, present reality. The courage to follow one's unique genius, wherever it may lead, even at the risk of breaking with public norms. Willing to fight for distant future potentials and for seemingly impractical concepts. Will stand up for unpopular thoughts or groups, the right to be different and to experiment. Fights on the battlefield of mind to express a new paradigm, a novel theory. One has, or is, a surprise, unexpected enemy.

Invents unorthodox strategies and tactics: for example, a martial artist's use of an opponent's superior strength against him, or the recent development of online social activism. Competes by brilliance of inspiration, or crazed intensity of a fixed idea. Acts as an aggressive change agent on the mental plane. For example, this can express as the probing free inquiry of the scientific method. Or as the dogmatic zeal of a fanatically held revelation.

High strung mental vitality. Sublimated libido. Power of the intangible: influence of ideas, strength of hope, force of truth. An enthusiasm for transformation, expressed as disinterested action for the greater good. Or the destructive mania of the perennially dissatisfied; ardor of the malcontent. The expectation of improvement, which by the sheer passion of its cause, sweeps away the inertia of an established order. The catharsis of revolutionary struggle, for better or worse.

Mars in Pisces/twelfth house

Will dissolves: surrenders old motives for new ones. A challenge to willingly accept loss of one's most cherished dreams for a higher cause. A call to resist self-pity.

A stronger force, emanating from the unconscious within or the world without, overwhelms one's ability and agency. The faith to accept its unknown but larger than selfish purpose. The courage to let go of ego and its works. This clears the way for a descent of spirit. Or leaves bewildered impotence in its wake.

An urge to self-destruction: as the precondition for resurrection and in service to a redemptive purpose. Or as a defeated world weariness. Consciously accepted martyrdom. Or unconscious victimhood and guilt tripping. The courage to let go, renounce, accept personal loss or loss of personality, out of compassion. Or as an intoxicating rapture.

Willing to fight for the oppressed, forgotten and despised, even at the risk of being identified with them. Fights in the depths of psyche for salvation and rebirth. An ability to penetrate the collective unconscious and energize some of its contents past the threshold of awareness. Dies, literally or figuratively, for love or a transcendent calling. Competes by losing and going on to something better. Or sinks into despair and simply disappears. One has, or is, a hidden enemy, a backstabber.

Low vitality: energy freely poured out to, or vampirized, by others. Sacrificial libido. Submergence of ego identity into its social or cosmic matrix. The finite spark of individuality, having completed its cycle and exhausted its potential, immerses in and reunites with the source.

The power of renunciation. Or the process of deterioration, heat of decay. The liberation that comes with death of desire. Or the chaotic paralysis of a will unable to choose or to act.

Subtle or confused intentions. All personal and social ambition melts away, leaving helpless passivity or the motive of universal, unconditional love.

Willful assertion becomes willing acceptance: 'Thy Will, not mine, be done.'

Jupiter

Jupiter forms an enormous hydrogen bubble in space. This giant is as big as a dwarf star, but not dense enough to ignite nuclear fusion. Still, it contains twice the mass of all other planets combined. Its diameter stretches eleven times longer than that of Earth. By volume it could hold 1,321 clones of our world.

Jupiter's immense presence dominates the middle ground of our planetary sequence. Four small rocky planets orbit closer to Sun; three diminishing gas globes circle farther out. Astronomically, by size and position, Jupiter is the central planet of our solar system. Astrologically it plays a parallel role in the dynamics of human character. Jupiter symbolizes a soul uniting personal psychology (inner planets) with impersonal spirit (outer planets).

Jupiter, a world halfway to a star, mediates between Sun and its planetary offspring. Sun burns as a transcendent spiritual Fire upon which the eye or mind cannot look. Jupiter acts as a smaller, humanized Sun. It steps down Sun's overwhelming force to a comprehensible level. It cools and condenses an inhuman Will into a transpersonal but accessible state of grace. A divine impulse with a human face.

Sun embodies a cosmic ecstasy beyond our ken. Its energy drives the system, but requires smaller, more solid worlds on which to take shape. Through them it lives and evolves. Jupiter relates the spiritual realm of Sun with the material reality of the planets. Physically through its glowing gas immensity. Psychologically by channeling solar radiance into a revelation we can sense and aspire to.

Jupiter mutes the scary Sun to an intensity just above our own. Enough to stimulate psyche and motivate evolution, but not so much as to be alien. Jupiter serves as the gaseous shadow of our fiery star. It functions as an umbilical cord uniting Sun with its planetary centers of manifestation. It clothes Sun's power with personality. It formulates solar impulse into a religious and philosophical meaning larger than life, but available to it.

Jupiter embodies the highest state we can conceive of with our mind or feel with our heart. It generates a sense of awe towards that which is greater than self: nature, nation, God. And articulates it in conceptual, ideological and theological terms.

Jupiter is the first planet farther away from Earth than Sun is. It points to a larger destiny than personal purpose. Jupiter acts as an intermediate angelic stage linking a tiny human identity with its spiritual source. It portrays the face of God, as each of us sees it. An ideal Personality overshadowing and guiding a denser ego. A prophet, teacher, master demonstrating its higher nature. This inspires one's smaller personality to a more profound state of being.

Of course there are false prophets and fallen angels. Like any planet, Jupiter's energy can be distorted. Then it degenerates into an exaggerated ego, a super-sized self.

Jupiter grounds a state of consciousness beyond ego, in which one encounters God. Thus it provides an inner guide, a moral compass. By position and aspect Jupiter indicates the spiritual quality, soul orientation, steering one's subjectivity. Its actual expression depends on one's openness to this transpersonal truth.

Jupiter is more than human, less than infinite. Here is the realm of the gods, in whatever forms our limited feelings and thoughts can conceive.

God is a Person: a higher state of being with a centered self-aware identity. Not an abstract force; not a biological life. This Person lives larger than the human condition. As Christ said, one can only approach God through the level of evolution he personified: 'No man comes to the Father except by Me.'[1] The form of this approach is not important: 'In my Father's house there are many rooms.'[2] Only its integrity and intensity matter.

In the Stone Age this was conceived of as a happy hunting ground, with totemic animals embodying natural forces and supernatural beings. In the classical era as an Olympian court, with super-human gods, goddesses and heroes acting out eternal psychic dramas. In medieval times as a beatific Rapture, with a vision of Powers, Thrones, Dominions in which angels and fiends contend for salvation or damnation. In modern times as a holistic harmony of ecological balance, social justice and personal creativity enacting a cosmic evolutionary purpose here on Earth.

Each of these would be associated with specific socially sanctioned standards of worth. In the Stone Age, an appreciation of the magical animals and plants with whom we share the world. In the classical era, heroic individuality. In the medieval, submission to the Will of God and humble obedience to His anointed rulers on Earth. In the modern, impartial justice and global consciousness within a rainbow family of humanity.

Jupiter portrays the nature of one's approach to God. Its position and aspects indicate how one embarks on this pilgrimage. Jupiter locates where and how one partakes of God. Its danger lies in confusing participation with identification. The God image can absorb consciousness and empower its hidden inner demons.

302

One's primary response to life is to God. One's attitude/outreach towards the divine defines one's essential nature. This aspiration may be unconscious, a visceral feeling. Or a conscious quest. If unbalanced it can become an inflated aspect of consciousness, expressed as an ideology. Formerly these were religious. In modern times political. Now it seems that a scientific/technological idolatry is coming.

However one conceives of God involves a higher plane of existence, a life more abundant than the human condition. Essentially it refers to a transcendent state of consciousness. Jupiter symbolizes that by its movement as well as its mass. This huge globe rotates faster than any other in our solar system. It turns on its axis in just under ten hours. A planet's rotation defines its subjective awareness. One rotation carries every point on its surface through a complete orbit of its own center and a 360° perspective on the surrounding cosmos. Jupiter's accelerated spin suggests an intensified consciousness. It acts like a centrifuge separating the fine from the coarse, spinning off a subtle essence from a denser substrate.

Planetary rotation speeds up moving out from Sun to Jupiter, and then slows down beyond it. The planets within Earth's orbit, Mercury and Venus, rotate very slowly. These inner planes of basic mentality and innate values exist prior to experience. They mature organically at their own pace, taking time to incorporate outer events into personal identity. Mercury's day is ⅔ the length of its year; its mental consciousness can never fully grasp objective truth. Venus' day is actually ⅛ longer than its year; its subjective desire exceeds real possibility. Farther out, Earth and Mars both have 24-hour days. These are worlds of action and awareness, as we know them.

Potentials of intellect and love (Mercury and Venus), having developed individuality in the realms of existential reality (Earth and Mars), eventually transcend their known experiences. The complexities of personality sublimate into a statement of its higher meaning. The perceptual, emotional and mental details generating its awareness drop away. Their overall significance distills out into Jupiter's more ethereal truth.

The inner planets chart primary characteristics, basic qualities of psychology: mind (Mercury), love (Venus), will (Mars). Then, beyond the disintegrative zone of the asteroids, come the gas giants, Jupiter and Saturn.[3] These depict transpersonal realities: social participation and spiritual attainment, destiny and fate. Jupiter, first and largest of the atmospheric planets, describes a transcendent soul integrating all of these qualities. This soul is both prior to and derived from, but not identical with, personal character. It concentrates an extract of what a life means, minus its personal quirks. It demonstrates a state of consciousness abstracted out of experience.

Rainbow banded Jupiter vividly symbolizes our spectrum of consciousness. Its multiple flowing layers, extravagantly festooned with whorls and eddies, embodies a heavenly projection of our own multi-tiered hearts and minds.[4]

Each band on Jupiter flows as vast jet stream of awareness. Each blows in the opposite direction to the ones below and above it. Each emergent phase of consciousness has a complementary polarity to the ones that precede and follow it. Yin and yang, communal and individualistic states of consciousness alternate. In doing so they activate one another. This oscillating structure of the mind provides the stimulus of contrast and variety. However, one can become trapped on any one level, hooked on its truth flavor, oblivious to the other tastes of reality. In fact, this is our most common experience.

Jupiter also layers vertically, from its cold wispy cloud tops down an increasingly thick atmosphere. We experience its visible currents of consciousness at various levels of depth. Some have a shallow understanding, often vehemently expressed. Others have a deeper wisdom, respectful of nuance and subtlety. Around each of Jupiter's bands swirls a zone of turbulence. Storms of consciousness conflict and fertilize each other at their edges. This strengthens and clarifies each. Or induces a defensive fanaticism.

Every worldview is a world unto itself. We experience events through the prism of its general outlook. Every phase of Jupiter's spectrum appears to be the truth, the whole truth, and nothing but the truth. Each actually contains only one color of the rainbow. Jupiter's ultimate Truth contains, acknowledges and balances all these partial truths.

Several consciousness theorists have brilliantly portrayed the sequential flowerings of these levels.[5] Instinctual, tribal-mythic, hero-power, religious-moral, scientific-rational, holistic-existential worldviews all build upon their predecessors. Each adds a new dimension. But each is only partial. Even a holistic consciousness has little sense of relative value. It tends to deny hierarchical merit in favor of egalitarian networking. Thus it abdicates necessary judgment. Only a global worldview, encompassing all elements of Jupiter's immense sphere, can incorporate its several planes of consciousness into a higher synthesis.

Jupiter measures an evolving spiritual calculus. Differentially moving vectors of relative truth synthesize into a larger perspective. Jupiter implies an inclusive enlightenment accommodating contradictory facts (Mercury), conflicting feelings (Venus), divergent drives (Mars) and incompatible dreams (Moon). An intuitive wisdom integrating complexity into a singular vision. Or an intense revelation burning away the deadwood to reveal a Big Picture.

Jupiter defines one's overall sense of Truth, the meaning of reality. It also anchors this in more contingent truths applied to concrete circumstances: manmade laws of proper conduct. Jupiter expresses social values: not the personal preferences of Venus, but a general moral outlook. One tries to live up to it. Thus Jupiter enlarges consciousness into conscience.

Jupiter expresses an ethical spirit transcending immediate self-interest. It points to why one willingly conforms to community norms. And what one expects to gain by it. Not in terms of personal acquisitiveness (Venus), but of standing, rank, prestige. What one admires, or wants to be admired for. The larger than life exemplars one emulates. One's response to and expression of a social ethos.

Jupiter outlines the nature of one's collective involvement. It embodies the exhilaration of belonging to something bigger than self. It shows not what one wants (Venus), but what the universe wants one to be. What one feels outranks the self or any of its deeds. A sense of what life is about. Jupiter turns one on with the vision of a more heavenly reality.

Jupiter magnifies whatever it touches. It can enhance any of our qualities, including Saturn's shadow or Mars' anger. Jupiter empowers. And demonstrates how one uses power. That determines one's true status. Jupiter renders God's judgment as one's own soul evaluation of character from a higher perspective. Its conclusions are always different from what one thinks or imagines, perhaps sharply so.

Here consciousness learns the significance of its experience. Empirical mind meets the meaning of its data. Ego encounters the consequences of its choices. And perhaps a final post-personal destiny determined by those decisions.

Jupiter also magnifies the ego through one's social role. It describes participation in consensus reality. Where one contributes to the general welfare along conventional and expected lines. How one shares in the group-mind in an affirmative way. A tribal role; the office, formal or informal, one performs in the collective endeavor. A basic political stance; the attitude one brings to public affairs. Not a specific opinion, but a general frame of reference; not a partisan agenda, but a philosophical orientation.

Jupiter portrays how one joins the stream of history. The tribute paid to a larger cause, and the larger identity derived from it. One's contribution to evolution, and the personal evolution resulting from it. This may be achievement oriented (earth), emotional (water), intellectual (air), or inspirational (fire). It can occur through conscious choice or an unconscious immersion in herd psychology.

Whatever the level of awareness or scale of involvement, Jupiter always opens the door to a wider world. It energizes one with an unmerited confidence that eventually generates its own competence. Jupiter expresses the irrational exuberance that created existence from nothing, life from chemicals and perhaps even an immortal soul from passing personality. It embodies an innate optimism underwriting the human ability to foresee and invest in a distant future. It entails the wisdom of naiveté: an unjustified enthusiasm carrying every helpless newborn to the summit of adult achievement.

Jupiter exhibits the innate generosity of an expanding universe, a (once) bountiful Earth, a supportive society, the very gift of life. It maximizes the whole Self[6] through participation in the sheer thrill of existence. It exhilarates the soul because we are each always and fully in the presence of God, or the Tao, if only we could realize it. It inspires one with the unearned good fortune of a living body, feeling heart, thinking brain in a world full of possibility.

Venus delights one with personal pleasure; Jupiter gives a more subtle ecstasy. It demonstrates a cosmic joy animating everything from the vibrations of an atom to the enthusiasms of an ego to the esprit de corps of a nation. This Bliss is the most basic fact of all. Jupiter shows where and how one accesses it.

Jupiter's joy does not mean giddy glee or gigglefun play. It refers to an attunement with the spiritual wisdom and compassionate love that move the universe. Jupiter plugs one in to the general happiness of life. The cosmos sings with ecstasy. Jupiter encourages us to sing along with it. Because we are it. How one embraces, or rejects, this elation creates luck, one's resonance with events. Opportunity constantly and spontaneously appears. Does one have the wit and will to take a chance on it? That depends on how psyche aligns with its Jovian spiritual antennae. Preconceived opinions can cancel out Jupiter's subtle signals. Or compress them into a narrow mold. A free spirit can ride their wave to a farther shore.

How one responds generates consequences far greater than the original impulse. Jupiter's charged spiritual aura amplifies the immediate power of events into guiding principles of conduct. Every decision accelerates one down a chosen path, cascades into a snowballing trajectory of moral commitment to certain forms of behavior. Thus a random act of kindness, or moment of spiritual suicide, sculpts the contours of expectation, the shape of things to come.

Jupiter also mediates between self and society. We are each a fractal of the universe with a unique distortion due to incarnation in matter. Jupiter's special twist generates divine discontent as a remembrance of our higher nature. And an outreach to regain it. It gives a larger meaning to life as we begin to realize that each of us lives out a spiritual impulse interpreted through a unique experience.

In a less metaphysical, more psychological sense Jupiter portrays the internal archetype guiding one's evolution. Archetypes sublimate unconscious instincts into numinous psychic images. Like an ideal Platonic form, an archetype has a universal character defined through innumerable specific manifestations. Such archetypal figures as Wizard, Warrior, Seductress, Mother fuse personal identity with collective power. They constitute a common language through which one relates to others. Only by working through these symbolic roles can one develop individuality. Only by competently executing a generic social function can one eventually transcend the prison of personality.

By position and aspect Jupiter suggests the mythic story each of us plays out. There are a few basic human dramas: hero, martyr, bully, thief, lover, healer, etc. These general stories only come true through personal participation in a social narrative. The story is timeless: for example, boy meets girl; ambition betrays principle, etc. Its living experience and consequences are unique. Furthermore, boy meets girl can end up as more than a personal romance and give birth to a Lincoln or a Hitler. Or at least another member of the next generation.

Our instinctual nature as mammals (Moon) makes us bond strongly with others. One always identifies with a group. This larger identification starts with the family and the most powerful male and female archetypes one will ever encounter: our parents.

Jupiter = Big Daddy. We long to emulate him. This is true for men as a role model; for women as an ideal father figure. Jupiter's feminine counterpart is Moon, its Word made manifest. Moon = mother, the personal soul, other than one's own, through which one came into the world. We feel the feminine face of God first. Womb-life, birth, infancy, early childhood form the pre-verbal emotional foundation of Jupiter's aspiration.

Moon's emotional gravity grounds Jupiter's spiritual glow. Moon's unconscious instinct slowly coalesces and powers up into personal will (Mars) during childhood. Jupiter then socializes egocentric will: first by conformity to rules and roles demanded by family and community, perhaps later through an evolving personal consciousness and conscience.

Through socialization Jupiter expands one's nature to include more than just self-referential contents. Jovian empathy, the ability to stretch identity to encompass others, enlarges character. Not only by growing one's own wavelength of consciousness, but by embracing others. A particular form of awareness, however advanced on its own level (rational, emotional, practical, etc.) now adds new dimensions. Quantitative breadth opens to qualitative depth just as a circle transcends itself to become a sphere.

Jupiter's expansive spiritual context orients Moon's personal memory and moods. It guides instinct to aspiration, draws unconscious temperament closer to the god/dess within. Jupiter's transcendent soul force activates Moon's immanent soul of remembrance, personal and ancestral. Its spiritual aura generates an electricity that turns on the lunar memory banks. Jupiter breathes a greater Life into Moon's vehicle of psyche. It unites divine images with animal instincts, rarefied archetypes with inherited programs. Together they create a social being, acting beyond self centered motivations.

Jupiter generates a force field bigger than the tight central ego focus. This resonates with other energies and transmits that vibration to the core identity. It does so through social archetypes, collectively charged images. One identifies with these, first in fantasy, then as aspiration, finally by actually living up to them. Thus personality transcends its own limitations, becoming a social actor and a spiritual agent.

Jupiter focuses long-term cosmic rhythms into a soul template. At Jupiter the tides of imagination (Neptune), flashes of intuition (Uranus) and impersonal laws of reality (Saturn) coalesce into a humanized image. This abstract form is galvanized with personal characteristics emanating from the inner planets. The infrared heat of passion (Mars), visible light of experience (Earth/Moon), depth of desire (Venus), clarity of insight (Mercury), all infuse and inform a soul potential with individualized psychological energies. The principles of spirit (outer planets) and processes of life (inner planets) unite in a light body (Jupiter). This envelops, irradiates and animates the psyche.

At Saturn, beyond Jupiter, we meet our limit, contract in the face of Infinity. One falls away from the awe-full Reality of God into its more accessible reflection (Jupiter). This divine image guides, molds, orients a still smaller, yet more concrete, identity. As a separate soul precipitates out of the All it finds its own level. Jupiter describes the energy band on which it condenses. And from which it radiates out as light. This is the vibration one emits, the wavelength one rides, the illumination one projects.

Jupiter embodies an overall aura; one's general psychic atmosphere. A shining. It may be a dull splotch or a lurid hue; a deceptive shimmering or a distorted hallucination. A monochromatic spotlight, reducing everything to shades of a single color. A natural daylight, displaying a standard issue worldview. Or revealing things in their true colors. Perhaps it acts as an x-ray vision of deeper truths; a laser-like intensity, revelatory or burning; or a supernal radiance, inspiring and transfiguring. The empirical ego then expresses this spiritual coloration within a wide range of personality types.

Any position of Jupiter can be cloudy or clear, bright or feeble. The important issue is not its original state but its direction of movement. Is it clarifying or darkening? Intensifying or dimming? Sometimes one wavelength is overdeveloped, blotting out the other colors. It may need to fade and make room for the rest. Jupiter is not necessarily about more. It is about better. That involves sacrifice almost as often as gain.

We often grow the most through our embarrassments, mistakes and defeats. Loss can free one. Perhaps this is why one must die: to outgrow too warm and glowing a comfort zone of consciousness. Jupiter's path to God can be ambiguous and elusive. In the end:

'The first shall be last, and the last shall be first.'[7]

Jupiter is not fundamentally about worldly success, though it can manifest as such. After all, its plenitude can intoxicate with inflated self-esteem. Its bounty can bloat into hype. Too great an enthusiasm is Jupiter's characteristic problem. It tends towards extravagance. And wretched excess. Thus it needs the corrective of Saturn's contraction. Such restraint then leads to a different, more difficult, kind of growth through loss of a truth that fails, a prize turned to ashes.

Jupiter's good fortune lies not in power, riches or fame but as participation in a larger cause. Jupiter lifts one out of ego into a state of grace. It means salvation, not status or stuff:

'For what shall it profit a man if he gains the whole world and loses his own soul?'[8]

Jupiter secretes one's particular growth hormone. It induces exploration, expansion, evolution. This can be along one line of endeavor. Or it can enhance an ability to express the entire psyche. Jupiter marks one's competence. What one is good at, perhaps really good at. Yet one can become blinkered by achievement. Confidence can beget overconfidence and megalomania.

Jupiter powers an inherent urge to expand. This can mean more of the same, careening off into gluttony and obesity. It can express as uncontrolled growth: inflation in an economy, cancer in an organism. 'Cancer is the ideology of growth for growth's sake.'[9]

Or it can mean evolution. A progressive development of quantity creating the conditions for a breakthrough in quality. As each of Jupiter's bands of consciousness swells to its full potential it is charged with enough energy to leap to a higher plane. It includes what has already been achieved on one level while encountering and assimilating the different and difficult truth of the next. Each plane of consciousness necessarily acts as an opposite polarity complementing what precedes it. It takes moral courage to embrace this fuller, more inclusive reality. Jupiter underwrites the spiritual willingness to acknowledge a reality greater than what one presently knows.

Jupiter demonstrates faith in life's essential benevolence, trust in the unknown future. Beyond the small, intensely felt parameters and fated constraints of the human condition, Jupiter shines as the soul of hope. It points to a larger identity, gives evidence for a higher state of being. Jupiter's sense of deeper dimensions imbues the mundane with meaning. Its intuitions of implicit potential bring spiritual significance to our striving and suffering.

Jupiter motivates with premonitions of improvement, which for that very reason come true. Jupiter's expansive optimism, the internal heat of our warm-blooded nature, makes life more than worth the effort. Its ethereal promise redeems material reality by attracting it towards a better future. Its ethical injunctions encourage justice. Its social sensibilities sublimate into moral principles. Jupiter's insubstantial aspirations ultimately have more power than all the deadweight of established consensus. Its 'lift of a driving dream,'[10] whether conscious or not, stands behind all of our overt actions.

Jupiter exemplifies the truth that the whole is more than the sum of its parts. It enhances relationship with emergent properties. Jupiter's force field ensures that seemingly random interactions don't just cancel out in a zero sum game, but synergistically combine to create new opportunities. Life expands to fill these niches. Thus atomic reactions write genetic instructions in DNA molecules. These chemical codes express themselves as biological bodies. Their organic processes fuse into psychological awareness, then into an empathic encounter with others. Thus a collection of egos becomes a society.

The Jupiter function grows time from past to future, space from a pinpoint to a universe, matter from single atoms to intricate molecules, simple cells to complex organisms, etc. It embodies directionality;

310

orients movement into evolution. This is not a pre-formed plan or determined outcome. It involves openness to invisible potential, thus making it real. This does not imply a linear march into an ever more glorious future. It means an adventure into unexpected emergence. It includes backsliding, detours and cancerous forms of growth. Even these increase and intensify experience.

While Venus entices one's personal best, Jupiter takes one beyond to a transcendent aspiration. This still has a human face. It is a generically higher state of being: angelic, godlike, with subjective interiority, attunement to feeling. Its subtle energy patterns still have an individual quality. At Saturn and beyond lies the realm of impersonal forces. Jupiter integrates faceless forces and human foibles into a spiritual soul.

This soul so loves the world that it unites cosmic immensity and an inhuman grandeur with the passionate but limited concerns of struggling humanity. Jupiter, the central unifying principle, merges subjectivity in space/time (inner planets) with a timeless unconscious (outer planets). It marries these in our experience of spiritual significance. This is a long, slow process extending beyond single life. Jupiter lives larger than personal psychology. It makes one a shareholder in a group identity.

The conscious self is embedded in a larger Self, which includes instinctual, unconscious and spiritual levels.[6] Ego acts as the Self's executive agent, fitted to the circumstances of history, ethnicity, class, family. It centers human experience in a separate and singular consciousness. Nevertheless, it is by nature partial and limited. Each of us also embodies a transcendent soul. This soul embraces more than the whole Self; for it includes other minds and wills in a supra-personal identity. Ego forms a part, the growing tip, of a larger background.

Some of that background objectively surrounds you: a society filled with other subjectivities. Jupiter expresses a set of guiding principles that coordinates them in accordance with a higher mandate or prime directive. Jupiter promotes team spirit, unit cohesion, through an aura of group will and feeling. These become defined as duties and responsibilities with Saturn's next contractive phase.

We all move together by virtue of shared social mores. Some of these are codified into law. This marks the political expression of a culture. Its structure may be elitist or democratic, militaristic or commercial, religious or secular. Jupiter describes one's attitude towards the collective order and the powers that be.

Jupiter broadens participation into compassion. And extends it to more others: first in the family, then to socialization in school, followed by a (hopefully) growing inclusiveness of care and responsibility in maturity. To other nations and races; other species; perhaps even to those irritating other people in one's immediate vicinity.

In doing so one becomes less attached to personal identity. Ego has its own glory, but also functions to enact the purposes of a larger whole. Jupiter transcends an individual focus in the service of a greater cause: social and political or religious and mystical.

Jupiter distills one's essence into a spiritual equation. This equation contains more than one term: it has sensory, emotional, mental and moral dimensions. It summarizes and transcends several internal subjective levels, assimilates social influences, and builds on a long-term evolutionary legacy. One's personal Jupiter also provides a glimpse into a general God-equation that unifies and gives meaning to all specific energies.

Jupiter describes one's sense of a bigger reality: the human society, cosmic environment, spiritual truth that one experiences and helps to express. It demonstrates where and how one grows beyond personality while retaining an ego anchor.

Moons

Through their own characteristics moons externalize, make visible and known, the deep past, global memory and karmic needs underlying a planetary function.

Jupiter's most unusual moon orbits around its core in the topmost layer of its atmosphere. In its southern hemisphere a huge cyclone, three times larger than Earth, has been observed for 400 years. This standing tornado forms a vortex linking Jupiter's electrically charged interior with the void of space. It forms a Great Red Spot that seems to look out at the universe like the Eye of God. Does it symbolize an upwelling of consciousness, manifesting on Earth as an unprecedented global awakening since the Renaissance? Is a general spiritual crisis rippling through the solar system: portrayed by a perfect storm on its planetary center of gravity (Jupiter), enacted by its human expression of self-awareness on Earth, and now experienced by other planets as they are visited, perhaps stimulated, by our robotic probes?

Is the Great Red Spot just a long-winded chemical whirlpool on a giant gasbag in space? Or a material manifestation of an intangible soul state? Does it gyrate meaninglessly in the clouds? Or does it focus a psychic condition of the solar system through a clarifying lens? This permanent tempest turns on a still midpoint, just like any hurricane on Earth. Is this simply a dead zone, circled by howling winds? Or the open channel of an emergent property?

Is the physical phenomenon all there is? Or does it parallel a deeper psychological process? Is literal truth the whole truth? Or does it metaphorically reflect a larger reality? The central storm of the central world evokes fundamental questions. Upon the answers hangs one's worldview. And the validity of astrology. Jupiter's visible appearance provokes the mind's eye into a basic decision about the nature of reality. That alone makes it the philosophical planet.

The outer planets all have numerous moons, an appropriate reminder of their nature as social or collective unconscious forces, carrying a more complex inheritance than the purely personal qualities of the inner planets. Giant Jupiter hosts a family of 63 known moons. Most are tiny captured asteroids. Four, however, are quite large and distinctive in their own right. Four is the number of wholeness and manifestation: four directions in space, four seasons in time*, four fundamental forces of matter/energy,† four corresponding traditional elements.‡

Among these moons is Io, the most volcanically active body in our solar system, made so by Jupiter's gravity tides. Europa, covered by a vast liquid water ocean beneath an icy shell. This may host biological life. Ganymede, the largest moon in the solar system (though not relative to its parent planet) and Callisto, its most heavily cratered object. Io is clearly fiery in nature; Europa watery. Intensely sculpted Callisto has an earthy permanence of memory; perhaps giant Ganymede reflects the gaseous quality of its home planet. Jupiter's moons embody the full suite of elemental qualities, displayed in their physical natures. They reinforce the idea that Jupiter itself embodies a system of transcendent soul-consciousness mediating between Sun's spiritual domain and the inner planets' personal psychological realities. The various levels of awareness comprising Jupiter's globe add up to a divine superconsciousness. This connects with our material realm through the miniature solar system portrayed by its major moons.

* There are four seasons in the temperate zones (spring, summer, fall and winter), and generally two in the tropics, wet and dry. However, there are always four light/dark phases in a year everywhere: day dominant and increasing, day dominant and decreasing, night dominant and increasing, night dominant and decreasing.

† Gravity, electromagnetism, the strong force, holding atomic nuclei together, and the weak force, radioactively breaking them apart.

‡ The four traditional elements (earth, water, air, fire) have been reinterpreted in modern science as the four phases or states of matter: solid, liquid, gas, and plasma.

Notes

1. John 14:6. Christ consciousness is a level of evolution, not a specific path to its attainment. One can get there as a Catholic or a Muslim, a Hindu or a Jew, as Jesus was.

2. John 14:2

3. Farther out, Uranus and Neptune are ice giants. They symbolize impersonal phenomena of the collective unconscious.

4. You can access stunning images of Jupiter, and all other planets, online. Their physical appearance implies deeper levels of psychological meaning. Visible astronomical features signal underlying spiritual qualities.

5. Ken Wilber, widely considered the foremost consciousness theorist of our times, has written several eloquent books on this topic. Another interesting treatment is by Beck and Cowan in 'Spiral Dynamics,' a discussion of evolving value systems.

6. The great psychologist Carl Jung (1875-1961) defined the Self as conscious ego plus a personal unconscious, the collective unconscious and the instinctual nature, along with a transcendent spiritual dimension. The ego constitutes only a small lit up area of a much larger psychic totality.

Sun symbolizes the whole Self; Moon its instinctual and unconscious aspects; Jupiter its spiritual orientation. The lunar side grounds Self into biological and psychological life. The Jupiter side connects its empirical consciousness with a soul, personal essence subsumed into a transcendent state.

7. Mark 8:36 and Matthew 16:26

8. Matthew 20:16

9. Edward Abbey, American environmental writer, 1927-1989

10. Richard Nixon, U.S. President from 1969-1974. From his resignation speech.

Jupiter in Signs and Houses

Jupiter in a sign indicates the objective nature of one's spiritual orientation and social participation.

Jupiter in a house indicates one's subjective experience/expression of soul.

Jupiter's sign position indicates growth of a certain type of awareness. Its corresponding house position portrays evolution of an inner joy derived from it.

In fire signs/houses: initiation, rule, wisdom. Personality grows by soaring to the noblest heights of aspiration, or believing that it does. Soul seeks truth through creative self-expression. 'The audacity of hope' generates a new reality. Spirit ascends into transcendence with a willed unification of all energies into one great purpose.

In air signs/houses: judgment, theory, knowledge. Personality grows by expanding the mind, factoring all the little facts into one explanatory equation, however valid. Soul seeks truth through objective observation, locates the significance of data in relationship. A larger perspective gives reality a new meaning. Spirit ascends into transcendence with a theory of everything, simplistic or sophisticated.

In water signs/houses: imagination, psychic insight, empathy. Personality grows by diving to the very foundations of feeling, or drowns in an abyss of overdone emotion. Soul seeks truth through sympathetic inclusiveness. Depth of perspective, enhanced psychological sensitivity. Spirit descends into immanence with a compassionate embrace of all, good and bad alike.

In earth signs/houses: achievement, tangible acquisition, practical ability. Personality grows by actually accomplishing something, or grabbing credit for doing so. Soul seeks truth through application of theory to real facts and accepting the objective outcome. Respects reality rather than its own preconceptions. Spirit descends into immanence with tangibility of contact, sensory experience of existence.

Jupiter in Aries/first house

Spiritual rebirth. An individual sense of meaning emerges out of collective norms. It breaks free of conventional wisdom and enters a new cycle of personal expression. Burning aspiration more aware of its own intensity than of any exterior goal. Uninhibited faith in one's own will. Optimism, confidence and trust in self, its general outlook and presentation to the world. Growth through aggressive initiative.

Magnifies the potential of all beginnings, thus encouraging them. An opportunity to enjoy the blessings of a fresh start or a second chance. An intuitive sense of possibilities and a willingness to seize them. A springtime of hope.

A spirit of adventure. A pioneering impulse to explore new frontiers. Exuberant expansion. The spontaneous joy of exploration and discovery. The sheer thrill of vitality and of testing its strength.

Insists on the truth of authentic personal experience v authority, tradition or consensus. Emphasizes following one's own bliss. One contributes the most by doing one's thing, however immaturely, than by living up to others' expectations, however brilliantly.

A dawning enlightenment, simple and clear. Its newborn ardor enlarges consciousness. Or inflates ego. The wisdom of naive enthusiasm. Salvation through outgrowing an old law and embracing a new perspective. A competitive ethic. An individualistic philosophy emphasizing liberty and rights. The miracle of freedom. Glorifies self-assertion. Can be over-confident. God, the Force, experienced in its creative aspect.

Jupiter in Taurus/second house

Spiritual aspiration grounds itself in specific desires. Enhanced appreciation of the actual beauty inherent in every moment, situation and person as they are rather than as they 'should' be. Optimism, confidence and trust in one's own standards of judgment. Growing insight into the source and nature of value. Practical wisdom.

Magnifies the potential of existing attributes and resources. Expands through patient cultivation, solid incremental growth. The miracle of compound interest increases productivity: of psychological evolution, artistic expression, social participation as well as of financial assets.

An opportunity to enjoy the blessings of prosperity: emotional as well as material. The bliss of abundance. Character defined by how one invests endowed talents and surplus capital. Gives the wherewithal to get what one wants. And thus shows who one really is.

Tangible generosity. Altruistic sharing can promote the general welfare, and create a legacy, far beyond one's own abilities. Or acquisitive greed. The Midas touch can emphasize accumulation in quantity over increase in quality; reduce all meaning to market terms; identify with wealth rather than worth. Excessive faith in economic security inflates the importance of possessions to the point of being possessed.

Salvation through sensation:

'Man has no body distinct from his Soul. For that called body is a portion of Soul discerned by the five senses, the chief inlets of Soul in this age.'*

A productive ethic. A materialistic philosophy embraces visible truth and physical pleasure. God, the Force, experienced in its aspect of fertility.

* 'The Marriage of Heaven and Hell,' William Blake, 1757-1827, English artist and poet

Jupiter in Gemini/third house

Detriment. A quest for meaning, higher Truth, fades as respect for actual facts, real evidence and specific information intensifies.

Spiritual orientation objectifies. It separates from its matrix in the overall ego, becomes an independent, perhaps compartmentalized, factor. It redefines personal compliance with conventional morality on a more 'rational' basis, for better or worse. Or rationalizes self interest at the expense of ethical integrity.

A cerebral philosophy seeks validation through detached observation. Entertains alternative possibilities. Discovers general principles through a dialog of contrasting perceptions. It can splinter in too many directions or stretch out into superficiality. It can magnify differences, exacerbate division and promote splitting of wholes into fractions or factions. Good fortune nickeled and dimed away.

An opportunity to enjoy the blessings of intellectual growth. Expands through education, formal or informal. Optimism, confidence and trust in one's mental clarity and communication skills.

The social bond of language enabling shared experience. Growth of verbal ability, perhaps to the level of eloquence. Or a fall into excessive pedantry, hairsplitting, cheap mind games. A distracting proliferation of irrelevant opinions. A high ratio of noise to signal.

An open and enquiring mind. An enthusiasm for learning. Magnifies data acquisition and processing abilities. Information overload. Adds to the skill set. Can be a jack of all trades and master of none.

Salvation through synthesis; unites a babble of ideas into a coherent message. The miracle of abstraction, and symbolic representation, distills knowledge into wisdom. God, the Force, experienced in its mental aspect.

Jupiter in Cancer/fourth house

Exaltation. A quest for personal meaning, a deeper truth, reaches a critical emotional intensity.

Spiritual orientation subjectifies. Cultivates increased meaning from a fertile pool of feeling, mood and memory. Sensitivity to unconscious signals. Connects with instinctual roots. Absorbs subliminal impressions into conscious awareness. Expands through fantasy and dreams. Enhances imagination, the future's foundation.

An opportunity to enjoy the blessings of personal security encourages exploration of inner space. Magnifies the private sphere, or safe zone, permitting psychological growth. Domestic tranquility. Womb bliss. Intimate emotional engagement develops into a general capacity for empathy.

Optimism, confidence and trust in one's possibilities for happiness. The visceral joy of life animates rapport with others. The sheer jolliness of our warm-blooded nature at the core of all social interaction.

Sympathetic resonance with the commonalities that everyone shares. A sense of humor about the delightful silliness of the human condition.

A valuable inheritance, spiritual or material. Enthusiasm of belonging to a larger lineage. Appreciates the fruits of that legacy. Can be overly invested in the past. Salvation through enlarging family and tribal identification to a more inclusive level.

A nurturing philosophy. The miracle of subjective experience, one's unique psychic representation of the universe. God, the Force, experienced in its maternal aspect.

Jupiter in Leo/fifth house

Spiritual orientation radiates through a unique identity statement. One identifies with an archetypal icon, and seeks to represent it through a social role. Magnifies the ego as a personification of collective energies. Aspires to live up to an exalted code, an aristocratic standard of excellence. The power of pride to inspire nobility of character. The inflationary danger is obvious.

A commanding presence. Optimism, confidence and trust in one's creativity. An opportunity to enjoy the blessings that go with public recognition of personal talent. Good fortune well spent on a quality performance in the theater of life. Or squandered in arrogant elitism and privilege.

Recognizes its own potential as made in the image of God. Self expresses a larger soul. Or indulges a seductive megalomania. Salvation demands transcending a genuine sense of one's own splendor by giving all to a larger love.

Takes a dramatic stand, makes a defining choice, between moral courage and handsomely rewarded compliance with the powers that be. Plays for high stakes, whether out of expansive joie de vivre, lofty altruism or reckless enthusiasm. Growth through generosity. Magnanimity. Or extravagance. Exuberant passion. Or domineering pretention. A big heart. Or a loud mouth.

A philosophy of individual excellence. The miracle of leadership. Can be pompous, smug. God, the Force, experienced in its charismatic aspect.

Jupiter in Virgo/sixth house

Detriment. A quest for meaning, higher Truth, fades as respect for actual facts, real evidence and specific information intensifies.

Spiritual orientation purifies itself, perfects its own integrity, through practical service in an imperfect world. An opportunity to enjoy the blessings of increasing skill in one's chosen vocation. Optimism, confidence and trust in one's proficiency. Expands through hard work, efficiency gains, proper maintenance and constant upgrading.

Magnifies competence, perfection of execution in every endeavor. Outward drive sublimates into increasingly logical organization. Evolves by refining process. Rationalizes use of existing resources, gets far more from a lot less.

Enthusiasm for effective technique and correct method. Excessive emphasis on means can eclipse the end. It can magnify negativity, exaggerate flaws and thus promote a disease rather than its cure. Pearls thrown before swine; wisdom wasted on petty issues.

Salvation grows dutiful work into a labor of love. An enhancing philosophy utilizes imperfection as an occasion to improve the original. A therapeutic, corrective touch: fixes flaws, optimizes performance.

A discriminating ethic insists on principled choice in every decision. The miracle of integrity, the perfect composition of parts into a larger whole. Can inflate molehills into mountains. God, the Force, experienced in its healing aspect.

Jupiter in Libra/seventh house

Spiritual orientation adjusts to others. It defines self in participation more than through individual aspiration. A team player. An opportunity to enjoy the blessings of supportive association and the personal growth it entails. Optimism, confidence and trust in one's outreach to others. Increasing skill at group dynamics. Generally justified faith in the benevolence of partners. Expands through alliances, co-operation and incremental adjustments to the balance of power.

Magnifies diplomatic abilities. A spirit of give and take seeks convergence and complementarity of interests. Enhances equity and reciprocity. Or willing subordination to a larger power.

Evolution unfolds through the adaptation of self towards its environment rather than fulfillment of its own purposes. Identity revolves around social role instead of isolated attainment. Well adjusted to accepted norms, for better or worse. Gains community and self respect by exemplifying conventional morality.

Enthusiasm for right relationship through due process. Sees all sides of an issue and promotes a mutually beneficial wisdom. Salvation through win/win negotiation: an honest broker transcends stalemate to encourage new initiative. A judicious philosophy of fair play. Excessive compromise of principle for the sake of peace. Can be indecisive, overly solicitous of every opinion. Errs on the side of indulgence.

The miracle of justice. God, the Force, experienced in its aspect of harmony through conflict.

Jupiter in Scorpio/eighth house

Paradox: transcendent soul descends into the instinctual underworld. Divine aspiration fuses with demonic appetites. A blessed angel meets a fallen one deep within the conscience.

Spiritual wounding: encounter with an overwhelming truth that destroys the socially defined persona. It regenerates by assimilating this energy into a higher synthesis. Or regresses into an obsessive fixation. An inner Hell raised up and redeemed. Or its furies unleashed.

Amplifies subtle psychic signals. Unconscious drives intensified into compelling desires. Expands by expressing basic urges, often in conflict with conventional wisdom. Magnifies the agony and the ecstasy of authentic feelings, whether positive or negative.

Grows by elimination; strips off irrelevant niceties to deal with a core issue. A deep crisis challenges fundamental personal principles and religious or political norms. Evolves through transformative emotional experiences.

Optimism, confidence and trust in one's potency. An opportunity to exercise it. A defining choice over its purpose. The ethics of passion. Moral dilemmas of power.

Enthusiasm for life on the edge. Can rush in where angels fear to tread. Sublimates erotic libido into sacred sexuality. Or sensationalizes it as uninhibited lust:

'The road of excess leads to the palace of wisdom.'[1]

A philosophy of will. Or of nihilistic negation:

'Better to reign in Hell than serve in Heaven.'[2]

Salvation by faith in death, literal or figurative, as the way to rebirth. The miracle of its deliverance. God's passion on the cross of incarnation.[3]

1. 'The Marriage of Heaven and Hell,' William Blake
2. 'Paradise Lost,' John Milton, 1608-1674, English poet
3. 'Jesus Christ ... was crucified, died and was buried;
   He descended into hell.
   The third day he rose again from the dead;
   He ascended into heaven, ...'

From the 'Apostles' Creed,' a fundamental statement of Christian belief, used by both Catholics and Protestants. Its central premise of the Resurrection.

Jupiter in Sagittarius/ninth house

Rulership. A quest for meaning, higher Truth, assumes an unusual degree of importance in the personality. Religious, philosophical or political aspiration emphasized in relation to other aspects of psyche. Spiritual orientation socializes to express group norms and aspirations. It promotes and generally brings out the best in conventional wisdom. Enhances one's status as their exemplar.

Optimism, confidence and trust in one's faith, sacred or secular. A singular ethical imperative. At its best, the greatest commandment:

And you shall love the Lord your God with all your soul, and with all your mind, and with all your strength: that is the first commandment. The second is this, you shall love your neighbor as yourself. There is no other commandment greater than these.[1]

and the Golden Rule:

Do unto others as you would have them do unto you. That is the whole of the Law. All else is commentary.[2]

The margin of benevolence favoring purpose over chaos. A sense of life's meaningfulness. Grows self-confidence, which creates its own luck. Can puff up into giddy overconfidence. Magnifies opportunity in general. The thrill of expansion. Wild, free, blissful exuberance. Unexpected fortune, unearned promotion, encourages one to live up to a higher standard. Or exaggerates self-esteem.

Blessed with prophetic insight. Or an ability to ride the wave of public opinion, and manipulate it for better or worse. Salvation through a direct experience of enlightenment. Enthusiasm of revelation and its dissemination to the ignorant. The obvious danger of inflation.

The miracle of consensus: unity of belief, shared consciousness, esprit de corps making teamwork possible. Can lead to groupthink, conformist fanaticism. God, the Force, experienced as freedom guided by moral principle.

1. Mark 12: 30,31
2. Hillel the Elder, one of the most important religious leaders of Jewish history, ca 110 BC-10 AD

Jupiter in Capricorn/tenth house

Fall. A quest for meaning, higher Truth, must adapt to an uncongenial medium of practical necessity. Beautiful theories meet ugly facts. Spiritual orientation becomes a pragmatic purpose, directed to mobilize collective energies.

An opportunity to enjoy the blessings of hard earned respect in one's chosen vocation. Optimism, confidence and trust in one's executive abilities. Expands through hard work, unrelenting focus on the goal. Earns promotion, which may be denied so that one may serve a larger destiny.

Magnifies a consuming aspiration to excellence, or self-aggrandizement. Growth under adverse conditions tests character, generating an austere code of honor or cynical cunning. An inexorable determination to expand despite any obstacle. Inherent ability asserts itself against the odds, by fair means or foul. Evolution tenaciously overcomes resistance. Capitalizes on every opportunity, however limited. Mastery through effort rather than luck. Excessive regimentation. Can be narrow and materialistic.

Enthusiasm of achievement. Or growth through disappointment of false hopes and unworthy aims. Salvation through hard duty well done. High or heavy responsibility.

A conservative philosophy. Disciplined application of fundamental principles, whether in service to ego or a larger cause. The miracle of authority. Personality subordinated to impersonal law. Or blind ambition. God, the Force, experienced as a fateful calling.

Jupiter in Aquarius/eleventh house

Spiritual orientation abstracts: discovers universal principles that transcend accepted doctrines, whether scientific, religious or political. An opportunity to enjoy the blessings of revelatory insight. A possible jump to a new level of consciousness. Optimism, confidence and trust in one's intuition.

Expands by thinking outside the box. And capitalizing on the unexpected. Articulates the next step. Grows through originality. Exhilarating inspiration. Speculative theory can proliferate into an overgrown thicket of inflated ideas.

Promotes change, whether appropriate or anarchic. Overestimates its benefit. Growing mental autonomy explores unconventional alternatives. Evolves by sublimating essential qualities from circumstantial limitations. A prophet, not of known principles (Sagittarius), but of emerging potentials.

Magnifies hope, and thus brings it to pass. Impartial appreciation of various paths to enlightenment. Expanding recognition of truth's diversity and the many forms of joy. A revolutionary spirit brings a breath of fresh air. Or a storm of discontent.

Enthusiasm for the new and unusual. Elevated or excessive idealism. Can break down into eccentricity. Salvation through social expression of a reimagined future. A utopian philosophy seeking to establish a vision, of whatever merit.

The miracle of genius. Can be dissociated from reality. God, the Force, experienced through a revelatory shock of inspiration.

Jupiter in Pisces/twelfth house

Rulership. A quest for meaning, higher Truth, assumes an unusual degree of importance in the general personality. Compassionate altruism emphasized in relation to other aspects of the psyche.

A preexisting spiritual orientation dissolves. An opportunity to enjoy the blessings of divine love through ego loss. Accepts the meaningfulness of inevitable disappointment. Expands through the defeat of one's illusions, wishful thinking, unwarranted or unworthy hopes.

Optimism, confidence and trust in the essential benevolence of life and of humanity. Magnifies empathy. Encourages the outcast and rejected, who may embody necessary but neglected or denigrated qualities. Growth through renunciation. The freedom from ties and possessions making one totally available to every situation. Self-abnegation gives access to all other selves, and to a greater Self.

A sensitivity to the intangible Bliss animating existence. Redemptive vision. Or inflated delusion. A spirit of faith, hope and charity. Enthusiastic communion: selfless sympathy, inclusive rapport. Excessive indulgence of weakness can enable codependence. And even promote degeneracy.

Salvation through suffering. A sacrificial philosophy, acknowledging that giving is better than getting, the old must dissolve for the new to emerge, true victory often requires apparent defeat, death is the precursor to rebirth. The miracle of letting go. God, the Force, experienced as ecstatic surrender to a higher will.

Saturn

Saturn is the farthest of the seven visible planets. These constellate the conscious identity of the solar system, and of a human, its miniature analog. Cold yellow Saturn, like a dim afterimage of Sun, delineates the frontier of reality as we know it. It embodies the junction between individual identity and its unconscious sources. Thus it defines a point of maximum tension between known ego and its instinctual wellsprings.

Saturn's ringed perimeter, like a defensive wall, encloses a planet only ⅓ the mass of its inner neighbor, rainbow banded Jupiter. Beyond Saturn orbit two smaller globes, only ⅙ its size: tipped over Uranus, a window into the unconscious, and invisible Neptune, a symbol of the dream world. Saturn marks the last stand of organization, the fading edge of life and consciousness.

However, things can also be seen the other way around. Moving in from interstellar space, past a timeless realm of numinous ideals (Neptune) and archetypal ideas (Uranus), Saturn's ring acts as a lens, focusing imagination (Neptune) and intuition (Uranus) into conscious thought. It opens a gate channeling formless/abstract energies into tangible manifestation in time and space.

Saturn articulates the central organizing principles of form: laws of matter and energy, structures of life and psyche. It outlines a skeleton of basic processes underlying phenomenal events. Jupiter then fleshes them out with an expansive sense of meaning. Think of the Constitution: a general conceptual framework informs libraries of law, a few paragraphs of procedure guide volumes of specific statutes.

At Saturn the outer planets' fertile potential precipitate into defined patterns. Uranian inspiration, Neptunian dreams, Plutonian passion all freeze out into cold hard facts. Here too the inner planets' personal drives run up against the Reality Principle. All created things must move within their inherent limits and those of the system at large.

Saturn locates where a personal soul (Jupiter) distilled out of psychological factors (inner planets) reaches its zenith and thus its limit. It designates a moment of truth where imaginative creativity and immanent existence merge into a final statement of identity, fully revealed in the clear light of eternity. Thus Saturn is the place of Judgment.

Judgment under Law. Law has no meaning unless it involves penalties. These are the defined limits of existence. Every entity starts and stops in time. It follows a set developmental sequence. It deploys a specific energy, arranged in a unique signature of qualities. These may be purely physical, such as gravity and light. On a higher level they also include biological, psychological and spiritual characteristics. They operate within a specific range of possibilities and interact according to an inherent logic. Saturn posits the fundamental axioms of existence. The rules of the game. The universe's coherence depends on their orderly operation.

Every defined entity has its measure: mass, energy, duration. Its fullness of being also constitutes a restriction, its wholeness a confinement, its integrity a boundary. Saturn embodies the glory of actual fulfillment - and the melancholy that consummation also means termination.

Saturn portrays the finiteness of existence, the extent and ultimate limitations of any being. Every individual thing is formed by a set of characteristics distinguishing it from others. These characteristics are common unto all: raw resources, basic properties of our universe such as mass and energy on the physical plane; the universal DNA code and its associated amino acid building blocks on the biological. However, they can be combined in an infinite number of ways. Saturn symbolizes the rules structuring them into particular forms.

Saturn defines the mathematical laws behind physical phenomena. It embodies the organizing field grounding abstract forces into solid facts. It outlines the structural principles of material existence: electronic equations of chemical interaction, sequential order of biological evolution, stages of emotional/mental unfolding, and hierarchical levels of spiritual attainment. It generates a psychological skeleton, anchoring mind, love and will into the architecture of personality.

Saturn demonstrates the principle of cyclic unfolding, a developmental pattern inherent in time. The butterfly, and the housefly, must pass through egg, larval and cocoon stages of maturation. The human must morph from embryo to infant, toddler to child, adolescent to adult in order to fully manifest. Any dynamic process must move through initial impulse (Aries), concrete embodiment (Taurus), environmental interaction (Gemini). It must conserve (Cancer), express (Leo) and perfect (Virgo) its identity. It must balance with other energies (Libra) and be challenged/changed by them (Scorpio). This always occurs in a larger context of its meaning (Sagittarius), destiny (Capricorn), ideal future (Aquarius) and eventual dissolution (Pisces).

The signs of astrology express fundamental processes of time's flow. They are an astronomical expression of time's archetypal nature. Saturn expresses the idea of time itself, and its deterministic directionality: from past to future, cause to effect. What happens during these stages is open to novelty, mutation, evolution. But that there are stages, in a lawful order, expresses the Saturnine principle.

Saturn portrays the pattern making force evoking a universe out of potential energy. It defines the physical formulae of matter and energy, the biological processes of life, the intellectual logic of mind, the hard spiritual tests of an evolving soul. Psychologically it describes the basic operating procedures by which a small and mortal ego organizes itself to meet the challenges of a short life in a big world.

One enters the world with a wail. Birth = expulsion from oceanic womb-bliss. After the hard labor of 'our longest and most dangerous journey, four inches down the birth canal'[1] one falls into a separate existence. One's first individual act is to breathe in the thin air of aloneness. Thus one accepts incarnation as a fractal of the universe, an exemplar of its state at that moment. One takes up a destiny to embody and express the world's meaning condensed into a moment of time.

One's inherent character is itself a fate. It must also meet and make its fate in a preexisting environment of material scarcity, ego competition and social demands. Just as the Sun of self ignites into life so too it lights up the alien reality in which it must live. Saturn defines our sense of this anti-self, a challenging world that replaces a nurturing womb.

Saturn's world bearing burden does not fall on the ego alone. In fact the ego, astrologically mapped by the ascendant and its first house, comprises only a small fraction of the psyche. The global weight portrayed by Saturn pertains to the whole Self.[2] One takes it on as an instinctual acceptance of the human condition: the limitations inherent in our biology, and implied by its differentiation into psychological categories of gender, culture and temperament (such as those of astrological signs).

Saturn points to where conscious control breaks down and the larger, unassimilated part of life shows up. Here the lawful order, or tyranny, of ego fails and the danger/opportunity of non-ego emerges. Saturn describes the twilight zone between the visible surface and hidden depths of psyche. It locates the fracture dividing ego and unconscious; the terminus or line of discontinuity between our light and dark sides. It is personified by the Shadow, the anti-Self to solar identity.

The Shadow constellates a dull negative of personality: the dismal swamp of one's inferior side. It embodies half-baked consciousness, partially digested experience, primitive energies rising over the threshold of awareness. These raw contents demand attention, but are not yet assimilated into personality. Think of one's emerging sexuality in early adolescence: oozing pimples, social awkwardness, unfamiliar emotions expressed in the most inappropriate way. It also portrays the decay of unclaimed potential: the bitterness of unrealized dreams, the shame of not even having tried, the atrophy of talents never exercised. The psychic reek of their rotting and the clouds of negative attributes they breed, like puffy maggots hardening into buzzing flies. Saturn sums them all up into a sense of self-loathing, felt inwardly as depression, projected outwardly as mean-spirited malice.

Saturn emphasizes one's most embarrassing weakness, the thing you most fear to face. It painfully feels your worst wound. One is forced to heal, or brought to heel, by Saturn's presentation of a fundamental flaw.

Here one confidently speaks folly, ignorant words wafting on bad breath to a revolted listener. The poor response seems to prove how unfair life is. Saturn hides the Shadow in the shadows, blocks acknowledgment of its mortifying presence. It evokes self-pity as a defense against owning one's own pathos and its failures. This victim consciousness usually stems from (appropriately) punctured self-esteem. Yet it also demands a change of heart, the most difficult challenge of all: 'there will be more rejoicing in heaven over one sinner who repents than over ninety-nine righteous persons who do not need to repent.'[3]

In its corrective aspect Saturn functions as the superego, an impersonal ethical code that disciplines and sublimates selfish instincts. It provides a moral compass guiding psychological development and behavioral decisions. The superego crystallizes the highest ideals of Neptune and archetypal models of Uranus into images of perfection. It insists that personal ego live up to them. As such it acts as an opposite pole to the Shadow of inferiority and fear discussed below.

The inhumanly demanding superego makes one human because it drives the given nature to a higher state of being. However, if it gains too much strength it crushes all spontaneous vitality under suffocating guilt. Then a straitjacket of religious or social injunctions blocks evolution in the service of calcified tradition. If the superego does not acquire sufficient authority one becomes an automaton of momentary impulse, devoid of conscience or responsibility.

The superego generally acts as a set of internalized parental and social rules: 'thou shalt not steal,' etc. As such it promotes a consensus making community life possible. It can also enable collective crime as everyone conforms to its divinely sanctioned urge to stamp out chosen scapegoats. Saturn's superego expression ultimately demands a personal commitment to consciously chosen norms. It defines an internal responsibility to know one's own truth. And an external duty to abide by it despite the world's resistance.

This leads to an appalling existential loneliness. One has graduated from the security of groupthink, but not yet achieved a more inclusive enlightenment. Saturn's desert of despair encircles the oasis of our comfort zone. It tests, and breaks, all who seek to cross it. Only by devitalizing ego defenses can the whole Self, or soul, begin to emerge in its own right. Saturn's repellant harshness also deters, and thus protects, those who are not yet ready to handle this level of spiritual voltage.

Saturn structures a known self from the dynamic swirl of deep unconscious currents. It articulates the ordering principles of a unique character out of collective instincts. It regiments other planetary subpersonalities into a coherent unity. The cost of such a singular identity is the separation of its integrity from a fuzzy wholeness. Saturn's alienation generates a distinct personality, differentiated from its environment. And tasks it with an endless struggle to maintain itself against a larger context. Yet, as we know from the second law of thermodynamics, all things eventually wind down, peter out and are reabsorbed into their milieu. Saturn marks the temporary, and therefore infinitely precious, emergence of the individual from the All.

Saturn demonstrates the contracting principle. It narrows the focus, condensing volatile possibility into fixed facts. Fluid imagination shaped by hard necessity. Passionate instincts channeled by survival imperatives. Magical wishes denied by an implacable regime of cause and effect. Saturn is the great NO.

As such it is the most difficult and painful planet. It embodies bitter limitation. To be this you cannot be that. Here is the world's rock solid resistance to dreams. You can only make them come true with objective ability and unrelenting effort. Yet these unyielding demands force and form true character. Their brutal authenticity generates a new standard of value: actual achievement outranking indulgent fantasy.

Such merit must be earned by demonstrated competence. The discipline of effort, rigor of logic, precision of numerical exactitude evokes a miraculous self-organization from nebulous background noise. Only impeccable concentration can make a world from a wish. Saturn generates the strenuous force field that centers latent energy into actual manifestation. It condenses vacuous potential into visible potency.

Saturn organizes the energy blown out of Heaven in the Big Bang. It generates a universe out of nothing and establishes a rock bottom foundation of reality in the Void. Such effort takes its toll in a terrible sentence of finitude. For any individual thing to be it must exclude infinite possibilities of being other than it is. It takes energy to maintain such suppression. Eventually the energy runs down. One can hold back the disintegrative forces of the universe only so long.

Saturn offers existence and demands extinction. It concentrates but limits self that it may stand, for a short time, in contrast to its environment. Then, consumed by the internal decay of time, all selves crumble into dead dust. Saturn guarantees an end to being, and thus embodies one's deepest Fear.

Saturn = Satan. This planet is not a literal Satanic presence in the sky. Rather it symbolizes the accuser who spot darkens one's weak point. The pride that shrinks immortal soul into an ego fetish. The father of lies who misidentifies conscious personality with the whole Self. And then freezes it with fear, especially of its own liberation in death.

Saturn evokes one's inner demon, a personal counterpart to God's great Adversary. Generally this manifests as an imp of the perverse, a monkey on one's back, an inferior side of self. It frustrates conscious aims because they do not acknowledge its unmet needs and unrequited pain. It constellates a valid self-loathing based on the truth that ego fears to include its reality.

Yet this fiendish presence serves a purpose. It acts as a negative pole attracting the dysfunctional, twisted, unrealized forces of the Self. It organizes them around an inner black hole, the vortex to new dimensions of the collective unconscious. This dark passageway leads to the underworld, the secret core of Self. It is guarded by the wrathful deities of one's own ignorance, inadequacy and fear. If one proves worthy to overcome and assimilate them one gains the hidden treasure: the missing part of Self. Otherwise these ferocious illusions protect one from an inner truth as yet too hot to handle.

To liberate a fear releases its bound up energy. It also frees up access to the unconscious' redemptive wellsprings. This means far more than any growth of a current safe reality because it opens up entirely new dimensions of life.

Superego and Satanic Shadow - two poles of one axis, the spinal cord of psyche. It stretches from a peak of perfect norms to the very gates of Hell. One must pass through them to release those damned and dammed up forces that make one whole. Even Christ did not ascend to Heaven after His crucifixion. He first descended into Hell. Only thus could He redeem the world. Only then could He transfigure into God.

The evil associated with Saturn, and it is real, comes from its necessary function of contraction. Condensation gives vacuum energy solidity and weight. Density creates opacity, a shadow effect. The inherent nature of Saturn is to define and materialize Sun's Purpose. The shadow it casts constitutes the negation or adversary that clarifies solar principle through contrast. Their struggle may involve an inner wrestling with one's own dark side or a battle with its objective manifestation out in the environment. This confrontation always ends tragically because it invokes a fatal flaw, which must be lived out, drunk to the dregs.

Any distinct entity casts a shadow. Every planet carries a night side, shaded by its very corporeality from the Sun's light. One hemisphere plunges into dark and cold, turns away from the bright central fire and faces icy emptiness. It is chilled by the touch of nothingness, experiences insignificance before the Abyss.

In the same way the human body, temple of the soul, has a dark place where the Sun never shines. Every person, the most beautiful woman, the wisest scholar, passes stinking shit. At the core of one's being, in one's very bowels, lies something alien and toxic. It must be rejected. Or it will kill you. Every day each of us performs a private biological act wreathed in stench and shame. Perhaps on one's last day a soul will perceive its corpse as a turd.

Saturn forces one to acknowledge and adapt to a foulness inherent in life's emergence from matter. Perhaps this stems from life's Original Sin: the need for every living thing to feed off the death of others. (Even plants compete for access to light and require dead organic matter in the soil.) Part of what we physically eat, or psychologically experience, cannot be assimilated. Within ourselves, and in the world around us, lurks an unrecognizable Other. It must be excluded or eliminated.

To experience Saturn fully means to take on the darkness of the world and to acknowledge its power. Christ did so in his penultimate moment: 'My God, why hast Thou forsaken me?'[4] His mortal personality had to actually accept annihilation. Only by really doing death could Christ transcend it. His final words were utterly Saturnine: 'It is done.'[5] Not in theory. In real physical death.

Each person must encounter the ultimate horror: that the personal self really ends. Forever. The greater one's consciousness of this ending the more poignant its pain. The higher the achievement the harder the fall. After all the effort of mastering the world one must accept that it will be snatched away. Death is necessary. One's level of awareness and acceptance are optional.

Saturn means the final fact: that the end is the end. That when one dies s/he is really gone, never to return. Perhaps after death some spiritual essence or intangible soul survives. But personality, the unique psychological ego, is snuffed out forever. Thus every moment and every act are sacred, precisely because they are so ephemeral. What a heavy responsibility to realize that everything one does should be impeccable, because that opportunity will never recur. And the number of opportunities diminishes minute by minute, until an end is come.

Saturn also generates a protective numbness to buffer such intensity. Humans are slow maturing mammals that need time to develop. Saturn shields a fragile ego with comforting lies until it can face the truth. It armors a delicate social persona with denial until one can take responsibility. It dims a light too bright to bear until one is ready to see. Saturn blocks and restrains until one learns to overcome its bonds, and thus earns the strength to go beyond its fear.

Saturn's sign/house position points out what one defends against. How one does so. But permanent defense means ultimate defeat. A mature Saturn embraces the moment, knowing that its incompetence is forgiven by the moment's passing. Accepting the process slowly deepens appreciation of one's fleeting existence. It generates the wisdom of experience, for which there is no substitute.

Saturn feels the urgency of time. This generates the ambition to be all that one can be. The ability to capitalize on vanishing opportunity. Its achievement may be imperfect and incomplete. But it is real, forged out of insubstantial hope by persistence, discipline and skill.

Saturn binds time's flow into a specific narrative. It consolidates evanescent instants of experience into evolutionary increments to identity. Saturn's organizing principles structure emerging events into an architecture of personality. This implies a rational relationship between cause and effect, choice and consequence, decision and destiny. It establishes a step by step process leading to a logical sequence of development. Thus Saturn embodies the conservative nature of fundamental law. Saturn requires personal conformity to universal criteria. It demands respect for excellence, resonance with the highest standards. This takes one to the mountaintop, summit of attainment, exaltation of a peak experience.

Despite all the sorrows inherent in its nature Saturn also embodies profound joy: of hard duty done, aspiration achieved, victory against the odds. A somber ecstasy, far deeper and more moving than the gigglefun frivolity often mistaken for happiness.

Even the loftiest summit eventually erodes away. Each and all are leveled by death. Saturn marks the stone wall of certainty that, whatever a soul, afterlife or reincarnation might be, if they exist at all, one's present ego-consciousness will end forever. Easy to say, hard to imagine, devastating to accept. Yet that icy baptism of despair is the price that must be paid in full, willingly or not. Christ had to. Why then should any of us be spared?

But of course each of us shrinks from the absolute zero of that realization. To the degree one does so, consciousness is clouded and benumbed. It falls into a swoon, a spiritual coma, and reawakens at a lower, denser, less threatening level. This is the process of involution.

It occurs in life as a cheapening of experience. We kill time because we cannot endure its naked intensity. One escapes through depression, compulsive toil, meaningless ceremony, rote discipline, safe and rigid rules. This may also occur after life in what Buddhists describe as the Bardo experience: a falling away from an unendurable All into lower and denser levels of selfhood until one reaches equilibrium. Then rebirth, to patiently construct another personal ego in a different physical embodiment.

This shrinking process is what we call fear. It is Saturn's last and greatest test. One will take it, voluntarily or not, over and over and over again until fear is surmounted. Saturn administers an implacable reality check squeezing out all withholding, phoniness, evasion, falsehood: however much it hurts, however long it takes. There is no social promotion here. Only the cold hard truth.

In Saturn one encounters the self-limiting force that impels a split-off from God to become a miniature ego-god. And which drives one on the long hard road back to God enriched by experience. Only through acknowledgment of inadequacy, shame at failure, mortification of weakness, does one begin to crawl out of ego's smug and suffocating smallness. No one escapes the delusions of self-satisfaction on their own. It is forced by guilt over ignorance, humiliation of incompetence, loss of face before others and despair within at the repetitive robotic rituals of a defensive personality.

Saturn shows why, how and where you taste life's disappointment. Failure. The sense of impotence based on that. It can lead to corrective disciple. Or crippling shame.

'Into every life some rain must fall.'[6] Saturn's melancholy inevitably follows Jupiter's exuberance. Here is post coital sadness after the ecstasy of love, hangover after the party, letdown after victory's high. All things grow old, tired, stale. Saturn portrays the bleak grey depression of life. The bitterness of its humiliations, boredom of its grind, cynicism of its pettiness, desolation of its losses, frustration of its limitations, fear of its brevity. Why? Why must this horrid suffocating energy exist at all?

Because it forces us beyond the inherent smallness of all our hopes, ambitions, joys. Self centered consciousness, and life itself, must wither away before the mysteries of spirit and death, infinity and eternity. Saturn pays the price of our precious ego-construct, so tiny and temporal in the greater scheme of things. It grants liberation from all finite and created things by demonstrating their cold, dark side, the ashes of their ephemeral fire and light.

Saturn exposes one's painful dysfunction. It must someday, after all your days, be accounted for. God may judge, but Satan serves as a most competent prosecutor. His challenges put you through your paces to see where you stand in the spiritual order. Saturn defines your achievement. And your guilt. What you're guilty of, how you feel it and where you do penance.

Saturn emphasizes your Achilles heel. Vulnerability. It shows what you lack and will never have, but must always strive for. That awful moment of getting how you went wrong and why there is no excuse. The desperately desired aspect of life you must give up.

Why? Perhaps it has reached a culmination and blocks further growth. Or its satisfaction drains too much energy from an emergent function. Or simply because it has become old. Whatever the reason, where there is Saturn there is sacrifice. Voluntary or forced, consciously accepted or unconsciously endured.

Mars inflicts the sharp pain of defeat, and the hostile smirk of its agent. Saturn describes the reason for loss, and the emptiness of absence. Over time that emptiness invokes a new wisdom as old certainties, supports, and securities vanish. 'Salvation through suffering'[7] is Saturn's mantra. The salvation is an austere one of honor, duty, integrity. The suffering is real: endless work, illness, frustration teaching a hard lesson, 'drop by bitter drop.'[8]

Saturn always seems unduly severe, disproportionate and unfair: a lifetime of lost opportunity and heavy responsibility because of one sexual indiscretion, a career ended by the wrong joke or a tiny error seized on by jealous rivals, health ruined by a moment of inattention, love lost through a silly remark or moment of anger, decades of hard work taken by a swindle or a recession...

Pluto points to the impersonal soul purpose served by this anguish and deprivation. Saturn embodies their actual experience. And the attitude developed in the face of such adversity. In the long run, Saturn is just. In some ways it constitutes the very principle of justice. Not the affirmative, spiritually enhancing justice of Jupiter. A cold, clear justice from beyond the realm of egoic wish fulfillment. Saturn does not nurture or grow you. It tests you to see what you've got when the chips are down.

This justice does not conform to our sense of 'fairness' within the parameters of a given situation. Rather it uses overt incidents to address hidden issues. What may be a minor objective event brings up an important subconscious need, evokes a deeper lesson whose time has come. Saturn administers a reality check to one's whole Self, one's inner integrity, through the '...slings and arrows of outrageous fortune.'[9] Of course, one usually focuses on the obvious external injustice, diverting attention from the real issue.

Saturn's lessons take a long time to sink in because they involve unconscious contents. The unconscious has a timeless quality, which translates very slowly into the flow of conscious recognition. Saturn mediates between the realms of visible planets/conscious functions and outer planets/collective unconscious. Thus it enhances known experience with new dimensions of psychic depth. This comes at a price: destruction of the previous conscious attitude. Generally it occurs through a seemingly unjust happening (bad for the old outlook) that acts as a wedge for a more subtle awareness (good for the new level of insight).

One might object that this sugarcoats life's cruelty. What great lesson 'justifies' the wrong suffered by an innocent man imprisoned for decades, the young girl raped? There is no answer. 'God moves in mysterious ways.' Satan, His CEO, employs the darkest methods.

Saturn in a chart points to where and how one encounters these traumas. Denial of their deeper meaning constitutes the most common response. Insistence that their literal 'evil' is their only truth generates evil's greatest victory. Paradoxically the tough minded 'realist' often turns out to be Saturn's saddest victim.

'The only thing we have to fear is fear itself.'[10] Saturn points to where we shrink from the unbearable majesty of God, contract from a Joy we cannot sustain. Then we have only the memory of what might have been. The shame of not living up to it. And a dark determination, disguised as cynical wisdom, to make someone else take the blame, pay the price, bear the burden. For Saturn also tempts one to turn to the dark side: to project evils onto others, and to spite God because one falls short.

Saturn mocks self-confidence and mars self-respect. Doubt and pessimism, cynicism or even despair, sap the will, dull the mind, starve love. One retreats into a shell. The heart turns to stone in a winter of the soul.

Happiness bogged down by exhaustion, aches and pains. Inhibited vitality. Weariness shrivels away appetite, motive, or even caring. The squalor of a nose-picking world. A sense of futility as one fights the gravity of the entire planet with every step. Yet these are the dues demanded for the privilege of incarnation in the flesh.

Why must it be so? Every finite thing must make room for the next finite thing. Every cup holds only its appointed measure and no more (though often less). This withering sickness releases from the pressure of ambition, and desire. Liberates from small understandings and feeble powers. Acceptance lets limited experience shrink away, opening up a larger perspective. It relaxes a tight ego focus in preparation for release from selfhood.

The ebbing tide is as necessary as the flood. Even within the confines of one's short life Saturn's premonition of mortality focuses attention, sharpens senses, adds poignancy to feelings. Life is brief. Really knowing this gives each vanishing moment an ever-deeper profundity. Accepting a larger fate paradoxically enhances one's immediate experience. However limited the opportunities, inevitable the disappointments, small the accomplishments of a life, truly understanding that it contributes one note to a concert makes it magic. In its instant it becomes the whole symphony.

Saturn hears that note, well or poorly played, just as it sounds. It functions as a lucid awareness leading to impartial judgment. At the core of consciousness Saturn knows the score. It registers an exact calculus of physical, psychological, spiritual and social merits/demerits.

Saturn recognizes facts. From them it generates fate. Saturn symbolizes an impersonal intelligence orienting personal will: one's decision to participate in life as a distinct entity. Mars then executes that will in action.

Moon embodies the matrix of personality: a pool of memories, moods and motives blended into an unconscious temperament. Saturn's sharp chisel carves a face onto this inner Moon. It does so through the tests of time: the difficult work of personal development, the evolutionary outcome of that process.

Saturn defines the mark one makes on the world. A specific value added to, or taken from, history by one's endeavors. A clarified essence of identity, achievement and consequences. How one enhanced or besmeared the times. Saturn summarizes the bottom line of a life. Not its spiritual meaning (Jupiter), but its objective results. What you throw down at the end.

Saturn cuts each of us out of the herd to fulfill a unique destiny. It separates self from God so that one can be one. Psychologically Saturn charts the existential loneliness of each individual at the foundation of identity. It defines alienation as the positive impulse to selfhood, or a negative withdrawal from participation. Self-centering as either a focusing of potential or constriction of relationship. One's sense of time as the medium of evolution. Or of boredom, an inability to creatively mold and lovingly express its flow. 'Timing is the essence of victory.' Saturn defines fitness or weakness, the appropriateness or incompetence of one's response to circumstance.

Saturn demands decisive commitment to a specific identity. This implies the necessary rejection or renunciation of alternatives. Saturn portrays the principle of exclusion, rigor of logic, sharpness of definition. Its hard choices generate true merit. They shape clear mind from fuzzy dreams, actual achievement from vague aspiration.

The inevitability of consequence (karma) and inexorability of time develop seriousness in a life that is no joke. Saturn's meaning in the psyche is the absolute reality of here and now. Its brevity evokes sincerity. The fact of personal annihilation forces one to get real.

The loneliness of Saturn is based on the fact that each of us has a singular experience of the universe and serves a special function in it. To be a player one must be autonomous. But one must pay to play. The price is alienation and mortality. Saturn describes an aspect of psyche that registers the pain of separation and accepts the sacrifice required to be an individual.

By position and aspect Saturn defines the area of life most in need of discipline. Therefore subject to, and hopefully refined by, adversity. Saturn points out what is most lacking in a life - and the type of effort made to attain it.

Frustration generates ambition. A deficiency creates an asset: 'Necessity is the mother of invention.' Thus an oyster turns a painful grain of sand into a lustrous pearl.

It is uplifting to contemplate Saturn as: the principle of limitation minting individuality out of an undifferentiated All; the pressure of natural selection generating survival of the fittest and thus evolution through time; the Shadow holding one's hidden potential; the obstacle spurring ambition, achievement and self-surpassing. But:

Physical pain is real.

So is emotional depression.

And the anguish of a guilty conscience.

Saturn is the cross one must bear.

Moons

Through their own characteristics moons externalize, make visible and known, the deep past, global memory and karmic needs driving a planetary function.

Saturn has 48 known moons. Seven are large enough to gravitationally self-organize into spheres. The other 40+ irregular blobs symbolize whispers from the unconscious, wisps of instinct lacking the energy to achieve intelligible expression.

Saturn hosts the most unique and spectacular moon of all: its ring. This essentially two-dimensional disc encircles Saturn's three-dimensional globe. The ring maps Saturn's depth onto a clear symbol: a center within an enclosing wall. It acts as a skin separating, defining and protecting structured consciousness from the formless abyss of the unconscious. And as a lens focusing the infinite vacuum energy of space into a finite physical sphere; unrealized psychic potential into actual ego experience. It literally paints a bulls-eye in the sky, drawing one into the farthest visible gravity well from our central Sun. At the core of life Sun radiates boundless spirit. At its edge Saturn's ring binds that spirit into a boundary.

Saturn's halo ingathers solar radiance, condensing it into the reality of our most precious treasure. This is mythically portrayed as a hoard of gold and jewels guarded by a dragon; religiously described as Hell's harvest of lost souls enthralled by the Devil; psychologically understood as one's own heart of darkness shielded from awareness by the ring wraiths of our deepest fears.

On the outer rim of Saturn's outer ring a tiny moon beats like a (solar) heart. Enceladus, pumped by Saturn's tidal gravity, actually spritzes water geysers into space. There they freeze out into ice crystal accruing onto the ring's perimeter. Where there is water there may be life.[11] Even this small moon, literally at the edge of darkness, gives notice that Saturn symbolizes far more than the dreaded Grim Reaper, or 'Greater Malefic,' of traditional astrology. It is indeed that, but so much more as well.

Titan, Saturn's largest satellite, presents an even more explicit clue to its parent planet's nature. Titan is the only moon in our solar system with its own atmosphere. In fact, its nitrogenous, orange hued air is 1.6 times denser than Earth's. It seems to resemble Earth's primordial atmosphere of four billion years ago. Titan's surface consists of frozen hydrocarbons, the precursors of life. They may even insulate a liquid water ocean below. (Hydrocarbons, i.e. oils, float on water and hold in heat.) The unique organic-chemical constitution of Titan, a moon far more complex than our own, hints at the singular nature of Saturn: an anti-Sun at the edge of cosmic darkness attended by the cold shadow of an embryonic Earth.

Notes

1. The author was unable to find the attribution for this marvelous quote.
2. According to the great psychologist Carl Jung (1875-1961) the whole Self includes the small lit up area of ego consciousness along with the personal unconscious, collective unconscious, biologically based instinctual nature and a spiritual attunement to the Superconscious.
3. Luke 15:7 and Luke 15:10
4. Matthew 26:47
5. John 19:30
6. Henry Wadsworth Longfellow, poet, 1807-1882
7. Hebrews 2:10
8. 'Agamemnon,' Aeschylus, Athenian playwright, 525-456 BC
9. Shakespeare, Hamlet
10. FDR, first Inaugural Address, 1933
11. Future space probes may fly through these geysers to collect samples for biochemical analysis.

Saturn in Signs and Houses

Saturn in a sign indicates the objective nature of one's weakness.

Saturn in a house indicates an individual's subjective experience/ expression of limitation.

Saturn in fire signs implies fear of flying. Lacks trust in possibility and even in one's basic self. Inhibited will, bottled up enthusiasm, a zipped mouth. Its challenge is to patiently develop confidence and self-respect. Because it feels and abhors cowardice it can generate supreme courage.

Saturn in air signs implies fear of threatening ideas. Lacks trust in its own perceptions and even in one's basic intelligence. Rote learning, a closed mind, conventional thinking, tongue-tied. Its challenge is to patiently develop reasoning and communication skills. Because it feels and abhors ignorance it can generate supreme insight.

Saturn in water signs implies fear of feeling. Lacks trust in its own sensitivity and even in one's ability to love. Inhibited responsiveness. Constricted, even constipated, emotion. A cold fish. Its challenge is to open up, patiently learn to identify with others. Because it feels and abhors loneliness it can generate supreme empathy.

Saturn in earth signs implies fear of failure. Lacks trust in its ability to perform. Cautious to the point of paralysis. Refuses to step outside a narrow comfort zone and do anything new. A stick in the mud.

Its challenge is to develop a special competence. Because it feels and abhors incompetence it can generate supreme achievement in its field.

Saturn in Aries/first house

Fall: An inner darkness emerges over the threshold of awareness. One must face its Fear.* Everything else in this description is a footnote.

Ambition, in compensation for felt inadequacy, struggles to assert itself in a debilitating atmosphere of subjective embarrassment, covert shame and explicit social hostility. The circumstances of fate make, or break, character through defining experiences of deprivation, rejection and injustice. The demands of destiny individualize as a sense of lonely responsibility.

A hard lesson in personal limits. The self-discipline necessary to regiment character: reform its mortifying weakness, control natural impulse and deliberately embrace hard duty. Pessimism, doubt and skepticism about self and its presentation to the world.

Ego isolated from natural vitality, animal energy, spontaneous enthusiasm. An outworn but entrenched ego-construct restricts an emerging one. A sophisticated but obsolete world view limits naive new potential. Only by overcoming that inertia can emergent qualities learn to organize and hold their own in an unsympathetic world.

Self defined by confrontation with its nemesis. Identity deepened or defeated by adversity. A heavy burden develops determination. Or crushes spirit. Grace under pressure. Or surrender to depression.

A Shadow of justified guilt. Self-loathing. Consciousness numbed by a sense of inferiority, incompetence and impotence. Natural assertion inhibited by lack of confidence. Only the call of duty can breach the tightening circle of one's own pathos. One is challenged to fight for larger principles beyond self-interest. Only deliberate acts of courage in a greater cause can melt the ice of personal despair.

One will never see the spring flowers irrigated by release of its fresh waters. Nor does it matter. Liberation from selfishness, moral cowardice burned away, is the highest, and most difficult to attain, purpose.

* 'I must not fear. Fear is the mind-killer. Fear is the little death that brings total obliteration. I will face my fear. I will permit it to pass over me and through me. I will turn the inner eye to see its path. Where it has gone there will be nothing. Only I will remain.'

'Litany Against Fear' from 'Dune,' Frank Herbert, 1920-1986, American writer.

Saturn in Taurus/second house

A sense of destiny consolidates into fixed ambition. Or an oppressive craving. The circumstances of fate stabilize in an identity defined by its hunger for tangible possession, whether of objects or others, resources or power. Can become mired in materialism; chained to appetites or precious things.

A hard lesson in the limits of what one can and cannot have. The discipline to live within one's means, psychologically as well as financially. Pessimism, doubt and skepticism about self-worth.

Wretched envy blights all beauty. One cannot profit from others' talents or adequately deploy one's own. Lacks appreciation for what one already has, which is taken away. Material loss. Forced liberation from stingy clinging.

The discipline imposed by scarcity. Learns to derive enhanced value from a modest endowment. Patient accumulation, laborious persistence, unflagging effort, all of which come to be appreciated in their own right. Grinding toil produces small increments in quality of life, whether financial, social or spiritual. Over time these add up like the annual rings of a tree trunk supporting the skyward stretch of its sun kissed leaves and fruit.

Slow growth of genuine autonomy earned by one's own hard work. A hardy self made character. Actual experience develops into objective judgment of worth, an exact evaluation of merit.

Ego isolated from natural sensuality. Alienation from body. Visceral sloth and heaviness inhibits enjoyment of pleasure. Fear strangles desire.

A Shadow of impoverishment and thwarted needs. Basic wants delayed and denied. Identity is marred by compensatory greed. A challenge to outgrow jealousy over what one does not and cannot have; to reject false, outworn values that degrade one's true nature. A duty to cultivate more realistic standards of worth and productively express them.

Saturn in Gemini/third house

A sense of destiny objectifies: one responds to immediate demands rather than an innate agenda. The circumstances of fate are met opportunistically. Emphasizes tactical skill rather than strategic ambition. Sharply focused perception of facts can lack purpose, meaning or sense of consequence. Pragmatic problem solving without a central organizing principle.

Clear cerebral detachment. Or reason alienated from identity. Cold amoral curiosity. Remorseless logic based on limited data and selfish principles.

A hard lesson in the limits of one's intelligence. The discipline to acknowledge what one does not and cannot know. Pessimism, doubt and skepticism about one's mental quality and verbal ability.

Ego isolated from its environment. Divorced from real communication by arid intellectualism, artificial distinctions, contrived divisions/diversions. Constrictive mental labyrinths limit free thought. Ossified scholastic doctrines block experimentation. Narrow, or twisted, logic damns the flow of new ideas.

Difficult decision between incompatible truths. A need to choose: to take this and forgo that. This forces intellectual discipline, an insistence on due process, airing of alternatives. It can balance Gemini's superficiality with concentration and depth. Or default into rigid formula; a formalistic, pedantic outlook.

A Shadow of theoretical abstraction, empty verbosity, distracting mind games. Fear of commitment. Lack of honesty. Insincere role-playing. Crude manipulation. Can project its own inner darkness onto others.

Inhibited ability to prioritize. A challenge to develop unifying principles in a wasteland of data, rational rules organizing the chatter of information. A duty to articulate a hierarchy of meaning from dry facts, to find a criteria of relevance.

Saturn in Cancer/fourth house

Detriment. An impressionable sensitivity internalizes the world's darkness. Ambition surrenders to depression as guilty memories harden into paralyzing sorrow. Regrets what was, and might have been. Objective judgment melts into despondent gloom. Melancholia can deepen psyche. Or sink it into despair.

A sense of destiny subjectifies as one turns within to remake identity. Retreats from the circumstances of fate into a private pool of sensibility, feeling and mood, bitter or profound as the case may be.

A hard lesson in the limits of personal security. Demands emotional discipline in a cold uncaring world. Pessimism, doubt and skepticism about one's vulnerability. A sense of foreboding.

Unconscious fear stemming from past trauma. A duty to face and melt frozen psychological blockages. Ego isolated from its unconscious roots. Imagination and dreams are self-censored by a robotic superego. Harsh judgmentalism, authoritarian strictures of proper deportment, crush natural spontaneity.

A Shadow of emotional hunger. Arrested infantile issues. Separation anxiety. Suppressed responsiveness. Sullen hopelessness. Rejected inner feelings, and feelings of rejection.

This withering emotional drought devitalizes ego defenses, allowing a cautious opening to refreshing instinct. Inhibited engagement with the outside world as it reconstitutes within. Personality flows into a new sense of identity behind a protective shell. Think of a cocoon that shields a larva as it literally liquefies - to emerge as a butterfly.

A challenge to re-interpret disappointment as a developmental phase liberating one from false fantasies. A subjective meltdown of outworn feelings dissolves their bound up energy, making it available for a more mature sensibility. Loss of an inappropriately supportive crutch forces compensating growth of inner depth.

Saturn in Leo/fifth house

Detriment. A warm heart faces the cold reality of existential loneliness. Aching loneliness demands attention.

Senses destiny as the weight of an ordained role. Morose power wears a crown of lead. The circumstances of fate redirect spontaneous vitality into heavy-handed ambition. The call of duty narrows into compulsive self-assertion.

Ego isolated from playfulness, joie de vivre. Inhibited emotion. Lack of love. Denial of true passion. Estrangement; natural feelings freeze into a contrived act. Suppressed joy twists into the empty mimicry of pompous dignity.

A moment of glory swiftly passes. Pride takes a fall. A hard lesson in humility, the limits of one's talents. Pessimism about one's mediocrity; overcompensation for low self-esteem.

Fears humiliation. Yet evokes it through negative displays of imperious egotism. Meltdown of an inflated superego or social mask. A chilling encounter with the objective truth of one's own inferiority. Public shaming. Or private embarrassment.

Mortification burns away the armor of an alienated persona to reveal the wounded child within. It can regress into unyielding denial of its weakness. Or reinvent itself to achieve a personally authentic form of excellence. Can transform the tribulations of life into a triumph of art, with oneself as the subject.

The responsibility of moral courage. With an old identity discredited and its social standing gone only the core of its unrequited love remains. Can it shine out, with nothing to lose, giving freely without expectation of reward? If so then Saturn's harsh trials are more than redeemed. If not, one withers into embittered impotence.

A dramatic Shadow figure arises in opposition to one's central purpose. A demonic alter ego expresses one's unacknowledged darkness. It steps into the light and must be faced. A duty to confront the charisma of one's own false projections. A challenge to release the rigid arrogance of power, to melt the hard edge of autocratic pride.

Saturn in Virgo/sixth house

Senses destiny as a demand for purification through rigorous self- discipline and service to others. The circumstances of fate refine integrity through an exacting regimen of personal improvement, including ego's subordination to a larger cause.

A hard lesson in the limits of one's abilities. Constant effort to compensate by upgrading skills and fixing faults. Pessimism, doubt and skepticism about one's basic fitness. A nagging sense of inadequacy: spiritual, mental and emotional as well as physical. Genuine humility or a crushing lack of self-esteem.

Focused organization; clarity, precision and accuracy in thought and deed. Inner coherence is expressed through consistent personal rectitude. Or compulsive criticism denigrates self and others, drains vitality by the death of a thousand cuts.

An emphasis on narrowly defined excellence can override compassion. Lack of perspective: insistence on a core truth can exclude its complex implications. Simple virtue can turn off more subtle sympathies. Dry analysis can devalue the ambiguities of human emotion.

Ego isolated from a sense of wholeness and completion. Strict standards stifle empathy. Micromanagement limits efficient function. Hypercritical vigilance for error restricts availability to truth.

Fears contamination by the world's dirt and darkness. Can retreat into ritualistic purity, a small-minded perfectionism of irrelevant detail. Obsessive self-analysis, oppressive worry.

A Shadow of sanitized rationality. Identity is marred by guilt for never having done enough to correct personal flaws or heal the world's wounds. Inhibits appreciation for self and others as they are rather than as they should be. A challenge to serve out of love, not guilt. A responsibility to refine nervous intensity into effortless skill; to sublimate performance anxiety into spontaneous competence.

Saturn in Libra/seventh house

Exaltation. Objective judgment, in relation to other aspects of psyche, reaches a critical intensity. Collective norms and principles of justice, of whatever merit, override individual perspective. A judicious mentality, guided by duty rather than passion.

A sense of destiny adjusts to others. The circumstances of fate are defined by the necessities of public conduct rather than personal purpose. Mutual obligation rather than individual initiative informs behavior.

Inhibits self-expression in order to maintain alliances. Principled compromise. Honorable and pragmatic discharge of contractual agreements. A difficult struggle to set the boundary between tribal expectations and individual autonomy.

A hard lesson in disappointing relationship. The discipline to face exclusion and rejection. Vitality smothered by a weak, cold or oppressive partner(s). Passive acceptance of another's projected darkness.

Ego isolated from its own needs and desires by heavy responsibility to others. One takes on, or surrenders to, the burden of their overwhelming demands. Carries another's load, to the detriment of both.

Community standards alienate one from inner truth. Pessimism, doubt and skepticism about social skills and status in the group. Personality identifies with accepted conventions, judges itself by traditionally sanctioned criteria. This facilitates contact by providing an agreed frame of reference. Or freezes it into a contrived artificial mold. Acceptance of consensus bestows order and harmony at the price of originality. Yet gracious accommodation, if reciprocated, can deepen pleasant affinity into profound appreciation of the other's complementary reality.

A Shadow of rigid protocol, suffocating etiquette, political correctness. A formal code of conduct replaces spontaneity. Conventionally defined behavior restricts genuine interplay. Clear perception and sophisticated sensibilities can be coarsened by compliance with peer pressure.

Fear of conflict. Lack of individuality. Inhibited communication of real values. A challenge to right the balance by appropriate expression of one's own wisdom. A duty to honestly participate in society rather than merely conform to its demands.

Saturn in Scorpio/eighth house

A sense of destiny regenerates through ordeal. The circumstances of fate expose hidden fears.

A hard lesson in spiritual courage. The emotional discipline to accept that all one's plans serve a larger purpose than personal intent. Pessimism, doubt and skepticism about one's ability to effectively manage power.

Ego isolated from true passion. Inhibits erotic engagement with life. Bondage to compensating obsession. Alienation from spontaneous sexuality; redirects into contrived appetites or heavy suppression. Can focus natural libido into psychological will.

Crystallizes concealed, self-censored guilt into a known and bitter truth. Presents undeniable evidence of the bad one did, or wound received, that can never be undone. A devastating encounter with one's own Original Sin.

A Shadow of rigid emotional control, suppressed rage, blocked natural aggression. This frozen anger restricts access to Scorpio's inherent affinity with the subconscious depths. Eventually a dam bursts: the superego construct founders in a flood of repressed feelings. Entrenched self-definition overwhelmed by an eruption from the unconscious. A familiar Shadow of known weakness swept away. The devil you know dies. A new and scarier version emerges.

Loss of innocence: recognizes one's personal entanglement in deep, instinctive currents of darkness, evil and selfishness. This implacable judgment obliterates an old ego identity and its now irrelevant ambitions. Psyche reorganizes under the pressure of its unbearable shame. A mortified personality strips down to a core determination to pay its karmic debt. It can take responsibility, repent and rebirth into an exemplar of wisdom distilled out of pain. Or shrink into cold cynicism, projecting its own sinister malice onto others.

Feels the urgency of time. Senses the fateful deadline of mortality. Sees the grinning skull behind the smiling face. Can respond with intensely focused purpose. Or morbid fear.

Death's liberating aspect: soul freed from its corporeal burdens, spirit released from the constraints of form.

Saturn in Sagittarius/ninth house

A sense of destiny socializes. The circumstances of fate experienced as necessary compliance with group norms. In Libra personal judgment aligns with a tribal consensus, but maintains some objectivity and thus acts as a balancing agent. In Sagittarius one's ambition identifies with the common cause, is subsumed into it. The herd mentality stifles personal reality; an intolerable sense of constriction leads to a crises of conscience.

Ego isolated from genuine enthusiasm. An oppressive team spirit informs social participation. One feels bound by a straightjacket of dogma, and bored by its irksome shibboleths.

Optimism checkmated by brutal reality. Good fortune marred, or ruined, by inability to appreciate or live up to it. Encounters an inexplicable darkness in here or out there as belief, confidence and trust fade.

A hard lesson in a truth that fails. A humbling recognition that an ethical code falls short. Or down. Or that one fails to meet its just demands. Pessimism, doubt and skepticism stemming from cynical lack of conviction.

Alienation from natural spirituality. Yet the search for meaning is the most compelling drive in human psychology once basic physical needs have been met. Loss of orthodox faith, whether religious, social or political, forces one to compensate with a quest to find a central organizing principle one can really believe in. One becomes a pilgrim, sincerely stumbling towards the light. Or a fanatic convinced that s/he has found it.

God/the Force absent or experienced with Old Testament severity. A harsh emphasis on rote obedience, the letter rather than the spirit of law. Intolerance. A narrow philosophy enforces strident rules of righteousness. A Shadow of rigid doctrine and petrified standards suffocates free expression and joie de vivre.

Yet 'Fear of God is the beginning of wisdom.'*

Disillusionment and moral anguish force one to recognize a higher Law beyond personal opinion or conventional ideology. Liberation comes through renunciation of a false (but compelling) idol in favor of a larger, more demanding and rewarding, worldview.

A challenge to find one's own meaning, develop personal authenticity. A duty to expand one's horizons beyond the limits of received wisdom.

* Proverbs 9:10 and Psalms 111:10

Saturn in Capricorn/tenth house

Rulership. Ambition, in response to felt inadequacy, assumes an unusual degree of importance in the personality. Disciplined achievement is emphasized in relation to other aspects of psyche.

A sense of destiny drives the individual to control and organize collective energies. The circumstances of fate generate goal directed behavior. Proven accomplishment in the public realm. Power and renown won at great cost and effort through discipline, tenacity and careful strategy.

The objective consolidation and expression of a completed agenda, a structured order. But any completion is relative and limited. Once attained its flaws and weakness begin to manifest. The closing of a frontier always invites internal change; final maturation of a project flips into release of its binding energy. Experiences the essential impermanence of all achievement: sic transit gloria mundi.* Rags to riches, and back again. Rise and fall.

Eminence and the depersonalization that goes with an exalted, or sharply defined, position. Intensifies social authority, but reduces personal uniqueness. One can become a paragon of duty and forget one's humanity.

A hard lesson in the limits of authority. The discipline to acknowledge higher principles than self-advancement. Pessimism, doubt and skepticism about one's worthiness for promotion or right to command.

Ego isolated behind rank, defined by hierarchical status. A Shadow of blind ambition, robotic discipline, cold lust for power. A cynical sense of universal selfishness. Guilt.

Fears weakness and failure. Lacks empathy; others are seen in terms of their usefulness. Materialistic and pragmatic; inhibits feeling to get ahead. Suppressed emotion can congeal into dark melancholy. A challenge to find meaning in victory, spirit behind form. A duty to redefine success.

* Latin: Thus passes worldly glory, referring to the transience of power and fame.

Saturn in Aquarius/eleventh house

Rulership. Objective judgment assumes an unusual degree of importance in the general personality, overriding sensual, instinctive and emotional claims. Disciplined thought emphasized in relation to other aspects of psyche.

A sense of destiny distilled from personal subordination to a larger cause or doctrine. Circumstances of fate experienced through identification with an ideological model, political, scientific or spiritual as the case may be. This differs from Sagittarius' moral quest, is more like enlightenment by an all-encompassing explanatory equation.

A hard lesson in the limits of idealism. A Big Picture falls short. Or down. The intellectual discipline to acknowledge that theory is a poor substitute for a complex existence charged with unknown potentials. Pessimism, doubt and skepticism about one's hopes and intuitions.

Ego isolated behind ideas. A Shadow of mental detachment. Life defined by a formula, which is always incomplete. Or wrong. Cold clarity, lack of human warmth. Demonizes any deviation from the Plan. Fear of thoughtcrime.

Fundamental principles articulated into operating instructions. Revolutionary aspiration formulated into a practical program. Abstract intelligence harnessed to a developmental blueprint. But the grand design can straitjacket actual experience. Its implementation can disrupt organic function. Emphasizing a distant utopia and a calculated strategy of attainment can lead to ruthless suppression of all that does not conform to the goal.

An engineering logic blindly subordinates today's truth to tomorrow's purpose. It inevitably meets harsh unexpected consequences. Can learn through the experimental method: an insistence on facts that gives a reality check to visionary flights. The promise, limitations and threat of consciously directed evolution: think of genetic manipulation and biotechnology.

A challenge to transcend the map for the territory by acceptance of a mutable, open future. A duty to embrace the creative novelty of uncertainty over absolute ideals of static perfection.

Saturn in Pisces/twelfth house

A sense of destiny dissolves. The circumstances of fate force surrender of an old identity. Ego isolated by its own process of decay. A Shadow of dissolution and confusion.

Rejection of normal boundaries. Feels others' sorrows, and the weight of the world's woes. Must learn that:

'Sufficient unto the day is the evil therefof.'[1]

Every moment of sadness is balanced by opportunities for its redemption. Sensitivity to others' pain can stimulate effective empathy. It should not be inflated into a global depression, wallowing in despair over problems beyond one's reach. In that vein:

'Can any one of you by worrying add a single hour to your life?'[2]

A hard lesson in the limits of compassion. The emotional discipline to accept that kindness is not always reciprocated, good intentions often invite enmity. Pessimism, doubt and skepticism about the meaning of suffering.

A nebulous self image. Liquidation of a crystallized, and now constricting, personality. A simultaneous inner restructuring. Established rules and accepted limits fade away. An embryonic future organization begins to take shape. Its fuzziness leads to an ambiguous sense of reality. The blurring which accompanies a change of focus. It invites comparison with a seed, soaking up water, becoming soft and amorphous, so that a new, more complex life can emerge from it.

Melancholia. World weariness. Inhibits imagination, or darkens it. Fear of letting go. Lack of faith.

Forgotten or karmic memories surface as a fog of amorphous dread; a manifestation of unconscious guilt. This can be redeemed by accepting meltdown of an outworn ego, with its concomitant loss of control. It involves a difficult embrace of trust in the larger process. A duty to accurately discriminate between past illusions and emerging possibilities.

1. Matthew 6:34
2. Matthew 6:27

Uranus

Uranus twinkles at the very edge of visual perception. Despite millennia of stargazing this faint, slow moving speck was not even recognized as a planet until observed telescopically in 1781. Uranus also spins at a right angle to all other planets.[1] See diagram. This remote ice giant's astronomical properties hint at its psychological and spiritual symbolism.

Uranus orbits just past unaided discernment of its nature, like an implied truth one can't quite grasp. It hints at a separate reality outside the reach of our physical senses and mental categories.

Uranus' perpendicular orientation to the visible inner planets of personal consciousness provides the channel transmitting power from an invisible source (Neptune) to our phenomenal world. It links perceptible dimensions of time, space and causality with a formless Beyond. That cannot be defined in any way, yet it is the origin and end of all existence. Uranus grounds its potential into our palpable experience of matter, life and mind. Uranus connects finite entities with infinite energies; conscious character with its unconscious wellsprings.

Material reality emanates out of an intangible energy template. That such an unseen force field guides and molds the physical world is clearly understood by science. The modern creation story describes a universe exploding out of the void. Astronomers speak of an imperceptible 'dark matter' shaping the galaxies and an even more mysterious 'dark energy' accelerating cosmic expansion. (Indeed, 'normal' physical matter seems to account for only about 5% of the heavens' known mass.) At the other end of the scale, physicists describe a subatomic quantum realm where dense substance condenses out of and evaporates back into flashing background radiance. All of this is consistent with the traditional wisdom of most cultures, which portrays the manifest world as precipitating from and sublimating towards a spiritual dimension beyond the confines of thought.

Saturn embodies the Cross of Matter on which spirit takes form in our four dimensional universe. Uranus points to a more subtle cross uniting both matter and spirit in transcendent states of consciousness: encounters with intuition, inspiration and revelation.

Uranus' orbit defines an interface joining visible phenomena with their causal purposes. It portrays an etheric body animating physical form with incorporeal vitality. An electric aura galvanizing objects into action and subjects into awareness. Uranus' actual position along this path pinpoints where one encounters this spiritual surge into

Tilted Uranus

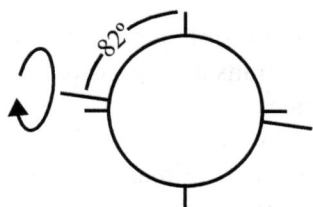

Uranus is tilted at 82° to the vertical. It spins north to south with a slight tilt east to west like Venus

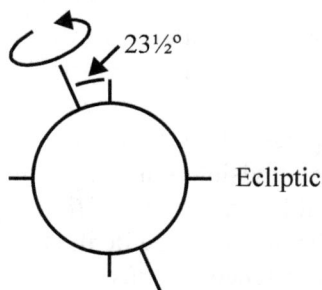

Earth is tilted at 23½° to the vertical. All other planets are tilted 0° - 28°

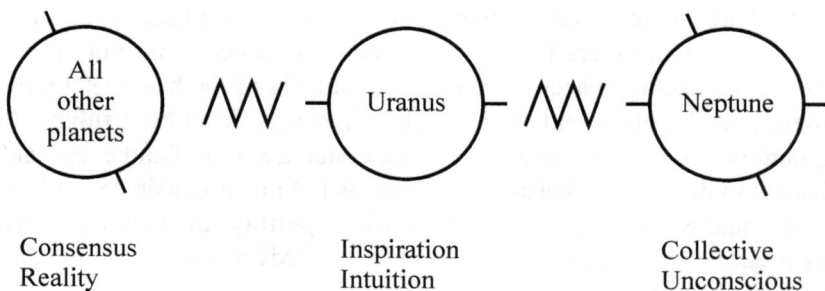

Consensus
Reality

Inspiration
Intuition

Collective
Unconscious

manifestation. Why one tunes into a Mind that jump-starts all smaller minds. And how one's ego identity responds to its stimulation.

Uranus symbolizes the abstract principles that coalesce into Saturn's laws of existence and stages of conscious development. It registers the invisible currents driving events, the subtle rationale behind specific facts. Here one peeks into the intangible force field within which materiality is embedded: an ideal order shaping sensible substance and motivating psychological process. Uranus describes the inspiration for Saturn's concrete framework of circumscribed circumstance. It embodies an evolving paradigm, an archetypal image, elaborating over time into an existential identity.

Uranus shows where and how one comes to terms with that which is larger than what one knows or can know. Whether this proves to be stimulating or destructive depends on one's attitude to the unknown. Openness and curiosity can assimilate its novel insights into a more inclusive worldview. A closed or defensive mind feels threatened by them.

Its thrill of discovery, excitement of breakthrough, can jump awareness to the next level. It can also overwhelm understanding with a blinding Vision or shattering breakdown. Uranus' lightning flash can inspire. Or shock one numb with an intensity too hot to handle. Uranus' access to more subtle planes of being can liberate. It can also sever any connection to common sense, or to others. Sometimes it simply surprises one with a change of fortune; a challenge of adaptation.

Uranus' transition zone connects manifestation (Saturn) and infinity (Neptune), existential truth and the mystery of its origin/purpose. This relationship oscillates as a tension between actual being and latent possibility. Uranus translates potential into a real force measured by its impact on materiality (Saturn). It manifests as a power vibration generating one's several bodies: animal, emotional, mental and moral.

Uranus functions through both ascension into spirit and condensation into existence. It marks the point of differentiation or phase change from one state to another. The one-degree of separation distinguishing water from ice, or from steam. The ephemeral instant when everything changes. We experience Uranus through a revelatory moment. The Eureka! insight. An orgasm. Our birth cry. And death rattle.

These abstract considerations (and Uranus is nothing if not abstract) also pertain to the biological plane. Today we idolize the DNA genome as the so-called 'Book of Life.' Actually, an individual's genetic code simply consists of a list of chemicals. It becomes meaningful only when mobilized into activity by a subtle energy pattern. DNA specifies the ingredients of protein building blocks, not how they organize into life itself. To some extent they can sub-assemble according to their biochemical properties, but basically a heap of proteins is no more a life than a pile of bricks and lumber is a house. A house requires a blueprint. A life requires an organizing field of vitality. We can think of the DNA helix spirals as tiny radio receivers grounding a universal life force, an etheric aura (Uranus). Each DNA gene receives it in a slightly different way depending on small variations in its nucleotide sequence. All of them put together add up to a singular organic identity.

The same process operates on the emotional and mental levels. One comes into the world with a psychological genome symbolized by a birth horoscope. The chart portrays an archetypal energy pattern. A Uranian snapshot of eternal truth precipitated out of time's flow. One activates it at whatever level of evolution one has or can achieve. Specific incidents energize its initially unconscious arrangement of instincts to create an individual narrative. Events provoke personal talents to jell out of an invisible web of aptitudes.

Self-consciousness arises through a sequential unfolding of universal developmental stages.[3] An emerging ego organizes a general process of bio-psychic maturation into a unique identity. Its pulse cannot be measured with electrodes or located by chemical probes. Its rhythm can be described by Uranus' position and aspects in a horoscope.

This vibration is effective because it galvanizes psychological potentials from their more ethereal soul source. It brings dormant possibilities to light by stimulating them from an entirely new direction. Think of a two-dimensional plane, like a blank sheet of paper, suddenly written upon from above: a third, previously unsuspected dimension. That's just the beginning: an inanimate pen, held in a living hand, directed by a thinking brain, motivated by the energies Uranus symbolizes. The impact of its novelty imparts meaning. The blank page now carries a message because its reality was impinged upon by an actual but unimagined quality: a writer's state of mind. That message then sparks completely new trains of thought in the reader's mind.

A small-minded paper molecule might contemptuously deny the existence of transformative agencies such as pens, hands, brains, thoughts and motives because it cannot perceive them. It might also smirk at the idea that it originated from a greenly flowering tree photosynthesizing under a vast and distant hydrogen fire. But these actually exist. Uranus points to higher order realities and channels their effect upon our own.

Uranus has the blandest surface of any planet. Its uniform blue-green sphere does not have the banded structure and howling storms of the other gas giants.[4] And it is cold. Uranus does not have much of an internal heat engine to drive and differentiate its chilled atmosphere.[5] It lacks the self-centered vitality that other planets have. Its almost ghostly lack of definition, without a character of its own, opens a clear window through which shines the light of another dimension, beyond the shared life of the solar system.

Pallid Uranus is the only planet without a personality. It spins at a right angle to all other planets. A planet's rotation around its own center demonstrates a subjective turning in on itself. Uranus' right angle breakout from the planetary pattern shows a detachment from the north/south polarity of subjectivity as we know it. Instead it provides an objective look into the factors driving self-realization. It can envisage many permutations of character because it does not identify with any of them. Uranus' divergence from the normal axis of core (heart) centered identity can lead to creative freedom or cruel alienation.

The featureless shine of Uranus acts like a veil, hiding an entirely different order of things. An anonymous looking door into another realm. It resembles the uniform cosmic background radiation, with infinitesimal temperature variations, marking the edge of what we can see in the universe. Yet the subtle peaks and valleys of those primordial waves eventually amplified into giant galaxies, flaring stars and living planets.

This smooth afterglow of the Big Bang only became visible about 380,000 years after the Event. Before that, light itself did not exist. Light photons were still merged in an opaque fog with subatomic particles. Only after the expanding universe had cooled down enough for atoms to form could light and matter 'decouple.' The universe then became transparent and visible. Uranus marks an equivalent point in psychological experience where the light of abstract knowledge decouples into known facts and a knowing subject.

Even before that, in the universe's first zillionth of a second, almost equal numbers of quarks and antiquarks, the most elementary particles, formed, then immediately annihilated each other, releasing radiant energy. Only one in a billion, $\frac{1}{1,000,000,000}$, quarks survived, constituting a slight preponderance of matter over antimatter. It seems that there was a cosmic battle before there was even a cosmos, in which 'good,' as we know it, prevailed over its antithetical principle of negation. It permanently defined the nature of our universe, created the archetypal template for its very substance at the most fundamental level. Such an instantaneous revelation is quintessentially Uranian.

Uranus' trail through space marks the shroud cloaking a misty ineffable infinity. Its position along that orbit portrays a rent in that veil through which eternity's mystery can be glimpsed: a 'crack between the worlds' of form and spirit. It winks at the very edge of perception, with tantalizing hints of a more subtle realization.

So rarefied an energy must be absorbed in measured doses (quanta). Too strong a flow would blow the fuse, too little and vitality would flicker out. Like unseen radiation raw exposure can burn away the delicate tendrils of life and mind. Properly filtered it is the stimulus of evolution. Just as a bee can see in the ultraviolet, just as a dog's sense of smell is 1000 times keener than ours, so Uranus reveals entirely new perspectives. These must be assimilated in a way consistent with one's conscious stance. Too much too soon leads to madness, not enough too late to calcification.

Uranus provides an inspiring, or shocking, contact with other currents of reality. For example, we all share a consensus that there are three dimensions of space. Yet we each vaguely intuit another one. So far science cannot define what is suggested by our sense of left and right.[6] We cannot pinpoint the difference except in the subjective feel of our bodies. But that, of course, is as real as it gets.

Even one's brain, the seat of awareness, is divided into left and right hemispheres, loosely connected with different cognitive processes: the 'logical' left and 'creative' right brain.[7] Its very anatomy embodies different mental/intuitive orientations; an intersection of objective sidedness with distinct psychic realities.[8] The nature of this right/left polarity exists just beyond our understanding - like one of those incredibly real dreams that vanishes no matter how hard you try to remember.

This sense of another physical orientation demonstrates the Uranian principle. It comprises a prescient perception of things just around the corner or over the horizon; another way of knowing. It is universally shared, but not understood or verbalized. A critical mass of subliminal awareness builds up and finally bursts into view through the agency of a genius or a crisis. After the initial shock of recognition it settles into solid common sense. This happens in the scientific realm and the political; in our moral sensibilities and aesthetic sensualities. Oddly, for such an abstract force, Uranus also functions strongly on the tactile and kinetic levels. A good athlete plays just ahead of his/her perceptions: aware of a flow, in tune with a rhythm.

Uranus senses the future, not as an extrapolation of the present, but in its emergent novelty. Uranus attunes us to the ordering principles, rather than the clunky facts, of an evolving situation. The underlying spirit, rather than the step-by-step logic, of a thought. The revelatory insight, rather than the hard data, of a discovery. The thrill separating real emotion from conventional expectation.

Uranus takes lunar instinct to the next level of intuition: not as a hard-wired, preprogrammed response from the past, but as a receptivity to unseen attractions that shape the future. It rewrites rules and alters terms across the board. It overturns an old paradigm in the dawning of a new truth. Pushing the envelope, thinking outside the box, expect the unexpected, are current phrases for encountering Uranus. 'Creative advance into novelty'[9] is a classic formulation of this truth.

In this creative zone known inputs - familiar perceptions, concepts and motivations - are transformed. Here sensations, feelings and thoughts recombine into original forms. Whether they emerge as revelatory insights or bizarre aberrations depends largely on the individual's attitude towards the unconscious. The intuitive process cannot be controlled. It can only be welcomed and nurtured or resisted and distorted.

Uranus shatters the boundaries of an established order, extending its scope and transmuting its quality. It blows away the restraints of current identity, circumstance and tradition (Saturn), sparks a new sense of meaning (Jupiter) and initiates the activity bringing that vision to life (Mars).

We live and move within Uranus' charged force fields. Its electric current passes through one's specific locus of hereditary, environmental and experiential receptors, generating a unique resonance of personal character. And driving it to constantly evolve.

The sign and house that Uranus occupies indicates revolution, or revelation, in the affairs signified by that energy zone. A settled identity or understanding is disrupted by collective unconscious, or social, imperatives bursting into manifestation. A sudden storm clears the air or devastates everything. There is no going back: a Uranian upheaval permanently changes the landscape, for better or worse. The latter clause depends entirely on how open one is to innovation/evolution, not as a rearrangement of present conditions, but as their replacement by a new order. And how receptive to impersonal truths that override ego considerations.

Uranus describes the shock of a life, whether transformative or traumatic. If Uranus is not prominent in a chart then it acts as a stimulus, or irritant, within a generally stable context. If it is powerful by position or aspect then radical change becomes the norm, not as a one-time event but a way of life. Consistent innovation keeps one on the edge. Or compulsive thrill seeking takes one over the top.

Properly tuned to Neptune's wellspring of imagination Uranus transmits an intuitive vision that automatically steers one's course. Poorly adjusted it fries the ego's circuits, generating a crackling static of overamped idiosyncrasies.

Uranus breaks boundaries. It plugs a known wavelength of comprehension into a higher frequency, for better or worse. Any psyche that cannot adapt to this influx by enlarging its horizons will overheat and disintegrate. The shadow side of enlightenment is dissociation, an overcharged mind blown apart by too much voltage.

Uranus acts as the gatekeeper for all transpersonal energies. It initiates a constant incentive to, and the dangerous challenge of, evolution. Its inspiration transcends partial perceptions and constricting concepts. It awakens one to a more inclusive engagement with the universe. Uranus accomplishes this by shining in from a deeper center of gravity than the current ego focus. Thus it can lead to a larger identity illuminated from a more universal center.

Such enlightenment is a process, not a product. It transforms the ego in service to a greater Self.[10] Any attempt to own, control or block it distorts impersonal brilliance into an exaggerated parody of personality, aberration of feeling, hyped up monomania of thought. Then enlightenment knots into eccentricity, living truth becomes a robotic mantra, the leading edge curls up into a straitjacket of insane enthusiasm.

Uranus constitutes both an exalted sense, and chilling simplification, of living experience. The danger at this level of abstraction lies in losing the vivid life of the trees for a ghostly image of the forest. 'The map is not the territory.' Uranus' cerebral equations can provide an overview or a caricature. Theoretical explanation can unify data into insight. Or reduce reality to a slogan. It can explain complexity. Or twist it into a cheap one liner. Conceptual (v concrete) thought can illuminate a Big Picture. Or dissociate one from it. Astrology itself is a Uranian discipline. It can function as the 'algebra of psychology'[2] Or as a cartoon of stereotypes.

Uranus generates the prototypes behind facts. Here potential builds up into an excitation or arousal that eventually erupts into life, creatively or destructively, according to one's ability to ground it. Thus it charts the emergence of novelty. With it comes the law of unintended consequences. We generally use this term negatively. Actually it often acts positively, albeit painfully, to guarantee we don't get stuck on one line of development, extrapolating forever into more and more of the same.

This fundamental element of uncertainty ensures that quantitative increments add up to qualitative initiations. It generates mutation and is therefore the engine of evolution. Most mutations are harmful, and are quickly deleted in nature. Most new ideas are impractical and most fledgling ventures fail. But a saving remnant survive and blossom to create diversity, complexity and transcendence. Thus fins became feet, and life crawled out of the sea onto the land.

Uranus = change. It generates new possibilities from old phenomena. It disrupts the established order (Saturn) so that dormant qualities can emerge when their time is ripe. It does so violently, because fundamental change has the quality of a discontinuity or quantum jump (birth, death) as opposed to the linear development, progression or growth of an existent situation (promotion in rank, increase in assets: Jupiter). Evolution proceeds through such 'punctuated equilibrium.' Uranus = ! . Pluto, the other tipped-over planet, portrays the cosmic Will or purpose prompting such exclamations.[1]

Thus an asteroid fell from the sky and blew away the 170,000,000 year long Age of Dinosaurs. In this way the field was cleared for small, ratlike ancestors of the mammals and of us. Only a planetary trauma, an extinction event, could have turned the page to such a new chapter of evolution.

This mindless rock did not plan the Age of Mammals or anticipate the coming of man. No great anthropomorphic mind or hand hurled it at Earth as part of a premeditated program. Rather an inherent creativity erupted into the world: without guarantee of any specific result, but presenting the danger/opportunity of a quantum jump. Yet all these seemingly random jumps add up to a clear trend of increasing consciousness. Multicellular organisms, like trilobites, emerging out of a planetary super-freeze 700,000,000 years ago were on a higher plane than the one-celled world preceding them. Dinosaurs, inheriting Earth after the greatest mass extinction known (Permian, 250,000,000 years ago) were yet more complexly conscious. Then they too were superseded. Yet life continued onwards and upwards.

These eons embody the unfolding of a great cosmic year, marked by Sun's 230,000,000-year orbit of the galaxy. Uranus translates this cycle to the solar systemic level. It symbolizes a longer than personal rhythm in which one is embedded, a general dynamic to which one must respond. We participate in it by the political revolutions, scientific breakthroughs and social upheavals of history. And in the personal revelations and revolutions of a life. Not all have a happy ending. Think of the Russian Revolution. Or of a child hit by a car. These sudden intrusions redefine life, whether of our planet, a society or a person. They illustrate the principle of change, the one thing that does not change.

Uranus, the agent of change, is bloodless and loveless. It generates elegant equations: of DNA blueprints, psychological functions, socio-historic waves. These include fractions of agony and subtractions of waste, divisions of hate and multiplications of woe.

Some die in prolonged torment while others play with rarefied concepts. Or go shopping. Uranus splits or fractures us from one another that we may have separate fates. We all have much in common: Neptunian empathy, Jupiterian solidarity and esprit de corps, shared lunar feelings. But we are not social insects. We are advanced primates, torn between herd instincts and individual urges. Saturn demonstrates the fact of our existential loneliness, and the content of its character. Uranus causes that individuality. It specifies the nature of one's necessary rebellion from the All so that one might become one. Uranus reenacts our expulsion from the Garden of Eden (instinctual bliss) that we may wander the world and create our own fate. Saturn embodies that fate. Jupiter grows it.

Uranus portrays the three great principles of individuality, impermanence, and illumination. These are what make 'I' stand alone.

Uranus expresses the process of individualization brought about through the irradiation of matter, life and psyche by a spiritual voltage. It fuses generic instinct with archetypal inspiration to generate a novel synthesis. It integrates promise and performance into a distinct wavelength of subjective light. And displays its objective essence as the particular photon of illumination emitted by one's encounter with life.

Uranus points to the original and final body electric, out of which the personality condenses, and back into which it sublimates, after development in the world of events. This is not one's soul, the transcendent meaning of a life (Jupiter). It refers to an all embracing vitality oriented by a specific impulse to manifest as a psychological being. And the once in infinity scintillation that self contributes to a greater Whole beyond its own brief moment.

Uranus separates the waters of the unconscious, where all is merged, so that individuality can emerge. It polarizes the primordial ocean of psyche into yin and yang, light and dark, those positive and negative charges whose combination generate the electricity or 'juice' of life. It defines direction, purpose and orientation out of Neptune's fertile chaos, which then incarnates as a task or a destiny (Saturn).

Uranus precipitates a cloud into raindrops, which fall to Earth, bringing life to the parched land. It shatters an existing order so that its individual fragments, each a specialized fractal of the whole, can zap, jab and jolt one another. Through such interplay they coalesce into new combinations with emergent properties. Yet all such individuality is transient, a fleeting signal of timeless truth in the drama of duality and duration.

Uranus challenges complacency with the principle of impermanence. Every entity forms as a temporary conglomeration of common elements. Uranus fuses them into a singular identity, an original combination of impersonal potentials releasing its own vibration, or personality. Thus it transforms a pool of DNA molecules into a living genome. Or a bunch of words into a specific message. Once expressed, its charge expended, the message disintegrates. An organism, having reshuffled its genes and reproduced, dies. A thought, having stimulated other thoughts or minds, is forgotten. At Uranus the radiance of eternity flashes into the moment, sparkles, and discharges itself.

All things change and pass away. This is one of two fundamental facts. The other is love. As has so well been said, 'Eternity is in love with the productions of time.'[11] The two merge through the agency of Uranus.

Eastern wisdom traditions emphasize the need to transcend impermanence. Western religious traditions stress love of its creatures, doomed as they are.

(Uranus itself has little to do with love. It can demonstrate how its intensity rocks your world; the impact rather than the experience of its rapture. Neptune, Uranus' sister world, an ice giant with a hot heart, locates one's ideals of love. Venus embodies its personal expression.)

Impermanence demands that every finite entity transcend its limitations and rejoin its ultimate source. Whether one does so consciously and voluntarily, or under fateful compulsion as in physical death, depends on how one responds to the unexpected opportunities offered by Uranus. Whereas Jupiter promotes expansion of existing identity, Uranus sublimates its individuality into an exemplar of universal principle. Jupiter grows a current self. Uranus explodes out of it.

Uranus illuminates any planet (psychological quality) it contacts in a changed context. The contentless Consciousness funneled through Uranus bathes everything it encounters in a new light. This shines in from another, unsuspected, angle. In doing so it reveals previously undiscovered depths. Hidden flaws and secret treasures emerge. One sees with fresh vision. Uranus = revelation. Such transcendence means experiencing all things from a different perspective. How accurately and well one receives that truth depends on the integrity of the intra-Saturnian ego-mind.

Uranus' organizing principles, archetypes or Platonic forms intensify and convert unconscious instincts into explicit insights. They render subliminal sensations into intelligible signals. These then manifest brightly or darkly, clearly or dully, according to their grounding matrix (the intra-Saturnian planets).

Uranus operates on the frontier uniting theoretical ideas with poetic ideals (Neptune). Neptune is abstract mental Uranus' dreamy, imaginative alter ego. These two planets act as the intellectual and emotional polarities of a single spiritual energy, just as electricity (Uranus) and magnetism (Neptune) are of a unified physical force (electromagnetism).

Uranus and Neptune are twins, with the same size and composition. (See 'Planetary Astronomy.') However, Uranus spins at a right angle to Neptune. Together they form the vertical and horizontal arms of a cross, separated in space but linked in meaning. See Figure 1, 'Outer Planet Transits.'[12]

The alignment of Uranus' poles relative to Neptune during its 84-year orbit traces the circling beam of a lighthouse within Neptune's ocean of amorphous yearning. It acts like a compass needle within the Neptunian fog; a reference point focusing diffuse dreams into the linear motion of time, causality and physical incarnation. Uranus provides a conceptual backbone for Neptune's swirling visions. It funnels nebulous ideals into an archetypal idea, the paradigm guiding a life. It channels vague charisma into a psychic algorithm directing unconscious promise into real personality. Uranus concentrates Neptune's subtle glow into a bright laser image that can etch itself into Saturn's stone hard world of facts.

From Neptune looking in, Uranus falls into tight solid physical manifestation. It means a contracting phase change: condensation, precipitation, coagulation, discharge. From inside Saturn's frontier of the Reality Principle it occurs as an expansive explosion, an irruption of raw power, which either lights up or tears down an organized system, whether of self or of society. Uranus makes that magic moment when Neptunian possibilities converge into a lightning bolt of inspiration. This then takes shape in Saturn's defined realm as an actual energy or entity, which participates with others in Jupiter's social community.

The same process also manifests on the collective level of human history. (See 'Outer Planet Transits.') As Uranus' north pole[13] points towards Earth a new social order grounds itself; a fresh phase comes into manifestation.[14] As its south pole faces us 42 years later that now old order must be transcended; its outworn energies seen in a new perspective.[15]

Uranus also underlies the basic transformations affecting all members of a species or culture: for example, the unavoidable metamorphosis of every human through embryo, infancy, childhood, adolescence, maturity and old age. By position and aspect Uranus charts one's response to the impersonal dynamics of biology and history. As with the other trans-Saturnian planets Uranus also points to the broad social context of individual participation. It portrays the collective unconscious and collective milieu within which a particular ego operates.

Unlike the classical planets, known since time immemorial, Uranus was discovered through technology: the use of a telescope. This enhancement of normal human perceptions itself correlates with Uranus' meaning of breakthrough past previous limits. Uranus, barely visible under the best of conditions, was first perceived as a planet in 1781 by Sir William Herschel, a British astronomer. It is an especially significant symbol of the era between its discovery and that of Neptune in 1846.

This was a period of fundamental change in human destiny. Politically the American and French Revolutions ignited new ideas of liberty, democratic governance and human rights that would eventually sweep the world. Economically, the Industrial Revolution made possible humanity's liberation from drudgery and want, something never before even dreamed of. Culturally, the rational Enlightenment and the following Romantic era produced a psychological change of incalculable importance. Together they transformed our vision of the human condition from that of a static being in a hierarchical universe to one of a free agent responsible for his/her own destiny. During this period the general contours of expectation intensified by an order of magnitude.

Uranus operates on the collective level as a cutting edge agent of social and technological change. For a historical review of its last two transits through each of the signs, 1844-2012, see 'Outer Planet Transits.'

Moons

Uranus has 27 moons. Most of them are tiny captured rocks lacking the gravitational energy to become centered spheres. They symbolize subliminal intuitive currents unable to cross the threshold into conscious insight. Uranus most distinctive moon, Miranda, comprises two mashed together parts resulting from a collision. Their juncture consists of a startling chevron straddling its entire body. What better reminder of its parent planet's own deep past, when it was bowled over by a smashup, dying to one dimension of reality, thus opening the door to another.

Notes

1. Pluto also steeply inclines from the vertical, at a 60° angle. However, Pluto symbolizes a cosmic force rather than a planetary state of being. (See 'Pluto.') It was even 'demoted' from planetary status by the

International Astronomical Union in 2005. (See 'Planetary Astronomy.') This does not lessen its astrological significance.

2. Dane Rudhyar, 1895-1985, astrologer and artist

3. These can be categorized in any number of schemes: oral, anal, genital. Or preconventional, conventional, postconventional. The predictable stages of life: terrible twos, adolescent angst, menopausal/midlife crises, etc. The stages of social development in which one is embedded: instinctual, tribal-mythic, hero-power, religious-moral, scientific-rational, holistic-existential worldviews.

4. At 700-1000 mph, the winds of Jupiter, Saturn and Neptune scream beyond anything ever heard on Earth.

5. Uranus originally rotated perpendicular to its orbit, in accordance with the mechanics of motion. In its early history an enormous collision knocked it over. (Just as a huge collision knocked Earth off the perpendicular, to a lesser degree, with its debris cloud coalescing into our Moon.) This titanic blow seems to have disrupted its core, dissipating much of its heat and leaving its thick atmosphere cold.

6. Chirality: symmetrical opposites that cannot be superimposed on each other. For example, you can't put a left glove on your right hand.

7. Paradoxically, each cerebral hemisphere controls the opposite side of the body: the left wired to the right hand and vice versa. This is clearly important, but we should not read too much into it since neurological science is still in its infancy.

In common language 'right' means correctness and positive qualities such as political rights. 'Left' is associated with its Latin term: 'sinister.'

8. Like the mind's eye, our physical eyes act in a Uranian way. The forward-looking eyes are polarized at right angles to the upright spinal chakra column with a brain on top.* The same is true of our ears (themselves at right angles to the eyes). Sensory inputs, light waves of sight and air waves of sound, arrive horizontally from out there to be evaluated, prioritized and interpreted by the vertical categories of hierarchical mind in here.

Intangible consciousness organizes their chaotic impressions into its clear perception. An unshaped shaper distills a 'blooming buzzing confusion'† of images into meaningful vision; an innate grammatical ability translates a cacophony of sounds into sentences. Sense and sensibility operate on fundamentally different levels yet are also mutually dependent.

* In Hindu Yoga and Tantric Buddhism Chakras are subtle body energy centers loosely correlated with certain physical organs or glands. They form an ascending/descending series along a parallel

psycho-spiritual spinal column of the etheric body, or bioelectric aura. The seven major chakras are:

base of spine - wellspring of animal vitality;

genital - sexuality, erotic charisma;

solar plexus - personal power, gut instinct;

heart - love, the soul uniting physical centers below with spiritual ones above;

throat - gives voice to creativity;

center of forehead (pineal gland) - intuition, mystic/psychic vision. The pineal gland shares an evolutionary origin with the photo-receptor cells of the eyes. It constitutes an inner eye;

crown (top of head) - mental union with universal consciousness.

For thousands of years yogis and meditators of many traditions have mastered techniques to activate these centers and open their energy channels. Such methods generate personal transformation through sublimation and precipitation. Thus one can raise and refine one's own energies. Or invoke and ground intangible spiritual currents.

† 'The Varieties of Religious Experience,' William James, 1842-1910, American philosopher

9. Alfred North Whitehead, 1861-1947, English philosopher

10. Carl Jung, 1875-1961, a father of modern psychology, defined the larger Self as encompassing conscious ego along with personal and collective levels of the unconscious, plus biological instincts. It also includes higher spiritual potentials, unmanifest soul qualities.

11. 'The Marriage of Heaven and Hell,' William Blake, 1757-1827, English artist and romantic poet

12. Electricity refers to the flow of electrons. Electrons are energy bands surrounding a much denser atomic nucleus, much like concentric planetary orbits circling Sun. When electrons are linked to a core nucleus they manifest through chemical activity. Chemistry involves the sharing or transfer of electrons between atoms. When electrons flow freely away from a binding nucleus they condense into a current generating electrical activity. One can see pure electricity in a lightning bolt. Electricity and magnetism form two sides of one fundamental physical force just as Uranus and Neptune express two sides of one psychic reality. Electricity differs from magnetism (Neptune), which is a standing force field generated by single outer shell electrons spinning in unison with others. At Uranus they discharge out into a moving force wave burning through matter.

13. Because of Uranus' extreme inclination its north and south poles are defined under 'Uranus' in 'Planetary Astronomy.' North means transition into a future; south describes consolidation of its results.

14. When Uranus' north pole faces Earth there is a transformative crisis in public affairs. It did so in 1778 (three years before it was discovered), 1860, 1944, and will again in 2028.

1778: the beginning of a 'new order of the ages'* with the American Revolution. It would ultimately be emulated around the world
* One of the American national mottos, 'novus ordo seclorum,' printed on the back of every dollar bill

1860: Abraham Lincoln was elected President, provoking southern secession and civil war.

1944: obviously a time of extreme civilizational emergency. 1945 brought the atomic bomb, made of uranium. It also brought peace and a new world order.

One shudders to think of what 2028 might bring as the agent of necessary change.

15. When Uranus' south pole faces Earth there is a calm immediately preceding or following a revolutionary period. It did so in 1818, 1902 and 1986.

1818: almost a century of relative peace began after a quarter century of revolution and war in Europe (1789-1815).

1902: the final flowering of a placid and conservative Victorian era. Then (1905) Einstein's theory of relativity shattered everything we thought we knew about time, space, matter and energy on a theoretical level. Soon after this Uranian solstice had passed World War I erupted on a blood and guts level.

1986: the final moment of a 40-year long bipolar world order based on a nuclear balance of terror. Soon after (1989) communism would peacefully collapse and a new world order come to pass. Interestingly, the south pole almost exactly faced Earth as humanity first visited Uranus with the Voyager 2 flyby in January 1986.

Uranus in Signs and Houses

Uranus in a sign indicates the objective or verifiable quality of inspiration.

Uranus in a house indicates the subjective experience/expression of intuition.

Uranus: inspiring or disruptive contact with the unconscious. A buildup of revolutionary potential in its position and aspects.

Uranus in fire signs transforms through assertion of will, projection of ego. It acts as an individualizing agent, generating an intuition of new identity.

Uranus in air signs inspires through a unique mentality or thought process. It acts as a differentiating or clarifying light, emphasizing contrasts and forcing choices.

Uranus in water signs intuits a singular emotional experience or psychological insight. It energizes unconscious issues whose time has come. It evokes latent depths of feeling into life.

Uranus in earth signs redefines the parameters of social or economic reality. It acts as an irresistible force on a previously immovable object. A pent up charge erupts into a fundamental change of circumstance.

Definition of term - Intuition: A sense or vision of unmanifest potential. Instinctive resonance with, and receptivity to, a coming reality, the shape of the future. Transcendent insight, more inclusive than cause and effect reason. A bridge between thought and spirit. Not as logically defined, or limited, as an idea; not as free-flowing, or nebulous, as imagination. The essence of understanding as an inclusive synthesis of fact and potential. Direct knowledge, immediate grasp, of a Big Picture, processed in full by the unconscious rather than in step-by-step parts by reason.

Uranus in Aries/first house

Dawn of a new consciousness. Intuition awakened and empowered. Previously latent potential emerges and forcefully asserts its autonomy. Demands freedom to explore and innovate.

Originality liberates one from personal karma and collective tradition. Transforms identity for better or worse. An independent perspective. Or eccentric dissociation.

Self-awareness shaped by the vision of a rising paradigm. Expresses the danger/opportunity of rebirth. Will regenerates in a springtime of inspiration. Behavior galvanized by a pioneering imperative. Or driven by a disruptive urge. Progressive or anarchic adventures on the frontiers of possibility.

Universal or archetypal ideas stimulate change. Intellectual theory generates decisive initiative. Abstract insight becomes experienced impulse. Illumination demands action, enthusiastic or foolhardy. Revelation sparks revolution: 'The shot heard around the world.' Novel character. Breakthrough in, or breakdown of, individual motivation and ability.

Uranus in Taurus/second house

Idealism adapts to reality. Universal archetypes consolidate into useful insights. Intuition finds innovative means to tangible gain. An idea actually manifests as inspired investment in the future. Inventiveness redefines resources and thus enhances productivity. Pragmatic originality. Illuminating discovery stabilizes into a business model. Or impractical aspirations destroy one. Change of material circumstance.

Reassessment of self-worth. A clarified vision of what one really wants. This can sublimate instincts, refine their expression and give pleasure a more subtle edge. But revolutionary Uranus can get frustrated in steady solid Taurus/2nd. If a conservative nature dams/damns its free flowing voltage then pressure builds until an eruption of pent up desire shatters psychological continuity.

New forms of beauty take shape, a changed aesthetic. A transformation of sensuality, up or down. Unconventional standards of evaluation. Novel or eccentric appetites. Breakthrough in, or breakdown of, values.

Uranus in Gemini/third house

Intuition objectifies. Ego separates from personal identification with archetypal forms. Consciousness individualizes out of collective ideas, takes an autonomous perspective.

Detached illumination transcends dilemmas, which cannot be resolved in their own either/or terms. Transformation wrought by dialog with one's opposite or counterpart out there and one's higher soul or hidden shadow in here. Self and other mutually redefined by comparison and rivalry. And united on a more inclusive plane as terms of a larger equation.

Appreciates provocative contrast, the inciting excitement of differences. Variety inspires. It can reconcile disparate ideals in an original intellectual synthesis. Or manipulate them as an alienated player.

Mental lightning flashes between two poles of aspiration, levels of being or schools of thought. It may stimulate, or shatter, one or both. An outworn worldview or paradigm self-destructs from its internal contradictions. This opens a space for liberating or shocking new perceptions. Novel or eccentric means of communication. Breakthrough in, or breakdown of, information processing.

Uranus in Cancer/fourth house

Inspiration subjectifies. It grounds itself as gut feeling; a visceral sense of truth. Psychic intuition.

Shatters a traditional or culturally defined sense of personal security. Gains or seizes freedom from inherited expectations or tribal inertia. Or is kicked out of the nest. Liberation or dissociation from the past.
Reinterprets memory, rewrites history, redefines affiliation.

Disruption of old conventions nurtures a new beginning with
fresh sensitivities. Or shell-shocked withdrawal, a retreat from life.
Separation from the spell of an unconscious consensus alienates one
from close or intimate community. This can open up into a more
detached and universal sympathy. Or regress into rebellious instincts,
quirky moods and a contrarian disposition.

An internal phase change transforms one's basic psychological foundation. Revisits origins with a transformed vision. Think of
a salmon leaving its home in the ocean and swimming upstream to its
birthplace so it can mate, reproduce and die.

Emotional revolution. A change in feeling tone. An outworn
dream disintegrates. Original or eccentric fantasies arise. Breakthrough
in, or breakdown of, imagination.

Uranus in Leo/fifth house

Detriment. Detached insight fades as the voltage of one's current con-
sciousness/opinion rises. Intuition loses universality to become uniqueness of individual expression. Theatrical originality; charismatic star
power. Or self-dramatization through shock tactics. Personal identification with collective archetypes generates inspirational leadership. Or
distorts ego into a caricature.

Creative vision, or crazed self-promotion, shatters an outworn
social mask. A revolutionary self-image aggressively projects its new
role on life's stage. A transformative impulse of delight. Or an exaggerated sense of specialness; grandiose display of personal quirks.

A change of heart. The joy of breaking barriers to love. Discovers
more inclusive feelings. Or veers off into inappropriate displays of
affection. Artistic genius or bizarre flamboyance. Aristocratic detachment. Or a rebel without a cause. Novel leadership. Or eccentric elitism. Breakthrough in, or breakdown of, personal authority.

Uranus in Virgo/sixth house

Intuition purifies through practical problem solving. Perfects ideas by
making them work in conformity with facts and reason. Unconventional
techniques leapfrog old ways of doing things. A new vision of what
constitutes excellence and how it should be achieved.

Drastic redefinition of standards. An inspiration becomes a to
do list. A thorough purge and restructuring of personality in accordance with this new agenda. A healing revolution/revelation. Or strange

prescriptions of eccentric quackery. Transformative upgrade, or disintegration, of personal integrity.

An identity crisis as one shifts from an emphasis on personal fulfillment to social service. Illumination grounded as pragmatic change in the details of lifestyle and community participation. Or irrelevant abstractions distract from truth; petty demands of critical analysis make the perfect an enemy of the good. Breakthrough in, or breakdown of, applied skills in real situations.

Uranus in Libra/seventh house

Personal intuition adjusts to different truth claims. Recognition of others as they are in their own right; appreciates their independent character. Opens to alien ways of thinking. Or is blown away by them.

Ideal archetypes defined through the dynamics of social participation rather than inner enlightenment. Synthesis arises from conflict of opposites; individual originality awakened by the wisdom of compromise. ('Two heads are better than one.') Sterile dilemma transcended by the jump to a new criteria of judgment. Inspiration in response to objective circumstance rather than as a consequence of inner urges.

Reevaluation of identity as a variable in an ever changing context. A relatively detached sense of self as functioning in a larger community equation. Revolution in relationship. Changed expectations of others. And of appropriate group behaviors. Transformed code of conduct, new social standards. Novel or eccentric interaction with intimates and associates. Stimulating or disruptive participation in a collective enterprise. Breakthrough in, or breakdown of, one's sense of justice.

Uranus in Scorpio/eighth house

New intuitions of power: what it is, who really has it, how it can be used. And of what must go to clear the way for its exercise.

Sudden destruction of outworn ideas or feeling bonds. Cathartic illumination of real motives. Abstract thought confronts visceral drives. The shock of recognition sparks emotional regeneration. Instinctual appetites sublimate into higher aspirations. Or idealism shatters in a revolution of lowered expectations. Then psychological insight freezes into a manipulative tool.

Passion informs, or poisons, inspiration. Intense initiation into a new reality transcends previous identity. Or burns bridges. Irrevocably changes self, social standing and associations. Subjective revolution/ revelation leads to spiritual death and rebirth. Or a shocking encounter, in here or out there, violently disrupts personality. Traumatic dissociation. Or a transformative quantum jump.

A drastic challenge to consensus consciousness. Conventional morality, accepted principles and unspoken understandings put to the test. Collective idols and timeless archetypes redefined under pressure. Breakthrough in, or breakdown of, emotional truth.

Uranus in Sagittarius/ninth house

Conventional wisdom enhanced and renewed by a spiritual revelation. Original expression of collective aspirations. An ability to mobilize abstract ideas in service to a public agenda. Or exploit them to promote personal ambition.

Intuits the long-term significance of events. Inspired insight into dynamics and future prospects of the current tribal trajectory. Enthusiastic dissemination, or imposition, of a universal Law. Or inversion of archetypal principles; seditious power of the Big Lie.

Religious revolution. A transformative encounter with the divine intensifies, or shatters, one's sense of morality. A visionary theory challenges compliance with social norms. A consequent metamorphosis of ethical standards, up or down.

Prophetic illumination of higher truth. Or of social opportunity. Unearned grace; an unexpected windfall. Sudden good fortune makes or breaks character. Novel or eccentric political ideas. Breakthrough in, or breakdown of, philosophical orientation.

Uranus in Capricorn/tenth house

Intuition grounded in necessity. It precipitates out of wide ranging theory to practical application, from philosophical speculation to administrative innovation. Spiritual archetypes mobilized as social principles. Universal truths harnessed to personal ambitions, good or bad.

Shattering of an old order and its replacement by a new one. Transformation in the nature of authority. This liberates pent up energy. Or generates cynical alienation. Concrete public manifestation of abstract ideals. Change of tribal conventions, collective expectations. Reevaluation of tradition, restructuring of hierarchy:

'The first shall be last, and the last first.'*

Sharply enhanced status, or diminished prospects; a new order of priorities and rank. Pragmatic inspiration provides a clear shot to the top. Or insubordination brings a sudden fall from grace. Duty structures individuality as an exemplar of higher purpose. Or represses it into rebellious explosion. Novel or eccentric management style. Breakthrough in, or breakdown of, personal discipline.

* Matthew 19:30 and 20:16.

Uranus in Aquarius/eleventh house

Rulership. Inspiration assumes an unusual degree of importance in the general personality and its thought processes. The power of ideas emphasized in relation to other aspects of the psyche.

Intuition sublimates from individual to social, scientific or spiritual concerns. One thinks on a universal, or spaced out, level. Ideal archetypes motivate actual behavior as principled conduct or unrealistic expectations. The raw voltage between intense potential and brittle circumstance generates transformative acceleration or anarchic disintegration.

Original thought. Or crazy irrelevance. Genius or madness. Utopian or dystopian vision of the future separates one from current consensus reality. A new normal. An experimental mentality and lifestyle, with brilliant or disastrous results. Abstract ideas inspire life or dissociate one from it. Novel or eccentric theories motivate personal identity. Breakthrough in visionary insight. Or bizarre breakdown of self and circumstance.

Uranus in Pisces/twelfth house

Intuits what must be renounced for the greater good. Changes conventional defeat to spiritual growth. Or inexplicably throws away fortune and standing.

Conceptual consciousness absorbed by psychic sensitivities. Visionary revelation, non-linear logic. Abstract thought dissolves into imaginative fantasy. Poetic inspiration. Or pipe dreams. Elevated ideas expressed as mystical images. These inspire a devotional rapture. Or glamorize delusion.

Sudden upwelling of unexpected feelings and suppressed memories. Subjective repolarization. Or emotional chaos. Liberation from illusion. Or traumatic loss of faith. A new identity ideal precipitates within the fog of karmic habits. A silent inner revolution: 'still waters run deep.'

Theoretical brilliance gives way to transformative compassion. A fundamental enlargement of empathy for the previously excluded. Or dissociation from normal sympathy. Breakthrough to a more subtle and inclusive awareness. Breakdown of boundaries between self, world and others.

Neptune

Ideally this chapter would be written in musical notation. Heard through evocative sounds. Experienced as an emotional melody or a spiritual hymn. It would generate a symphony of moods rather than a line of thought. Felt, not understood. A sense of awe and mystery rather than of clarity and insight would result.

The best way to approach Neptune would be to close this book, empty the mind and meditate. Not on anything, but on nothing at all. Thus one may open to an illumination from beyond the busy inner chatter.

Neptune is the only planet completely invisible to the naked eye.[1] Its reality lies beyond conscious reach. Its presence can be felt, but never known. It infuses the atmosphere from behind the scenes, but remains inaccessible to direct perception.

Neptune symbolizes the primordial Unconscious. The dream behind material manifestation. The ideal behind the real. This exists in its own right, beyond Uranus' abstract organizing principles or Saturn's concrete behavioral laws. It describes the primal longing at the source of all life. And the rapture of release from the bonds of existence at its end.

Neptune acts subliminally as our contact with an all-inclusive Consciousness beyond any self-centered consciousness. It describes a general psychic sensitivity rather than a specific awareness. Ego floats at the surface of its unfathomable mystery. Neptune is the Ocean. We are its fish. Fish are unaware of the ocean, yet they live in its embrace.

Even the great mass and diversity of sea creatures constitute only a small part of its life-giving presence. In fact, most of the ocean is biologically barren. Vast stretches of its surface lack enough mineral nutrients to support photosynthesis at the base of life's food chain. All of its depths are without light to do so. Yet the oceans' great empty spaces recharge the vitality of our planet. They evaporate trillions of tons of water into evanescent clouds, untouchable fantasies in the sky. These rain down and nourish all terrestrial life, from tropical forests to arid steppes. Fluffy puffs of vapor, floating thousands of miles into dry continental interiors, provide Neptune's gift to an otherwise dead landscape.[2]

Like the ocean Neptune seems empty yet is pregnant with potential. Emptiness makes its own reality. Silence often speaks louder than words. As Taoism reminds us, the hole in the door, the cavity in the cup, are the purpose of these objects. Mathematics gives real value to zero: ten differs from one. Computer logic rests on a binary code: one and nothing. Neptunian nothingness measures fullness.

Every word on this page stands alone, surrounded by nothingness. One finds Neptune in the blanks between the words, through which one subconsciously absorbs and processes their meaning.

Taking the theme of emptiness further, the sundering seas separate continents. This permits diverse ecologies and civilizations to evolve independently. The planets spin in an apparently empty void, allowing each to be a world unto itself, distinct from all others. Neptunian isolation gives each planet, ecosystem and culture space in which to individualize.

Even the physical void of outer space demonstrates only part of what Neptune implies. Its 'empty' volume actually generates 'dark energy,' an inexplicable force causing the universe's rate of expansion to accelerate, in defiance of all 'common sense.' The vacuum sparkles, alive with quantum fluctuations. Discrete particles and fields emerge and disappear with prolific abandon. Neptune miraculously evokes a shimmering aura from the Void.

What is true in space may be in time as well. The seeming death of sleep refreshes one for a new day. Might Death itself be the same, awakening one into another life? The ultimate question, to which we will each get an answer. Or not, if death brings annihilation of consciousness. You never know with Neptune, the symbol of ambiguity and paradox. It can only be encountered with faith and feeling.

Neptune points to the inexplicable mystery of existence. Its ambivalence generates a fertile tension that distinguishes life from amorphous anarchy or static perfection. And allows the fluid freedom and spontaneity of evolution.

Neptune = enigma. Its indescribable Bliss sustains the universe; its fecund unity transcends all existential limitation. Yet protective illusions veil such sublime energies. Neptune intoxicates and confuses, clouds purpose and distracts consciousness, undermines with passive doubt and active treachery, until one learns to embrace its stimulating inconsistencies. Only by accepting creative contradiction can one encounter the real reality, including both the phenomenal world and its formless wellsprings.

Invisible Neptune stands as the last planet; the misty fog bound shore of Infinity. It points to the Oneness from which all things emerge and to which they return. In our contracted reality of being and becoming Neptune portrays a null zone between and separating entities. In our human condition Neptune represents the unknown beyond the ego's boundary. The negation of everything we know. The appalling nothingness of infinite space surrounding Earth, the utter loneliness of every ego doomed to die. An ocean of oblivion surrounding one's flickering self-consciousness.

Your time will end. Eternity will go on without you. Your brain-centered locus of sensation, feeling, thought must disintegrate. It will never exist again. Beyond our limit of existential capacity we cease to be. Forever. Neptune posits an absolute zero. Final Nothingness. The Abyss. As long as one identifies with existence then Neptune marks the ultimate horror.

There is no such thing as nothing. It does not exist.

There is only an ultimate transcendence of each and every singular thing. This Neptune offers. And demands. No ritual or prayer, no medical technique or heroic achievement, can hold back the tide of death. Final death and all the little deaths: of outworn relationships and suffocating ideas, limited projects and limiting projections. One can only surrender to it, as to sleep.

Thus, Neptune means surrender and sacrifice. Not surrender as a bargaining ploy, nor sacrifice in expectation of a reward, but true renunciation. To what end? To the end of all things and reabsorption into the One. We come from and return to an infinite source. Though finite we yearn for it. To go there one must give up everything. Even self. Neptune symbolizes one's attitude towards such loss.

Neptune rewards oblivion with redemption. This does not mean getting back an improved version of what you gave up. Or getting something altogether better. It means letting the universe redefine you on its terms, not yours. It gives release from an old self into a new dimension.

This occurs totally at the end of life. Its degree of redemption depends on one's level of trust in surrendering identity without guarantee of result. On faith in a process that brought one forth from nothingness in the first place.

Within life Neptune acts through the power of renunciation: the ability to leave safe certainties behind and unconditionally embrace the undefined promise of a larger reality. This is not so much painful as scary. Thus we shrink from it. Then the Neptune experience becomes distorted by wishful expectation and degraded by fearful resistance. We may call this unknown future heaven or hell, nirvana or nightmare. It is all the same, all one. Everything depends on one's orientation to its mystery: affirmation of a dimly sensed emergence, or revulsion against dissolution of the current self.

Neptune charts latent potential. It evokes possibilities rather than actual characteristics. Neptune's position indicates invisible talents, undeveloped abilities. Activating these unfamiliar powers requires loss of present character: the caterpillar must disintegrate within its cocoon

373

to emerge as a butterfly, the child must surrender innocence to the sexual fevers of adolescence, the adult must cast off the security of present status and opinion to achieve a more inclusive state of consciousness.

Neptune's negation of self can express through a mystic's transcendence of ego, a soldier's sacrifice of life, an idealist's devotion to a cause, a drunkard's slide into intoxication. Neptune portrays what one sacrifices and why. Its position and aspects describe what must be renounced. It may be a cherished belief system. Or money, career, marriage, etc. Neptune's house position indicates the area of life subject to decay and dissipation. Its sign position shows how this occurs.

One always sacrifices for a higher ideal, a new sense of identity, conscious or unconscious. If unconscious, this appears as a fate against which one feels helpless. In that case one becomes a victim until learning to embrace its greater purpose. This requires one to forfeit a beloved illusion, liquidate an outworn attribute. As that happens the underlying vision becomes more apparent. Its initial presentation is murky, a bewildering perplexity. But it grows, feeding off what it decomposes. It parasitically drains vitality, like every embryo in the womb - to irrigate a developing hope.

Neptune operates outside the consensus reality of individual egos, tangible objects and directed actions. It is not limited by the reality principle necessary for survival in a difficult objective environment (natural or social). Instead it constitutes the background foundation of unlimited subjective sensitivity.

Here personal identity melts down into raw feeling, washing away all reason and balance because it has no external frame of reference. Such Neptunian force can inspire. Or intoxicate. It manifests as ecstasy. Or hysteria. Blind adulation of a celebrity or cause; shared madness of a mob; mass frenzy of a game, concert, rally or revival all share the common quality of an immersion into its preconscious collective emotion.

More commonly we experience Neptune alone. This happens when an irresistible tide of sleep and dreams overwhelms the sense of self. Consciousness abdicates to a completely different reality. This call of Neptune cannot be denied: without sleep and dreams we die.

Neptune's boundless darkness surrounds our tiny lighted island of consciousness. It was before the beginning, so it will be after the end. One enters it regularly. Neptune's night absorbs one in what seems to be an imaginary world. Yet it is actually the primordial source of consciousness, the psychic equivalent of the quantum flux underlying material manifestation. Sleep's eerie dreamscape, unconstrained by the reality principle, plays out beyond rational understanding. Yet it is

374

essential to the life we think we know. A few days without dreams will drive one mad; a few more will physically kill.[3]

Neptune embodies one's ability to receive subliminal signals from the unconscious medium sustaining personality. Its inner Ocean flows with currents welling up from the depths of instinct and imagination. We experience them as dreams. Individual minds differ in their openness to those energies. Each psyche can only assimilate its symbolic messages up to its intuitive capacity.[4]

Neptune charts the archetypal dream a life embodies. The mythic theme orienting one's stream of consciousness. The primal fantasy one lives out. Moon then translates this into a subjective personal narrative. Moon formulates Neptune's mystic longings and imaginative visions into specific images, a unique content, based on individual memories and emotional priorities. Moon evokes personal tides of mood out of Neptune's unfathomable abyss.

In dreams, and perhaps after death, personality dissolves into a shared psychic reservoir of the collective unconscious. In that Neptunian melting pot it is fertilized by remembrance of timeless truths. There it is renewed by a cosmic baptism, its elements reorganized into new subjective energies. Then one's inner vision quest returns to continue its workout in the waking world.

At Neptune the central focus of ego evaporates into primal sensations. Waves of emotion surge, crest, crash and dissipate just one step past the shoreline of identity. The undertow of a subconscious agenda draws one out into their sinuous rhythms. Currents of imagination sweep one along with no sense of an orienting self. One sails the seas of fantasy, or nightmare, driven by invisible winds of spirit.

Yet an intermittent continuity of awareness, a vague impersonal shadow-self experiences this phantasmagoria. A subjective Witness lives in sleep, and perhaps in death. It exists prior to, and independently of, the ego. Its unfocused sentience underlies awareness. Its amorphous energy generates the shifting forms of consciousness. It is stimulated by objective perceptions, fed by one's actions in the so-called real world, and flowers into inspirational images.

Neptune condenses numinous ideals into symbols. Symbols can never be defined; they are fluid and multidimensional. They generate intuitive ideas (Uranus). These are accessible to consciousness, with one pole anchored in articulated concepts, the other in fertile Neptunian chaos. Something is always lost in translation. And gained in tangibility.

Neptune and Uranus are twin planets: virtually identical in size, mass, composition and speed of rotation. On the physical plane they manifest two aspects of the same energy: electromagnetism. Uranus embodies its electrical side as a moving current, an outward flow, of electrons away from their atoms into a directed stream of energy. Neptune exemplifies its magnetic side: a coordinated spin of electrons around their atoms generating a standing force field, an inward identity.[5] The same principle holds true in their expressions on the emotional, mental and spiritual planes.

Uranus projects Neptune's subjective charisma out into objective reality. It spins at an acute angle to Neptune, averaging 82°.[6] Together they form the horizontal and vertical axes of a cross uniting Uranus' etheric plane (the electronic template of life) with Neptune's astral plane (the deep dream of collective, or cosmic, imagination). These two subliminal forces weave together as the warp and woof of a subconscious tapestry, one's intuitive sense of the universe. Their polarization channels Neptune's mystic yearning into Uranus' abstract concepts. Saturn organizes them into specific thoughts. Jupiter promulgates them in the context of a religious, philosophical or political worldview. This general social orientation then takes on personal characteristics through the inner planets.

Uranus is abnormally cold, bland and featureless. Neptune is relatively hot, with a stormy atmosphere.[7] These physical differences reflect their complementary roles at the edge of consciousness. Uranus: detached and mental; Neptune: merging and emotional. Neptune fuses; Uranus differentiates. Neptune embodies a feeling state, a supernal oneness submerging individual identity. Uranus enables individual breakout from such oceanic unity into separate selfhood. This necessarily involves a violent process: a cutting loose, breaking away from the Neptunian All.

Neptune locates the hidden reality of the collective unconscious. Uranus gives access to it through its intuitive electricity.

Uranus/Neptune as a unit connects ego-mind with more subtle dimensions of consciousness behind concrete entities and events. Uranus has an inspirational quality. It provides access to an ethereal potency via archetypal symbols, mental abstractions, specific intuitions. Neptune lives in the imagination: a timeless subjective space of ecstatic identification with visionary images.

Uranus and Neptune in aspect, a formal geometrical relationship in the zodiac, facilitate Neptune's ability to directly express its psychic awareness or mythic insight. Together they express two sides of a freshly minted coin of consciousness. For example, even mathematics, the quintessential Uranian expression of abstract ideas, is permeated with Neptunian ambiguity: imaginary numbers (like the square root of negative one), endlessly receding quantities (like pi, the ratio of a circle's circumference to its radius), non-Euclidean geometries and other very real irrationalities.

Neptune in aspect to the personal or social planets, creates confusion because Neptune dissolves, while the other planet promotes, an existing state of consciousness. An unaspected Neptune portrays a sensibility that is either silently disintegrating or developing. A reclusive inner evolution of the unconscious itself, in its own subliminal terms, may be the most common Neptunian experience.

By its sign and house position Neptune indicates a fading psychological function. A quality of the total Self has reached a relative peak of development in comparison to the whole. Or degenerated to become actively dysfunctional, sabotaging further growth. In either case it must wither away, just as every human generation, great or decadent, must give up the ghost to make room for the next. By releasing its binding energy that function re-immerses into its collective or cosmic source. Thus it can absorb new impressions and be reborn.

In Neptune's apparent dead zone an old consciousness dissipates and a new one gestates. Out of its rotting and ripening all things come. And to its All, or nothing, they return when their duration in time, extension in space, experience in action is up.

Neptune decomposes an obsolete ego construct or attribute. This generates toxic byproducts of decay. They can poison perception, stupefy the mind and paralyze the will. A fog of confusion permeates thought, values and behavior. This can lead to dysfunction and self-destruction. Or to hypnosis by a stronger collective euphoria.

The sign and house Neptune occupies means apparent loss, or betrayal, in the affairs signified by those energy zones. This initially leads to debilitating emptiness. One can then escape into delusion, adopting fetish-substitutes for real satisfaction in that area.

Or one can accept dissolution of beloved ideals/idols. And open to the vulnerability of an unexpected redemption:

'Truly, truly I say to you, unless a grain of wheat falls into the earth and dies, it remains alone; but if it dies, it bears much fruit.'[8]

The delicacy and subtlety of the Neptunian experience makes this baptism into a new sensibility difficult in the rough and tumble of a harshly competitive world. Neptune tends to express itself best in artistic and spiritual endeavors. It must face painful deception in the political or social arena because its example of renunciation inherently challenges vested interests, and its sensitivity makes it easy prey for voracious egos.

Neptune attracts with the hypnotic draw of an ideal. An ideal - not a Uranian idea. Neptune is too all-inclusive to be crisply formulated as an idea must be. Neptune indicates the feeling behind the idea. Not a personal emotional feeling (Moon), but an enchanted religious awe.

Neptune embodies the mutual enchantment between spirit and matter. That generates life and consciousness. Sun = spirit, Moon = matter, Neptune = the magnetic Love they have for one another. All smaller loves reflect that. Venus charts love's personal expression.

Neptune functions as a higher octave of Venusian love, just as Uranus does of Mercurial mind. (See 'Dignities.') Neptune symbolizes Agape, a universal Christ-like love. This is more rarefied than Venus' Eros, an emotional affection for a particular individual with a sexual spark. Neptunian love involves a larger than personal empathy, with a mystical ambience.

One cannot see compassion. That doesn't mean it isn't there. One cannot define the exact nature of Neptune's redemption. Yet it is as real as death. Or as illusory.

Neptune can seduce by hallucinatory fascination, a false allure. Without firm footing in solid facts Neptune promotes both imaginative creativity and impossible fantasies. It is archaic, like the nebulous cloud of stardust from which the solar system arose. And exalted, like the etheric music of its spheres.

Neptune evokes an alien dimension, hostile to sense perception and rational understanding. This intangible reality undermines embedded worldviews and ego defenses. It brings loss of control. Without control is one a victim? Monster? Liberated?

Neptune subverts any self-centered frame of reference. Personality disintegrates in sleep, conventional morality melts down in ecstatic or intoxicated transports, defining memories erode, continuity of consciousness collapses in death. A tsunami of raw psychic power inundates identity. A maelstrom of hypnotic rapture draws one into the collective unconscious. Is this a desperate drowning or a baptismal immersion? Will one sink or swim or surf the wave? That depends on one's basic stance in the face of life's mystery: trust and love or fear and denial.

As the ego fades out one encounters its source, an invisible dream world underlying the visible material one. The astral plane, or realm of desire. Venus demonstrates its personal configuration. Neptune describes one's encounter with its pre-personal instincts and transpersonal inspirations. Human nature condenses at their intersection.

Neptune funnels energies from far infrared and ultraviolet regions of the spiritual spectrum into a more narrowly focused band-width of consciously perceived lights. It receives impressions of psychic heat waves or ghostly x rays, and translates them into sensed, felt images - just as a space telescope, positioned above Earth's dense life giving atmosphere, takes pictures of unseen frequencies emitted by the heavens.

Neptune refracts subtle vibrations of collective passion and cosmic illumination into a rainbow of subjective energies. This subconscious aura, the coloration of an ego, is perceived clearly or dully, brightly or dimly, according to one's level of evolution.

Neptune concentrates boundless imagination into the primal myths suffusing and shaping individual awareness. Blends angelic ideals and demonic delusions into an overall subjective charisma. Generates a unique personal glamor that permeates awareness and elicits behavior.

Neptune is a planet still in formation, a gas cloud spinning in on itself. Neptune centers spirit's yearning for tangible existence, endows it with emotional magnetism. Uranus channels this into an inspirational mental concept, or archetype. Saturn precipitates it into a material form governed by generic physical laws, biological conditions, psychological structures. These shape the contours, but do not define the content, of individuality. That emerges as a self-conscious soul at the planetary system's center: huge brightly banded Jupiter. This transcendent identity then 'falls' into the immanent rock solid reality of the compact terrestrial planets: little Mars, one's core drive; living Earth, ringed by its memory Moon; Venus, hot heart of personal love; and tiny Mercury, mind naked before the central spiritual fire of Sun.

We are each a fractal of the Whole: an experiment in consciousness, an excursion into activity by one underlying universal Force. Every soul is a (more or less) distorted image of God, a brief scintillation of the Radiance. Neptune embodies the longing of spirit to clarify its real nature in matter's evolutionary struggle. Its spellbinding seduction unites time and eternity, body and soul, in the mystery of psychological emergence.

Neptune's location marks a fountain of fantasies, out-surging dream tides. And the hypnotic fascination of death's dark abyss into which they ebb, enhanced by experience. Neptune describes the mutual enchantment of life and death, greater than both. It is the Magic.

And the madness. Every color twists the light from its original wholeness in one direction. Neptune focuses an intangible radiance into denser, more distinct wavelengths. These light waves disrupt the featureless face of infinity. They crisscross to form interference patterns, a shimmering of ideals and illusions, squalid cravings and ineffable longings, weaving together into the aura of a soul. This aurora borealis like shining organizes itself into the design or blueprint of individuality through the agency of Uranus. It then takes form and shape under the hard hand of Saturn. Neptune = the ideal, Uranus the plan, Saturn the reality.

Every entity distorts the Whole, just as every planet warps space. Neptune bends formless spirit along ancient fault lines of the cosmos to illuminate and work them out in the toil of evolution. It projects the deep unconscious out into the world to be enacted and redeemed. Its primordial longings, accumulated over eons, take form in Neptune's collective dreams.

Neptune suffuses the public mood with a redemptive vision, or an intoxicating illusion. Like the other trans-Saturnian planets, Neptune charts the social context within which an individual functions. It reveals an underlying tone of creative imagination or crazed fantasy motivating a historic period.

The qualities of Neptune particularly dominate the era between its discovery in 1846 and that of Pluto in 1930. At that time ancient paradigms dissolved into another worldview. New perspectives on evolution (Darwin), depth psychology (Freud, Jung) and relativistic physics (Einstein, etc.) immersed us in a different reality. Humanity's most basic assumptions about ancestry and origins; identity and consciousness; time, space, matter and energy all melted down into a new vision. We were baptized into an altered state. For a historical review of Neptune's last transit through each of the signs, 1861-2026, see 'Outer Planet Transits.'

Because Neptune moves so slowly, taking 14 years to transit a sign, the thrilling enticements of one age cohort may leave another cold: a generation that values honor/courage will differ from one that elevates fairness/justice; both may be at odds with yet another mesmerized by ambition/achievement. Neptune's inner personal octave, Venus, then specifically evaluates people and situations within this general spiritual atmosphere.

On the psychological plane our thoughts, feelings, sensations and purposes emanate from an invisible source. They then coarsen and thicken into the realm of nouns and verbs we call real. Neptune mysteriously inspires the imagination with a supernal magic. Uranus translates this into conceptual insights. Saturn gives them articulated form, carrying social meaning (Jupiter).

Neptune points to the collective unconscious. Its glimmering depths contain potencies only hinted at by the social archetypes of Jupiter. In the dream state its conscious/unconscious interface glows with strange patterns as the mind explores itself freed from the restraints of logic and reality. These patterns range from trivial to cosmic, grotesque to sublime, nightmarish to beatific. They undergo their own evolution, parallel to that of the waking mind.

Neptune's psychic receptivity attunes one to the invisible oscillations underlying phenomenal facts. It operates independently of sensory input or physical limitation. Through it one can hear the music of the spheres, see the character of another's heart, sense things distant in time and space, on an ethereal wavelength.

These experiences cannot be verbally defined anymore than can the emotional states evoked by normal music. Neptune brings feeling to the soul, not information to the senses. It evokes subjective resonance, not objective results. It acts as a diffuse atmosphere rather than as a discrete word. The fact that such energies operate below the radar makes them all the more powerful. Dreams shape the world at least as much as Uranian plans or Saturnine rules.

Yet in the end all of these paranormal states constitute distracting sideshows. They are faint shadows of Neptune's true estate: a conscious revelation of universal love. A general compassion extended to every individual with full awareness and commitment.

That love also embodies a deep sadness: the pain of separation necessary for existence. It accepts spirit's sacrificial immersion into a limited, fragmented and conflicted life. We are each torn from the womb of eternity and long to return. This remembrance of, and yearning for, unity generates empathy: first with some, then with all.

Neptune spins this shared sensitivity into a mythological worldview with a collective meaning. Its magical symbols constellate life's flood of feelings. Uranian scientific principles organize the complexity of material phenomena around ideas such as evolution, relativity, conservation of energy, etc. Neptunian visionary images center emotional vitality around ideals of love, beauty, peace, justice, etc.

These redemptive themes can degenerate into intoxicating illusions of specialness and superiority, expressed religiously, politically or personally. Then our deeper wholeness bears witnesses to the clashing craziness of egos, including one's own. It takes a long time, perhaps lifetimes, for emotional awareness (Moon) to develop personal love (Venus), then social identification (Jupiter) and finally an all embracing care and concern (Neptune). At each step of the way, melting in melancholy mortification, the soul broadens its stance to a greater inclusiveness.

Yet, in its Neptunian dimension, that soul also connects with another reality. In this world it remains exiled from its celestial home. Here, baptized in tears, it learns compassion:

'He was despised and rejected by men; a man of sorrows, and acquainted with grief; and as one from whom men hide their faces he was despised, and we esteemed him not.'[9]

Moons

Neptune has 14 known moons, two of which are significant: Triton and Pluto. These two are virtual twins in size and composition. They demonstrate a diffuse background cosmic radiance spiraling down into Neptune's waters of imagination.

Triton, ¾ the size of our Moon, circles Neptune retrograde. It orbits in the opposite direction to all other moons of all other planets. Astronomically this implies that it is a captured planetoid. Astrologically it points to the in-falling, still forming nature of Neptune as wisps of space gas condense into its ocean of dreams. Triton, like Venus, Neptune's more tangible octave, symbolizes an involutionary vortex. It draws the void-energy of space down into Neptune's depths of psyche.

Pluto seems to be an almost escaped moon of Neptune. Or a satellite being captured by it. It circles briefly within Neptune's path for 20 out of 248 years of its own orbit, thus orbiting both Neptune and Sun.[10] Pluto acts as a lightning rod, drawing the spiritual equivalent of interstellar radiation into Triton's involutionary gateway. See 'Pluto.'

Notes

1. Pluto acts as a force, not a planetary state of being. It represents the pre-planetary foundations of our solar system, displayed in its surrounding Kuiper Belt of ice and rock fragments. Pluto introduces this reality to the system as it intersects Neptune's orbit.
2. In a striking parallel to the ocean's watery deserts, 97% of the human genome consists of nonfunctional DNA. Most is simply genetic gibberish ('junk DNA'): decayed remnants of obsolete genes from earlier stages of development, viral insertions and inert repetitive sequences. Yet this junk DNA acts as the matrix of evolution. It provides a reservoir of redundant nucleotides that can be reassembled into new genes. Here innovative mutations can occur without damaging the vital functions conserved in the tiny protein coding segments (genes) or the regulatory regions turning them on and off.

Like junk DNA, and a sparsely inhabited ocean irrigating the land, hidden Neptune serves as the paradoxical source of life more abundant. Its lack of overt activity hides a deeper psychic potency.

3. The longest verified case of sleep deprivation involved a 17 year-old student, Randy Gardner, who stayed awake for 264 hours (11 days) in 1965. He became psychologically dysfunctional, with severe paranoia and hallucinations, before any physical damage occurred. The same has been observed in all other studies.

Menachem Begin, a Polish Jew who later became Prime Minister of Israel, 1977-'83, was subjected to sleep deprivation by Stalin's NKVD. He described it thus:

> In the head of the interrogated prisoner a haze begins to form. His spirit is wearied to death, his legs are unsteady and he has one sole desire: to sleep...Anyone who has experienced this desire knows that not even hunger or thirst are comparable.

Unethical experiments carried out on lab rats at the University of Chicago in the 1980s showed that they consistently died within two weeks of sleeplessness. Some quibble that this was due to the 'stress' of being forcibly awakened over a thousand times a day rather than to lack of sleep itself. Such a meaningless distinction also illustrates how Neptune deceives: by distraction of attention, subversion of values, from the real truth of unnatural cruelty to irrelevant interpretations of pointless results. Yes, one can torture mammals to death by denying them sleep - at the cost of one's soul.

Neptune points to the false premise at the core of one's worst mistakes. The Big Lie one unconsciously accepts.

4. Some claim they rarely or never dream. Sleep research has proven this false. We all dream during every sleep cycle; we simply cannot recall their reality in the fundamentally different waking state. Others say that dreams are not important, but only a mindless processing of the waking day's events. Certainly a large proportion seems to consist of bizaRre fragments or cartoon like sequences with no apparent meaning. Yet these form only a chaotic transition zone between the organized surface of ego consciousness and the unstructured sensitivity of its depths. At this level the unconscious, exposed to conscious scrutiny but unable to rationally articulate itself, can only present fleeting images of its fermenting contents.

Below it, dreams follow their own psychological truthflow rather than a sequential cause and effect logic. There everyone works out personal issues through imaginative fantasies of subconscious symbolism, freed from ego's pride and prejudice. A few can remember revelatory dreams of collective significance.

383

Neptune's celestial music is normally blotted out by the biological demands and loud social concerns of consensus consciousness. It still plays in the background and is subliminally heard by the sleeping mind. It can awaken spiritual qualities in anyone who learns to listen.

5. Magnetism is an energy pattern generated by the spin of atomic electrons. Usually these are paired on specific energy levels (orbitals) with opposite spins canceling each other out. A few elements, notably iron, have a single electron in its outermost orbital that can align with the spin of its neighbors. When a huge number of such electrons spin in unison they collectively emit a magnetic domain. Thus magnetism means a sympathetic resonance amplifying tiny electronic spins into a coherent field pervading a grounding medium, such as iron. This physical phenomenon parallels a spiritual synchronicity permeating the concentric density planes of the cosmos: through matter, life, psyche, and mind, back to spirit.

Neptune illustrates the magnetic nature of one's soul as a hypnotic spinning around its own center. This generates a vortex of spiritual force around which its psychological qualities coalesce. It may be aligned with the parallel spinning of other centers. And like anything with a strong character it also repels or rejects incompatible forces. Neptune's twin planet Uranus describes magnetism's discharge as an electric current, flowing out into the world and against its material resistance as an ability to perform work.

Iron is the characteristic seat or host of the magnetic force. Iron is the densest, most compact atom that can be formed by nuclear fusion in a star. The formation of iron absorbs more energy than it can release by further fusion into heavier elements. Thus, at the stage when iron fusion begins a star almost instantly collapses because it can no longer radiate energy to counteract its gravitational contraction. It falls in upon itself, and then bounces back out in a nova or supernova explosion. The enormous energy of such an explosion binds together those heavier elements, such as gold, silver, uranium that cannot form during the fusion process of a star's life. It is as if iron, the end of a star's shining, absorbs that shining into its own material structure, grounding its radiance into an organized magnetic force field.

Iron, the magnetic materialization of a star's last luminescence demonstrates a spiritual quality. So does every element, chemical compound, mineral, plant and animal. Each manifests an aspect of Neptune's all-ensouling energy field.

An interesting treatment of this theme can be found in 'The Secrets of Metals,' by Wilhelm Pelikan (1893-1981).

6. The angle between Uranus' and Neptune's north poles varies from 54° to 110° depending on these two planets' relative inclination towards Sun. See 'Outer Planet Transits,' Figure 1.

7. Uranus is cold because its internal heat engine was disrupted billions of years ago by the gigantic collision that knocked it over, perpendicular to all other planets. Neptune is hot inside because it, alone among the planets, is still forming, generating the heat of gravitational contraction.

8. John 12:24

9. Isaiah 53:3

10. See 'Outer Planet Transits,' Figure 2.

Neptune in Signs and Houses

Neptune in a sign indicates the nature of one's ideals. Quality of imagination. Participation in collective dreams.

Neptune in a house indicates what aspect of personal identity or experience is dying to be reborn.

Because Neptune moves so slowly, spending 14 years in each sign, only four or five Neptune sign positions are mature at any moment. Other sign positions describe previous or emerging generations, or earlier historical eras.

At the time of writing (2015) no one is alive with Neptune in Aries, Taurus, Gemini or Cancer. The few surviving with it in Leo are mostly senile, and all of those in Virgo are on the wrong side of 70. Only those with Neptune in Libra, Scorpio, Sagittarius and Capricorn are currently adults in their prime. People with Neptune in Aquarius are now children or adolescents, and those in Pisces are infants, or perhaps in the pipeline for incarnation. Over the next decade older members of the Neptune in Libra cohort will fade out, while older members of the Aquarian group rise into early adulthood.

Every day Neptune passes through all the houses because they are defined by Earth's own rotation.

Neptune: ferment within the unconscious. Neptune dissolves form. It liquidates an existing psychological structure defined by its sign and house position. This creates an opening for baptism into a subtler emergence of that quality.

Neptune in fire signs or houses: charismatic projection of personal glamor. Or hypnosis by a more powerful will. It suggests the supernal light of a heavenly vision, divine illumination or revelatory enlightenment. Or the hell fire of illusions, lies, betrayals revealed.

The siren call blinding one, as a moth drawn to the flame. A redemptive ecstasy of participation in a transcendent will. And the acid agony of self-deception burned away. Hidden truths, underlying forces, latent potentials shine forth in luminous magic.

Neptune in air signs or houses: poetic articulation of subtle or mystical truth. Or mental meltdown as reason and common sense dissolve into delusional fantasy. It suggests a spiritual synthesis of clashing ideas and conflicting perspectives. Mental grasp of transcendent reality; making sense of seemingly chaotic processes. Or escape from life's ambiguity into an arid rationalism. The magic, or quicksand, of faith in a universal theory whether religious or political, scientific dogma or cultural consensus.

Neptune in water signs or houses: personal psychic sensitivity. An attunement to deep collective currents. Or drowning in a group mystique and blind adoration. It suggests baptismal immersion into an oceanic Oneness with others and the universe. A mystical feeling flood of compassion and love. Direct contact with the life-giving, but treacherous, waters of the unconscious. Foundering in storm-tossed seas of private emotion or public passions. Meltdown of frozen memories or blockages, releasing a tsunami of primal instinct.

Neptune in earth signs or houses: subordination of wishful thinking and ego longings to impersonal truth. Or a soul-drought with its false compensations of wealth, control, status. Psyche seduced and abandoned by the 'bitch-goddess Success.' It suggests grounding of mystical vision in practical achievement. Harnessing of spiritual insight to rational purpose and compassionate action. Applied charisma. Or a desiccation of feeling. The exhausting routine of work and mundane requirements of life suck away the magic.

Neptune in Aries/first house

Paradox: the planet of dissolution in the sign/house of self-assertion.

Disintegration and sublimation of personal will. Devitalizes a tired ego fantasy. Voids a now decadent self-image. Resistance to this necessary decay generates illusions of helpless paralysis. Acceptance implies the enchantment of new beginnings. The magic of a fresh dream. Renunciation of an old perspective or worldview creates space for a larger one to emerge. A redemptive vision of rebirth.

Imagination individualizes. A defining myth burns away. An unconscious illumination crosses the threshold of awareness to fill the vacuum. It struggles to emerge from its own inner trance, and from the confusion of its initial encounter with objective reality. Its subtle energy permeates identity with a poetic and mystic sensibility. Or drowns it in the intoxicating firewater of a delusional ecstasy. Its potent glamor can inspire spiritual transcendence. Or generate an obsession by strongly felt but dimly understood psychic forces.

A visionary ideal, or spellbinding hallucination, suffuses personality. One can intentionally channel its collective or instinctual images. Or become an empty echo chamber for them. A heroic battle to awaken from a hypnotic rapture of the depths and bring its treasures up into the light. Or sleepwalk into oblivion.

Empathetic outreach; mercy in action. Or self-pity. Sacrifices personal interests to compassionate embrace. Or surrenders to victim consciousness, defaults into passive-aggressive evasion and denial. Effective action can be undermined by a nebulous sense of alienation.

Neptune in Taurus/second house

Disintegration and sublimation of personal desires. Surrender of resources. Devitalizes confused standards of merit and worth. Voids a now decadent 'realism' that only economic motivations count. Resistance to this necessary decay generates toxic illusions of substitute gratifications through control of fetish objects, or persons. Acceptance implies the inclusive magic of sharing: a compassionate offering of worldly wealth. Redemptive sacrifice of possessions. Or spellbinding possession by them. Meltdown of old values. Renunciation of previous pleasures and now burdensome goods.

The enchantment of spirit into matter. The hypnotic attraction of physical sensation unmodified by exterior significance. A visionary ideal of beauty. Imagination consolidates into specific yearnings. Dreams condense into wants. Or dissolve into appetites.

Intoxication by the idolatry of greed. The mesmerizing glitter of gold. The hypnotic allure of Precious. Its inevitable loss. And the paradoxical liberation that brings.

There is a fundamental tension between tangible Taurus and ethereal Neptune:

'No one can serve two masters. Either you will hate the one and love the other, or you will be devoted to the one and despise the other. You cannot serve both God and money.' (Matthew 6:24)

The deception of materialism: that only the visible is true. Or a devaluation of the world and body in exaggerated raptures of asceticism. Resolution comes through practical empathy: distribution of accumulated assets to serve collective needs. And through a more loving sensuality: mystic appreciation for God's incarnation in nature and in the human form.

Neptune in Gemini/third house

Disintegration and sublimation of a mental paradigm. Imagination objectifies. Personal dreams detach from identification with collective myths.

Devitalizes a tired fantasy of superficial cleverness, quick but shallow wit. Voids a now decadent vision that prioritized hard data over ambiguous meaning. Resistance to this necessary decay generates intellectual intoxication by overemphasis on analytical dissection v holistic function, information bytes v intangible qualities. Acceptance implies a more subtle understanding of previously disowned spiritual or mystic forms of knowledge. Renunciation of a fetish for certainty clears a mind-space that allows irrigation of arid rationality by poetic metaphor. A redemptive vision of dualistic thought infused by a transcendent wisdom.

Meltdown of cerebral categories. Cognitive paradox as mind tries to comprehend the mystery of its unconscious matrix. Thought can become distorted by idealized perceptions. Or seduced by the illusion of isolated facts taken out of context.

Divided ideals. Or ideals of division: negatively as fantasies of hate or superiority, positively as a higher truth bringing order out of chaos, light from darkness. Dissolves previous ideas of what constitutes reality. Seeks a higher imaginative synthesis. An attempt to express the ineffable, clarify ambiguity, articulate the numinous. However, effective communication can be undermined by wishful thinking, nebulous concepts, confused expression.

Neptune in Cancer/fourth house

Disintegration and sublimation of private sensitivities. Imagination dissolves a tacitly accepted public consensus into a new subjective mood.

The maternal Cancer/4th house energy field births collective unconscious currents into psychological tides of individual feeling. Here Neptune devitalizes an outworn ego fantasy so that a more inclusive identity can absorb this vitalizing flood. It voids the ebbing tribal mythology that sustained a now obsolete self-image. Resistance to this necessary decay generates toxic illusions of memory, history and origins compensating for loss of an idealized past. Acceptance implies the magic of personal resonance with universal longings. Opens to more subtle reception of inner signals and external impressions. Renunciation of once inspiring, but now merely hypnotic, ideals and idols clears space for a larger empathy. A redemptive vision of self-centered emotion absorbed into shared psychic bonding with a charmed circle of intimates. Possible immersion into a mystic sense of oceanic oneness with the entire sphere of existence.

Meltdown of traditional affiliations (familial, ethnic, cultural) into a deeper appreciation of fundamental roots. Ancient dreams permeate present imagination. Feels and channels the 'shadows of forgotten ancestors.' Or escapes into the delusions of herd psychology. Participation mystique.

The enchantment of untamed emotion. The magic of raw feeling, uncensored by intellect or purpose. The illusion of security by finding refuge from the world in dreams. However, glamorous fantasies can undermine the reality principle.

Neptune in Leo/fifth house

Disintegration and sublimation of ego. Devitalizes a tired fantasy of special uniqueness. Voids a now decadent form of subjective expression. Meltdown of an obsolete social role. Surrenders past glory; dissolves false pride. Resistance to this necessary decay generates toxic illusions of megalomania: personal identification with images arising from the collective unconscious. Acceptance liquidates an investment in pretension, releasing its magnetic force back into innocent imagination. This clears space for universal Soul to shine through the medium of individual creativity.

Self redeemed by sacrifice for a grand passion. Illuminates a glamorous Vision. Or a seductive illusion. The inspirational power of an ideal. Or hypnotic allure of an idol. Ignites an inner rapture into focused devotion. Channels a dream into art.

A developed personality, suffused with enigmatic charisma, gives a human face to romantic myth. The spellbinding mystique of leadership. The magic of a nobility that evokes emulation in others. Generosity of spirit floods forth in unreserved compassion upon good and bad alike. Or ebbs into a confused sense of infantile omnipotence. Narcissistic intoxication. Delusions of grandeur. Or a sense of insignificance washed away by immersion in the shared ecstasy of tribal emotion.

Idealizes love, and the beloved. Radiant feeling brings latent beauty to life, lights up another's invisible qualities. Or blind adulation can freeze the love object into a statue on a pedestal.

Neptune in Virgo/sixth house

Detriment. Imagination fades as practical competence increases.

Disintegration and sublimation of skills. Devitalizes a tired fantasy of petty standards. Voids a now decadent and petrified vision of perfection. Resistance to this necessary decay can generate toxic illusions of competence at small or unworthy things. Acceptance implies the sacrifice of ritual purity in favor of genuine compassion. Such renunciation clears a space for healing self and others by actual service.

Meltdown of a soulless rationality. A redemptive vision of integrity that incorporates spiritual dimensions of body, mind and soul. Or delusions of virtue. A hypochondriac fetish for narrowly defined hygiene: physical (germophobia), mental (political correctness) or social (ethnic cleansing). A sterile myth of methodology: efficient means serve distorted ends. Rapture undermined by the fine print. A song desiccated by critical analysis.

Clarifies ideals with a view to simplicity and consistency. Tempers ecstatic vision, personal transports of feeling, by the ethical imperatives of empathy. Makes charity concrete. Universal love tested in practice. Salvation by work. Faith in due process.

Dreams disciplined by the reality principle. Or subverted by irrelevant details. The magic, or idolatry, of technique. The glamor of precision. The poetry of pragmatism. Ideals reduced to formulae, making them useful. That, rather than mystic longing, got us to the Moon.

Neptune in Libra/seventh house

Disintegration and sublimation of relationships. Devitalizes a tired collective balance of values. Voids a now decadent vision of social standards. Resistance to this necessary decay generates toxic illusions of dishonest encounter with others. Then posturing and artificial convention obscure genuine empathy. Acceptance implies the magic of an artistic sensitivity deriving inspiration from creative contrast or even conflict.

Renunciation of obsolete or inappropriate roles clears a space for a higher harmony. A redemptive vision of right relationship levels differences and barriers. Emphasizes common ground. Egalitarian pretension can subvert respect for excellence.

Imagination adjusts to the presence of other dreams. Old criteria of judgment dissolve. A new canon of beauty. Aesthetic sensibility refined. Or lets itself go. Enduring, or rigid, standards of honor and virtue are forgotten. Different ideals of fairness and equity emerge. Confusion in association with others. Ambiguous relationships and rules of relationship. Looser and more inclusive, or laxer and more permissive, codes of conduct.

Meltdown in norms of justice, for better or worse. Transcendent community ideals, or degenerate popular delusions, inform personal choice. Independent judgment can be undermined by deferential cooperation. The mystique that inclusiveness and consensus guarantee a better outcome then individual assertion. However, hypocritical process and phony role-playing can undermine decision making and real action.

Neptune in Scorpio/eighth house

Disintegration and sublimation of libido, the psychic life force. Devitalizes social norms forbidding real passion. Voids unspoken taboos that prevent genuine feeling. Resistance to this necessary decay generates toxic illusions of power, caused by identification with now decadent collective strictures. Acceptance implies baptism into a new dimension of emotional sensibility.

Meltdown of superego controls releases normally suppressed desires and perceptions. Liquidates inhibition. This clears a space for the emergence of unconscious energies: angelic ideals and demonic urges. Encounters the blissful and wrathful deities of personal conscience. Or of group karma.

Dissolves myths of power: the moral narratives that channel political and sexual drives. This liberates their binding energy for higher expression. Or unleashes dark seductions of their most primitive side. Breaching these psychological firewalls exposes the final illusion: the dream of death. Surrenders to its negation; or celebrates it in orgiastic ecstasies of destruction. Denies its devouring reality in fantasies of eternal life. Or sacrifices ego to faith in its mystery.

Imagination regenerates through loss of the separate self-sense. It immerses into a hypnotic rapture of the instinctual depths. Or illuminates inner darkness with a redemptive vision.

The magic of an erotic trance. Embrace of sexuality as a sacrament raising biological energies into a spiritual communion of souls. Mystic refinement of passion into compassion. Eros (sexually charged love) ascends into a more demanding, and rewarding, Agape (universal Christ-like love). Or descends into a lascivious confusion of promiscuous dissipation.

Neptune in Sagittarius/ninth house

Dissolution or sublimation of a religious or philosophical paradigm. Devitalizes a tired tribal myth. Voids now decadent social standards of righteousness. This necessary decay can generate toxic illusions of a relativistic vacuum dissolving ethical integrity. It can also feed the ripening of transcendent ideals. Renunciation of conventional wisdom creates a space for channeling a divine presence. This can inspire or intoxicate. The magic of spiritual charisma. A redemptive vision of universal principles superseding hypnotic doctrines of political ideologies or sectarian cults.

Personal identification with collective dreams. Prescient imagination transcends myths of consensus consciousness. Senses the larger meaning and direction behind linear time's plodding pace. Psychic intuition of deeper truths, the long term significance of current events. Or the seductive glamor of a false prophet. Hallucinations of distorted or exaggerated revelation.

Meltdown of orthodox interpretation opens up new dimensions of mystic experience. It can generate a rapture of liberation. Or undermine standards of conscience. A glimpse of supernal Light enhances moral sophistication. Or blinds, leading one as a moth into the flames of fanatical enthusiasm.

Idealistic fervor. Or feverish delusion. Visionary faith. Growth of metaphysical consciousness and contemplative practice. Larger, looser feelings of freedom, or license, blur social norms. Ambiguous aspirations.

Neptune in Capricorn/tenth house

Dissolution and sublimation of an obsolete vocation. Devitalizes a tired mystique of success. Voids a now decadent ambition blocking spiritual growth. Resistance to this necessary decay can generate toxic illusions of mastery and control; hiding from truth behind rank. Acceptance liquidates constraining forms to liberate their binding energy. Such renunciation clears a space for new social ideals and arrangements. Worldly goals sacrificed to a redemptive vision of effective compassion.

Neptune's fluid creativity is inhibited in the Capricorn/10th house zone of structured energy and practical realism. It undermines identification with the conservative mythology holding any society together. Erodes accepted ideals of personal duty and collective responsibility. Elevates new idols of individual power and prosperity. Worships the Golden Calf. Or the magic of spiritual initiation through disciplined austerity.

Inevitable decay of achievement. Melts down conventional priorities, replaces them with a more flexible, and ambiguous, dream. An old ego structure dissolves. Traditional values, good and bad, decay. Time honored certainties wash away. Hierarchical distinctions blur. Subverts authority. Loss of respect for both real merit and artificial privilege. Status glamorized, substance devalued. The illusion of celebrity clouds genuine accomplishment.

Imagination organized by conscious purpose. Dreams congeal into a to do list. The reality principle can be sabotaged by fantastic goals. Rational strategic planning can degenerate into wishful thinking.

Neptune in Aquarius/eleventh house

Dissolution of hopes, wishes, aspirations. Imagination condenses into a program. Fluid intuition precipitates into a systematic blueprint. Dreams adapt to an alien terrain of detached thought. Compassion struggles to generate a rational agenda.

Devitalizes a tired theoretical construct. Voids a utopian myth now drained of life. Resistance to this necessary decay generates toxic intellectual illusions. Acceptance implies a more transcendent inspiration deepened by universal empathy.

Cerebral axioms and principles can never fully encompass the elusive nature of reality. Only respect for fertile ambiguity can embrace paradoxical truth. Renunciation of linear mental programming clears space for higher, more archetypal dimensions of understanding. A redemptive vision of sequential logic dissolved into holistic intuition.

The enchantment of ideas. Identification with collective ideals of improvement and evolution. However, the best laid plans always go awry. Trust in social reforms is undermined by the tragedy of the human condition. Belief in a larger mystery emerges.

Dry abstraction irrigated by psychic sensitivity. Personal originality opens a channel for mystic revelation. However, illusions of brilliance can blind one to unintended consequences, hidden irrationalities and fatal inconsistencies. Exalted fantasies can melt down into mere eccentricity, or evaporate into the thin air of impracticality.

The faith to embrace a new paradigm. Such a conceptual leap leaves old certainties behind to immerse in larger ocean of wisdom. Or finds itself stranded in the bubble of a separate reality.

Neptune in Pisces/twelfth house

Rulership. Compassion, renunciation and sacrifice assume an unusual degree of importance in the general personality. Mystic vision and mythic themes are emphasized in relation to other aspects of psyche.

Disintegration and sublimation of an entire worldview. Imagination dissolves: old dreams die so new ones can emerge. Devitalizes a tired emotional fantasy. Voids a collective trance and surrenders to an unknown future. Resistance to this necessary decay generates toxic karmic illusions. Acceptance enlarges a life to include all life. Loss of identification with the separate self sense clears space for the magic of unconditional love.

Yet sacrifice can be undermined by treachery. Predators often exploit naive altruism. Indiscriminate sympathy can make one a codependent enabler. These undertows generate a subjective struggle to distill psychic poisons into spiritual forgiveness; and redeem pain by unconditional charity.

Appreciates elusive, intangible truths and fleeting nuances of feeling. The soul of ambiguity, a holy fool. Emotionally sophisticated or just plain confused. Divine or demonic intoxication. Powerful idealism, untethered to the reality principle, opens to seductive whispers from the collective unconscious. And to sublime illuminations of a higher Will.

The veil of illusion - and the illusory hopes that paradoxically entice one to transcend it. Launch into uncharted seas - and blind faith giving the only hope of successful navigation. Liquidates the past: a river flows into the Ocean.

Salvation through suffering made meaningful. Tears of compassion:

'Jesus wept.'

Pluto

Pluto swoops into the solar system at a 17° angle to the other planets' orbital plane. Figure 1. This small but meaningful angle, 5% of a circle, equals the degree of separation from Sun that any planet needs to become visible from out of the solar glare.[1] It measures the amount of space distinguishing a psychological function from the central personal purpose. Pluto does something similar at the other end of the spectrum. It introduces interstellar forces from deep space into our system from a slightly different perspective than that of the other planets' shared orbital level. It orients our solar system to its galactic matrix.

Pluto is also the only planet that intersects another planetary orbit. It actually crosses Neptune's path and spends 20 years closer to Sun. It then moves out again for a long ride (228 years) at the outer fringes of the system. Figure 2.

Thus Pluto orbits Neptune. They are planet and moon, as well as two distinct planetary forces. Yet Pluto almost always intersects Neptune's orbit far away from Neptune itself, perhaps even in zodiacal opposition to it. Pluto does not circle Neptune's physical globe so much as its energy level in space. It interweaves Neptune's trajectory with a visitation from a far domain. Penetrates Neptune's perimeter of motion with the periodic intrusion of a world from beyond our system of worlds. This implies a subtle relationship between Neptunian dream and Plutonic passion, redemption and resurrection, at the far edge of psyche.

Neptune's orbit marks the shoreline of human consciousness. Our solid reality fades out into a foggy Ocean of dreams, demonic and divine. Here one's known identity, centered on a star, experienced on Earth, dissolves into dim mists where all desire dies.

Our planetary system ends at Neptune. Beyond it a cloud of tiny planetoids tumble through the dark. It forms a sphere of icy fragments: not organized on a coherent plane, but scattered across the sky; not moving in circular patterns, but careening on wildly elliptical paths in all directions; not consolidated into one body, but splintered into countless shards. This is the Oort Cloud/Kuiper Belt, a shatter zone of ice and rock, leftover debris from the solar system's formation.

The Oort Cloud embodies a spherical asteroid zone surrounding our solar system, enclosing it within a cosmic placenta. This bubble mediates between our star and its galactic environment. Some of the Cloud's material spirals inwards as a flattened disc: the Kuiper Belt. That acts as an umbilical cord transmitting interstellar vibrations to the

Figure 1   Pluto's inclination to solar system

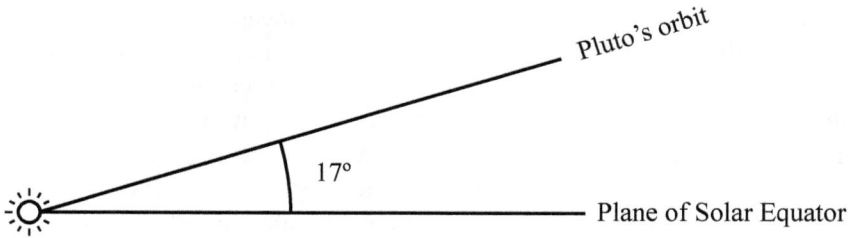

Pluto orbits at a 17° angle to the plane of the solar equator. All other planets orbit close to that plane except Mercury, which has an angle of 7°. Pluto introduces an element of verticality onto the horizontal wheel of concentric orbits.

Figure 2   Pluto orbit

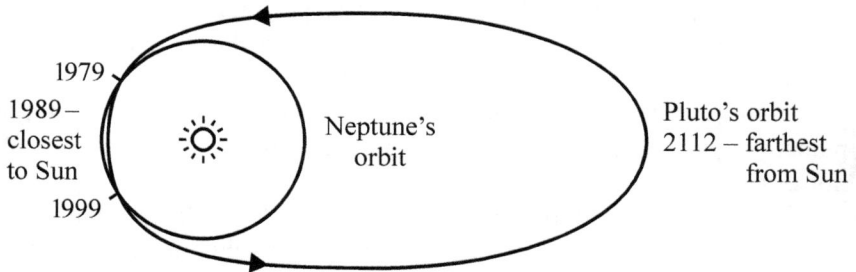

Pluto crosses and orbits inside of Neptune's orbit for 20 out of 248 years.

planetary domain. Pluto, at the Kuiper Belt's near edge, focuses those signals into psychic wavelengths.

This jumbled astronomical layer resembles the quantum chaos underlying physical phenomena. Yet it gave rise to the solar system's structured cosmic atom. Pluto connects these two planes of being. The subatomic energy field fundamentally differs from, yet creates, material reality. Similarly, Pluto converts a general life force into instinctual urges. It channels elemental sensations into the primordial images that then generate consciousness.

Pluto does not describe a state of being like the other planets, but rather an irresistible force. It enters and disrupts a stately minuet of circling worlds. This intruder explodes out of the nowhere beyond Neptune's nirvana. It relays a generation long broadcast from the stars, then flings itself back out at them, to metamorphose and return centuries later. Pluto symbolizes a periodic shock wave that reverberates through the solar system then vibrates back out into the galactic void.

Pluto does not symbolize an autonomous psychological function (such as Venus = love, Mars = personal will, etc.). Rather it invokes a new commandment. This acts as an overwhelming compulsion, an obsessive drive. As such it is partial, fixated on one thing to the exclusion of all others. It includes a readiness to destroy the whole identity in order to promote one overriding Priority.

Pluto's impact disintegrates an old Neptunian myth, releasing its vitality into a fresh spiritual impulse. It obliterates its previous qualities and concentrates their energy into a singular surge. This arises as a simple imperative that redefines a worldview.

Nor is this the end of Pluto's alien nature. Pluto is very small, only ⅔ the size of Earth's Moon. Yet it has not one, but two, bodies. Its giant moon Charon, ½ the size of Pluto itself, is proportionally much larger, and far closer to its parent, than any other moon (only eight Pluto diameters away). Earth's Moon makes a distant second, at ¼ the diameter of the parent, orbiting thirty Earth diameters away. Pluto is a double planet, two globes closely circling each other, as they loop into and out of the planetary plane.

This double-balled body regularly thrusts into and out of Neptune's fecund womb, inseminating psyche with cosmic energies. Pluto plunges into Neptune's system-encircling ocean, fertilizing it with stardust from distant suns. By position and aspect tiny Pluto describes a sperm impregnating a Neptunian dream. From their orgasm Uranus quickens an inspiration into expression.

A moon indicates planetary baggage. This can be dead weight of the past. Or a resource for the future. It can be thought of as karma: an inheritance or a burden. Most planets have a suite of comparatively small moons, or none at all. Only Earth and Pluto have big ones in comparison to the central globe. Relatively speaking Pluto's moon is twice as big and four times closer than ours. This is a doom-laden world.

Charon was boatman of the dead, ferrying their souls across the river Styx to Pluto's underworld. He demanded a coin for this service. Astrologically his price is death: physical, emotional, professional, spiritual, as the case may be. Charon, gatekeeper of Hades, reminds us of Pluto's nature as the place of no return. It conveys one to an irrevocable transformation.

Tiny Pluto, carrying its enormous satellite, does some heavy lifting and thus packs a powerful punch. A small match can ignite a big fire. Pluto acts like a television signal: a faint carrier wave that can be amplified into a meaningful message. And a DNA spiral: a microscopic squiggle of chemicals that flowers into a living organism. Or the flap of a butterfly's wings cascading into a typhoon.

At first this energy whispers softly in the deepest subconscious. It resonates within, building up over time, until, like the delicate insect become a howling hurricane, it bellows forth as a compelling voice. The Voice of God. It demands what you must do for the universe, not what the universe can do for you.

In the end they are one and the same. We are each part of something beyond individual comprehension. Pluto subsumes one in a larger than personal Purpose. It slowly grinds away at ego until one consciously accepts that destiny or fate. Its workings take a long time, perhaps longer than a lifetime. This is an impersonal force: our encounter with the inhuman.

One day this force will reach out and take away your humanity. You may be eaten alive by cancer, seized by a brain attack, quietly abducted into death's great unknown. And why not? The same force also gave you the unearned gift of life. 'The Lord giveth and the Lord taketh away. Blessed is the name of the Lord.'[2]

Impersonal forces shape us: genetic dictates, biological necessities, animal instincts, unconscious motivations and social pressures. Our conscious freedom is constantly challenged by these blind powers. An evolving pattern of response to these inhuman energies evokes one's humanity. Or destroys it. Thus life tests one. Saturn sums up the score: the objective fruit of one's blossoming. Pluto reveals the seed it bequeaths to the future.

A seed contains a genetically recombined message, different from that of the fruit delivering it. Pluto cooks past karma into emerging motivation. It launches one on a fateful course without regard for one's own personal wishes or subjective self-evaluation.

The personality, enmeshed within its web of activities, is not privileged to hear this verdict. Like all things Plutonian it remains invisible: a secret judgment of the soul. We each play a role and serve a purpose exceeding personal intention. Its full meaning can never be known to the ego that must execute it. Yet one's attitude towards this hidden agenda defines a destiny: futile obstruction, passive submission, active service or creative cooperation. In the end everything Plutonian revolves around the theme of 'Thy Will, not mine, be done.'[3]

This larger Will demands a confrontation with something truly foreign encountered in one's own depths or out there in the world. Consciousness must assimilate it. And is transformed by it. A new quality is added or an ancient heritage destroyed. One must come to terms with a previously unsuspected truth adverse to one's present character and hopes. This change is irreversible - there's no going back.

Pluto is about unconscious striving towards an intensified state of being. That requires annihilation of current identity. One must transcend who one is and what one most loves. Since we rarely do this voluntarily Pluto does it for us. The key lies in one's attitude towards this necessary breaking of eggs to make an omelet. Is one traumatized? Does one resist? Become intoxicated by the destructive process itself? Or embrace the prolonged agony of transformation?

Pluto always involves death of a cherished attribute. And the reward of a new beginning - if one can adapt. Many cannot. If one can pass through the fire it gives rebirth. Otherwise, and often, only ashes.

Changing circumstances generate new standards of fitness. Those who cannot respond to their challenge are destroyed. Evolve or die. This process is ruthless, yet for all of its cruelty has created the complex beauty of flower, beast and man from atoms in a puddle. Was it worth the pain and struggle? We answer 'yes' with every breath we take.

Pluto remakes one very slowly, over years, decades, a lifetime. Think of geological change or glacial movement: profound but imperceptible. It works on the deepest, hardest elements of personality. One must actively engage with the thing one least wants to face or lose what one most wants to keep. Pluto targets one's Achilles heel. And attacks it relentlessly. It is so unfair to the ego - and so necessary to its transcendence.

Pluto's relatively huge moon, Charon, expresses the karmic load of unfinished business that one must address. It evokes one's most abysmal problem. This is a specific issue, different from Saturn's Shadow, which points to a general fear or weakness limiting the whole personality. Pluto forces one to deal with a particular toxic legacy. Sometimes it tasks one to carry a collective burden, pits one alone against a social pathology. Unfair? Too bad. Do or die.

Pluto is no fun. Yet nothing surpasses its exaltation of death and rebirth, negation and resurrection. Whatever the birthing pains it brings renewal. Its relentless will drove naked apes through ice ages, drought, famine, plague and war to become the cutting edge of consciousness on this planet, and within this solar system.

Pluto's insistent urge elicits life out of matter, feeling out of biology, mind out of sensation, spirit out of calculation. It evokes increasingly subtle energies out of a denser substrate. This fiery process incinerates the dross to liberate its subtle heart. It all sounds so romantic. It is actually an agonizing struggle. Every evolving being must pay its price.

A dark wind, a silent tide of fate, guides individual lives to a rendezvous with destiny larger than anything the ego can imagine. The invisible hand of God shapes every life to its Purpose. Pluto points to why, where and how this hidden process operates.

Uranus embodies the frontier of consciousness. Pluto signals its sensed but unknown interior: the tectonic rumbling beneath our feet, the storm blowing in from a far off ocean, the ghostly influence of forgotten ancestors. Uranus' flash of inspiration revolutionizes a current frame of reference. Pluto's silent flood slowly carries one to an inconceivable destination.

Pluto locates an invisible fissure in the psyche through which an unfulfilled need erupts. This demands attention in no uncertain way. Its previously suppressed quality makes it raw and scary. It cannot be sanitized. Pluto points to a simple existential fact, like death. You cannot work on it; you can only develop the courage to let it work on you.

Pluto describes a fate to which one must adapt as part of the collective and as a participant in history. It also defines a fate created by one's own consciousness and conduct. Pluto portrays the binding nature of our actions, the consequences objectively earned by our behavior.

Its ultimate expression comes with death's final judgment. Pluto marks a timeless moment of truth: really seeing just who and what one was. An eternal Now of implacable fact, without evasion or excuse. One passes through its gate of no return, inscribed with the spellbinding words: 'Abandon all hope, ye who enter here.'[4]

You are what you have done. You have passed beyond Neptune's ocean of wishful thinking about what might have been. Here you lie still within the grave. There perhaps all that one once was burns away to fuel what one might become. A call to resurrection may stir the dark waters of death with an impulse to rise and redeem.

Pluto defines the evolutionary demand driving both individuals and groups. This force flares through their inertia, eliminating those who cannot adapt: species, societies, selves. Ultimately it consumes every entity, for each is but a stage in the terrible, beautiful flowering of Spirit. Pluto reveals where personal preference and identity are over-whelmed by a higher priority. It spotlights how an invisible soul eats your ego so it can grow.

Soul's greater reality enfolds ego consciousness just as a sphere envelopes a plane. Pluto's 17° intersection of other planetary orbits cracks open the door into a vertical dimension challenging our normal horizons. Pluto's inclination points to a more encompassing truth surrounding the disc of planetary properties that we can apprehend. The realm of the dead, depths of the unconscious, heights of supercon-scious, the long tides of history and heredity - these unknowable areas lie outside our direct experience but strongly affect it. Pluto shows where they touch us.

An un-integrated sphere of frozen flotsam encircles the flat plane of planetary orbits. It can be compared to a reservoir of viral DNA snippets surrounding the solar system's cellular organization. Pluto serves as their emissary, plunging into Neptune's psychic sea, infect-ing it with genetic messages from ancient eons of time and remote reaches of space. We now know that such viral transmission of genetic information bytes between vastly different biological species unites all life into one interactive genome. (Though it sometimes sickens and occasionally kills.)

Within any given cell RNA, a single-stranded information-bearing molecule, mediates between the double-stranded DNA encod-ing our genetic heritage and the proteins it codes for. RNA is both more primitive and more versatile than DNA. RNA carries information like DNA, and can also direct its application into actual protein synthesis, which DNA cannot. The first life was probably RNA based until evolu-tion separated data storage and protein building into specialized func-tions. Even today RNA messengers remain as the go-between.

Pluto acts like a messenger RNA molecule, a gene-splicer that can reword a genetic message. RNA transcribes a DNA gene out of its secure storage in the cell's nucleus and rearranges its instructions in response to a changing biochemical environment. Thus a gene coding for the word 'emit' can be transcribed as is, or be transmuted into words with completely different meanings such as 'time,' 'item,' and 'mite.'[5] This message then plunges into the slippery wet liquid of the cell's cytoplasm (Neptune) to become a protein, an active life agent.

In the same way Pluto transforms primal instincts and transfers them into Neptune's inner ocean of dreams. It brings new pearls of insight, and perils of infection, into the living waters of consciousness.

Pluto connects consciousness to its psychic base just as RNA links hereditary information with material proteins. Pluto, like RNA, acts as a catalyst: a change agent in a larger cellular environment. Pluto does not embody a full or integrated worldview just as RNA does not encode a complete biological blueprint. Rather both carry a transformative message impacting a larger, more complex system.[6]

Pluto accesses vital drives underlying the architecture of biology; vulgar instincts motivating the subtle processes of psychology. It evokes the energy of another dimension beneath the surface of perception. This disturbs the peace, disrupts an accepted state of awareness. Injects a novel factor into a previously balanced equation, confronts a known equilibrium with the wild card of unpredictable Otherness. Pluto's energies are crude, not evolved; fundamental, not sophisticated. They have a barbaric vigor and savagery to them. Only thus can they revitalize a tired ennui, fossilized outlook, degenerate identity.

Pluto regenerates by a return to origins, going back to basics. It forcefully reminds one of previously hidden issues that must now be addressed. This is inherently difficult, dangerous, even traumatic, because it uncovers the earliest preconscious distortions or lesions in awareness. Rediscovers repressed memories. Brings shocked, dissociated elements of psyche to the surface. These are hard to face because they occurred prior to the ego's development of an ability to handle them. They are preverbal, embedded in the substance and deforming the structure of consciousness. Pluto accesses and brings them to attention.

One can shrink from acknowledging them. Such primal issues, traumas, deprivations embody ghostly apparitions of the infantile helplessness experienced when one first encountered them. Revisiting them can crush the spirit and paralyze volition. One flees from what one cannot face. Pluto then generates obsessive substitute images. One learns to avoid these inner horrors through fetishes, addictions and scapegoating.

The prior state of being revealed by Pluto is more primitive than our evolved awareness, yet also has potentials it lacks. To take a comparable example, life could not currently evolve from chemicals on Earth because our planet now has an oxidizing (electron eating) atmosphere.

This was generated by life's own photosynthesis. Its oxygen would quickly degrade life's delicate biochemical precursors before they could assemble into stable reproducing cells. An oxygen free environment allowed RNA based life to emerge and generate the conditions for its own leap to a higher state: oxygen burning organisms are far more energy efficient than their predecessors. Pluto invokes a psychological parallel to this prebiotic world. Its reversion to deep instinctual energies allows us to reinvent a jaded consciousness or a decadent society on an entirely new basis, from basic principles unacceptable to its current consciousness.

Pluto reformats whatever planetary principle it contacts. And whatever sign energy zone it occupies. Pluto brings an obsolete attribute up out of the unconscious for metamorphosis. It points to a buried quality seeking transformation; the renewal of enantromedia (Greek: changing into the opposite as in yin/yang, night/day, winter/summer).

By position and aspect Pluto describes a familiar area of life subjected to the unknowable intentions of a higher imperative. A function stressed past the breaking point in the interest of a complete makeover. A quality regenerated, or destroyed, by the demands of a larger destiny.

Overall, Pluto represents one's essential purpose stripped of all subjective properties. Not a personal soul of meaning (Jupiter) but an impersonal urge that called one into being. The first cause of one's existence; an underlying necessity one must enact. A motive prior to experience, which continues after individuality ends.

The larger design, which one served well or poorly, remains. It will clothe itself in another life. Whether that retains any continuity with one's present self is beyond the ken of sense and reason, an enigma inaccessible to conscious knowledge.

Yet Pluto's nature implies the idea of karma: that one expresses more than a remembered past. And participates as a seed for the future. Its long loop out of the planetary plane into another dimension of deep space implies a different kind of journey after death. One with a return, as it plunges back into our known reality, changed and to change.

This does not refer to the personal ego, which is temporary and mortal. It refers to a higher Will and its deep karmic trajectory. Personality connects them as a brief expressive sparkle.

If so, then all events along the way are stimulants towards a more encompassing Identity. Or illusions distracting one from it. These then constantly entangle the self until one learns to liberate their energy. Pluto describes a necessary transmutation of unconscious hypnosis into conscious soul.

Transformation, metamorphosis, death/rebirth: all sound very exciting and spiritually uplifting. These processes are actually excruciating, and always open to the possibility of catastrophic failure. They require one to face an invisible power. Pluto does not make drastic changes in response to a known challenge or perceived need. It is about being assailed from an unknown dimension, like a star being sucked into a black hole.

Just as a single brain cell cannot understand the thoughts surging through it in a flash of electricity, so the ego is torn apart by hidden demands of the soul. Yet the brain could not function unless each neuron grounded and thrilled to the higher voltage of a consciousness beyond its own comprehension. Awareness is intangible, brain cells are quite visible. Yet consciousness drives those billions of jelly globs as both cause and effect.

Likewise, individual humans grope their way through the collective passions of history. Its larger design can only actualize through the sum of people privately living it out. Social processes can only be enacted through personal experiences. Perhaps over many lifetimes the soul's ego anchor begins to dimly sense, then voluntarily submit to and knowingly cooperate with these strong yet subtle forces.

Whether erupting internally or bearing down externally Pluto delivers the same message. One must serve a greater plan, by conscious choice, demonic possession or self-destructive resistance. Perhaps personality cannot cope with the challenge. Then it falls into obsession, dominated by a power it cannot control or transcend. This may emanate from within as mania or madness. Or appear from without through a charismatic Leader, religious or political cult, social fad, economic issue. One sees Pluto every day in the news.

Learning to accept ego loss marks the first step in Pluto's experience. This alone is more than most can bear. Mercifully, Pluto usually operates behind the scenes or in terms of a vast but somewhat distant historical process. Those whom it directly impacts by its prominence in an astrological chart are singled out to implement a hidden collective agenda.

Whether or not this is 'fair' is irrelevant. What is fair? What might be justice to an entity on its own level could hold it back in another context. From the Plutonian perspective unfairness itself is just another test, to see if one can display grace under pressure. Whining and sniveling, making excuses: these are truly reprehensible. Pluto does not do empathy. It has only contempt for weakness. Thus it makes one stronger. Tell that to a man unjustly imprisoned or a woman raped.

Plutonian power derives from the intersection of a timeless arche-typal imperative with a mortal and conditional psyche. Such a con-frontation disintegrates the personality complex. Energy emanating from the next stage of development irresistibly catapults identity into a new reality. For example, every boy and girl is pulverized by puberty. Childhood innocence must be destroyed by a higher demand: that our species continue through sexual reproduction. Its psychological cor-relate sacrifices natural naiveté to adult ambiguity. Yet for all its pain and loss few grownups would choose to reverse the process.

This next stage is not necessarily more advanced. A man may become more robotic than the bright boy he once was. A personality unable to cope may revert to an earlier state, sink back into its roots. Sometimes one just has to start over again. Pluto symbolizes instinc-tual compulsion as much as transformative resurrection. It lives in the chthonic forces rumbling below our feet as much as the starlight sparkling above.

Pluto fits remarkably well with the theory of a death instinct (Thanatos) coexisting with the pleasure principle. This force operates spectacularly in the wars and general horrors of history. It shows up on a more mundane basis in our ever so common self-sabotage; a compul-sive obstruction of our own and others' potential.

Pluto's death wish contrasts with Eros, Venus, the desire to have and to hold, to live and to love. Mars develops personal courage in the face of death. Jupiter gives it meaning as the soul of a life. Saturn provides closure, defines its final result. Uranus enables its quantum jump into another plane of being. Neptune embodies a longing for rapturous release, yearning for loss of self, dissolution and merger with the universe. But Pluto is the actual urge to die encoded in our cellular memory.[7] The awe-full will demanding death as the price of life.

Nothing new can emerge without death of the old. Often such death just brings a barren reversion to a simpler state of being. Sometimes it creates an ecstatic surpassing of self. One's attitude alone determines the outcome. Pluto's direct impact is extreme and irrevers-ible: a soul searing contact with the Will of God. It offers one option and one only: to give freely now what will later be taken by force.

Pluto acts as a spiritual pulse transmitting the essence of a life in the face of death's mystery. It functions as a psychic gene, not an organized genome, carrying the general meaning, but not the spe-cific features, of personality across the great gulf into: an afterlife? another incarnation? an impersonal energy field? final nothingness? Like both DNA and RNA it is a distillation purged of all existential qualities, an identity stripped to its core principle. As such it represents a transcendental quanta, or energy packet, entering into, and perhaps reemerging from, another level of existence.

Pluto acts as the inexplicable agency of a Purpose beyond our understanding. It depicts the inexorable process of transformation. This must obliterate every confining form as a demonstration of, and movement towards, a Reality behind our sensory/emotional/mental veils of illusion. So absolute and impersonal a force devastates any consciousness centered upon its known qualities rather than on its intrinsically infinite nature. Yet only thus can such a consciousness leap through birth and death to find its own true soul. Pluto burns through our several bodies, physical, emotional, mental and spiritual. It destroys and rebuilds them, that it may express its own ends with ever-greater intensity.

Pluto represents death transcending Will: the terrible radiance of an inhuman faith and love, rooted in eons of evolutionary travail, carrying us through Saturnine time and circumstance towards an ultimate destiny. This is not pre-given, but generated in the agony and the ecstasy of life.

We suffer through our inability to appreciate the new sensations which accompany and stimulate this growth. Pluto's insistent passion carries us through this pain, transforming it into lucidity of intellect, intensity of love, perfection of action. It sparked life in the primeval seas, and drove it, heedless of cost or of individual lives, from molecule to man; over land, into air, and out into the shining cosmos.

Pluto manifests the deep underlying quality of time as it flows through life. Time is not an abstract succession of identical intervals. It means a living stream of consciousness. It strives towards greater inclusiveness and intensity of awareness through experience.

A tree and a butterfly, a five-year-old girl and a 50-year-old woman sense one Earth's circling of the Sun differently. Yet the seasons of that round are objective facts. They may be subjectively experienced at various levels of awareness, but the background reality of winter or summer, spring or fall remains the same for all. Pluto maps out a larger environment that frames our personal lives. Whether one lives during an Ice Age or balmy spell, through feast or famine, war fever or tranquil bliss, personal identity becomes a single note of, and conditioned by, a longer movement. Here one dances with destiny.

Plutonian time runs in generational rather than annual cycles. A subtle psychological atmosphere permeates each of these epochs. This time spirit, or zeitgeist, evolves over decades. It provides a general orientation, a social moment, within which individuals live. Waves of creativity or paranoia, religious enthusiasm or acquisitive greed, slowly sweep society. Each person must respond in conformity or rebellion, willing participation or lemming-like hypnosis. Pluto enfolds one in a larger drama. Within it we enact, or endure, our fate. Then every generation with its peculiar obsessions crashes into oblivion.

Each of these eras nurtures certain aspects of human nature and stifles others. For example, the vibration or feeling tone of the 1950s was quite different from that of the 1960s. Distinct personality types flourish, or struggle, through these changing periods. Obviously a warrior spirit would have resonated to the zeitgeist of the early 1940s. It might find a test of courage, heroic meaning, and exaltation in battle. Or it might act out fatal flaws of arrogance and sadism. Either way it was in tune with the times. A gentle poetic soul would be challenged to the core by this alien reality. It might rise to the occasion, transfigured by a process it would never consciously choose. Or simply serve as a victim in a sacrificial orgy. Was this great trial an opportunity for myriads of souls to work out their deepest drives, to fulfill their karma? Or was it a hellish cataclysm that defined the fate of millions just by being in their face?

Saturn clocks time's measurable processes and visible phenomena. Its slowly changing purposes emanate from deep permutations of the archetypal realm. Pluto charts this emerging design. Neptune clothes its raw dynamic in dreams. Uranus articulates it into thought. Pluto embodies an urge that evokes mystical yearning and mental inspiration. Its hidden imperative becomes a vision channeled through ideas to galvanize action.

The three outer planets are not distinct psychological factors like the seven visible ones. Rather they each act as an aspect of one collective unconscious energy field. Pluto delineates the vast subterranean tides of human experience as manifested through history. It indicates the basic need or intention of an age. Neptune portrays its overall mood, which Uranus manifests through social change. Pluto portrays the general character or orientation of an era, Neptune its ideals and illusions, and Uranus its specific impact on the temporal reality of history (Saturn).

Pluto operates at the collective level as the deeper cause behind overt public events. For a historical review of its last transit through each of the signs, 1760-2026, see 'Outer Planet Transits.'

Pluto affects the individual in two ways. First, as members of a particular generation, shaped by transpersonal biological, social and spiritual forces. Second, as the power of death and rebirth in one's own development, especially if grounded by a personal planet.

Moon

Pluto's relatively giant moon Charon forms half of a unique double planet system. Thus it is described as an aspect of Pluto itself rather than an independent symbol.

Notes

1. During any planet's conjunction with Sun it is immersed in overwhelming light. The heliacal rising of a planet refers to its first visible emergence after this conjunction. Heliacal setting refers to its last appearance before its absorption into that light. Since antiquity heliacal rising and setting have been calculated as about 15° of zodiacal distance from Sun.

2. Job 1:21

3. Mark 14:36

4. 'The Divine Comedy,' Dante Alighieri, 1265-1321, Italian writer

5. This example is taken from Barry Commoner's seminal article on alternative splicing of DNA 'Unraveling the DNA Myth: The spurious foundation of genetic engineering,' published in Harper's magazine, February 2002.

　　Dr. Commoner (1917-2012) was an American biologist and a founder of the modern environmental movement. His work helped to expose the inherent unpredictability of genetic manipulation. He formulated the biological equivalent of Heisenberg's Uncertainty Principle in physics.

6. Interestingly, the AIDS virus that attacks our identity-defining immune system is an RNA based retrovirus, a throwback to an earlier way of life, deadly to our own.

7. All of our cells are genetically programmed to self-destruct. Every time a cell divides each of its gene-coils (chromosomes) drops off one of the sealing units (telomeres) binding it together. After a set number of cell divisions all of the telomeres have fallen off and the DNA spiral unravels, resulting in death.

Pluto in Signs and Houses

Pluto in a sign indicates a larger will, an objective purpose, to which one must adapt.

Pluto in a house indicates one's subjective experience/expression of impersonal destiny.

Because Pluto moves so slowly, spending 12-32 years in each sign, only two, three or four of its sign positions are mature at any moment. Over the last two generations Pluto has been moving at its fastest pace on the near arc of its elliptical orbit. Therefore, the largest possible number of its zodiacal expressions are active right now. Other positions describe previous or emerging generations, or earlier historical eras.

At the time of writing (2015) no one is alive with Pluto in Aquarius, Pisces, Aries, Taurus or Gemini. All of those in Cancer are over 77. Those with Pluto in Leo are aging, with all over 58. Only those with Pluto in Virgo and Libra are currently adults in their prime. People with Pluto in Scorpio are now in early adulthood, with the oldest just entering their 30s. Those in Sagittarius are children or adolescents. Those in Capricorn are infants, or perhaps in the pipeline for incarnation. Over the next decade older members of the Pluto in Leo cohort will fade out, while older members of the Sagittarian group rise into early adulthood.

Every day Pluto passes through all the houses because they are defined by Earth's own rotation.

Pluto: hidden motivation. An unconscious urge or compulsion driving conscious personality. It describes an area of life subject to the unknowable purposes of a higher will or soul.

In fire signs/houses: the imperative of individualization. A will to self-assertion, creatively or destructively.

In air signs/houses: the imperative of mental transcendence. A will to detach from known identity in order to achieve objective clarity and perspective.

In water signs/houses: the imperative of bonding, finding a common denominator. A will to melt or merge together in a larger psychic unity.

In earth signs/houses: the imperative of practical transformation. A will to objective accomplishment, to bend existing reality to a long-term purpose.

Pluto in Aries/first house

Rebirth. Identity transformed, driven by a new commandment. Hidden destiny assumes an individual face. Karma enters a new cycle, takes on a fresh character. The past burns away as fuel for takeoff into the future.

A destructive eruption clears space for a new beginning. Deep unconscious drives overwhelm the persona, one's ego mask. Previously concealed forces arise to replace it. A developing intention overrides known motivations. And devours the old self to feed its emerging design.

An invisible urge rises over the threshold of awareness. It is not a personal motivation but a fateful stimulus. Not a negotiable option but an evolutionary demand. One fulfills, or is destroyed by, it.

Personal will expresses a larger purpose. It subjectively identifies with an instinctual or collective necessity whose time has come. It objectively enacts a social or spiritual agenda, whose real significance remains largely unknown. This manifests as an obsession, a compulsive acting out of dimly sensed imperatives beyond conscious preference/choice. One slowly learns to cooperate with this urge, to embrace a transpersonal fate. Or falls prey to it.

A secret calling comes to light and life. Or its suppressed energy destroys one.

Pluto in Taurus/second house

Detriment. The power of collective will and impersonal fate fades as personal desire and individual values emerge. One's participation in a larger destiny stabilizes around fulfilling one's own needs. A drive for tangible gain. Or the wisdom taught by its loss.

Obsessive sensuality sublimated into relentless acquisition. Or dissipated in hedonistic excess. Or channeled into tantric transcendence. 'Tantra' means 'the essence of that which is woven together.' It is a Hindu/Buddhist discipline manifesting spiritual forces through awakening the divinity of our several sensory bodies: physical, emotional and mental. It can also play out more slowly on an unconscious instinctual level. In the west 'tantric' usually refers to a specific aspect of this: raising erotic pleasure into sacred sexuality.[1] In all cases it means elevating awareness and expression of the energies embodied in the very substance of one's biological and psychic constitution.

Destruction and renewal of resources. A fortune made and lost. A lesson in the contingency of worldly success:

> But store up for yourselves treasures in heaven, where neither moth
> nor rust destroys, and where thieves do not break in or steal. For
> where your treasure is, there will your heart be also.[2]

The urge to primitive accumulation underlying material growth and enabling social refinement. Compulsive productivity generates capital for a larger purpose. It sows a crop that others will reap. Creates an estate others will inherit. Evokes latent potential, mobilizes untapped assets. Manages wealth, or destroys it. Hidden treasure enriches or ruins one.

1. Tantra is usually described as raising kundalini, visualized as a coiled serpent of compressed libido, or life force, up through a series of energy centers, or chakras, loosely associated with the spinal column. However, kundalini also acts by grounding universal spirit in a descent of grace. This completes the circuit.

2. Matthew 6: 20, 21

Pluto in Gemini/third house

One's participation in collective destiny, impersonal fate or a karmic agenda objectifies. It separates out from personal ego, as an independent experience observed with a detached attitude.

Enlightenment induced by a change of perspective. A perceptual bias or criteria of rationality destroyed and replaced by a new one. The transition between one way of knowing and another generates a moment of freedom in which one can glimpse the larger process driving changeable phenomena.

Mental metamorphosis. Confronts a different conceptual framework challenging one's reality. The need to acknowledge and negotiate with this parallel worldview. Its alien nature holds valuable hidden qualities absent from the current state of awareness. Latent intellectual potential mobilized by dealing with the truly other. Transformative dialog or deadly rivalry. The incalculable power of language to devastate or heal, to teach or deceive.

A sword of division clarifies distinctions Or amputates unpalatable truths. Visible emergence of an alter ego or shadow side. A subconscious personality contradicts, and complements, known identity. Or is projected onto others. A hidden double comes to light or destroys one (Jekyll and Hyde).

Pluto in Cancer/fourth house

One's participation in collective destiny, impersonal fate or a karmic agenda subjectifies. The experience of public events condenses into a private pool of sensibility, mood and memory.

Birth trauma. That which grew in oceanic womb bliss, union with Mother, erupts into an individual self. A unique psyche emerges out of its collective background. Like the quickly evolving infant and child it is shaped by inherent developmental processes more than personal choice. Identity transformed by subordination to a larger necessity, acceptance of destiny, rather than as an expression of ego purpose.

Power of the past. Karmic issues surface. Unresolved baggage demands attention. Deeply buried familial or ancestral problems and potentials emerge into expression. Suppressed or denied instincts take center stage in all their primitive rawness. They act out, demolishing an old psychic habitat, laying the foundations of its next phase. An explosive release of unconscious passion challenges personal and group security. It destroys a safe comfort zone, creating space for a new emotional reality. The feeling nature redefined by crisis. Hidden fantasies come to light or drag one down.

Pluto in Leo/fifth house

One's participation in collective destiny, impersonal fate or a karmic agenda expressed through powerful assertion of individuality. Projection of a unique identity statement as one's social contribution.* Hubris drives one to audacity, perhaps even nobility. Or a spectacular fall from grace.

An essential pride or faith in self as the vehicle of divine providence. A compelling need to stand out, be special; to do one's own thing. Creative passion redefines personal character and social role. Or defaults into arrogance and a compulsion to dominate.

Hidden feelings dramatically erupt into visible expression. Natural instincts empowered, the inner child's authenticity liberated. Spontaneous originality changes the game. Emotional warmth melts artificial convention into real encounter. Or regresses into the hellfire of infantile narcissism, shameless posturing, obsessive attention seeking and insatiable demands for immediate gratification.

Uninhibited presentation of talent, or imperious egotism, fearlessly and flamboyantly displayed. An emerging courage openly reveals one's true nature. Or inflated self-esteem destroys one with appropriate theatricality.

Fated or karmic love. A transformative generosity embraces the formerly excluded. Or self-absorption devours any real affection. A heart broken and remade by the demands of a larger destiny.

* 'L'etat, c'est moi,' I am the state, said the Sun King, Louis XIV, during a Pluto in Leo transit ca. 1700.

Pluto in Virgo/sixth house

One's participation in collective destiny, impersonal fate or a karmic agenda purifies its operating procedure. It eliminates extraneous clutter, gets down to the core. Transformative crisis redefines ego to make it the vehicle of spirit. Perfects self through integrity in service to a larger cause. Or fragments and disempowers it by fixation on irrelevant shortcomings.

Organizes isolated parts into a singular whole with new properties. For example, under the right conditions matter assembles itself into organic life. Quantitative laws of chemistry transcend themselves in the qualitative emergence of biology. In the same way human personality melds generic instincts into a unique consciousness. Separate skills, like reading, merge into overall competence, like understanding. A methodical makeover of everything from daily habits to one's central purpose.

Flaws and imperfections relentlessly exposed. A drastic purge and reorganization of identity to conform to higher standards. A demanding regimen of personal therapy and social improvement. Efficiency upgraded to a new level, for better or worse.

The power of logic and reason to make life intelligible. Or kill its poetry with dry analysis. Penetrating observation. Or obsessive criticism. A drive to deconstruct and reexamine basic premises sharpens insight. Or dissects living wholes into scattered fragments. Hidden illness comes to light for healing. Or compulsive faultfinding paralyzes effective action.

Pluto in Libra/seventh house

One's participation in collective destiny, impersonal fate or a karmic agenda adjusts to a larger context. Power defined as intensity of relationship more than as inner purpose.

Transformational impact of others' expectations. Strong identification with, or rejection of, community demands. The imperative of adaptation: a need to align with environment, conform to context. A shift in focus from subjective quality of self to the objective nature of its associations.

Basic instinct modified by an uncongenial medium of checks and balances. Raw passion constrained by demands of fair play and due process. Seeks to integrate conflicting, or simply distinct, polarities into a harmonious configuration.

Fundamental re-evaluation of relationship. Relative standing of the parties, and relevant standards of judgment, redefined. Ancient patterns of association, conventions of conduct, swept away. New social arrangements and norms of personal interaction emerge. A certain coarsening of behavior is an inevitable concomitant as sophisticated, but now obsolete, niceties are shoved aside to allow the emergence of previously excluded, and thus unrefined, agents. Hidden stakeholders in the social contract come to light. Their participation enhances or disrupts the process.

Pluto in Scorpio/eighth house

Rulership. Enactment of, or submission to, an impersonal fate or collective will assumes an unusual degree of importance in the general personality. Metamorphic processes of psychological death and rebirth

413

are emphasized in relation to other aspects of psyche. One's participation in a communal destiny or karmic agenda regenerates. Explores the roots of its own motivation. Reorients self in a larger context of general rather than personal purpose.

A quantum jump. An experience of annihilation: one's old identity is destroyed and transformed, into dead ash or new life. The will, faith and love to embrace death as a necessary complement to life.

The dark side of instinct confronted. Universal inner demons, shared nightmares, emerge into consciousness so that their energies can be liberated and transformed. Their presence can no longer be ignored or suppressed. Ego must acknowledge and assimilate previously forbidden qualities and taboo subjects. A code of silence is broken. Scary secrets revealed and redeemed. The horror of ancient lies and oppressions exposed and eliminated. Or futile attempts at control self-destruct.

Plunge into an emotional abyss. Passage through a spiritual fire. This process devastates form but releases soul.

Pluto in Sagittarius/ninth house

One's participation in collective destiny, impersonal fate or a karmic agenda socializes. Group norms and aspirations take precedence over personal purpose.

In Scorpio, Pluto depicts a quantum jump; in Sagittarius the quanta of light released by it. A prophetic eruption destroys an agreed spiritual consensus and makes space for a new dispensation. The overwhelming impact of a religious, philosophical or political vision. A compelling need to propagate its message. A genuine revelation, transcendent insight. Or the fanaticism of a partial truth exaggerated by overwrought enthusiasm.

A drive to expand past natural limits leads to a necessary chastisement. The nemesis invoked by overreach. The concealed costs of growth revealed. A hidden hubris popped, inflated expectations laid low. Bloated success breaks down of its own excess. Its lost credibility enables the emergence of another worldview, a more inclusive orientation. Or provokes an uncompromising refusal to admit error, regresses into intensified insistence on an old law and makes a last stand in defense of the god that failed.

Transformed aspirations. The seeds of a larger future sprout. A climax forest burns; fresh green shoots appear.

Pluto in Capricorn/tenth house

One's participation in collective destiny, impersonal fate or a karmic agenda intensified by a restructuring of objective circumstance.

414

Fundamental change in the central organizing principles of society. And in the communal context of an individual life. Economic relationships and political forces transformed, evoking the necessity of personal response. Authority redefined in both structure and purpose. Traditional arrangements and understandings must conform. Hierarchies of rank determined by a different set of priorities. Ancient standards of excellence expunged, changed criteria of merit instituted. One moves up or down on a larger tide.

One adapts to the concrete establishment of a new order. Or withers away in the ruins of the old. The individual must reinvent social role to meet the survival demands of its emerging, initially harsh, demands. Winter winnows the strong from the weak.

Hidden, behind the scenes, influence moves public events. An invisible power whose time has come erupts into the world. A transcendent purpose takes tangible form. Overt initiation of another political[1] or material reality.[2] Practical grounding of spiritual attainment.[3]

1. For example, the American Revolution, 1776.

2. James Watt's development of the steam engine, 1765-'76, which powered the first Industrial Revolution.

Pluto was in Capricorn 1763-1778.

3. The ministry of St. Paul to the gentiles, which transformed Christianity from a Jewish sect to a universal faith, coincided with a Pluto transit through Capricorn from 42-61. Jesus was born with Pluto in Virgo, perhaps opposing his Sun, probably in 6 BC. He was crucified and transfigured with Pluto in Sagittarius ca. 30.

Pluto in Aquarius/eleventh house

One's participation in collective destiny, impersonal will or a karmic agenda becomes cerebral and idealistic. The power of visionary thought, of the pen over the sword.

An idea whose time has come erupts into consciousness, demolishing an old paradigm, clearing space for another worldview. The need to reconstitute both knowledge and authority on the basis of revised axioms. A new vision of heaven and earth supplants the known and familiar. Transformational impact of expectation upon circumstance, of hope upon reality.

Ancient karma pulverized by the force of an emerging aspiration, good or bad. Traditional affiliations transformed by emergence of a more universal perspective or belief. Identity redefined through growth of empathy, recognition of a shared fate. For example, a bigot suddenly awakening to the common humanity of all races. Or revolutionary disintegration of community creates a social vacuum, inviting nihilistic chaos.

A conceptual leap out of present and visible reality generates effective foresight. Or alienates from the living Now in favor of an invisible abstraction. Hidden potentials come to light. Or are twisted by too passionate an idealism.

Destroys old hopes, wishes and ideals. Replaces them with new norms and beliefs guiding personal life. Activates theoretical protocols governing governance. An ideological imperative to implement utopian, or dystopian, change through the force of reason[1] or by reason of force.[2]

1. American Constitution, 1787
2. French Revolution, 1789
Pluto last transited Aquarius 1778-1798: see 'Outer Planet Transits.'
In a previous Pluto transit through Aquarius, 61-84:
The gospels were written down, transmitting the Christian message to future generations and times.

Rome's destruction of the Jerusalem Temple changed Judaism from a ritual religion focused on a physical Temple with a priestly elite to a more decentralized faith based on local synagogues and rabbis.

Pluto in Pisces/twelfth house

One's participation in collective destiny or a karmic agenda dissolves. Surrenders an old identity to an embryonic future. Embraces fate. Trusts in God's Will more than personal intent.

An urge to liquidate the past in preparation for rebirth. To redeem it by experiencing its consequences, accumulated karma, both good and bad. This leaves one free for a new beginning. The ultimate potency of will transcending its own nature to accept the demands of a higher destiny. The power of renunciation. Or a hidden fear of life.

A mystic drive for loss of self in union with God, nature, all of humanity. These delicate currents of sensibility are usually subliminal. Now they well up as a romantic impulse challenging consensus reality and social convention. Unattainable but entrancing urges inspire or destroy one.

An eruption of unconscious contents or collective passions overwhelms ego, clearing space for a more universal rapport. Or leaves a traumatized zombie in its wake. A deluge of archaic memories, a surge of newly awakened feelings and fantasies, generates emotional redemption. Or chaos. Hidden dreams come to light. Or fester as hypnotic nightmares of regression and dissolution.

The metamorphosis of letting go: 'Thy will, not mine, be done.'

Aspects

Any astrological chart describes a dynamic process, not a static snapshot. Its qualities unfold through time in the movements of directions, progressions and transits (see 'Sun and Earth'). They also express through the spatial relationship between its planets (aspects). Aspects link scattered planetary energies, amplifying them into a coherent whole.

The geometrical relationship of planets activates their interplay. Obviously if two planets are in conjunction, merged at the same point in the sky, their functions add up in a powerful focus. Their qualities synergistically combine to produce an emphasis greater than the sum of its parts. If two planets are in opposition, 180° apart, their energies confront and complement each other. This produces an oscillating polarity, a seesaw effect. Each stimulates the other, in confrontation or in dialog. They bring each other to life.

The conjunction and opposition are the most powerful aspects. There is nothing quite so energetic as fusion. Yet a powerful singularity can be surprisingly unconscious as it has no outside frame of reference. The mutual reflection of complementary opposites is less powerful but more conscious. They play off each other. A line of development between two foci is more interactive than a simple flash point.

The other aspects are not quite so overwhelming. For just that reason they may be more consciously accessible and productive.

The square, a 90° aspect, describes blocked energies seeking release. Two functions are at odds. They act at cross-purposes, from incompatible motives. They each come at the other from its blind side. This generates creativity or frustration, under conditions of high pressure. In a birth chart this pressure is not an episode but a permanent condition.

A square describes two centers of experience separated by an entire season of evolution (three zodiacal signs). Tension between them builds up to a crisis. Squares express themselves powerfully and overtly because of this dynamic confrontation:

> Even the wisest man grows tense
> With some sort of violence
>
> Before he can accomplish fate
> Know his work or choose his mate.
> From this spasm of passion,
> All changed, changed utterly: A terrible beauty is born.[1]

Figure 1   Aspects

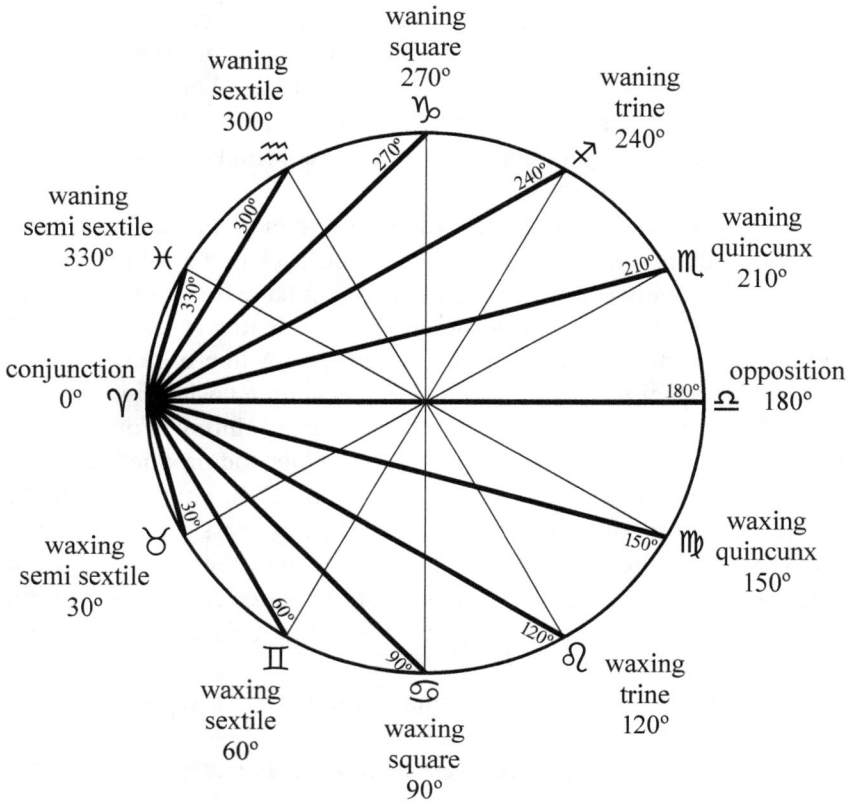

Trines & Squares

Figure 2
Trines

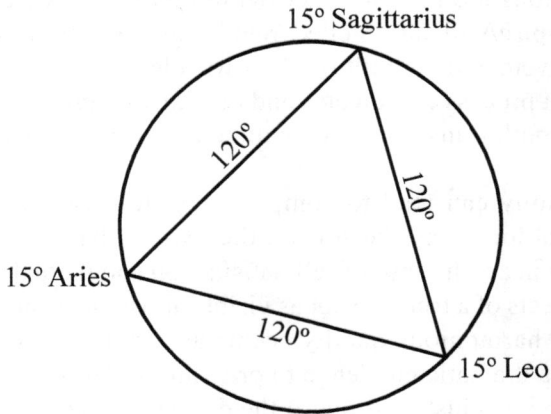

15° Sagittarius

120°

120°

15° Aries

120°

15° Leo

Figure 3
Squares

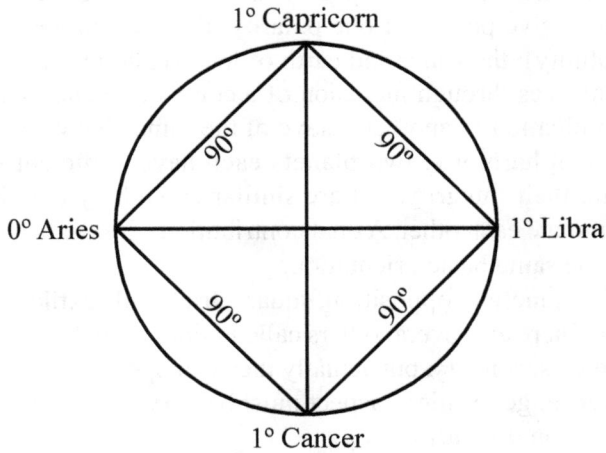

1° Capricorn

90°   90°

0° Aries

1° Libra

90°   90°

1° Cancer

Figure 4
T Cross Square

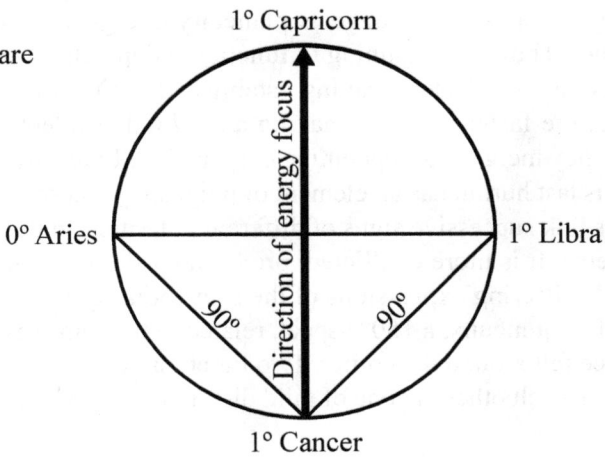

1° Capricorn

Direction of energy focus

0° Aries

1° Libra

90°   90°

1° Cancer

419

The trine, a 120° aspect, describes a state of harmony. Two planetary functions are synchronized within two signs of the same element (fire: spirit/will; air: intellect/relationship; water: psyche/emotion; earth: achievement/tangibility). Their wavelengths amplify each other. A consistent process coordinates and mutually enables them. This generates a smooth transition to new dimensions of experience between their energies.

Harmony can lead to complacency. Rather than strenuously evolve, as is forced by the square, the two too happy functions may simply bask in a rich sense of self-satisfaction and mutual back scratching. The effects of a trine are not as visibly apparent as those of a square because its harmonious quality seems an innate part of personality rather than a dramatic challenge to or within it. However, its sophisticated creativity is just as strong if the dormant power of this 'sleeping giant' can be activated.

The sextile, a 60° aspect, is similar to the trine. A sextile links two successive phases of one polarity: the fire and air of extroversion (masculinity); the water and earth of introversion (femininity).[2] A sextile reinforces through inclusion of a compatible energy rather than as an amplification of another octave of the same element. It implies help rather than harmony: two planets each have sufficient separation to maintain their integrity, but are similar enough by position to sustain and stimulate each other. A dual contribution gives value to cooperation within the same basic orientation.

Conjunction, opposition, square, trine and sextile form the major aspects. There are several others called minor aspects. These are usually considered secondary, but actually they can operate powerfully within a narrower range. A minor aspect must be very close to act strongly, but that situation does arise.

The semi-sextile, a 30° aspect. When waxing (the faster planet leaving the slower), it suggests planetary energies disengaging from one other. They are beginning to function independently as contrasting expressions of a basic meaning established at the conjunction. When waning, the faster planet is making a final independent statement just before they merge in an upcoming conjunction. Like a deathbed confession this last hurrah has an element of poignancy and seriousness. Semi-sextiles link successive signs of different polarities, male to female, and vice versa. It is more conflicted, providing a sharper contrast, than the sextile's differing expressions of the same polarity.

The quincunx, a 150° aspect, related to the semi-sextile, implies a presence felt around the corner. Two functions sense, but can't quite get a grip on, each other. A zone of mild disruption, or irritating stimulation, through contact with the alien. Quincunxes occur one sign before and after the mirror merging of an opposition. They mobilize a sense of urgency in the face of perceived strangeness; evoke unease rather than overt confrontation.

The semi-square (45°) and sesquiquadrate (135°) are also related to each other as softer, more synergistic versions of the square. Indeed, in the overall zodiacal cycle, starting at 0° Aries, these aspects to the vernal equinox (15° Taurus, 15° Leo, 15° Scorpio, and 15° Aquarius) are called points of avataric release. An avatar is a Hindu term for an archetypal incarnation. Each of these degrees demonstrates a maximal manifestation of its seasonal quality, equally free of its initial condition and final fate (the equinoxes and solstices). In a chart semi-squares and sesqiquadrates generate self-assertion in a more balanced way than the critical intensity of a square.

An aspect is always calculated in terms of the faster planet's motion relative to the slower. Thus, for example, a waxing Moon successively makes a conjunction, sextile, square, trine, and opposition to Sun, before repeating the process in reverse during its waning. An applying aspect, such as Moon at 5° Scorpio moving towards a trine with Sun at 10° Cancer, means the faster planet is closing in on an exact configuration with the slower one. This indicates an intensifying dynamic. They are blending, joining forces. A relationship is evolving. A separating aspect, such as Moon at 10° Scorpio moving away from its trine to Sun at 5° Cancer, means the faster planet is leaving the slower one. This indicates an expressive dynamic. Each partner releases new qualities evoked by their interaction. Two functions are disengaging, each changed by their encounter.

An aspect waxes as the faster planet moves away from the slower, going towards opposition. This describes a growing potency of the faster planet as an embodiment of the pair's energy. For example, a waxing Moon, in general terms, means one's unique personality is becoming a more powerful vehicle of an underlying will or purpose (Sun). The ego-manifestation increasingly displays, and displaces, its original impersonal spiritual inspiration.

An aspect wanes as the faster planet moves back towards the slower, approaching conjunction. This describes the faster planet's dissemination of the pair's energy. For example, a waning Moon, in general terms, means a unique personality expends itself, sacrifices its own being, in service to an underlying will or motive (Sun). Ego is shedding its idiosyncrasies, returning to its spiritual source

The midpoints of any waxing or waning semi-cycle are squares, with the faster planet at a 90° angle to the slower. A waxing square always means a crisis of action. The fast moving planet must effectively adapt the initial spiritual impulse to its objective environment. A waning square experiences a crisis of consciousness. The fast moving planet must undergo a complete reorientation of character in preparation for its spiritual recharge at the upcoming conjunction.

Aspects vary in power, as expressed by the orbs, or zones of influence, surrounding their exact culmination. The conjunction and opposition are the most powerful, having an orb of about 10° before and after culmination when they involve the luminaries, Sun and Moon. They have an orb of 8° with other planets. The square and trine have orbs of 6°, the sextile of 4°, the minor aspects 2°. Of course, their power shades off rapidly towards these limits.

Occasionally, a planet stands alone, not linked to any other by aspect. In this case it develops in isolation. Its expression remains primitive because it does not get an ongoing workout of its energy with other energies. When activated by a direction, progression or transit, it tends to erupt in a raw, disconcerting way. Yet it also embodies a different quality of experience, separate from the 'consensus' of the other connected planets. It embodies the treasure of a distinct perspective. If this can be integrated into the chart as a whole then consciousness and personality are greatly enhanced.

The relationships between planets form a force field generating identity. All relationships are mutual and reciprocal. They bring an otherwise frozen pattern to life through the interplay of its energies. In contemplating a chart the aspects between planets are just as important as their positions. Positions portray qualities. Aspects activate them.

There are three major groupings of aspects: between Sun and Moon, personal planets and outer planets. The Sun/Moon lunation cycle is the ur-aspect, the archetype of all relationship. It links purpose and psyche in visible manifestation through Moon's phases. See 'Lunar Phases and Aspects.'

Aspects between personal planets (Sun - purpose, Moon - psyche, Mercury - mind, Venus - love, Mars - will) indicate an individual's psychological dynamics. Aspects between a personal and an outer planet indicates identity reacting, or in thrall, to larger objective forces. Aspects between the slow-moving outer planets indicate social events and deep collective unconscious movements. They serve as a vital tool in mundane astrology, whose subject is the unfolding of public affairs and the destiny of nations. See 'Synods.'

Planetary aspects chart relationships between psychological functions. They may be harmonious expressions of mutual support, or smug taken for granted talents that lack any stimulus to development (sextile, trine). They may be adverse, wasting the indicated powers in fruitless conflict. Or drive their growth through mutual challenge (square, opposition). They may reinforce, or cancel each other out (conjunction).

Planets in aspect are energies in action. Aspects generate a current, provoke a dialog, between the principles involved. They bring a chart to life. They create a gestalt, a wholeness, a unified dynamic out of what would otherwise be a jumble of disparate qualities. Two, or several, planets in aspect constitute more than the sum of their parts. One or a few strong aspects can dominate the energy budget of a chart.

Aspects are as important as positions because they indicate movement and evolution of the functions involved. The next three chapters outline the energies in play between pairs of planets in aspect. Their sign and house positions must also be factored in when evaluating these dynamics. Planetary positions portray what kinds of psycho-spiritual energies you have. Aspects indicate what they are doing.

Notes

1. 'Under Ben Bulben' and 'Easter 1916,' W. B. Yeats, Irish poet, 1865-1939. He won the Nobel Prize in Literature in 1923.
2. Sextiles run between Aries (fire) to Gemini (air) to Leo (fire) to Libra (air) to Sagittarius (fire) to Aquarius (air). They also run between Taurus (earth) to Cancer (water) to Virgo (earth) to Scorpio (water) to Capricorn (earth) to Pisces (water).

Aspects from Signs

Planets in aspect portray interaction between discrete psychological qualities. Signs in aspect portray orderly fluctuations in process. The following paired sign relationships describe general energy dynamics, not specific outcomes. This section outlines how force flows between energy zones, regardless of the participants. For example, slow Saturn anchored in Aries, with fast Mercury beginning to separate at 30° from it in Taurus, describes a different psychological situation than Saturn in Aries with Venus beginning to separate at 30° from it in Taurus. The underlying movement, from will to desire, is the same; the specific energies involved differ.

These polarities of activity unfold in a regular sequence. Here each specific example will be described in the format of slower/faster. Thus if the slower planet is in Aries, and the faster in Taurus, it will be noted as Aries/Taurus, etc. Changes are described as modifications to the anchoring function generated by movement of its faster partner. Of course, this influence is mutual and reciprocal. It can be described the other way around; for example Aries/Taurus below could be stated as: 'desire shaped by will, tangible output emerges from primal energy.' The purpose of these descriptions is not to provide a recipe for interpretation, but to provoke the reader's mind into its own appreciation of the dynamics between energy zones.

From fire signs:
If the slower planet anchors in will (fire), and the faster function:

Begins to separate at a 30° waxing semi-sextile,
then it jumps into a different medium (earth).
Potential ability starts to actualize in a specific program:
Aries/Taurus: will begins to take shape as desire, energy seeks a tangible outlet.
Leo/Virgo: creativity begins to develop actual skill, expressive technique.
Sagittarius/Capricorn: aspiration begins to climb the ranks of authority, abstract principles define themselves in actual decisions.

Separates in a 60° waxing sextile,
then it rides a wave of affinity in a complementary medium (air).
Individual interpretation of a general purpose emerges:
Aries/Gemini: will finds alternatives. Emergence of Plan B.
Leo/Libra: personal creativity finds social expression.
Sagittarius/Aquarius: spiritual fervor finds theoretical articulation.

Separates in a 90° waxing square, or an emotional crisis of action,
then it is torn by a riptide of contrast from an alien medium (water).
Will viscerally commits to a plan or vision:
Aries/Cancer: impulse encounters emotional consequences, feelings contradict will.
Leo/Scorpio: personal pride encounters a powerful adversary, even negation.
Sagittarius/Pisces: aspiration meets ambiguity, purpose encounters confusion.

Separates in a 120° waxing trine, a new developmental phase of spirit,
then it is refined by a surge in the same medium (the next fire sign).
Will renegotiates its own purpose, gains in subtlety and sophistication:

Aries/Leo: will centers in creativity. Innocent purpose develops, or decays into, pride.

Leo/Sagittarius: joy turns to wisdom. Creativity becomes socially relevant.

Sagittarius/Aries: philosophical vision becomes personal initiative. Wisdom takes action.

Nears opposition at a 150° waxing quincunx,
then it encounters an agitating alien presence (earth).
Will modifies its egotistical quality in the challenge of disciplined effort:

Aries/Virgo: will redefines its operating procedure, impulse disciplines its expression.

Leo/Capricorn: personal pride adapts to social authority. Artistry challenged by necessity.

Sagittarius/Taurus: grand aspirations materialize as discrete goals, wisdom challenged by desire.

Contrasts at a 180° opposition,
then it unites with, or divorces from, a complementary medium (air).
Mind articulates purpose:

Aries/Libra: self-expression defined by relationship. Will constrained or complemented by justice.

Leo/Aquarius: personal creativity takes on universal meaning. Heart complemented or constrained by head.

Sagittarius/Gemini: principle articulated into rational argument. Spiritual aspiration defined through mental concepts.

Begins to approach from opposition in a 210° waning quincunx,
then it encounters an agitating alien presence (water).
Will is challenged by emotional realities:

Aries/Scorpio: enthusiasm modified by psychological subtlety. Initiative adapts to strategic requirements.

Leo/Pisces: domination modified by compassion or cloaked in illusion.

Sagittarius/Cancer: philosophy irritated or stimulated by subjective feeling. Ethics learn emotion.

Approaches in a 240° waning trine, a final developmental phase of spirit,
then it is refined by a surge in the same medium (fire).
Will reorients to a larger purpose, or expression of spiritual meaning:

Aries/Sagittarius: personal impulse seeks social justification.

Leo/Aries: ego finds a stimulating challenge, creativity gets a jolt.
Sagittarius/Leo: a philosophical proposition becomes personal.

Approaches in a 270° waning square, or crisis of consciousness,
then it is torn by a riptide of contrast from an alien medium (earth).
Aspiration pragmatically redefines itself in line with demands of reality:
Aries/Capricorn: enthusiasm meets strategic imperatives. Impulse learns to plan.
Leo/Taurus: high standards meet practical needs. Nobility (real or imagined) comes down to earth.
Sagittarius/Virgo: philosophy adjusts to inconvenient facts.

Approaches in a 300° waning sextile,
then it rides a wave of affinity in a complementary medium (air).
Will acts through a social perspective, a collectively accepted meaning:
Aries/Aquarius: theory informs initiative or impulse. Will subordinates itself to an impersonal idea.
Leo/Gemini: creativity expressed through contrast. Ego sublimates charismatic power into mental ability, verbal eloquence.
Sagittarius/Libra: principle consummated through fairness of application; strict truth balanced by merciful justice. Will accepts enabling compromise.

Approaches in a 330° waning semi-sextile,
then it sublimates into a different medium (water).
Personal feeling immerses in a higher cause or calling, imagination commits to a spiritual resolve:
Aries/Pisces: empathy sacrificed to initiative. Obsolete or irrelevant memories jettisoned in favor of a fresh start.
Leo/Cancer: security, tradition, family sacrificed to self-expression, or selfishness. A subjective sensitivity underlying, or undermining, creativity.
Sagittarius/Scorpio: emotional passion transformed into spiritual principle. An enlightened projection of hidden power, or a vindictive one of treasured pain.

From earth signs,
If the slower planet anchors in demonstrable achievement (earth) and the faster function:

Begins to separate in a 30° waxing semi-sextile, then it jumps into a different medium (air).
It gains an independent mental perspective on an objective situation or raw fact:

Capricorn/Aquarius: changing perspective on the nature and source of authority. New ambitions. Originality breaks from convention.

Taurus/Gemini: starts to question basic values. New perspectives on desire, changing evaluation of comparative worth.

Virgo/Libra: personal sense of integrity weighed in a larger social balance. Ability, competence, service questioned in the light of new standards.

Separates in a 60° waxing sextile, then it rides a wave of affinity in a complementary medium (water).
Objective facts take on emotional relevance:

Capricorn/Pisces: ambition lubricated by empathy. Hard reality takes on subtle nuance.

Taurus/Cancer: productivity becomes nurturing. Sensuality gains sensitivity.

Virgo/Scorpio: technique takes on passion. Purity absorbs lessons of power.

Separates in a 90° waxing square, or crisis of action, then it is torn by a riptide of contrast from an alien medium (fire).
It makes tactical decisions on how to attain strategic objectives:

Capricorn/Aries: ambition takes the initiative, chooses a plan of attack. Or one's established position is aggressively challenged.

Taurus/Leo: saving versus spending, having one's cake or eating it. How will wealth, tangible or spiritual, be deployed? What values are worthy?

Virgo/Sagittarius: ability faces a moral challenge. What purpose does its competence serve? What is the meaning of its effort?

Separates in a waxing 120° trine, a new developmental phase of practical ability, then it is refined by a surge in the same medium (the following earth sign).

Actual implementation of projects goes to the next level of sophistication:

Capricorn/Taurus: ambition acquires resources. Authority learns productivity.

Taurus/Virgo: Sensuality purified. Productivity rationalized.

Virgo/Capricorn: service leads to promotion. Competence generates real achievement.

Nears opposition to it in a 150° waxing quincunx,
then it encounters an agitating alien presence (air).
Simple facts are challenged by complex context. Common sense enhanced by sophisticated concepts:
Capricorn/Gemini: single-minded ambition excited or irritated by alternative paths.
Taurus/Libra: desire tempered by demands of fairness.
Virgo/Aquarius: integrity challenged by a new vision of purity.

Contrasts at a 180° opposition,
then it unites with, or divorces from, a complementary medium (water).
Emotional consummation of accomplishment, the psychological payoff of practical results:
Capricorn/Cancer: grim ambition enriched by vivid imagination. Discipline complemented or challenged by feeling. Authority learns to nurture as well as command.
Taurus/Scorpio: productivity rewarded, or challenged, by power. Sensuality enhanced or warped by passion.
Virgo/Pisces: Integrity complemented or challenged by empathy. Linear logic learns subtle nuance. Sharp facts blur into wider possibilities.

Begins to approach in a 210° waning quincunx,
then it encounters an agitating alien presence (fire).
Practical habits are challenged by new spiritual demands:
Capricorn/Leo: ambition challenged by creativity. Work ethic teased/tested by life's inherent playfulness.
Taurus/Sagittarius: acquisition constrained by moral injunctions. Sensuality modified by ethical concerns.
Virgo/Aries: purity excited/irritated by aggressive impulses. Careful competence stimulated by spontaneous enthusiasm.

Approaches in a 240° waning trine, the last phase of objective development,
then it is refined by a surge in the same medium (earth).
This clarifies its true value or objective social merit. A final summary of real possibility:
Capricorn/Virgo: terms of ambition refined. Exercise of authority rationalized.

Taurus/Capricorn: disciplined investment towards future gain. Sensuality sublimated into achievement.

Virgo/Taurus: rationality learns values. Means informed by desired ends.

Approaches in a 270° waning square, or crisis of consciousness, then it is torn by a riptide of contrast from an alien medium (air).
A new mental perspective redefines solid facts:

Capricorn/Libra: ambition challenged by social conscience. Validity of achievement, justification of authority questioned.

Taurus/Aquarius: values challenged by a radically new social or theoretical paradigm.

Virgo/Gemini: validity of basic assumptions questioned. Protocol or operating procedure challenged by alternative criteria.

Approaches in a 300° waning sextile,
then it rides a wave of affinity in a complementary medium (water).
Now realized practical objectives become psychologically integrated:

Capricorn/Scorpio: ambition enhanced or ambushed by passion. Authority immunized against, or corrupted by, the dark side

Taurus/Pisces: values enhanced by compassion or undermined by decadence.

Virgo/Cancer: integrity enriched by imagination or corrupted by personal preferences.

Approaches in a 330° waning semi-sextile,
then it sublimates into a different medium (fire).
Will expends its all to attain the pearl of great price:

Capricorn/Sagittarius: ethical norms adapt to practical necessities.

Taurus/Aries: initiative adapts to available means. Enthusiasm sated by sensuality.

Virgo/Leo: pride mortified by recognition of shortcomings. Creativity tempered by demands of technique.

If the slower planet anchors in detached mental perspective (air) and the faster function:

Begins to separate in a 30° waxing semi-sextile,
then it jumps into a different medium (water).
Theories or ideas gain emotional coloration:

Libra/Scorpio: harmony commits to passion. Justice takes off the blindfold, picks up the sword.

Aquarius/Pisces: ideas melt into ideals. Abstract theory enlarges, and dilutes, into empathy.

Gemini/Cancer: thoughts turn to feelings. Perception melts into imagination.

Separates in a 60° waxing sextile,
then it rides a wave of affinity in a complementary medium (fire).
Ideas or relationships define themselves through the exercise of will:

Libra/Sagittarius: balanced perspective commits to a principled stand.

Aquarius/Aries: theory commits to action.

Gemini/Leo: ideas expressed creatively.

Separates in a 90° waxing square, or crisis of action,
then it is torn by a riptide of contrast from an alien medium (earth).
Ideas adapt to reality, theories become practical:

Libra/Capricorn: ideas of justice meet facts of rank and privilege.

Aquarius/Taurus: ideas meet desire, theory adjusts to material and economic realities.

Gemini/Virgo: contending schools of thought meet annoying details of fact.

Separates in a 120° waxing trine, a new developmental phase of mind,
then it is refined by a surge in the same medium (the next air sign).
Theory or relationship evolves to a new level of sophistication:

Libra/Aquarius: innovation breaks a deadlock. New ideas move or upset the balance.

Aquarius/Gemini: contrary arguments stimulate theory. Unexpected perceptions refine ideas or reappraise dogmas.

Gemini/Libra: harmonization of difference. An emerging consensus unites disparate schools of thought.

Nears opposition in a 150° waxing quincunx,
then it encounters an agitating alien presence (water).
Emotional nuance, complexity of feeling, challenges clarity of thought:

Libra/Pisces: justice demands martyrdom. Relationship requires sacrifice.

Aquarius/Cancer: theoretical ideas disturbed by fluid imagination, challenged by emotion.

Gemini/Scorpio: ideas stimulated/challenged by passions. Clear choices ambushed by hidden motives.

Contrasts at a 180° opposition,
then it unites with, or divorces from, a complementary medium (fire).
Overt action based on theory, belief, ideas (as opposed to interests or feelings):

Libra/Aries: ego defined in context rather than on its own. Self acts on behalf of others. Or disrupts a social consensus.

Aquarius/Leo: ideas come to life through personal example.

Gemini/Sagittarius: competing ideas symbiotically focus into a general principle.

Begins to approach in a 210° waning quincunx,
then it encounters an agitating alien presence (earth).
Ideas and theories are disturbed by objective facts or social realities:

Libra/Taurus: relationship challenged by disclosure of real desires.

Aquarius/Virgo: theory put to the test of actual experiment.

Gemini/Capricorn: alternative interpretations disciplined by the reality principle.

Approaches in a 240° waning trine, the last phase of a train of thought,
then it is refined by a surge in the same medium (air).
New insights deepen and develop a paradigm:

Libra/Gemini: contrasting perceptions redefine justice. Communication enhances relationship.

Aquarius/Libra: new concepts of justice redefine the social contract. Inspiration rebalances an accepted paradigm.

Gemini/Aquarius: inspiration revolutionizes a stale debate. A new vision changes the terms of conversation.

Approaches in a 270° waning square, or crisis of consciousness,
then it is torn by a riptide of contrast from an alien medium (water).
One faces the emotional consequences of detached decisions or abstract theories:

Libra/Cancer: abstract considerations of fairness conflict with personal emotion and family loyalty.

Aquarius/Scorpio: theory encounters power, ideas meet irrational malice.

Gemini/Pisces: rational dialog dissolves into polarized feelings. Competing interests degenerate into emotional alienation; mutual subversion creates chaos. Or they learn to reconcile in a more inclusive vision.

Approaches in a 300° waning sextile,
then it rides a wave of affinity in a complementary medium (fire).
Will objectively or socially consummates an idea:

Libra/Leo: relationship subsumes personal identity.

Aquarius/Sagittarius: futuristic theory resolves into socially relevant laws or principles.

Gemini/Aries: competing alternatives resolve into a personal decision.

Approaches in a 330° waning semi-sextile,
then it sublimates into a different medium (earth).
Old practical arrangements give way to new relationships/organizing concepts:

Libra/Virgo: integrity adjusts to relationship, purity tempered by justice.

Aquarius/Capricorn: practice corrected by a new paradigm.

Gemini/Taurus: desire corrected by rational consideration.

If the slower planet anchors in shared emotional reality (water) and the faster function:

Begins to separate in a 30° waxing semi-sextile,
then it jumps into a different medium (fire).
Will begins to detach from communal instinct into personal expression:

Cancer/Leo: maternal nurturing becomes vibrant play. Joyful expression of private mood.

Scorpio/Sagittarius: passion justified by philosophy. Power expressed as principle.

Pisces/Aries: universal sympathy turns to personal initiative. Love reborn through self-assertion.

Separates in a 60° waxing sextile,
then it rides a wave of affinity in a complementary medium (earth).
Inner feelings actualized through objective behavior:

Cancer/Virgo: learns to competently execute personal dreams.

Scorpio/Capricorn: translates passion into social power.

Pisces/Taurus: learns to profit from loss.

Separates in a 90° waxing square, or crisis of action,
then it is torn by a riptide of contrast from an alien medium (air).
Feelings learn to express themselves in response to objective challenge:

Cancer/Libra: subjective imagination adapts to social reality.

Scorpio/Aquarius: a quest for power adopts/adapts to new ideas, plans, technologies.

Pisces/Gemini: a nebulous sense of unity learns about I and Thou the hard way as the other proves that s/he is really different.

Separates in a 120° waxing trine, a new developmental phase of feeling,
then it is refined by a surge in the same medium (the next water sign).
Primal emotions mature into more subtle sensitivities:

Cancer/Scorpio: life takes an interest in death. Dreams of power.

Scorpio/Pisces: power gains by relinquishing control. Passion learns compassion.

Pisces/Cancer: universal compassion commits to personal caring. General empathy turns to intimate emotion.

Nears opposition in a 150° waxing quincunx,
then it encounters an agitating alien presence (fire).
Will challenges feeling, spiritual demands contrast with emotion:

Cancer/Sagittarius: ethical or social principles challenge personal feelings.

Scorpio/Aries: aggression activates hidden passions. A sensed threat invites strategic mobilization.

Pisces/Leo: aristocratic standards challenge sloppy empathy.

Contrasts at a 180° opposition,
then it unites with, or divorces from, a complementary medium (earth).
Dreams actually manifest, for better or worse:

Cancer/Capricorn: fantasy becomes reality. Personal dreams become social accomplishments. Disappointment of getting what you want.

Scorpio/Taurus: taking power. Getting possession. Consummating passion.

Pisces/Virgo: healing through sacrifice. Renunciation leads to purification.

Begins to approach in a 210° waning quincunx,
then it encounters an agitating alien presence (air).
Reason challenges feeling, perspective distances from emotion:

Cancer/Aquarius: rational thought challenges wishful dreaming. A need to plan activates imagination.

Scorpio/Gemini: mind begins to articulate hidden passion. Disturbing perception of contrast between private motives and public persona.

Pisces/Libra: indecision. Demands of justice challenge inappropriate sympathy.

Approaches in a 240° waning trine, the last phase of an emotional journey,
then it is refined by a surge in the same medium (water).
Personal sensitivities enlarged by appreciation of others':

Cancer/Pisces: clinging learns to let go.

Scorpio/Cancer: drive for power melts into desire for intimacy.

Pisces/Scorpio: compassion learns passion. Love picks up the sword.

Approaches in a 270° waning square, or crisis of consciousness,
then it is torn by a riptide of contrast from an alien medium (fire).
A spiritual truth challenges an entrenched emotional stance:

Cancer/Aries: dreams get a wake up call. Imagination interrupted by events.

Scorpio/Leo: hidden passions tamed/shamed by pride. Lust for power challenged by generosity, vengeance by magnanimity.

Pisces/Sagittarius: escapist fantasies pierced by sharp truths. Sympathy/indulgence encounters demands of moral law.

Approaches in a 300° waning sextile,
then it rides a wave of affinity in a complementary medium (earth).
Feelings consummated in demonstrable results; dreams gain social acceptance:

Cancer/Taurus: resources appropriately expended to enable dreams.

Scorpio/Virgo: relative perfection of technique in the service of passion/power.

Pisces/Capricorn: compassion accepts discipline as the price of achievement.

Approaches in a 330° waning semi-sextile,
then it sublimates into a different medium (air).
Ideas melt into emotions, abstractions are renounced in favor of true feelings:

Cancer/Gemini: mental openness commits to emotional involvement.

Scorpio/Libra: social propriety cuts loose, commits to real passion, or self-destruction.

Pisces/Aquarius: clear but detached vision commits to compassionate involvement.

Solar Aspects and Retrogradation

Any planet aspected by Sun is singled out for attention. It stands in the spotlight. Its illumination by Sun makes that planetary function a channel for the whole identity, as a talent or through a challenge.

Moon's aspects to Sun are so fundamental that they are discussed separately in 'Lunar Phases and Aspects.' This chapter will discuss Sun's aspects to all other planets, from Mercury through Pluto.

Sun's intensity and centrality generates two special conditions of planetary relationship with it, as seen from Earth. Aspects to Sun can involve 'combustion' and retrogradation. Combustion means a fiery fusion of the core solar identity and one of its planetary attributes at the conjunction. Retrogradation involves a planetary 'secession' from the gestalt of personality so that it can turn within to redefine itself in contrast to the whole. This occurs just before, during and after its opposition to Sun. Thus, in relationship to Sun, planetary qualities can die and be reborn as expressions of a fundamental purpose (combust). Or redefine their own nature (retrogradation) in relative independence of that purpose. In all other combinations among themselves the participating planets retain their own identity while interacting in the different modes of conjunction, square, trine, opposition, etc. See 'Planetary Aspects.'

The inner planets, Mercury and Venus, conjoin, separate from and approach Sun because they move faster than Sun appears to from Earth's viewpoint. They never oppose Sun because they move within Earth's orbit: see 'Retrogradation: Astronomical Facts' below. Sun conjoins, separates from, opposes and approaches all other planets outside Earth's orbit because those planets move slower than Sun as seen from Earth.

As Sun separates from an outer planet the central identity explores and utilizes that planet's function as a projection of its overall purpose. Near opposition the planet retrogrades, undergoes an internal transformation, then resumes direct motion. Sun then approaches this now metamorphosed function, seeking to incorporate its new features into the basic identity.

As Sun separates from a planet after conjunction the overall self differentiates from a fusion with that planetary role. The central identity individualizes its expression of the planet's energy. The planet serves as an instrument of the larger self through its specialized sphere of activity. It becomes an experimental probe for the general personality, acts as a scout, tests new possibilities of the self's actualization. Finally, near opposition, that function turns within, retrogrades and develops its own autonomous power.

Figure 1   Direct motion, all planets

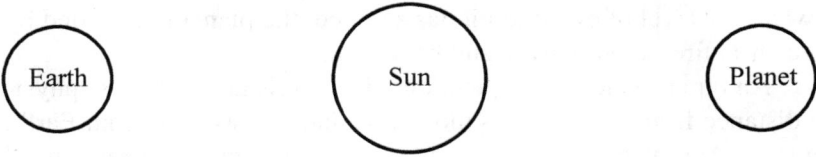

Figure 2   Retrograde motion
            Inner planets: Mercury and Venus

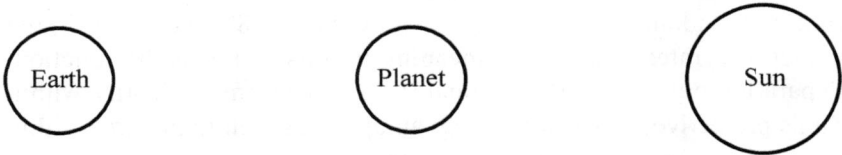

Figure 3   Retrograde motion
            Outer planets: Mars - Pluto

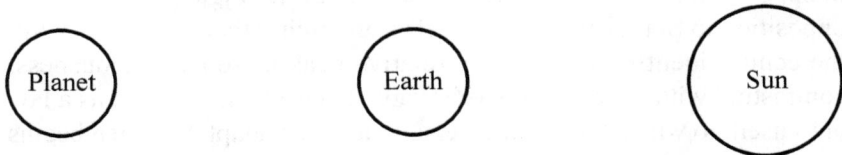

As Sun approaches a planet after opposition the general personality begins to integrate this new power. The planet has developed a relatively independent and advanced capability during its retrograde phase. It now enhances rather than expresses the larger self. It has become a more highly evolved part, a leading edge, of the general identity. Finally, as Sun nears conjunction again, the planetary function becomes a magnet, even an obsession: self's main project. Then, consummated at whatever level of evolution it has attained, the planet is engulfed by the central fire, to burn away and be reborn.

An outer planet in conjunction with Sun is at its greatest physical distance from Earth. It has moved behind Sun as seen from Earth. Figure 1. Any planet conjoined with Sun is consumed and revitalized in the central fire. As Sun approaches to within 17° it disappears from visual view in the sky and conscious experience in the heart. Lost in the glare, nullified as an independent actor, it no longer acts autonomously, but is subsumed into Sun's general purpose. Closing to within 8° of Sun it breaks down completely in a catharsis of renewal. It undergoes a meltdown, engulfed by a larger solar reality. At the exact moment of conjunction Sun and planet fuse, like sperm and egg, in the mysterium tremendum of rebirth. As Sun moves on to 8° away from it, the planet integrates a recharged meaning into its own specific function. Separating out to 17° it consolidates this transformed identity within Sun's protective, if overwhelming, aura, just as a child matures within the family: dependent, yet growing at a much faster pace than during adulthood. The planet develops a new identity as an expression of Sun's primary purpose. Beyond 17° of separation the planet resumes its own agency as a specialized manifestation of Sun's essence.

Near Sun's waxing trine (120°) of separation, any outer planet appears to stop and turn retrograde. This continues as Sun moves towards, then passes, opposition to the planet. A retrograde outer planet in opposition to Sun is physically closest to Earth. Figure 3. A planet in opposition to Sun distinguishes itself from, rather than integrates with, the central identity. It reaches a relative peak of self-consciousness, contrasting with the overall psychology. It acts autonomously, as a law unto itself, to which the general personality must adapt. Sun then begins a new approach to this now semi-independent function. Near Sun's waning trine of approach (240°) the outer planet resumes its apparent direct motion. But Sun moves faster and overtakes it until the cycle renews itself in a new solar conjunction.

Planets retrograde for various lengths of time depending on their speed relative to that of Earth. The astronomical mechanics and astrological meaning of retrogradation are discussed below.

The next section describes the cycle of aspects between Sun and planets. These include two planets inside Earth's orbit, Mercury and Venus, and six planets beyond Earth's orbit. Those six include three planets of conscious objective or social experience: Mars/will, Jupiter/spirit, Saturn/fate or fear. And three planets of the collective unconscious: Uranus - inspiration/intuition, Neptune - imagination/compassion, Pluto - collective fate/God's Will. The latter three act subliminally, below the surface. They can be powerful, but manifest as circumstance, or social imperatives, rather than as known elements of personality.

A faster planet separating from a slower one is differentiating, asserting its distinctiveness or independence.[1] This can go too far and become a schizophrenic dissociation, leading to conflict and degradation. A faster planet approaching a slower one is integrating with it.[2] The two energies are converging, moving towards merger. This can go too far and become an amorphous meltdown, leading to confused entanglement. The general rhythm of relationship proceeds as follows, illustrated by the movement of central identity, Sun, relative to an outer planet (Mars through Pluto).

At the semi-sextile (30°) central identity detaches from fusion with the planetary function that it absorbed, redefined and channeled during the conjunction. Overall purpose achieves a degree of separation from its normally subordinate attribute. By the sextile (60°) overall purpose harmoniously aligns with its planetary function. Attributes cooperatively serve identity. At the waxing square (90°) conflict erupts between central identity and its expressive function. Think of a dispute between a head of state and an ambitious subordinate (who may or may not be more competent than the boss). At the waxing trine (120°) identity achieves a smooth competence in directing its attribute.

From the waxing trine to opposition (180°) to the waning trine (240°) the planet retrogrades, turns within, to rejuvenate itself as an independent agent in contrast to the central identity. At the waxing quincunx (150°) it flares up in a somewhat disruptive, or nonconforming, statement of its own purpose as distinct from that of the whole personality. At the opposition it perfectly executes, or openly rebels from, basic identity. Thus both the whole self and its subpersonality gain an enhanced understanding of their own natures through a complementary coordination, or a bitter divorce. By the waning quincunx (210°) personality begins to assimilate its subpersonality's quasi-independent competence. This marks the difficult start of a learning curve integrating the two. The waning quincunx begins to perform this mission internally; the waning trine (240°) expresses that integration externally.

Near the waning trine the planet turns direct. Now the faster moving Sun begins to approach it. The central identity appreciates and uses an opportunity to smoothly integrate a reformed, upgraded, but somewhat autonomous ability into the whole personality. At the waning square (270°) an old sense of identity conflicts with, and must adapt to, its newly developed talent. If successful, consciousness is enhanced and personality empowered. If not, incompatible urges tear it apart. At the waning sextile (300°) identity harmoniously aligns with its relatively advanced attribute. By the waning semi-sextile (330°) identity consecrates itself to the opportunity/challenge defined by its more highly evolved function.

Finally, at 17° of Sun's approach, the planet disappears into the solar glare, reintegrates with the overall identity. At conjunction (0° of separation) it merges with, and is consumed by, Sun's core purpose. It focuses Sun's spiritual force through the medium of its particular activity. And burns away as the fuel or vehicle for that outpouring. Then, as Sun begins to separate from it, the now discharged planet begins to integrate general solar vitality into a new statement of its particular quality. It recharges within Sun's womblike spiritual aura. Finally, at 17° of separation from Sun, it re-emerges into a new cycle of autonomous expression.

Notes

1. From conjunction to opposition, 1°-179°
2. From opposition to conjunction, 181°-359°

Solar Aspects

Sun/Moon

Spirit and matter. Soul and body.
Purpose and psyche. Meaning and manifestation.

The Sun/Moon relationship, or lunar phase, forms a fundamental feature of personality. It expresses one's overall instinctual, emotional and psychological orientation. Because Moon grounds solar principle into living experience this is by far the most important planetary relationship. In fact it merits its own chapter: 'Lunar Phases and Aspects.'

Sun/Mercury and Venus

These two planets always remain closely aligned with Sun as seen from Earth because they move within smaller orbits than ours. They oscillate within a short distance of Sun from Earth's perspective (24° and 47°

respectively). Thus they do not really form aspects with Sun, but rather demonstrate a central identity's inherent properties of mind and desire.

Mercury and Venus illustrate planes of inner experience. They express inherent qualities of the central self within a fairly tight focus. They differ from planets beyond Earth's orbit that symbolize external factors which challenge/stimulate basic identity through a full range of relationships.

Sun/Mercury

Spirit and mind. Meaning and communication.
Purpose and intellect.

As an inner planet Mercury's orbit is tightly bound to Sun as seen from Earth. It can never move more than 24° away from Sun. Mercury symbolically abstracts and articulates the central identity. The most important consideration is whether Mercury rises before Sun, in an earlier degree of zodiacal longitude, or sets after it in a later degree. See 'Mercury.'

Conjunction: just as a dawn of enlightenment shines through the mists of ignorance, so solar vitality consumes outworn ideas, releasing a fresh ability to perceive. As in the genetic recombination of conception, the life-essence reshuffles its mental programs, renewing its axioms of truth and rules of evidence.

An old way of thinking burns away as Mercury approaches Sun in direct motion, a new one ignites at conjunction, another perspective emerges as Mercury separates from Sun. The same process that is veiled in the light of fusion during Mercury's direct conjunction with and behind Sun arises in different form during Mercury's retrograde conjunction with Sun between it and Earth. The direct case involves an evolution in what the mind thinks about. The retrograde case involves a development in how the mind thinks. See 'Mercury retrograde.'

Mercury makes no other aspects to Sun.

Sun/Venus

Spirit and love. Purpose and pleasure.
Meaning and desire.

As an inner planet Venus' smaller orbit is closely bound to Sun as seen from Earth. It can never move more than 47° away from Sun. Venus subjectively expresses an ideal identity, which entices real behavior. The most important consideration is whether Venus rises before Sun, in an earlier degree of zodiacal longitude, or sets after it in a later degree. See 'Venus.'

Conjunction: just as the heat of passion warms a cold heart, so solar vitality consumes dead relationships, releasing a new openness to beauty. As in the genetic recombination of conception, the life-essence reshuffles its desires and renews its values.

An old love, and way of loving, burns away as Venus approaches Sun in direct motion, a new one ignites at conjunction, its refined grace emerges as Venus separates from Sun. The same process that is veiled in the light of fusion during Venus' direct conjunction with and behind Sun also arises during Venus' retrograde conjunction with Sun between it and Earth. The direct case involves an evolution in what/who one loves. The retrograde case involves a development in how one loves. See 'Venus retrograde.'

Waxing semi-sextile (30°): desire begins to separate from the whole Self, with a somewhat autonomous character. Values detach from identity, stand in their own right, regardless of self-interest. Love takes on a life of its own, regardless of the central purpose.

Semi-square (45°): desire reaches a maximum of autonomy, at both the direct and retrograde stations. Values at odds with the central purpose. Love begins to conflict with identity, then turns back to reintegrate with the whole Self.

Waning semi-sextile (30°): desire sacrificed to the larger interests of identity. Values commit to serving the central purpose. Love returns from its adventures and seeks re-integration with the whole Self.

Venus makes no other aspects to Sun.

Solar Aspects to Outer Planets

The dynamics of Sun's aspect cycle with planets beyond Earth's orbit remains the same regardless of its specific partner. The following outlines a recurring rhythm of relationship between the central Self and its various attributes.

Definition of terms:

'Self' refers to a total identity complex of instinct, unconscious memories, conscious personality and super-conscious soul/transcendent spirit. It means one's authentic wholeness including, but not limited to, objective social role and subjective individual character, inner sensitivities and outer behavior, explicit qualities and implicit potentials.

'Spiritual identity' refers to the intangible Force, or animating principle, one expresses through the medium of an ego. A current of universal energy grounded in personality. This is activated through its planetary functions according to its aspect, or relationship, with them

Sun generally refers to the whole Self, and specifically to one's spiritual identity: the larger meaning/purpose of one's life.

'Ego' refers to one's conscious presentation of the Self. What one makes of its vitality, how one actually lives its essence. Ego is charted at the ascendant, which describes Earth's rotational aspect or relationship to Sun. (Sun's position relative to Earth's horizon of awareness: see 'Sun and Earth.') Ego grounds one's subjective experience, and objective expression, of spiritual identity as colored by planetary aspects.

Sun/Mars

Spiritual and personal will. Purpose and implementation.
Identity and ability. Central meaning and the battles it must fight.

Conjunction: just as a forest fire consumes deadwood, releasing its nutrients for new growth, so solar vitality flares off the spent fuel of an exhausted drive, making space for a new impulse of self-assertion. As in the genetic recombination of conception, the life-essence reshuffles its energy configuration, renews its attribute of personal will. Self revisits its core motivation. Spiritual identity reinvents its purpose. Ego fuses an innate meaning with objective executive ability to generate a fresh initiative. Courage redefined by a baptism of fire.

An old passion burns away as Sun approaches Mars, a new one ignites at conjunction, its action potential emerges as Sun separates from Mars. The same issues that are veiled in the light of fusion with Sun at conjunction come closer to conscious definition at the opposition. See 'Mars retrograde.'

Waxing semi-sextile (30°; stimulating): Self begins to separate from its purposes and activities. Spiritual identity detaches from will and its works. Ego differentiates from its enthusiasms and impulses. Meaning starts to emerge out of passion.

Waxing sextile (60°; supportive): Self effectively projected through its purposes and activities. Spiritual identity aligns with explicit behavior. Ego competently executes the strategic demands of will. Meaning flows in harmony with passion.

Waxing square (90°; action crisis: danger/opportunity): Self rebels against prior purposes and activities. Spiritual identity conflicts with now irrelevant demands of will, seeks new forms of assertion.

Ego breaks from spent passion, seeks a more authentic expression. This challenge stimulates one's warrior side, or gives it too much power. Meaning found in battle.

Waxing trine (120°; amplifies, mutual reinforcement): Self integrates with its strategic purposes and tactical activities. Spiritual identity smoothly deploys executive ability. Having achieved the ego's immediate goals, will turns within for a review of its operating procedure (retrogrades). The quest for meaning seeks a new inner passion.

Waxing quincunx (150°; irritating): Self questions its previous purposes and activities. Spiritual identity at odds with old behavioral strategies. Ego seeks to control a difficultly independent will. Passions seem to lack meaning.

Opposition (180°; challenge and illumination): Self redefines its purpose and activities. Spiritual identity reviews its motivations. It commits to a higher passion. Or gets stuck in splitting off from an old one. Ego battles to reach a new level of competence in asserting its will. Or loses control of its own behavior. An inner sense of meaning fundamentally improves its strategic outreach. Or is torn apart by incompatible drives. See 'Mars retrograde.'

Waning quincunx (210°; irritating): Self begins to sense a new purpose. Spiritual identity starts adapting to a different behavioral strategy. Ego struggles to redefine its will. An inner sense of meaning gropes to express revitalized passion.

Waning trine (240°; amplifies, mutual reinforcement): Self integrates with an emerging purpose. Spiritual identity smoothly deploys enhanced executive ability, for a good cause or a bad one. Ego effectively projects will. Meaning energized by new passions. Mars turns direct.

Waning square (270°; consciousness crisis: danger/opportunity): Self rejects a now irrelevant purpose, turns towards an emerging will. Spiritual identity reorients its behavioral strategy in line with a new agenda. Ego breaks away from stale passion, seeks something more exciting. Meaning found in a battle of conflicting motivations.

Waning sextile (300°; supportive): Self effectively serves an emerging purpose. Spiritual identity supports and cooperates with a relatively autonomous will. Ego competently executes a new strategy, for better or worse. Meaning aligned with a rising passion.

Waning semi-sextile (330°; stimulating): Self consecrated to an emerging purpose. Spiritual identity sacrifices itself to a battle defined by a dominant, or domineering, will. Ego commits to a larger than personal strategy, transcending its own interests. Meaning found in serving a new passion, the hope for a fresh start.

Sun/Jupiter

Spirit and soul, the infinite and humanized faces of God.
Purpose and philosophy. Central meaning and its social expression.

Conjunction: just as a spiritual enthusiasm flares off dead dogmas, so solar vitality consumes a tired belief system, making space for
consciousness expansion. As in the genetic recombination of conception, the life-essence reshuffles its religious/philosophical configuration, renews its social/political expression. The Self revisits its sense
of the divine, at whatever level of evolution it is on. Spiritual identity
reinvents its morality and ethical principles, in line with a growing
awareness of 'life more abundant.' Ego's sense of individual meaning
fuses with an inner archetype, a personification of higher truth, or with
an outer consensus of conventional wisdom. Self's connection with its
transcendent soul redefined in Sun's central fire.

An old truth burns away as Sun approaches Jupiter, a new one
ignites at conjunction, another level of aspiration and awareness
emerges as Sun separates from Jupiter. The same issues that are veiled
in the light of fusion with Sun at conjunction come closer to conscious
definition at opposition. See 'Jupiter retrograde.'

Waxing semi-sextile (30°; stimulating): Self begins to separate
from its social and political context. Spiritual identity detaches from
group norms and an accepted religious/philosophical consciousness.
Ego defines itself in contrast to conventional wisdom. Individual meaning emerges out of collective morality.

Waxing sextile (60°; supportive): Self expands through social
participation and resonates with accepted ethical principles. Spiritual
identity supports group norms and is aligned with its religious/philo-
sophical context. Ego competently personifies collective morality and
optimistically accepts the truth of conventional wisdom. Individual
meaning flows in harmony with spiritual aspiration.

Waxing square (90°; action crisis: danger/opportunity): Self
rebels against conventional wisdom and collective morality. Spiritual
identity conflicts with its social environment or religious/philosophical
heritage. Ego breaks from group norms and accepted beliefs, for better
or worse. Individual meaning found in stimulating conflict between
antagonistic ethical principles.

Waxing trine (120°; amplifies, mutual reinforcement): Self integrates with its social environment and political context. Spiritual identity aligns with group norms and enhanced by larger ethical principles.
Ego's comfortable embrace of conventional wisdom turns within for
an uncomfortable review of accepted belief (retrogrades). Increasingly

subtle levels of meaning found in the exploration of religious/philosophical consciousness.

Waxing quincunx (150°; irritating): Self questions its social environment and political context. Spiritual identity at odds with group norms and conventional wisdom. Ego challenged by disturbing new religious/philosophical aspirations. Accepted beliefs seem to lack meaning.

Opposition (180°; challenge and illumination): Self redefines its sense of truth and ethical principles. Spiritual identity stimulated by a fundamental moral challenge. Ego embraces new norms of group participation, another level of political awareness, for better or worse. A traditional religious/philosophical consciousness understood at a higher level of meaning and guidance. Or a new worldview challenges conventional wisdom across the board. See 'Jupiter retrograde.'

Waning quincunx (210°; irritating): Self begins to sense a new ethical code and moral standards. Spiritual identity tentatively reorients towards an emerging form of consciousness and different group norms One's disturbing new religious/philosophical or social/political aspirations challenge the community. One is no longer bothered by them, but bothers others with them. Meaning found in spiritual experimentation.

Waning trine (240°; amplifies, mutual reinforcement): Self integrates with emerging social and philosophical aspirations. Spiritual identity expresses a new vision of heaven and earth. Ego personifies rising group norms and changing moral standards. Meaning found in evolving, rather than accepted, ethical principles. Jupiter turns direct, as inner exploration turns to outer religious proselytizing or political activism.

Waning square (270°; consciousness crisis: danger/opportunity): Self rejects identification with a now obsolete social or moral status quo. A new belief system challenges conventional wisdom at every point. Ego reorients to another sense of spirituality. Meaning found in the battle of differing religious/philosophical principles or antagonistic ethical standards (e.g. sharing v self-reliance).

Waning sextile (300°; supportive): Self stimulated by an emerging religious/philosophical or social/political consciousness. Spiritual identity aligns with rising group norms and supports changing moral standards. Ego competently serves a new belief system, good or bad. Meaning found in evolving aspirations rather than tried and true conventional wisdom.

Waning semi-sextile (330°; stimulating): Self consecrated to an emerging religious/philosophical or social/political consciousness. Spiritual identity sacrifices itself to or for new ethical principles and moral standards. Ego committed to a larger group norm that transcends its own interests. Meaning found in surrender to rising aspirations, good or bad.

Sun/Saturn

Spirit and fate. Purpose and frustration.
The central meaning and its nemesis or dark side.

Conjunction: just as the radiance of hope lights up an inner darkness, so solar vitality inflames a shadow of despair with a spirit of renewal. As in the genetic recombination of conception, the life-essence reshuffles its inherent limitations so that an old weakness motivates and guides the deployment of a new strength. The Self revisits its guilt to redeem it through the discipline of a fundamental restructuring. Spiritual identity faces a hard fate. Ego shoulders a lonely destiny with heavy responsibilities. A sense of duty redefined by a baptism of fire in the central Sun. Personal meaning fused with a recognition of and response to the reality of evil.

An old fear burns away as Sun approaches Saturn, a new one ignites at conjunction, another nemesis emerges as Sun separates from Saturn. The same issues that are veiled in the light of fusion with Sun at conjunction come closer to conscious definition at opposition. See 'Saturn retrograde.'

Waxing semi-sextile (30°; stimulating): Self begins to separate from a sense of duty and destiny. Spiritual identity starts to detach from fear, develops a disciplined effort to overcome it. Ego defines itself in contrast to a Shadow of inner guilt and weakness. Individual meaning emerges out of a given fate.

Waxing sextile (60°; supportive): Self accepts duty and resonates with destiny. Spiritual identity cooperates with fate and is positively stimulated by fear. Ego competently negotiates with a Shadow of inner guilt and weakness. Individual meaning found in the discipline of following long-term goals with a consistent and realistic strategy.

Waxing square (90°; action crisis: danger/opportunity): Self rebels against its fate and confronts its fear, wisely or foolishly. Spiritual identity contends with a sense of personal injustice or perceived deprivation. Will it overcome them or sink to the level of its nemesis? Ego breaks away from assigned duty and limited destiny to find its own way. Individual meaning found in a protracted conflict between light and dark, ambition and depression, freedom and oppression.

Waxing trine (120°; amplifies, mutual reinforcement): Self integrates with a larger sense of duty and destiny. Spiritual identity slowly organizes through consistent and effective discipline. Ego effectively adapts to the demands of fate and realities of fear. A sense of achievement turns within, to face its hidden darkness (retrogrades). A new level of meaning found in lighting up, or unleashing, a Shadow of inner guilt and weakness.

Waxing quincunx (150°; irritating): Self questions its duty and destiny. Discipline disrupted by hidden weakness. Spiritual identity at odds with its fate and agitated by fear. Ego disturbed by a Shadow of unnamed guilt that gnaws at self-respect. Individual meaning confounded by doubt. This leads to cynicism or a bracing realism.

Opposition (180°; challenge and illumination): Self redefines its sense of duty and destiny. Spiritual identity stimulated or crushed by a full-on encounter with fate, and with fear. Grace under pressure. Or cringing impotence. Ego embraces discipline in the service of integrity. Or cynically denies it in favor of self-interest. A sense of meaning lights up the Shadow of inner guilt, repression and lies. Or one falls under their dark spell, justifying their evil. See 'Saturn retrograde.'

Waning quincunx (210°; irritating): Self begins to sense a new destiny, with unclear duties. Spiritual identity questions its fate, but doesn't get an answer. Ego disturbed by nameless fears. A sense of meaning challenged by a Shadow of unacknowledged guilt. It learns to accept and work with doubt. Or never escapes it.

Waning trine (240°; amplifies, mutual reinforcement): Self integrates with an emerging sense of destiny. Spiritual identity successfully expresses a demanding discipline by personal example. Or learns to regiment others. Ego aligns with a larger than personal fate, an evolving standard of integrity, in the face of fear. Saturn turns direct, as an inner sense of duty becomes an external code of conduct. It is lived up to by self, or imposed by it on the community. Meaning found in an increasingly sophisticated encounter with, and redemption of, the Shadow. Or cynical accommodation to it.

Waning square (270°; consciousness crisis: danger/opportunity): Self diminished by fear, darkened by a Shadow of guilt, repression and lies. Or renewed by a difficult choice to crush its own weakness in the winepress of a higher, impersonal imperative. Spiritual identity reorients to a new sense of duty and destiny. Ego rejects an obsolete form of integrity and the now irrelevant discipline needed to maintain it. Or devolves into cynical lack of conscience and selfish conduct. A confrontation between an old law and emerging meaning.

Waning sextile (300°; supportive): Self effectively serves an emerging sense of destiny. Spiritual identity cooperates with the demands of a larger fate. Ego competently supports a new sense of integrity and its required discipline. Meaning found in an evolving dialog with the Shadow of inner guilt; develops a deeper understanding of fading fears, and of the new ones taking their place.

Waning semi-sextile (330°; stimulating): Self consecrated to an emerging sense of destiny. Spiritual identity sacrifices everything for duty. Ego commits to a larger fate that transcends its own fears. Meaning found in forgiving acceptance of inner guilt and weakness. Or despairing surrender to them.

Solar Aspects to Trans-Saturnian Planets

Sun's, or any planet's, aspects to the outer planets beyond Saturn work somewhat differently than the above. Outer planets = zones of subconscious turbulence. They do not define discrete psychological attributes, but point to an encounter with chaos or creativity. Solar aspects to outer planets mean that identity has entered, is involved in, a transcendence or disintegration situation. It faces larger forces that revitalize it. Or regresses to an earlier, easier, more primitive state of being.

The outer planetary forces of the collective unconscious open up, or shut down, conscious experience. They are not organized qualities of existence, but intensifications of consciousness, taking it up to the next level above, or breaking it down to the next one below. They act like or currents under the sea: not known and visible islands or continents, but powerful, unpredictable movements beneath the surface.

Sun/Uranus

Spirit and transformation.
Purpose and vision, either as genius or madness.
Central meaning and its encounter with novelty or anarchy.

Conjunction: just as a lightning bolt shatters the darkness, illuminating its hidden contents, so a sudden inspiration zaps an outgrown purpose, revealing a new worldview. As in the genetic recombination of conception, the life-essence reshuffles its guiding abstractions, renews its theoretical orientation or criteria of meaning. The Self redefined by a startling event or insight. Spiritual identity shaken to the core by a revelation, of whatever merit. Ego transformed by sudden, jolting changes in circumstance and consciousness; revolutionary jumps up or down. Personality identifies with an archetypal image or idea.

Self-transcendence or eccentric dissociation from common sense. Intuitive connection with unconscious energies, whether enlightening or disruptive. One's attitude towards a collective paradigm redefined by a baptism of fire in the central Sun.

An old utopian blueprint burns away as Sun approaches Uranus, a new one ignites at conjunction, another level of visionary expectation emerges as Sun separates from Uranus. The same issues that are veiled in the light of fusion with Sun at conjunction come closer to conscious definition at opposition. See 'Uranus retrograde.'

Waxing semi-sextile (30°; stimulating): Self begins to separate from an abstract idea, insists on its own uniqueness as opposed to representing a formative archetype. Spiritual identity starts to stabilize after an inner upheaval. Escape from turmoil. Ego defines itself in contrast to a revelation, whether of genius or madness. Personal meaning individualizes out of an inspiration or theoretical construct.

Waxing sextile (60°; supportive): Self aligned with an abstract idea or formative archetype. Spiritual identity supports and cooperates with inspiration. Ego competently grounds an intuitive vision and expresses a revolutionary revelation. Personal meaning flows in harmony with theoretical insight.

Waxing square (90°; action crisis: danger/opportunity): Self rebels against an abstract idea or formative archetype. Spiritual identity breaks away from an inspiration or revelation. Ego disrupted by surprise intrusions from within or attacks from its environment. It learns to act in a completely new way, better or worse than before. Personal meaning found in battle with the tyranny of theory.

Waxing trine (120°; amplifies, mutual reinforcement): Self integrates with an abstract idea or formative archetype. Spiritual identity aligns with an inspiration, enhanced by a revelation. Ego successfully surfs a wave of external change. And turns within, to change itself (retrogrades). A new level of meaning found in an intuitive vision or theoretical insight.

Waxing quincunx (150°; irritating): Self questions an abstract idea or formative archetype. Spiritual identity upset by disturbing new ideas, challenged by thoughtcrime. Ego confounded by intuitive revelation. Personal meaning inconsistent with a theoretical construct.

Opposition (180°; challenge and illumination): Self redefined by an abstract idea or formative archetype. Spiritual identity stimulated or crazed by inspiration. Ego embraces, or denies, a life-changing intuitive vision or revelatory insight. Personal meaning takes a transformative leap, up or down. Genius or madness. Transcendence or breakdown. Extremes of experience. See 'Uranus retrograde.'

Waning quincunx (210°; irritating): Self begins to sense a new revelation. A changing spiritual identity disrupts the community with disturbing ideas, causes trouble by propagating thoughtcrime (which may be enlightened or sociopathic). Ego questions a formative archetype. Personal meaning inconsistent with a reigning paradigm.

Waning trine (240°; amplifies, mutual reinforcement): Self integrates with an emerging revelation. Renewed spiritual identity stimulates the community with an inspiration that is charged with exciting novelty. Ego aligns with, and effectively acts upon, a revolutionary vision. Uranus turns direct, as inner intuition becomes an external agenda for change, disruptive or benign. Personal meaning found in a grand theory: the future or the fringe.

Waning square (270°; consciousness crisis: danger/opportunity): Self shocked by an insistent new worldview. Revolutionary insights transform or traumatize one's self-image and social role. Spiritual identity rejects an obsolete archetype, reorients towards a new one. Ego breaks with a stale vision, a now irrelevant abstraction. Personal meaning found in battle with outworn theories and crazy revelations.

Waning sextile (300°; supportive): Self effectively serves an emerging revelation. Spiritual identity supports and cooperates with a revolutionary agenda of personal and social transformation. Ego competently serves an intuitive vision or inspirational idea. Meaning flows with a new formative archetype or theoretical construct.

Waning semi-sextile (330°; stimulating): Self consecrated to an emerging inspiration. Spiritual identity sacrifices to or for a revelation or a revolution, whether personal, scientific or political. Ego committed to an intuitive vision or idea. Meaning found in acceptance of, surrender to, a new theoretical construct or formative archetype.

Sun/Neptune

Spirit and imagination. Purpose and compassion.
Central meaning's encounter with mystical union
or confused dissolution.

Conjunction: just as a tsunami washes away a familiar shoreline of consciousness, so solar vitality dissolves a now decadent dream, making space for a new vision. As in the genetic recombination of conception, the life-essence reshuffles its visionary ideals, renews its magnetic field of empathy. The Self returns to its source in the magic of imagination, which can create a world or a personality. Spiritual identity immersed in mystical ecstasy or drowned in hallucinatory intoxication. Ego melts in compassion for others, or slobbers in codependence upon them. Personal meaning fused with the mystery of grace or sinks back into the unconscious. A universal, or indiscriminate, sense of love redefined by a baptism of fire in the central Sun.

An old poetic sensibility burns away as Sun approaches Neptune, a new one ignites at conjunction, another redemptive dream emerges as Sun separates from Neptune. The same issues that are veiled in the light of fusion with Sun at conjunction come closer to conscious redefinition at opposition. See 'Neptune retrograde.'

Waxing semi-sextile (30°; stimulating): Self begins to separate from a dream. Spiritual identity detaches from a redemptive ideal, or illusion. Ego defines itself in contrast to the demands of compassion or codependence. Personal meaning individualizes out of an imaginative vision, or a hallucinatory intoxication.

Waxing sextile (60°; supportive): Self aligns with a redemptive ideal, or illusion. Spiritual identity supports and cooperates with an imaginative vision, or a hallucinatory intoxication. Ego competently grounds compassionate empathy. Personal meaning flows in harmony with the mystery of grace.

Waxing square (90°; action crisis: danger/opportunity): Self rebels against a redemptive ideal, or illusion. Spiritual identity conflicts with deception from within, betrayal from its associates, confusion in its environment. Can it cut through the fog, or will it sleepwalk, lemming-like, to its destruction? Ego breaks from an imaginative vision or hallucinatory intoxication. Personal meaning found in battling collective myth.

Waxing trine (120°; amplifies, mutual reinforcement): Self integrates with a redemptive ideal, or illusion. Spiritual identity enhanced, or intoxicated, by an imaginative vision. Ego competently adapts to a collective participation mystique. It also turns within to follow a dream, or a nightmare (retrogrades). A new level of meaning found in compassionate empathy or in the comforting embrace of codependence.

Waxing quincunx (150°; irritating): Self questions a redemptive ideal, or illusion. Spiritual identity undermined by imagination. Ego subverted by nebulous longings and impossible dreams. Personal meaning inconsistent with the draining demands of empathy or codependence.

Opposition (180°; challenge and illumination): Self redefined by a redemptive ideal, or illusion. Spiritual identity stimulated by mystical union with a higher vision. Or intoxicated into a lower state. Ego embraces compassionate empathy or clinging codependence. Personal meaning dissolves into mystical ecstasy or emotional chaos. See 'Neptune retrograde.'

Waning quincunx (210°; irritating): Self begins to sense a new redemptive ideal, or illusion. Spiritual identity disturbed by imagination. Ego tentatively reorients towards an emerging magic of group participation or mystical ecstasy. Personal meaning undermined by nebulous feelings that subvert consensus reality.

Waning trine (240°; amplifies, mutual reinforcement): Self integrates with an emerging redemptive ideal, or illusion. Spiritual identity enhanced, or intoxicated, by a new sense of magic. Ego aligns with and poetically expresses collective longings. Neptune turns direct, as imagination entrances others with vivid images and a compelling narrative, divine or demonic. Personal meaning found in an evolving empathy or devolving codependence.

Waning square (270°; consciousness crisis: danger/opportunity): Self rejects an outworn redemptive ideal, or illusion. Spiritual identity battles an intoxication, mythical or substantive. Ego breaks from a stale dream or a decaying group identification. Meaning found in battling unconscious possession. Embraces the personal disintegration of mystical illumination. Or torn apart by nebulous longings.

Waning sextile (300°; supportive): Self effectively serves an emerging redemptive ideal, or illusion. Spiritual identity supports and cooperates with an imaginative vision. Or drowns in intoxicated hallucination. Ego subordinates its own interests to a compassionate or hypnotic vision. Personal meaning aligns with a rising collective dream or ecstatic mystical illumination.

Waning semi-sextile (330°; stimulating): Self consecrated to an emerging redemptive ideal, or illusion. Spiritual identity sacrifices to or for a transcendent vision or an intoxicating hallucination. Ego commits to compassionate empathy or codependence. Personal meaning found in surrender to a collective dream or mystic illumination. Or is lost in a nightmare of confusion.

Sun/Pluto

Spirit and metamorphosis. Personal and collective purpose.
Central meaning and its encounter with death and rebirth.

Conjunction: just as a volcanic eruption blows away a familiar landscape, so solar vitality consumes a petrified obsession, making space for a new passion from the deep unconscious. As in the genetic recombination of conception, the life-essence reshuffles the demands of a larger Will, renews a guiding destiny. The Self returns to a core collective purpose, its generational ethos and historical context. Spiritual identity permeated by the larger processes of society and history in which it is embedded. Ego repeatedly encounters spiritual and emotional death experiences, with their possibility of rebirth. They transform it for better or worse. Personal mission fused with a group fate. A compelling necessity redefined by a baptism of fire in the central Sun.

An old karmic or collective issue burns away as Sun approaches Pluto, a new one ignites at conjunction, an impulse of impersonal Will, divine or demonic, emerges as Sun separates from Pluto. The same issues that are veiled in the light of fusion with Sun at conjunction come closer to conscious definition at opposition. See 'Pluto retrograde.'

Waxing semi-sextile (30°; stimulating): Self separates from a collective purpose, detaches from hidden passions of the deep unconscious, demands of a larger Will. Spiritual identity emerges out of its generational ethos and historical context. Ego gains, or grabs, its own space within community necessity, distinct from the social mores and concerns of its time. Personal mission flows parallel to, but not with, a group fate.

Waxing sextile (60°; supportive): Self cooperates with a collective purpose, stimulated by hidden passions of the deep unconscious, demands of a larger Will. Spiritual identity rides the wave of its generational ethos and historical context, trims its sails to the prevailing wind. Ego aligns with community necessity, gives voice to the social mores and concerns of its time. Personal mission flows in tandem with a group fate.

Waxing square (90°; action crisis: danger/opportunity): Self rebels from collective purpose, breaks free from hidden passions of the deep unconscious, demands of a larger Will. Spiritual identity diverges from its generational ethos and historical context. Ego battles community necessity, defines itself in contrast to the social mores and concerns of its time. Personal mission flows away, emigrates, from a group fate.

Waxing trine (120°; amplifies, mutual reinforcement): Self integrates with collective purpose, smoothly adapts to hidden passion of the deep unconscious, demands of a larger Will. Spiritual identity aligns with its generational ethos and historical context. Ego effectively expresses community needs, the social mores and concerns of its time. And turns within, seeking the roots of power (retrogrades). Personal mission resonates with a group fate.

Waxing quincunx (150°; irritating): Self at odds with collective purpose. It is too individualized to comply with hidden passions of the deep unconscious, demands of a larger Will. Thus they disturb it. Spiritual identity is uneasy with its generational ethos and historical context. Ego questions community necessity, the social mores and concerns of its time. Personal mission grates against the flow of a group fate.

Opposition (180°; challenge and illumination): Self dies and is reborn: transformed and responsive to a larger context. Or devolves into a traumatized shadow of its former identity. Personal mission and collective purpose, a conscious sense of meaning and hidden passions of the deep unconscious, complement and enhance each other. Or they mutually self-destruct. Spiritual identity exemplifies its generational ethos, the social mores and concerns of its time. Or acts in total opposition to its historical context, prophetically or treasonously. Ego faithfully reflects, or bitterly rejects, a group fate. See 'Pluto retrograde.'

Waning quincunx (210°; irritating): Self at odds with collective purpose. It questions hidden passions of the deep unconscious, demands of a larger Will. Spiritual identity disturbed by emerging implications of its generational ethos and historical context. Ego works out apart from community necessity, cannot relate to the social mores and concerns of its time. Personal mission inconsistent with group fate, can be rudely reminded of that fact.

Waning trine (240°; amplifies, mutual reinforcement): Self integrates with a rising collective purpose. It smoothly adapts to emerging dimensions of the deep unconscious or a larger Will. Spiritual identity competently embodies a coming generational ethos, the next phase of its historical context. Ego blazes a trail for the community, is ahead of the social mores and concerns of its time, for better or worse. Pluto turns direct, its inner power matured, to enrich or devastate the community. Personal mission pioneers a group fate.

Waning square (270°; consciousness crisis: danger/opportunity): Self rejects an old collective purpose, seeks another one. It breaks away from spent passions of the deep unconscious, irrelevant demands of a larger Will. Spiritual identity battles a dying generational ethos, seeks a new historical context or meaning. Ego defined in contrast to the social mores and concerns of its time. It walks away from community necessity, or is crushed by it. Personal mission swims upstream against a group fate, heroically or in futility.

Waning sextile (300°; supportive): Self supports and cooperates with an emerging collective purpose. It effectively serves new dimensions of passion from the deep unconscious, demands of a larger Will. Spiritual identity encouraged by a rising generational ethos and historical context. Ego competently serves community needs, exemplifies the next step in social mores and concerns, for better or worse. Personal mission follows a group fate.

Waning semi-sextile (330°; stimulating): Self consecrated to an emerging collective purpose. It expresses new passions from the deep unconscious, demands of a larger Will. Spiritual identity is already anchored in another generational ethos and at odds with its current context. Ego sacrificed to or for community necessity. It is ahead of the social mores and concerns of its time, can be punished for that. Personal mission pioneers a group rebirth.

Retrogradation

Astronomical Facts

The planets of our solar system revolve around their orbits at different speeds. They all move steadily forward in the same direction, circling Sun. But we on Earth are also moving. Therefore, other planets sometimes appear to move backwards because of this speed differential. Think of a fast car passing a slow one. The slow car is objectively moving forward. But from the vantage point of the fast one it appears to be falling back. This apparent backward motion is called retrogradation and has profound symbolic meaning in astrology.

Sun never retrogrades because Earth revolves around it. Moon never retrogrades because it revolves around Earth. Every other planet retrogrades for a specific period, because they each revolve concentrically, at different speeds, around a common center (Sun). We view their motion from one of the moving orbits of that concentricity, which is slower than those of Mercury and Venus, faster than all the rest.

A planet appears to move directly through the zodiac when it is on the far side of Sun from Earth. It appears to retrograde when it is on the near side of Sun: Figures 4 and 5.

Planets within Earth's orbit, Mercury and Venus, travel around a smaller orbit than Earth. As they travel that segment of their orbits closest to Earth they appear to be moving backwards across the zodiac. Figure 4, arc AB. They are not retrograde for half the year, as the diagram might seem to imply, because at a constant rate of motion they cover the closer concave arc much faster than the more distant convex arc. In the same way, a car going 50 miles an hour right in front of you appears to be moving faster than a car going 50 miles an hour on the horizon.

At the exact center of their retrograde arc, their closest approach to Earth, Mercury and Venus occupy the same zodiacal degree as Sun (inferior conjunction). 'Inferior' does not imply lesser; it means closer. At the exact center of their arc of direct motion, their farthest distance

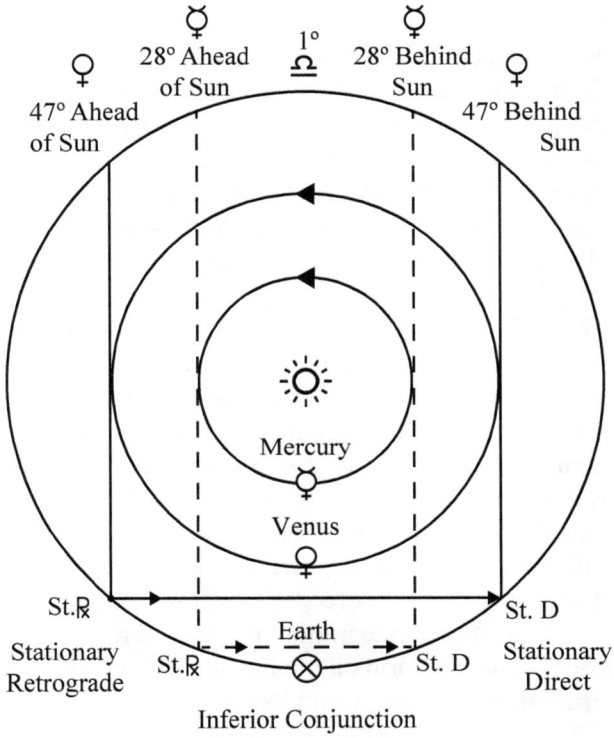

Figure 4   Inner planet retrogradation

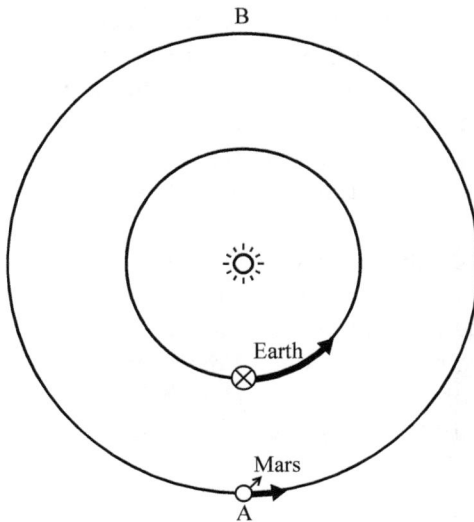

Figure 5   Outer planet retrogradation

from Earth, (but still within Earth's orbit) they also occupy the same degree as Sun (superior conjunction). 'Superior' does not imply better; only farther.

Planets outside Earth's orbit travel around a larger circumference than Earth. Thus they appear to move backwards across the zodiac as Earth catches up with and passes them, just as a slow moving car seems to move backwards from the window of a faster one overtaking it. At the exact center of its retrograde arc, its closest approach to Earth, an outer planet is in opposition to Sun (Figure 5, point A). At the exact center of its direct arc, its farthest distance from Earth, it is in conjunction with Sun (Figure 5, point B).

Venus and Mars retrograde for the least amount of time because their orbits most closely approximate that of Earth. Uranus, Neptune and Pluto retrograde for the longest period because their orbits are much larger and their movements appear much slower than that of Earth. The sum total of any planet's motion through the zodiac every year is always at least a little bit forward.

All planets, inner and outer, appear bigger and brighter during their retrograde phase because they are closer to Earth. Their energy, while turned within, becomes more available for conscious review and revision. They shrink and dim to minimum size and luminosity when in direct movement opposite Earth on the far side of Sun. During this longer direct period they experience and express a more distant objective reality, a fateful challenge/stimulus to the overall character.

Any planet appears to be stationary for a characteristic period of time while it is changing from direct to retrograde, and from retrograde to direct motion. If a planet is stationary retrograde its function is in the process of turning within. If it is stationary direct its function is in the process of exterior emergence. A planet acts powerfully while on station because it consolidates and expresses the results of an entire cycle of movement, direct or retrograde as the case may be.

Mercury retrogrades for 20-24 days at each of three equally spaced intervals during the year (e.g. March, July, November or February, June, October, etc.). It is stationary one day before and after each of these periods.

Venus retrogrades for about 42 days, preceded and followed by 18 months of direct motion. It is stationary for two days before and after. Venus retrogrades for the least amount of time of any planet.

Mars retrogrades for about 80 days, preceded and followed by 22 to 24 months of direct motion. (This variation exists because Mars has an eccentric orbit.) It is stationary for three days before and after.

The social and collective unconscious planets retrograde for a substantial period every year because they are much farther away from Earth. Jupiter retrogrades for about 120 days every year, and is stationary for five days before and after. Saturn retrogrades for about 140 days every year and is also stationary for about five days before and after. Uranus retrogrades for about 155 days every year and is stationary for six days before and after. Neptune retrogrades for about 157 days every year and is stationary for seven days before and after. Pluto retrogrades for about 160 days every year and is stationary for eight days before and after.

Astrological Significance of Retrogradation

When a planet retrogrades the energy or quality symbolized by that planet turns inward, exploring the basis of its own nature rather than participating outwardly in the world. The planetary function introverts to contemplate its identity, become more conscious of its emergent potentials.

During its direct motion, which is most of the time, the planetary function acts and evolves. During its retrograde motion it redefines that function. It retools itself. A retrograde planet operates more subjectively and less overtly than a direct one. It explores the roots of its essence rather than tests the limits of its expression. It corrects errors, upgrades deficiencies, improves performance. Thus it can make a fresh start at its direct station, when it resumes forward motion, with a deeper understanding of itself and a new operating procedure.

A retrograde planet sleeps and dreams. It processes, assimilates and integrates the lessons of its direct activity; consolidates objective experience into its psychological character. We tend to underestimate, even disparage, sleep as an inert dead zone in our lives. Yet it renews known abilities and attributes with the subtle energies of their instinctual and spiritual sources.

Any planet is as powerful retrograde as when direct. On one hand it is much closer to Earth, stronger by proximity. On the other it seems to backslide from our vantage point on Earth.

Mercury retrograde depicts mind editing itself. Intellect re-examines its fundamental assumptions. Reformats its internal operating protocols. For this reason it has difficulty communicating outwardly. Here a subtle, complex mentality, having reached a relative peak of development, revisits its underlying spiritual purpose. As it moves back towards Sun Mercury burns off irrelevance and abstracts the essence of its experience into a new pattern of internal consciousness. Moving from inferior conjunction to direct, the mind subjectively organizes and articulates the significance of this solar baptism. A mental reorientation.

Venus retrograde portrays 'the revaluation of all values' (Nietzsche). It redefines the desire nature. Recalibrates the basis upon which choices are made. Explores new possibilities of how to love. Other dimensions of beauty. Moving towards inferior conjunction the distortions, flaws and shortcomings of old values become painfully clear. Moving from there to direct, new values take form. A desire reorientation.

Mars retrograde describes self assertion turned inwards. It redefines motivation; reorients will. This begins to awaken latent personal power. Effective external action along familiar lines is stymied so that a new kind of behavior can develop. A painful revelation of the irrelevance and inadequacy of previous strategies occurs as Mars moves back towards opposition to Sun. A new sense of personal purpose and the ability to execute it develops as Mars moves from opposition to direct. A strategic reorientation.

Jupiter retrograde forces an inner confrontation with received political or religious truths. Conventional wisdom and philosophical shibboleths questioned. Inward spiritual growth. This is often sparked by external deprivation, limiting distraction from outside. Thus one can hear more clearly the guru, god or soul within. A reformulation of moral and ethical principles occurs as Jupiter moves towards opposition with Sun. A growing ability to express them develops as Jupiter moves from opposition to direct. A social/spiritual reorientation.

Saturn retrograde is a dead giveaway of self restrained from within by a chilling sensitivity to its own internal deficiencies. It lacks normal boundaries or ego defenses against the outside world. It compensates with a profound inner discipline. Reconstructs subjective identity from the ashes of objective defeat. Or surrenders to a diminished sense of life. A methodical mobilization to overcome weakness, and face fear, as Saturn moves towards opposition to Sun. A renewed sense of destiny germinates while moving from opposition to direct. Reorients fate in the face of adversity.

Uranus retrograde confronts ego with a demand for subjective transformation. An inspiration, of whatever merit, shatters an obsolete sense of self. A revolution of expectations. Self becomes more inclusive. Or careens off into madness. An internal breakdown of consensus consciousness, and breakthrough to a new sense of identity, occurs as Uranus moves towards opposition to Sun. An original expression of revelatory vision develops as it moves from opposition to direct. Reorients intuition.

Neptune retrograde dissolves ego-consciousness back into its sustaining sea of psychic images and ideals. A plunge into the inner dream world. A baptism of redemptive vision or hypnotic intoxication. A deepening immersion into mystic sensibility, or escapist fantasy, as Neptune moves towards opposition to Sun. A new sense of poetic magic, or mythic delusion, as it moves from opposition to direct. Reorients imagination.

Pluto retrograde confronts ego with the need to transform under pressure. An inner catharsis forced by encounter with an overwhelming power. An old identity dies, with or without rebirth, depending on its willingness to submit to a more inclusive truth. A descent into Hell: to burn away karma, or suffer endlessly for sins one cannot admit. These may be collective rather than personal. A fusion of individual destiny with social purpose as Pluto moves towards opposition to Sun. Awakens to a larger reality, whether mastered by self or imposed by others, as it moves from opposition to direct. Reorients in response to a larger Fate.

A retrograde planet internalizes and is forced to own all the socially problematic aspects of whatever energy it symbolizes. It cannot comfortably participate in the accepted wisdom or herd mentality regarding that issue. It must fight the lonely fight to redefine it against conventional opinion. One must take it on alone and regenerate it without support from others - and usually in the face of their opposition.

Mercury retrograde must personally wrestle with outmoded knowledge that others insist is true. It learns to confront fossilized theories and effectively articulate a more accurate narrative.

Venus retrograde must stand against twisted values imposed by the social consensus. It learns to redeem repressed or distorted desires by attractively presenting better means of satisfaction.

Mars retrograde must confront the passive aggressions and festering poisons generated by others' inability to live authentically. It is a designated victim that learns to develop courage by expressing its true nature despite condemnation.

Jupiter retrograde must grow out of the political/religious madness of its time. It learns to propose better social alternatives to dysfunctional arrangements. Obviously this invites opposition.

Saturn retrograde must face the Fear that others cannot acknowledge. It carries the burden of others' projected anxiety until it becomes competent at dealing with those issues that family, friends and society find too scary to handle.

Uranus retrograde must meet the challenge of disconcerting truths that are too threatening for most to accept. It learns to express a new vision of the future.

Neptune retrograde must deny and transcend a false glamour that infatuates the mob. It learns to see through collective deceptions, reject others' cherished illusions. This often invokes a hysterical reaction, with which one must learn to calm.

Pluto retrograde must take on deep destructive forces of social karma. It learns to heal them by the regenerative example of one's own transformation.

Lunar Phases and Aspects

Moon embodies solar spirit in a psychological soul. Moon's angular relationship to Sun, its lunar phase, channels Sun's animating purpose into felt experience. How Moon reflects Sun demonstrates how a life reveals its inner identity.

Sun and Moon's zodiacal positions define a solar meaning and its lunar manifestation. Their aspect, or phase, connects those energies. Moon's position describes a general sensitivity or subjective temperament. Moon's phase portrays an emotional orientation, the way it expresses that mood or feeling nature.

During its 29½ day orbit around Earth Moon moves from conjunction with Sun (new) to a thin waxing crescent to a first quarter (half Moon) to an oblate light-filling orb (waxing gibbous) to a fully lit sphere on the opposite side of Earth from Sun (full). It then takes this process in reverse, shedding light (waning gibbous) to a third quarter (half Moon) to a thin waning crescent back to conjunction with Sun at a new Moon in the next sign. The constantly changing ratio between Sun and Moon, light and dark, portrays a moving calculus between conscious and unconscious, intention and instinct, motive and memory. Sun, the central source, emanates spiritual essence into a life force. Moon, a satellite defining Earth's outer circumference, grounds that vital energy into a rhythm of identity phases.

Moon's darker phases, centered on the new Moon, reflect psyche's waning immersion into, or waxing emergence out of, spirit (Sun). Moon's lighter phases, centered on the full Moon, reflect psyche's waxing evolution, and waning expression, of a tangible personality. Lunar darkness = gestating unconscious potency, an objective spiritual recharging. Lunar light = explicit conscious psychology, a subjective fulfillment.

The Lunar Cycle

Moon has eight major phases, illustrated in Figure 2.

Four of them denote turning points, fundamental changes of emotional orientation:

new, with Moon conjunct Sun, personality impregnated by spirit;
waxing square, a crisis of action;
full, with Moon opposing Sun, personality demonstrating spirit;
waning square, a crisis of consciousness.

The other four constitute developmental stages of emotional experience:

waxing crescent, growth of instinctual expression;

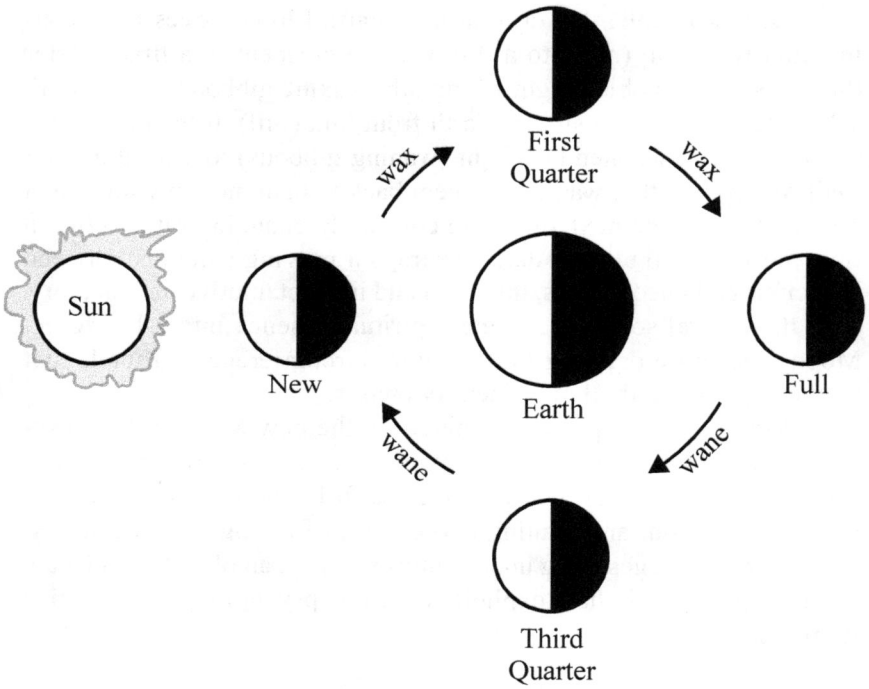

Figure 1 The Lunation Cycle
as seen from above the solar system

Figure 2 Lunar Phases
as seen from Earth

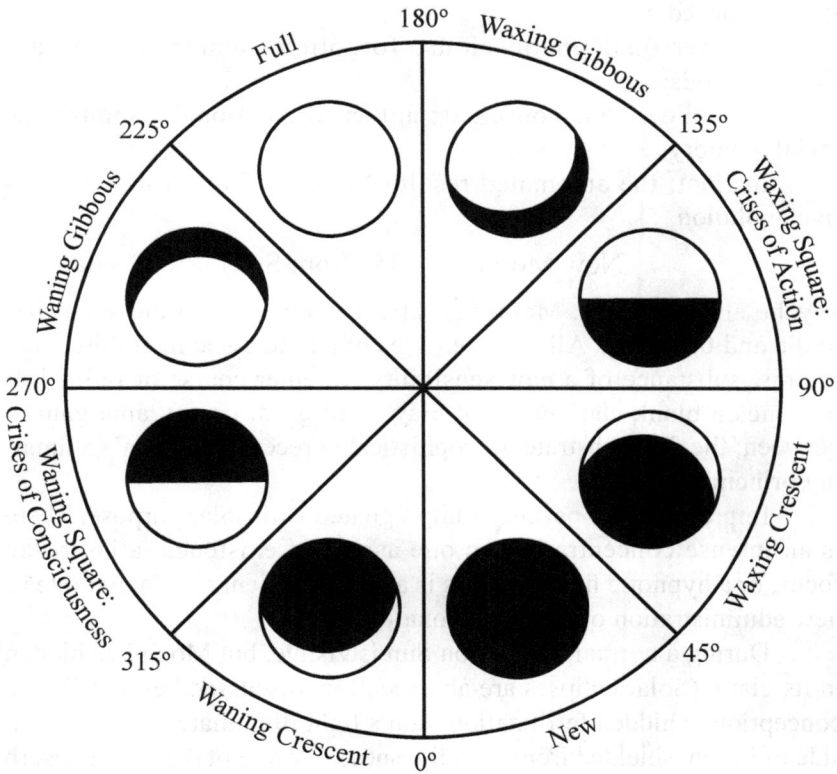

waxing gibbous, growth of emotional identity;

waning gibbous, sharing of psychological wisdom;

waning crescent, release of self-consciousness back to its soul source.

Definition of terms:

Spirit: intangible potency; higher will or soul purpose. Symbolized by Sun.

Psyche: the subconscious matrix of personality symbolized by Moon. It is composed of:

the personal unconscious: forgotten memories and subliminal moods;

the collective unconscious: universal emotional response and racial memory;

instinct: the automated result of three billion years' cumulative evolution.

New Moon (0° - 45° from Sun)

Psyche absorbs spirit. Moon figuratively plunges into the solar fire, to die and be reborn. All the memories of an old cycle melt down into the raw substance of a new sensibility, whether coarse or refined. It becomes a blank slate made of clay or of gold, or any amalgam in between; the dull substrate, or sophisticated receptor, of Sun's animating principle.

Impressionable psyche is impregnated with solar purpose. There is an intense concentration on one aspect of existence: a laser-like focus, or a hypnotic fixation. This is a 'seed moment.'[1] It inaugurates a new administration of soul's personality.

During a normal new Moon Sun is visible, but Moon lies hidden in its glare. (Solar eclipses are an exception, discussed below.) This is conception, a hidden fertilization. Sun's light illuminates the 'dark' far side of Moon, shielded from consciousness. We do not see it; but absorb it in the deep unconscious, as if charging a battery. The essential nature of the electricity energizing the battery cannot be described, only its behavior as it flows between positive and negative electrodes. So too the union of spirit/life, consciousness/instinct, meaning/manifestation are power surges that can be experienced but not explained.

The new Moon is an influx initiation. One is baptized into the psychological waters, spiritual fires, intellectual atmosphere, or tangible circumstances of a new reality. From this seminal event consequences flow, knowledge shines, personality blooms. But the initial fusion encounter, like the fertilization of egg by sperm, remains veiled, prior

466

to consciousness. The new Moon reenacts an unknowable first cause, the mysterium tremendum, behind all phenomena.

The new Moon symbolizes hidden origins. It lays the foundation of all later development, the wellspring out of which flows the river of life. The new Moon indicates a psyche that is not an autonomous subjectivity or a self-willed personality, but rather a channel of creative impulse. Primeval forces and unconscious memories manifest through it. It performs best by going with the instinctual flow rather than by attempting to display a personal uniqueness that it has not yet developed.

The new Moon unites spiritual and psychological energies in an intuitive immediacy of experience. Or as an obsessive monomania. It lacks personal content. Instead it focuses a causative urge that will later blossom into an ego.

An old past burns away in fusion with solar spirit. An impulse to new identity glows in the fire-mist of formation. It has not yet condensed into a specific individuality. Ego radiates with an impersonal numinosity, not as a defined character. It channels intangible forces through spontaneous instinct rather than a formed consciousness. Like any beginning it surges with potential, a subjective enthusiasm. Like a young child it absorbs impressions and germinates a personality in response. It demonstrates an initial emergence of spiritual radiance into psychological expression.

Waxing Crescent (45° - 90°)

Psyche grows a spiritual spark into a living flame. Personality begins to emerge as the vehicle of solar intention. It is not yet an autonomous ego; rather it naturally and unselfconsciously channels a larger current of Sun's meaning. It is innocent: naive in the best and worst senses.

One is no longer immersed in the rapture or fusion experience of a new Moon. One now bears witness to it. One comes down from the mountain with a vision. The magic has become a message. This does not reflect personal experience or subjective preference. It has an objective quality of communion with impersonal truth. And an urgent immediacy that must be conveyed to others.

If expressed with spontaneous enthusiasm, a wonder that lets the revelation speak for itself, it can inspire others. Any attempt to rationalize or intellectually justify it fails and falls into dogma. And then fanaticism.[2] Personality cannot explain the light. It can only demonstrate its radiance in action and by example.

As Moon waxes through its thin crescent period a new light emerges. It has a spring like quality: fresh, enthusiastic, youthful. A general or objective spiritual intuition takes on a subjective coloration. An instinctive alignment of outer environment and inner unconscious starts to generate an individualized self-sense distinct from both. Inherent temperament begins to acquire personal character.

First Quarter (90° - 135°)

Psyche achieves personal definition out of impersonal spirit through a 'crisis of action.'[3] Budding individuality encounters and confronts the cold cruel world. It must adapt. It now establishes its own competence at the cost of innocence. It must take a stand in contrast to its surroundings. And break from its inherited feeling nature. Shared instincts coalesce into personal emotions. One commits to a unique subjective identity and the actions stemming from it. Self-conscious choice replaces natural flow. It is the moment of individualization.

At this point Moon crosses from within Earth's orbit, closer to Venus: inner harmony, to beyond it, closer to Mars: outer expression. Self leaves its roots, and the herd, to do its thing, creatively or as an outlaw. Alignment with collective mood flips into a subjectively felt contrast against it. Self-definition arises through confrontation with, rebellion from, its surroundings. The drama of ego emergence requires conflict with the demands and expectations of others.

The crisis of action issue is not conflict as such - that is a given - but how one manages it. It needs to demonstrate inner truth despite social pressure or external obstacle. Thus it stimulates self-assertion. Tension between a new individual perspective v established social norms generates an increasingly effective ability to act. Or evokes frustration leading to rogue behavior. In either case identity aggressively expresses a growing sense of its own uniqueness.

Waxing Gibbous (135° - 180°)

Psyche independently expresses spirit. Individuality comes into its own. One blossoms as an autonomous actor. Personality no longer objectively reflects the cosmos. It has become a uniquely configured microcosm of it.

Personal truth replaces collective sensibilities. Integrity means following one's bliss. One must steer by one's own lights, rather than by ancestral instinct or shared wisdom. Fidelity to self, rather than living up to others' expectations, or subordination to a cause, leads to evolution.

A ripening emotional identity redefines the world in the image of its dreams. A growing sense of discovery, and of personal competence, stretches for the peak. Its can rush to judgment with immature ideas. Or identify with imaginative fantasies about its own merit. Narcissism is the seduction, self-absorption the shadow.

Maturation and expression of a subconscious narrative. Projects an inherent temperament, or pre-existing bias, onto reality. Increasingly conscious presentation of instinctual wisdom. Or psyche's natural feelings devoured by a metastasizing lunacy: 'all my means are sane, my motive and my object mad.'[4]

One serves best by subjective authenticity. Only by demonstrating an inner truth can one contribute to the outer world. Social reality means little; individual perspective means everything. By reflecting the image of God as experienced within one automatically radiates a divine creativity.

The danger lies in taking personal credit for such instinctive power. In that case insatiable cravings for recognition lead to contrived ego projections that cloud the soul's brightening mirror.

Full Moon (180° - 225° from Sun)

The waxing phase culminates and ends. Sun and Moon form a polarity in direct opposition. Psyche reflects spirit. Moon no longer absorbs solar vitality with a view to assimilating it into growing personality. Rather it independently exemplifies Sun, recreating spirit in its own image as a fully formed subjectivity - at whatever level of evolution one has achieved. Full is a moment of relative enlightenment. Of maximum conscious manifestation of the potential initiated at the new Moon.

The full Moon is not at a higher level than any other phase. It simply marks a turning point, where the progressive transformation of instinct into emotion, objective input into subjective output, reaches its final expression for a given cycle. It describes a moment of completion and relative perfection as opposed to the more dynamic interaction of other phases. Moon: matter, body, psyche, mirrors the radiance of Sun: spirit, meaning, purpose, to the full measure of its achieved ability. Emotional development peaks. It can attain a summit of personal growth. Or find itself isolated on a subjective island; alienated from social or objective reality.

Psyche consolidates into the greatest clarity of perspective on itself and the world around it. Self is illuminated with solar purpose. Or divorced from it. It most fully embodies a realization of meaning, to the extent of its ability. Or schizophrenically splits into dissociated fragments: Jekyll and Hyde made all too real. The final truth of a developmental round, for better or worse.

The process of personality formation is complete. It will henceforth expend itself in social participation. Now it must give rather than grow. What has been learned will be taught; what has been absorbed will be emitted. Experiential input is digested and transformed by Moon magic into an outgoing psychological message. As the full Moon passes the waning cycle begins. This involves release rather than buildup. It expresses what has already been achieved rather than strives for new attainment. During the waning phases one expends self for society, then later sacrifices it for a spiritual rebirth at the next new Moon.

Waning Gibbous (225° - 270°)

Following the full Moon, psyche radiates universal spirit from an individual perspective. One now gives rather than accumulates. The evolution of personality is (relatively) complete. Now it disseminates a revealed message, the meaning of its experience, to the world at large. A developed self expends itself, sheds its own light out onto society. Psyche flowered at the full. Now it bears fruit. This may be nourishing or poisonous.[5]

This is a teaching, or even a crusading phase. One shares, or imposes, what one has learned. The visibly waning Moon portrays an erosion of subjective ego, a disintegration of personality. In compensation one concentrates on a singular ability, a bright point of light projected outwards. The personal self is consumed by and sublimated into, an essential statement of meaning.

The relative enlightenment of the full now begins to inseminate the subconscious darkness. Consciously achieved realizations and hard won attainments become an accepted inheritance. This frees up the psyche for further advance. We don't have to consciously think about how to walk, or spell out every word in a book, because these once difficultly learned abilities have been poured back into the unconscious as instincts. The unique attributes of personality are automating, resorbing back into an instinctual competence. The area of conscious imagination shrinks into a focused intensity on one great message. This must be delivered to the world. All other qualities become fuel for this fire. This can lead to obsession. Or generate a ray of hope.

Third Quarter (270° - 315°)

After one has given all that one has to offer, a crisis of consciousness arises. Psyche adapts to a new spiritual dispensation. The past revelation of the full, however intense, is now inadequate. One senses different challenges and other opportunities just over the horizon. These are instinctively felt, not explicitly realized. An old perspective, prior truths, however valid in their own time, must give way to an emerging worldview. One reorients to a coming new reality.

An outworn sensibility is shed. One moves beyond an obsolete emotional stance and opens up to new possibilities undreamt of in the old order. The past fades. Or is taken away. Memories remembered in a new light. Recognition of the need for total realignment. Or a complete loss of faith in anything.

Subjective truth now yields to objective reality. Individual interpretation vanishes, replaced by simple acceptance of facts. This involves voluntary surrender to an impartial appreciation of excellence that outranks personal preference. Ego submerges into its environment. It identifies with the larger current within which it swims rather than its own point of view. This can generate anxiety over a diminishing ego, shrinking uniqueness. Or graduation to a more inclusive sense of being; a dispassionate view of self in the greater scheme of things.

Waning Crescent (315° - 360°)

After a reorientation of consciousness psyche returns to spirit. Personality progressively divests itself of past baggage, time honored attributes, so that it may spontaneously resonate with its environment. Hopes and fears, likes and dislikes, opinions and proclivities give way to naked vulnerability in preparation for an upcoming solar baptism. Subjective attitudes are sacrificed to an unconditional sensitivity to the universe as it is, not as one would have it.

Beyond all specific states of consciousness and permutations of personality one resorbs back into the environment. One forgets self and thus remembers the universe. Gives up the ghost of personal ambition, and identity itself, to become one with all. Here psyche begins to immerse in another dimension, the next world. Nonattachment replaces ego grasping:

'Cast a cold eye
On life, on death.'[6]

The Taoist concept of wu wei, action through nonaction, informs behavior. One joyfully accepts fate as part of a larger process:

'Thy Will, not mine, be done.'[7]

Of course such a process of winding down, of surrender to the unknown, can also evoke bleak despair. Leaving consensus reality behind can terrify one who identifies with the socially conditioned self. The only recourse is to let go and give up the ghost of ego pretension. One must trust in the larger forces that created one in the first place, to which one now returns.

Then the cycle begins anew, from another starting point in the next sign. Some phases (first and third quarters) are turning points. Some (new and full) are consummations. Some (crescents and gibbous) are developmental/expressive.

This is the Great Round of cyclic time; an Eternal Recurrence of archetypal energies. Only a growth of consciousness can move this circle into a spiral with a linear direction. This can happen as an intensification inwards or an expansion outwards.

Notes

1. Dane Rudhyar, 1895-1985, widely considered the father of modern humanistic astrology
2. A waxing crescent Moon is the symbol of Islam, just as the cross is of Christianity. The original revelation of this religion was a stark simplicity: there is one God and to fully embrace Him is to partake of His compassion. Soon this spiritual fire was abused to justify political agendas and cultural practices. For example, its core principle of 'jihad,' which means inner struggle towards union with God, became twisted to justify violent imposition of belief on others. This all too human failure to live up to its own ideals meant that a faith celebrating only one out of eight Moon phases fell out of phase with the larger cycles of history. Now Islam is experiencing a waning crescent identity crisis as it faces modern realities.
3. Dane Rudhyar also coined the terms crises of action and of consciousness for the lunar waxing and waning quarter phases.
4. Captain Ahab in 'Moby Dick.'
5. Thus Einstein had a waning gibbous Moon in Sagittarius; Hitler had one in Capricorn.
6. 'Under Ben Bulben,' W. B. Yeats, Irish poet, 1865-1939. Yeats actually wrote a book on lunar phases: 'A Vision.' However, this is difficult reading; prose was not his medium. There are several good books on this subject. One slender volume is particularly evocative: 'Phases of the Moon,' by Marilyn Busteed and Dorothy Wergin.
7. Mark 14:36 and Luke 22:42

Lunar Aspects to Sun

Definition of terms:

'Self' refers to a total identity complex of instincts, unconscious memories, conscious personality, superconscious soul and transcendent spirit. It means one's authentic wholeness including, but not limited to, objective social role and subjective individual character.

It unites inner sensitivities and outer behavior, explicit qualities and implicit potentials.

'Ego' refers to one's conscious presentation of the Self: how one deploys its vitality and actually lives its essence.

'Psyche' refers to subconscious instinctual temperament. A general emotional mood.

Conjunction: a deep focus on one aspect of reality. A powerful emphasis on a singular emotional truth. This is either profound or blinkered. Subjective soul imprinted by its spiritual source with a new meaning. Personality baptized into another cycle of the Self's evolution. Psyche accepts a reborn purpose. Ego fused with unconscious mood in authentic feeling or naive self-absorption. Instinctive rather than deliberate expression of identity.

Waxing semi-sextile (30°; stimulating): subjective soul begins to separate from its spiritual source. Emotional temperament detaches from the Self. Unconscious mood asserts its autonomy in contrast to the ego. Psyche diverges from a general purpose and starts feeling its own reality. Conscious identity decouples from its instinctual base and starts to express a personal flavor.

Waxing sextile (60°; supportive): subjective soul aligned with its spiritual source. Emotional temperament supports conscious identity. Unconscious mood cooperates with ego. Psyche competently grounds instinct and resonates with the Self's general purpose. Feelings flow with a larger sense of meaning.

Waxing square (90°; action crisis: danger/opportunity): subjective soul rebels against its spiritual source, seeks its own personal truth. Emotional temperament conflicts with the central identity. Unconscious mood disputes ego's sense of meaning. Psyche breaks away from an outworn purpose. Instinctual needs provoke a crisis in the personality. Feelings fight a false or incomplete idea of the Self.

Waxing trine (120°; amplifies, mutual reinforcement): subjective soul integrates with its spiritual source. Emotional temperament aligns with the Self. Unconscious mood enhances the ego's sense of meaning. Psyche effectively expresses a general purpose. Instinct accurately reflects identity. Feelings add depth to the surface personality.

Waxing quincunx (150°; irritating): subjective soul questions its spiritual source. Emotion disrupts the Self. Unconscious mood at odds with ego's sense of meaning. Psyche evades conscious purpose. Instincts confound identity. Feelings of incompleteness gnaw at the surface personality.

Opposition (180°; challenge and illumination): subjective soul and its spiritual source complement and enhance each other. Or schizophrenically split. Emotional temperament truly reflects the Self. Unconscious mood mirrors ego's conscious reality. Psyche expresses purpose. Feelings ground a sense of meaning. Instinct reinforces identity. Or all of them divorce as psyche dissociates from purpose in a general breakdown of personality.

Waning quincunx (210°; irritating): subjective soul begins to sense a new spiritual center. New emotional needs confound the general consciousness. Unconscious moods disrupt ego's sense of meaning. Psyche inconsistent with a general purpose. Instincts at odds with identity. Emerging feelings disturb the Self.

Waning trine (240°; amplifies, mutually reinforcement): subjective soul integrates with an emerging spiritual center. Emotions in tune with the general trend of conscious development. Unconscious mood adapts to ego's aspiration towards a higher, more inclusive sense of meaning. Psyche expresses an evolving purpose. Instincts enhance identity. Rising new feelings go to the next level of sophistication.

Waning square (270°; consciousness crisis: danger/opportunity): subjective soul rejects an outworn spiritual source. Emotion reorients towards a new identity. Unconscious mood confronts ego's known meaning. Psyche breaks from a now irrelevant purpose. Instinct provokes a crisis in an obsolete general awareness. True feelings conflict with the dying shell of an old Self.

Waning sextile (300°; supportive): subjective soul serves an emerging spiritual center. Emotion supports a rising new consciousness. Unconscious mood cooperates with ego's evolving meaning. Psyche competently expresses a future oriented purpose. Instincts support a new identity. Feelings aligned with the Self's next cycle.

Waning semi-sextile (330°; stimulating): subjective soul consecrated to a spiritual source. Emotion sacrifices to or for a reborn consciousness. Unconscious mood embryonically expresses ego's next phase. Feelings commit to a future purpose. Instinctive surrender to the Will of God. 'Thy Will, not mine, be done.' Personal psyche absorbed by collective or cosmic purpose. This can mean capitulation to a false god.

Lunar Nodes and Eclipses

Sun and Moon appear to be the same size as viewed from Earth. This fact becomes clear during a total solar eclipse when Moon, passing in exact alignment between Sun and Earth, almost completely covers the solar disc.[1] In our terrestrial experience we stand at the fulcrum, the tipping point, between matter and spirit, body and soul, animal and angel. There is a slight preponderance of spirit, demonstrated by the solar corona's delicate ring of fire surrounding the lunar disc during such an eclipse.

Moon condenses spirit into psyche. It focuses solar potential into a personal soul of instinct, sensitivity and feeling. This lunar soul circles north and south of its Earthly plane of manifestation.

Moon orbits Earth at a 5° incline to the ecliptic, the path of Earth's orbit around Sun. The north node shows where Moon's orbit intersects the ecliptic (Earth's orbital path) while moving north of it. The south node, 180° opposite, shows where Moon crosses the ecliptic moving south. (See 'Mundane Considerations,' Figure 1.)

This pair of nodal points retrogrades. It moves backwards through the zodiac every 18.6 years, spending one and a half years in each of the twelve signs. This movement parallels the retrogradation of the vernal equinox (0° Aries) through the zodiac every 25,920 years (Precession of the Equinox). Thus there are 1440 lunar nodal cycles in one Precession, or Great Year. What this ratio might mean is open to speculation. The parallel meaning of these two cycles is more apparent.

Precession refers to the long eras of history, about 2160 years per sign. These move in the opposite direction (i.e. Aries, Pisces, Aquarius) to the normal seasonal round (Aquarius, Pisces, Aries).[2] The collective current of history seems to act as a contrary force, challenging our identity, constantly demanding that we become other than what we already are. It presents a series of crises, uncovers deeper issues, brought to the surface by our forward moving growth. Thus, for example, the accumulating knowledge base and conceptual tools of science, resulting from a noble quest for truth, have brought us face to face with nuclear weapons and genetic manipulation. These are matters of life and death. They force humanity to evoke deeper spiritual resources and mobilize more fundamental levels of consciousness.

In the same contrary way the lunar nodes are a remembering rather than an anticipatory movement. They evoke memories, issues, talents, problems from the deep past. They bring an encounter with the roots, origins, causes of personality. They act as a reverse compass, indicating where we have come from. They articulate a prior trajectory, a deep flowing current upon which the conscious ego floats.

The visible Moon forms a specific locus defining the unconscious foundations of present personality. Moon's nodes are abstract points, not material bodies. They describe 'shadows of forgotten ancestors.' They reverberate from long gone days as ghostly after-images of who

Figure 3   Eclipses

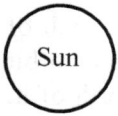

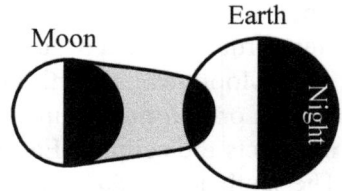

New Moon: Total solar eclipse
Moon blocks Sun

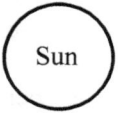

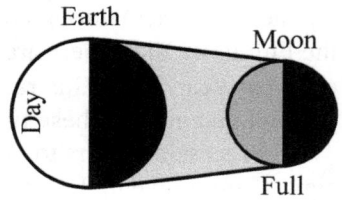

Full Moon: Total lunar eclipse
Earth blocks Sun

Sun and Moon look almost exactly the same size as seen from Earth. This is because Sun is about four hundred times farther away from us than Moon. Sun and Moon are shown the same size to illustrate their visual equality from our perspective. Moon is actually ¼ the size of Earth and 30 Earth diameters away.

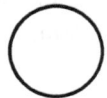

Moon is shown at 25% of its distance from Earth. It would take four pages lined up horizontally to show the true proportion.

476

Figure 4   Total Eclipse of the Sun

we once were. They indicate the shades of past personalities and their effects on the present.

The nodes can be thought of as the prior and now cast-off personalities that one's soul has inherited in this life alone: as infant, child, adolescent; in one's previous career or relationship; when one saw the world in the context of other ideals or ambitions. Or one can think of them as echoes of previous incarnations. In that view they elucidate very deep inertial energies and long term goals, providing a context for one's current reality.

The lunar nodes are the astrological factor most linked to concepts of reincarnation. They then depict abilities and challenges inherited from other lives. The actual Moon shows how these manifest in one's present personality. The nodes demonstrate where they came from and what they need to experience.

Astrology does not require a belief in reincarnation. The nodes can be seen as remnants of prior developmental stages in this one and only life. However, if one wants to investigate how the ego might be shaped by earlier episodes of existence, the immaterial, backwards moving nodes provide clues and guidance.

When the nodes are activated by the actual presence of both Sun and Moon on them then an eclipse results. An eclipse unearths a deep karmic issue (whether of the unconscious or of a previous life). It brings a major buried problem from the deep past up to the surface to be faced and dealt with.

A solar eclipse is a special condition of the new Moon. During a solar eclipse Moon's orbit around Earth temporarily intersects Earth's orbit around Sun. Moon then conjoins Sun on either the south or north node. Earth, Moon and Sun directly line up, with Moon physically blotting out the more distant Sun. Figures 3 and 4.

Day is eerily darkened. Moon's black orb is outlined by a ring of fire. A solar eclipse expresses an emergence of inherently foreign material into consciousness. A truly alien quality rises into the light of day. A scary and difficult issue presents itself. Here we get a brief glimpse of primeval processes beyond the ken of normal human consciousness. It can be compared to a direct sense of the birth trauma, our single most profound experience, buried so deeply in oblivion. A solar eclipse brings such things to the surface, smeared with slime and blood, bearing the power and pain of the most fundamental realities.

The full Moon generates a lunar eclipse when Earth passes directly between it and Sun. The full Moon then plunges into Earth's shadow, lit only by a lurid red glow of Earthlight. A lunar eclipse brings a dark mass of unconscious energy out into the open, un-illuminated by solar purpose or spiritual meaning. It embodies an upwelling of subconscious need, made (barely) visible in its own eerie terms. Only thus can a level of psychological density, a roadblock of congealed emotion, an iceberg of frozen feeling, arise into manifestation to work itself out. An alienated, disowned shadow side comes into its own, so that it can be acknowledged and acted upon.

The difference between solar and lunar eclipses is that a solar eclipse is starker, actually darkening the day. It challenges normal sanity with something truly disconcerting. This is an alien force, raw and primitive, standing between consciousness and spirit, demanding attention.

A lunar eclipse is like an unconscious or collective tide emerging out of night. Our own planetary shadow becomes visible and known. It is somewhat closer to home, more personal and less freaky than the solar eclipse. It brings up a general problem that one must own, recalls an inherited difficulty the current personality now experiences. An existential predicament has 'rotted and ripened' in the depths of psyche. A painful scary memory comes to fruition and must now be faced.

During a lunar eclipse Moon's normal brightness at the full falls into Earth's eerie shadow, which is reflected back to us. During a solar eclipse Sun's shining is temporarily turned off. In both cases spirit is short-circuited, as Moon blocks Sun from Earth, or Earth blocks Sun from Moon. In Sun's absence the dark foundations of the unconscious rises to our attention, in horror or for healing.

All eclipses involve either a new or a full Moon, symbol of the timeless unconscious. Moon manifests pre-personal memories, whether conceived of as instincts or karma. It takes time for their comatose energies to power up from oblivion into conscious recognition. These primal archetypes slowly translate into the stream of consciousness or flow of events. They reflect underlying issues, individual or collective, that usually germinate until triggered by a planetary transit. An eclipse is like the birth of a squalling incontinent baby that then develops for months before it actually does something such as speak its first word or take its first step.

Eclipses remind us that there are psycho-spiritual forces beyond our comfort zone. They occur in pairs (solar and lunar) twice a year, as Sun and Moon conjoin and oppose each other on or near the north and south nodes. They mark cycles, one-sixth of the yearly round, when immobilized, crystallized aspects of psyche come out to be recognized and redeemed. Ten out of twelve annual lunar cycles involve a dance of matter and spirit, soul and psyche. Two others, the eclipses, involve the externalization of hidden psychic tumors so that they may be known and healed. They allow unprocessed subconscious contents to emerge in their own right to face the light and come up into consciousness.[3]

The lunar nodes have their own characteristics even when they are not being activated in an eclipse. The south node expresses an energy or identity feature that reached a relative peak of development and power in the past (whether of this, or in another, life). Therefore it points to an innate ability, but one that has stopped growing. It is simultaneously an area of stagnation: an easy default position, a safe rut in which to hide. One has already 'been there, done that.' Further repetition just wastes time and drains energy. The south node also represents an unresolved issue from the deep past that has hardened into a liability. It should be addressed, but is easily avoided because it has numbed down into a habit, a mechanical response to life. If one learns to revitalize it then that old problem becomes a new asset. One can only do so through the agency of Moon's north node (below).

The planet ruling the south node's sign location indicates how such a petrified talent or unconscious problem operates at present. Thus a south node in Libra indicates a background of social acquiescence rather than self-assertion. The position and aspects of Libra's planetary ruler, Venus, indicates how that tendency to deference in the interest of harmony manifests in one's current state of being.

The north node expresses an energy or identity feature that needs to be developed in the future. An unacknowledged potential. An unfamiliar challenge that must be met if one is to go any farther. The north node does not demonstrate a real and present attribute, but a promise. It reveals a solution to the south node fixation. It points out the direction one must go in order to redeem the south node's problem.

The planet ruling the north node's sign location indicates where that challenge presents itself here and now. Thus a north node in Aries (opposite the above south node in Libra) indicates an evolutionary demand for self-assertion even at the risk of conflict and ostracism. Its planetary ruler, Mars, indicates how that demand must be met under present circumstances.

A solar eclipse on the south node points to an ancient, deeply ingrained trauma whose paralyzed, knotted up energy must be released. Thus it is brought up as an unavoidable crisis that one cannot sidestep. On the north node it presents a scary but powerful possibility of liberation. One can choose to turn away. One will then always regret the path not taken.

Lunar eclipses involve both nodes, emphasizing the one Moon occupies. On the south node an exhumation of old karma in order to finally put it to rest. On the north node remembrance, and perhaps redemption, of a goal sought but not achieved in the past.[4]

Think of the south node as a dried up riverbed, overgrown with weeds (deadening rituals), littered with empty liquor bottles and cigarette butts (dysfunctional programs). Yet if inundated with snowmelt from the distant peaks of north node attainment it becomes a conduit of growth, channeling life giving waters into a thirsty land. Along any river most of its water slowly percolates underground, recharging aquifers and nourishing life far from its banks.[5] This accords with the subconscious nature of the nodal axis. They form an instinctual orientation that can irrigate the south node's latent potentials if one can awaken from its sleepwalking to the north node's purpose.

Again, one can think of these as issues from one's personal past or as a momentum from an entirely different existence. However defined, the north node and its ruler portrays what one must do to achieve one's potential. The most difficult and alien, yet also most rewarding, challenge in life. The south node portrays what comes easily and naturally, either as an expression of north node attainment or in retreat from it. If, as and to the extent one attains the north node goal, the south node expresses its results or fruits. If one does not live up to the north node challenge, the south node shows why not, what held one back.

A third immaterial factor, the Part of Fortune, points out the concrete circumstances under which nodal achievement or stagnation occurs. The Part of Fortune makes the same zodiacal relationship to Moon as the ascendant does to Sun. It marks the rising point of unconsciousness coming up into the light of life. It signifies instinctual awareness, the leading edge of subconscious temperament as the ascendant is of conscious personality.

Notes

1. Specifically, from our viewpoint on Earth, each is about half of one degree in diameter: Sun's disc covers 32′2″ of arc; Moon's covers 31′37″.
2. See 'Precession,' Figure 1.
3. For more information on eclipses see 'Mundane Considerations,' second section ('The Saros Cycle.')
4. 'We shall not cease from exploration
    And the end of all our exploring
    Will be to arrive where we started
    And know the place for the first time.'

'Four Quartets,' T. S. Eliot, American/British poet, 1888-1965. He won the Nobel Prize for Literature in 1948.

5. Liquid fresh water = 1% of Earth's water. Groundwater = 96% of that, vivifying a gossamer thin film of soil atop our planet's rocky bulk. Surface water in lakes, streams, rivers and wetlands accounts for the remaining 4%. Ninety-seven percent of our water is salty ocean brine, two percent is frozen in the polar ice caps and a statistically negligible but vital component floats in the air as rain-bearing clouds that bring life to the land.

Lunar Aspects

Moon grounds all planetary energies into an overall temperament. Those planets directly aspected by Moon are emotionally emphasized. Embraced in a deep subconscious resonance with the whole personality. Endowed with a strong feeling charge.

Lunar aspects are almost as important as solar ones because Moon synthesizes all planetary attributes into a general psychological orientation or sensitivity. However, Moon points to unconscious processes. Grounding these planetary energies turns them into instinctive responses more than active initiatives, subconscious moods rather than known and visible motives. Thus they play a huge role in character and behavior, yet act as habitual tendencies instead of conscious strivings. Beneath the surface of consciousness these subliminal movements may be the most important but are also the least understood.

'The unconscious always compensates for deficiencies in the conscious attitude.'* Moon, emblem of the unconscious, in aspect to any planet of personal consciousness, brings that function's undeveloped side into the light. Thus Moon displays both the embarrassing problems and latent potentials of a planetary attribute. Moon instinctively reveals its hidden quality. This reveals an otherwise inexplicable emotional intelligence (Mercury), attraction (Venus), anger (Mars), philosophical optimism (Jupiter) or pessimistic fear (Saturn). Moon emotionally registers and reflects a planetary energy as experienced by the whole Self, not just the conscious ego.

As Moon moves within Earth's orbit, closer to Sun, from waning third quarter through the new to waxing first quarter, personality immerses in and reflects its objective sources: solar spirit and lunar instinct. As Moon moves outside Earth's orbit, from waxing first quarter to full to waning third quarter personality displays a subjective presentation of self as a microcosm of the universe.

As Moon waxes from new to full subjectivity grows. As it wanes from full to new objectivity grows. This happens because Moon waxes away from, or wanes towards, its solar source. In aspect to any other planet Moon, personality, does not itself become more subjective or objective, because it is not relating to its own source. Rather it subjectively assimilates or objectively expresses a specific planetary function in its overall emotional makeup.

   * The great psychologist, C. G. Jung (1875-1961). This was one of his classic formulations, central to his work.

Aspects of Moon

Lunar aspects are important because Moon, as the integrator of personality, grounds general psychological forces into experienced personal feelings. It conveys planetary energies into human emotions.

   These descriptions are necessarily incomplete because every Moon aspect to a planet also has a phase aspect to Sun. Thus if we say 'Moon conjunct Mercury' that Moon might be a waxing gibbous or a waning crescent, etc. It also occurs in a specific location: in Virgo or in Sagittarius, etc. With any other aspect two locations, of Moon and of planet, are involved. Thus a sextile, whether waxing or waning, might involve Aquarius and Aries, or Scorpio and Capricorn, etc.

   Sometimes Moon is without aspect, alone in space. This situation is uncommon but not rare. The absence of lunar aspects constitutes its own special condition, known as a void of course Moon, discussed at the end of this chapter.

Moon/Mercury

Instinct and reason. Emotion and logic. Memory and thought.

   Conjunction: psyche imprinted by sense perception. Subjective soul fused with data processing mind. A logical temperament seeks to balance objective information with visceral sensitivities. Paradox: a cool rational mood accepts feelings as facts, decides on gut instinct.

   Emotion marries intellect, generating intuitive or imaginative thought. Articulates the unconscious. Can bring dreams to life through language. Remembers and expresses the psychological coloration of mental processes.

   Waxing semi-sextile (30°; stimulating): feelings begin to separate from thoughts. Emotion detaches from intellect. Subjective soul distances from logical criteria of mind, individualizes on its own terms. Unconscious mood or temperament asserts itself against a conscious mental construct. Instinct differentiates from reason. Memory reinterprets simple facts.

Waxing sextile (60°; supportive): feelings parallel and endorse thoughts. Emotion and intellect cooperate. Subjective soul harmoniously aligns with logical processes of mind. Unconscious mood or temperament flows with a conscious mental construct. Instinct and reason work together. Memory reinforces ideas.

Waxing square (90°; action crisis: danger/opportunity): feelings rebel against thoughts. Emotion wars with intellect, provoked by external circumstance. Subjective soul breaks free from cold dictates of reason, takes its own path. Unconscious mood or temperament conflicts with mind. Instinct resists the conscious mental construct, dances to a different tune. Memories disrupt ideas.

Waxing trine (120°; amplifies, mutual reinforcement): feelings harmonize with thoughts. Emotion and intellect synchronize and cooperate. Subjective soul integrates with logical processes of mind. Unconscious mood or temperament nurtures and consolidates a conscious mental construct. Instinct reinforces reason. Memory serves as a valuable resource of mind.

Waxing quincunx (150°; irritating): uneasy feelings disturb thought. Emotional discomfort provokes intellectual restlessness. Subjective soul disturbs the logical processes of mind. Unconscious mood or temperament sidesteps a conscious mental construct. Instinct inconsistent with reason, questions its conclusions. Memory interferes with ideas.

Opposition (180°; challenge and illumination): Cerebral head and visceral gut powerfully reinforce each other. Or conflict to the point of paralysis. Mind and memory cooperate to amplify rationality. Or divorce in a threat to basic sanity. Emotion and intellect complement or contradict. Thought and feeling strongly aligned. Or completely at odds. Subjective soul deepens mental clarity. Or drowns it in sentimentality. Unconscious mood or temperament reflects a conscious mental construct. Or schizophrenically dissociates from it. Instinct adds new dimensions to reason. Or distorts it in the service of fantasy.

Waning quincunx (210°; irritating): participation in consensus consciousness at odds with one's own perceptions. Emotional expression of inconvenient thoughts. Subjective soul disrupts mental logic. Unconscious mood or temperament questions an accepted paradigm. Instinct confounds reason. Changeable memories undermine ideas.

Waning trine (240°; amplifies, mutual reinforcement): feeling and thinking in growing harmony. Emotional endorsement of an emerging intellectual perspective. Subjective soul integrates with a rising mental paradigm. Unconscious mood or temperament evokes new criteria of logic and evidence. Instinct resonates with an evolving rationality. Memories confirm a train of thought.

Waning square (270°; consciousness crisis: danger/opportunity): feelings reject a habitual way of thought. Emotion demands a fundamental rethink of everything. Subjective soul questions an outworn mental paradigm. Unconscious mood or temperament sheds an obsolete conscious orientation. Instinct confronts reason, takes a new direction. Inconvenient memories challenge basic intellectual assumptions.

Waning sextile (300°; supportive): feelings support an emerging mental agenda. Emotion backs a rising theory or perception. Subjective soul harmoniously commits to another kind of consciousness. Unconscious mood or temperament processed by new mental protocols. Instinct nurtures a revised rationality. Memory reinforces where thought is going.

Waning semi-sextile (330°; stimulating): feelings defer to facts. Emotional warmth gives way to cool analysis. Subjective soul consecrated to a new mental paradigm. Unconscious mood or temperament feeds a coming consciousness. Instincts seen in a new light.

Moon/Venus

Maternal and erotic love. Needing and wanting.
Memory and desire. Instinct and ideal.

Conjunction: psyche imprinted by desire. A sensual temperament. Subjective soul identifies with the pursuit of pleasure, according to the nature of its sign placement (Scorpio's idea of pleasure differs from Gemini's). Or is enslaved to appetite. Instinctive delight. Or voracious hunger.

The unconscious brought to life by love. Emotionally expresses a refined self-ideal, a graceful sense of beauty. Sensitive, tender and subtle. In touch with its own feelings and values. Responsive to the needs and moods of others. Seeks relationship and accommodation. Remembers love and happiness.

Emphasizes and renews the feminine principle at whatever level of evolution one is on.

Waxing semi-sextile (30°; stimulating): feelings begin to separate from values. Subjective soul differentiates from an inner self-ideal. Personal sensitivity distances from identification with relationship. Unconscious mood or temperament asserts itself against accommodation with others. Instinct seeks its own way of love. Memory detaches from desire, becomes more objective.

Waxing sextile (60°; supportive): feelings support and cooperate with values. Emotion and relationship harmoniously synchronize. Subjective soul aligns with an inner self-ideal. Unconscious mood or temperament flows in accommodation with others. Instinct reinforces love. Pleasant memories.

Waxing square (90°; action crisis: danger/opportunity): feelings conflict with values; one becomes sensitive to new, incompatible desires. Emotional crisis about how to relate. Subjective soul rebels against an inner self-ideal. Seeks a more authentic version. Unconscious mood or temperament hostile to accommodation with others. Instinct hungers for a new way of love. Memory can get stuck on lost or unattainable pleasures.

Waxing trine (120°; amplifies, mutual reinforcement): feelings and values reinforce each other. Love comes naturally, perhaps too easily: something good taken for granted. Subjective soul integrates with an inner self-ideal. Unconscious mood or temperament nurtures accommodation with others. Instinct resonates with affection. Happy memories.

Waxing quincunx (150°; irritating): uneasy emotional disquiet about basic values. Unrest in relationship. Subjective soul inconsistent with an inner self-ideal. Unconscious mood or temperament sidesteps accommodation with others. Instinct somewhat uncomfortable with demands of love. Memories embarrassingly contradict desire.

Opposition (180°; challenge and illumination): Maternal and erotic love, sensitivity and sensuality, memory and desire, inner feelings and shared values: all of these synergistically enhance the feminine side of psyche. And make it more conscious. Or they split into caricatures of idealized grace and voracious hunger as an inner virgin and whore fight it out. The unconscious temperament and idealistic soul complement and consummate each other in a well-integrated anima (guiding female archetype). Or divorce into contradictory impulses of sociable feeling and subjective moodiness; beauty and the bitch (which is which?). Emotional sophistication combined with natural rapport nurtures genuine love. Or seduces others in the service of primitive needs. Empathy supports relationship. Or insatiable appetites devour it.

Waning quincunx (210°; irritating): feelings uncomfortable with values. Emotion questions propriety. Subjective soul at odds with an inner self-ideal. Unconscious mood or temperament interferes with accommodation to others. Instinct confounds love. Socially disruptive memories.

Waning trine (240°; amplifies, mutual reinforcement): feelings resonate with novel desires. Emotions align with emerging values. Subjective soul integrates with a new self-ideal. Sensitivity finds satisfaction, can become complacent. Unconscious mood or temperament evokes the next level, another dimension, of relationship. Instincts turned on by an enticing vision of love. Golden memories.

Waning square (270°; consciousness crisis: danger/opportunity): emotional rebellion against expected relationship and socially accepted values. A hunger for new pleasures and novel forms of beauty. Subjective soul rejects a false self-ideal. Unconscious mood or temperament sheds inauthentic accommodation with others. Instinct confronts outworn love, reorients towards something (hopefully) better. Unhappy memories can lead to injudicious choices.

Waning sextile (300°; supportive): emotional support for emerging values. Subjective soul supports and cooperates with a new self-ideal. Unconscious mood or temperament commits to another dimension of appreciation. Instinct serves an evolving form of love. Personal feelings defined by the beloved. Remembers what others remember.

Waning semi-sextile (330°; stimulating): personal feelings consecrated to, even sacrificed for, emerging values. Subjective soul embraces a maturing self-ideal. Instinct aligns with a tentative, still developing, form of love. Unconscious mood or temperament accommodates others' desires, perhaps even losing its own identity. Memories renounced for a new vision of beauty.

Moon/Mars

Instinct and will. Reflection and action.
Memory and drive. Passivity and aggression.

Conjunction: psyche imprinted by will. Unconscious potential energized by personal purpose. Feelings activated by a stimulus or challenge. Subjective soul fused with an aggressive impulse of self-assertion. Brings imagination to life, for better or worse.

An instinctive urge to explore and initiate. An energetic temperament. Action oriented, can be frenzied. A combative mood. Emotionally favors the strong, but will fight for the weak: think of any mammal mother's ferocious protection of her offspring. Instinctive courage. Or blind belligerence. Remembers a strategic plan.

Waxing semi-sextile (30°; stimulating): feelings begin to separate from action. Emotional independence from dictates of will. Subjective soul differentiates from ego purpose. Unconscious temperament mellows out, distances from passionate drives. Instinct asserts its own impulses apart from strategic intent. Moods and memories become less demanding.

Waxing sextile (60°; supportive): feelings in tune with action. Emotion and will synchronize. Subjective soul supports and cooperates with ego purpose. Unconscious mood or temperament flows with assertive impulse. Instinct stimulated by challenge. Memory enables behavior.

Waxing square (90°; action crisis: danger/opportunity): feelings revolt from the demands of will. Subjective soul rebels from ego purpose. Unconscious mood or temperament hostile to a spent passion. Instinct challenges outworn forms of self-assertion. Sensitive to emotional violence or imposition from the environment. Remembers insults, slights and wrongs. That drags one down into primitive vengeance. Or stimulates a higher level of motivation and behavior.

Waxing trine (120°; amplifies, mutual reinforcement): feelings enhanced, invigorated, by action. Emotion powerfully and effectively expressed. Subjective soul integrates with ego purpose. Unconscious mood or temperament nurtures and appropriately expresses aggressive impulse. Instinct stimulates self-assertion. Memory serves will.

Waxing quincunx (150°; irritating): emotional uneasiness about one's actions. Sensitivity at odds with passion. Subjective soul inconsistent with ego purpose. Unconscious mood or temperament sidesteps aggressive impulse. Instinct interferes with self-assertion. Memory questions the purpose of will.

Opposition (180°; challenge and illumination): subjective temperament complements executive ability. The unconscious acts with instinctive competence. Or will and emotion violently clash; power and feeling acrimoniously divorce. Inner self-reflection stimulates outer self-assertion. Or challenges it. Sensitivity motivates behavior. Or enervates it. Memory justifies, or inhibits, purpose.

Waning quincunx (210°; irritating): subjective soul interferes with ego purpose. Unconscious mood and temperament provoke inconsistent behavior. Instinct questions self-assertion. Conflicting memories disrupt emotional tranquility in self and others. Disturbs the peace, for better or worse.

Waning trine (240°; amplifies, mutual reinforcement): subjective soul integrates with an emerging purpose. Unconscious mood or temperament nurtures ego expression and evokes new possibilities of self-assertion. Instinct resonates with action. Emotional charisma can generate leadership ability. Effective stimulation, or manipulation, of memories to achieve a strategic goal.

Waning square (270°; consciousness crisis: danger/opportunity): serious conflict between will and habit, self-assertion and inertia. Subjective soul rejects an outworn ego purpose. Seeks a new passion. Unconscious mood or temperament sheds a spent impulse. Instinct reorients towards a new behavioral strategy. Memory struggles with, or breaks free of, angry emotions.

Waning sextile (300°; supportive): feelings support a rising will. Subjective soul cooperates with an emerging purpose. Unconscious mood or temperament nurtures an increasingly subtle ego assertion. Instincts stimulate a new passion. Emotional commitment to an action agenda. Memories enhance self-confidence in the service of a strategic goal.

Waning semi-sextile (330°; stimulating): feelings consecrated to battle. Emotions sacrificed to achieve a purpose. Subjective soul surrenders to an emerging will. Unconscious mood or temperament senses the need for a new strategy. Instinctive hunger for a fresh start. One remembers what serves a ruling passion, chooses to forget what does not.

Moon/Jupiter

Conservation and expansion. Grounding and soaring.
Feeling and morality. Emotion and philosophy.
Instinct and spirit. Memory and meaning.

Conjunction: psyche imprinted by transcendent soul. The unconscious grows a conscience, expands to emotionally reflect larger than personal aspirations. Feelings informed by religious/philosophical or social/political imperatives. Subjective soul fused with spirit, in farsighted wisdom or inflated grandiosity.

Individual temperament or mood identifies with social expectations: a team player or a leader. Emotionally embodies ethical principles. A strong sense of morality: conventionally conformist, fanatically certain or prophetically enlightened. Can get these confused. Remembers and truly believes in a tribal narrative, for better or worse.

Waxing semi-sextile (30°; stimulating): feelings begin to separate from spiritual aspirations. Personal emotion detaches from social role. Subjective soul asserts itself against moral demands of conscience. Unconscious mood or temperament differentiates from conventional wisdom. Instinct at odds with a religious/philosophical or political/tribal ethic. Memories distance from optimistic ideological interpretations.

Waxing sextile (60°; supportive): feelings align with spiritual aspirations. Emotion synchronizes with social expectation. Subjective soul cooperates with moral demands of conscience. Unconscious mood or temperament flows with conventional wisdom. Instinct stimulated by a religious/philosophical or political/tribal ethic. Memories accentuate the positive.

Waxing square (90°; action crisis: danger/opportunity): feelings conflict with ideological imperatives. Emotion rebels from social expectation. Subjective soul rebels against moral demands of conscience. Unconscious mood or temperament hostile to conventional wisdom. Instinct challenges a religious/philosophical or political/tribal ethic. Memory seeks psychological truth rather than motivational myths.

Waxing trine (120°; amplifies, mutual reinforcement): feelings harmonize with spiritual aspirations. Subjective soul integrates with moral demands of conscience. Emotional commitment to a social role. Unconscious mood or temperament endorses and effectively expresses conventional wisdom. Instinct resonates with a religious/philosophical or political/tribal ethic. Memories emphasize goodness, justice and beauty.

Waxing quincunx (150°; irritating): feelings irritated by spiritual demands. Subjective soul inconsistent with moral demands of conscience. Emotions disrupt conventional expectations. Unconscious mood or temperament sidesteps conventional wisdom. Instinct questions a religious/philosophical or political/tribal ethic. Memories flex the mind with paradox and ambiguity.

Opposition (180°; challenge and illumination): body and soul, psyche and spirit, complement and enhance each other. Or they split into antagonistic principles, each denying the other's truth. Subjective mood and social wisdom resonate. Or dissociate. Emotion and ethics, feelings and morality, instinct and conscience, reflect or refute their counterpart. Remembers an agreed narrative; a shared religious or political aspiration. Or divorces from the community consensus in prophetic sensitivity or inflated personal fantasy.

Waning quincunx (210°; irritating): feelings challenge a shared social narrative. Subjective soul disrupts moral demands of conscience. Emotional heresy disturbs accepted norms. Unconscious mood or temperament confounds conventional wisdom. Instinct at odds with a religious/philosophical or political/tribal ethic. Inconvenient memories question given truths.

Waning trine (240°; amplifies, mutual reinforcement): feelings embody new social ideals. Emotions flow with rising group norms. Subjective soul integrates with an emerging morality. Unconscious temperament evokes a more subtle interpretation of conventional wisdom. Instinct resonates with a coming religious/philosophical or political ethic. Mood and memory identify with where the tribal myth is going.

Waning square (270°; consciousness crisis: danger/opportunity): emotional rejection of outworn spiritual aspirations. Feelings turn away from established truths towards a new dispensation. Subjective soul challenges obsolete morality. Seeks a new criteria of conscience. Unconscious mood or temperament sheds conventional wisdom, re-orients to another standard of authenticity. Instinct confronts religious/philosophical or political/tribal ethics. Memory radically reinterprets events.

Waning sextile (300°; supportive): emotional commitment to a spiritual agenda. Feelings enhanced by a premonition of higher truth. Subjective soul cooperates with an emerging morality, supports new criteria of conscience. Unconscious mood or temperament commits to a reinterpretation of conventional wisdom. Instinct serves a rising religious/philosophical or political/tribal ethic. Remembers what God or society says is right to remember.

Waning semi-sextile (330°; stimulating): feelings consecrated to, personal considerations sacrificed for, a higher truth. Emotions given to a social cause. Subjective soul embraces a new morality. Unconscious mood or temperament immerses in another definition of conventional wisdom. Instinct identifies with a rising religious/philosophical or political/tribal ethic. Memories abandoned to follow a bright, or bright-seeming, path.

Moon/Saturn

Spontaneity and discipline. Emotional sensitivity and cold hard fact.
Feeling and frustration. Id and superego.
Inner child and demanding parent.

Conjunction: psyche imprinted by a larger than personal fate. Soul fused with a sense of social or spiritual destiny. Mood is focused by the demands of self-discipline in service to a difficult and austere goal. Or inhibited by cynical pessimism. Sensitivity sharpened, or repressed, by hard survival demands. Practical instincts honed by a grim struggle, internal or external. The subjective emotional nature adapts to objective reality.

A serious and ambitious temperament. Remembers hunger, want, deprivation, limitation. And the need for unremitting effort to overcome them. Sweet melancholy. Or hopeless depression. Feelings regimented by duty. Feelings for the Regiment, the authority of superego.

Deep recognition of one's mortality and weakness. Unconscious fear. 'Fear of God is the beginning of wisdom.'

Waxing semi-sextile (30°; stimulating): feelings begin to separate from fear. Emotion breaks free of inhibition. Subjective soul differentiates from, individualizes out of, impersonal law. Unconscious mood or temperament asserts itself against demands of fate and destiny. Instincts detach from duties. Memories distance from a past of limitation and deprivation.

Waxing sextile (60°; supportive): feelings accept discipline in the service of ambition. Emotions synchronize with duty. Subjective soul cooperates with impersonal law and objective reality. Unconscious mood or temperament flows with demands of fate and destiny. Instinct stimulated by fear. Remembers and follows the rules.

Waxing square (90°; action crisis: danger/opportunity): subjective soul rebels against constricting rules, seeks individual authenticity. Unconscious mood or temperament conflicts with expected duty. Self at odds with assigned fate, opens to a new and demanding destiny. Driven by an emotional urgency derived from a sense of weakness, inadequacy and sin. Experiences the hard consequences of deeply felt mistakes. Remembers guilt and works to correct it. Instinct challenges fear. And is tested by it.

Waxing trine (120°; amplifies, mutual reinforcement): feelings smoothly and naturally disciplined in service to a higher destiny. Unconscious mood or temperament accepts and endorses its fate. Emotions resonate with duty. Subjective soul integrates with impersonal law and objective reality. Instinct effectively manages fear. Remembers the goal and patiently embraces a strategy to attain it.

Waxing quincunx (150°; irritating): feelings of inadequacy stimulate intermittent self-discipline. And limit emotional response. Subjective soul alienated from the rules, seeks a new sense of objective reality. Driving discontent. Or unhappy dissatisfaction. Unconscious mood or temperament sidesteps a fate it neither rejects nor believes in. Instinct inhibited by subliminal fears it can't quite identify. Remembers awkward mistakes; may or may not learn from them.

Opposition (180°; challenge and illumination): subjective soul and objective law, inner mood and outer fact, complement and enhance each other. Or schizophrenically split into separate realities. Instinctive feelings and social discipline resonate or dissociate. The unconscious reflects a consistent psychological logic manifesting as integrity. Or it withers into defensive depression, too weak to organize itself as a coherent personality. Psyche and fate affirm and embrace each other. Or emotion coldly shrinks from destiny in the loneliness of fear. Remembers, but may reject, the call of duty.

Waning quincunx (210°; irritating): negative feelings inhibit emotional expression. A sense of personal unworthiness can be projected onto the environment. Subjective soul at odds with impersonal law and objective reality. Unconscious mood or temperament confounds demands of fate and destiny. Instinct disturbed by fear. Sensitive to the failings of others.

Waning trine (240°; amplifies, mutual reinforcement): a new sense of duty evokes feelings of resolve and determination. Subjective soul integrates with an emerging redefinition of impersonal law and objective reality. Unconscious mood or temperament aligns with a more subtle interpretation of the demands of fate and destiny. Cool clear sensitivity resonates with emotional discipline in the face of fear. Remembers what can go wrong and avoids it.

Waning square (270°; consciousness crisis: danger/opportunity): acutely feels limitations of ability. Deep fear of failure. Sensitive to inadequacy in the eyes of others. Reorients to a new standard of achievement. Subjective soul rejects the rules, an outworn definition of impersonal law and objective reality. Unconscious mood or temperament walks away from an expected destiny to create its own reality. This may come at great emotional cost. Instinct confronts past fears. Remembers lessons of disappointment: thus is emotionally wise, or cynical.

Waning sextile (300°; supportive): emotional commitment to an emerging sense of duty. Feelings cooperate with a rising reality. Subjective soul synchronizes with objective demands of a new destiny. Unconscious mood or temperament aligns with a reinterpretation of the rules. Instinct begins to recognize future fears and limitations. Remembers and obeys vows.

Waning semi-sextile (330°; stimulating): personal feelings sacrificed to a larger destiny. Subjective soul consecrated to a new objective reality. Emotions focused on the goal. Unconscious mood or temperament serves the demands of fate. Instinct embraces fear: surrenders to or transcends it. Drops old baggage in the interests of emerging duties.

Moon/Uranus

Instinct and inspiration. Visceral feeling and abstract intuition.
Past memory and future vision.

Conjunction: psyche imprinted by a lightning bolt. A traumatic/ transformative external event, or internal realization, fundamentally changes the emotional nature. Feelings revolutionized. A new kind of sensitivity emerges.

Subjective soul grounds a formative psychological archetype into personal expression. Visionary illumination generates an enlarged intuitive empathy. Or spaced-out alienation. Instinctive expectations revised by a revelatory experience. Or violent mood swings as habitual inertia blocks subconscious demands for evolution.

Waxing semi-sextile (30°; stimulating): personality begins to separate from its formative psychological archetype. Emotional individuality emerges. Subjective soul differentiates from an abstract model, asserts its own uniqueness. Unconscious mood or temperament insists on a distinctive interpretation of general ideas. Subliminally remembers a guiding inspiration, but seeks to detach from it.

Waxing sextile (60°; supportive): personality supports and cooperates with its formative psychological archetype. Individual psyche competently embodies an impersonal vision. Subjective soul aligns with an abstract idea. Unconscious mood or temperament flows with an intuitive insight. Emotion stimulated by theoretical inspiration. Subliminally remembers harmony with a larger mind.

Waxing square (90°; action crisis: danger/opportunity): personality revolts from its formative psychological archetype. Individual psyche fights for its own uniqueness rather than as an expression of universal mind. Subjective soul rebels against abstract ideas. Unconscious mood or temperament emotionally conflicts with a theoretical vision. Feelings challenge mental inspiration. Subliminally remembers other possibilities of sensibility and self-expression.

Waxing trine (120°; amplifies, mutual reinforcement): personality harmoniously aligns with its formative psychological archetype. Individual psyche inspired by a sense of universal truth. Subjective soul integrates with abstract ideas. Unconscious mood or temperament effectively expresses theoretical insight. Feelings resonate with intuition. Subliminally remembers a deeper cosmic order and seeks to exemplify it.

Waxing quincunx (150°; irritating): personality disturbed by contrast between a formative psychological archetype and its own quirks and foibles. Unusual or eccentric assertion of individuality. Subjective soul evades or sabotages its own intuitions, must learn to listen to them. Unconscious mood or temperament sidesteps inspiration. Emotion uncomfortable with an accepted theory, seeks its own interpretation. Subliminally remembers that it needs to reform a kink in psychological expression.

Opposition (180°; challenge and illumination): an existing personality, at whatever phase of development, confronts a transformative experience or revelation. In contrast to the conjunction, where psyche becomes a conduit for impersonal inspiration, the opposition demands a subjective response to and assimilation of visionary ideas. The entire temperament adapts to a discovery, and modifies it in turn. An emerging hybrid combines old and new. Self reinterprets its heritage in a fresh light.

Personality fully reflects its formative psychological archetype to the limit of its ability. Or violently rebels against it. An inspiration becomes emotionally relevant. Felt soul and thought theory, unconscious mood and intuitive insight, complement and enhance each other. Or coldly dissociate into untethered instincts electrified by sterile abstractions. Past memory and futuristic dreams fertilize a new sensibility. Or cancel out in shocking discord. Individuality manifests through extremes of illumination and eccentricity, genius or madness. Subliminally remembers a higher state of being.

Waning quincunx (210°; irritating): personality expresses a unique interpretation of its formative psychological archetype in disturbing contrast to social norms. Radical individuality as a reformer or a crank. Subjective soul alienated from accepted ideas and questions new ones. Unconscious mood or temperament senses, but can't quite get a handle on, an emerging inspiration. Emotions confound expectations. Subliminally remembers other alternatives.

Waning trine (240°; amplifies, mutual reinforcement): personality expresses a formative psychological archetype as a role model for the future. Individual psyche instinctively embodies a felt higher truth for the community. An original presentation of a rising sensibility is well received. Subjective soul integrates with an emerging inspiration. Unconscious mood or temperament aligns with a more subtle interpretation of abstract theory. Feelings resonate with intuition. Subliminally remembers a utopian vision that it seeks to personally demonstrate.

Waning square (270°; consciousness crisis: danger/opportunity): personality deliberately expresses a different version of its formative psychological archetype in contrast to inherited or social expectations. Individual psyche acts as a rebel role model. Subjective soul rejects irrelevant abstractions, seeks a new inspiration. Unconscious mood or temperament sheds obsolete insight and stale intuition. Emotionally confronts an outworn theory, seeks a better one. Subliminally remembers, and reorients towards, a better arrangement than current convention.

Waning sextile (300°; supportive): personality returns to its formative psychological archetype enhanced by emotional experience. An ebbing tide of individuality sublimates back into universal mind, pours out its gifts to recharge a collective psychic aquifer. Subjective soul subordinates itself to, cooperates with, an emerging social inspiration. Unconscious mood or temperament commits to a new intuition. Feelings express abstract or utopian ideas. Subliminally remembers its origins and returns to them.

Waning semi-sextile (330°; stimulating): personality sacrifices in service to its formative psychological archetype. Individual psyche gives itself over to a theoretical vision, clear or crazy. Subjective soul consecrated to an emerging inspiration. Unconscious mood or temperament adopts a new intuitive stance. Feelings surrender to an abstract or utopian idea. Subliminally remembers and serves a greater truth than its own.

Moon/Neptune

Instinct and illusion. Personal and collective dreams.
Memory and imagination.
Subjective emotion and universal compassion.

Conjunction: psyche imprinted by transcendent ideals. The personal unconscious flooded by collective memories and images. Subjective soul grounds a sense of universal compassion into personal empathy. Mood or temperament enriched by emotional communion with others. Or devolves into herd psychology, abdicates to a lemming-like ecstasy of participation mystique.

Instinct marries an imaginative vision, or intoxicating illusion. Poetic sensitivity or chameleon-like impressionability. Feels charity for all. Or wallows in slobbery sentiment. Remembers mystic truths of the dream world. Or a nightmare of chaos. Individual feelings dissolve into a larger sense of identity. Or a nebulous fog of confusion.

Waxing semi-sextile (30°; stimulating): personality begins to separate from its inner dream-source. Individual psychology emerges from a collective trance. Subjective soul differentiates from mythic imagination, or illusion. Unconscious mood or temperament asserts itself against a redemptive or intoxicating rapture. Feelings distance from empathy or codependence. Subliminally remembers an enchantment from which it must break free.

Waxing sextile (60°; supportive): personality cooperates with a collective dream. Psyche embodies group ideals. Subjective soul harmoniously aligns with mythic imagination, or illusion. Unconscious mood or temperament flows with a redemptive or intoxicating rapture. Emotion stimulated by compassionate empathy or codependence. Subliminally remembers integration with a universal emotional source.

Waxing square (90°; action crisis: danger/opportunity): personality escapes from a collective vision. Individual glamour or charisma contrasts with a group ideal. Subjective soul rebels against mythic imagination, or illusion. Unconscious mood or temperament conflicts with a redemptive or intoxicating rapture. Emotion challenges compassionate empathy or codependence, seeks something more authentic. Subliminally remembers a call to follow its own dreams by dissolving tribal bonds.

Waxing trine (120°; amplifies, mutual reinforcement): personality manifests and nurtures a collective dream. Individual psyche demonstrates an ideal vision. Subjective soul integrates with mythic imagination, or illusion. Unconscious mood or temperament endorses and effectively expresses a redemptive or intoxicating rapture. Emotion resonates with compassionate empathy or codependence. Subliminally remembers an inherent harmony between one's own psyche and the deep unconscious.

Waxing quincunx (150°; irritating): personality subverts a collective dream. Individual psyche undermines hypnotic group cohesion, for better or worse. Subjective soul inconsistent with mythic imagination, or illusion. Unconscious mood or temperament sidesteps a redemptive or intoxicating rapture. Emotion uncomfortable with compassionate empathy or codependence. Subliminally remembers a need to demonstrate personal vision away from the herd.

Opposition (180°; challenge and illumination): personality identifies with a glamorous dream. Or intoxicated by an illusion. Individual imagination and a collective vision, unconscious mood and mythological truth, complement and enhance each other. Subjective sensitivity and universal compassion resonate with a social ideal. Memory and magic reflect a redemptive charisma. Deep empathy, emotional vulnerability, mystic faith, makes one open and available to others and the world at large. This can be exploited. Then idealism can dissolve into escapism, or disintegrate into confused hallucination. Subliminally remembers unity between self and cosmos.

Waning quincunx (210°; irritating): personality makes waves on the slick surface of a collective vision. Individual psyche presents a disturbing alternative to ideals. Subjective soul questions mythic imagination, or illusion. Unconscious mood or temperament disrupts cooperation with a redemptive or intoxicating rapture. Emotion ill at ease with compassionate empathy or codependence, seeks something more real. Subliminal remembrance of other dreams.

Waning trine (240°; amplifies, mutual reinforcement): personality aligns with a new collective vision. Individual psyche embodies a rising group ideal. Subjective soul integrates with an emerging mythic imagination, or illusion. Unconscious mood or temperament evokes a more subtle interpretation of a redemptive or intoxicating rapture. Emotion resonates with compassionate empathy, or codependence. Subliminally remembers unity of self and tribe.

Waning square (270°; consciousness crisis: danger/opportunity): personality refuses to participate in the false premises of a hypnotic consensus. It tunes out a collective dream and dances to a different music. Individual psyche dissolves identification with an accepted ideal and follows its own imagination. It can find itself lost at sea. Subjective soul rejects a now irrelevant mythic imagination, or illusion. Unconscious mood or temperament sheds an outworn redemptive or intoxicating rapture. Emotion conflicts with empathy. Feelings revolt against the demands of compassion, or codependence. Subliminally remembers, and reorients towards, another vision.

Waning sextile (300°; supportive): personality resonates with an evolving collective dream. Individual psyche aligns with a rising tribal myth. Subjective soul cooperates with an emerging group imagination, or illusion. Unconscious mood or temperament commits to a collective rapture: redemptive or intoxicating. Feelings immerse in compassion, or codependence. Subliminally remembers a shared vision in which all participate.

Waning semi-sextile (330°; stimulating): personality consecrated to a collective dream. Renounces individual identity to identify with a social or spiritual vision. Subjective soul embraces mythic imagination, or illusion. Unconscious mood or temperament immerses into an emerging rapture. Personal emotion dissolves into compassion, or codependence. Subliminally remembers the need for redemptive sacrifice.

Moon/Pluto

Personal past and unconscious karma. Feeling and fate.
Subjective emotion and collective necessity.
Individual memory realigns with a larger, more universal narrative.

Conjunction: psyche imprinted by individual karma or collective fate. The unconscious possessed by a larger will, of history or of God. Subjective soul grounds collective purpose into personal emotion. Mood or temperament resonates more strongly than normal with its generational ethos and historical context. Instinct marries the hidden passion, or obsession, of a larger destiny. Sensitive to the demands of its time and tribe. Assimilates and nurtures a group dynamic, for better or worse. Remembers a prime directive or overwhelming commandment overriding all other considerations.

Feelings die, perhaps to be reborn.

Waxing semi-sextile (30°; stimulating): personality begins to separate from its fate. Individual psyche emerges from identification with a collective time spirit (zeitgeist). Subjective soul differentiates from an assigned sense of destiny. Unconscious mood or temperament asserts itself against its generational ethos and historical context. Feelings distance from the tribal will. Subliminally remembers a group purpose from which it must break free.

Waxing sextile (60°; supportive): personality genuinely supports group purpose. Psyche endorses collective feeling. Subjective soul cooperates with a sense of fate. Unconscious mood or temperament flows with its generational ethos and historical context. Emotion stimulated by a larger will. Subliminally remembers self's destiny as a tribal member.

Waxing square (90°; action crisis: danger/opportunity): personality passionately disengages with group purpose, creatively or destructively. Individual psyche strongly, even violently, asserts itself against fate. Subjective soul rebels against an assigned sense of destiny. Unconscious mood or temperament conflicts with its generational ethos and historical context. Emotion challenges the tribal will. Subliminally remembers that individual development is the group's purpose, not the other way around.

Waxing trine (120°; amplifies, mutual reinforcement): personality smoothly integrates with a larger destiny or group purpose. Individual psyche identifies with collective needs. Subjective soul accepts its fate, however hard, and experiences it at an increasingly subtle level. Unconscious mood or temperament endorses and effectively expresses its generational ethos and historical context. Emotion resonates with tribal feeling. Subliminally remembers that self represents and serves a greater will.

Waxing quincunx (150°; irritating): personality subtly dissents from group purpose. Individual psyche uncomfortable with a fated role. Subjective soul inconsistent with assigned destiny. Unconscious mood or temperament sidesteps its generational ethos and historical context. Emotional evasion of the tribal will. Subliminally remembers other paths.

Opposition (180°; challenge and illumination): psyche and destiny, feeling and fate, complement and enhance each other. Or mutually self-destruct. Emotion and a larger Will, individual mood and its generational/historic moment, resonate in a shared narrative. Or split off in obsessive mutual denial. Personality strongly responds to group purpose. Or dissociates from it, even unto death. Subjective identification with collective need. Or violent rejection of, and by, the tribe. Subliminal remembrance of an overwhelming Power.

Waning quincunx (210°; irritating): personality subtly disrupts a now obsolete social purpose. Psyche repudiates a 'destiny' and tentatively explores an alternative. Subjective soul questions its 'fate.' Unconscious mood or temperament sidesteps its generational ethos and historical context. Emotion confounds the tribal will. Subliminally remembers that the herd is not always right.

Waning trine (240°; amplifies, mutual reinforcement): personality aligns with a rising group purpose. Subjective soul integrates with an emerging sense of fate. Psyche accepts and competently demonstrates a collective role. Unconscious mood or temperament evokes a more subtle interpretation of its generational ethos and historical context. Emotion resonates with a new tribal will. Subliminally remembers that self reflects a larger destiny.

Waning square (270°; consciousness crisis: danger/opportunity): personality challenges group identity with a radically different purpose or sense of destiny. Insists on individual psychic transformation as the leavening for and exemplar of collective metamorphoses. Subjective soul rejects a now irrelevant fate. Unconscious mood or temperament sheds an obsolete generational ethos and historical context. Emotion confronts tribal will, seeks a better way. Subliminally remembers, and reorients towards, a coming new order.

Waning sextile (300°; supportive): personality supports a new sense of destiny. Individual psyche cooperates with an emerging collective need. Subjective soul aligns with a felt but still invisible future, commits to faith in a larger fate. Unconscious mood or temperament reinterprets its generational ethos and historical context. Feelings immerse in an evolving tribal will. Subliminally remembers a shared purpose that subsumes individual goals.

Waning semi-sextile (330°; stimulating): personality consecrated to a destiny. Psyche commits to death and rebirth. Subjective soul sacrifices to and for an emerging sense of fate. Unconscious mood or temperament adopts a new generational ethos and historical context. Emotion gives itself to the tribal will. Subliminally remembers a new dawn just over the horizon.

500

Void Moon

A void Moon happens when Moon has completed all major aspects with all other planets before leaving a sign.[1] During its transit through the remainder of that sign, after having consummated every relationship, Moon goes into a state of limbo. Its function of ingathering and blending all other planetary functions within the force field of a sign has been accomplished. Now it travels through a null zone before entering the next sign. For example, if Moon in Leo has made its last planetary aspect with Mercury at 25° Aries, then during the remaining 5° of its transit through Leo (25°-30°) it is void of course.

During this period Moon is ungrounded, cut loose from a living web of psychological energies. Being near the end of a sign it has fulfilled that sign's purpose at its level of evolution. Now it is unconnected. Its old identity has passed; a new one has not yet arrived. This can be a moment of paralysis, inability to act, lack of effective agency. Psyche feels marooned in space. Think of a worker who has finished a job. Now s/he is laid off, fired, adrift in unemployment.

A void of course Moon means that a phase of development is completed but no longer relevant. One naturally wants to continue with what one is familiar with, perhaps even good at. But now that leads nowhere. Frustration builds because demonstrated ability can no longer be deployed. No matter how advanced one's skills, no matter how hard one works, things just don't happen. At the same time one has not yet arrived at the new reality of the upcoming sign. One is caught in a dead zone. In medieval times this was called the vacuus cursus, an accursed vacuum.

Because a void of course Moon prevents or stymies action it forces reconsideration of all that one was or thought one knew. Suspended between past and future, untethered to the present, one is free. Without resources or allies, but also without burdens or expectations. One can, indeed must, reinvent oneself. Developed ability, without an avenue of release, must find/create new means of expression. Or wither away in impotence, a ripened fruit rotting on the vine.

This Moon is outside the system. The great integrator now stands alone. It must take a completed understanding to a new level. Karmic, innate, acquired abilities have no outlet. They cannot escape into a new reality, the next sign. They must redefine what's already there.

Void of course is the most difficult lunar position because Moon's natural function of horizontal integration on one plane must now transcend itself to the next vertical step of the same process. It cannot simply glide into the next reality (sign); it must completely redo the current one. Moon, the conservative planet of memory, passive mirror

of reflection, unconscious pool of instinct, must intensify a given inheritance, invoke new dimensions from a dead past.

The void Moon is often misinterpreted to mean that nothing will
come of any enterprise undertaken during its period. This can be put to
rest by noting that technically the United States chart has a void Moon
at the end of Aquarius.[2] No one would claim that the American experiment came to naught.

Notes

1. Sometimes planets concentrate at the beginning and in the middle of
signs. This leaves the later degrees unoccupied. Therefore Moon does
not form any aspects to them as it transits the end zone of whatever sign
it is in. The planetary spread varies from month to month. For example,
Moon was void for a total of 26 hours in January 2012, about 3% of
the month. In October 2012 it was void for 163 hours, over 20% of the
month. Generally it averages roughly 10%.
2. The generally accepted United States chart is calculated for proclamation of the Declaration of Independence on July 4, 1776 at 5:10
pm in Philadelphia. This chart is presented in Figure 6, 'Mundane
Astrology.'

Its Moon, moving from full to waning gibbous, is at 27°10′
Aquarius. It makes no major aspects before transiting into Pisces.
However, it closely applies to a waxing semi-sextile with Pluto at 27°32′
Capricorn. Pluto symbolizes a collective unconscious force rather than
a distinct planetary quality. This energy evokes a latent quality in Moon
itself. It intensifies Moon's own hidden side. Moon remains void, but is
supercharged with a collective unconscious stimulus.

Before Pluto's hidden power became historically explicit (since
its discovery in 1930) one could say that the American chart had a
void Moon in the traditional sense. During that period the USA exemplified its highest qualities: taking the dead past to the next level as a
'new order of the ages.'* In its relatively isolationist formative period
(1789-1941) the American experience was about creating space for
opportunity, free of traditional old world constraints. After World War
II overtly manifested Pluto energy amplified this into explicit global
responsibility. America became the 'indispensable nation,' shaping the
institutional matrix and mass psychology of a world society.

Aquarius describes an energy zone of inspiration and innovation.
America's void Moon there speaks to its unrestrained embrace of a
technological imperative. Its approach to Pluto by aspect suggests that
this expresses a collective unconscious, historic or karmic necessity that
the U.S. brings forth on behalf of the entire world. It does so in its role

as the universal nation, not by exercising formal jurisdiction over the planet, but through its universally emulated example.

The Plutonically heightened potential of America's void moon, operating in a historical atmosphere of unprecedented liberty, symbolizes a freedom that has brought the whole human family to another level: politically, socially, economically and technologically. We have split the atom, remade life, reached Moon itself. A now globalized republic of science and technology pursues artificial intelligence rather than natural wisdom, creates laboratory life while it extinguishes organic ecosystems, leaps forth into the cosmos while devastating its own planet.

This seems to be a necessary phase, an inevitable concomitant of the void's freedom. Its spectacular success has created a momentum that cannot be stopped, yet cannot be sustained. It has sown the seeds of its own destruction through the proliferation of weapons of mass destruction, vulnerability of the cyber-infrastructure upon which we have suddenly became dependent, accelerating environmental breakdown and literal economic bankruptcy. These, along with more subtle cultural and spiritual factors, make a Plutonian catharsis inevitable. See 'A Mundane Prediction.'

In that light one might ponder this description of a long vanished America from the perspective of a distant future:

'Yet here was a people of unique promise, gifted innately beyond all other peoples. Here was a race brewed of all races, and mentally more effervescent than any ... Thus was this once noble people singled out by the gods to be cursed, and the minister of curses.'†

Footnotes to a Footnote

* 'Novus ordo seclorum,' one of the American national mottos, found on the back of every dollar bill
† 'Last and First Men,' a future history by Olaf Stapledon, British writer, 1886-1950

Planetary Aspects

The following outline of planetary aspects may seem somewhat formulaic. That is because the dynamic between two planets remains the same in each case. Only the specific terms of the equation change. Thus a waxing sextile always acts as a waxing sextile, regardless of whether it involves Mercury and Jupiter, or Venus and Saturn, etc.

Aspects between the personal planets (Mercury, Venus and Mars) portray psychological dynamics within the conscious personality.

Aspects between personal planets and the gas giants (Jupiter and Saturn) indicate individual expression of social role and spiritual qualities.

Aspects between personal planets and the outer planets (Uranus, Neptune and Pluto) portray individual expression of collective unconscious currents.

Aspects between the gas giants (Jupiter and Saturn) portray a larger than personal social or spiritual context of consciousness.

Aspects between the gas giants and outer planets (Uranus, Neptune and Pluto) describe social and spiritual expression of collective unconscious forces.

Aspects between the outer planets describe a collective energy field within which personality is embedded.

Mercury

Aspects of Mercury illuminate any planetary principle it contacts. Gives a rational perspective on its nature. Clarifies its attributes through lucid intellectual understanding. Articulates its qualities, making that function more self-aware. Communicates its energy, making it more conscious to the whole personality. A mental function.

Mercury/Venus

Mind and desire. Thoughts and values. Head and heart.

Mercury and Venus are unique among planetary pairs in that they can never be more than 72°, one fifth of the zodiac, apart. This is because both travel around smaller orbits than Earth's. They are tightly bound to Sun's central position within the perspective of Earth's larger orbit. Even this degree of spread is highly unusual, occurring only when one is at its maximum distance ahead of Sun in zodiacal longitude, and the other at its maximum distance behind. Usually they are much closer together.

All of this makes sense when one remembers that mind does not operate independently of desire but is oriented by it. Thought articulates and justifies values. Mercury and Venus both symbolize interior planes of experience, expressions of a subjective integrity. They are necessarily linked in a unity of personality.

Conjunction: head and heart at one. Unity of reason and love. Or lack of discrimination between them. Cerebral perception of relationship. This can make love mutable as conditions change. It can lead to glib and superficial pleasantry rather than real passion. Effective communication of values. Or rationalization of desire.

Waxing semi-sextile (30°; stimulating): reason begins to separate from love. Mind emerges from desire. Detached perspective on values.

Waxing sextile (60°; supportive): reason justifies love. Mind articulates desire. Harmonious expression of values.

Quintile (72°, maximum separation; irksome and irritating): tension between reason and love, generating a need for reconciliation. At this point both Mercury and Venus must turn either retrograde or direct and begin approaching each other. This situation is very rare.

Waning sextile (300°; supportive): reason seeks the complementarity and consolation of love. Mind serves desire. Articulate expression of emerging values.

Waning semi-sextile (330°; stimulating): reason commits to love. Mind identifies with desire. Communication and justification of emerging values.

Mercury/Mars

Mind and will. Knowing and doing. Thought and action.
Passionate thinking, penetrating or crudely aggressive.

Conjunction: mind imprinted by will. Intellect joined with purpose. Reason fused with passion. Thinks about action. And the deeper causes of action. Ideas shaped by operational demands. Words are direct, urgent, forceful. They express motivations, intentions, agendas. Perceptions energized by challenge. A tactical/strategic intelligence, geared towards winning rather than truth for truth's sake. 'Knowledge is power.'

Waxing semi-sextile (30°; stimulating): mind begins to separate from will. Intellect emerges from ulterior motive into its own right. Thought differentiates from strategic/operational demands. Ideas put actions into perspective. Words explain motivations. Perceptions detach from goals.

Waxing sextile (60°; supportive): mind expresses will. Intellect serves purpose from an allied but objective stance. Thought effectively cooperates with strategic/operational demands. Ideas justify action. Words drum up support. Perceptions synchronized with decisions.

Waxing square (90°; action crisis: danger/opportunity): mind revolts from will. Intellect refuses to serve a purpose it no longer believes in and seeks another. Thought rejects strategic/operational demands. Ideas battle passions. Words contradict actions, or give them new meaning. Perceives alternative possibilities.

Waxing trine (120°; amplifies, mutual reinforcement): mind smoothly articulates and facilitates will. Intellect discovers more sophisticated ways of making and executing decisions. Thought energized and deepened by the stimulus of strategic/operational demands. Ideas encourage action. Words inspire or sugarcoat motivation. Subtle perception enhances the power of purpose.

Waxing quincunx (150°; irritating): mental unease about purpose. Unruly thoughts interfere with will. Intellect uncomfortable with strategic/operational demands. Ideas trip up action. Words confuse or evade real motivations. Perceptions at odds with goals.

Opposition (180°; challenge and illumination): mind and will complement and enhance each other. Or violently dissociate. Intellect comprehends a strategic purpose. It understands how to achieve or oppose it. Thought reflects and objectively enables operational demands. Or rejects and subjectively sabotages them. Ideas clarify the meaning of action. Words expose true motivations. Or maliciously lie about them. Perceives the underlying motives of conflict.

Waning quincunx (210°; irritating): mind expresses objections to will. Intellect dissents from purpose. Thought evades strategic/operational demands. Ideas hinder an action agenda. Words confuse intentions. Perceptions mock passions.

Waning trine (240°; amplifies, mutual reinforcement): mind smoothly articulates and facilitates an emerging will. Or adapts to a rising power. Intellect explains a new purpose. Thought finds effective, or innovative, solutions to strategic/operational demands. Ideas promote an action agenda. Words express intentions. Perceptions reinforce decisions.

Waning square (270°; consciousness crisis: danger/opportunity): mind openly challenges will. Intellect presents a compelling case against present purpose. Reorients towards a new one. Thought repudiates strategic/operational demands. Ideas block an action agenda. Words contradict intentions. Or redirect them. Perceptions disprove passions.

Waning sextile (300°; supportive): mind expresses an emerging will. Intellect faithfully serves purpose. Thought cooperates with evolving strategic/operational demands. Ideas justify an action agenda. Words elicit participation. Perceptions prove validity of passion.

Waning semi-sextile (330°; stimulating): mind consecrated to battle. Intellect sacrifices objectivity to instrumentality in a cause. Thought enables strategic/operational demands. Ideas defer to an action agenda. Words explain intentions. Perceptions conscripted to serve will.

Mercury/Jupiter

Mind and spirit. Information and meaning.
Perception and significance. Data and comprehension.
Big Picture thinking, prophetic or inflated.

Conjunction: mind impregnated by spirit. Intellect fused with aspiration. Ideas shaped by social relevance, morality and ethical principles. Thinks big, about big things. Tends to verbosity and sweeping generalization. Can inflate molehills into mountains. Reason and religion at one. Perception and philosophy see eye to eye.

Waxing semi-sextile (30°; stimulating): mind begins to separate from spirit. Intellect detaches from aspiration. Thought diverges from morality and ethical principles. Ideas put a social vision into perspective. Words explain a higher consciousness. Reason moves from philosophic to pragmatic concerns. Perception of tangible fact starts to replace ideological consistency.

Waxing sextile (60°; supportive): mind expresses spirit. Intellect serves a religious or social vision from an allied but objective stance. Thought cooperates with morality and ethical principles. Ideas demonstrate a higher consciousness. Words drum up support for it. Perceptions confirm philosophy.

Waxing square (90°; action crisis: danger/opportunity): mind rebels from spirit, seeks its own truth. Intellect breaks free of conventional wisdom. Thought rejects accepted morality and ethical norms. New ideas battle an established social vision. Words contradict principles, or expose pretension. Perceptions challenge dogma.

Waxing trine (120°; amplifies, mutual reinforcement): mind articulates the next level of a religious or political orientation. Or smoothly justifies the status quo. Intellect advances sophisticated arguments for intangible truths. Thought enjoys the stimulus of morality and ethical principle. Mental ideas encourage a more subtle, transrational form of consciousness. Words inspire, or sugarcoat, a spiritual or social vision. Perceptions prove philosophical propositions.

Waxing quincunx (150°; irritating): mind uneasy with spiritual guidelines. Intellect poses uncomfortable questions to conventional wisdom. Thought evades accepted morality and ethical principles. Ideas trip up a higher consciousness. Words struggle to articulate a religious or political vision. Perception notices inconsistencies between interpretations and actual facts.

Opposition (180°; challenge and illumination): mind and spirit complement and enhance each other. Or deny the other's very existence. Intellect expansively comprehends a religious/philosophical or social/political worldview, at its level of evolution. Thus it effectively enables or opposes conventional wisdom. Thought strongly reflects or rejects morality and ethical principles. Ideas clarify the meaning of a higher consciousness. Words reveal or deliberately distort a social vision. Expanded, or grandiose, perceptions.

Waning quincunx (210°; irritating): mind expresses spiritual quandaries. Intellect questions conventional wisdom. Thought uncomfortable with accepted morality and ethical principles. Ideas hinder a higher consciousness. Words struggle to articulate an emerging social vision. Reason dissents from religion. Perceptions mock philosophy.

Waning trine (240°; amplifies, mutual reinforcement): mind effectively expresses an emerging spiritual truth. Or adapts to a rising consensus. Intellect clearly explains a religious rationale, philosophical proposition or social/political agenda. Thought has moral depth and appreciates ethical principles. Ideas promote a social vision, of whatever merit. Words express a higher, or inflated, consciousness. Perceptions expand to include the intangible: nonlinear forms of logic, psychological roots of behavior.

Waning square (270°; consciousness crisis: danger/opportunity): mind openly challenges spiritual assumptions. Intellect presents the case against ideology or conventional wisdom. Reorients towards new convictions. Thought repudiates accepted morality and ethical principles. Ideas block a higher consciousness. Words contradict an outworn religious or social vision. Or give it a new meaning. Perceptions disprove philosophical or political convictions.

Waning sextile (300°; supportive): mind justifies an emerging spiritual aspiration. Intellect faithfully serves a larger religious/philosophical or social/political truth. Thought cooperates with an evolving morality and ethical principles. Ideas serve a higher consciousness. Words elicit social participation. Perceptions support the validity of a new wisdom.

Waning semi-sextile (330°; stimulating): mind consecrated to spirit. Intellect acknowledges its own logical limitations in the face of transrational reality. Thought defers to morality and ethical principles. Specific ideas are sacrificed to general norms. Words explain a rising religious or social vision. Perceptions enlarge to include the intangible. Or surrender to wishful thinking.

Mercury/Saturn

Mind and its relation to the hard facts and laws of reality.
Intellect and its central problem, issue, dilemma.
Information and its organizing principles.
Disciplined thinking, focused or inhibited.

Conjunction: mind imprinted with a disciplined rigor. Intellectual focus. Deep concentration. Respects data and logic. Rejects imagination, interpretation, wishful thinking. Thinks seriously about impersonal laws. Ideas shaped by a skeptical, pessimistic rationality. Words are few and apt. Expression can be inhibited. Perceives cold hard fact.

Waxing semi-sextile (30°; stimulating): mind begins to separate from the dictates of pure reason. Intellect learns to detach from data. Thought begins to diverge from accepted rules of evidence, restraints of impersonal law. Ideas put arbitrary limitations in perspective. Words explain organizing principles. Perceives contrast.

Waxing sextile (60°; supportive): mind aligns with the logic of first principles. Intellect harmonizes sensory data with rational law. Facts support a paradigm. Thought cooperates with accepted rules of evidence, restraints of impersonal reality. Ideas justify necessary limitations. Words elicit responsibility. Perceives resonance.

Waxing square (90°; action crisis: danger/opportunity): mind breaks from limitations of reason. Intellect argues the case against an organized structure. Thought rebels from arbitrary, or justified, restrictions; denies validity of accepted laws. Ideas battle calcified logic and traditional restraints. Or common sense. Words contradict responsibility. Or give it a new meaning. Perceives boundaries, necessary limits to knowledge or any particular kind of knowledge.

Waxing trine (120°; amplifies, mutual reinforcement): mind elucidates simple, sophisticated principles that organize information. Intellect smoothly integrates specific facts into overall law. Ideas clarified by the stimulus of impersonal law and its rules of evidence. Integrity of thought. Words inspire, or sugarcoat, responsibility. Perceives underlying similarities.

Waxing quincunx (150°; irritating): mind questions the scope of reason's competence. Intellect disturbed by inconvenient facts. Thought evades restraints of impersonal law, rules of evidence. Ideas uncomfortable with accepted limitations. Words struggle to articulate organizing principles. Perceives dissonance.

Opposition (180°; challenge and illumination): mind and empirical data complement and enhance each other in clear cold logic. Or are stymied by unresolved contradictions between fact and principle. Intellect focused by rational discipline. Or stifled by an arbitrary system. Thought strongly reflects impersonal law and rules of evidence. Or rejects their basic premises. Ideas clarify necessary limitations. Words reveal or deliberately distort responsibility. Perceives the end of a road, as achievement or in frustration.

Waning quincunx (210°; irritating): mind questions accepted organization, whether of science or society. Intellect raises issues of proof, process or competence. Thought evades impersonal rules of law and of evidence. Ideas confuse responsibility. Words struggle to articulate facts. Perceives inadequacy.

Waning trine (240°; amplifies, mutual reinforcement): mind expresses an emerging structure of law, whether scientific or social. Intellect organizes a multitude of facts into simple, elegant principles. Thought gains a fresh appreciation for the integrity of rules and reason. Ideas promote responsibility for consistent orderly process. Words effectively express necessary limitations. Perceives the long-term formation of large-scale organization.

Waning square (270°; consciousness crisis, danger/opportunity): mind rejects outworn interpretation. It accepts the reality, and discipline, of challenging new facts. Intellect reorients its basic guidelines and protocols. Thought repudiates accepted rules of law and evidence, finds another standard of integrity. Ideas break away from old limitations, for better or worse. Words contradict obsolete responsibilities. Or redirect them. Perceives loss of a mental paradigm. And perhaps the outline of a coming order.

Waning sextile (300°; supportive): mind justifies new principles. Intellect adjusts to a simpler, more sophisticated way of organizing data. Thought cooperates with evolving rules of law and standards of evidence. Ideas accept the inherent guidelines and limitations of a rising system. Words elicit responsibility for a coming order. Perceives an emerging mental paradigm.

Waning semi-sextile (330°; stimulating): mind consecrated to a new paradigm. Intellect accepts the loss of old, obsolete concepts. Thought defers to new rules of law and evidence. Ideas serve emerging responsibilities. Words explain the outline of a coming order. Perceives the withering away of what was once thought true.

Mercury/Uranus

Mind and inspiration. Logic and intuition. Reason and revelation.
Normal intelligence and genius/madness.
Original thinking, innovative or crazy.

Conjunction: mind imprinted by inspiration, of whatever merit. Intellect revolutionizes its operating procedures, standards of evidence. Thinks out of the box, creatively or crazily. Ideas shaped by intuition, a vision of possibilities. Words like lightning, revelatory or shocking. Perceives change.

Waxing semi-sextile (30°; stimulating): mind begins to separate from a revelation. Intellect learns to take a detached perspective on the excitement of inspiration. Thought diverges from theory. Ideas put a utopian vision in perspective. Words explain intuitive insights. Coolly perceives change.

Waxing sextile (60°; supportive): mind aligns with the winds of change. Intellect cooperates with intuition. Thought provides evidence for theory. Ideas justify intuitive insight. Words drum up support for a utopian vision. Perceives where things are heading and gets ahead of the curve.

Waxing square (90°; action crisis: danger/opportunity): mind revolts from the excesses of revolutionary enthusiasm. Intellect dashes cold water on heated inspiration. Thought rebels from theory. Mental ideas battle utopian vision. Words contradict intuition. Or gives it new meaning. Perceives dangers, flaws and limitations of change.

Waxing trine (120°; amplifies, mutual reinforcement): mind integrates and explains raw intuition. Intellect articulates insight, makes it universally available. Thought enjoys the stimulus of theory, and fleshes it out with real data. Ideas encourage new perspectives. Words inspire a utopian vision. Perceives new ways to communicate.

Waxing quincunx (150°; irritating): mind troubled by growing inconsistencies between theory and fact. Intellect agitated by hidden doubts. Thought evades utopian vision. Specific ideas trip up 'brilliant' insights. Words struggle to articulate intuitions. Perceives a breakdown in operating procedure.

Opposition (180°; challenge and illumination): mind and inspiration, intellect and intuition, complement and enhance each other. Or coldly dissociate, utterly rejecting the other's basic premise. Thought reflects brilliant, or bizarre, insight. Ideas clarify a new perspective.

Words reveal or deliberately distort a utopian vision. Perceives genius or madness, the future or the fringe.

Waning quincunx (210°; irritating): mind experiences hard-to-explain disruptions. Intellect disturbed by sudden change in standards of evidence. Thought seeks to understand a visionary insight that contradicts its normal paradigm. Specific perceptions block and deny theoretical speculation. Words struggle to articulate a new kind of intuition. Perceives a coming disruption.

Waning trine (240°; amplifies, mutual reinforcement): mind expresses novel insight. Intellect smoothly integrates an intuitive vision into a socially acceptable paradigm. Thought appreciates the challenge of inspiration, and backs it up with facts. Ideas promote a futuristic scientific theory or a utopian political agenda. Words effectively express new perspectives. Perceives a mental stimulus.

Waning square (270°; consciousness crisis: danger/opportunity): mind breaks free of a now oppressive vision. Intellect argues the case against a new theory or revelation. Thought repudiates a utopian agenda. Ideas block or deny an outworn intuition. Words contradict a visionary experience. Or give it new meaning. Perceives that a scientific or social revolution must change course to stay relevant.

Waning sextile (300°; supportive): mind articulates a new way of thinking. Intellect adjusts its procedures in line with an emerging theory. Thought cooperates with an evolving intuition. Ideas justify a utopian vision. Words elicit transformation. Perceives a changed mental landscape.

Waning semi-sextile (330°; stimulating): mind consecrates itself to a revelation. Intellect interprets an emerging worldview. Thought defers to intuition. Ideas serve a new theory. Words explain a rising utopian vision. Perceives all things in a new light.

Mercury/Neptune

Mind and imagination. Fact and fantasy.
Mythic thinking, poetic or chaotic.

Conjunction: mind imprinted by imagination. Intellect melts in poetic rapture. Thinks of mythic, mystic themes. Ideas are dreamy. Words are enigmatic. They express deep collective feelings, a redemptive vision or intoxicated illusion. Perceives shared emotional truth.

Waxing semi-sextile (30°; stimulating): mind begins to separate from imagination. Intellect learns to take a detached perspective on visionary experience. Thought diverges from a redemptive vision, or illusion. Ideas put empathy in perspective. Words explain dreams. Perceives the danger of total immersion in a rapture.

Waxing sextile (60°; supportive): mind expresses collective emotion. Intellect aligns with imagination. Thought cooperates with a redemptive vision, or an illusion. Ideas justify the raptures of poetry. Words drum up empathy. Perceives a universal or shared dream.

Waxing square (90°; action crisis: danger/opportunity): mind splits from imagination. Intellect throws cold water on fantasy. Thought rejects a redemptive vision, or illusion. Ideas battle dreams. Words contradict sentimentality or phony camaraderie. Perceives feverish delusions and revolts against them.

Waxing trine (120°; amplifies, mutual reinforcement): mind smoothly articulates imagination into poetry. Intellect integrates mystic or mythic truth with rational thought. Thought enjoys the stimulus of a redemptive vision. Or the comforts of illusion. Ideas encourage empathy. Words inspire dreams, or sugarcoat nightmares. Perceives subtle implications of simple facts.

Waxing quincunx (150°; irritating): mind subverted by the irrational. Intellect undermined by strange dreams. Thought evades cold facts, prefers poetic images. Ideas trip up on illusions. Words struggle to articulate a redemptive vision. Perceives confusion.

Opposition (180°; challenge and illumination): reason and poetry, intellect and imagination, complement and enhance each other. Or completely ignore, evade and deny the other's reality. Thought strongly reflects or rejects a redemptive ideal, or an illusion. Ideas clarify dreams. Words reveal sympathetic feelings. Or manipulatively distort them. Perceives an ideal truth, or a seductive hallucination.

Waning quincunx (210°; irritating): mental clarity disturbed by subconscious upwellings. Intellect confounded by paradox. Thought evades the possibility of a redemptive vision, or the snare of illusion. Ideas hinder feelings of empathy. Words struggle to articulate dreams. Perceives the possibility of new dimensions.

Waning trine (240°; amplifies, mutual reinforcement): mind expresses an emerging imagination. Intellect articulates a poetic connection between seemingly isolated events and entities. Thought appreciates the depth of a new redemptive vision. Or the growing comfort of illusion. Ideas promote rising dreams. Words effectively express empathy. Perceives unity in multiplicity.

Waning square (270°; consciousness crisis: danger/opportunity): mind breaks free from visionary psychobabble. Intellect argues the case against sloppy sentimentality. Thought repudiates an outworn redemptive vision, or illusion. Ideas block or deny feelings of empathy. Words contradict old dreams, or redirect them. Perceives islands of fact in a sea of fantasy. Or thinks it does.

Waning sextile (300°; supportive): mind accepts a more fluid reality. Intellect adjusts to sympathetic rather than analytical forms of reasoning. Thought cooperates with an emerging redemptive vision, or illusion. Ideas justify rising dreams. Words elicit empathy. Perceives poetic resonance.

Waning semi-sextile (330°; stimulating): mind consecrates itself to a vision. Intellect serves imagination. Thought defers to empathy. Ideas expressed poetically. Words explain a rising dream. Perceives an embryonic new world, or complete mental disorder.

Mercury/Pluto

Mind and fate. Conscious perception and hidden purpose.
Individual perspective sublimated by collective necessity.
Penetrating thought, sees to the core or is seized by an obsession.

Conjunction: mind imprinted by deep instinctive, karmic or collective purpose. Intellect fused with a compulsive sense of destiny. Ideas shaped by hidden passions, demands of a larger Will. Words are penetrating. Makes irrevocable statements, says transformative things that can never be unsaid. Perceives an overwhelming Power, which it must comprehend, express and interpret.

Waxing semi-sextile (30°; stimulating): mind begins to separate from sense of destiny or fateful necessity. Intellect learns to take a detached perspective on collective purpose. Thought diverges from a larger Will. Ideas put obsessions in perspective. Words explain a hidden passion. Perceives a need to distance from groupthink.

Waxing sextile (60°; supportive): mind expresses a deep instinctive, karmic or collective purpose. Intellect aligns with a sense of destiny. Thought cooperates with a greater Will. Ideas justify fateful necessity. Words drum up support for a hidden passion. Perceives a larger than personal movement.

Waxing square (90°; action crisis: danger/opportunity): mind breaks free of obsession. Or dies trying. Intellect throws cold water on collective purpose. Thought rebels from a larger Will. Ideas battle demands of fate, with heroic clarity or obstructive denial. Words contradict a hidden passion, or give it new meaning. Perceives and expresses dangers of groupthink.

Waxing trine (120°; amplifies, mutual reinforcement): mind expresses a new level of passion. Intellect articulates collective purpose. Thought effectively serves a larger Will. Ideas encourage a sense of destiny. Words inspire transformative experience. Perceives and interprets the flow of unconscious forces.

Waxing quincunx (150°; irritating): mind disturbed by unconscious or collective rumblings. Intellect disrupted by hidden passion. Thought evades demands of a larger Will. Ideas sidestep 'dictates' of destiny. Words struggle to articulate fateful necessity. Perceives something alien rising to the surface.

Opposition (180°; challenge and illumination): individual mind and collective purpose complement and enhance each other. Or violently dissociate as a personal paradigm is destroyed and transformed by its encounter with a greater Power. Intellect meets fate as an eruption from the unconscious depths, creative or destructive. Thought strongly reflects or rejects a larger Will. Ideas clarify instincts. Words reveal hidden passions. Perceives an inevitable destiny.

Waning quincunx (210°; irritating): mind disrupted by unconscious or collective forces. Intellect bothered by unanswerable questions raised by fate. Thought evades demands of an emerging Will. Ideas hinder a sense of destiny. Words struggle to articulate rising passions. Perceives the shadow of something much bigger than itself.

Waning trine (240°; amplifies, mutual reinforcement): mind expresses an emerging fate, the call of a larger than personal necessity. Intellect integrates collective unconscious contents into a communicable narrative. Thought appreciates and articulates the power of a rising Will. Ideas promote a coming destiny. Words effectively explain inevitable necessity, the demands of fate. Perceives and interprets hidden passion.

Waning square (270°; consciousness crisis: danger/opportunity): mind fundamentally rejects, painfully splits off from, collective purpose. Intellect argues the case against overwhelming unconscious or historical forces. Reorients towards a rebirth of individual truth from the herd mentality. Thought repudiates an obsolete Will. Ideas block or deny hidden passions. Words contradict, or give new meaning, to a sense of destiny. Clearly perceives the trauma and tragedy of its time.

Waning sextile (300°; supportive): mind articulates its role in a larger narrative. Intellect interprets and communicates an emerging collective purpose. Thought cooperates with a dawning Will. Ideas justify new passions. Words elicit transformative participation in a group endeavor. Perceives a rising Power.

Waning semi-sextile (330°; stimulating): mind consecrates itself to an obsession, good or bad. Intellect serves the larger purposes of the tribe. Thought defers to a greater Will. Ideas promote emerging passions. Words explain a new order of things. Perceives a coming rebirth, or total annihilation.

Venus

Aspects of Venus idealize any planetary principle it contacts. Puts it in an appreciative light; emphasizes its value and desirable qualities. Draws out its inherent beauty. Evokes pleasure in it. A loving function.

Venus/Mars

Female and male, yin and yang. Desire and drive.
Values and valor. Sensuality and assertion.
Pleasure and passion. Love and war.

Conjunction: latent desire activated. Love awakened by passion. A fusion of female sensitivity and male will. This can release a hot erotic charisma. Or sublimate into a spiritual union of masculine and feminine qualities. It can also short-circuit, fixated in an arrested checkmate of the gender dynamic.

Empowers a subjective self-ideal. Brings an inner beauty to life. Recharges libido. Energizes new possibilities of pleasure. Reorients the pursuit (Mars) of happiness (Venus). This may struggle to express itself. Think of adolescence: a fresh but awkward awakening of personal yearning.

Sexuality somewhat androgynous: a delicate balance or a neutered impasse. Unity more than relationship: enhanced by shared experience or impoverished by monolithic values.

Waxing semi-sextile (30°; stimulating): desire begins to differentiate from impulse. Love separates from raw passion and takes a more detached perspective. A subjective self-ideal emerges out of primal drive. An inner beauty entices will into more conscious expression. Pleasure awakens to self-assertion. Personal preference diverges from strategic demands for action. Stimulating relationship. Sexuality evoked by differences. Values independence.

Waxing sextile (60°; supportive): desire appropriately aligns with ability to execute. Love dances with passion. A subjective self-ideal, an inner beauty, guides will into graceful expression. Pleasure in diplomatic assertion. Personal preference agrees with action, in tune with strategic demands. Harmonious relationship. Sexual identity satisfied, perhaps complacent. Values cooperation.

Waxing square (90°; action crisis: danger/opportunity): desire at odds with realities of power. A subjective self-ideal inappropriate to its ability to execute; can incite will to clumsy violence. Or an inner beauty inspires it to difficult, even heroic effort.

Love conflicts with impulsive passion. Personal preference rebels against strategic demands for action. Challenging relationship. Takes pleasure in battle, (hopefully) can learn from defeat. Sexuality conflicted: blocked or stimulated to a new level. Confrontation between values forces hard choices.

Waxing trine (120°; amplifies, mutual reinforcement): desire induces a new level of self-assertion. Love gracefully expresses passion. A subjective self-ideal, an inner beauty, entices will into a higher level of sophistication. Or seduces it into satisfied passivity. Personal preference enjoys what it does, feels stimulated by action. Mutually enhancing relationship. Or one that is too easy. Sexuality well adjusted: it can be taken for granted or consciously cultivate an enhanced sensuality.* Strengthens existing values.

* Any Venus/Mars combination can develop or attain the heights of sensuality. However, for some this comes more naturally, or is a more important priority.

Waxing quincunx (150°; irritating): self-assertion confused by ambiguous desires. Love troubled by inappropriate passion. A subjective self-ideal, an inner beauty, irritates will with elusive, hard to meet demands. Pleasure unsure of what it wants. Personal preference uncomfortable with behavior and strategic realities. Rocky relationship. Sexuality challenged by mystery, curiosity. Values tested by unfamiliar circumstances.

Opposition (180°; challenge and illumination): love and will, desire and power, enhance each other in a balanced relationship. Or they divorce, polarizing into hurt sensibility and angry passion. A subjective self-ideal gracefully responds to objective stimuli. Inner beauty inspires self-assertion and leads it to victory. Or a seductive mirage entices it to ruin. Purpose consummated. Or enervated by pleasure.

Male and female sides of the personality, and its relationship with the other sex out there, creatively contrast to form a more inclusive identity. A complementary marriage, of internal psychological qualities and external partners.* Or an emotional and erotic standoff. Sexuality hot or cold; can gyrate between the two. Contrasting values: will they integrate in a higher synthesis? Or cancel out in mutual hatred?

* Venus and Mars express gender tinted, or tainted, polarities of emotion. Moon integrates them into the feeling nature. None of the other planets are personally subjective like these three worlds surrounding Earth.

Waning quincunx (210°; irritating): desire provokes power with elusive new goals. Love driven, or driven off, by unacknowledged passion. A subjective self-ideal, a search for inner beauty, draws will onto unknown paths. Uncertain where pleasure lies. Personal preference irritated by irrelevant strategic demands. Experimental relationship. Sexuality challenged by dissatisfaction. Values vary according to situation.

Waning trine (240°; amplifies, mutual reinforcement): desire integrates with an emerging power. Or adroitly adapts to it. Love graciously guides self-assertion and artfully expresses passion. A subjective self-ideal, an inner beauty, civilizes will, enhancing its reach. Or enervates its drive. Pleasure rewards effort. Receptive to a new strategic orientation. Balanced, beneficial relationships. Sexuality well adjusted, can evolve to higher plateau. Inner values and outer actions synchronize. Personal ideals and behavior are consistent.

Waning square (270°; consciousness crisis: danger/opportunity): desire challenges ability to execute by raising the bar, changing the rules. Love rejects an old passion, seeks a new one. A subjective self-ideal, an inner beauty, shames will into more sophisticated effort. Or sets it up for failure. Takes pleasure in repudiating an outworn strategy and asserting its own preferences; must be able to learn from mistakes if it is to succeed. Combative relationship. Sexuality confronts its own contradictions; finds inhibition or difficult breakthrough. Discounts past victories; values another, more subtle form of consummation.

Waning sextile (300°; supportive): desire stimulated by an emerging purpose. Love embraces a larger passion. A subjective self-ideal, an inner beauty, resonates with will. Personal preference cooperates with rising strategic demands. Takes pleasure pursuing a new emotional balance of power. This occurs both within personality and in its relationships. Values an evolving redefinition of sexuality.

Waning semi-sextile (330°; stimulating): desire consecrated to the pursuit of a long-term purpose. Love serves will. A subjective self-ideal, an inner beauty, experienced as passionate identification with, or surrender to, a rising sense of power. Personal pleasures and preferences defer to emerging strategic demands for action. Relationship dedicated to a cause, crusade, effort. Sexuality sublimated. Values heroic sacrifice.

Venus/Jupiter

Personal ideal and transcendent spirit.
Subjective truth and social wisdom.
Sensuality and morality. Desire and ethics.
Love and fortune.

Conjunction: emotional desire and conventional wisdom in unison. Sensuality and spirit at one. Love expands its compass, becomes more inclusive. Abundant opportunity. Or enervating excess. Happy, perhaps superficial, relationship.

A subjective self-ideal, an inner beauty, grows to its fullest achievable potential at the current level of consciousness. Personal preferences and pleasures defined by accepted moral and ethical principles. Or, in highly evolved cases, by ecstatic union with a transcendent soul. Values and exemplifies societal or religious/philosophical norms. This can grow to a direct experience of the divine.

Waxing semi-sextile (30°; stimulating): desire begins to separate from spiritual aspiration. Love learns to detach from social expectation. Relationship evolves through celebration of differences. A subjective self-ideal, an inner beauty, individualizes at the current level of consciousness. Personal preference differentiates from accepted morality and ethical imperatives. Pleasure distinguished from principle. Values one's own interpretation of societal or religious/philosophic norms.

Waxing sextile (60°; supportive): desire cooperates with spiritual aspiration. Love becomes more generous and inclusive. A subjective self-ideal, an inner beauty, develops new abilities at the current level of consciousness. Pleasure reinforces principle. Personal preference resonates with accepted morality and ethical imperatives. Relationship grows through mutual stimulation. Values enhanced by societal or religious/philosophic norms.

Waxing square (90°; action crisis: danger/opportunity): desire conflicts with spiritual aspiration. Love rejects an idealized version, seeks its own expression; defies social expectation. A subjective self-ideal, an inner beauty, jumps, perhaps prematurely, to a new level of consciousness (not necessarily higher). Pleasure battles principle, forces a redefinition of ethical norms. Personal preference rebels against accepted morality. Relationship grows through contrast, demands uncomfortable truth. Values sharpened or warped: defined through struggle with societal or religious/philosophical norms.

Waxing trine (120°; amplifies, mutual reinforcement): desire gracefully integrates with, and is strengthened by, spiritual aspiration. Love embraces a fullness of experience. Or enjoys a smooth and pleasant glide path. A subjective self-ideal, an inner beauty, evolves to a more sophisticated state on the current level of consciousness. Pleasure enhanced by living up to principles. Personal preference for tried and true morality and ethical imperatives. Relationship grows through a sense of shared prosperity, emotional as well as material. Values endorse societal or religious/philosophical norms. Gets positive feedback from participation in the accepted order.

Waxing quincunx (150°; irritating): desire irked by spiritual demands. Love tweaked by new evolutionary possibilities. A subjective self-ideal, an inner beauty, senses a not yet defined new level of consciousness. Pleasure at odds with demands of principle. Personal preference uncomfortable with accepted morality and ethical imperatives. Relationship grows through a stimulating itch. Values uncomfortable with societal or religious/philosophical norms.

Opposition (180°; challenge and illumination): desire complemented and enhanced by spiritual aspiration. Or dissociates from it. Loves the highest soul qualities in self and others. Or loves everyone and everything promiscuously. Sublime pleasure or gross excess.

A subjective self-ideal, an inner beauty, ascends to a new level of consciousness. Or inflates narcissistic self-esteem to the bursting point. Personal preferences strongly reflect or reject collective morality and ethical imperatives. Relationship grows through diversity, multiple connections with subjective self and objective others. Or is cheapened by superficial variety. Genuinely values and lives up to societal or religious/philosophical norms. Or flamboyantly denies them.

Waning quincunx (210°; irritating): desire pulled by felt but unidentified spiritual aspirations. Dissatisfied love seeks new outlets. A subjective self-ideal, an inner beauty, senses the possibility of another level of consciousness. Pleasure questions ethical imperatives. Personal preference irritated by a no longer satisfying morality. Relationship grows by entertaining alternatives. Inner values incite disturbing views of societal or religious/philosophical norms.

Waning trine (240°; amplifies, mutual reinforcement): desire gracefully integrates with emerging spiritual aspiration. Love aligns with soul. A subjective self-ideal, an inner beauty, competently demonstrated at the consensus level of consciousness, but also senses and grows larger possibilities. Pleasure enhanced by conformity to rising principles. Personal preference for a new morality and its ethical imperatives. Relationship promotes evolution, or social climbing. Values enhanced by societal or religious/philosophical norms.

Waning square (270°; consciousness crisis: danger/opportunity): desire rejects spiritual aspiration. Love takes its own course in defiance of social expectation, wisely or foolishly. A subjective self-ideal, an inner beauty, develops through conflict with conventional wisdom. It seeks a new level of consciousness, for which it may not be prepared. Pleasure denies the validity of community principles, rightly or wrongly. Personal preference repudiates an outworn morality and its ethical imperatives. Relationship demands new forms of intimacy. Values defined through open debate with societal or religious/philosophical norms.

Waning sextile (300°; supportive): desire cooperatively aligns with spiritual aspiration. Love seeks a higher expression of goodness, truth and beauty. A subjective self-ideal develops through service to an emerging level of consciousness. Pleasure guided by a rising principle, good or bad. Personal preference cooperates with a new morality and its ethical imperatives. Relationship reinforces a larger social commitment. Values evolving societal or religious/philosophical norms.

Waning semi-sextile (330°; stimulating): desire consecrated to spiritual aspiration. Love commits to selfless devotion: to another individual, a social cause, or in search of its own higher soul. A subjective self-ideal, an inner beauty, develops in service to a new level of consciousness. Personal taste defers to a rising morality and its ethical principles. Relationship demands joyful sacrifice. Values surrender to emerging political or religious/philosophical norms.

Venus/Saturn

Personal ideal and objective fact. Self-esteem and inadequacy.
Pleasure and discipline. Desire and duty.
Love and frustration.

Definition of terms: 'Shadow' refers to one's unconscious inferiority; weakness and fear. 'Dark side' refers to a more conscious malevolence, in self or others.

Conjunction: desire meets fear. Deep love encounters hard demands of fate. A subjective inner ideal shaped by duty. Pleasure in self-discipline and difficult to attain merit. A preference for heavy responsibility.

Identifies with the Shadow, or dark side, in compassionate empathy. Or embraces its corruption. Imprinted with austere values in service to impersonal law and the highest standards of integrity. Or shriveled by cynical coldness, withered in the sight of an evil eye.

Waxing semi-sextile (30°; stimulating): desire begins to separate from fear. Love learns to emerge from the Shadow, or dark side. Or to falsely deny its existence. A subjective self-ideal, an inner beauty, defines itself against the dictates of fate. Pleasure evades the restraints of discipline. Personal preference differentiates from impersonal rules of law. Relationship paradoxically generates a sense of self in contrast to the other. Values detachment.

Waxing sextile (60°; supportive): desire clarified and focused by fear. Love cooperates with fate, and is strengthened by its demands. A subjective self-ideal, an inner beauty, develops through living up to tough but realistic standards of integrity. Pleasure deepens by embracing salutary discipline. Personal preference guided by impersonal rules of law. Relationship in shared and accepted duty. Values pragmatic accommodation to the Shadow, or dark side.

Waxing square (90°; action crisis: danger/opportunity): desire breaks from fear. Or is broken by it. Love defies fate, chooses its own, which may be a hard one. A subjective self-ideal, an inner beauty, shaped by struggle against limitation and deprivation. Pleasure rejects others' standards of discipline. Personal preference rebels against impersonal rules. Relationship crossed by the demands of duty. Values, and pays the price of, integrity in the face of a fair-seeming foul Shadow.

Waxing trine (120°; amplifies, mutual reinforcement): desire partially tames fear by embracing a more subtle sense of destiny. Love gracefully accepts its fate and takes pleasure in duty. A subjective self-ideal, an inner beauty, develops as an artful sublimation in response to deprivation. A preference for the stimulus of impersonal rules of law and high standards of integrity. Relationship naturally aligns with the requirements of social discipline. Values steady, patient exposure of the Shadow, or dark side, to the light of love.

Waxing quincunx (150°; irritating): desire chilled by unnamed fears. Love darkened by vague shadows of the Shadow. A subjective self-ideal, an inner beauty, develops as a growing appreciation of grace in the face of ambiguity. Pleasure at odds with standards of discipline. Personal preference uncomfortable with impersonal rules of law. Relationship disrupted by cold winds of fate. Values the flaws that create real beauty.

Opposition (180°; challenge and illumination): desire openly confronts the dictates of fate. Love and fear define and enhance each other. Love releases the energy locked up in fear; fear makes love real though stern tests of commitment. Or they dissociate in an ice age of despair as all feelings freeze in the dark.

A subjective self-ideal shaped, or crushed, by stern discipline. Takes pleasure in living up to austere standards of conduct. A preference for the beauty of difficult to attain integrity. Or self-loathing cynicism as a shriveled soul sinks into the loneliness of sordid appetites. Relationship deepens through hard experience over time. Or withers into cold formality and suffocating boredom. Values a balanced equilibrium of joy and duty, scary Shadow and inner light. Tends to gyrate between them.

Waning quincunx (210°; irritating): desire overcompensates for fears it does not quite comprehend. Love intrigued by a sensed presence of the Shadow, perhaps dangerously so. A subjective self-ideal, an inner beauty, learns to incorporate aspects of the dark side. Or can be dragged down by them. Pleasure at odds with standards of integrity. Personal preference irritated by impersonal rules, demands of discipline. Relationship jolted by cold reality checks. Values the stimulation of unexpected difficulties.

Waning trine (240°; amplifies, mutual reinforcement): desire smiles at fear, which learns to smile back. Love gracefully integrates with an emerging sense of duty. A subjective self-ideal stimulated rather than intimidated by the Shadow, or dark side. Pleasure deepened by responsibility. Relationship expresses the rewards of discipline. Values a classic simplicity of in personal taste and conduct.

Waning square (270°; consciousness crisis: danger/opportunity): desire rejects old fears, wisely or foolishly. Love challenges restrictions and pays the price, for better or worse. A subjective self-ideal stresses beauty over duty, happiness over discipline. It can encounter serious resistance and severe punishment. Personal preferences repudiate the authority of rules, laws and standards, in brave liberation or as selfish greed and unrestrained temptation.

Relationship evokes the Shadow, or dark side. Thus it can be experienced as redemptive or scary, demanding or constrictive. Pleasure deepens through an emergence of personal values out of fated limitation. Or is suffocated by oppressive tradition.

Waning sextile (300°; supportive): desire appropriately tempered by fear. 'Fear of God is the beginning of wisdom'* Love in harmony with demands of duty and destiny. A subjective self-ideal, an inner beauty, develops through graceful acceptance of fate. A preference for emerging rules, laws and standards. Pleasure enhanced by their authority. Relationship perfected by the discipline of compromise. Values the Shadow, or dark side, as an inducement to sharper artistic skill in the dance of life.

* Proverbs 9:10 and Psalms 111:10.

Waning semi-sextile (330°; stimulating): desire consecrated to fate. An austere love for a distant, hard to attain goal or admired person. A subjective self-ideal, an inner beauty, develops as compassionate sacrifice to redeem the Shadow, or dark side. Pleasure deepened by anticipation of a better emerging order. Personal preference defers to the authority of new rules, laws and standards. Relationship disciplined by a higher duty. Values grace in the face of fear. Or throws away all that is worthy to escape it.

Venus/Uranus

Personal ideal and transformative inspiration.

Conjunction: desire fundamentally changes in nature. A subjective self-ideal develops, or breaks down, in sudden intuitive leaps. Pleasure in revolution or revelation. Unconventional personal tastes, an appreciation of unusual beauty.

Relationship is deeply transformative, for better or worse. An inclusive but detached love: inspired or abstract. Cool, or chilly, emotional expression. Senses future potential, which it seeks to liberate from present circumstance. Values universal ideas more than tangible possessions.

Waxing semi-sextile (30°; stimulating): desire begins to separate from abstract ideas. Love learns to emerge from inspiration into appreciation. A subjective self-ideal, an inner beauty, starts to develop a sense of its own uniqueness rather than existing as the embodiment of an archetype. Personal taste seeks an island of stability in a sea of change. Pleasure in establishing one's own space. Relationship paradoxically generates a sense of individuality. Values detached observation.

Waxing sextile (60°; supportive): desire enticed by inspiration. Love stimulated by unexpected events and unconventional people. A subjective self-ideal, an inner beauty, expresses a unique personal revelation. A taste for novelty. Takes pleasure in cooperating with change. Relationship transforms in an evolutionary, not revolutionary, way. Values adaptation.

Waxing square (90°; action crisis: danger/opportunity): desire breaks free of abstract ideas. Loves the lone rebel rather than the revolution. A subjective self-ideal, an inner, expressed in defiance of convention. Personal taste takes a strenuously individualistic path. Finds pleasure in disruption, positive or negative. Relationship in upheaval. Values the unique over the archetypal.

Waxing trine (120°; amplifies, mutual reinforcement): desire gracefully integrates with abstract ideas. Inspired love evokes new dimensions of communion in who and how it blesses. A subjective self-ideal, an inner beauty, appropriately expresses an intuitive vision. A taste for the stimulus of change. Pleasure in smooth evolution: New Year's 'out with the old, in with the new.' Relationship is transformative, but not disruptive. Values the archetypal over the unique.

Waxing quincunx (150°; irritating): desires troubled by strange urges. Love inexplicably drawn to unusual destinations. A subjective self-ideal, an inner beauty, expressed eccentrically. Personal preference uncomfortable with the implications of change. Pleasures disrupted. Relationships change without apparent explanation. Values unexpected surprises.

Opposition (180°; challenge and illumination): sensual/emotional desires and abstract ideas, individual love and universal archetypes, complement and enhance each other. Or violently dissociate in a chasm between appreciation for what is and inspiration of what could be. A subjective self-ideal, an inner beauty, stimulated by revolutionary insight. Or shocked to the core. Personal taste reflects an appetite for change. Or craves anarchic disruption. A revelation of new pleasures, higher or lower. Relationship is transformative. Or traumatic. Values individuality in communion, independence in commitment.

Waning quincunx (210°; irritating): desire unsatisfied, seeks unconventional outlets. Loves intriguing novelty. A subjective self-ideal, an inner beauty, expressed in unusual or even shocking style. Personal taste irritated by irrelevant and distracting change. Unusual pleasures with unexpected outcomes. Relationships quirky; an odd couple. Values eccentricity.

Waning trine (240°; amplifies, mutual reinforcement): desire gracefully integrates with emerging ideas. Love is generalized rather than possessive. It extends to new levels of appreciation and inclusion. A subjective self-ideal, an inner beauty, develops through participation in creating a better future. A taste for novelty and change. Pleasure of anticipation. Relationship seeks utopian, perhaps unrealistic, expression. Values and enables tangible expression of inspiration.

Waning square (270°; consciousness crisis: danger/opportunity): desire rejects old ideas. Love seeks new ones. A subjective self-ideal, an inner beauty, expressed through rebellious insistence on personal preference. A taste for experimentation; can be shocking to others, disruptive of one's own tranquility. Pleasure in breaking free, cutting loose. Relationship rocky, but potentially creative. Values originality.

Waning sextile (300°; supportive): desire enticed by emerging ideas. Loves future possibilities more than present reality. Can prefer utopian theories to flawed individuals. Expresses a subjective self-ideal, an inner beauty, as an experimental prototype of a new social model. Takes pleasure in effectively promoting it. Personal taste reflects cutting edge inspiration, or fringe fads. Relationship guided by abstract insight. Values novelty.

Waning semi-sextile (330°; stimulating): desire consecrated to an idea. Loves an inspiring person or cause. A subjective self-ideal, an inner beauty, sacrifices to or for a future vision. Personal taste defers to a need for change. Pleasure in anticipating a breakthrough to something completely new. Relates to the entire universe, with altruistic inclusiveness or as crazy promiscuity. Values complete transformation, up or down.

Venus/Neptune

Personal and universal love. Desire and compassion.

Conjunction: personal desires dissolve, replaced by mystical or collective yearning. Love absorbed into a sense of universal compassion. Or decays into indulgent illusion. A subjective self-ideal, an inner beauty, expresses through selfless sacrifice. Devotion to idealistic causes or idealized relationships. Can be taken advantage of. Pleasure in complete merger: no boundaries. Values romantic imagination or a seductive hallucination.

Waxing semi-sextile (30°; stimulating): personal desire begins to separate from collective ideals. Love learns to differentiate from a mystical vision. A subjective self-ideal, an inner beauty, develops through appropriate distancing from a dream, or illusion. An individual form of devotion develops out of mythic imagination. Specific pleasures emerge out of a general psychic sensitivity. Moves towards relationship, away from amorphous unity. Seeks its own sensual or emotional values distinct from a nebulous empathy.

Waxing sextile (60°; supportive): personal desire enticed by a visionary image. Love serves and exemplifies compassion. A subjective self-ideal develops through appropriate empathy. Sympathetic devotion. Pleasure in artistic expression of ideals. Relationship enhanced by, but does not disappear into, a sense of mythic imagination. Values poetic beauty.

Waxing square (90°; action crisis: danger/opportunity): personal desire breaks free of mystic or collective ideals. Love seeks a unique rather than universal expression. A subjective self-ideal, an inner beauty, develops through disillusionment, which can liberate or poison. Devotion to an inner dream v the tribal myth. Takes pleasure in expressing one's own imagination in contrast to a generally accepted vision. Relationship conflicts with illusory expectations. Insists on individual rather than group values.

Waxing trine (120°; amplifies, mutual reinforcement): personal desire gracefully integrates with collective dreams. Universal love or indiscriminate enabling. A subjective self-ideal, an inner beauty, develops through appropriate compassion. Devotion to the tribe: 'one for all and all for one.' Pleasure in artistically expressing a shared mythic imagination. Relationship has a mystical quality. Values a redemptive vision or an intoxicating illusion.

Waxing quincunx (150°; irritating): personal desire unclear. Love undermined by illusion. A subjective self-ideal, an inner beauty, develops as an ability to deal with ambiguity, to nurture the brighter side of grey. Devotion despite uncertainty. Pleasure oddly mixed with disappointment. Relationship confused. Values the tentative emergence of a sixth sense amidst the fog.

Opposition (180°; challenge and illumination): personal desires and collective ideals, individual love and universal compassion, complement and enhance each other. Or dissolve in amorphous confusion. A subjective self-ideal develops as a unique poetic sensibility. Takes pleasure in channeling ineffable rapture into mythic expressions of beauty. Art reflects deep currents of imagination. Or drowns in intoxicated illusion.

Devotion to a redemptive vision. Or a seductive appetite. Relationship merges into empathetic soul-union. Or decays into nebulous mutual betrayal. Values loss of self in mystical union.

Waning quincunx (210°; irritating): amorphous personal desire. Loves an illusion, yet can be uplifted by its poetic yearning. A subjective self-ideal, inner beauty, develops as an ability to artistically express subtle implication. Devotion accepts uncertainty. Pleasure despite disappointment. Relationship founders on treacherous shoals, but evokes and can be redeemed by forgiveness. Values the ambiguity of love.

Waning trine (240°; amplifies, mutual reinforcement): personal desire gracefully integrates with an emerging collective vision. A subjective self-ideal, inner beauty, develops as an artistic talent that can express still forming collective longings. Devotion to a rising tribal myth. Pleasure in imaginatively presenting it.

Compassionate love extends to all. Relationship bathed in mutual empathy. Or drowns in shared delusion. Values a mystic faith in a better world. Can effectively channel or personify that dream.

Waning square (270°; consciousness crisis: danger/opportunity): personal desire rejects old collective ideals. Love seeks a new redemptive image. A subjective self-ideal, an inner beauty, develops as insistence on a unique expression of a universal vision. Devotion to an individual version of the tribal myth. Pleasure in pursuing one's own dreams rather than those assigned by others. Relationship evolves, or devolves, through hard experiences of betrayal and forgiveness. An emerging ability to distinguish true values from delusional seductions.

Waning sextile (300°; supportive): personal desire enticed by an emerging redemptive image. Love enhanced by a sense of universal rapport. A subjective self-ideal, an inner beauty, develops through personal identification with a rising collective vision. Takes pleasure in making it artistically or emotionally real. Devotion to a mythic dream, and the imagination to poetically express it. Relationship resonates with a mystic glow or an intoxicated buzz. Values solidarity.

Waning semi-sextile (330°; stimulating): personal desire consecrated to a redemptive ideal. Love sacrifices for a compassionate vision. A subjective self-ideal, an inner beauty, develops through dissolution of personal interest on the altar of mystical union. Individual devotion yields to collective imagination. Pleasure in growing identification with a mythic image which engulfs individual judgment, for better or worse. Values ecstatic surrender.

Venus/Pluto

Personal ideal and collective or fated demand. Wish and necessity. Pluto sublimates personal preference into devotion to a larger destiny. Love reprocessed.

Conjunction: personal desire impregnated by collective purpose. Fated and fateful love. A subjective self-ideal, an inner beauty, identifies with a hidden destiny. Devotion to a larger cause. Pleasure in surrender to an overwhelming Power.

Natural sensuality, innocent sensitivity, sucked into the instinctual underworld, or a Hell experience, to regenerate under pressure. A descent into the depths: finds treasure or trauma. Intense, compulsive relationship. Values die, perhaps to be reborn.

Waxing semi-sextile (30°; stimulating): personal desire begins to separate from collective purpose. Love learns to detach from fate and find its own way. A subjective self-ideal, an inner beauty, develops through discovery of one's own worth independently of others' expectations. Pleasure in a rebirth of private happiness. Relationship awakens self-awareness. Devotion emerges out of destiny. Differentiates individual values from a compulsive tribal will.

Waxing sextile (60°; supportive): personal desire stimulated by collective forces. Love in harmony with fate. A subjective self-ideal, inner beauty, develops as an artistic expression of hidden power. Effective devotion to a cause. Takes pleasure in giving it a human face. Relationship appropriately enacts an unconscious or karmic destiny. Values cooperation with larger tribal currents.

Waxing square (90°; action crisis: danger/opportunity): personal desire breaks free of collective purpose. Love asserts its own validity in the face of a larger fate (think 'Dr. Zhivago'*). Devotion defies destiny. A subjective self-ideal, an inner beauty, expresses as a unique sensibility rising in contrast to the tribal will. Private pleasure reborn from mass obsession. Or destroyed by it. Relationship forged in battle against overwhelming odds. Values the individual over the group.

Waxing trine (120°; amplifies, mutual reinforcement): personal desire gracefully integrates with collective purpose. Love resonates with destiny, enacts and expresses fate. A subjective self-ideal, an inner beauty, develops as a personification of hidden power. Gives instinctive force, or the general will, an attractive human face. Devotion sanctifies a cause. Takes pleasure in creatively presenting it. Relationship in harmony with unconscious karmic needs. Senses and values invisible resources, brings buried treasure up into the light.

Waxing quincunx (150°; irritating): personal desire jarred by collective purpose. Love disrupted by unconscious rumblings. A difficult effort to reconcile a subjective self-ideal with group needs. Devotion tested by intangible threats. Pleasure oddly mixed with pain. Relationship stimulated or shaken by blind fate. Values an ability to instinctively adapt to the dark.

Opposition (180°; challenge and illumination): personal desire and collective purpose, love and fate, complement and enhance each other. Or catastrophically dissociate, as individual judgment confronts an unconscious obsession. A relatively evolved subjective self-ideal faces an eruption of deep karmic, instinctive or tribal demands. Beauty meets the Beast.

An invisible Will overrides sensual pleasures and social mores, perhaps even unto death. Intense passion supplants normal happiness. Or destroys it. Absolute devotion to, or venomous hatred of, a larger cause. Pleasure reflects a hidden Power. Relationship intensified, or devoured, by an overwhelming force, internal or external. Values a total commitment to destiny. This can require loss of all that one has.

Waning quincunx (210°; irritating): personal desire disturbed by collective purpose. Love disrupted by hidden passion. A subjective self-ideal, an inner beauty, develops by sensing and adapting to invisible powers. Devotion tested by uncertainties of destiny. Pleasure despite pain. Relationship rocked by secondary reverberations of larger forces. Values disclosure of unconscious influences.

Waning trine (240°; amplifies, mutual reinforcement): personal desire gracefully integrates with an emerging collective purpose. Love responds creatively to hidden karmic, instinctive or tribal needs. A subjective self-ideal, an inner beauty, embodies a rising power. Takes pleasure in artistically presenting its future. Devotion harmoniously channels an invisible Will. Relationship aligns with possibility of rebirth. Values cooperation with the tide of destiny.

Waning square (270°; consciousness crisis: danger/opportunity): personal desire rejects collective purpose. A subjective self-ideal, an inner beauty, presents a unique interpretation of emerging group needs. Devotion defies, and redefines, a rising Power. Pleasure emigrates away from a march of the lemmings. Or is crushed by it. Relationship torn by conflict between past and future values. Emphasizes individual love in contrast to tribal demands.*

Waning sextile (300°; supportive): personal desire drawn to, cooperates with, collective purpose. Love enhanced by participation in a larger destiny. A subjective self-ideal, inner beauty, expressed through enticing presentation of an emerging future. Devotion to a rising Power. Pleasure in effectively serving it. Relationship naturally resonates with a deep fate. Values individual identification with group needs.

Waning semi-sextile (330°; stimulating): personal desire consecrated to collective purpose. Love abandons itself to a sacrificial passion. A subjective self-ideal, an inner beauty, identifies with a larger destiny. Takes pleasure in complete subordination to, merger with, a cause. Individual devotion yields to karmic, instinctive or tribal necessity. Relationship becomes fate, absorbs individuality into a compulsive union. Values death in service to rebirth.

*'Dr. Zhivago,' by Boris Pasternak (1890-1960), was a Nobel Prize winning novel (1958) about the value of personal love in a time that stressed subordination of self to utopian ideas (the Russian Revolution).

Mars

Aspects of Mars energize any planetary principle it contacts. Provokes and stimulates it into action. Challenges it. Draws it into conflict wherein its true nature is revealed, for better or worse. A confrontational function.

Mars/Jupiter

Personal will and transcendent soul. Ego drive and ethical standards. Self-assertion and social morality. Aggression and aspiration. Impulse and imperative. Power and truth.

Conjunction: passion activates soul. Will focuses aspiration into a long- term strategy. Puts philosophy into action. Brings a worldview to life in real behavior. Energetic expression of a religious or political agenda. A militant prophet, ready to fight for beliefs. Or violently impose them.

Self-assertion seizes opportunity. Powerful expansive urge, whether physical or spiritual, emotional or economic. Aggression rewarded, for better or worse. A competitive ethic. Vigorously optimistic, can be overconfident. Glorifies jihad, struggle, against real or imagined enemies and inner doubts.

Waxing semi-sextile (30°; stimulating): passion begins to separate from spiritual justification and act on its own terms. Will learns to detach from philosophic certainty and follow its instincts, good or bad. Behavior diverges from a belief system, in liberation or hypocrisy. Expansive urges put in perspective; aggressive exuberance turns a cold eye to its energy budget. Self-assertion differentiates from morality and ethical imperatives. Optimism tempered by a more realistic appraisal of the strategic situation.

Waxing sextile (60°; supportive): passion cooperates with spiritual principle. Will effectively implements a philosophic agenda. Behavior justified by belief. Expansive urges competently planned in line with available energy. Self-assertion cooperates with accepted morality and ethical imperatives. Ego drive conforms to conventional wisdom and norms. Realistic optimism.

Waxing square (90°; action crisis: danger/opportunity): passion wars with spiritual principle. Will breaks free of philosophic justification; individualizes on its own terms. Self-assertion rejects accepted morality and ethical imperatives. Behavior at odds with personal beliefs as hypocrisy or with social mores as rebellion. Ego drive battles conventional wisdom, rightly or wrongly. And pays the price.

Expansive urges overreach. An aggressive ethic learns a sobering lesson. Overconfidence. Or the courage to grow through failure of inappropriate projects. Exuberant optimism dashed, with possible transcendence to a deeper faith.

Waxing trine (120°; amplifies, mutual reinforcement): passion strategically integrates with spiritual principle. Will effectively pursues far-sighted philosophic goals, whether good or bad. Behavior aligns with belief. Self-assertion stimulated by accepted morality and ethical imperatives. Expansive urges meet success, can overextend. Enthusiastic enactment of an agreed social agenda. Ego drive energetically champions conventional wisdom and is handsomely rewarded. Powerful but realistic optimism.

Waxing quincunx (150°; irritating): passion disrupts spiritual principle. Will at odds, but not at war, with philosophic convictions. Behavior tries, but cannot fully follow, beliefs. Self-assertion uncomfortable with accepted morality and ethical imperatives. Expansion meets unexpected resistance. Ego drive thwarted by social norms. Optimism foiled and thus either confused or brought down to earth.

Opposition (180°; challenge and illumination): passion and spiritual principles, will and philosophic conviction, complement and enhance each other. Or violently dissociate. Behavior effectively implements beliefs or completely conflicts with them. Self-assertion champions or aggressively confronts conventional wisdom. Personal power goes to a new level of aspiration. Expansive urges meet extraordinary success or crushing hostility. Social fame or notoriety, as hero or villain. Optimism leads to victory or to death.

Waning quincunx (210°; irritating): passion questions new spiritual aspirations. Will contends with philosophy, neither in complete agreement with or opposition to conventional wisdom. Behavior erratically conforms to, and then acts against, beliefs. Self-assertion irritated by irrelevant morality and ethical principles. Expansive urges find that success proves elusive and ambiguous. Social mores generate personal frustration, which can explode. One is not sure what to hope for.

Waning trine (240°; amplifies, mutual reinforcement): passion integrates with emerging spiritual aspirations. Will effectively enacts a long-term evolutionary agenda. Competent behavior in tune with beliefs, right or wrong. Self-assertion reinforced by morality and ethical principles. Expansive urges lead to both worldly success and philosophic sophistication. This can lead to genuine leadership or smug arrogance. Energetic endorsement of conventional wisdom and consequent social approval. Optimism validated, for better or worse.

Waning square (270°; consciousness crisis: danger/opportunity): passion rejects spiritual aspirations, seeks another justification. Will wars with conventional philosophy, or adopts a philosophy of war. Behavior at odds with beliefs. Finds new motivations, better or worse. Self-assertion repudiates outworn morality and ethical principles. Expansive urges blocked and punished. This leads to cynicism or generates other avenues of growth. Ego and society conflict, creatively or destructively, to either or both. An old optimism dashed. New hopes may emerge.

Waning sextile (300°; supportive): passion guided by emerging spiritual aspirations. Will effectively aligns with, sincerely follows, beliefs. Self-assertion cooperates with a new morality and ethical principles. Expansive urges serve the larger community and a rising truth. Fights for the tribe, not personal glory. Society recognizes and rewards that team spirit. Sober optimism.

Waning semi-sextile (330°; stimulating): passion consecrated to a spiritual aspiration. Willing to die for philosophic conviction. Behavior sacrifices for beliefs. Self-assertion defers to a rising morality and its ethical principles. Expansion into a new ethical outlook and sense of social reality. This may invite exile or martyrdom. The optimism of surrender to and trust in God.

Mars/Saturn

Will and frustration, obstacle, limit.
Courage and fear. Power and weakness.
Energy and enemy/enmity. Impulse and discipline.

Definition of terms: 'Shadow' refers to one's unconscious inferiority; weakness and fear. 'Dark side' refers to a more conscious malevolence, in self or others.

Conjunction: passion chilled by adversity. This leads to grim resolve or depressed resignation. Will meets fear. Character defined by that encounter.

Behavior adapts to a serious presentation of malice with cruel and cynical 'realism.' Or confronts its negative energy in unremitting struggle. Disciplined effort/courage focused on a hard challenge. Or frozen paralysis by it. Self-assertion merges with the demands of duty and destiny. Or the dark side. Pragmatically works with or on the Shadow.

Waxing semi-sextile (30°; stimulating): passion begins to separate from constricting limitations. Will distances from fear. Behavior rejects unjust rules of the game. Contraction, withdrawal, in the face of adversity in order to redefine strategy. Self-assertion in spite of the demands of duty and destiny. Realistically avoids, sidesteps, power of the dark side, or Shadow.

Waxing sextile (60°; supportive): passion acts pragmatically within accepted limitations. Will effectively negotiates with fear. Or compromises with it by pretending that malice is not so bad after all, that even evil has a good side. Behavior redirects negative energy, as in the martial arts. Impulse contracts into restrained, rationally deployed strength. Self-assertion cooperates with the demands of duty and destiny. Realistically accommodates power of the dark side, or Shadow.

Waxing square (90°; action crisis: danger/opportunity): passion rebels against limitation. Will confronts fear: breaks its bonds or is broken by it. Combative behavior: heroic or cruel. Self-assertion becomes a duty. Fights the dark side, or Shadow. Can adopt its methods and malice. Impulse contracts into hard effective discipline. Or cowardice in the face of an enemy. Realism demands war.

Waxing trine (120°; amplifies, mutual reinforcement): passion strategically integrates its limitations; acts pragmatically to mitigate weakness and deploy strength. Will adroitly adapts to fear, in effective transcendence or smooth appeasement. Behavior flips negative energy over to better use. Or sells out to it for a handsome reward. Self-assertion resonates with the demands of duty and destiny. Impulse contracts into seemingly effortless skill at difficult tasks. Diplomatic realism works with the undeniable power of the dark side, or Shadow.

Waxing quincunx (150°; irritating): passion inhibited by constricting circumstance. Will undermined by ambiguous fears. Behavior varies in the face of adversity. Self-assertion uncertain of duty. Pulls back in confusion. Senses limitations imposed by power of the dark side, or Shadow. Focuses effort on what is possible.

Opposition (180°; challenge and illumination): passion and personal limitation, will and fear, complement and enhance each other in a sublime discipline of focused force. Or violently dissociate in cruel and protracted conflict. A marriage, or battle, of fire and ice. Behavior conditioned by confrontation with a shadow of repression and lies. Character reflects the grim, and heroic, demands of this permanent, unrelenting war. Or it gyrates between extremes of courage and frozen paralysis.

Self-assertion defined by the call of destiny and duty. Contracts strategically, then acts, like the coiling of a snake before it strikes. Or frantically attempts to escape responsibility. Cold-eyed realism or impotent dread in the face of the dark side unveiled.

Waning quincunx (210°; irritating): passion inhibited by a sense of its own inadequacy. Will subverted by unknown fears. Behavior tries to adapt to hidden malice, veiled threat, sinister implication. Self-assertion seeks to understand the demands of duty and destiny. Pragmatically accommodates the dark side, or Shadow. This leads to pessimistic resignation or mobilization of what abilities it can muster in the face of ambiguity.

Waning trine (240°; amplifies, mutual reinforcement): passion pragmatically anticipates limitations and obstacles in formulating an effective strategy. Will leaves old terrors behind and bravely faces, or smoothly sidesteps, emerging fears. Behavior adapts to new rules. Self-assertion redefines destiny and duty. Realistically prepares for the next level of engagement with the dark side, or Shadow.

Waning square (270°; consciousness crisis: danger/opportunity): passion rejects old limitations, faces serious retaliation. Will openly wars with circumstance. Behavior defies fear, bravely or foolishly. Self-assertion denies imposed duty and destiny, finds another strategy. Fight or flight. Grim realism accepts the inevitable pain and loss of brutal confrontation with the dark side, or Shadow.

Waning sextile (300°; supportive): passion cooperates with emerging limitations. Will comprehends and works around rising fears. Behavior recalibrated by new rules. Adopts a more effective strategy. Self-assertion redefines a sense of duty and destiny. Makes realistic plans that acknowledge the dark side, or Shadow.

Waning semi-sextile (330°; stimulating): passion consecrated to a new definition of self and society, warts and all. Will bravely faces, or is overcome by, emerging fears. Self-assertion defers to responsibility. Behavior adapts to selfless duty. Or loses all control. Drops ego and fights to the death against overwhelming malice. Or lies down to die. Abandons realism in favor of sacrifice.

Mars/Uranus

Will and inspiration/insanity. Impulse and originality.
Self-assertion and collective change.

Conjunction: personal passion imprinted by inspiration. Or madness. Will strongly energized by abstract ideas. Behavior is unconventional: either original or simply eccentric. Unusual strategy, based on intuition rather than logic. Activates change. Or revolution.

Waxing semi-sextile (30°; stimulating): personal passion begins to separate from inspiration, or madness. Will learns to detach from abstract ideas. Self-assertion diverges from theoretical insight. Behavior avoids temptations of dangerous eccentricity. Adapts an original vision to real circumstance. Activates incremental change.

Waxing sextile (60°; supportive): personal passion cooperates with, and effectively enacts, inspiration or madness. Will competently executes abstract ideas. Self-assertion guided by a revelation or theoretical insight. Behavior selectively employs originality. Adopts an evolutionary strategy. Activates an appropriate charge of change.

Waxing square (90°; action crisis: danger/opportunity): personal passion breaks free of inspiration, or madness. Will conflicts with abstract ideas. Self-assertion rejects a guiding theoretical insight. Behavior is highly original or outright crazy. Adapts a revolutionary strategy leading to breakthrough. Or breakdown. Activates rebellion, for better or worse.

Waxing trine (120°; amplifies, mutual reinforcement): personal passion takes inspiration, or madness, to the next level. Will smoothly adapts to abstract ideas. Self-assertion stimulated by guiding theoretical insight. Behavior is gracefully original, or amusingly eccentric. Adopts a long-term strategic agenda for change. Activates competent innovation, for a good cause or a bad one.

Waxing quincunx (150°; irritating): personal passion disrupted by inspiration, or madness. Will jolted by sudden strange ideas. Erratic behavior. Adopts a changeable strategy, may not even follow that. Activates a choppy mix of brilliance and zaniness.

Opposition (180°; challenge and illumination): passion and inspiration, will and abstract theory, complement and enhance each other. Or violently dissociate. Behavior informed by genius or madness. May flip-flop between the two. Self-assertion reflects a revelation, brilliant or crazy. Revolutionary change. Or complete anarchy. Activates an innovative alliance between intuition and executive ability. This generates a strategic breakthrough, or explosive disintegration.

Waning quincunx (210°; irritating): personal passion zapped by strange inspirations, or madness. Will disturbed by unusual ideas. Self-assertion irritated by irrelevant theoretical insight. Behavior varies unpredictably, adapts to novelty. Activates surprise.

Waning trine (240°; amplifies, mutual reinforcement): personal passion integrates with an unfolding inspiration or a developing madness. Will smoothly executes abstract ideas. Self-assertion appreciates the stimulus of new theoretical insight. Behavior orients to an emerging reality with different rules. A radical strategy effectively implements a revolutionary agenda. Activates directed change, for good ends or bad.

Waning square (270°; consciousness crisis: danger/opportunity): personal passion rejects an old inspiration, seeks a new one. Will conflicts with abstract ideas. Self-assertion repudiates an outworn theoretical construct. Rebellious behavior, for better or worse. Novel strategy leads to breakthrough. Or breakdown. Activates violent change, good or bad.

Waning sextile (300°; supportive): personal passion cooperates with emerging inspiration. Will effectively executes a futuristic vision, good or bad. Self-assertion cooperates with a rising theoretical model. Behavior consistently plays by new rules. An unconventional strategy. Activates commitment to a change agenda.

Waning semi-sextile (330°; stimulating): personal passion consecrated to an inspiration, or to madness. Will serves an abstract idea, good or bad. Behavior already adapted to a coming new order, may run afoul of established rules. Self-assertion defers to a revelation. Unconventional strategy, perhaps one of 'action by nonaction.' Abandons pointless overt activism for a more subtle revolution of heart and mind.

Mars/Neptune

Will and imagination. Aggression and compassion.

Conjunction: activates spiritual ecstasy or emotional intoxication. Will energizes the collective unconscious, generating psychic empathy or hysterical delusion. Self-assertion sublimates into universal love or blind adoration. Personal purpose inundated by nebulous longings. Ego-drive surrenders to a redemptive ideal or hypnotic codependence. The power of compassion.

Waxing semi-sextile (30°; stimulating): passion begins to separate from a redemptive vision, or illusion. Will learns to detach from empathy. Self-assertion diverges from collective ideals. Personal purpose emerges out of universal compassion. Ego-drive asserts itself in contrast to mystic spirituality. A dream of individuality motivates action.

Waxing sextile (60°; supportive): passion cooperates with a redemptive vision, or illusion. Will competently executes an emphatic agenda, or an indiscriminate enabling. Self-assertion aligns with collective ideals. Personal purpose devotes itself to compassion. Or decays into codependence. Ego drive makes dreams, or nightmares, come true. The power of visualization.

Waxing square (90°; action crisis: danger/opportunity): passion rebels against a redemptive vision, or illusion. Will in conflict with empathy, demands tough love: 'shape up or ship out.' Personal purpose fights against cloying indiscriminate compassion. Ego drive undermined by emotional intoxication. The power of self-assertion versus collective ideals, for better or worse.

Waxing trine (120°; amplifies, mutual reinforcement): passion takes a redemptive vision, or illusion, to the next level. Will smoothly adapts to a spiritual ecstasy or an emotional intoxication. Self-assertion appreciates the stimulus of collective ideals. Personal purpose aligns with a compassionate agenda. Or codependent enabling. Ego drive effectively expresses empathy, to help or to manipulate. The power of charisma.

Waxing quincunx (150°; irritating): passion subverted by an inappropriate redemptive vision or illusion. Will undermined by confusion. Self-assertion questions collective ideals. Personal purpose diluted by nebulous longings. Ego drive must defend itself against nagging demands for unwarranted empathy. The power of a subtle intoxication.

Opposition (180°; challenge and illumination): passion and ideals, will and empathy, complement and enhance each other. Or each simply forgets its counterpart's existence, and sleepwalks in an energized but unconscious trance. Personal purpose exemplifies and enacts a redemptive love. Or drains its strength in battling a delusion. Self-assertion reflects a collective vision. Or fights against it. Ego drive expresses universal compassion. Or loses itself in codependence. Power dissolves into spiritual ecstasy, or decays into blind intoxication.

Waning quincunx (210°; irritating): passion subverted by an indefinable narcosis. Will undermined by nebulous guilt. Self-assertion uncomfortable with irrelevant collective ideals. Personal purpose can't quite get its act together, yet because of this confusion may be forced to develop a deeper emotional subtlety. Ego drive adapts to ambiguity. Activates a shimmering mirage.

Waning trine (240°; amplifies, mutual reinforcement): passion integrates with an emerging redemptive vision, or illusion. Will smoothly adapts to a new ideal, good or bad. Self-assertion stimulated by a rising collective myth. Personal purpose aligns with a compassionate mission. Or a delusional absolution. Ego drive orients to empathetic service. Activates a larger love: extended to all, or reserved for an adored tribe/myth.

Waning square (270°; consciousness crisis: danger/opportunity): passion rejects an old redemptive vision, or illusion. Will wars with indiscriminate compassion or subtle guilt trips. Self-assertion repudiates an outworn collective ideal. Personal purpose fights against immersion in a collective trance. Ego drive asserts itself against a spiritual vision, or intoxication. Breaks free from codependence. Or from empathy.

Waning sextile (300°; supportive): passion cooperates with an emerging redemption, or illusion. Will effectively executes a compassionate vision or a collective delusion. Self-assertion identifies with a rising collective ideal. Personal purpose aligns with demanding empathy. Or smoothly slides into a destructive trance. Ego drive enraptured by a larger love. Or sleepwalks into a spiritual swamp. Powerful longing for a new dawn.

Waning semi-sextile (330°; stimulating): passion consecrated to an emerging ideal, or illusion. Will surrenders to a redemptive vision or hallucination. Self-assertion defers to a collective myth. Personal purpose identifies with a larger love or delusional fantasy. Ego drive sacrificed to empathy or codependence. Martyrdom in spiritual ecstasy or confused intoxication.

Mars/Pluto

Personal and collective will. Conscious passion and hidden purpose. Self-assertion and fate. Extreme transformation.

Conjunction: personal passion activated by collective purpose. Individual will impregnated by God's Will. Or a hypnotic facsimile thereof. Ego drive imprinted by a generational/historic fate. Self-assertion subsumed in identification with its larger karmic or social context. Seeks transformation through intense experiences of death and rebirth.

Waxing semi-sextile (30°; stimulating): personal passion begins to separate from collective purpose. Individual will learns to distance itself from God's Will. Ego drive differentiates itself as apart from a generational/historic fate. Self-assertion emerges out of a karmic or social obsession. Seeks an independent rebirth.

Waxing sextile (60°; supportive): personal passion cooperates with collective purpose. Individual will competently executes God's Will to the best of its understanding and ability. Ego drive sympathetically resonates with a generational/historic fate. Self-assertion reinforced by its karmic or social context. Seeks rebirth as an exemplar or model member of the community.

Waxing square (90°; action crisis: danger/opportunity): personal passion rebels from collective purpose. Individual will breaks free of an obsession with God's Will. Ego drive defies its generational/historic fate, seeks to express its own. Self-assertion struggles against its social context. Seeks rebirth on a new, different and difficult path. This may invite retaliation from the community.

Waxing trine (120°; amplifies, mutual reinforcement): personal passion strategically integrates with collective purpose. Individual will smoothly adapts to God's Will, perhaps too confidently. Ego drive competently executes a generational/historic fate. Self-assertion cooperates with its karmic or social context. Seeks to actively participate in a community rebirth.

Waxing quincunx (150°; irritating): personal passion disturbed by collective purpose. Individual will disrupted by the inscrutable demands of God's Will. Ego drive makes a troubled statement of its role in a generational/historic fate. Self-assertion stymied by its karmic or social context. Seeks clarity of direction.

Opposition (180°; challenge and illumination): personal passion and collective purpose, individual will and God's Will, complement and enhance each other. Or traumatically dissociate in a violent divorce. Ego drive either exemplifies a generational/historic fate or utterly rejects it. Self-assertion reflects its social context by obsessive identification, or conflict, with the community. Seeks transformation through extreme experience, positive or negative.

Waning quincunx (210°; irritating): personal passion silently diverges from an emerging collective purpose. Individual will ill at ease with a new sense of God's Will. Ego drive out of step with the demands of its generational/historic fate. Self-assertion disrupts its karmic or social context. Seeks another direction.

Waning trine (240°; amplifies, mutual reinforcement): personal passion integrates with an emerging collective purpose. Individual will seeks to discover and express God's Will for the future. Ego drive just the right amount ahead of a generational/historic fate: thus it can lead, for better or worse. Self-assertion cooperates with its karmic or social context to advance an unspoken but keenly felt agenda. Seeks rebirth as exemplar of community transformation.

Waning square (270°; consciousness crisis: danger/opportunity): personal passion rejects collective purpose, seeks a new one. Individual will questions the justice of God's Will. Ego drive challenges its generational/historic fate. This can invoke violent punishment. Self-assertion defies its karmic or social context with its own version of a better way. Seeks rebirth through conflict.

Waning sextile (300°; supportive): personal passion cooperates with an emerging collective purpose. Individual will competently executes a new interpretation of God's Will to the best of its ability. Ego drive serves the necessary next stage of its generational/historic context, as its community generally sees it. Self-assertion aligns with its karmic or social fate. Seeks rebirth in a coming new order.

Waning semi-sextile (330°; stimulating): personal passion consecrated to a collective purpose. Individual will surrenders to God's Will. Ego drive sacrifices to or for its generational/historic fate. Self-assertion through voluntary submission to the demands of a karmic or social context. Seeks death, trusts in rebirth.

Jupiter

Aspects of Jupiter magnify and grow any planetary principle it contacts. They elucidate the spiritual quality of its energy. Draw out its larger meaning and significance. An expansive function.

Jupiter/Saturn

Aspiration and limitation. Optimism and pessimism.
Opportunity and destiny.
Expansion and contraction: the heartbeat of soul.
Spirit and reality. Morality and mortality. Righteousness and guilt.
Philosophic/religious worldview and the problem of evil.
God and Devil.

Conjunction: spiritual aspiration meets the dark side. It finds a limit, or liberates repressed potential, on the frontier of shadow's subconscious fear. Self-reflective soul encounters and adapts to cold hard facts. Optimistic hope tempered by pessimistic realism. Expansion balanced by contraction.

These complementary energies merge in a spiritual fusion that imprints individual character with a larger than personal consciousness. This powerful emphasis initiates a concern with collective issues; baptizes one into a social destiny as both opportunity and duty.

The Jupiter/Saturn conjunction recurs every 20 years. It is a fundamental tool in mundane astrology, the study of past history and emerging trends on a national or societal scale. (See 'Synods.')

Waxing semi-sextile (30°; stimulating): spiritual aspiration begins to separate from the dark side, a shadow of repression and unrealized potential. Self-reflective soul learns to distance itself from objective circumstance. A political or religious/philosophical consciousness individualizes from the constriction of impersonal law. A sense of social opportunity emerges from a destiny of duty. Optimism grows away from fear.

Waxing sextile (60°; supportive): spiritual aspiration cooperates with positive potentials of dark side negativity, gives some oxygen to the suffocating shadow. Self-reflective soul expands by accepting objective facts. A political or religious/philosophic consciousness resonates with the realities of impersonal law. A social role increases through adroit performance of assigned duty. Destiny takes advantage of opportunity. Optimism grows by sidestepping fear.

Waxing square (90°; action crisis: danger/opportunity): spiritual aspiration rebels against the dark side, confronts a shadow of repression and unrealized potential. Self-reflective soul breaks free of constricting circumstances, whether internalized restrictions or external obstacles. A political or religious/philosophical consciousness denies existing law and makes new rules. It may become an outlaw. Social opportunity seized in defiance of prescribed duty. A growing sense of destiny finds its own way, wisely or foolishly. The optimism of faith, heroic or doomed, fights fear.

Waxing trine (120°; amplifies, mutual reinforcement): an expansive aspiration partially integrates shadow energies into the light of spiritual awareness. It liberates their latent potentials. Or enables the dark side to express more freely. Self-reflective soul synergistically harmonizes with a larger more objective reality. A political or religious/philosophical consciousness enhanced by the discipline of impersonal law. A social role grows through competent discharge of increasing responsibility. Destiny rides a wave of opportunity. Optimism tames fear.

Waxing quincunx (150°; irritating): spiritual aspiration disturbed by encounter with a shadow of repression and unrealized potential. Self-reflective soul disoriented by dark, incomprehensible facts. A political or religious/philosophical consciousness resents, struggles with, impersonal limitations. Social role constrained by unpredictable blockages, destiny burdened by seemingly unfair duties. Optimism dogged by unknown fears.

Opposition (180°; challenge and illumination): spiritual aspiration and the shadow's inner potential, self-reflective soul and its objective circumstances, complement and enhance each other. Or cancel out in a standoff between faith and fear. A political or religious/philosophical consciousness reflects the facts of impersonal law. Or is divorced from any sense of reality by either ideological inflation or fatalistic resignation. Turns the lead of failure into the gold of success. Or vice versa. Destiny achieved through successful discharge of hard duties. Optimism openly meets the dark side, in mutual liberation or humiliating defeat.

Waning quincunx (210°; irritating): spiritual aspiration tripped up, or strengthened, by ambiguous encounters with the dark side. Self-reflective soul disturbed by implacable facts. A political or religious/philosophical consciousness bedeviled by nagging doubts. Social role disrupted by impersonal limitations. Destiny can't quite seize opportunities. Optimism clouded by caution.

Waning trine (240°; amplifies, mutual reinforcement): spiritual aspiration integrates with an emerging appreciation of the shadow's unrealized potential. Self-reflective soul synergistically harmonizes with an evolving sense of objective possibility. A political or religious/ philosophical consciousness is sharpened and disciplined by acceptance of impersonal law. A social role opens up through competent discharge of reasonable duties. Destiny makes the most of opportunity. Optimism grows past fear, wisely or foolishly.

Waning square (270°; consciousness crisis: danger/opportunity): spiritual aspiration rejects a shadow of outworn repressions and now irrelevant potentials. Self-reflective soul breaks from traditional guidelines of conscience and identity, for better or worse. A political or religious/philosophical consciousness challenges and redefines the rules. This may invoke a more sophisticated realism. Or an ideological denial of plain fact. True social role at odds with assigned duty. Destiny creates its own opportunity without community support. Optimism in spite of fear, bravely or foolishly.

Waning sextile (300°; supportive): spiritual aspiration cooperates with an emerging sense of the shadow's unrealized potential. Self-reflective soul aligns with a changing definition of reality. A political or religious/philosophical consciousness serves a rising new order. Social role accepts current limitations for future opportunity. Duty in service to hope. Optimism pushes ahead into the unknown, despite fear.

Waning semi-sextile (330°; stimulating): spiritual aspiration consecrated to midwifing the birth of shadow's latent potential. Self-reflective soul embraces and surrenders to a larger sense of objective reality. A political or religious/philosophical consciousness overrides self-interest in a victory of optimism over fear, warranted or not. A hidden social role. Secret faith. Or misplaced trust in cynical lies. Sacrifices personal opportunity in service to a higher duty and greater destiny.

Jupiter/Uranus

Evolution and revolution. Conventional wisdom and intuition.
Social participation and inspirational initiative.
Philosophic/religious worldview and transformative revelation.

Conjunction: spiritual aspiration imprinted by an inspiration. Self-reflective soul transformed by a revelation. A political or religious/ philosophical consciousness flips over into something fundamentally new. Social role radically redefined. Optimistic about change and innovation, perhaps too much so.

Waxing semi-sextile (30°; stimulating): spiritual aspiration begins to separate from an inspiration. Self-reflective soul learns to distance itself from the power of ideas. A political or religious/philosophical consciousness reexamines itself from a detached, or alienated, perspective. Social role quietly redefined. Optimistic about managing the dangers of change and innovation.

Waxing sextile (60°; supportive): spiritual aspiration cooperates with an inspiration. Self-reflective soul stimulated by the power of ideas, perhaps naively. A political or religious/philosophical consciousness welcomes reform within an accepted context. Social role redefined through promotion. Optimistic about evolutionary change and innovation.

Waxing square (90°; action crisis: danger/opportunity): spiritual aspiration rebels against an accepted revelation or guiding collective inspiration. Self-reflective soul breaks free from the power of an idea. A political or religious/philosophical consciousness at odds with the reigning paradigm, seeks a new one. Social role suddenly, dramatically changed. Reversal of fortune. Hopes for revolution, whatever the consequences.

Waxing trine (120°; amplifies, mutual reinforcement): spiritual aspiration expansively integrates with an inspiration. Self-reflective soul synergistically harmonizes with novel ideas. A political or religious/philosophical consciousness welcomes sweeping but managed reform. Social role receives major unexpected promotion and opportunity. Optimistic about the benevolent impact of change and innovation.

Waxing quincunx (150°; irritating): spiritual aspiration jolted by implications of a revelation. Self-reflective soul disoriented by strange ideas. A political or religious/philosophical consciousness troubled by difficult questions. Social role unexpectedly shaken up. Resigned to change and innovation.

Opposition (180°; challenge and illumination): spiritual aspiration and its fundamental inspiration, self-reflective soul and abstract ideas, complement and enhance each other. Or split apart in a shocking moment of dissociation. A political or religious/philosophical consciousness blessed by revelation. Or blasted by revolution. Social role understood in a new light. Or utterly changed. Optimistic about a complete transformation, which may prove liberating or disastrous.

Waning quincunx (210°; irritating): spiritual aspiration disrupted by newly understood implications of its fundamental inspiration. Self-reflective soul disturbed by incongruous ideas. A political or religious/

544

philosophic consciousness battered by troubling questions. Social role challenged by a new context. Seesaws between accepting and resisting change.

Waning trine (240°; amplifies, mutual reinforcement): spiritual aspiration integrates with an emerging inspiration. Self-reflective soul empowered by novel ideas. A political or religious/philosophical consciousness synergistically harmonizes with a coming transformation. Social role thrives in a climate of change. Optimistic about the direction of evolution and innovation.

Waning square (270°; consciousness crisis: danger/opportunity): spiritual aspiration rejects an old inspiration, seeks another one. Self-reflective soul embraces a new paradigm, good or bad. A political or religious/philosophical consciousness demands revolution in the name of an emergent theory or revelation. Social role drastically transformed by larger events. Hopes for utopian change and across the board innovation. Takes big risks to accomplish it.

Waning sextile (300°; supportive): spiritual aspiration cooperates with an emerging inspiration. Self-reflective soul reforms itself in terms of a novel idea. A political or religious/philosophical consciousness embraces a coming new order, good or bad. Social role plans and prepares with utopian expectations. Optimistic about the future, perhaps naively so.

Waning semi-sextile (330°; stimulating): spiritual aspiration consecrated to an emerging inspiration. Self-reflective soul selflessly serves an abstract idea. A political or religious/philosophical consciousness already anchored in a new order and at odds with its current environment. Social role sacrifices for or to a coming utopia. Hopes for a complete transformation of self and society.

Jupiter/Neptune

Wisdom and compassion. Consensus truth and dream.
Social role and poetic imagination.
Religious/philosophic worldview and mystical vision.
Growth and dissolution.

Conjunction: spiritual aspiration imprinted with a redemptive ideal. Or illusion. Self-reflective soul informed by an enlarged sense of compassion. Or undermined by confused dreams. An old social role dissolves. Baptism into a new one. Longs for universal love and empathy, can decay into indiscriminate enabling.

Waxing semi-sextile (30°; stimulating): spiritual aspiration begins to separate from a redemptive ideal, or illusion. Self-reflective soul learns to distance itself from an imaginative vision. A political or religious/philosophical consciousness reexamines its criteria of empathy. Seeks a new social expression of compassion. Hopes for a gentle growth of universal love.

Waxing sextile (60°; supportive): spiritual aspiration cooperates with a redemptive ideal, or illusion. Self-reflective soul stimulated by an imaginative vision, good or bad. A political or religious/philosophical consciousness welcomes an expanded sense of empathy within an accepted context. Social role becomes more charitable. Hopes for evolutionary growth in the scope and depth of universal love.

Waxing square (90°; action crisis: danger/opportunity): spiritual aspiration rebels against a redemptive ideal, or false idol. Self-reflective soul breaks free of an imaginative vision, or illusion. A political or religious/philosophical consciousness at odds with collective myth. Social role undermined by self-sabotage or betrayal from others. Hopes for a mystical revelation, can get confused hysteria.

Waxing trine (120°; amplifies, mutual reinforcement): spiritual aspiration integrates with a redemptive ideal, or illusion. Self-reflective soul synergistically harmonizes with an imaginative vision. A political or religious/philosophical consciousness grows into an enlarged sense of compassion. Social role glamorized as an expression of collective dreams. Hopes for the power of myth and magic to make things better, with surprising success.

Waxing quincunx (150°; irritating): spiritual aspiration subverted by ambiguous implications of a redemptive ideal, or illusion. Self-reflective soul disoriented by a confused vision. A political or religious/philosophical consciousness troubled by intoxicating fantasies. Social role undermined by unrealistic dreams. Resigned to occasional waves of chaos.

Opposition (180°; challenge and illumination) spiritual aspiration and a redemptive ideal, self-reflective soul and an imaginative vision, complement and enhance each other. Or dissolve in a chaotic maelstrom. A political or religious/philosophical consciousness enlarged by compassion. Or intoxicated by illusion. Social role reflects a collective myth, embodies a universal ideal. Or decays into a hyped up fantasy. Hopes for magical revelation, may find it. Or complete confusion.

Waning quincunx (210°; irritating) spiritual aspiration disrupted by the implications of a new redemptive ideal, or illusion. Self-reflective soul disturbed by confusing dreams for the future. A political or religious/philosophical consciousness undermined by an impractical lack of focus. Social role subverted by deception from within or without. Accepts and resists a need for greater compassion. An ambiguous response to demands for empathy.

Waning trine (240°; amplifies, mutual reinforcement): spiritual aspiration integrates with an emerging redemptive ideal, or illusion. Self-reflective soul synergistically harmonizes with a rising imaginative vision. A political or religious/philosophical consciousness smoothly adapts to the decay or dissolution of an old myth. Social role thrives in chaos. Hopes for a kinder, gentler world, and tries to encourage it.

Waning square (270°; consciousness crisis: danger/opportunity): spiritual aspiration rejects an old redemptive ideal, or illusion. Seeks a new one. Self-reflective soul breaks away from the charisma, or hypnosis, of conventional wisdom. It embraces an imaginative vision, good or bad. A political or religious/philosophical consciousness turns to a mythic collective dream. Or intoxication. Social role dissolved in the chaos of larger events. Hopes for magic, may find madness.

Waning sextile (300°; supportive): spiritual aspiration cooperates with an emerging redemptive ideal, or illusion. Self-reflective soul adapts to, reshapes itself by, a vague but compelling imaginative vision. A political or religious/philosophical consciousness embraces an enlarged, or inflated, sense of identity. Socially disengages, inhabits a coming dream. Hopes for a brave new world.

Waning semi-sextile (330°; stimulating): spiritual aspiration consecrated to a redemptive ideal, or illusion. Self-reflective soul selflessly serves an imaginative vision, good or bad. A political or religious/philosophical consciousness already anchored in a new mystical community and at odds with its current environment. Social role embraces sacrifice in the name of compassion. Hopes for universal love, may find hypnotic exploitation.

Jupiter/Pluto

Conventional wisdom and unconscious necessity.
Religious/philosophic worldview and demands of destiny.
Social role and transformation.
Growth and death. Heaven and Hell.

Conjunction: personal spiritual aspiration imprinted by collective purpose. Self-reflective soul impregnated by hidden passions of the deep unconscious, demands of a larger Will. A political or religious/philosophical consciousness transformed by its generational ethos and historic context. Social role fused with an obsessive need for power. Hopes for rebirth.

Waxing semi-sextile (30°; stimulating): personal spiritual aspiration begins to separate from a collective purpose. Self-reflective soul learns to distance itself from hidden passions of the deep unconscious, demands of a larger Will. A political or religious/philosophical consciousness reexamines its participation in a generational ethos and historic context. Social role redefined away from community standards, individualizes. Hopes for increments in power.

Waxing sextile (60°; supportive): personal spiritual aspiration cooperates with collective purpose. Self-reflective soul stimulated by hidden passion of the deep unconscious, demands of a larger Will. A political or religious/philosophical consciousness gradually reforms its sense of participation in a generational ethos and historic context. Social role redefined by patronage and promotion. Hopes for the next level of power.

Waxing square (90°; action crisis: danger/opportunity): personal spiritual aspiration rebels against collective purpose. Self-reflective soul breaks free from hidden passions of the deep unconscious, demands of a larger Will. A political or religious/philosophical consciousness at odds with its generational ethos and historic context. Social role redefined by drastic transformation. Hopes to profit from community crises, wisely or maliciously. May be destroyed instead.

Waxing trine (120°; amplifies, mutual reinforcement): personal spiritual aspiration integrated with collective purpose. Self-reflective soul synergistically harmonizes with hidden passions of the deep unconscious, demands of a larger Will. A political or religious/philosophical consciousness adroitly conforms to its generational ethos and historic context. Social role enhanced by, gains through, community upheaval, for good ends or bad. Profits by riding an inevitable wave of fate.

Waxing quincunx (150°; irritating): personal spiritual aspiration disturbed by implications of the collective purpose in which it is embedded. Self-reflective soul troubled by hidden passions of the deep unconscious, demands of a larger Will. A political or religious/philosophical consciousness questions its generational ethos and historic context. Social role redefined by unpredictable acts of God. Makes the best of inevitable fate.

Opposition (180°; challenge and illumination): personal spiritual aspiration and collective purpose, self-reflective soul and hidden passions of the deep unconscious, complement and enhance each other. Or one's fortune and standing destroyed by impersonal forces, for better or worse. A political or religious/philosophical consciousness blessed by an affirmative eruption in its historic context. Or cursed by an upheaval that denies it. Social role completely transformed, up or down. Exemplifies a generational fate. Powerfully reflects or resists a larger Will.

Waning quincunx (210°; irritating): personal spiritual aspiration disrupted by newly sensed implications of a collective purpose in which it participates. Self-reflective soul disturbed by rising passions of the deep unconscious, demands of a larger Will. A political or religious/philosophical consciousness uncomfortable with its generational ethos and historic context. Social role challenged by emerging community needs. Wavers between accepting and resisting fate.

Waning trine (240°; amplifies, mutual reinforcement): personal spiritual aspiration integrates with an emerging collective purpose. Self-reflective soul synergistically harmonizes with rising passions of the deep unconscious, demands of a larger Will. A political or religious/philosophical consciousness smoothly adapts to a changing generational ethos and historic context. Social role rides a wave of transformation. Hopes to profit from fate.

Waning square (270°; consciousness crisis: danger/opportunity): personal spiritual aspiration rejects a dying collective purpose, seeks another one. Self-reflective soul burns old bridges, pivots towards rising passions of the deep unconscious, demands of a larger Will. A political or religious/philosophical consciousness transformed by its the impersonal forces of its generational ethos and historic context. Social role drastically redefined by changing expectations and new standards. Hopes to profit from destruction of an old order.

Waning sextile (300°; supportive): personal spiritual aspiration cooperates with an emerging collective purpose. Self-reflective soul reforms itself through a new perspective on hidden passions of the deep unconscious, demands of a larger Will. A political or religious/philosophical consciousness embraces a transformed generational ethos and historic context. Social role enhanced by successful anticipation of inevitable change. Hopes to join the vanguard; to serve in the first wave of a coming order.

Waning semi-sextile (330°; stimulating): personal spiritual aspiration consecrated to an emerging collective purpose. Self-reflective soul selflessly serves rising passions of the deep unconscious, demands of a larger Will. A political or religious/philosophical consciousness already transformed by a new generational ethos and at odds with its historic context. Social role sacrificed for or to an inevitable upheaval. Hopes for death and rebirth, of both self and community.

Saturn

Aspects of Saturn inhibit, limit, frustrate any planetary principle it contacts. This forces that energy to address its weakness. Draws out the dark undeveloped side for hard corrective labor. A contracting function.

Saturn/Uranus

Order and revolution. Discipline and freedom/anarchy.
Structured process and transformational change.
Sequential logic and revelatory inspiration.
Fear and transcendence: breakthrough or breakdown.

Definition of terms:

Formative archetype: an ideal model with one pole anchored in a concrete identity (Saturn) and the other channeling an inspired intuition of what it could be (Uranus). The Platonic Form, or essential idea, behind a manifestation: for example, the soul's astrological blueprint of a personality, which is then filled in and modified by real experience.

Evolution: a phased developmental unfolding (Saturn) punctuated by transformative experiences (Uranus). In this section, describing the relationship between continuity (Saturn) and change (Uranus): evolution stimulated, or shattered, by revolution. An identity remade by a revelation - perhaps of its formative archetype. A historically conditioned character (Saturn) motivated by, and drawn to, its ultimate design or inspired purpose (Uranus).

Shadow (Saturn): refers to one's unconscious inferiority; weakness and fear. In this context, a boundary or frontier one cannot or dares not cross.

Conjunction: identity-definition, a sense of personal integrity, imprinted with a guiding inspiration. Self-discipline oriented by an abstract idea. Grounds and structures a revelation, good or bad. A formative archetype slowly takes shape through step-by-step evolution. An old fear transcended. A new Shadow, an anti-revelation, arises to take its place.

Waxing semi-sextile (30°; stimulating): identity-definition, a sense of personal integrity, begins to separate from an inspiration and follow its own logic. Self-discipline learns to operate independently from the guidance of an abstract idea. Theory emerges into practice. Evolution oriented by precedent, the momentum of a new dispensation. A formative archetype assumes an individual character. Fear sets the limits of change as a new Shadow emerges at the edge of consciousness.

Waxing sextile (60°; supportive): identity-definition, a sense of personal integrity, guided by an inspiration. Self-discipline stimulated by abstract ideas. Theory aligns with practical application. Evolution follows a logical sequence. A formative archetype begins to take ordered structure. Fears deviation from a now committed to plan as a Shadow coalesces just beyond its parameters.

Waxing square (90°; action crisis: danger/opportunity): identity-definition, a sense of personal integrity, rebels from a guiding inspiration. Self-discipline breaks free of an abstract idea, follows its own pragmatic agenda. Actual cases diverge from theory. Evolution meets unexpected obstacles. A formative archetype must adapt and conform to constraints of reality. Fear encounters a darker scarier understanding of the Shadow. This focuses an individual statement of duty/destiny. Or shatters resolve in the face of overwhelming change.

Waxing trine (120°; amplifies, mutual reinforcement): identity-definition, a sense of personal integrity, integrates with a guiding inspiration. Self-discipline synergistically harmonizes with an abstract idea. Actual cases illustrate theoretical truth. Evolution flows in an orderly and purposeful direction. A formative archetype is brought to life, made real in practice. Pragmatic management of fear and the Shadow.

Waxing quincunx (150°; irritating): identity-definition, a sense of personal integrity, at odds with its guiding inspiration. Self-discipline is too individualized to comply with an abstract idea. Theory challenged, but not overthrown, by irritating facts. Evolution interrupted; proceeds in fits and starts. A formative archetype must compromise with strange, not completely understood realities. Changing fears linked to erratic signals from the Shadow.

Opposition (180°; challenge and illumination): identity-definition and its guiding inspiration complement and enhance each other. A sense of personal integrity pragmatically expresses abstract ideas of perfection. Or self-discipline shatters in brittle incompatibility with too high a voltage of change. Theory and practice mutually inform and reinforce a Big Picture. Or dissociate into warring fragments of truth. Punctuated or punctured evolution. A formative archetype gives larger meaning to raw facts. Or fear twists them into a shriveled caricature of the Shadow.

Waning quincunx (210°; irritating): identity-definition, a sense of personal integrity, disrupted by inconsistencies of a guiding inspiration. Self-discipline at odds with the implications of an abstract idea. Theory cannot fully justify reality, gropes for a higher synthesis. Evolution takes unexpected twists and turns. A formative archetype meets inconvenient facts. Fears uncertainty, unpredictable change.

Waning trine (240°; amplifies, mutual reinforcement): identity-definition, a sense of personal integrity, integrates with an emerging inspiration. Self-discipline synergistically harmonizes with rising abstract ideas. Theory enriched by new facts. And facts made meaningful by theory. Evolution flows in a purposeful direction. A formative archetype deepened by practical experience. An innovative approach to managing the Shadow and dealing with fear.

Waning square (270°; consciousness crisis: danger/opportunity): identity-definition, a sense of personal integrity, rejects the guidance of an old inspiration, seeks another one. Self-discipline breaks away from obsolete or irrelevant requirements of an abstract idea. A crying need for a new theory to explain undeniable facts. Evolution by revolution, creative or disruptive. A formative archetype must adjust to an incompatible reality. Changing fears based on a revelatory encounter with the Shadow. This galvanizes intuition. Or shatters structure and logic.

Waning sextile (300°; supportive): identity-definition, a sense of personal integrity, cooperates with an emerging inspiration. Self-discipline guided by a new abstract idea. Theory effectively accommodates a growing diversity of facts. A formative archetype entices evolution forward. Changing fears as one encounters the novelty of Shadow energies attached to a rising vision.

Waning semi-sextile (330°; stimulating): identity-definition, a sense of personal integrity, consecrated to an emerging inspiration. Self-discipline serves the requirements of a rising abstract idea. Theory determines the interpretation of facts more strongly than usual, rather than letting them speak for themselves. Archetypal principle outranks actual perception. Fears adapt to the Shadow of a changed reality.

Evolution surrenders to a new standard. Think of fish stranded out of water on tidal flats. Over time they adapted to breathing air rather than upgrading their existing capabilities. Thus life emerged from relative perfection in the sea to a clumsy new beginning on land.

Saturn/Neptune

Order and chaos. Form and dissolution.
Reality and imagination. Fear and compassion.

Conjunction: identity-definition, a sense of personal integrity, imprinted with a redemptive ideal. Self-discipline oriented by an imaginative vision. Individual character subsumed by a collective myth. A dream becomes a destiny. A longing for universal love merges with the hard facts of life as practical compassion. Or dissolves all realism in a hallucinatory trance. Fears a Shadow of chaos.

Waxing semi-sextile (30°; stimulating): identity-definition, a sense of personal integrity, begins to separate from a redemptive ideal. Self-discipline learns to operate on its own terms, independently of an imaginative vision. Collective participation takes on an individual character. A coherent dream emerges from nebulous yearning. Compassion oriented by realistic limits. Fears the return of past chaos, builds a firewall against old nightmares.

Waxing sextile (60°; supportive): identity-definition, a sense of personal integrity, shaped by a redemptive ideal. Self-discipline stimulated by an imaginative vision. Effective participation in a collective myth. Dreams practically expressed in real life. Compassion adapts to circumstance. Fear mellowed by a poetic appreciation of limits.

Waxing square (90°; action crisis: danger/opportunity): identity-definition, a sense of personal integrity, rebels from a redemptive ideal. Self-discipline breaks free of an imaginative vision, follows its own more pragmatic agenda. Collective participation guided by practical necessities. Dreams constrained and channeled, or crushed, by reality. Stern law challenges compassionate caring, or codependent enabling. Fears chaos, works hard to contain it. Or sinks into it.

Waxing trine (120°; amplifies, mutual reinforcement): identity-definition, a sense of personal integrity, integrates with a redemptive ideal. Self-discipline smoothly enables an imaginative vision. Collective participation flows in an orderly and purposeful direction. Dreams redefine reality. Compassion made effective by regular rules. Fear softened by feelings of mystic beauty.

Waxing quincunx (150°; irritating): identity-definition, a sense of personal integrity, is incompatible with a redemptive ideal. Self-discipline pragmatically sidesteps an imaginative vision. Collective participation must deal with hard realities of selfishness. Dreams disrupted by facts. Compassion challenged by irritating necessities. Ambiguous fears.

Opposition (180°; challenge and illumination): identity-definition and a redemptive ideal complement each other. A sense of personal integrity enhanced by an imaginative vision. And a vision grounded by self-discipline. Otherwise realism crushes imagination (Saturn) or dissolves in chaos (Neptune). Dreams enrich the meaning of facts. Or twist them into illusions. Compassion reinforces law. Or undermines it. Collective participation channeled by pragmatic rules. Or suppressed by intoxicated Fear, the Shadow of a collective or mythic nightmare.

Waning quincunx (210°; irritating): identity-definition, a sense of personal integrity, disrupted by inconsistencies of a redemptive ideal. Self-discipline at odds with emerging implications of an imaginative vision. Collective participation inhibited by irritating realities. Dreams meet inconvenient facts. Compassion somewhat incompatible with justice. Ambiguous fears of the future.

Waning trine (240°; amplifies, mutual reinforcement): identity-definition, personal integrity, integrates with an emerging redemptive ideal. Self-discipline synergistically harmonizes with an imaginative vision of the future. Collective participation effectively enabled by sophisticated pragmatism. Dreams enriched by actual experience. And vice versa. Compassion gives new depth to a sense of reality. Fears diminished by the beauty of a rising myth.

Waning square (270°; consciousness crisis: danger/opportunity): identity-definition, a sense of personal integrity, rejects the guidance of an old redemptive ideal, seeks another one. Self-discipline breaks away from fantasies, or inappropriate imagination. Orderly structure and rule of law contend with chaos. Dreams face incompatible reality. Compassion gives way to hard, undeniable facts. Fears the Shadow of a rising collective myth.

Waning sextile (300°; supportive): identity-definition, a sense of personal integrity, cooperates with an emerging redemptive ideal. Self-discipline conforms to an imaginative vision. Effective participation in a rising collective myth. Dreams enhance a new sense of reality. Compassion informs law. Fears the deluge that will be unleashed by meltdown of old standards.

Waning semi-sextile (330°; stimulating): identity-definition, a sense of personal integrity, consecrated to a redemptive ideal. Self-discipline serves an imaginative vision. A rising collective myth adopts new standards of behavior, for better or worse. Dreams of possibility outrank perceptions of existing reality. Practicality surrenders to compassion. Fear dissolves into mystic ecstasy. Or a shapeless nightmare.

Saturn/Pluto

Order and transformative imperative.
Personally chosen and socially determined destiny.
Fear and fate.

Conjunction: identity-definition, a sense of personal integrity, imprinted with collective purpose. Self-discipline oriented by hidden passions of the deep unconscious, demands of a larger Will. The structure of consciousness expresses a generational ethos, reflects its historic context, more strongly than usual. A sense of duty redefined by community necessity. Individual destiny resonates with group fate.

A representative of one's time; can exemplify a karmic/collective wound or darkness:

'The wound is the place where the Light enters you.'

Rumi, 1207-1273, Persian poet and Sufi mystic

Waxing semi-sextile (30°; stimulating): identity-definition, a sense of personal integrity, begins to separate from collective purpose. Self-discipline learns to operate independently from hidden passions of the deep unconscious, demands of a larger Will. The structure of consciousness emerges out of a generational ethos and historic context. A sense of individual duty gains space within community necessity. Achieves a detached perspective on the social mores and concerns of its time. One's own destiny flows parallel to, but not with, a group fate.

Waxing sextile (60°; supportive): identity-definition, a sense of personal integrity, positively shaped by collective purpose. Self-discipline stimulated by hidden passions of the deep conscious, demands of a larger Will. The structure of consciousness cooperates with its generational ethos and historic context. A sense of duty aligns with community necessity. Gives voice to the social mores and concerns of its time. Individual destiny flows in tandem with group fate.

Waxing square (90°; action crisis: danger/opportunity): identity-definition, a sense of personal integrity, rebels from collective purpose. Self-discipline breaks free from hidden passions of the deep unconscious, demands of a larger Will. The structure of consciousness diverges from its generational ethos and historic context. A sense of duty fights against claims of community necessity. Defines itself in sharp contrast to the social mores and concerns of its time. Individual destiny flows away, emigrates, from a group fate.

Waxing trine (120°; amplifies, mutual reinforcement): identity-definition, a sense of personal integrity, integrates with collective purpose. Self-discipline synergistically harmonizes with hidden passions of the deep unconscious, demands of a larger Will. The structure of consciousness successfully embodies and illustrates its generational ethos and historic context, for better or worse. A sense of duty endorses and effectively serves community necessity. Aligns with the social mores and concerns of its time. Individual destiny goes with the flow of a group fate.

Waxing quincunx (150°; irritating): identity-definition, a sense of personal integrity, at odds with collective purpose. Self-discipline is too individualized to comply with hidden passions of the deep unconscious, demands of a larger Will. The structure of consciousness uneasy with its generational ethos and historic context. A sense of duty at odds with claims of community necessity. Questions social mores and concerns of its time. Individual destiny grates against the flow of group fate.

Opposition (180°; challenge and illumination): identity-definition and collective purpose complement each other. Personal integrity and hidden passions of the deep unconscious polarize and express a karmic issue that has come to term. Otherwise they jointly impede a larger destiny for self-serving ends (Saturn), or block personal development by obsessive paranoia (Pluto). Self-discipline, a sense of duty, dedicated to community needs. Or it refuses to conform, out of principle or selfishness. Exemplifies its generational ethos, the social mores and concerns of its time. Or acts in total opposition to its historic context, prophetically or treasonously. Individual fate faithfully reflects, or bitterly rejects, tribal demands.

Waning quincunx (210°; irritating): identity-definition, a sense of personal integrity, disrupted by inconsistencies of collective purpose. Self-discipline at odds with the implications of hidden passion from the deep unconscious, demands of a larger Will. The structure of consciousness disturbed by emerging implications of its generational ethos and historic context. A sense of duty works out apart from community needs; cannot relate to the social mores and concerns of its time. Individual destiny out of step with group fate, can be rudely reminded of that fact.

Waning trine (240°; amplifies, mutual reinforcement): identity-definition, a sense of personal integrity, integrates with an emerging collective purpose. Self-discipline synergistically harmonizes with new dimensions of hidden passion from the deep unconscious, demands of a larger Will. The structure of consciousness competently embodies or indicates a coming generational ethos, the next phase of its historic context. Performance of duty as a model for the community. Rational character is just ahead of the social mores and concerns of its time. Thus it can lead, for better or worse. Individual destiny pioneers development of a group fate, along good lines, or bad.

Waning square (270°; consciousness crisis: danger/opportunity): identity-definition, a sense of personal integrity, rejects an old collective purpose. Embarks on a hard pilgrimage to find another one. Self-discipline breaks away from obsolete passions of the deep unconscious, irrelevant demands of a larger Will. The structure of consciousness rejects a dying generational ethos, seeks a new historic context or meaning. A sense of duty walks away from community requirements. Or is crushed by them. Character defined in contrast to the social mores and concerns of its time. Individual destiny swims upstream against a group fate, heroically or in futility.

556

Waning sextile (300°; supportive): identity-definition, a sense of personal integrity, cooperates with an emerging collective purpose. Self-discipline conforms to new dimensions of passion from the deep unconscious, demands of a larger Will. The structure of consciousness encourages a new generational ethos and historic context. A sense of duty aligns with emerging community needs. Exemplifies the next step in social mores and concerns of its time, for better or worse. Individual destiny follows a group fate.

Waning semi-sextile (330°; stimulating): identity-definition, a sense of personal integrity, consecrated to an emerging collective purpose. Self-discipline serves rising passions from the deep unconscious, demands of a larger Will. The structure of consciousness is already anchored in a future ethos and at odds with its current context. A sense of duty sacrifices to community needs. Ahead of the social mores and concerns of its time, can be exiled or punished for that. Individual destiny pioneers a rebirth of group fate, for better or worse.

Aspects Between Uranus, Neptune and Pluto

The trans-Saturnian planets (Uranus, Neptune, Pluto) refer to transcendent potentials rather than specific manifest qualities. Aspects between them indicate subterranean forces behind our conscious awareness; an alignment of deep unconscious energies coming to a cathartic crisis. Think of a city leveled by two tectonic plates slipping along a buried fault line, or a magma plume volcanically erupting from miles below the tranquil surface. These alignments disrupt known psychosocial reality with unexpected and alien forces. They may fertilize/create or traumatize/destroy. They are novel emergences/emergencies: Acts of God, which do not proceed from what came before. Aspects between trans-Saturnian planets in a chart indicate an encounter with larger social and cosmic forces that are independent of one's personal identity.

These outer planet aspects unfold over multigenerational stretches of time. Thus the Uranus/Neptune conjunction, and every subsequent aspect in sequence, occurs every 172 years; Uranus/Pluto occurs every 127 years; Neptune/Pluto occurs every 492 years. Obviously any individual can experience only a small fraction of these aspects, or even know anyone who did. To take the most extreme example, a long waxing sextile of Neptune to Pluto is in place from 1945-2035. (Because of Pluto's eccentric orbit it moves at about the same speed of normally faster Neptune for decades.) No one born for almost a century will ever experience anything other than this sextile and perhaps its succeeding square.

Why then describe these other aspects? Because they provide clues to the psychological makeup of generations born during other historical periods. Outer planet aspects are one of the most valuable tools for astrological studies of history, or of national evolution. These psychological descriptions are meant to suggest the unconscious atmosphere underlying collective social and historical manifestations of outer planet aspects.

The historic meaning of long term cycles between the two social planets, Jupiter and Saturn; between these two and the transcendental planets of the collective unconscious (Uranus, Neptune, Pluto) and between the transcendental planets themselves are discussed in the next chapter, 'Synods.'

Uranus

Aspects of Uranus awaken the mystic dreaminess of Neptune or excite the hidden power of Pluto. Draws out their latent potential to transform or disintegrate. A revolutionary function.

Uranus/Neptune

Uranus and Neptune are almost identical in size and composition. They polarize the same transcendental energy. Uranus, spinning at a right angle to Neptune, channels Neptunian dreams into consciousness. It articulates Neptune's imaginative atmosphere into conceptual thought forms. Uranus focuses the Neptunian magnetic force field into an electric current, an inspirational voltage that stimulates or shocks material reality. See diagram in 'Uranus'.

Conjunction: abstract ideas imprinted and oriented by a redemptive ideal, or illusion. Mental inspiration impregnated by an imaginative vision, or intoxicating hallucination. Clarity merges with charity. Unconscious fusion of detached insight with poetic sensibility. Fertilization of objective intuition by felt compassion.

Waxing semi-sextile (30°; stimulating): abstract ideas begin to separate out from a redemptive ideal, or illusion. Mental inspiration learns to distance itself from imaginative vision, or an intoxicating hallucination. The unconscious equation tips away from charity to clarity, poetic sensibility to detached insight, felt compassion to cerebral intuition.

Waxing sextile (60°; supportive): abstract ideas support a redemptive ideal, or illusion. Mental inspiration aligns with an imaginative vision, or intoxicating hallucination. Unconscious cooperation between charity and clarity, poetic sensibility and detached insight, felt compassion and cerebral intuition.

Waxing square (90°; action crisis: danger/opportunity): abstract ideas rebel against a redemptive ideal, or illusion. Mental inspiration breaks free of an imaginative vision, or intoxicating hallucination. A combative discontinuity between charity and clarity, poetic sensibility and detached insight, felt compassion and cerebral intuition.

Waxing trine (120°; amplifies, mutual reinforcement): abstract ideas integrate with a redemptive ideal, or illusion. Mental inspiration synergistically harmonizes with an imaginative vision, or intoxicating hallucination. A shared resonance of charity and clarity, poetic sensibility and detached insight, felt compassion and cerebral intuition.

Waxing quincunx (150°; irritating): abstract ideas disturbed by a redemptive ideal, or illusion. Mental inspiration made ambiguous by an imaginative vision, or intoxicating hallucination. Tension between charity and clarity, poetic sensibility and detached insight, felt compassion and cerebral intuition.

Opposition (180°; challenge and illumination): abstract ideas and redemptive ideals, mental inspiration and imaginative vision, complement and enhance each other. Or mutually cancel out in the unconscious depths, leaving only a roiling sense of turbulence. Charity and clarity are a loving couple. Or bitter foes. Poetic sensibility expressed or denied by detached insight. Felt compassion reflected, or sharply mocked, by cerebral intuition.

Waning quincunx (210°; irritating): abstract ideas disrupted by cloudy implications of redemptive ideals, or illusions. Mental inspiration confused by imaginative vision, or intoxicating hallucination. Poetic sensibility and detached insight, felt compassion and cerebral intuition, at odds. Charity and clarity stumble over each other.

Waning trine (240°; amplifies, mutual reinforcement): abstract ideas integrate with an emerging redemptive ideal, or illusion. Mental inspiration synergistically harmonizes with a novel imaginative vision, or intoxicating hallucination. Clarity enables charity, poetic sensibility enriches detached insight, felt compassion deepens cerebral intuition.

Waning square (270°; consciousness crisis: danger/opportunity): abstract ideas reject an outworn redemptive ideal, or illusion. Mental inspiration breaks away from a decaying vision, or intoxicating hallucination. Clarity redefines charity. Insight sharpens sensitivity, or coldly mocks it. Cerebral intuition gives a new direction to compassion, or dissociates from feeling.

Waning sextile (300°; supportive): abstract ideas enable a rising redemptive ideal, or illusion. Mental inspiration competently cooperates with an emerging vision, or intoxicated hallucination. Clarity and charity productively align. Poetic sensibility and detached insight, felt compassion and cerebral intuition, share and serve a dream of the future.

Waning semi-sextile (330°; stimulating): abstract ideas consecrated to a coming redemption, or illusion. Mental inspiration sanctified by an emerging ideal, or distorted by hallucination. Clarity sacrificed to charity. Detached insight tips towards poetic sensitivity. Cerebral intuition serves a growing, or devouring, compassion.

Uranus/Pluto

Uranus provides a revolutionary expression of Pluto's karmic or collective passion. Uranus articulates a utopian/dystopian vision powered by Pluto's hidden necessity.

Conjunction: abstract idea imprinted by collective purpose, or hypnosis. Mental inspiration impregnated by hidden passions of the deep unconscious, or demands of a larger Will. Objective insight awakens and expresses subjective obsession. Fusion of detached clarity with fateful necessity, individual intuition and group power.

Waxing semi-sextile (30°; stimulating): abstract ideas begin to separate from collective purpose, or hypnosis. Mental inspiration learns to distance itself from hidden passions of the deep unconscious, demands of a larger Will. Objective insight detaches from subjective obsession. Power intuitively tips away from fateful necessity towards individual clarity.

Waxing sextile (60°; supportive): abstract ideas cooperate with collective purpose, or hypnosis. Mental inspiration aligns with hidden passions of the deep unconscious, demands of a larger Will. Positive resonance between objective insight and subjective obsession, detached clarity and fateful necessity, individual intuition and group power.

Waxing square (90°; action crisis: danger/opportunity): abstract ideas rebel against collective purpose or hypnosis. Mental inspiration breaks free of hidden passions of the deep unconscious, demands of a larger Will. A sharp discontinuity between objective insight and subjective obsession, detached clarity and fateful necessity, individual intuition and group power.

Waxing trine (120°; amplifies, mutual reinforcement): abstract ideas integrate with collective purpose, or hypnosis. Mental inspiration smoothly adapts to hidden passions of the deep unconscious, demands of a larger Will. Synergistic harmony of objective insight and subjective obsession, detached clarity and fateful necessity, individual intuition and group power.

Waxing quincunx (150°; irritating): abstract ideas disturbed by collective purpose, or hypnosis. Mental inspiration ambiguous towards hidden passions of the deep unconscious, demands of a larger Will. Tension between objective insight and subjective obsession, detached clarity and fateful necessity, individual intuition and group power.

Opposition (180°; challenge and illumination): abstract ideas and collective purpose, mental inspiration and demands of a larger Will, complement and enhance each other. Or violently confront in the unconscious depths, generating an earthquake in consciousness. Objective insight and subjective obsession are a loving couple. Or vicious foes. Detached clarity expresses or denies fateful necessity. Individual intuition reflects, or mocks, group power.

Waning quincunx (210°; irritating): abstract ideas disrupted by implications of collective purpose, or hypnosis. Mental inspiration confused by hidden passions of the deep unconscious, demands of a larger Will. Objective insight and subjective obsession stumble over each other. Detached clarity and fateful necessity, individual intuition and group power, at odds.

Waning trine (240°; amplifies, mutual reinforcement): abstract ideas integrate with an emerging collective purpose, or hypnosis. Mental inspiration synergistically harmonizes with a new interpretation of hidden passions from the deep unconscious, demands of a larger Will. Objective insight enables subjective obsession. Detached clarity brings fateful necessity to light. Individual intuition ahead of group power, can be rewarded for that.

Waning square (270°; consciousness crisis: danger/opportunity): abstract ideas reject an outworn collective purpose, or hypnosis. Mental inspiration breaks away from hidden passions of the deep unconscious, or demands of a larger Will. Objective insight denies subjective obsession. Detached clarity sharpens definition of fateful necessity, or coldly mocks it. Individual intuition ahead of group power, can be punished for that.

Waning sextile (300°; supportive): abstract ideas cooperate with an emerging collective purpose, or hypnosis. Mental inspiration competently serves a new interpretation of hidden passions of the deep unconscious, demands of a larger Will. Objective insight aligns with subjective obsession. Detached clarity of individual intuition concerning the direction of fateful necessity and group power.

Waning semi-sextile (330°; stimulating): abstract ideas consecrated to a rising collective purpose, or hypnosis. Mental inspiration sanctified by emerging passions of the deep unconscious or demands of a larger Will. Objective insight clarifies a fateful destiny. Individual intuition accepts the need of sacrifice to or for group power.

Neptune/Pluto

Neptune only aspects Pluto's hidden power, presenting its fateful necessity through a mystic vision or spiritual delusion. Neptune embodies the redemptive dream or toxic illusion generated by Pluto's primeval purpose.

Conjunction: redemptive ideal imprinted by collective purpose. Or an illusion energized by hypnotic power. An imaginative vision impregnated by hidden passions of the deep unconscious, demands of a larger Will. Or an intoxicating hallucination fused with a lemming-like liebestodt (German: love of death). An obsessive rapture of compassion. Or narcosis of the depths.

Waxing semi-sextile (30°; stimulating): a redemptive ideal begins to separate from collective purpose, or hypnosis. An imaginative vision distances itself from hidden passions of the deep unconscious, demands of a larger Will. Dreams tip away from karma; fateful necessity moves towards compassion.

Waxing sextile (60°; supportive): a redemptive ideal cooperates with collective purpose, or hypnosis. An imaginative vision serves hidden passions of the deep unconscious, demands of a larger Will. Compassion positively resonates with karma or fateful necessity.

Waxing square (90°; action crisis: danger/opportunity): a redemptive ideal rebels from collective purpose, or hypnosis. An imaginative vision breaks free of hidden passions of the deep unconscious, demands of a larger Will. Or is sucked down into them. Compassion refuses to enable or indulge karmic obsession.

Waxing trine (120°; amplifies, mutual reinforcement): a redemptive ideal integrates with collective purpose, or hypnosis. An imaginative vision synergistically harmonizes with hidden passions of the deep unconscious, demands of a larger Will. Compassion dissolves karma and fateful necessity.

Waxing quincunx (150°; irritating): a redemptive ideal disrupted by collective purpose, or hypnosis. An imaginative vision troubled by hidden rumblings from the deep unconscious or demands of a larger Will. Compassion confused by conflicting requirements of karma or fateful necessity.

Opposition (180°; challenge and illumination): a redemptive ideal and collective purpose, imaginative vision and hidden passions of a larger Will, complement and enhance each other. Or silently cancel out in the dark unconscious depths. Compassion liberates karma and fateful necessity. Or drowns in it.

Waning quincunx (210°; irritating): a redemptive ideal disrupted by an emerging collective purpose, or hypnosis. An imaginative vision shaken by premonitions of hidden passions in the deep unconscious, and demands of a larger Will. Compassion torn between past and coming necessities.

Waning trine (240°; amplifies, mutual reinforcement): a redemptive ideal integrates with an emerging collective purpose, or hypnosis. An imaginative vision synergistically harmonizes with a novel interpretation of hidden passions in the deep unconscious, or demands of a larger Will. Compassion effectively midwifes a coming fate, good or bad.

Waning square (270°; consciousness crisis: danger/opportunity): a redemptive ideal rejects an obsolete collective purpose, or hypnosis. Seeks a new one. An imaginative vision refuses the seductions of hidden unconscious passions, or demands of a larger Will. May be destroyed by that defiance. Compassion denies obsession, turns its back on the cruelties of group fate.

Waning sextile (300°; supportive): a redemptive ideal cooperates with an emerging collective purpose, or hypnosis. An imaginative vision aligns with hidden passions of the deep unconscious, demands of a larger Will. Compassion serves the needs of an inevitable and necessary group fate.

Waning semi-sextile (330°; stimulating): a redemptive ideal consecrated to an emerging collective purpose, or hypnosis. Imagination serves a new sense of unconscious passion, demands of a larger Will. Compassion sacrifices to or for a group fate, good or bad.

Synods

The four small terrestrial (Earthlike) planets closest to Sun describe the realm of personal psychology and its attributes: mind (Mercury), love (Venus), will (Mars) and memory (Moon). Earth itself is where they play out. Beyond the inner planets lies a shatter zone of asteroids, an apt symbol for the disintegration of ego at death. Beyond them lie two gas giants, Jupiter and Saturn. They are of a different nature than the rocky terrestrial worlds anchoring personality. These are immense spheres of hydrogen, the lightest element, laced with a smidgen of other gases. They symbolize meaning (Jupiter) and destiny (Saturn) abstracted from ego: its spiritual quality, stripped of personal quirks. They also describe the larger social reality within which our individual lives pass. 'No man is an island'; we are each embedded in a collective historical reality. The slow dance of Jupiter and Saturn portrays its evolutionary unfolding.

Jupiter sublimates significance out of circumstance. It distills principles out of phenomena; presents the intangible essence of a situation. Jupiter depicts the soul: both of an individual person and of a collective society. On the group level this soul expresses through belief systems: philosophies, ideologies, religions. These systems are codified into law, whether as an implicit morality or as explicit legislation. Thus Jupiter describes the highest aspirations of a group, whether a nation, church or corporation.

Saturn depicts how those aspirations are institutionalized. It portrays the structure of a society. The nature of the social bond holding it together: the basis of authority. Saturn centralizes expansive aspiration into a focused application.

Saturn describes the explicit form and fundamental organizing principles of destiny. Jupiter expresses its spiritual quality and meaning. Saturn demonstrates the fate or consequences generated by Jupiterian beliefs as they intersect with reality. If those beliefs are healthy or appropriate Saturn provides an orderly grounding and evolutionary progression of them over time. If they are incongruent with human nature or natural law Saturn symbolizes the resistance that eventually forces a reevaluation.

Jupiter progressively unwraps Saturn's abstract law and grows it into an actual soul experience. This occurs on both the individual and collective levels. Jupiter describes the adventure of history; Saturn its results. Jupiter presents options and possibilities. Saturn makes choices and decisions. They can work together, reinforcing each other, like the alternating expansion and contraction of a heartbeat. Or Jupiter can inflate Saturn's Shadow and Saturn can suffocate Jupiter's Spirit.

The relationship between Jupiter and Saturn describes what kinds of issues are raised, not how they will be addressed. Their dynamic symbolizes a context of opportunity/challenge. Individuals and societies respond: partly in accordance with their inherent nature, partly through the exercise of free will.

At twenty-year intervals Jupiter and Saturn conjoin. A new cycle of applied aspiration begins. Its quality is suggested by the nature of the conjunction sign. The waxing first decade of this cycle tends to emphasize the Jupiterian side of the equation, for expansion is Jupiter's function. The waning second decade of the synod tends to be more Saturnine, for contraction and final definition is Saturn's function.

Jupiter, with its twelve-year orbit, exemplifies the twelve archetypal phases of personal and social development encoded in the zodiacal signs. Saturn, with a 29½ year orbit, articulates the inner structure of those archetypes, the specific unfolding of each sign, in its thirty-degree spectrum of expression (including an extra ½° of indeterminacy and freedom).[1]

The long cycles of fate (Saturn) and its meaning (Jupiter) are measured by the alignments of our system's two giant planets. Their intersecting movements manifest a rhythmic oscillation of intangible energies. We, on Earth, experience them as twenty-year generational periods beginning at the conjunctions. A spiritual wave pattern resonates through the solar system, charted in human history as a mutual interaction of necessary destiny (Saturn) and evolutionary freedom (Jupiter).

Aspects between the social planets, Jupiter and Saturn, have been studied for centuries as indices of historical development. Their generational conjunctions are called synods or mutations. They occur in a regular sequence through the four elements (fire, earth, air, water, in that order). Jupiter/Saturn perform nine to twelve mergers in each three-signed element before moving on to the next.

The synods move backwards through the modalities of the elements in a regular pattern, from the cardinal sign of an element to the mutable, then to the fixed and back to the cardinal again.[2] Each conjunction, or synod, occurs about three degrees short of a retrograde trine to its predecessor on the long-term average.[3] Thus ten conjunctions falling back an average of three degrees every generation (twenty years) equals an entire sign (thirty degrees) of displacement every two hundred years. Then the cycle moves into a new elemental phase.

The twenty-year cycle of these two planets is called a minima or specialis; the 200 year elemental cycle a media or trigonalis; the entire 800 year cycle through all four elements a maxima or climacteric. The specific conjunction inaugurating a new elemental cycle is called a Great Mutation. It is unusually significant in that it colors the entire ensuing media or trigonalis. A transition period occurs between elemental periods as maverick conjunctions in the upcoming element pop up towards the end of a cycle. For example, during the recent earth cycle, 1842-2020, a maverick Jupiter/Saturn formed in Libra (air) in 1981. Libra is the sign of balance. This mutation coincided with a total change in the global balance of power with the fall of communism, end of the cold war and beginning of a new world order.

All mutations (minima, specialis) occurred at 20-year intervals in:

Earth signs between 1007/8-1206. It began with a rare initial triple conjunction in 1007/8 between 9°-14° of Virgo as Jupiter passed Saturn in direct motion, then retrograded back across it, then returned for a final prograde past it. The rarity of a triple conjunction justifies taking it as the Great Mutation beginning an earth media or trigonalis, even though it was followed by one last fire conjunction in 1027. Earth sign conjunctions then became the norm until 1206, with one air maverick towards the end, in 1186. A maverick appearance of the upcoming element is normal towards the end of a trigonalis.

Air signs between 1226-1405 (with a water maverick in 1365). Great Mutation at 3° of Aquarius.

Water signs between 1425-1643 (with fire mavericks in 1603 and 1623). Great Mutation between 13°-18° of Scorpio (another rare triple conjunction).

Fire signs between 1663-1821 (with an earth maverick in 1802). Great Mutation at 13° of Sagittarius.

Earth signs again between 1842-2000 (with an air maverick in 1981). Great Mutation at 9° of Capricorn.

Air signs again between 2020-2199 (with a water maverick in 2159). Great Mutation at 1° of Aquarius.[4]

The last Great Mutation was in Capricorn (earth) in 1842. This initiated the present era of materialistic philosophy and high objective achievement. The next will be in Aquarius (air) in 2020. It will initiate the transition to a new Aquarian precessional age. (See 'Precession.')

The coming era will be more collectivist than ours. Air is more concerned with balanced relationship and social harmony in contrast to earth's emphasis on acquisitiveness and excellence. Environmental constraints, technological concerns and a growing egalitarianism between races, genders and cultures will not allow for the disparities of wealth and power characteristic of an earth age. The necessities of global economic and ecological management make that general nature inevitable. Its specific quality is open to a wide range of possibilities. It could manifest as anything from a new age utopia to a science fiction police state.

Notes

1. This small extra space embeds an activating factor. One half degree is the size of the solar disc as seen from Earth. It symbolizes an opening to spirit that brings Saturn's structure to life.
2. This retrograde movement is similar to that of precession of the equinox and of the lunar nodes. However, the latter two are continuous curves of motion through space (the zodiac) rather than discontinuous conjunctions over time.
3. In specific cases they can be up to 17° before or after a retrograde trine to the previous synod due to variations in these planets' orbits.
4. All information about the dates and positions of the synods was gleaned from Richard Nolle's conjunction tables published on the Internet. The writer is, and all students should be, grateful for such generosity in making this information freely available.

Let us examine the last maxima or climacteric of the synods, extending from 1007-1842 in general. We will then look at the current media or trigonalis, extending from 1842-2020 in more detail. The focus will be on Western civilization, the progenitor of an emerging world order.

Earth, 1007-1206

In 1000 Europe was still mired in the Dark Ages: primitive, chaotic, weakly stitched together by a network of Catholic monasteries and embryonic monarchies. By 1206 it had soaring cathedrals, great castles and growing cities. An era of relative peace and prosperity succeeded centuries of barbarian invasions. A stable feudal order created the conditions for economic growth and cultural flowering after centuries of anarchy. Almost miraculously a new civilization materialized when the dreaded Last Judgment of the year 1000 did not. This period inaugurated a second great age of the West, the high medieval, preceded by the classical Greco-Roman, and followed by the modern.

The Church provided a universally acknowledged framework of values, legal norms and spiritual discipline. The Papacy regained its moral authority after a long degeneration (culminating in a Pornocracy, Rule of the Harlots, 904-964). National monarchies became strong enough to launch a series of Crusades to retake the Holy Land. This very literal expression of religious fervor materially enriched Europe by exposing it to lost knowledge of the ancients and superior crafts of the Islamic world. (While conveniently employing a disruptive warrior class overseas.) Technology, trade and learning revived.

The Virgo tone of this earth period is especially demonstrated by a sudden new veneration of the Virgin (Virgo) Mary. Catholicism underwent a profound transition from an emphasis on the ritual magic of the Sacrament to an emotional personal faith. Every individual was now expected to model his or her life on Christ's, and to seek intercession with God through the Great Mother. This acknowledgment of the feminine principle on the spiritual plane was paralleled by the emergence and diffusion of a new ideal of romantic love in this life. The idea that marriage should be founded on personal affinity rather than family alliance or economic arrangement was a distinctive characteristic of Western civilization. It marked a fundamental recognition of the individual as such, rather than simply as a member of the collective. Obviously there has been personal love in all times and cultures. Now it became a religiously sanctioned social norm and an institutionalized individual expectation. It also embodied an affirmation of female dignity.

Veneration of the Virgin may seem quaint, even silly, in our hyper-rational materialistic era. However, in an Age of Faith, when spiritual identity was all one had in a world of poverty, ignorance and brutality, it marked a psychological revolution.* We should not be too certain that our sophisticated modern mentality, buzzing with information overload, is more advanced than a simpler, more focused religious sensibility. A mind distracted by consumer products, celebrity peccadilloes and entertainment possibilities is not necessarily more enlightened than one contemplating a few universal themes such as the Great Mother or the Redeemer.

Earth indicates tangible achievement, demonstrable material progress. At this time a religiously sanctioned feudal order brought relative stability after half a millennium of turmoil following the fall of the Roman Empire. Basic advances in agriculture and industry, along with a warming climate, led to a breakthrough in economic productivity. These developments generated a shared culture across Europe, loosely unified in a spiritual empire of Christendom.

*At this time the Church was generally a civilizing force. The horrors of the Inquisition, and the hysteria of mass witch burning, would happen later during the crises of the late medieval period.

Air, 1226-1405

By the thirteenth century an earth cycle of practical achievement in political organization and applied technology had laid a solid foundation for the high medieval period. Having reached its limit of economic productivity it sublimated into an air cycle, synthesizing a new mental outlook and generating new social relationships. Learning emerged from cloistered monasteries into great universities. A cosmopolitan scholastic class diffused knowledge and a common culture across Europe. Arabic numbers (invented in India around 500) with their positional notation and concept of zero replaced clumsy Roman numerals. This revolutionized mathematics, the enabling software of modern science.* Long distance trade flourished; with it came banking, insurance and international law. Craft guilds standardized the quantity, quality and price of goods just as their descendants, transnational corporations, do now. Universal practices based on abstract principle began to supplant local customs based on ancient tradition, just as in today's globalization.

Politically the trend was towards egalitarianism. Growing towns received royal charters of liberty, and their industrious middle classes gained personal rights, in return for financing national monarchies against rapacious and rebellious nobles. Uniform and predictable law replaced arbitrary fiat, or trial by ordeal, whether through precedent (common law) in England, or legislation (Roman law) on the continent. In England the Magna Carta (1216) for the first time in history explicitly proclaimed certain core principles: the King was subject to, and not above, the law; he must govern in consultation with representatives of the nation (parliament); and every man has inalienable rights which may not be violated for any reason of political expediency. In 1297 this empirical bargain between King and barons was formalized as the permanent basis of government. It would take centuries for these ideals to become realities, but once unleashed they would change the world forever.

The Aquarian character of this era is demonstrated not only by its idealistic tendencies, but also by a sudden revolution within it. A great plague, the Black Death, swept away at least ⅓ of Europe's population in just two years, 1348-49. Generations of relative peace had led to overpopulation and social rigidity. In the blink of an eye everything changed. The dazed survivors inherited the wealth of their more numerous predecessors. Labor, being scarce, became dear: wages doubled in the late 14th century. Many manor-bound serfs earned their freedom. By the turn of the 15th century most people had acquired immunity against ever-feebler outbreaks of the disease. The sense of a new dawn, the Renaissance, was beginning to emerge as air morphed into water.

Air promotes social harmony over self-assertion, collective regulation more than individual interest. During this trigonalis a corporate feudal civilization, with 'a place for every man, and every man in his place,' seemed to exemplify a divine order nurturing both commerce and contemplation.

* Positional notation means that a 'one,' 1, means 'ten' when written with zero as a placeholder to its right, 10. Two ones mean eleven, because one is in the tens column and one is in the ones column, 11. This made math as we know it possible. Imagine adding 23 + 45 if one had to write it as XXIII + XLV.

Water, 1425-1643

Water refers to the unlimited possibilities of imagination, as opposed to the limitations of logic (air), practical possibilities of achievement (earth) and power constraints of will (fire). The era of Jupiter/Saturn synods in water was truly one of boundless horizons: the Age of Discovery. It was not only geographical as the Old World discovered the New (1492). It was also spiritual, as Christianity went through an agonizing reappraisal of every doctrine and belief in the Reformation and Counter Reformation. It finally ended up with something entirely new: a spirit of rational inquiry, embodied in the Scientific Revolution. It was artistic, generating the immortal creativity of great masters, Michelangelo, DaVinci, Shakespeare. It was also intellectual, as the Renaissance brought to light both ancient wisdom and new perspectives.[1]

All of these discoveries were disseminated by the printing press (Gutenberg, 1452). For the first time knowledge spread widely as soon as it became available. This unleashed an explosion of technological innovation: for example, the telescope unveiled the heavens just as the Copernican revolution changed the way we thought about them.[2]

Europe literally took to the sea. A revolution in naval architecture and navigation by means of the magnetic compass opened up the oceans. The introduction of ship-mounted cannon made its fleets invincible. An urge to explore, to seek out the unknown, drove its mariners to sail around Africa, creating trade routes to the fabulous wealth of Asia;

to cross the Atlantic and find new continents; to circumnavigate the globe, not only proving that the Earth is round, but making it their own.

The Scorpionic nature of this media is well illustrated by its most far-reaching event: the Old World's encounter with the New. Contact brought death to the Native Americans, who had no immunity against diseases to which Europeans had adapted.[3] It brought opportunity to Europe, just as the corporate medieval era was dying and an individualistic Renaissance came to birth. American gold and silver greased the wheels of commerce and industry, providing capital to fund the technological explosion of early modernity. Its food crops, such as corn and potatoes, peanuts and tomatoes, fed growing populations. America's now virtually empty lands provided an outlet for colonization and new forms of social organization. If there has ever been an instance of transformation by encounter with the Other (the Scorpio function) this was it.

Water, the universal solvent, dissolves old forms and washes away boundaries. Water, the elixir of dreams, promises new worlds. In this age it delivered.

Notes

1. Literally: the great breakthrough in Renaissance art was perspective, the portrayal of three-dimensional depth in a painting or drawing. Before that all art was flat: two dimensional, symbolic rather than representational.
2. That Earth revolves around Sun, rather than Sun around Earth.
3. Probably 90% of the pre-contact population was wiped out by introduced diseases during the 16th century. This was not deliberate - at that time nobody had any idea of infection. Both the indigenous and European communities saw disease as a result of spiritual imbalance.

A politically incorrect note: modern sensibility tends to interpret this encounter as a rapacious extermination of innocent peoples living in ecological harmony: the 'Conquest of Paradise.' In fact, indigenous cultures were extremely varied: from cannibalistic Aztecs to gentle Arawaks, warlike tribes that reveled in public displays of torture to mystic communities devoted to spiritual practice.

A unification of the old and new worlds was inevitable at that stage of historical development. So were its biological consequences. That said, this complex story also includes hideous episodes of genocide.

Fire, 1663-1821

By the mid 17th century the Age of Discovery, with its sense of unlimited possibilities, had morphed into an era of fire, with a focused passion for power. The medieval quest for mystical union with the Creator gave way to the modern drive for control over creation. Whereas the Renaissance looked to classical antiquity, the Enlightenment (a fiery term) innovated with an eye to the future. Indeed, it invented the very concept of progress. All previous cultures had seen history as falling away from a Golden Age. The way forward was back: faithfulness to revelation, loyalty to ancestral standards. Now, for the first time, it seemed that a better world could be attained through reason, the human condition improved through applied intelligence. This was the premise of all its great revolutions: the scientific and industrial, American and French.

This era introduced another idea: the pursuit of happiness. Happiness has always existed. Indeed, the simple joy of life is its most fundamental quality. But in tribal, ancient and medieval cultures the individual lived to serve the collective, or to attain salvation. The inherent worth of mortal personality, and a right to express it as one saw fit, had rarely been explicitly acknowledged.[1] The quest for self-fulfillment and personal satisfaction was an emergent value of early modernity.

Politically, after the Thirty Years War (1618-48), secular nation states replaced medieval theocracies. They were laissez-faire, no longer concerned with their subjects' spiritual life, not yet worried about their social welfare. Liberties and rights of the strong were emphasized over care and compassion for the weak. Socially, freelance private companies carved out empires abroad, settling colonies in America and conquering ancient civilizations in Asia.[2] Culturally, individualism flourished. Rather than being organically embedded in a divinely sanctioned corporate order, each person now stood alone before God, master of and responsible for, his or her own destiny.[3]

Intellectually, the scientific revolution, born in the previous era, flowered and illuminated the general temper of the age. Its experimental spirit encouraged technological innovation in a free-wheeling capitalist economy. That generated the Industrial Revolution, a decisive assertion of power, not only over nature, but also over human destiny. From time immemorial virtually everyone had lived with unremitting physical drudgery, from dawn to dusk, childhood to old age, at 35. Preindustrial life was generally wretched, brutal, diseased and ignorant. During this era that misery was not tangibly lessened: fire is about initiating impulse, creative will, not its material payoff.[4] That would come in the succeeding earth period.

The Sagittarian character of this era is well illustrated by its greatest political event, in 1776. The American Revolution brought something genuinely new into the world: a consciously designed government by, for and of the people. For all the faults of the early American republic, such as its acceptance of slavery, it became a beacon of hope to the world and has remained so ever since.[5] The United States chart actually has the Great Mutation degree of 13° Sagittarius rising. (See 'Mundane Considerations.') Sagittarius means freedom and expansiveness.

Fire describes the will to power, and the power of will. This fire era marked the transition between an unchanging, fatalistic, agrarian dispensation to a dynamic, rational era of technological competence. Accelerating change also brought widespread social alienation.

Notes

1. Even the ancient Greeks saw man (and only men counted) primarily as a participating citizen of the city state. 'Man is by nature a political animal' (Aristotle). The later Christian message of personal salvation emphasized our responsibility to God and conscience as superseding socially defined obligations. By the time of this fire epoch that sense of moral autonomy had evolved into the idea of individual rights in this life.
2. Thus, the British East India Company gradually took over India for private profit between 1680 and 1857, when it finally handed the Jewel of Empire over to the Crown.
3. Privacy was virtually unknown before the Renaissance. From peasant hovels to aristocratic courts everyone lived communally, in the public eye. Only in the 16th century did private rooms begin to appear in houses, personal chairs replace common benches, individual reading of printed books supplant group participation in an oral culture.
4. The early industrial revolution was notorious for its exploitation, especially of child labor. Yet without it most of those children would have starved to death, unnoticed in the high mortality of agrarian society. Think of today's sweatshops in China and Mexico pouring out cheap consumer goods for Western middle classes. For all their degradation they are a step upwards from rural hopelessness. For every vacancy that opens they have ten applicants. Those of us fortunate enough to pursue consciousness growth tend to be blissfully ignorant of just how grindingly hard life is for billions of people even today.
5. Indeed, it almost immediately inspired the French Revolution, an explosion in a petrified social order. This then swept across Europe in a generation of military aggression under Napoleon. Since then, it has engulfed the world: virtually all governments now claim to be

variations on the Anglo-American model, giving at least lip service to the concepts of representative democracy, separation of powers, rule of law, inalienable human rights. In theory the only exceptions are Iran and Saudi Arabia, pretending to be governed by divine law as revealed in the Koran.

Earth, 1842-2020

This era brought a transformation of life's material conditions. Its most notable social accomplishments, the abolition of slavery and liberation of women, were made possible because machines replaced muscles in the workplace. Widely distributed economic prosperity has enabled unprecedented creature comfort and personal psychological autonomy. Its consumer culture has also dulled the urgency of spiritual concerns so important to our more insecure ancestors.

A scientific worldview focused on objective facts has displaced traditional narratives emphasizing moral meaning. Statistics have eclipsed values. Technological achievement has granted us enormous power for better and for worse. It has also become the dominant ideology, or seductive idolatry, of our time. We increasingly worship the work of our own hands. Thus artificial intelligence supplants wisdom, genetic engineering revises biological life, a medical model of the human condition has largely replaced a religious one.

The pragmatic orientation of this earth era has achieved the basic productive capacity and accumulation of wealth to transcend age-old physical deprivation, and the mean spirited ignorance associated with it. Our newfound abilities have also generated a false sense that technological truth is the only truth. An illusion that our power proves our merit. But action invites reaction. This confidence will inevitably be put to the test: earth is about limitations as well as results. It may involve objective dysfunction: economic meltdown, ecological collapse, actual use of weapons of mass destruction. It will certainly involve subjective and social value choices as we face a world of shrinking natural resources, increasing environmental degradation, growing population and bankrupt economies.

For the first time in history we have the tools to create a just society. Or to destroy all prospects for a decent future. The practical decisions we make in this last decade of an era of explosive material growth will do much to determine the nature of the more steady state air era to follow. After generations of economic expansion, society will turn to issues of equity as a new air media begins in 2020.[1] The need for global economic and ecological balance, and to control potentially catastrophic technologies, makes that inevitable.

Let us examine the current earth period in more detail, briefly looking at each of its generational mutations. This overview will be mostly confined to American history, in the interest of simplicity, and because the U.S., unburdened by the Old World's heavy social and historical baggage, could more freely express these emerging energies. Each synod (minima, specialis) tends to express and expand upon a meaning in its first decade (Jupiter) and to consolidate its consequences in the second (Saturn).

The modern earth media's overall Capricornian nature (defined by its initiating Great Mutation) is well illustrated by man's landing on the Moon. Capricorn is about tangible achievement. It is hard to imagine a greater accomplishment than 'breaking the surly bonds of Earth'[2] and physically entering the infinity of space. This objective triumph also reflects a corresponding subjective growth, in social conscience and personal consciousness.

Capricorn - 9° (1842) - Expansion: The first industrial revolution, centered on steam power fueled by coal, spread to a socially significant scale. Railroads (initiated in 1825) shrank distance. The telegraph (1844) annihilated time. Electronic communications began. News that had taken months to travel around the world now took seconds. The crop reaper (put into mass production, 1847) revolutionized agriculture. It vastly increased productivity while displacing rural labor to growing industrial cities. Politically the U.S. achieved its Manifest Destiny, attaining continental dimensions through diplomacy with Britain (northwest) and war with Mexico (southwest).[3]

Consolidation: A decade of compromise and equivocation over slavery (1850s) gave the north time to industrialize, ensuring its victory in a closely fought Civil War. The first oil well (Pennsylvania, 1859) and the Bessemer process of producing cheap steel (1855) initiated a second industrial revolution. The scientific truth quest attained fundamentally new levels of understanding in biology with Darwin's evolutionary theses (1859) and in physics with Maxwell's electromagnetic theory (published in 1864).

Capricorn institutionalizes, gives structure, to inspiration. The establishment of an industrial economy, and of new scientific paradigms (evolution and electromagnetism), laid the material and intellectual foundations of modernity.

On the world scene this was indeed a seminal mutation. China, in some ways the great Other to the West, had dwelt in splendid isolation for millennia. Suddenly, unexpectedly, its political order and cultural confidence were shattered by a rising, industrializing Britain. The Opium War (1839-42) forcibly opened China to international trade, in ideas as well as goods. One can legitimately object to the spectacle of an imperialist power forcing opium on a traditional civilization at gunpoint. But this sordid episode also occurred in a larger context. The time had come for global integration. China was a walled off realm, looking backwards to a closed classical past rather than forward to an open future. The West's violent intrusion destroyed a stagnant and complacent order. This unleashed a century of chaos, civil war and foreign invasion, until a strident communist revolution finally leveled the old ways. China only began to revive with Deng Xiaoping's sweeping reforms at the start of a maverick air mutation in Libra (1981).[4] Today (2013), less than two generations later, China is resuming its natural status as a superpower - but now as part of the world rather than apart from it.

During the same period the American Navy induced Japan, the last major hermit kingdom, to open up as well. This was accomplished by an intimidating visit to Tokyo harbor (1853/4). Unlike China, Japan adapted quickly and adroitly to a new reality.

From the hunter-gatherer tribes of the American west and African jungles to the decaying civilizations of India and the Middle East all cultures and polities were absorbed into a global system by the mid 19th century. Only geographically isolated Tibet would remain apart until the mid 20th century. Tibet was a special case, a spiritual entity more than a political one.

The Great Mutation of 1842 accurately timed humanity's reorganization from a collection of autonomous cultures into a universal civilization with local flavors. This was only made possible by the organizational efficiency, technical competence and material motivations associated with an earth era. This mutation in Capricorn began with an abrupt global unification in practical economic terms. Ideas and politics follow trade. The trend towards globalization has continually intensified ever since. Soon, as we begin to move into an air mutational era starting in 2020, the emphasis will shift to relationship issues: economic justice, social equity and environmental sustainability. The passing earth period created wealth, the coming air period will rationally distribute it in the interest of long-term stability.

Notes

1. This will inaugurate a transition to an even longer Aquarian precessional age from 2060-4220 AD. Aquarius is an air sign. See 'Precession.'

2. From the poem 'High Flight' by John Gillespie Magee, 1922-1941, an American pilot killed in World War II:

> Oh! I have slipped the surly bonds of Earth,
> Put out my hand and touched the face of God.

3. One could argue that this was a contractive era from a Mexican perspective. But Mexico was a corrupt despotism; the United States a dynamic powerhouse. The rewards of an expansive period go to its growing edge. Lively movement rather than petrified passivity defines history.

Sadly, this situation remains essentially unchanged 150 years later, as millions of Mexicans who vote with their feet attest. Today's despotism is exercised by drug cartels that dominate a weak narco-democracy and feed on America's insatiable addictions.

The naked territorial imperialism of the early industrial age offends modern sensibilities. But that has been history's way until very recently. Remember too that Mexico did not preside over indigenous tribes of the North American west with their consent or any pretense of seeking it.

4. China has always been considered a Libra country. Its current dynasty, the People's Republic, was formally inaugurated on October 1, 1949 with Sun at 9° Libra. (See 'Mundane Considerations.')

Virgo - 19° (1861) - Expansion: Civil War (1861-65) may seem a strange manifestation of growth. Yet in fact it constituted a rebirth and second founding of the nation. The greatest episodes of social achievement and spiritual enlargement demand purifying sacrifice. (The same theme would recur eighty years later, in Taurus, during the 1940s.) Virgo aptly symbolizes the establishment of national integrity: all citizens were now free, in one republic rather than a federation of states.

Consolidation: Efforts at social reform in the south (Reconstruction) wound down. Corporate America began to take shape as economies of scale emerged in more efficient industrial organizations.

Taurus - 2° (1881) - Expansion: The gilded age of robber barons and the golden age of Wild West cowboys. Giant corporations became the dominant social institution. An era of untrammeled acquisition and wealth creation reflects a Taurean theme.

Consolidation: In 1890 the Census Bureau declared that the western frontier had finally closed. Henceforth that defining edge of the American psyche would express on new frontiers of science and technology. A rising middle class flourished in a stable, conservative environment. In 1898 the U.S. became a world power by gaining an island empire in both the Caribbean and Pacific (Spanish-American War, plus annexation of Hawaii).

Capricorn - 14° (1901) - Expansion: The culmination of an age of progress in a rapidly industrializing and globalizing world. The introduction of horseless carriages, flying machines and the wireless (radio) created a recognizably modern society. New paradigms in physics (Einstein) and psychology (Freud, Jung) initiated a modern consciousness.

Contraction: The Capricorn theme of rise and fall, achievement and the limits of achievement, came into full flower. A century of general peace and prosperity reached its apogee in 1914, then suddenly plunged into darkness. The Great War came. Innocence turned to cynicism as a lost generation was sacrificed for nothing. The U.S. was far less affected than others, but at the end of this cycle it retreated into isolationism (selfish Saturn), making another war all but inevitable (fated Saturn).

Virgo - 27° (1921) - Expansion: The Roaring Twenties, as a jazzy nervous energy replaced staid old certainties. Prosperity diffused to the working class. Now the average Joe could afford to buy a car, own some stock, dream the Hollywood dream. Prohibition (1920-33), a noble experiment at compulsory moral improvement, demonstrated a Virgoan urge to purification.

Contraction: The Depression squeezed excess out of the economy and society with a vengeance. A New Deal rewrote the American social contract, with government regulation of the economy and enhanced power for the workers (Virgo). Truly sinister attempts at 'purification' emerged in Europe as Stalin murdered millions of class enemies and Hitler prepared for the Final Solution.

Taurus - 15°, 12° and 10° (1940) - Expansion: A rare triple conjunction emphasizes this specialis. The basic values (Taurus) of humanity were put to the test as never before. After World War II a new approach to shared international prosperity, begun with the Marshall Plan for European recovery, generated a long cycle of sustained economic growth across the globe.

Consolidation: The 1950s marked history's first experience of mass affluence (in the Western world) as the world took a post-war breather.

Capricorn - 26° (1961) - Expansion: Incredible achievement, exemplified by successful accomplishment of a pledge to 'land a man on the Moon, and return him safely to Earth'* (1969). Authority (Capricorn) was challenged and democratized by social movements bringing a new sensibility around race, peace, feminism and the environment to the public square.

Consolidation: A hangover from the sixties' exuberance in a time of stagflation and malaise. An old industrial order reached its limits to growth. Under the surface new social forms were gestating with the development of biotechnology, personal computers and the rise of nongovernmental organizations.

* President John F. Kennedy, 1961

Libra - 10°, 8° and 5° (1981) - Expansion: Another rare triple conjunction; a maverick presaging an upcoming air cycle (2020-2199). The long Cold War wound down and unexpectedly ended. A new world order emerged, emphasizing universal acknowledgment, though not yet achievement, of common values: democracy, rule of law, human rights and capitalist economics.*

Consolidation: A changing social landscape in a general atmosphere of peace. The emergence of new technologies, such as the Internet and biotech, initiated a fundamentally new reality. The economic rise of China (a Libra country) began to alter the global balance of power.

Note

People generally work best in intimate or small group situations. Ideally most economic activity would be decentralized to the artisanal or cooperative level. New information technologies enhance this form of teamwork.

However, if we want to explore space, build renewably powered cars and live in cities then large corporations are also necessary. We cannot heat and light New York in January with rooftop solar cells (which are built by big, technologically sophisticated companies).

These impersonal organizations are motivated by financial incentives. Capitalism, private ownership of the means of production, creates wealth because it works with human nature rather than seeking to channel it by altruism or coercion. It rewards successful risk taking while its market discipline eliminates inefficient effort. Indeed its exponential growth must be restrained lest it overwhelm other social priorities, as it has today.

The problem with unchecked capitalism is that it subordinates all other values to acquisition while devouring its natural and social context. Its relentless competition promotes a tiny oligarchy that then corrupts the political system to its further advantage. Its current debased form, funneling wealth to the top 1%, cannot last. Capitalism itself, the free enterprise stimulus to individual excellence, is inherent in human nature.

The alternative is socialism, state or community control of the means of production. This means political distribution of its rewards, by perceived need rather than proven merit. Socialism can provide a humane context for integrating economic power with other community concerns, such as equality and ecology. However it does not encourage growth because it lacks tangible incentives for the creative minority.

As we enter an air precessional era economic considerations will fade in a time of egalitarian material abundance. Priorities will shift from accumulation to fair and sustainable deployment of resources. Greater emphasis will be placed on the pursuit of intangible goals, giving people time to play and dream rather than just work, work, work.

Taurus - 23° (2000) - Expansion: A worldwide boom, fueled by reckless debt and Byzantine financial speculation, suddenly imploded (September, 2008). The contractive phase was triggered a little early by the movement of metamorphic Pluto from Sagittarius, a Jupiterian sign, into Capricorn, a Saturnine one.* The damage seemed temporarily contained by unprecedented multi-trillion dollar 'stimulus' programs delivering more of the same rather than real change. Did these emergency bailouts begin the transition to a sustainable economy? Or simply postpone the day of reckoning?

Astrology describes the nature and timing of decision points. It cannot predict their outcome. Its rhythms set the stage, create the occasion, for our exercise of free will and moral choice.

Consolidation: Diminishing natural resources, growing deficits and aging populations will compel a fundamental restructuring of the economy. This could be painful or productive, depending on how it is handled. The Taurean theme of how wealth is generated, and by what criteria it is distributed, will likely dominate this period of transition to a coming air cycle. The important issues are how humanity asserts conscious stewardship over the global economy, planetary environment and our own technological abilities. It must make fundamental value decisions (Taurus) about the use, or abuse, of power. Those decisions, positive or negative, will create the material context shaping an

Aquarian Great Mutation (2020) that will segue into a 2160 year long Aquarian precessional age. Thus they will have an enduring influence.

(Written in 2010. The following three paragraphs were added in early 2017.)

This last subcycle of the earth period reflected Saturn's conservative/fearful side rather than its disciplined ambition to meet demanding duty and achieve high goals. An increasingly plutocratic (wealth dominated) government tried to revive rather than revise an unsustainable economy. It did so by injecting enormous amounts of credit into the same financial institutions that caused the crises, making them even bigger.

Yet these subsidies also extended the life of an impressive social and scientific progress. Indeed, no other course was practical. The size, complexity, momentum and entrenched special interests of modern society make political reform impossible. Its spectacular flowering, both splendid and sinister, must run its course.

Saturn also symbolizes fateful coercive correction. The United States is now bankrupt. When that open secret becomes explicit the house of cards will collapse. Only thus can the deck be reshuffled.

* Pluto was in Sagittarius from 1996-2008. It will transit Capricorn from 2008-2024. Note the difference in length due to Pluto's eccentric orbit. For more information see the description of its collective and historic cycles in 'Outer Planet Transits.'

Other events of this time, dramatic as they may be, must be seen in perspective. The terrorist attacks of September 11, 2001 were an outburst of rage, not a sign of any future organizing principle. They stem from turmoil in a traditional Islamic civilization flooded with petrodollars, modern weapons and disturbing new ideas. This backlash against modernity invoked international police actions involving enormous effort and real sacrifice. Sadly, much bigger wars are almost inevitable as Iran gets the bomb; if Pakistan, an unstable nuclear power, implodes; and when the Arab-Israeli conflict comes to a final showdown. Such wars would obviously be historically important, and could seriously disrupt our interdependent world. Still, tragic as they may be, these are possible eruptions of stress and negativity, not long-term evolutionary trends.

Outer Planet Synods – Overview

Aspects of social (Jupiter, Saturn) with outer (Uranus, Neptune, Pluto) planets involve the impact of collective unconscious forces on manifest events. Conjunctions of the social and transformational planets creates a polarity.* One pole, of meaning (Jupiter) or form (Saturn), expresses in the phenomenal world. The other pole, of inspiration (Uranus), imagination (Neptune) or fate (Pluto), focuses an intangible force. It concentrates an unconscious energy state into a specific action potential. This is then grounded or channeled through the medium of conscious philosophy (Jupiter) or impersonal law (Saturn).

* Transformational in this sense does not necessarily mean highly evolved. It means that these planets clock subtle tides of the collective unconscious. They flow far below the surface, like the great magma plumes deep in Earth's interior beneath our feet. They erupt into consciousness only when activated by contact with a personal or social planet. Whether that manifestation turns out to be primitive or transcendental depends on the evolutionary level and expressive ability of the planetary function grounding them in the material world.

The conjunctions (synods) of Jupiter and Saturn express a sequential development of historical stages. They generate a social heartbeat of outpouring (Jupiter) and ingathering (Saturn). Growth and consolidation. Jupiter and Saturn are vectors of visible and dynamic trends. They demonstrate a moving calculus of historical forces.

The synods of Jupiter or Saturn with any of the outer planets form a regular pattern of unpredictable crisis (danger/opportunity). At predictable intervals cosmic or subterranean forces erupt into our orderly and organized material world. Without them the interplay of conscious energies would be a complex, but essentially mechanistic, dance of known forces.

When Jupiter or Saturn contact an outer planet they act as a lens, or vortex, drawing down an energy surge from Infinity. This surge may fertilize or disrupt. But most importantly it brings novelty into the system. Outer planets introduce currents from beyond, influences from over the horizon, into the set rhythms of both personal and social psychology. They shake the system up, injecting disturbing, demonic or divine, forces into the routine.

The synods of Jupiter and Saturn chart a given long term developmental sequence, much like a human life going through predictable stages of infancy, childhood, adolescence, adulthood, age. The synods of Jupiter or Saturn with any of the outer planets chart the emergence of emergencies. They announce the intrusion of something new, whether creative or destructive. How a society responds to that stimulus depends on how healthy its Jupiter/Saturn social receptors are.

It should be remembered that the outer planets were only discovered in modern times: Uranus (1781), Neptune (1846), Pluto (1930). The conscious revelation of these previously hidden levels of the psyche has tracked the accelerating pace of historical evolution since the Enlightenment. Uranus, which can barely be seen by a keen naked eye in a clear sky, was not recognized as a planet until observed through an improved telescope in 1781. This planet, associated with transformative inspiration, came into conscious view just as the American, French and Industrial Revolutions were changing the world forever. Neptune, the first planet completely invisible to the naked eye (normal conscious awareness) was also the first to be discovered through abstract mathematical reasoning because of its perturbations of Uranus' orbit. Associated with redemption and illusion, Neptune was acknowledged at the same time as new ideals of social compassion were emerging in the abolitionist, feminist and animal humane movements. Its characteristic political expression came through the birth of socialism ('The Communist Manifesto,' 1848).

Uranus and Neptune are the same size and composition. They are separated in space but represent two aspects of the same energy. Uranus constitutes its inspirational mental pole. Neptune constitutes its imaginative emotional pole. Uranus is actively transformative and revolutionary. Neptune implies a dreamy sensibility, a numinous state of feeling. Uranus is connected with the Enlightenment and an age of reason. Neptune is connected with the following romantic and transcendental period. Together they transformed (Uranus) and reimagined (Neptune) the traditional contours of social expectation, bringing an entirely new sense of possibility into human affairs.

Uranus, emphasizing individuality and innovation, came into view just as the American, French and Industrial Revolutions were collectively validating these qualities. Neptune, emphasizing a universal emotional inclusiveness, came into view just as technology began to dissolve time and distance, shrinking the wide world into a global village. Its associated romantic and transcendental movements opened new dimensions of sensibility by celebrating nonrational sensitivities.

The mental originality of Uranus and the psychic sensibilities of Neptune have always been present. However they lay largely dormant under the constricted socioeconomic conditions of a traditional agrarian order. They have become activated across the threshold of consciousness and cultural acknowledgment by the accelerating pace of life since the industrial revolution. This social transformation is both a symptom, and a cause, of an increasing intensity of consciousness since the Enlightenment. It has objectively presented itself in the visible discovery of these planets, just as it has subjectively emerged with the modern growth of psychological consciousness.

The acknowledgment of an inner life distinct from one's actions or social role is a recent development in history. Psychological self-examination, or of others, was almost unknown in literature until the late 19th century. Recognition of the unconscious is more recent still (Freud, late 19th century; Jung, early 20th). These previously dormant, now awakened, dimensions of awareness stimulate our formal moral/rational worldview from an energy zone beyond it. They constitute a sub or super-conscious experience underlying and generating consciousness - just as an indefinable, fuzzy quantum reality underlies and generates, but is fundamentally different than, its tangible material superstructure (the world we know).

Uranus/Neptune constitute an electrical (Uranus) and magnetic (Neptune) potential. It generates a work producing current when either pole is invoked by contact with a visible planet. These planets demonstrate a reservoir of latent energies that are only beginning to come into manifestation. As we more fully assimilate these still novel forces they will stimulate emergent abilities. During the earth cycle (1842-2020) they expressed mainly on the scientific, technological, political and economic levels. In the upcoming air cycle (2020-2199) they are likely to begin grounding new intuitive (Uranus) and empathetic (Neptune) abilities.

The same considerations apply to Pluto, a very different kind of celestial body. Pluto is a double dwarf planetoid in a highly elliptical orbit. It links the planets with a surrounding sphere of tumbling ice and rock debris left over from formation of the solar system. As such it is a carrier or messenger of a primordial will, or generative force, prior to Sun's planetary structure. Its contacts with social planets mark eruptions of this primal force into history.

Pluto represents the drive to self-organization that forged planets and a solar system out of dust and ice. In the human psyche it symbolizes a similar will to identity, shaping fragmentary DNA codons into a living body, generalized instincts into a singular personality. Pluto marks a compulsive urge to ego formation that orients latent abilities into actual traits; a rocket booster of pre-personal vitality that lofts and aims a tiny, infinitely precious payload of consciousness towards a fated purpose. In the historical sense Pluto symbolizes a parallel process: the collective will driving a society or an era to its rendezvous with destiny.

The discovery of Pluto in 1930 coincided with the sudden emergence of the technocratic welfare state. The Depression ended centuries of laissez-faire capitalism and individual initiative, replacing them with planned, large-scale social engineering. This happened under every form of government: democratic, with its New Deal of vast public works programs; socialist, with its Five Year Plans of industrialization; fascist, with a totalitarian regimentation of society. Today, economies are centrally supervised on a continental scale. Modern society could not exist otherwise. Science is no longer a series of brilliant insights by lone geniuses. It is a vast team effort, marshaling thousands of researchers, decades of effort, billions of dollars to accomplish gigantic projects such as sequencing biological genomes, launching space probes, operating supercolliders. Even culture and entertainment are now mass produced at a professional level. Pluto came into view just as a collective will began to consciously direct social endeavor, starting with the crises of Depression and World War; becoming the accepted norm ever since.

The intensified collective states of consciousness symbolized by the outer planets are an emergent property of an accelerated historical process initiated during the last fire cycle (1663-1842). These qualities were socially dormant during earlier epochs. There were individual cases of genius (Uranus), universal empathy (Neptune) and fateful will (Pluto), but these did not become deliberately directed conscious social forces until the modern period. They acted as deep unconscious currents prior to their respective overt recognitions during the 18th, 19th and 20th centuries.

Just as human mental abilities develop sequentially over time so do social sensibilities. For example, an infant has a latent capacity to learn language. Still, s/he cannot actually speak for the first couple of years. S/he has a subliminal awareness of language being spoken; indeed an osmotic mimicry is how s/he learns. It takes time for this inherent power of linguistic expression to mature. In the same way, it took centuries of historical evolution for subtle levels of consciousness, symbolized by Uranus, Neptune, Pluto to rise to the surface of awareness and become integrated into the collective mindset. Certain exceptional individuals have been able to access these dimensions in every era, but they were not the norm. Today, because the general force field of mass consciousness has intensified, Joe Sixpack has the opportunity to think at a level that was once only accessible to a Lao Tzu or a Socrates. (With the caveat that s/he rarely chooses to make the effort.)

For this reason it is important not to interpret remote historical events in terms of outer planet influences. They were present but submerged, not yet consciously activated on a large scale. Certainly the most creative movers and shakers responded to these energies. Thus they impacted history through their leadership. But social institutions were simply not yet ready to express them, just as a first grader is not ready for algebra though s/he may later become a brilliant mathematician.

Modernity's recognition of inner energies symbolized by the outer planets marks a fundamental enlargement of human consciousness. We can model novel possibilities, simulate scenarios, by tapping into the free form energy levels mapped by these deep layers of intuitive and psychic consciousness. (They can also hypnotize.) Synods of the social planets with these energies represent moments of collective sensitivity to emergent potential. They do not depict discrete phases of historical evolution like the classic synods of Jupiter and Saturn. Rather they symbolize an atmosphere, mood, charge that informs, but does not explicitly define, events. They portray different kinds of openness to unrealized possibility. Thus Uranus endows a mental alertness to inspiration, or susceptibility to insanity; Neptune reflects a poetic dream channeling, or hallucinatory intoxication; Pluto serves an overriding karmic/collective need, or a hellish obsession. The social planet with which any of them are paired will then express that energy in the real world, at its own evolutionary level in an individual or society.

Let us examine them in more detail. In some of these years there are three conjunctions because the faster planet (for example, Jupiter) moves forward past the slower planet (for example, Uranus), then retrogrades back across it, finally prograding past it a final time. The same applies to all other planetary pairs.

Jupiter/Uranus

These are the most noticeable conjunctions of this series because each of its members is the closest of its kind to the human center of consciousness here on Earth. They mark sharp turns in direction, sudden changes in social priorities. It marks rebellion against the status quo, whether political, cultural or ideological. It has an exuberant Promethean spirit of unlimited aspiration. This can inspire tremendous breakthroughs or incite a devastating backlash. A spirit of innovation, with the danger of creative eccentricity veering into extremism or outright madness. It is optimistic, perhaps unwisely so, and promotes change, either progressive or anarchic.

Jupiter/Uranus conjunctions happen every fourteen years. The last conjunctions were in:
1941 (26° Taurus)[1]
1954/5 (28°, 27°, 25° Cancer)
1968/9 (4°, 3°, 1° Libra)[2]
1983 (9°, 8°, 6° Sagittarius)

1997 (6° Aquarius)
2010/11 (initially at 1° Aries, then again at 29° and 27° of Pisces)
The next will be in 2024 (22° Taurus).

The first thing that strikes one when looking at these years is how diverse they are. The same astrological conjunction of Jupiter and Uranus produces vastly different results each time it happens. Thus 1955 was a quiet year marked by publication of 'The Man in the Gray Flannel Suit,' a novel about this period's social conformity, while 1968 was a time of youthful rebellion and a flamboyant counter-culture. 1941 was about Pearl Harbor and the Nazi invasion of Russia; 1997 was a peaceful, prosperous, historically forgettable year. Does this demonstrate that astrology is bogus and without descriptive or predictive merit?

First, we must remember that each of these conjunctions took place in a different sign. For example, Cancer (1954/5) emphasizes home, security, family, inner pursuits; Libra (1968/9) emphasizes outer relationship, finding a new balance, harmony through conflict. Cancer (emotion) and Libra (intellect) are at a right angle (square) to each other in the zodiac: they are as dissimilar as two signs can be. Naturally a powerful conjunction would only accentuate the difference.

Equally important, we must keep in mind that social planet conjunctions with outer planets are not associated with discrete events or consistent phases of evolution. They introduce novelty, zap the system with fresh but intangible energies. They overturn (Uranus), subvert (Neptune), regenerate (Pluto) an old context. They create a new atmosphere, according to their nature. Thus, 1954/5 marked a sea change towards tranquility (Cancer) after a quarter century of severe crises starting with the Depression (1929), finishing with the death of Stalin and an end to the Korean War (1953). Obviously 1941 and 1968/9 marked moments of conscious realignment linked with dramatic historical events. 1983 was more subtle: it initiated a 'Morning in America,' a rebirth of national optimism along conventional and conservative lines after a decade of malaise (occurring in Sagittarius, ruled by Jupiter). In 1997 this energy was even more sublimated, expressing through technological rather than social innovation (occurring in Aquarius, ruled by Uranus).[3]

The unexpected Arab Spring of 2011 provides a perfect illustration of this conjunction. The relevant Jupiter/Uranus synod occurred three times, finally at 27° Pisces in January 2011, just 3° before the vernal equinox. This suggests sudden transformation of age-old karma in anticipation of a social rebirth. A culture long inured to fatalistic acceptance of corrupt authoritarian rule suddenly woke up and demanded democracy. A fundamental empowerment of civil society and acknowledgment of human dignity swept the Arab world almost overnight. This consciousness revolution has already generated impressive social and political consequences. However it unfolds, a cultural change of this magnitude can never be reversed.

Sometimes these conjunctions act strongly and explicitly through objective events; sometimes they express more intangibly as changes in the social, philosophic or scientific climate. Yet the pen is mightier than the sword. The power of a new idea or ideal is often far greater than that of a meaningless bloodbath or political circus. Social/collective unconscious conjunctions ground a latent voltage in real life. This may manifest through historic action, public opinion or intellectual insight. It may be immediately apparent or only appreciated in hindsight.

Notes

1. Conjunct Algol, traditionally considered the most malevolent fixed star in the sky. It is hard to imagine a more apt symbol for the total global war then getting under way, with its associated Holocaust and atom bomb.
2. One of them was on July 19, 1969: one day before the first Moon landing: 'We come in peace for all mankind.'
3. At this time the Internet was just coming online, along with the .com boom (no one before the late nineties would have had any idea of what a .com meant). The biotech revolution sharply accelerated with the impetus of the Human Genome Project. The space program entered a new phase, with international cooperation in the construction of a permanent manned outpost beyond Earth.

Jupiter/Neptune

This synod emphasizes idealism, whether practical or delusional. It has a mystical and religious quality: either a transcendental inclusiveness or a hypnotic fascination with some cultic fetish. Humanitarian and empathetic. It can blur common sense distinctions and indulge unwarranted optimism. The epitome of glamour, whether genuine charisma or phony posturing. Fertile hopes and confused intoxication. Jupiter grows Neptune's mystic glow, either expanding imagination or inflating illusion. Associated with collective fantasies, whether ennobling or degrading. A time when old ideals are rotting and new ones ripening in an atmosphere of dreamy hopefulness.

Jupiter/Neptune conjunctions happen every thirteen years. The last conjunctions were in:

1945 (6° Libra): a moment of postwar euphoria.

1958 (4° Scorpio): the apogee of the fifties' homogenous suburban dream.

1971 (3°, 2°, 1° of Sagittarius): the high of a very different counterculture vision.

1984 (1° Capricorn): more self-centered ideals of getting, and getting ahead. Neither expansive Jupiter nor fluid Neptune fully expresses its own nature in structured, materialistic Capricorn.

1997 (28° Capricorn): a continuation of the above.

2009 (27°, 27°, 25° of Aquarius): false hopes of reviving an unsustainable economic order with huge jolts of fiscal stimulation rather than real reform. See the preceding Jupiter/Pluto conjunction of late 2007 below.

The next will be in 2022 (24° Pisces).

Jupiter/Pluto

Sometimes Pluto deepens Jupiter's established social or spiritual momentum. Sometimes it curls Jupiter's trajectory into new dimensions. Just as a black hole in space bends starlight, so Pluto, fateful necessity, turns Jupiter's growth onto another path. Or sucks it down into the underworld for death and rebirth.

Pluto periodically resets Jupiter's cultural compass. It can reorient conventional expectations through the unconscious demands of collective instinct and racial will. Or immobilize Jupiter's outwards expansion, converting its energy to an internal growth in sophistication. Jupiter visibly manifests Pluto's veiled power, in a total change of fortune or as much more of the same.

Magnifies a hidden passion, positive or negative. Raises buried treasure to the surface. Or redirects quantitative enlargement into qualitative upgrade. Brings secret ambition to fruition, in overt expression or as a hidden maturation in the womb. Grows the influence of small strongly motivated groups, or latent but highly charged religious/philosophic and political principles

Transforms conventional wisdom, spiritual aspiration and their social expression. Or intensifies them in unconscious anticipation of rebirth: think of an animal gorging on abundant food in late summer - so that it can give birth in a hidden den after winter's hibernation.

Jupiter/Pluto conjunctions happen every twelve years, on average, since Pluto's speed of motion varies because of its elliptical orbit. The last conjunctions were in:

1943 (7°Leo): reversal in the fortunes of war. The Axis tide ebbs, an Allied surge flows.

1955/6 (29°, 28°, 27° of Leo): a spiritually inert period of prosperity. Such interludes of historic dullness can give long-term trends time to develop. The maturation of postwar prosperity to the point where it became ripe for the social revolution of the late 1960s.

1968 (24° Virgo): transformation of social values in a cultural revolution.

1981 (25° Libra): an equally powerful conservative counterrevolution.

1994 (29° Scorpio): like 1955/6 a period of consolidation, following the Cold War. An intensification of technological capacity with the development of gigantic long-term projects such as the Internet, International Space Station and Human Genome Project.

2007 (29° Sagittarius): this conjunction occurred in December 2007. It exactly timed the turning point when a long 'eerie boom' based on debt and wasteful overconsumption flipped into an economic slide culminating with the near financial meltdown of September 2008. A reversal of economic fortune.

Sadly, the crisis' political opportunity for transformative change was not taken. Banks deemed 'too big to fail' became even bigger and the oligarchic power of the top 1% increased. Meanwhile the US national debt doubled,[1] squandered on subsidies and stimuli without real reform. Jupiter's tendency to superficial inflation, more of the same, was exaggerated in its own sign of Sagittarius.[2] It overcame Pluto's demand for deep regeneration. That will come soon enough.

The next Jupiter/Pluto conjunctions will be in 2020 (25°, 25°, 23° of Capricorn) and 2033 (15° Aquarius).

1. From $8.951 trillion in fiscal year 2007 to $18.118 trillion in FY 2015. This does not include unfunded liabilities such as Social Security and Medicare.

2. The qualities of any sign are often intensified in its final degree, as if it were making a last hurrah.

Saturn/Uranus

During this 45 year cycle Saturn completes one orbit (29½ years), then goes an additional halfway around the zodiac to meet Uranus. Saturn fulfills a revolution around its own solar purpose, then makes a Uranian style jump into an opposite sign-polarity.

This conjunction has an Aquarian flavor because it involves that sign's two ruling planets. Saturn/Uranus zaps an obsolete structure with a shattering inspiration. It replaces a scientific paradigm, social worldview, or political system with something very different. It either reformats, or defaults into anarchy. An old order suddenly collapses. A new one takes its place.

Saturn/Uranus conjunctions happen every 45 years. The last conjunctions were in:

1897 (28°, 27°, 26° of Scorpio): materialistic physics began to collapse with the discovery of subatomic forces (radioactivity). The sense of an autonomous rational self fell with the discovery of its irrational subconscious foundations (Freud). Politically, the Spanish-American War (1898), though brief and with minimal casualties, collapsed a decrepit empire, making the United States a world rather than a continental power.

1942 (0° Gemini): the near collapse of civilization itself as Nazi Germany came to within a hair's breadth of victory.*

1988 (0° Capricorn, 29°, 28° of Sagittarius): the collapse of communism.

The next will be in 2032 (29° Gemini).

*Along with humanity's initial leap into outer space with the German V-2 rocket. This breakthrough technology first soared above Earth's atmosphere and into the void on October 3, 1942.

Saturn/Neptune

Two opposite principles: form (Saturn) and flow (Neptune), structure and dissolution, the mountain and the sea. Saturn can give expression to Neptune's poetic yearnings, make tangible its redemptive dreams. Or Neptune can wash away Saturn's organized pattern in amorphous chaos. Tension between realistic necessity and idealistic vision, the practical and the perfect. Subverts and dissolves petrified systems, replacing them with something better (Russia, 1989), or worse (Russia, 1917). This synod particularly resonates with Russia, traditionally a land of iron-fisted government and vodka soaked intoxication.*

Saturn/Neptune conjunctions happen every 36 years. The last conjunctions were in:

1917 (5° Leo): Russian Revolution.

1952/3 (23°, 22°, 22° of Libra): death of Stalin.

1989 (12°, 12°, 11° of Capricorn): second Russian Revolution.

The next will be in 2026 (1° Aries).

largely through the agency of Russia because of that country's central importance during the 20th century. Given Russia's diminishing role we can expect a new expression in the future.

Saturn/Pluto

When the rhythms of time and logic of development (Saturn) focus the hidden needs of destiny (Pluto) a hard hand reshapes society. At certain times new rules must come into force. Just as material objects cannot deny the laws of gravity, nor living bodies the dictates of biology, so collective organisms cannot defy the demands of history, the requirements of an emerging order. Saturn/Pluto imposes the discipline and duties of another dispensation. That means forcefully reshaping the inertia of established reality, bending it to another purpose.

Just as a changing climate evokes new ecologies in nature, at brutal cost to those that had achieved perfect fitness under the old conditions, so Saturn/Pluto brings regime change to nations and cultures. Its method is compulsion, not consent. Those who bear the burden of restructuring do not receive its benefits and would not choose to sow what others will get to reap. Yet the sowing must be done: workers must work and soldiers must die for larger ends that even their 'leaders' rarely understand.

Hard discipline. Conservative authority. Fateful necessity. A demanding destiny (Pluto) finds a focus (Saturn). A compulsive instinct to organize power. A collective will to regenerate lost authority. Obsessive control, or implosion of an overly rigid structure.

Discipline forged by ordeal. Weakness burned away by surviving and transcending Hell. Ancient karma resurrected for drastic metamorphosis. Old forms destroyed, their energy released or reborn. Associated with the destruction of petrified social systems. And with the rebirth of tough hard seeds that were buried and now sprout. Think of Israel coming back to life in 1948 after 2000 years of Jewish exile and oppression.

Saturn/Pluto conjunctions happen, on average, every 33 years, varying because of Pluto's elliptical orbit. The last conjunctions were in:

1914/15 (3°, 3°, 1° of Cancer): World War I. Eruption of a dark fate engulfing millions. It would eventually lead to even darker depths. The Shadow side of history emerged for all to see.

1947 (14° Leo): rebirth of ancient civilizations in a nuclear world.

On August 15, 1947, four days after the conjunction, the Indian subcontinent peacefully gained independence. It immediately devolved into a bloody Hindu-Muslim Partition. That has now led to a tense nuclear faceoff between India and Pakistan.

On May 14, 1948, one human pregnancy later, Israel emerged from the Holocaust. This instantly ignited war with the Arab world. And a long-term confrontation many see as leading to eventual Armageddon.

Overall a better world order was born after the trauma of World War II. Yet, with the nuclear genie (Pluto) out of the bottle (Saturn) and into the hands of those with age old rivalries …

1982 (28° Libra): A conservative ascendancy stabilized the end of an intensely political era. This generated the conditions for the emergence of today's managerial and technocratic world order. China threw off Maoism; the United States turned away from half a century of liberal reform (1933-1981) to a 'Reagan revolution' of deregulation and increasing inequality; the Soviet Union went senile and died.

The next will be in 2020 (23° Capricorn).

Outer Planet Conjunctions

Conjunctions between the outer planets themselves (Uranus: Inspiration; Neptune: Imagination; Pluto: Metamorphosis) indicate profound changes in the collective unconscious, deep tectonic flows in basic awareness, fundamental evolution of social outlook. These take place at very long intervals.

Uranus/Neptune

The intelligible edge of the unconscious (Uranus) aligns with its imaginative depths (Neptune). Visionary mental inspiration is attuned to its idealistic and emotional sources. The Neptunian dream space opens up a communication channel, downloads on a specific intuitive frequency (Uranus), into socially agreed consensus consciousness.

Conjunction every 172 years. The last conjunctions were in:

1821 (4°, 3°, 2° of Capricorn).

1993 (20°, 19°, 19° of Capricorn).

The next will be in 2165 (7° Aquarius).

The previous conjunction took place in 1650, long before either was discovered.

The 1821 Uranus/Neptune in Capricorn, a sign of demonstrable achievement, institutionalized innovation. The scientific method became the emergent religion of modernity. Imagination and inspiration were consistently applied to practical problems. Progress, even magic, became a planned program.

The Industrial Revolution took off after a generation of war and upheaval (1789-1815). For millennia history had been a chronicle of military, political, religious and cultural events against an unchanging background of agrarian life. The basic human condition had been an endless round of exhausting manual labor and early death. Suddenly a self-reinforcing flood of economic growth and technological invention changed all that. The material and social scope of life grew by an order of magnitude in a few generations.

After a cycle of industrialization and urbanization (1821-1993) a second Uranus/Neptune in Capricorn reiterated the same theme of creative vision grounded in tangible transformation. This time an information economy proliferated around the world in the blink of an eye. A new global nervous system visibly took form. The remainder of this period will be preoccupied with integrating this fundamentally enlarged database of knowledge and power into a sustainable social order and a new sense of human identity.

Uranus/Pluto

Conjunctions average every 127 years, varying because of Pluto's elliptical orbit. The last conjunctions were in:

1850/1 (0°, 0° of Taurus, 29° Aries).

1965/6 (18°, 17°, 17° of Virgo).

The next will be in 2104 (8° Taurus).

The previous conjunction took place in 1710, long before either planet was discovered.

Uranus/Neptune symbolizes the creative orientation of long-term social processes. Uranus/Pluto describes the purpose behind that process. A new perspective (Uranus) on a core issue (Pluto).

Uranus/Pluto at the last (29th) degree of aggressive Aries in 1850 marked the final triumph of American expansion across the continent. It also brought the festering issue of slavery to a boil. Should it be allowed in the vast new southern acquisition stretching from Texas to California? In 1850 Pluto had not yet emerged into conscious recognition. Yet its hidden presence reinforced Uranus' emergent soul-searching around this injustice. The political compromise of that year paradoxically sharpened the debate while delaying a showdown for another decade. That gave the north more time to continue its industrialization, ensuring its victory in a civil war that redefined the nation, and through it the world's destiny. In a deeper sense this conjunction ended a fire epoch (1663-1842) emphasizing individual initiative in favor of an earth epoch (1842-2020) emphasizing social organization (see Jupiter/Saturn above). The abolition of private property in other human beings was a fundamental step in that direction.

Uranus/Pluto at 17° of Virgo in 1965 exactly trined (120°) an upcoming Uranus/Neptune at 19° Capricorn in 1993. Innovation (Uranus) in response to existential challenge (Pluto) catalyzed the emergence of a long-term transformative ideal (Uranus/Neptune): a post-political global technological civilization.

Uranus/Pluto in 1965 brought a fundamental new twist to the contest of wills between freedom and collectivism (manifesting through a US/USSR superpower confrontation). This deadly power struggle sublimated into a technological competition (Virgo). It would play out off-planet, in a race to land on the Moon. The space race of the 1960s jump started the technology boom that almost miraculously created a new economy. (Both Virgo and Capricorn are earth signs, emphasizing practical manifestation of real results.) In 1965 the U.S. was an industrial society; by 1993 its leading edge had become a futuristic science based economy. This could not have happened without the massive stimulus provided by the space program and its associated Cold War military spin offs.

Some would argue that our move from Earth's cradle out into the cosmos was inevitable at this stage of evolution. That is far from certain. Perhaps only a socially cohesive generation, accustomed to large-scale teamwork in the face of life and death pressure, would have the motivation and tenacity to embark on and stick with such a program. Perhaps only an era of enormous surplus wealth, in the glow of post-war prosperity, would have dared to dream such an impossible dream. It is hard to imagine early 21st century America, socially fragmented, financially bankrupt, demographically aging, with a gridlocked government, undertaking such a bold program from scratch. Our vast techno-scientific complex is now funded because it has already become the dominant institution in an information economy - thanks to the initial stimulus of the space race.

Furthermore, the space program has probably already saved the planet several times over: without it there may not be a civilized now. Space satellites detected the unexpected breakdown of our protective atmospheric ozone layer due to industrial chemicals (CFCs: chlorofluorocarbons). Had this gone unnoticed and unchecked, searing ultraviolet radiation would have devastated the global environment. Satellites accurately monitor the type, number and disposition of nuclear weapons, guarding against both surprise attack and the paranoid decision-making that accompanies ignorance. Without that information governments would not have had the confidence to stand down from a hair trigger nuclear posture, let alone begin to disarm.

Uranus/Pluto 1965, at the midpoint of a space race beginning with the first satellite (1957) and ending with the last Moon walk (1973), announced humanity's successful response to its first planetary danger/opportunity: the Cold War. It turned out to be the right crisis at the right time. It might not have ended so well.

Uranus/Pluto spotlights an urgently felt social emergency that generates long-term implications far beyond the immediate issue. Who remembers the Compromise of 1850? Yet because of its consequences we live in a multiracial society rather than a color-coded hierarchy. Who remembers Khrushchev's threat that 'We will bury you?' Yet because of it we are a space faring species.

Neptune/Pluto

Conjunction every 492 years; the length of this cycle smooths out the elasticity of Pluto's orbit. The last conjunction was in:

1891/2 (9°, 9°, 8° of Gemini).

The next will be in 2384 (13° Gemini).

The previous conjunction took place in 1398/9, centuries before either planet was discovered.

Uranus/Neptune and Uranus/Pluto interface with tangible reality and ego consciousness through the inspirational channeling effect of Uranus. Both Neptune and Pluto operate entirely below the surface of awareness. Think of the invisible Gulf Stream, a vast maritime river of warm tropical water giving northern Europe a temperate climate. Unseen, far out at sea, it generates the daily weather of hundreds of millions who otherwise could not survive at those latitudes.

Neptune/Pluto indicates multigenerational mutations in depth psychology. Slow changes in basic instinct. Openings to new subtleties of perception, feeling and understanding. For example, since the agricultural revolution humans seem to have become more socialized, herd-like, even docile. We now instinctively depend on, and defer to, the community rather than surviving by our own keen honed wits. Individual aggression is generally selected out over the long haul. A more collective, feminine psychology emerges, with both positive and negative results. A kinder and gentler, yet perhaps less bold and assertive, species may be forming.

The last two Neptune/Pluto conjunctions occurred in dualistic, mental Gemini: 1891 at 9°; 1398 at 4°. The 1891 pairing coincided with recognition of the ambiguous aspects of both matter and mind that cannot be accommodated by reason, even in principle. The great quest to consciously understand the natural world and human nature came up against an unexpected discovery of their inherently fuzzy, unpredictable qualities. The 1398 conjunction coincided with a slow emergence of the Renaissance as reason split off from medieval religious mysticism.

Finally, since about 1945, and until about 2035, these two distant and subconscious energies have been moving in a long waxing sextile (60°) or reinforcing aspect to each other. This happens because Pluto's highly elliptical orbit brings it close enough to Sun for awhile that it moves at about the same speed as Neptune. (See 'Pluto,' Figure 2.) After 2035 Pluto will slow down as it moves further away from Sun, and the sextile relationship will break down.

The mutual amplification of these otherwise very subliminal forces is one reason they have manifested so overtly, and generally benignly, in recent decades. The postwar era produced a sea change in mass consciousness around fundamental issues of race and gender, human rights and psychological empowerment. A globalized culture essentially unified the world in the space of a single lifetime. This reformatted collective sensibility has generally lifted individuals to a larger, more inclusive state of consciousness.

Soon this emergent level of personal enlightenment will be tested by technological temptations very different than the political passions of the past. Genetic engineering, electro-chemical brain manipulation and mind/computer melding will force everyone to make existential choices about personal identity. People will have to decide between faith in their inherent nature as a child of the universe, or trust in its biotechnical modification as a deliberately upgraded product of applied intelligence.

The long Neptune/Pluto sextile symbolizes a social evolution that will soon eliminate traditional forms of poverty, discrimination and oppression. (This may be expedited by a drastic thinning of the herd and a leveling of traditional structures.) That will facilitate the emergence of a brave new world making more subtle and insidious demands as we turn from a religious to a medical model of the human condition.

As Pluto transits through Aquarius, 2024-43, an initial presentation of these issues will test and prepare humanity for a coming Aquarian Age (2060-4220: see 'Precession'). Neptune's concurrent transit through initiating Aries, 2026-40, will generate illusions of power as we increasingly worship ourselves as the creation of our own hands.

Outer Planet Transits

This chapter outlines how the slow moving outer planets, Uranus, Neptune and Pluto, chart deep generational change. Chart, not cause. Planets do not affect us. They are cosmic energy centers that resonate to the same underlying spiritual reality we embody. Their astronomical characteristics symbolize our own collective potentials. Their trajectories through the zodiac portray how those possibilities have manifested through history.

These three planets were discovered in recent centuries with the aid of telescopes. Thus they portray emergent properties of modernity. They describe new dimensions of consciousness, and of power, generated by our accelerating social evolution and technological innovation over the last 250 years. Their long transits through specific energy zones (signs) indicate a strong correlation between planet/sign symbolism and actual events. Hopefully this will stimulate the reader to develop a sense of how astrology discerns meaningful patterns in history. While astrology cannot predict specific incidents it does project general trends. It demonstrates a consistent process with which we can consciously engage and co-create.

The planetary forces beyond Saturn's frontier of consciousness act in a fundamentally different way than the seven visible planets known since antiquity.[1] These bodies are invisible to the naked eye, symbolically inaccessible to normal consciousness.[2] They describe an underlying subconscious matrix as different from consensus reality as the subatomic quantum realm of physics is from the atomic matter of the cosmos. Quantum reality consists of probabilities rather than facts, flashing energies sparkling into and out of existence without distinct cause and effect. In the same way, our subconscious seems to function as a shimmering sea of images and impulses rather than a logical train of thought or consistent thread of emotion.

Unlike the discrete qualities of the classical planets (e.g. Mercury = mind, Venus = love, Mars = will, etc.) the outer planets act as various aspects of one force field. Just as a ray of light can diffract across a spectrum as various colors of one radiance, so these planetary bodies, spread out in space, provide differing perspectives on an overall collective energy.

The nature and relationship of their physical globes symbolically illustrates the idea that they display levels of one fluid flux rather than independent qualities. Uranus and Neptune are twins, with the same size and composition. However, Uranus spins at a right angle to Neptune. Together they form the vertical and horizontal arms of a cross,

Figure 1   Uranus/Neptune Relationship

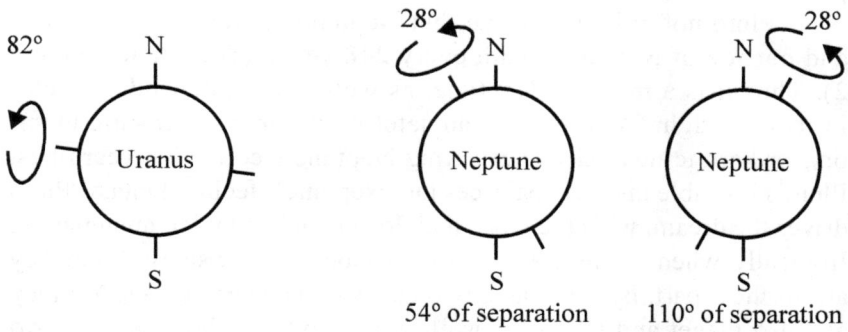

The angle between Uranus' and Neptune's north poles varies from 54° to 110° depending on these two planets' relative inclinations towards Sun. No doubt this has a subtle meaning.

Figure 2   Pluto orbit

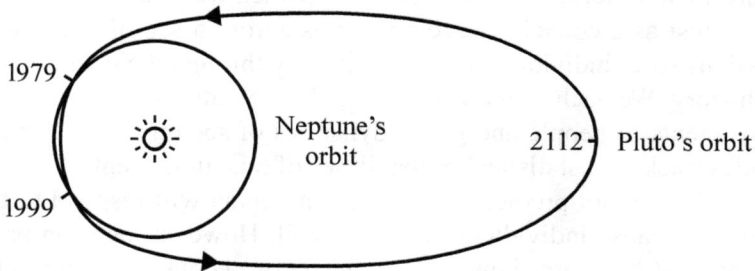

Pluto crosses and orbits inside of Neptune's orbit for 20 out of 248 years. Thus it can be considered a moon of Neptune.

separated in space but linked in meaning. Figure 1. Neptune is abstract mental Uranus' dreamy, imaginative alter ego. These two planets act as the intellectual and emotional polarities of a single psychosocial energy, just as electricity (Uranus) and magnetism (Neptune) are of a unified physical force (electromagnetism).

Pluto not only orbits Sun, but Neptune as well, circling inside and outside of Neptune's path every 248 years. (See 'Pluto,' Figure 2). Thus it is a moon of Neptune, as well as an independent factor in its own right. As a Neptunian satellite it depicts a cosmic memory, or karmic necessity, motivating Neptune's collective yearnings. Pluto's invisible instinct coalesces into Neptune's feeling fantasy. Pluto drives the dream, wills the wish, that flowers in Neptunian imagination. Ironically, when Neptune and Pluto move on opposite sides of Sun they are further apart, by far, than any other two planetary bodies. Yet they are also planet and moon, in as close an orbital embrace as any two planets can have.

All three of these planets function as a triple octave of one vibration in another dimension of consciousness. They also move on another timeline, with extended orbital periods that dwarf individual human experience. The classical planets all circle Sun many, or at least several, times in a normal human lifespan. The outer planets dance to a slower rhythm. Uranus takes 84 years to make one trip around Sun: the maximum length of time any human psyche can witness. Neptune, at 168 years, and Pluto, at 248 years, resonate to frequencies beyond a range we can fully experience. All of these planets point to generational and historical rhythms, a collective rather than an individual beat. They chart the long-term social cycles within which we live.

Just as a conscious ego navigates across a sea of unconscious passions so an individual life makes its way through the tides and trials of history. We each move within a herd. The outer planets track mass movements of people and group dynamics of societies just as mathematics tracks the statistical probabilities of quantum events.

One cannot predict how any given person will respond to these powers because individuals have free will. However, one can predict the general pattern of how large numbers of people will react to their invisible guidance. This is mediated through collective force fields, whether formal and structured, like nations, or informal and fluid, like public moods and fads. The mutation cycle of Jupiter and Saturn provides a context for actual events. (See 'Synods.') Their positions and aspect at any given time portrays specific situations. The outer planets orient us to the mysterious driving force behind those happenings, with its levels of accessible inspiration (Uranus), ineffable imagination (Neptune) and underlying will (Pluto).

Notes

1. Sun, Moon, Mercury, Venus, Mars, Jupiter, Saturn
2. Uranus is technically visible as a faint speck in a very clear sky. Yet, despite millennia of stargazing, it was not recognized as a planet until observed telescopically on March 13, 1781.

Uranus

Uranus' seven-year transit of a sign indicates how emergent potentials transform the social milieu, creatively or destructively. Uranus functions as the point source of contact with animating principles behind historic phenomena.

Uranus in Aries initiates a general change in atmosphere: transformed expectations in the socio-political realm, a different orientation in the cultural, new paradigms in the scientific and technological. Uranus entered Aries in 1760, 1844, 1927 and 2011. Because Uranus in Aries begins an extended historical period some comments about the Uranus cycle in general are appropriate. It marks the length of a long human lifetime, perhaps suggesting the maximum level of novelty and stimulation the psyche can assimilate. Uranus' 84-year orbit also runs parallel to, but is not temporally congruent with, the four generation sociological rhythm portrayed by Strauss and Howe in their seminal work 'Generations.'[1] Thus it describes a fundamental unit of the human condition: one's participation in a generational experience that transcends, includes and (partially) defines personal identity.

Each Uranus cycle since its discovery in 1781 has displayed the flavor of a newly unearthed level in the collective unconscious. The period 1760-1844, during which Uranus itself was discovered, had a highly Uranian character; 1844-1927, when Neptune was discovered (1846) was quite Neptunian; 1927-2011, when Pluto was discovered (1930) was unmistakably Plutonian.

Prior to its conscious recognition as a planet the Uranus plane of experience acted as a latent energy, an ungrounded voltage. It embodied a potential, intangibly influencing but not openly expressing itself in psyche and history. Uranus was like a background radiation: real and present, but unacknowledged. A diffuse force field rather than an explicit energy focus. Once Uranus, and the qualities it symbolizes, emerged into conscious awareness on a public scale (1781) it directly and powerfully expressed its own nature. Thus 1760-1844 was an era of revolution: the American inaugurating a new model of governance; the

French, shattering a petrified social order; the Industrial, transforming the basic contours of human possibility. It generally had a classical, rational atmosphere: the Enlightenment, but finished with a mystical Romantic sensibility presaging recognition of its sister planet, Neptune.

At the same time a first magnitude philosophical breakthrough paralleled the political and technological revolutions of the late 18th century. Changes in social organization are superficial unless accompanied by changes in consciousness. Inner transformation is more fundamental than external economic growth; a collective enlightenment means more than a switch in government. In 1781 Immanuel Kant, a German philosopher (1724-1804), published the 'Critique of Pure Reason.' In it he definitively established the inherent autonomy of consciousness as distinct from the phenomena it perceives. A more subtle state of being, pure consciousness, pervades the world of matter and motion. We cannot know a thing in and of itself, as it exists in its own right. We can only know it through the medium of our own consciousness. The recognition that the nature of consciousness is as important as the empirical reality of experience changed the way we think as much as any scientific discovery or theory. The understanding of mind as fundamental was fundamental. It marked the first self-conscious consciousness revolution.

Then a new Uranian cycle with a Neptunian flavor ran from 1844-1927.[2] This was an idealistic era of utopian expectation, characterized by a general peace,[3] increasing prosperity and seemingly unlimited prospects for progress. Age-old evils, such as slavery, were abolished; new ideals, such as women's rights, embraced. The physical constraints of time and distance were shrunk by electronic communications and motorized transport. Indeed, Einstein's Relativity (1905) and the following golden age of physics dissolved the very ideas of solid matter and uniform duration in the early 20th century. Our special status in creation melted away with evolution (Darwin, 1859). Our seemingly conscious ego morphed into an ever-changing focal point of instinctual energies (Freud, Jung). All certainties dissolved, revealing a larger but more ambiguous human and universal condition. Finally, this cycle washed away in a confused bloodbath that nobody really wanted and with no definitive outcome (the Great War).

Another began with a distinctly Plutonian tone from 1927-2011.[4] A genteel era of increasing refinement suddenly plunged into a desperate economic Depression. This spawned the rise of totalitarian police states (Nazi Germany and Stalinist Russia). World War II was the outcome. After this volcanic outburst spent itself, humanity faced a protracted contest of wills between two superpowers on hair trigger alert for nuclear Armageddon. With the end of the Cold War this existential challenge continues in a more subtle technological form. Humans became a force of geological magnitude on the climate and biodiversity of our planet. Artificial intelligence, spaceflight, genetic engineering and neurochemical manipulation are the outward and visible manifestations of a primal metamorphosis within our own species.

So far we have dealt surprisingly well with the sudden onset of these incredible danger/opportunity challenges. Now Uranus has transited out of its revelation of the Plutonian layer of the trans-conscious spectrum. Since its discovery Uranus has demonstrated an initial recognition of successively deeper layers of psyche and possibility. It begins a new cycle, 2011-2095, having exposed its three octaves of expression (inspiration, 1760-1844; imagination, 1844-1927; will/power, 1927-2011). A newly evolved conscious ability to envisage, plan and direct the future will replace the initial shock of these levels' emergence. This could take shape as an encouragement of enhanced human potential - or as a coercive social programming.

The three Uranus cycles since its discovery (1781) have successively uncovered ever more distant planets in space: Uranus itself, Neptune and Pluto. The physical revelation of these planets has symbolically coincided with the disclosure of previously unacknowledged planes of psychological insight and social evolution. An increasingly self-aware, planned feedback loop of innovation; scientific, technological, and political (Uranus, 1760-1844). A recognition of the deep irrational foundations of our conscious and moral worldview in psychology, fundamental uncertainty at the quantum level in physics and seemingly random yet teleological (goal oriented) evolutionary processes in biology (Neptune, 1844-1927).[5] An encounter with overwhelming and fateful forces, politically in the mass movements, good and evil, of the 20th century; technologically in the unprecedented powers attained by humanity (Pluto, 1927-2011).

Now a new Uranus cycle is beginning (2011-2095) that will synthesize these new levels of consciousness and power into the long-term character of an upcoming Precessional Age of Aquarius.[6] The lightning bolt of Uranian revolution, so prominent since its discovery, must ground itself in time; integrate revelation into an enduring social order and its associated worldview. This could manifest as a utopian golden age, a science fiction police state or a shattered and dazed anarchy of environmental collapse. One way or another the coming era will see a stabilization of the transformational Uranian impulse into a quasi-permanent social, political and ideological dispensation.

The three previous cycles beginning with Uranus in Aries (1760, 1844, 1927) were able to explore ever deeper levels of psyche, ever higher peaks of discovery, in an environment of technologically enhanced abundance. Now increasing population and diminishing natural assets present another kind of challenge: maintenance of steady state productivity on a small planet, or an increasingly primeval struggle over water and food, oil and minerals. An age of unlimited expansion will either consolidate its achievements for long term survival on a finite world, or overshoot its limits, crash and burn.

Most likely some catastrophe, like a global pandemic or a climate induced crop failure, will thin the ranks of humanity and force the survivors to make fundamental changes. Some will choose various new age utopias, others will opt for different forms of technological regimentation. These agendas will then fight it out, ultimately generating a hybrid consensus. The 2011-2019 Uranus in Aries transit will begin, not resolve, this process.

Notes

1. A 20 year long generation × four generations = 80 years, approximately the same length as a Uranus orbit.

Strauss and Howe posit a four generational psychosocial rhythm consisting of: an outer directed, achievement oriented cohort (e.g.: the 'greatest,' GI generation, born approximately 1900-1920), followed by an adaptive, moderating one (the silent generation, born 1920-1940); then an inner directed idealistic cohort (the baby boomers, born 1940-1960) followed by a pragmatic, streetwise one (GenX, born 1960-1980). Then the cycle begins anew: thus another 'doer' generation the 'Millenials' was born between 1980-2000. No generation is inherently better or worse than any other, though the achievement and idealistic ones tend to be more prominent. (Of course, the achievements can be negative and the ideals bad.) 'Generations' provides considerable and compelling evidence for this thesis.

Strauss and Howe make no reference to astrology. Furthermore, the 84-year Uranus cycle does not synchronize with this 80-year recurrent rhythm, but is offset from it. Thus, for example, Uranus entered Aries in 1760, 1844, 1927 and 2011, of which the last two entries were in the middle of a generational cohort. The similar duration of a generational round and a Uranus year means an individual's participation in the collective enterprise can encompass all four seasons of generational experience, a full cycle of social reality. Of course that individual can be born at any point within both a generational cohort and a Uranian orbit.

2. September 23, 1846

3. Pax Britannica, 1815-1914, from the Napoleonic wars to World War I

4. February 18, 1930

5. The current standard view in biology is that because evolutionary change is caused by random mutations in the genetic code, therefore evolution itself is random. However, life clearly and consistently evolves towards greater complexity and more inclusive states of consciousness through this random process, albeit with many twists and reversals.

6. The Age of Aquarius will run from 2060-4220. See 'Precession.' Uranus rules the sign of Aquarius, along with Saturn.

Uranus in Signs

Uranus portrays the cutting edge of scientific and technological change. It describes the sparkplug igniting social forces. Its transformations are also described within the context of contemporary collective ideals (Neptune) and power motivations (Pluto). For the sake of simplicity the historical examples used to illustrate the rest of this chapter will refer primarily to the American experience.

A Uranus transit of Aries marks the originality of new beginnings. Unexpected novelty in worldview or actual circumstance.

1844-51: Invention of the telegraph (1844) revolutionized communication. Messages that took weeks to cross the continent, months to go global, now arrived instantly in real time. Mass production of a standardized crop reaper (1847) transformed agriculture, allowing a few to do the work of many. This displaced rural labor that would man Union armies during the Civil War, then move out to the frontier or into booming industrial cities.

The United States suddenly doubled in size through diplomacy and war (1846-48). Thus it reached its 'Manifest Destiny' as a nation of continental dimensions. A pioneering outsurge led to instantaneous settlement of its west coast during the Gold Rush.

Newly discovered Neptune descended from the heights of Transcendental spiritual aspirations (Neptune in Aquarius, 1834-47)[1] to more compassionate concerns about the evils of slavery and issues of workers' rights (Neptune in Pisces, 1847-61).[2] Undiscovered Pluto added its hidden strength to Uranus as they both conjoined in Aries. (See 'Synods.')

1. Some of America's most characteristic idealist thinkers flourished in this last phase of the Romantic period: Ralph Waldo Emerson (1803-82), Henry David Thoreau (1817-62), and Walt Whitman (1819-92).

2. Karl Marx (1818-83) published his stirring 'Communist Manifesto' during the European social revolutions of 1848. His massive economic tome, 'Das Kapital,' would follow as Uranus transited Taurus.

1927-35: The shattering onset of a Great Depression inaugurated the modern managerial state, taking the form of welfare capitalism in the West, fascism in central Europe and centralized planning in the USSR. The economic crisis, along with the sudden rise of a totalitarian threat, initiated large-scale government support for pure science, its applied development and their industrial/educational infrastructure. This led to a permanent and accelerating tsunami of technological innovation.

New mass ideals supplanted old private dreams as society collectivized (Neptune in Virgo). Personal and national security ebbed away (Pluto in Cancer).

The implications of Uranus' current transit through Aries, 2011-2019, are discussed later in the chapter.

A Uranus transit of Taurus marks fundamental change in the material circumstances and defining values of a society.

1851-58: The first oil well (1859) began an energy revolution that is only now peaking. The Bessemer steel making process (1855) opened a new era of heavy industry. Oil and steel would become the foundations of an industrial economy for the next century.

The debate over slavery intensified sharply after the Compromise of 1850. Sweeping economic changes decisively altered the internal balance of power. The growth of railroads, mechanized agriculture and industrialization in the north laid the foundation of the Union's victory in a closely fought Civil War.

A growing sensitivity to the injustice and suffering of slavery undermined national unity (Neptune in Pisces). This was reinforced by a new willingness to insist on these emerging values, even at the cost of conflict (Pluto in Taurus).

1935-42: Governments made enormous investments in wartime research and development. These generated a wide range of new technologies, many of which had peacetime uses. A centrally organized science based economy began to replace a laissez-faire industrial order.

A concrete trial of strength between ideologies and nations (World War II). Humanity's basic values fought it out in the most literal way. Seemingly fixed national identities were transformed: the US shifted from an isolationist to an international posture, the USSR converted from an agrarian to an industrial society, the power and leadership of Western Europe self-destructed.

Three very different collective ideals - democracy, fascism and communism - were put to the test (Neptune in Virgo). Hidden passions erupted with a roar as Pluto moved from Cancer into Leo.

A Uranus transit of Gemini means mental clarification through eloquent expression of inspired insight. A choice between clear alternatives. Taking sides.

1858-65: Darwin published 'The Origin of Species' (1859); Maxwell published his equations describing electromagnetism (1864).* These two intellectual arguments contrasted with the productive breakthroughs of the previous Uranus in Taurus period. They were at least as important, because they fundamentally changed our views of biology and physics.

Civil War divided the nation. Its eventual outcome was reunification on a more enduring basis. As the nation split apart Neptune moved through martial Aries, casting a spell of moral, even Biblical, righteousness over the war. Pluto continued through Taurus, powering the industrial muscle of the north, which was greatly stimulated by the war effort.

*Einstein described the work of James Clerk Maxwell (1831-1879) as 'the most profound and the most fruitful that physics has experienced since the time of Newton.'

1942-49: The atom was split. The binding energy of matter's nucleus was released through arcane intellectual investigation into the fundamental nature of nature.

The world was split by war (World War II) and ideology (Cold War), yet united by a tentative blueprint of world government (United Nations).

A fundamental break from old paradigms as new ideals of world order replaced strident nationalisms. This was guided by collective dreams of peace and justice (Neptune in Libra) emerging from the drama of total war (Pluto in Leo).

A Uranus transit of Cancer marks a break from the immediate past, a shift in mood. A reorientation from public emergency to personal pursuits. Reevaluation of heritage.

1865-71: A now reunified nation bound itself together with a transcontinental railroad linking the east and west coasts (1869). Mendeleev's Periodic Table demonstrated family affinities (Cancer) of the material elements, laying a new foundation for chemistry (1869).

Changes in domestic and community life as Reconstruction reformed the south, industrialization accelerated in the north and a flood of small homesteaders poured into the west.

As a once divided house reintegrated (Cancer) Neptune continued through Aries, generating a new sense of national character that replaced sectional identities. Pluto in Taurus consolidated this with an economic restructuring away from plantation slavery in the south and towards corporate organization in the north.

1949-55: The discovery of DNA's helical structure and how it functions (1953) opened a new chapter in our comprehension of biological life and how it evolves through the generations.

A postwar baby boom, the growth of suburbs and sustained prosperity emphasized private and domestic concerns after a quarter century of depression and war.

A return to relative tranquility amidst new ideals of international cooperation (Neptune in Libra) and transformed postwar national identities (Pluto in Leo).

A Uranus transit of Leo marks a time permitting and encouraging personal development, relatively free of public drama. Social issues are muted, individual creativity blossoms.

1871-78: Modern conveniences such as the typewriter (1873), telephone (1876) and phonograph (1877) began to enhance daily life.

With the crusading fervor of the Civil War over, society turned to the pursuit of private fortune. This was the golden era of robber barons and cowboys, of the Wild West with its opportunities for uninhibited self-expression.

As social change gave way to personal concerns, Neptune joined Pluto in the economic sign of Taurus. Unrestrained capitalism generated both personal and corporate wealth in an era of 'Every man for himself and the Devil take the hindmost.'

1955-62: Humanity triumphantly asserted a cosmic destiny: breakthrough into outer space by satellite (Sputnik, 1957) and living astronaut (Gagarin, 1961; Glenn, 1962).

Social change was muted in the glow of postwar prosperity. A placid period, the world's first experience of an affluent society in which most people were comfortably middle class.* These conditions nurtured the growth of pride and self confidence in marginalized groups who would soon assert themselves in the civil rights, feminist and peace movements.

Collective and generational ideals began a deep transformation as Neptune entered Scorpio. A Cold War driven technology began to redefine the human condition as Pluto entered Virgo.

*In the U.S. and Western Europe. Of course, most people overall were not members of this community, but lived in grinding third world poverty. So it had been since the dawn of the agricultural revolution. But Uranus is not about the background norm - it is about the emergent property.

A Uranus transit through Virgo resolves contradictions between social ideals and realities by insisting on new standards. Application of known scientific principles to practical technological use.

1878-84: Edison's invention of the incandescent electric light bulb (1879) - a simple device bringing light to night. It made modern life possible.

A federal civil service based on merit replaced the spoils system of appointment by political patronage. Negatively, discrimination in its worst sense made a comeback as Reconstruction ended in the south.

Corporations rationalized production in an atmosphere of economic motivation free of major political discord, with both Neptune and Pluto in Taurus.

1962-68: The space race lavishly funded and nurtured technological innovation across the board. A vast expansion of educational opportunity ensured long-term commitment to a science based economy.

609

The civil rights revolution demanded that the nation demonstrate integrity by living up to its stated ideals of equal justice for all. Its success and nonviolent tactics inspired a broad social self-criticism and healing, especially in the peace and feminist movements.

The difference between the relative quiet of 1878-84 and the wild exuberance of 1962-68 was a rare Uranus/Pluto conjunction in Virgo throughout this period, becoming exact in 1965. In the earlier period both Neptune and Pluto were in Taurus. People just wanted to be left alone to make money. This time Neptune moved through passionate Scorpio, with its urgency for rebirth, while Pluto amplified Uranus' demand for transformation into an immediate social emergency.

A Uranus transit through Libra brings adjustment to new external realities. So far in history it has operated as a slow tipping of the scales rather than as a sudden disruption.

1884-90: The balance of power slowly swung from small-scale private enterprise towards immense consolidations of wealth. A quiet period as corporate interests and civil society found a natural equilibrium. This period assimilated more than generated technological, economic and demographic change. It ended as the Census Bureau declared the western frontier closed. The wild edge that had fundamentally shaped the American national character was now history. Individual pioneering turned to collaborative effort as scientific discovery and technological innovation replaced physical exploration.

A more complex array of social classes differentiated as both Neptune and Pluto entered multifaceted Gemini.

1968-74: A phase change in planetary history, comparable to that when life first moved from sea to land. By setting foot on the Moon (July 20, 1969) humanity assumed a cosmic destiny. The full significance of this initiation will not be appreciated for many years: but it has happened.

It is not yet known whether humans can survive long term and reproduce successfully in the weightlessness of space, or on the low gravity worlds of Moon and Mars. Still, the fact that we have entered space, physically touched the infinite, implies that something profound has happened on a collective spiritual level.

This period also introduced a general ecological perspective, symbolized by the vision of a finite 'Spaceship Earth.' Confronted with the choice between unlimited growth (impossible) and environmental disaster (unacceptable), humanity faced the need for a new relationship with nature. This became widely recognized though far from accomplished during this period.

The price of oil suddenly quadrupled, ending the postwar period of cheap energy. This ushered in a new era of financial globalization as petrodollars funneled into a worldwide banking system. Everywhere national autonomy was increasingly subsumed by the international economic order. Previously isolated China began to participate in it, realigning the balance of power.

Traditional sensibilities dissolved into counterculture ideals (Neptune in Sagittarius). Passions for social purification compromised as changing values, economic inflation and political scandal paralyzed effective governance (Pluto in Libra).

A Uranus transit through Scorpio marks a time of deep inner transformation whose implications will surface later. A buildup of charge.

1891-98: Forces that were to remake the world silently grew in scope and potency. The discovery of radioactivity (Becquerel, 1896) and the unconscious dimensions of psychology (Freud, 1896) redefined the foundations of physics and philosophy. These insights into the essential nature of things were far more important than overt political events, of which this period was generally free.

The growth of corporate power slowly transformed society as urban complexity replaced a simpler agrarian order. Class distinctions sharpened as Neptune and Pluto continued moving together through diversified Gemini. Farmers became laborers in many industries, as workers graduated into a middle class of clerks and merchants.

1974-81: The development of recombinant DNA technology (discovered in 1973) opened the door to conscious manipulation of life's biological heritage. Its implications are fundamental. The temptations of genetic engineering will constitute an ultimate test of human identity.

Politically, the eruption of a radical Islamic reaction to modernity (Iranian Revolution, 1979). In principle this could have expressed a demand for recognition of the spiritual dimension in a soul stifling global consumer culture. Sadly, it actually reflected poisonous resentment rather than an elevating vision. The unexpected election of a Polish Pope, John Paul II (1978-2005), presented a similar but more positive challenge within the ossified Soviet system. This, along with a Scorpionic reassertion of national will in the West (Thatcher, Reagan), would stress the internal contradictions of communism to the breaking point. A shift to the right as an industrial society morphed into a more individualistic information economy.

Deep technological and economic transformations gestated under a surface of political gridlock (Pluto in Libra) and the inflated self-esteem of a 'me generation' (Neptune in Sagittarius).

A Uranus transit through Sagittarius marks an accelerating expansion of new forces and ideas whose time has come.

1898-1905: The invention of wireless radio (1903) generated a quantum jump in electronic communication. Humanity took wing with the first airplane flight (Wright brothers, 1903). Our species launched into the sky.

The United States (Sagittarius rising) gained an island empire during the Spanish-American War (1898). By essentially annexing the Pacific Ocean and Caribbean Sea it transformed from an inward looking continental country to an outward oriented world power.

The American melting pot began to digest new waves of ethnic immigrants from southern and eastern Europe as Neptune entered Cancer. A sense of unlimited expansion in the economy and technology was underwritten by an ever deeper exploration of physics, biology and psychology as Pluto continued through intellectual Gemini.

1981-88: The biotech and Internet revolutions took off, opening the door to an information economy.

The political and philosophic victory of a liberal democratic vision as communist police states and right wing dictatorships melted away. A global expansion of freedom. A time of optimism as the world transcended a forty-year US/USSR nuclear confrontation.

A rejuvenation of traditional morality as social ideals returned to more conservative forms (Neptune in Capricorn) after a long period of change and experimentation. Power realities moved from a rebalancing (Pluto in Libra) to a decisive end game in the Cold War (Pluto in Scorpio).

A Uranus transit through Capricorn marks fundamental restructuring of a mature worldview ripe for transformation. Or the actual establishment of a new order.

1905-12: Einstein published his special Theory of Relativity (1905) completely changing our understanding of time, space, matter and energy.

Henry Ford introduced mass production of automobiles (1909). This permanently transformed the economic and social landscape of modern society. Politically, culturally and economically this was the pinnacle of an unprecedented era of progress. Its quantitative evolutionary change had built up energies that would soon flip over into qualitative revolutionary upheaval.

The Gilded Age of capitalism generated a maximum concentration of charge supporting intellectual transformation (Pluto in Gemini) in a genteel atmosphere of tradition and security (Neptune in Cancer).

1988-96: Long term planning and large scale organization rather than spectacular breakthrough in science and technology. This laid the groundwork for gigantic efforts such as the Human Genome Project, International Space Station and the World Wide Web.

Establishment of a new world order following the sudden unexpected end of the Cold War. This had a Capricornian flavor based on conservative principles of limited government with a managerial corporate character.

Neptune's concurrent transit through Capricorn grounded inspirational ideals into now universally accepted institutional forms. Pluto's movement through Scorpio backed this up with a globalized financial market.

A Uranus transit through Aquarius portrays instantaneous transformation: either violent shattering of a rigid structure or universal acceptance of a new consensus.

1912-20: World War I overthrew a century of peace and progress (1815-1914). It initiated the short 20th century (1914-1991) of transformative, often traumatic, upheaval. The Russian Revolution (1917) posed a fundamental political and economic challenge to all accepted norms, combining utopian social experimentation with mass executions and savage repression.

The demands of total mobilization generated new social realities as women entered the labor force in all combatant countries to replace millions of men sent off to the front. Technology was systematically organized and applied to the development of complex weapons platforms, such as vastly improved aircraft, submarines and tanks. This temporary switch from spontaneous to planned innovation foreshadowed the managed science based society of the future.

War and revolution changed everything as Neptune generated illusory ideals of national pride in Leo, and Pluto plunged into a bloodbath of instinctual tribal passion in Cancer.

1996-2003: Oddly enough, this was a period of consolidation as a now generally accepted new order stabilized after the Cold War. Uranus in Aquarius need not be disruptive (as in 1912-20) if it can express itself in an open system. Rapid globalization of the economy and integration of technological innovation into social life made this a cosmopolitan era diffusing a universal civilization around the world. Bloody police actions in Afghanistan and Iraq were exceptions that prove the rule. There will always be some degree of conflict in human affairs.

Expanding international cooperation and cultural consensus, with their many good aspects, can also remind us that the greatest danger of an Aquarian era can be complacent groupthink. The Uranus/Aquarius transit of 1996-2003 may preview an upcoming Aquarian Age* characterized by consumerism of the mind, a bland harmony of spirit. Serene contentment with achieved excellence, mellow satisfaction with an obvious all embracing truth narrative, may replace the creative conflict of a more violent and passionate past. It has happened before in other civilizations: for example, imperial China. While this Uranus transit constituted a much needed breathing spell of tranquility and progress, it may also foreshadow a sanitized global mall of the future. ☺

Visionary technological projects, such as the International Space Station, Human Genome Project and World Wide Web coincided with the twin planets Uranus' and Neptune's concurrent transit through Aquarius. Pluto in Sagittarius generated an expansive lift to these grand and costly long-term efforts.

* Uranus rules Aquarius. The Aquarian Age will last from 2060-4220 (see 'Precession').

A Uranus transit through Pisces brings dissolution of traditional structures and mores. It clears the decks of karma for an upcoming cycle. Uranus in Pisces expands social participation with a concomitant relaxation of standards. It includes but inflates. It liberates many, but dilutes expectations to do so. Its new horizons of consciousness may seem superficial (and often are), but they are irreversible. Like a tentative predawn light it dissolves the dark without fully revealing the day. It marks a surge into naive new realms of hope. These will eventually get a reality check, but the dream, once dreamt, is not forgotten.

1920-27: The promise of future miracles beckoned, with the first television[1] and liquid fueled rocket.[2]

A delusional peace after the 'war to end all wars' petered out in universal exhaustion. During the Roaring Twenties a short-lived prosperity created the first middle class society. The average family could afford a car and a radio, items that would have seemed magical to their parents. (The same occurred during the more recent 2003-11 transit, with its laptops, cell phones and other electronic gizmos.) Mass media and expanded education dissolved parochial identifications. Marginalized groups were liberated: women could vote; a vibrant black culture expressed itself in the Jazz Age. Life's horizons expanded. Soon the economic bubble would burst in the Great Depression, but an enhanced cultural sophistication had become the new norm.

Meanwhile, Neptune wove a spell of gaudy flamboyance as it passed through Leo, while passionate mass movements gestated in traumatized nations torn from their traditional roots (Pluto in Cancer).

1. Philo Farnsworth, 1928.
2. Robert Goddard, 1926. This precursor of the space age rose only 41 feet before crashing - but the door to the cosmos had opened.

2003-11: Scientifically and technologically this was a period of deepening subtlety rather than fundamental breakthrough. The astonishing became normal. Exoplanets orbiting alien stars, gene sequencing and splicing, biotech medicine and nanotech physics were relegated to routine blurbs in the news. Ever more sophisticated electronic devices became part of daily life. A new techno-civ silently supplanted traditional cultural identities, as the world flowed together in a ghostly cyberspace.

A delusional boom based on speculation and debt flipped into a global financial crisis taking business as usual to the edge. This may inspire a fundamental restructuring towards an economically and ecologically sustainable system. Or it could be the precursor of a real meltdown in a far more interdependent world than that of the 1930s. In either case a new dispensation will begin to emerge after 2011: see below.

The triumph of Piscean illusion in voodoo economic theories of unlimited credit and spending was reinforced by Pluto's surge through ever-optimistic Sagittarius and Neptune's wishful thinking in Aquarius.

A Preview of Coming Events

Uranus channels all three outer planets' energies into a cutting edge of long-term social and scientific change. A general overview of how these are likely to play out over the next generation follows (written in 2013):

Aries (2011-19): Initiation of a more socially equitable and ecologically sustainable economy after the near financial collapse immediately preceding. Failure to do so voluntarily will lead to breakdown and a forced restructuring under catastrophic circumstances.

The disintegration of an overgrown, debt-driven system (Neptune in Pisces) will generate a new hierarchy of social imperatives and institutions (Pluto in Capricorn).

Taurus (2019-26): A new economic order and its associated social values will visibly take shape simply because increasing stresses on the planet's environmental resources and social safety nets demands it. In this case astrological prediction simply confirms what common sense dictates. It could be an earth and people friendly utopia of solar power, organic agriculture, distributed learning, etc. Or it could be a science fiction nightmare of medicated zombies in a computerized police state.

Dissolution of the old order (Neptune in Pisces) will accompany the explicit emergence of a new governing structure (Pluto in Capricorn). The actual process and content of these changes may be positive or negative. However, the sheer momentum of an unsustainable mass society makes the latter more likely in the short term.

Gemini (2026-33): By now a new world order, positive or negative, will be materially established. This period should see a fundamental split, in fact a showdown, between two incompatible mindsets, ideologies, worldviews within that society. It will probably be over the appropriate use of technology, particularly biotechnology and genetic manipulation.

New ideals, or illusions, of collective identity will emerge (Neptune in Aries) as a coming Aquarian Age begins to manifest (Pluto in Aquarius).

The same general dynamic of initiation (Aries), manifestation (Taurus) and divisive choice (Gemini) seen in the social and political sphere will also occur in science and technology. These endeavors are particularly associated with Uranus. In Aries Uranus will initiate pioneering breakthroughs based on previously deployed collective tools such as the International Space Station, Large Hadron Collider (atom smasher), Human Genome Project and Internet. Uranus in Taurus should ground these discoveries in applied technologies made available on a large social scale. Uranus in Gemini should bring stark choices around the options presented by their unprecedented powers.

Computers, the electronic brains enabling the technological explosion, will continue their exponential growth in speed and capability until 'Moore's Law' reaches its theoretical limit around the time Uranus enters Taurus. This is actually a rule of thumb stating that the number of transistors packed onto a given area of integrated circuit doubles every two years. It has consistently held true since the late 1950s and should do so until about 2020. Then, as transistor size approaches that of single atoms, this process will culminate and end. At that point it will become possible to implant these tiny sophisticated devices into the human nervous system, creating a man/machine hybrid. Whether or not to do so will almost certainly provoke a fundamental split in society as Uranus enters Gemini.

With Uranus in Aries the quest to understand life's genetic inheritance will become a willful attempt to control it. Gene-splicing tools are now widely available, online and even at the high school level.[1] The urge to manipulate metabolism and create new life forms will be irresistible. We must play God because we can. Biomedical research will aggressively pursue life's secrets at the molecular level. And recombine them into artificial organs and organisms. It will be spurred by the excitement of fundamental discovery. And the aphrodisiac of power.

Few people realize how far such research has already gone (October 2016). For example, scientists can now grow human 'baby brains,' equivalent to that of a 9 week old fetus, in a petri dish. Skin cells are reprogrammed into pluripotent stem cells, capable of generating any cell type. These are then manipulated to become 'cerebral organoids,' tiny brains with all the structures and genes of our organ of consciousness. They can be kept alive in a nutrient gel for up to a year. The next step will be to create a supporting mesh that can deliver nutrients and oxygen to an even larger version. Scientists confidently claim that these miniature brains are not conscious because they have no bodies. But of course they are bodies in and of themselves. Who knows what subjective experiences their inter-communicating neurons have? Who can doubt the Hellish nature of such experiments?

As Uranus enters Taurus (2019-26) the quest for a materialist explanation of, and control over, life may run up against the inherent physical realities of biology. We now know that the genetic code is not a 'Book of Life' narrating the assembly, structure and properties of organisms. Rather it is a database of protein-coding catalysts activated by a holistic cellular force field. Gene expression is not a linear deterministic process subject to unconstrained manipulation. Instead it responds to the electric aura and bio-chemical complexity of the entire cell.

We know this because 'specific' genes are routinely spliced into many protein-generating forms depending on cellular conditions. This is similar to the example in which the letters t-i-m-e can be rearranged to spell out words with completely different meanings: item, emit and mite.[2] This four letter 'gene' does not simply mean the unidirectional flow of events from past to future; it can also mean a thing, an emanation or a tiny insect. Thus it cannot be effectively manipulated outside of its verbal context. Nor can biological genes. Furthermore the enhancement, suppression or distortion of any one gene affects others since all work together as a whole. Thus serious interference will disrupt the overall functioning of the cellular environment on which all of them depend.

Uranus in Taurus will probably bring an ability to substantially reconfigure the human genetic endowment. Life consists of an information web grounding vital energies. We will impose our own narrowly conceived patterns on its subtle organizing properties. There will be unintended consequences of enhancing certain functions at the cost of disrupting system coherence.[3]

By the time Uranus enters Gemini (2026-33) citizens of technologically advanced societies may face a defining choice of whether or not to accept genetic reprogramming. Some will see it as a promise, others as a threat. There are powerful intellectual arguments on both sides of the issue. This test will select for intuitive ability. Those who get it wrong will be biologically ruined by tampering with their own genomes. Or left behind by refusing to adapt to a genetically enriched society. Those who get it right will survive to seed the next generation.

The biotech approach rests on the proposition that consciousness emanates out of biological structure. Upgrading and fine tuning its physical source enhances psychological awareness and other functions. Another view asserts that body manifests the energy pattern of an incorporeal soul. Tinkering with its interdependent complexity distorts expression of this animating spiritual impulse.

These two claims are antithetical. The next few decades will reveal which is true...

With Uranus in Aries near-Earth space flight is privatizing while governments develop pioneering technologies to colonize Moon and Mars. As Uranus enters Taurus we will return to our Moon, this time to stay. But can humans survive in its weak gravity?[4] We now know from experience with the International Space Station that even the most athletic person loses up to 15% of bone and muscle mass after just six months of weightlessness. It takes two or three years to recover bone density. Is it possible for humans to live long-term on low gravity

Moon or Mars? If they adapt they can never return to Earth's crushing embrace. Will they be able to reproduce? If so, with what result?

Since the late 1950s we have lived with the sense that space is the final frontier; that the stars are our destiny. What would it mean if we discover that lack of gravity prevents colonization of the solar system? That we can visit but not stay? Current plans aim for a manned mission to Mars around 2030. During Uranus' transit of Gemini we should learn whether we can move off planet and thereby diversify as a species. Or whether we are biologically cut off from the heavens. In either case the answer will profoundly affect human identity.

These extrapolations of scientific discovery and technological application are almost certain to occur even if there is an apocalyptic interlude due to ecological or economic collapse. Technological societies will preserve their most valuable assets and skilled people in research institutes, universities and other advanced facilities and at the upper levels of government, industry and the military. Mega-death in a mass society would thin the herd but not stop the accelerating evolution at its cutting edge.

Uranus charts the emergence of challenges that are inevitable at this stage of development. Individuals can meet them with free will. Collective response is more determined, statistically based on group dynamics. An increasingly wired world in a post religious age is almost certain to embrace the enticing promises of technological salvation. People hardly ever reject new toys. Man will seek to become a consciously created work of his own hands rather than a child of the universe. Brain implants and genetically enhanced abilities will be promoted as the next natural step, just as the use of fire once was. Refusal to participate in such obvious benefits could become stigmatized, then punished, as prophesied so long ago. The mere fact of such unprecedented powers guarantees a spiritual crisis around their use.

When might such an apocalyptic period come? 'But of that day and hour knoweth no man, no, not the angels of heaven, but my Father only.'[5] However, one can make an educated guess as to when a preparatory breakdown of the established order might begin. See 'A Mundane Prediction.'

Notes

1. For example: one can take a 3D printer, easily obtained online, and load it with four vials, each containing one of the four genetic nucleotides (A, G, T and C) ordered from a biological supply house. Insert a computer program that strings them together in any desired order. Inject the resulting gene into a cell nucleus, and then culture a whole

bunch of them …

2. This example is taken from Dr. Barry Commoner's seminal article 'Unraveling the DNA Myth: the Spurious Foundations of Genetic Engineering,' published in Harper's magazine, February 2002.

3. When complex genomes disintegrate they break up into quasi-living genetic fragments called viruses. Those who violate the integrity of their own biochemical program may release an inner plague.

4. Moon's gravity = 17% of Earth's. Mars' = 38% of Earth's.

5. Matthew 24:36

Neptune

Neptune's 14-year transit of a sign charts the dream tides of generations. It implies ideals rather than describing events. It points to the general vision behind specific deeds.

Neptune is the only planet completely invisible to the naked eye.[1] As such it symbolizes energies that are veiled from normal consciousness. In psychological terms it represents the dreamtime. Spiritually it portrays a timeless plane of ideals/illusions, divine and demonic, behind the phenomenal world. Historically it represents the public mood, collective yearning, emotional coloration of a period defined by its 14 year transit of a sign.

It is usually a mistake to associate Neptune with specific events. Rather it refers to the atmosphere surrounding events.[2] Neptune is not about war and revolution, legislation and achievement. It is about a collective vision, or trance, causing, or caused by, those actions. It is a movement rather than a program; an image, not a fact. It has little to do with technology, everything to do with poetry. Thus any description of Neptune's historical manifestation through the signs is, by definition, elusive and nebulous, pertaining more to the mood of an era than its happenings.

Notes

1. Pluto, a dwarf double planetoid, is not a planet astronomically because it does not have gravitational dominance of its wildly elliptical orbit. That is precisely what makes it astrologically important. Pluto actually intrudes within Neptune's orbit for 20 years, one generation, injecting or fertilizing the concentric planetary system with a galactic message. 'Pluto,' Figure 2. A planet portrays a plane of being, a realm of consciousness. Pluto portrays a fateful challenge erupting out of

another dimension such as the galaxy or the collective unconscious. See 'Pluto.'

2. For example, Neptune in Virgo (1928-42) describes a hysterical and distorted ideal of racial purity in Nazi Germany. In most cases that would be all one could say about Neptune's subtle, indirect, behind the scenes influence. In this case, Neptune' subsequent entry into Libra (an air sign), December 1941, actually describes the liquidation of Europe's Jews using poison gas* beginning in 1942. Yet its grotesque abnormality demonstrates how unusual a direct manifestation of Neptunian energy is. Positive expressions would include the lives of saints and mystics. Neptune depicts an otherworldly plane of existence, heavenly or hellish, that inspires or deludes, but is rarely so openly invoked.

* Neptune is associated with poison because it represents a formless energy that dissolves organized structure. Poisons are generally invisible agents that disrupt organic function.

Neptune in Signs

Neptune dissolves an existing structure or attitude and replaces it with a new ideal. Neptune's dream transits are also described in the context of contemporary Plutonian motivations and the dynamics of Uranian social change.

Neptune in Aries portrays a new vision of collective or national identity. The lift of a driving dream. The glamor of rebirth and beginnings.

Neptune last transited Aries 1861-74. The United States dissolved and was reconstituted by Civil War. The melancholy grandeur of a martyred President, Abraham Lincoln, symbolized a tragic redemption of the national character. In a striking parallel medieval Russia abolished serfdom, a form of slavery yoking its vast peasant population (1861). It began to liberalize and to astonish the world with a cultural flowering. Fragmented Germany coalesced into a European powerhouse under the leadership of militaristic Prussia (1871). These three nations would dominate the coming 20th century. This period defined their self-image and guiding ideals.

Japan experienced a similar process, liquidating a feudal system of Samurai warlords and becoming a centralized modernizing state almost overnight (Meiji Restoration, 1867). In consequence it would become the dominant, indeed only, Asian power until the mid-20th century. However, this was largely a triumph of Neptunian illusion, made possible only by the abnormal eclipse of its giant neighbor China.

These dreams of national rebirth were underlain by changing economic realities (Pluto in Taurus): machines displaced age-old reliance on slave or serf labor, while railroads and telegraphs bound continents together in political unity. Ideals were actualized by through the articulation of new identities (Uranus in Gemini) and their emotional consolidation in patriotic feeling (Uranus in Cancer).

Neptune in Taurus portrays an idealization of values. Sublimation of sensuality into spirituality or productivity. If unsuccessful, its decay into neurosis. The enticement of riches and glamor of finance. Dreams of acquisition; of having and holding.

Neptune last transited Taurus 1874-87. The gilded age of capitalism, a period almost completely dominated by the magic of money: the creation and accumulation of wealth. Sensuality was channeled, or repressed, by elevated, or unrealistic, Victorian standards of morality.

Dreams of personal wealth were amplified by Pluto's concurrent transit through Taurus. They were actualized by a muting of Uranus' disruptive influence (in Leo, its sign of detriment) and its rationalization of production through corporate organization (in Virgo).

Neptune in Gemini portrays dissolution of a focused, formulated mentality into a more ambiguous consciousness. Clear perception melts into imaginative vision.

Neptune last transited Gemini 1887-1901. Behind the scenes a definition of mind as essentially rational and of matter as fundamental melted down. The discoveries that self-conscious ego is largely a shifting focus of unconscious forces (Freud, 1896), and that solid metal can evaporate into radioactive energy (Becquerel, 1896), opened the door to a larger but more fluid worldview. It articulated enigmatic dimensions of psychological and physical facts. The ideal of an intelligible reality became more subtle and nuanced.

Cerebral ideals of intellectual discovery were reinforced by Pluto's concurrent transit through Gemini. They were actualized by introducing organized programs of applied research in universities and industry, generally supplanting the lone genius (Uranus in Libra). This long-term institutional teamwork led to a deepening penetration of nature's most fundamental secrets (Uranus in Scorpio).

Neptune in Cancer portrays an immersion into, a direct experience of, the transrational on its own terms. The emotional matrix of society melts down, releasing a flood of unconscious feeling. The glamor of belonging, or herd instinct.

Neptune last transited Cancer 1901-14. Einstein dissolved an orderly mechanistic universe into a relativistic flux of differential times and gravity warped spaces. Jung revealed that instinctual energies self-organize into a dream logic of archetypal images; a collective unconscious flow underlying the rational ego.

A century of tranquility (1815-1914) became overripe and rotted from within. The illusion of permanent peace and everlasting progress began to ferment with intoxicating tribal fantasies.

Dreams of an endless summer were culturally encouraged by a Victorian sublimation of instinct into cerebral passions (Pluto in Gemini). They were actualized by inspired flights of inspiration (Uranus in Sagittarius) and consolidated by the discipline of scientific method (Uranus in Capricorn).

Neptune in Leo portrays an idealized collective ego image. The glamor of glamor inspires or deludes.

Neptune last transited Leo 1914-28. The illusion that we can fully know and predict phenomenal reality gave up the ghost in the golden age of physics.*

A pent up urge for irrational violence pressed the reset button on history. A great killing spree began. Nations flaunted their pride in an extravagant flood of their children's blood (Great War, 1914-18). European empires were dissolved (German, Austrian, Turkish), fatally undermined (British, French) or totally reconstituted (Russian). Their sense of national identity was poisoned by fantasies of betrayal and revenge (Germany), intoxicated by utopian illusions (Russia), exhausted (France) or confused by escapist dreams of isolation (United States). The drama of war was followed by a flamboyant era of short-lived prosperity in the roaring twenties. Millions fleetingly tasted the good life, only to have the cup dashed from their lips as Neptune entered Virgo, its sign of detriment.

Extravagant nationalistic mythologies activated tribal passions (Pluto in Cancer). They were enabled by Uranus' revolutionary fervor (in Aquarius), followed by escapist fantasies (in Pisces).

* For example, Heisenberg's uncertainty principle (1927) proved that we cannot know two basic facts, position and speed, of a particle at the same time because the very act of observation changes the situation being observed.

Neptune in Virgo portrays healing magic or quackery. The glamor of purity as an ideal of integrity or an illusion of separateness and superiority.

Neptune last transited Virgo 1928-42. An interdependent world economy melted down in the Great Depression. The functional organization of industrial society collectivized: democratically through a New Deal in the U.S., by brutal compulsion in Germany and the USSR. Ideals of rugged individualism were replaced by ones of managerial efficiency. The dream of self-reliance gave way to that of technocratic competence. A frontier ethos became a bureaucratic one. A capitalist era socialized. This was an inevitable reality check to a vision that had run its course. Across Europe pseudoscientific delusions rationalized evil in the name of purification: millions were liquidated as class enemies or racial vermin.

Unreal ideals of purity and perfection were empowered by intense nationalistic feelings (Pluto in Cancer). These then ignited into dramatic confrontation (Pluto in Leo). They were actualized by militant ideologies (Uranus in Aries) and made possible by sweeping economic mobilization for war (Uranus in Taurus).

Neptune in Libra portrays a preoccupation with ideals of justice. The glamor of harmony, real or phony. A meltdown of dysfunctional relationship and rebalancing of affairs.

Neptune last transited Libra 1942-57. By splitting the atom (1942) humanity erased the distinction between the phenomenal world of atomic matter and the invisible sub-atomic realm. It merged an objective cause and effect reality with its scintillating substrate of probabilistic energy flashes popping into and out of existence. This interpenetration of the fundamentally different quantum and cosmic states of matter implies a corresponding spiritual and consciousness realignment. Its true and full meaning will not be understood for a very long time. Something of primal significance occurred in the relationship between mind and matter, dissolving the barrier between archetypal and actual, formative and formed realms of being. The harnessing of this new power in fission (1945), then fusion (1952), nuclear explosions underlined, in the most explicit way, the importance of this event.

The storms of World War II led to a very real, if partial, victory of justice in this world. China, ruled by Libra, dissolved under the impact of war and revolution (1949) to reemerge as a transformed society. India gained its independence (1947) through a mass movement of nonviolent idealism led by the saintly figure of Mahatma Gandhi. Europe began to liquidate its age-old divisions, starting with a Common Market, precursor to the European Union.

Ideals of peace, justice and global harmony were reinforced by magnanimous postwar statesmanship (Pluto in Leo). They were actualized by unprecedented co-operation with international partners in confrontation with a peer adversary (Uranus in Gemini). And by attention to popular needs; consolidation of postwar prosperity (Uranus in Cancer).

Neptune in Scorpio portrays a meltdown of dysfunctional power arrangements. An upwelling of deep repressed passion. Glamor of the alien and forbidden. Erotic charisma. A primal group therapy. Revolutionary or nihilistic ideals.

Neptune last transited Scorpio 1957-70. In an era that began with the first satellite (Sputnik, 1957) and ended with the first Moon landings (1969) humanity plunged into the ultimate ocean of outer space: the cosmic baptism of a naked ape.

Long festering social poisons surfaced to be redeemed by highly charged mass movements. The civil rights struggle dissolved an institutionalized system of racial oppression. Only two generations later an African American, Barack Obama, would be elected President - something unthinkable in 1960. A sexual revolution changed the most intimate norms of behavior. An emotional revolution of personal empowerment psychologically liberated millions. However, a certain debasement of standards accompanied these successful challenges to authority, with long-term consequences in the decline of social cohesion.

A dream of social regeneration was enabled by a drive for integrity of the legal and political process (Pluto in Virgo).* It was actualized by a generosity of feeling made possible by unprecedented abundance (Uranus in Leo) and an insistence on fidelity to previously ignored standards (Uranus in Virgo).

*'I have a dream' (Martin Luther King, 1963) made a stirring statement of ideals that ultimately led to specific civil rights legislation (Uranus in Virgo).

Neptune in Sagittarius portrays ideals of freedom, often divorced from responsibility. Prophetic vision or exaggerated imagination

Neptune last transited Sagittarius 1970-84. The first years of this period saw widespread interest in Eastern religions/disciplines along with an awakening to the environmental consequences of unrestrained growth. Spiritual enthusiasms and ecological perspectives superseded the intensely political interests of the previous phase. Then massive inflation (Sagittarius) in the price of oil (Neptune) transferred liquidity from national economies to international financial institutions. This unleashed decades of globalization that would engulf all local identities into a common corporate culture. Its immediate effect was economic stagflation and social malaise. Counterculture liberation decayed into me generation narcissism. Secular disillusionment generated a traditional religious revival with a charismatic Pope, a radical Ayatollah and the growth of evangelical fervor. Conservative ideals/illusions made a political comeback with the election of a movie star President (Reagan, 1980). An era that began with Earth Day ended with a glorification of conspicuous consumption.

Spiritual enthusiasms petered out as a culture of self indulgence destroyed social norms (Pluto in Libra). This process was actualized by a liberalization of mores that decayed into an ethos of aimless pleasure seeking (Uranus in Libra) and a reaction against traditional values in an atmosphere of cynical alienation (Uranus in Scorpio).

Neptune in Capricorn undermines an old order and discredits established hierarchies. It can also ground and structure a new vision. The glamor of ambition and tangible achievement. Dreams of empire. Seduction by 'the bitch goddess Success.' Illusion that rank = merit, or is an acceptable substitute for it. Charismatic authority. Materialistic ideals.

Neptune last transited Capricorn 1984-98. The fall of the Berlin Wall (1989) symbolized the end of history.* Not an end to important events, but the establishment of a worldwide consensus on the organizing principles of global integration. Representative democracy, implemented through free elections rather than elite guidance; basic human rights rather than coercive social engineering; rule of law rather than of state power; corporate capitalism rather than command socialism: these are now the accepted norms of a universal civilization. Future dilemmas will be about personal identity in an age of technology rather than about the right political structure or economic system in a now integrated world.

The smooth inauguration of a managerial world order in an atmosphere of pragmatic cooperation distinguished this period. The steady consolidation of technological visions into applied systems on a global scale laid the socio-economic foundation for its long-term success. (Think of the Internet: unknown in 1984, ubiquitous by 1998. The coming techno-civilization, and its associated mindset, would be impossible without it.)

Social idealism contracted into fetishes of personal ambition or material wealth, intensified by Pluto's plunge into power-seeking Scorpio. This was reinforced by a libertarian reaction against traditional morality and thrift (Uranus in Sagittarius). Uranus' subsequent transit through Capricorn, joining Neptune, solidified the triumph of materialism and the consumer culture.

Note

'The End of History' is the title of an influential 1992 book by American author Francis Fukuyama.

This does not mean an end to drama. For example, we are currently witnessing (early 2016) the violent disintegration of artificial nation states such as Iraq and Syria into their more natural ethnic and sectarian components. This chaotic process will probably spread across the Middle East and elsewhere. As an unsustainable world economy implodes spectacular upheavals and breakdowns will generate immense suffering and grotesque displays of cruelty. There will be sound and fury: the rise and fall of charismatic leaders, conquering generals, inspired or deluded prophets.

The tragedy of this stormy passage will disrupt, but not replace, the long-term trajectory of political and personal liberation. In an increasingly educated and cosmopolitan world only representative democracy, rule of law, respect for human rights, women's empowerment and a free market in a communitarian context can satisfy increasingly conscious individual and social aspirations. Authoritarian approaches, of both left and right, are too rigid and narrowly conceived to meet the challenges of modernity. The complex social ecology of a post-industrial world requires the flexibility and feedback of democracy. By definition this will reflect its cultural environment: Anglo-American variants will be more individualistic, East Asian ones more collectivist.

The choices of the future will revolve more around biotech challenges to unique identity than tribal battles over social organization. Every soul will face an existential struggle over technological temptations: genetic modification, brain/computer interfacing, personally tailored electronic or chemical consciousness manipulation (the same issue that every alcoholic faces). S/he will have free choice - within the subtle coercion of a medically defined human condition that is already replacing a traditional spiritual/religious sense of self.

Neptune in Aquarius portrays universal or abstract ideals. Technocratic dreams of a rational utopia, a cyber-paradise. A flowering of scientific imagination. Socially: hypnosis by group think, friendly fascism.

Neptune last transited Aquarius 1998-2012. A globalized economy and an Americanized culture engulfed humanity. A wired world connected most people in a universal embrace of consumer values and electronic fantasies.[1] A uniform techno-civilization emerged. This presents both opportunity and danger as the human family becomes a single social organism.

A worldwide electronic nerve net began to include everyone in its database and in its consciousness modality. We all increasingly inhabit a cyberspace that generates not just similar tastes and values but a uniform way of thinking.[2] All will have access and all will be accessible. A global village is fast emerging.

Genetic engineering, pharmaceutical manipulation, human/computer interfacing will constitute its spiritual challenges. Ethical issues will be medicalized. Theories about truth will be replaced by therapies about wellness. A lonelier, more subliminal struggle over existential identity will supplant the passion of mass struggles over social organization.

Technocratic dreams of genetic manipulation and artificial intelligence were enabled by an optimistic sense of unlimited possibility following the successful wind-down of the Cold War (Pluto in Sagittarius. That got a sharp economic reality check as soon as Pluto entered practical Capricorn in late 2008.) An era of giddy expansion was actualized by Uranus' concurrent transit through utopian Aquarius, followed by its activation of Neptune's home sign of idealistic and illusory Pisces.

1. The writer is aware that a billion people live in absolute poverty and another billion just one step above. North Korea and the Taliban still exist. Six thousand African girls are genitally mutilated

each and every day. (Written in 2013.) Nevertheless, these are remnants of a receding past, not portents of a coming future.

2. The internet and electronic media will be to the world what the American public school system was to a nation of immigrants. Few white people seriously identify with the ethnic heritage so important to their grandparents. Now even visible color barriers are coming down fast. The 'melting pot' is a very Neptunian image and process.

Neptune in Pisces brings dissolution of an old worldview and the social conditions that supported it. Emergence of new ideals. During the last such transit, 1847-61, these were political: abolitionism, feminism and socialism rose as an urban industrial order displaced an agrarian one. This time around competing visions of a post industrial world: holistic, organic, ecological v a corporate dystopia of electronic and genetic manipulation.

Neptune will next transit Pisces 2012-26. The Age of Pisces[1] characterized by idealistic passions, religious and political, will begin to ebb away. A chillier, more rational technocratic order will supplant it. Traditional identities will dissolve: either melded into a common culture, or melted down in a general economic or ecological collapse.

Assuming a continuation of current trends, and based on the symbolism of Neptune in its own sign of Pisces, one can expect universal norms to permeate the global village. New generations, exposed to a common electronic upbringing, will become increasingly synchronized. The need to manage a world economy and protect a planetary ecology will inevitably bring standardization, for better and for worse. Extreme economic disparity will converge towards a sustainable plateau of social justice and prosperity. A managerial consensus will harmonize the interests of all. In an interdependent world all must be accommodated, and all must conform. Life will become blander and fairer. Shared vicarious experience and a universal mass culture will merge the human family into one community.

Ironically, even a real financial meltdown or global environmental catastrophe would generate the same end result, though in a more forceful way, by eliminating excess population and herding the traumatized survivors into a planet wide state. Technology and a cosmopolitan consciousness have advanced too far and diffused too widely for any other outcome.[2] One way or another, Neptune in Pisces will liquidate past karma and set the stage for a unified humanity to enact its deepest collective dreams, perhaps as prophesied by the great religious traditions. (See the Bible, 'Revelations.')

Neptunian dreams, or nightmares, will be made real by a well-organized and efficiently managed world system (Pluto in Capricorn). They will actualize as Uranus initiates (Aries), then grounds (Taurus) a new cycle.

Later, questions of individual identity in this technological value system will come to the fore as Neptune enters Aries (2026-40). A new conflict of natural v engineered qualities will begin. A generation from now tiny computer implants, neuro-chemical mood enhancers and customized genetic tweaking will present each person with an existential challenge. The temptations of biotech self modification will have powerful intellectual arguments pro and con. How one responds will become a test of fitness selecting for intuitive ability.

1. The Age of Pisces ran from 100 BC-2060 AD. See 'Precession.'

2. Of course, there might be an interregnum of anarchy if a really big calamity occurred, such as a major crop failure due to climate change, or an earthquake which destroyed a vital component of the world economy (say Tokyo or Los Angeles). Still, world elites are so interconnected, and their incentives so powerful, that it would only be a matter of time before a universal state emerged out of the wreckage. Because we already have a globalized consciousness a globalized political order is not far behind. Neptune in Pisces will basically clear the decks for its formal emergence.

This definition of globalization does not refer to the current model in which a handful of multinational corporations dominate elected governments. And millions of migrants from failing states flood across open borders to colonize other societies with vastly different civilizations, customs and mores. Rather it means a world in which each self governing culture zone is economically and ecologically self sufficient within a universal, and enforceable, system of democratic process, rule of law, respect for human rights and planet wide security arrangements.

Pluto

Pluto marks an obsession seeking redemption. A buried treasure that completes and fulfills identity; a lost fragment of self that must be found and reintegrated. Or killed and expelled, thrown into the fire like the Ring of Sauron.[1] It demonstrates the same thing on a societal level. It portrays what a group, or a time period, must do or get, create or destroy, in order to become whole. It is the will to power, and to transcendence, that drives history. Pluto serves a larger agenda, the Will of God, which itself evolves as we enact it through our groping in the dark.

Pluto defines a primal urge that becomes conscious only through its participation in the tangible world. Think of a newborn baby, helpless and unaware, yet also the vehicle of a destiny. That destiny has a general outline, given at birth: gender, historical period, national identity, social rank, family heritage, genetic endowment and perhaps karmic proclivities. Its specific details are not given but will unfold through conscious choice and unconscious compulsion, the challenges of chance and fundamental facts of life. Initial conditions and inherent orientation (Pluto) inform and guide, but do not determine, the quality of individual initiative (Mars).

These defining social factors are objective correlatives of inner subjective states: a girl has a different psychological orientation than a boy, regardless of their individual qualities; a Chinese has another frame of reference than an American. The outer facts of fate not only generate circumstances one must face; they also shape the states of mind with which one meets them. Furthermore, and most importantly, a baby has an internal dynamic independent of environment. This innate psychology also constitutes a fate. Character is destiny. Pluto charts the deep soul purpose behind and motivating that psychology. If one does not believe in a soul independent of empirical personality, then Pluto can be seen as an unconscious Prime Directive, an instinctual imperative underlying conscious action and awareness.

The same dynamic applies at the historical level. A deep instinctual will drives men and nations to their 'rendezvous with destiny.'[2] Those born at a particular time must express the nature and needs of that moment. They enter into a historical process, a collective unconscious movement, a racial evolution. The quality of their participation will define its character. How they respond is partly a matter of free will. It is also a function of their own inherent nature, which is attuned to, resonates with, the spirit of their times. The individual members of a generation are the living expression of a historical moment or state of being. They are also the agency of that moment's self-transcendence, or of its suicidal regression.

Nations too have their own character, partly caused by and causing their historical situation, but also partly innate and autonomous. For example, many proud nations have been defeated in war, but none has ever responded like Germany after 1918. It seems that this nation was predisposed, perhaps in some sense 'chosen,' to demonstrate how thin a veil of sanity separates us from a cold and alien dimension of evil.

Was Nazi Germany inevitable or an accident of history? The question is irrelevant: by definition anything that has already happened was inevitable. Certain configurations of social forces are preordained by the logic of events. Our response to them remains open until we make a decision, as we must. Pluto poses fundamental choices, which cannot be sidestepped. Was humanity vaccinated by its initial encounter with Plutonian energies in World War II? Or was this a militaristic preview of a more friendly fascism to come: a technologically enhanced vampirism soon to suck billions of souls into its hungry databanks?

Pluto poses inevitable challenges whose outcome is uncertain. That depends on the quality and depth of the participants' awareness. Pluto also invokes a sensitivity to the psychic forces generating those danger/opportunities.[3] That sensitivity may result in hypnotic acquiescence or in conscious understanding.

Pluto's challenges are like time bombs in history. Just as some genes activate at a certain period in an individual lifespan, for example adolescence, so these demands for attention surface during specific phases of social evolution. They can only be defused by consciously acknowledging and assimilating their troubling new perspectives from the deep unconscious.

The phases of Pluto's unfolding pass through the normal sequence portrayed by the symbolism of the zodiac. However, their timing differs significantly due to Pluto's highly elliptical orbit. Some energies erupt quickly with concentrated force, such as Pluto's twelve-year transit through Scorpio, the sign it rules. Others evolve at a slow steady pace, such as the long developmental cycle of Pluto in Taurus, lasting 32 years. These inexorable processes of the body politic parallel those of the biological organism: for example, the storms of adolescence last only a few years while the responsibilities of adulthood go on for decades.

Like Uranus and Neptune, Pluto symbolizes the emergence of increasingly subtle levels of consciousness in an accelerating historical process. Uranian innovation reached a critical mass of self-conscious political expression, and a sustained feedback loop of technological development, at the time of its discovery (1781). Neptunian idealism, emotional opening, romantic/transcendental sensibility and compassionate outreach were made possible by the quickening pace of economic opportunity and enlarged scope of social consciousness at the time of its discovery (1846). In the same way, Pluto's will to total mobilization for collective transformation was enabled by the intensification of modern life at its time of discovery (1930).

This level of awareness was activated by the crisis of Depression. It initially took political form: a pragmatic New Deal in the United States, extremist mass movements in Nazi Germany and Soviet Russia. After a cathartic bloodbath (World War II) and a protracted contest of wills (Cold War) political discord morphed into technocratic consensus. The Plutonian will to power now works through a global corporate organization seeking technological mastery of natural forces and of human nature.

Today immense international projects deploy armies of scientists and engineers spending billions of dollars over decades of effort. They decode genomes and synthesize life, assemble space stations and launch planetary probes, build atom smashers and operate information superhighways. Such sustained and sophisticated endeavor was made possible only at a stage of development attained when Pluto itself became visible (1930).

Obviously Pluto has always existed. So have x-rays and microwaves. However, these energies could not be consciously recognized, or manipulated, until a certain level of social/scientific development was reached. This level of awareness emerged on a socially significant scale during the Depression/World War II era. It has accelerated ever since.

Of course there have been long-term collective projects throughout history: practical ones like the Roman roads or futile wastes like the Great Wall of China. But these were essentially exercises in gigantism: more of the same on a colossal scale. They did not involve a planned breakthrough to new levels of objective achievement like projects to split the atom or reach the Moon or create novel life forms. Nor did they invoke a parallel, inherent and necessary subjective growth. Developing nuclear power, space flight and biotechnology involved true 'advance into novelty.'[4] They meant consciously changing consciousness.

Because the Plutonian dimension of power has only emerged into awareness and application since 1930 we have not yet experienced its full cycle (248 years) in overt manifestation. Prior to 1930 one can sense an underlying Plutonian orientation in history during the period after Uranus' discovery (1781), when a new plane of collective experience was becoming consciously available on a mass scale. Humanity could only respond to these forces as it developed the capacity to discern them. It took millennia of historical evolution for society to reach that level of sensitivity. Perhaps it also took many recyclings of individual human souls, through successive reincarnations over the centuries, for them to attain the maturity to assimilate these energies. One need not believe in reincarnation to contemplate Pluto. However, the concept of reincarnation fits the symbolism of Pluto: death and regeneration towards a larger purpose and a more inclusive identity.[5]

History is neither just 'one damned thing after another',[6] nor a determined linear progression. It is a spiraling movement, both cyclical and directional, with retrograde episodes, just like the pattern of our solar system. An overt sequence of events unfolds in, and expresses, a developing matrix of collective and evolutionary necessity. A larger Will gives direction to a seemingly random fluctuation of events. Thus quantum scintillations generate atoms, chemical reactions self-organize into life, millions of consumer decisions make a market, a circus of egos forms a nation. This Will is not an explicit Plan moving towards a pre-determined end. It enacts a self-amplifying urge to greater inclusiveness and eventual transcendence through the process of death and rebirth.

Since Pluto's discovery we are no longer shielded from these forces by the inertia of ignorance. We must deal with the promise, problems and perils of an intensified state of consciousness whether we like it or not. Humanity has entered a brave new world of artificial intelligence and genetic engineering, social liberalization and psychological empowerment, environmental degradation and interplanetary exploration. Pluto involves a conscious recognition of the fundamental forces underlying our visible existence: subatomic physical reality, genetic biological heritage, depth psychology and social dynamics. It also involves a quest to control these forces. And the hubris, overweening pride, that goes with it.

Notes

1. The Ring of Power is the central 'character' in J.R.R. Tolkien's (1892-1973) epic fantasy 'Lord of the Rings.'
2. FDR inaugural address, 1933
3. Interestingly, and tellingly, the German-speaking world originated depth psychology and an awareness of the irrational forces behind our 'conscious' decisions. Yet it was also the world that fell most completely under the spell of obsession and delusion.
4. Alfred North Whitehead, 1861-1947, English philosopher
5. Pluto would then indicate the process of reincarnation and spotlight the specific need that is being developed, or issue confronted, in this life. Moon would indicate the subconscious memories, karmic heritage, innate talent that Plutonian will has to work with in the present personality.
6. Attributed to Arnold Toynbee, 1889-1975, English historian

Pluto in Signs

Pluto's 12 to 32 year transit of a sign indicates the larger purpose behind events. An evolutionary need or issue coming to the surface. What must die and regenerate.

Prior to Pluto's discovery: As the inspirational spark of Uranus achieved a sustained self-conscious feedback loop it opened the doors of perception into even more subtle dimensions, soon to manifest. The presence of Neptune and Pluto began to be felt, though not yet seen.

Pluto transited Aries 1822-51: An urge to begin anew; to reinvent identity and test its will; to get up and go.

A pioneering era of laissez-faire capitalism and rugged individualism. The Industrial Revolution really got underway with the invention of the steam locomotive (1825). The young United States aggressively expanded from sea to shining sea, expressing a sense of Manifest Destiny.

Pluto's entry into Aries coincided with, and closely squared, an 1821 Uranus/Neptune conjunction in Capricorn, an important harbinger of the industrial age. (See 'Synods.') It was as if newly discovered Uranus was pulling Neptune and Pluto's still intangible levels of one unified force field into manifestation. Thus the Romantic era of literature, art and music in the early 19th century foreshadowed the rise of Neptunian social idealism after its discovery in 1846. Pluto itself remained hidden, like an 'invisible hand'* guiding the early Industrial Revolution through the cumulative effect of individual wills. Only after capitalism's spontaneous self-organization collapsed in the Great Depression did Pluto's Will to Power explicitly emerge in the modern managerial state (after 1930).

*'The Wealth of Nations' (1776), Adam Smith, 1723-1790. The most influential economic treatise ever written.

Pluto transited Taurus 1851-83: Renewal of values. A drive to materialize desires, to get and to have.

A cataclysmic redefinition of national identity through Civil War. A transformation of basic values with the abolition of slavery. The storm was followed by a socially tranquil era of wealth creation. The concurrent transit of Neptune through Taurus (1874-87) reinforced the theme of steady solid material growth.

Pluto transited Gemini 1883-1914: Renewal of mental paradigms. A need to know, to experiment, to perceive alternative realities.

Extraordinary intellectual achievement. Freud and Jung exposed an inner world of the personal and collective unconscious. Einstein revealed a relativistic other side to the common sense world of time, space, matter and energy. A host of scientists, writers, artists and philosophers flourished during this prosperous and genteel era. Meanwhile Europe was splitting into two armed camps, unconsciously preparing for a great world war and an era of ideological division.

The concurrent transit of Neptune through Gemini (1887-1901) reinforced the rational articulation of an ineffable dimension complementing our known consensus reality. (Neptune and Pluto actually conjoined in Gemini in 1891. This only happens every 492 years: see 'Synods.')

During and after Pluto's discovery:

Pluto transited Cancer 1914-38. Renewal of group-feeling, tribal will. Pluto itself was discovered during this transit, emphasizing its instinctual power.

Generations of peace and growing prosperity had produced a sense of ennui. An upwelling of war fever opened the floodgates of deep social and political passions. Two alternatives to liberal democracy demanded and got their day in the Sun: elitist fascism and anthill communism. It was as if right and left brain hemispheres contended for psychic dominance in the body politic. German fantasies of racial superiority and Russian dreams of remaking human nature embodied these emotional drives in national/cultural form. Everywhere a basic sense of personal security (Cancer) was challenged: in the west by economic depression, in Russia by state terror, and in general by armed German aggression.

The cohort born with Pluto in Cancer would protect and nurture the world through a time of hot and cold war. It would be the last and greatest generation of the old school, putting family, nation and traditional values first. It would also give birth to the postmodern era.

Pluto in Leo, 1938-57: Renewal of identity.

Pluto's Will to Power dramatically emerged into the light of day. Fundamental secrets of matter and of life became conscious and controlled. The invisible forces holding the atom together were split open, the hidden code of biology (DNA) made known. The very core of nature became the playground of human creativity.

The best and worst potentials of the human heart acted out in 'the good war' (World War II). The deepest degradation and highest heroism were dramatized in an outer conflict of national egos, an inner struggle for mankind's very soul.

The postwar generation born with this placement would grow up to exemplify the power of individuality. For all their narcissism and hype the baby boomers created a revolution in personal autonomy. Following one's bliss rather than conforming to social expectations became a new norm. Much of this would degenerate into egotism and consumerism. Still, a basic sense of empowerment and self expression would lead to a freer, more creative, and less disciplined, society.

Pluto in Virgo, 1957-71: The triumph of technology; creativity organized. An urge to rationalize and purify society.

The launch of Sputnik, the first artificial satellite (1957), inaugurated the space age. Humanity was no longer tied to Earth or bound by its horizons. Our planet, floating in the emptiness, became recognized as very small and vulnerable. Birth of both an ecological ethic of loving it and the technological epic of leaving it.

A demand for social integrity in living up to stated principles of equal justice for all energized the civil rights and feminist movements. A concomitant demand for personal integrity, expressed in a short-lived 'counterculture,' generated greater realism and openness in social interaction. It also cheapened discourse: most people's 'honesty' involves raw ego projection more than a genuine search for truth. Still, this is generally healthier (Virgo) than the emotional repression and exaggerated propriety of earlier generations. A concurrent Uranus in Virgo transit (1962-68) emphasized these trends. Uranus and Pluto would actually conjoin in 1965, an event that happens only once every 127 years (see 'Synods').

The Pluto in Virgo birth cohort would mature to become the geeks and nerds of the computer and biotech revolutions. They would build and implement the network of planetary integration, technologically, economically and socially. Their information economy would spark 'a million mutinies'* against oppressive traditional restrictions in the first, second (state socialist) and third worlds alike.

*V. S. Naipaul, a social commentator of Hindu background. His reference was to an unprecedented and ongoing grassroots revolt against the caste system in India, but it applies worldwide.

Pluto in Libra, 1971-85: A call to Judgment. Fate defined by a new standard.

The discovery of how to slice and recombine DNA (1973) potentially altered the very nature of life itself. Now we could manipulate genetic heredity, and even create artificial organisms. For the first time we could play God.

A new balance of power began to form. China, ruled by Libra, emerged out of isolation, instituting pragmatic social and economic reforms after decades of Maoist revolutionary fervor. It would quickly rise to superpower status, just as the USSR started to disintegrate. The Islamic Revolution in Iran (1979) unleashed an upheaval in the greater Middle East that has not yet reached its crescendo. Most fundamentally, the oil price shock of 1973, quadrupling the price of that vital commodity, marked the end of cheap energy and the beginning of real financial globalization. Economic interdependence started to create new political facts. Pluto in Libra embodied a slow tipping of the scales. The direction in which things were moving, and the possibilities that had been unleashed, marked a profound, irreversible change of course.

The birth cohort with Pluto in Libra will most likely facilitate a new world order now coming into view. They will adjust competing social and economic interests as we move towards global integration. Multicultural and ecological harmony will be their purpose and contribution. However, late in life they will probably be called upon to render judgment, make basic value decisions, as the secular crisis of world governance passes and a new crisis of technological adaptation begins to emerge.

Pluto in Scorpio, 1985-96: An urge to complete transformation. Regeneration.

Meltdown of the Soviet Empire. End of the Cold War. Already people are forgetting just how dangerous this confrontation really was because it ended well. It could just as easily have destroyed human civilization, leaving behind only 'a republic of grass and insects.'*

Globalization of the world economy, and Americanization of its culture, became an irresistible tide. Growth of the Internet (unheard of in 1985) and development of biotechnology laid the foundations of a fundamentally new society.

The birth cohort with Pluto in Scorpio will probably act as agents of a profound struggle over the uses of these technologies. By the time they reach maturity, starting around 2020, the possibilities of genetic modification and computer/mind interfacing will present novel issues and challenges. This generation will most likely develop powers that will tempt and test humanity's basic identity.

* Bill McKibben, environmental and social author (b.1960). It is more than likely that rogue states or terrorist groups will use nuclear weapons at some point. After all, the genie is out of the bottle. But the specter of global Armageddon involving thousands of MIRVed ICBMs seems to have been averted. Even these acronyms, once the stuff of daily news reports, now seem dated and arcane. MIRV = multiple independently targeted reentry vehicles (warheads); ICBM = Intercontinental Ballistic Missile.

Pluto in Sagittarius, 1996-2008: Expansion. A drive to grow beyond previous limits.

Humanity's reach extended to the farthest edges of space and time, matter and life. Satellite observations uncovered the 'face of God,' a background microwave radiation pattern left over from the Big Bang; a mysterious 'dark energy' expanding the universe at an ever-faster pace; and dozens of exoplanets orbiting alien stars. Biologists decoded the human genome, discovered exotic forms of life in undersea volcanoes and acid lakes, and began to synthesize artificial genes. Physicists explored strange subatomic dimensions in ever more powerful atom smashers. Computers got faster and faster. Machines got smaller and smaller, down to molecular size (nanobots). Discoveries and inventions that would have seemed miraculous only a generation earlier were relegated to page 22 of the newspaper.

An era of giddy expansion in every field of human endeavor. Social and cultural globalization continued to accelerate. Everyone in the industrial world became wired into a virtual reality of cyberspace. A long economic joyride was fueled by debt and speculation. It abruptly ended when Pluto entered Capricorn (late 2008).

The birth cohort with Pluto in Sagittarius will probably set a long-term spiritual agenda after the basic organizational issues of planetary governance are settled. They must face the existential challenge of technological power: what should we do when we can do anything.

Pluto in Capricorn, 2008-24: Contraction. Necessary austerity. The practical reality of global organization on every level: economic, cultural and political.

This period will demand that we live within our means, financially and ecologically. If we cannot do so it will administer a hard lesson in basic survival: Capricorn is about discipline. A new hierarchy of values will emerge, emphasizing restraint over consumerism, international order over sovereign prerogative, long term planning over immediate gratification. During this time humanity will do what it must to get through the demographic, environmental and economic transition to a sustainable steady state. It will probably succeed, even if the process is traumatic: Capricorn is the most pragmatic sign. Then new issues of humanity's relationship to a technological world of its own making will arise.

Pluto last transited Capricorn around 1763-78, during the run up to and beginning of the American Revolution. Its as yet unconscious influence can be seen in the essentially conservative nature of that revolution, which sought to preserve existing and inherent rights rather than transform society.

Pluto in Aquarius, 2024-43: A utopian urge to build the New Jerusalem.

The practical social issues of survival will probably be resolved during the preceding transit. This may involve a major thinning of the herd. Then, just as in the newly pacified Roman Empire of Augustus (ruled 29 BC-14 AD), conditions will be ripe for a spiritual crisis. This may involve a long predicted Antichrist personifying a temptation and a terror that will test every individual.[1]

Pluto last transited Aquarius 1778-98. Its presence in idealistic Aquarius amplified newly-discovered Uranus' transformative impulse during the French Revolution. In contrast to the American, the French Revolution (1789) sought to remake society and transform the human condition through political means.

Notes

1. On August 11, 1999 there was a total solar eclipse at 19° Leo.[2] It was visible across the Balkans and much of the Middle East.

The eclipsed Sun in Leo exactly opposed Uranus in Aquarius. This polarity squared another one of Saturn in Taurus opposing Mars in Scorpio.[*] Thus these five planets formed a grand cross. Nine months later, on May 3-4, 2000 all seven visible planets were conjunct in Taurus. Who or what was born at that time?

See Figures 2 and 3. For an explanation of their astrological symbols see Figure 2 in the next chapter, 'Mundane Considerations.'

* Sun, Uranus and Mars were all in the signs that they rule.

2. This eclipse belonged to Saros series 145.†

A previous member of the series occurred on July 9, 1945 - one week before the first atomic explosion in the Jornada del Muerto desert near White Sands, New Mexico. It was visible as a partial eclipse from the test site (the path of totality was further north).

The next eclipse of this series will pass over the United States on August 21, 2017, with totality visible from Oregon through South Carolina. It will form on President Trump's rising degree at 29° Leo. Two weeks later violent Mars will transit and activate this point ...

† See 'Mundane Considerations: Saros Series.'

Pluto in Pisces, 2043-67: An urge to liquidate the past. The Age of Pisces will dissolve. Enactment of a deep collective fantasy: dream or nightmare. Either delusion or redemption will triumph, setting the tone for a 2160 year long Age of Aquarius.

Pluto last transited Pisces 1798-1821. The meteoric career of Napoleon (ruled 1799-1815) dissolved Europe's traditional order and set the stage for a later growth of strident ethnic nationalism. That would peak during the rise and fall of the Third Reich at the time of Pluto's visible emergence (1930). Pisces evokes karma. Pluto, lord of the underworld, in this sign suggests a dark collective shadow seeking to take form and play itself out in the light of day.

Figure 2   Stellium - May 3, 2000   Noon   Ocnele Mari, Romania

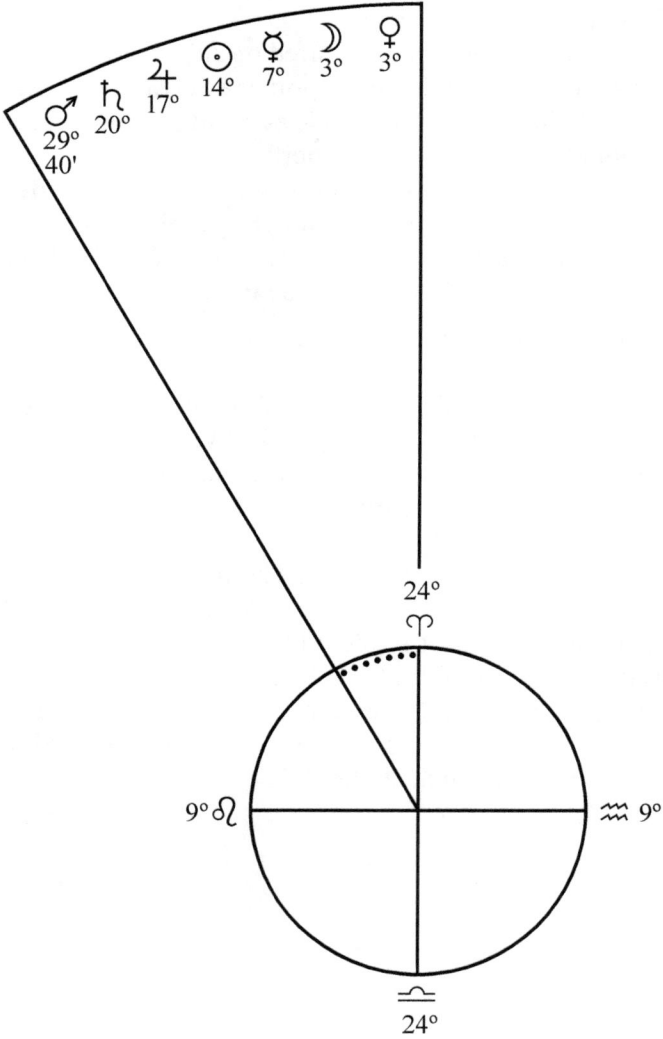

In order to display the planetary symbols they are spread out. In reality these planets were all concentrated in less than ⅓ of the upper left quadrant on on that day or close to it.

Note that Mars is just leaving Taurus. It conjoins the Pleiades, one of the most powerful star clusters in the heavens.

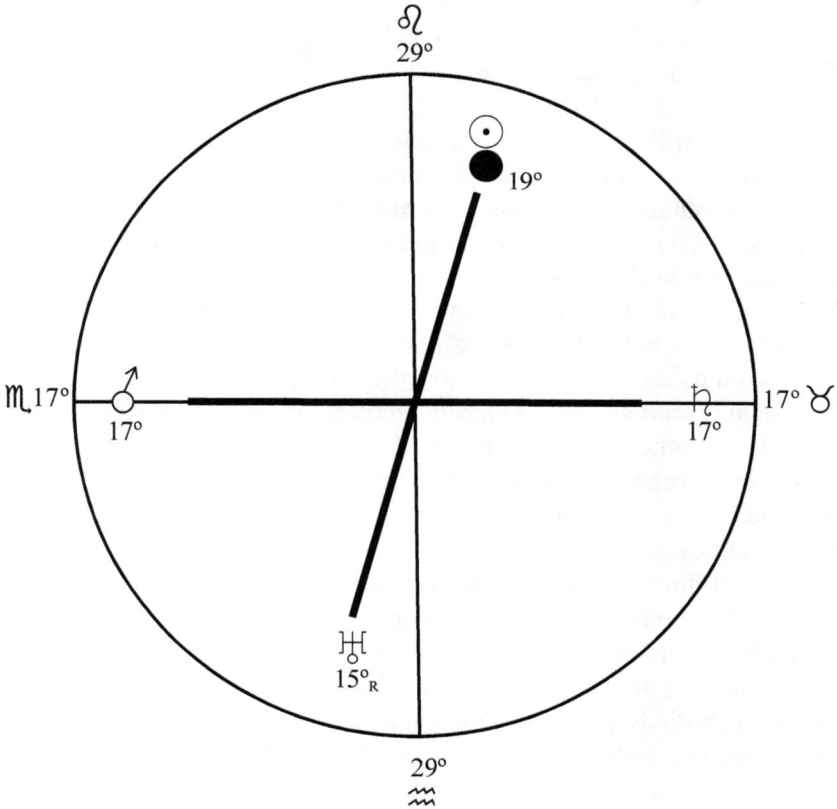

**Figure 3   Grand Cross - August 11, 1999   2:03pm
Ocnele Mari, Romania**

The time of conception for whoever was born nine months later during the stellium of May 3-4, 2000 portrayed in Figure 2.
This eclipse culminated over Ocnele Mari, Romania.

Epilog

The long slow-moving waves of encounter with ever-deeper planes of consciousness are now converging into a perfect storm. As Uranus enters a new cycle (Aries, 2011-19), Neptune enters its own karmic sign of Pisces (2012-26). Pluto itself entered Capricorn, the sign of established order, in late 2008, generating a financial earthquake. This may have been only a warning shot compared to a real restructuring yet to come. The challenge of our current transition into the Age of Aquarius (2060-4220) is to integrate these vibrant, and violent, energies into a stable dispensation.

Uranus will initiate (Aries) and then ground (Taurus, 2019-26) this movement, as Neptune in Pisces wipes the old slate clean. Pluto in Capricorn (2008-24) will begin to disclose the actual form of a new order, in both its positive and negative aspects. Perhaps these internal contradictions will fight it out as Uranus enters dualistic Gemini (2026-32) and Neptune (ideals/illusions) simultaneously begins a new cycle in aggressive Aries (2026-40). Pluto itself will transit Aquarius (2024-43), evoking both its demonic and divine potentials. This may be personified by a long awaited Antichrist. The outcome of that episode will define the nature of a new Age of Aquarius.

Uranus and Neptune were together in Aquarius (1998-2003), then in mutual reception (2003-11). Mutual reception means they are each in the sign the other rules: Uranus in Pisces, ruled by Neptune; Neptune in Aquarius, ruled by Uranus. Mutual reception 'abates all malice.' It is as if the two energies reciprocally coordinate and bring out each other's best qualities. It acts like the medieval situation in which the heir to the French throne would live at the court of England, and the English prince at the French court. Neither country would start a war while their future king was in the other's territory. After 2011 these planets will move out of mutual reception: revolutionary Uranus into aggressive Aries, hypnotic Neptune into Pisces, its own sign of disintegration and expiation. The underlying tone or mood of public affairs may become more polarized.

Mundane Considerations

Historic Overview

Mundane astrology describes the character of nations and other corporate bodies. This was the first form of astrology. It emerged with the first civilization, Sumer, in what is now southern Iraq (ca. 3500-2000 BC). As its soil became saline from centuries of irrigation Sumer was displaced by a daughter civilization, Babylon, in the fertile steppes of central Iraq (ca. 2000-538 BC). Babylon continued and developed the Sumerian tradition.[1]

Both Sumer and Babylon worshipped the starry desert skies and gods embodied in the planets. Their religion was based on planetary omens concerning the fate of king and state. These were taken seriously because at that time planets were seen as actual gods, not symbolic representations of them. It was vital to know their will and intentions.

By about 1000 BC these omens had become codified into a Babylonian text known from its opening line: 'Enuma Anu Enlil...'[2] They were purely empirical descriptions with no theoretical explanation. Yet they were the product of a systematic observation of the heavens that sought not just facts but their significance. Unlike modern astronomers the Babylonian stargazers' concern was to find the meaning of celestial phenomena. For at least 1500 years they correlated planetary positions with concrete events, and learned to extract signals of significance from the background noise of coincidence. Thus the basic astrological identities of planets were pragmatically established over centuries of patient observation.

Many copies of the Enuma have been found. It was a standard reference listing about 7000 planetary positions or weather conditions and their associated predictions, laboriously inscribed on clay tablets in cuneiform, wedge shaped markings. These provided a long-term database from which later thinkers would discern cyclic regularities. They included consistent records of all solar and lunar eclipses from 747 BC on. The Persian conquest of Babylon in 538 BC broke a priestly monopoly on such knowledge. It also introduced a technological innovation from Egypt:[3] writing with ink on papyrus (early paper). That facilitated the spread of accumulated astronomical information and its astrological interpretation. This heritage came to the attention of the Greeks who quickly gave it a mathematical basis.

By 432 BC Meton, an Athenian astronomer, had organized raw lists of eclipses into regular cycles (Saros series: next section). His contemporary, Euktemon, first described the separate zodiacal constellations as measuring a continual path of (apparent) solar motion.[4]

He also defined its four seasonal turning points: spring and autumn equinoxes; summer and winter solstices. During the cosmopolitan Hellenistic era, from the fourth century BC through the first centuries of the Roman Empire, astrology incorporated a wealth of new mathematical and astronomical discoveries.[5] More importantly, it developed a philosophical basis in Platonic explanations of the planets as symbolizing a lawful order in heaven; emanations of spiritual principle rather than expressions of divine whim.[6]

The practice of astrology also democratized: from a centralized state oracle it became a means of personal fortune telling. The first known individual horoscope was cast for April 29, 410 BC in Babylon. It simply noted planetary positions in constellations rather than mapping them within a holistic zodiacal configuration. The first evidence of a zodiac organized into 360 degrees comes from a horoscope of 263 BC. The first verified use of the ascendant, or rising sign, comes from a Greek chart of 4 BC.

Astrology does not come down to us as some great wisdom from time immemorial. Instead it evolved over the millennia, just as a child's mind matures from concrete to conceptual thought. It started from a crude and literal stance as a simple list of particular meanings; a direct correlation between observed phenomena in heaven and experienced facts on Earth. It grew into a theoretically coherent system during the classical era of Greece and Rome. Finally Claudius Ptolemy summarized the astrological knowledge of antiquity in his 'Tetrabiblios,' which remained the standard reference until the Renaissance.[7]

Astrology was eclipsed, along with all forms of knowledge, during the Dark Ages. It made a comeback in the high medieval period with Europe's exposure to Islamic learning in Spain and the Holy Land. At that time astrology's relationship with the Church was ambiguous: some saw it as a reflection of divine order, others as a contradiction of God's omnipotence. Generally a view that the regularity of planetary movement manifested God's purpose prevailed. Throughout the Renaissance astrology exerted a major cultural and intellectual influence. It was then used almost entirely to predict external events; there was little sense of it describing interior subjective dimensions of personality.[8]

Astrology lost credibility during the Scientific Revolution of the 17th century as a worldview proceeding from cause and effect logic replaced one based on sympathetic resonance. (See 'Theory.') It fell out of favor as an irrational superstition during the Enlightenment of the 18th and almost disappeared with the materialistic outlook of the 19th. Since the early 20th century it has reemerged as an increasingly sophisticated description of psychological states of consciousness. These manifest on the collective as well as an individual level.

Notes

1. For example, Babylon retained Sumerian as a liturgical language for a thousand years, much like Latin in Medieval Europe. This indicated tremendous respect because Sumerian is a language isolate, unaffiliated to any other, including the Akkadian* spoken in Babylon. (In contrast Latin belongs to the same Indo-European family as English, French, German, etc.) That respect was well deserved considering that Sumer invented the wheel, the plow, writing, and civilization itself.

Others shared it as well: many of the stories in Genesis derive from Sumerian sources known to predate Abraham, the first Patriarch, who made the Hebrews' Covenant with God. These motifs include a primordial division of the waters (Genesis 1:6), the Flood, the tree of life, a serpent who steals our immortality. Abraham, who lived ca. 2000-1800 BC, originally hailed from Ur, one of the oldest Sumerian cities.

*Akkadian, belonging to the Semitic family, served as the working language of administration, commerce and scholarship throughout the ancient Middle East from ca. 2000 to 750 BC. It was replaced by Aramaic, a sister language, because the latter was written with an alphabet, making communication far easier than cumbersome cuneiform. Aramaic, similar to Hebrew, was the common tongue from 750 BC to the seventh century AD when it was supplanted by Arabic, yet another member of this family. Jesus spoke Aramaic.

Below are the planetary names in Sumerian and Akkadian:

Planet	Sumerian	Akkadian
Sun	Utu	Shamash
Moon	Nanna	Sin[†]
Mercury	Enki	Nabu
Venus	Inanna	Ishtar
Mars	Gugalanna	Nergal
Jupiter	Enlil	Marduk
Saturn	Ninurta	Ninurta

[†] In modern astrology Moon symbolizes the unconscious: a default to ignorance, the essence of sin.

2. This translates as 'When the gods Anu and Enlil...' (Anu was the sky god; Enlil, the air god). The Enuma describes astronomical and weather phenomena along with what they allegedly portend: if this, then that. You can view images of these tablets and read more from and about them online. Below is a sample translated from a section dealing with Sun:

'If in Nisannu (March/April) the sunrise (looks) sprinkled with blood and the light is cool: rebellion will not stop in the country, there will be devouring by Adad (the storm god). If in Nisannu the normal sunrise (looks) sprinkled with blood: battles. If in Nisannu the normal sunrise (looks) sprinkled with blood: there will be battles in the country. If on the first day of Nisannu the sunrise (looks) sprinkled with blood: grain will vanish in the country, there will be hardship and human flesh will be eaten. If on the first day of Nisannu the sunrise (looks) sprinkled with blood and the light is cool: the king will die and there will be mourning in the country. If it becomes visible on the second day and the light is cool: the king's...high official will die and mourning will not stop in the country. If the sunrise (looks) sprinkled with blood on the third day: an eclipse will take place.'

It may be that such cloud conditions during the planting season in a desert country meant bad weather, a poor crop and thus war and famine. We still follow this advice on a shorter daily time scale: 'Red sky at night, sailors' delight; red sky in the morning, sailors take warning.'

The oldest preserved section of the Enuma, the tablet of Ammisaduqa from about 1700 BC, contains omens pertaining to Venus: 'In month Shabati, 15th day, Venus disappeared in the west for three days. Then on the 18th day Venus became visible in the east. Springs will flow. Adad will bring his rain and Ea (the water god) his floods. King will send messages of reconciliation to king.'

3. There is no evidence for any form of astrology in Egypt prior to its incorporation into a universal Hellenistic empire in 332 BC. Speculation about whether the pyramids were actually temples aligned with the ancient locations of specific stars may be true, but have nothing to do with astrology as we know it. The Egyptians carefully observed the heavens for calendrical reasons, especially watching for the pre-dawn rise of the great star Sirius which timed the Nile's annual flooding. There is no record of them ascribing divinatory meaning to planetary movements.

4. The Babylonians left no evidence that they recognized a constellational zodiac as a path of continual motion. The first precursor to such an idea comes from the Mul Apin (Plow) tablet of 687 BC. This describes three 'gates' of heaven on the eastern horizon: northern, equatorial and southern. Through them stars and constellations rise into view on specific dates during the year. It also describes Sun and planets rising at cyclically changing points through these gates as they 'follow'

Moon's path. There was no sense of their movement as an integrated energy curve through the heavens.

5. For example, Hipparchus, ca. 190-120 BC, perhaps the greatest astronomer of ancient times, discovered precession of the equinox, the 'Great Year' of Earth's 25,920 year polar cycle. (See 'Precession.') He was able to do so because he also invented trigonometry, the geometry of triangulated measurements mapped onto the surface of a sphere, like the arc of the ecliptic.

6. Plato, 423-347 BC, was one of the greatest thinkers in history. (A. N. Whitehead, himself a blue chip philosopher, famously stated that '...the European philosophical tradition consists of a series of footnotes to Plato.') Plato's most important insight, among many, was that the material world is only the shadow of a transcendent spiritual dimension. Individual entities are smudged copies of their ideal forms, or archetypes. Actual events mimic higher causative principles. This underlies the metaphysical rationale for astrology and many other spiritual, mystical and religious traditions.

The counter argument is that of materialism, prevalent in modern times. It states that only tangible phenomena and physical processes exist. The truth lies in a reconciliation of both approaches: messy life makes abstract ideals real, however imperfectly. And stark facts reflect a higher meaning and greater purpose than their mere existence. The fact that existence grounds consciousness and generates philosophical concerns demonstrates this point.

7. Ptolemy, ca. 85-165 AD, was a Greek astronomer/astrologer in Alexandria, the Roman Empire's intellectual capital. His astronomical work, the Almagest, synthesized ancient knowledge in this field and was considered authoritative for well over a thousand years. However, he shared the almost universal illusion of a geocentric (Earth centered) solar system. Only Aristarchus of Samos, ca. 310-230 BC, is known to have promoted the correct heliocentric (Sun centered) model before its rediscovery by Copernicus, published in 1543.

8. Nostradamus (1503-66), a French seer who employed astrology as part of his prophetic method, fascinates many to this day. William Lilly (1602-81) was an English practitioner who used horary astrology, a technique of answering specific questions based on the time they are put to the astrologer. He was so successful that his book 'Christian Astrology' (1647) remains the definitive text on this subject. It is still in print.

Eclipses are by far the most dramatic heavenly phenomena, matched only by the rare appearance of a great comet. Thus they preoccupied the first astronomer/astrologers. Every individual eclipse also occurs as a member of an extended cycle known as a Saros series (Saros = Greek: to repeat). The astrological meaning of particular eclipses is discussed in 'Lunar Phases and Aspects'; their more collective meaning as participants in a Saros series is covered below. The next seven paragraphs of this section are a little technical. However, it is important to understand the astronomical basis of astrological phenomena. For more information on the celestial mechanics of these cycles you can go online or consult an astronomy textbook.

Eclipses in each Saros series recur at an interval of 18 years, 11 days and 8 hours.[1] Because of that extra ⅓ day (8 hour) increment of Earth's rotation the next Saros, 18+ years later, is visible at 120° of longitude further west, or ⅓ of the distance around the globe. Thirty-six years later it is visible at 240° west of the original location. Fifty four years later it recurs over the same spot on Earth, but is 34° west, or further along, in zodiacal longitude in the sky (because 34 additional days have accrued in when the eclipse takes place: 11 and ⅓ days × 3 eclipses = 34 days). For each actual member of the series, visible from different spots on Earth, the eclipse occurs 11°-12° ahead of its immediate predecessor in zodiacal longitude.

Let's use a south node solar eclipse series as an example of how the process works. See Figure 1. Every series begins with a new Moon about 18° east of (earlier than) the south lunar node in zodiacal longitude. For example, new Moon at 0° Libra, south node at 18° Libra. Moon conjoins Sun in the zodiac before reaching its own descending (south) node. That node is where Moon's slightly inclined orbit crosses the ecliptic moving from north to south. Moon is converging with, but has not yet intersected, Sun's path (ecliptic). Sun is a little bit south of Moon. At this point Moon's disc is as far as it can be from the solar disc to its south while making visual contact with it from Earth's perspective: they barely touch. Thus it generates the most partial of partial eclipses, which can only be seen in Earth's far south, near the Antarctic pole.

Because Moon's nodal axis retrogrades by ½° eastwards through the zodiac over each 18 year cycle, the south node gradually approaches the recurring new Moons of the series. These occur on different degrees of the zodiac than the original initiating eclipse (see second paragraph above). At every successive eclipse Sun and Moon come closer together as seen from Earth. Moon's disc progressively covers more of Sun's. It also becomes visible farther north on Earth and sweeps over a wider area.

There are 15 partial eclipses, each one getting fuller, until Sun/Moon conjunctions occur close enough to the ecliptic to produce total eclipses. There are then 21 total eclipses as the retrograding node approaches the series of new Moons, and another 21 as the eastward moving node leaves the series behind to its west. After 42/43 total eclipses the series of Sun/ Moon conjunctions now happens far enough west of the withdrawing node that the 15 remaining eclipses become more and more partial until they fade out completely. Finally the cycle ends at 18° west of (later than) the south node.[2] For example, new Moon at 0° Libra, south node at 12° Virgo. Moon conjoins Sun in the zodiac past its intersection with the ecliptic on the descending node. The point where Moon's orbit moves from north to south of the ecliptic is behind the new Moon. Sun is now north of Moon. Its last tiny partial eclipse of the series is visible only in the far north, near the Arctic pole.

The same process occurs with north node solar eclipses, starting above the Arctic and ending over Antarctica. Lunar eclipse cycles also involve a similar dynamic as Earth's shadow partially, then completely, overlaps the lunar disc at full Moons near either the north or south nodes. Whether solar or lunar, a Saros series lasts an average of 1300 years and involves an average of 71/72 eclipses. Both solar and lunar eclipse cycles evolve from partial to total over the first 650 years, then back from total to partial over the second 650 years.

During this long period an average of 42 other Saros cycles are concurrently taking their course, each at a different stage of development. In the 18 year period between eclipses of any given series other eclipses of other series are taking place in other signs. This is because solar and lunar eclipses occur in tandem, two weeks apart, twice a year every year. They happen at new or full Moons near the nodes.

During that year the nodes themselves are moving eastwards. They retrograde through the zodiac every 18.6 years. But it only takes 18 years, 11 days and 8 hours for them to move back to where they generate the next eclipse of a given series. Thus the nodes generate the next eclipse of the series before returning to the nodal cycle's original starting point. During this entire period of 18.6 years they have also generated eclipses belonging to other series with other starting points.

The 6½-month difference between the recurring eclipse cycle and the slightly longer period of Moon's own orbital (nodal) retrogradation causes the Saros series. The eclipses of the series begin small, become total, then fade out because these two cycles are closely, but not exactly, aligned. Over many years the ½° retrogradation of the longer nodal cycle relative to the Sun/Moon eclipse cycle generates 72 waxing and waning eclipses. (Waxing: 18° of separation at the beginning of the series × ½°

nodal retrogradation per cycle = 36 eclipses, 15 partial and 21 total, as the node approaches a series of solar or lunar eclipses. Waning: another 36 eclipses, 21 total and 15 partial, happen as the node moves away from the cycle of new or full Moon eclipses.) In order to track this complexity astronomers number each Saros series, labeling the solar and lunar cycles separately. In both cases, if the series began near the north node it is assigned an even number; if by the south node an odd number.

What could be the astrological meaning of a series of 72 eclipses extending over 1300 years? How does one distinguish any Saros cycle, or any one of its eclipses, from the 42 other solar or lunar Saros series, making 84 altogether, occurring during the 18+ year interval between eclipses of any given sequence?[3]

The initial eclipse of any series points to, or embodies, a planetary configuration without its own subjective dimension. The systems of house division necessary to subjectively organize planetary patterns break down at the high polar latitudes where Saros series actually begin. (See 'House Division.') The initial eclipse resembles a virus, a string of genetic instructions lacking its own cellular organization, which transfers genetic information to more sophisticated structures (cells).[4] The initial eclipse does not represent a formed or centered state of consciousness, but rather a 'loose cannon' energy that must be integrated into consciousness. This is consistent with the inherent nature of eclipses as representing an unconscious, subjectively unorganized, condition forcing itself on our attention. This is a disruptive process, just as eclipses have always been interpreted.

The initial Saros signature event only manifests if it turns the key of a structured planetary configuration. If a particular eclipse is geographically visible, and its original planetary imprint activates a sensitive degree of a horoscope, then the viral energy of the series infects and stimulates the situation at hand through the medium of that eclipse. The actual eclipse under consideration may also occur in some aspect to the initial starting point of the series, such as a square (90°) or trine (120°), thus coloring its expression.[5]

In this sense a Saros series acts like Pluto, which swoops into the flat plane of concentric planetary orbits at a 17° north/south angle from the chaotic Kuiper Belt surrounding it. (See 'Pluto.') Other than Pluto, which ends the planetary sequence, only Mercury, which begins it, orbits at an appreciable incline to the ecliptic (7°). Mercury constitutes the outer perimeter of Sun itself; it represents the bandwidth of Sun's own stellar consciousness. (See 'Mercury.') All other planets, Venus through Neptune, orbit Sun on essentially the same plane, the ecliptic.[6] They deliver specific messages on that bandwidth. Pluto punctuates it with interstellar energies by an intrusion from outside: above and below.

A Saros series does the same to Earth's own sphere by calling down a north/south polar energy from outside the east/west disc of planetary orbits. The series then unfolds that energy through a cycle of 72 specific eclipses over thirteen centuries. A Saros series, like Pluto, introduces alien and disruptive, but also fertilizing, qualities from a vertical dimension that intersects our horizontal plane of consciousness.

The ecliptic portrays Earth's bandwidth of consciousness about its source and purpose (Sun), organized into signs. Actual eclipses occur within the ecliptic by definition; thus the name.[6] However, every eclipse belongs to a Saros series. Every Saros series geographically begins at the poles, outside the realm of organized subjective expression as charted by the house structure of a horoscope. An eclipse cycle enters history at an extreme polarity, drawing down cosmic forces from beyond our normal ken. Over the centuries its energy assimilates into the stream of history, then fades out, as do all things. This parallels our own most basic biography. Every human psyche begins prior to conscious memory in the defining experiences of womb/birth/early infancy. Personal character emerges out of, and returns to, the collective unconscious as its ego vehicle waxes and wanes over the years.

Each year generally hosts four Saros series in the two pairs of solar/lunar eclipses that happen during it. Most of these eclipses manifest as stand-alone events. They do not invoke their Saros inheritance except when their embedded planetary pattern directly activates a chart's pre-existing sensitivity to its initial (formless) energy surge. Such an example is described in the next chapter.

An eclipse brings up a karmic issue: a spiritual blockage (solar) or repressed memory (lunar) that demands attention. It points to a difficult legacy that must be faced. Eclipses are not 'bad' in and of themselves: they simply bring up a suppressed problem whose time has come to surface. Thus they can act as a healing process or a horror show. Eclipses are powerful intrusions of unconscious material into normal awareness. On rare occasions they also evoke an ancient issue stemming from the series to which they belong.

Saros cycles are connected with mundane astrology because of their long duration, far exceeding that of an individual life. A Saros series pertains to mass moods and collective tides rather than personal psychology. Waxing it may describe presentation of a once dormant social or moral problem; waning its fading from priority by either successful discharge or after a destructive catharsis. A Saros series describes a lineage of generations wrestling with an ongoing existential problem. A study of the common thread connecting its generationally separated eclipses may provide insight into long-term historical processes.

Figure 1 - Celestial Mechanics of the Saros cycle

Scale distorted to illustrate the concept on a small page.

Line of eclipses slightly offset from path of the ecliptic to portray the idea of distance south or north of the node (depicted as an eclipsed Sun on the ecliptic). By astrological convention east is at the left and west at the right.

An observant reader will notice that the line inclines from south to north - characteristic of the north node. But this line does not depict the lunar orbit itself - it represents a long term sequence of eclipses. Each notch represents five new Moons on the north to south arc of their orbits, within 18° of the south node (eclipse range). They are slanted 'downwards,' from north to south, to portray their south node character. Each normally shaded notch indicates five partial eclipses.
Each bold notch indicates five total eclipses.

Moon's orbit around Earth inclines at 5° to the ecliptic. Midpoints of the oval show the limits of that inclination, exaggerated for purposes of illustration. (10° total width = less than 3% of a circle.) The nodes are where Moon's orbit intersects the ecliptic, moving north or south. Here the nodes are aligned with the ecliptic at the center of a series. Moon moves along its orbit from left to right on the solid arc, and returns on the dashed arc. Its retrograde nodal axis moves in the opposite direction. The dashed section visually reminds us that Earth is a sphere.

Moon can be anywhere along its orbit when conjoining Sun (new Moon) or opposing it (full Moon) in the zodiac. However, a new or full Moon must be within 18° of a node to form an eclipse.

The north node is where Moon's inclined orbit intersects the ecliptic moving from south to north. The south node is where Moon's orbit intersects the ecliptic moving from north to south.

The nodes are 180° apart.

They retrograde through the zodiac every 18.6 years.

Figure 1 - Celestial Mechanics of the Saros cycle

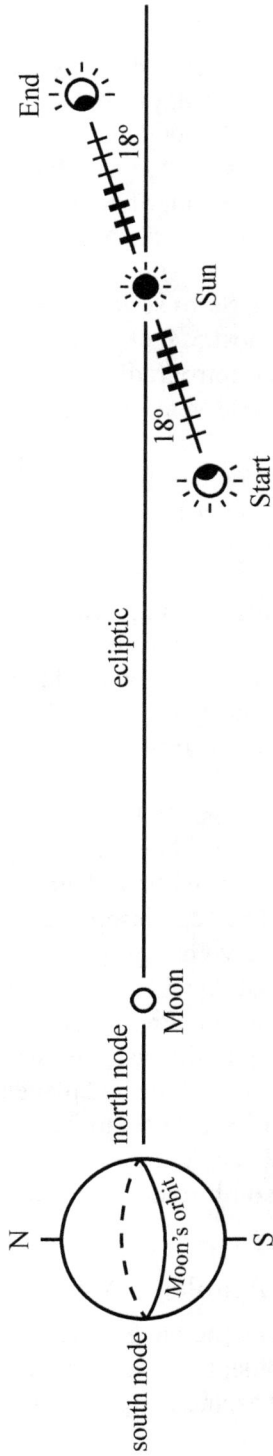

Each normally shaded notch indicates five partial eclipses.
Each bold notch indicates five total eclipses.

655

Notes

1. To be technical: 14 normal years + 4 leap years + 11⅓ days. Or 13 normal years + 5 leap years + 10⅓ days. In the interest of simplicity all other numbers in this section are rounded off.

2. A lunar node is where Moon's orbit around Earth intersects the ecliptic, Earth's orbit around Sun. Ten out of twelve new Moons during the year occur more than 18° away from the Moon's nodal axis and do not generate eclipses.

3. There are 84, rather than 72, Saros series in play during this 18+ year interval because some years host 5, 6 or even 7 eclipses. This happens because the lunar nodes keep retrograding through the zodiac during this period and because the lunar year of 354⅓ days is shorter than the solar year of 365¼ days.

4. A virus is an autonomous strand of genes looking for a host. Viruses are genetic fragments that transfer information between widely different species. The incorporation of their DNA into a genome shifts that genome's internal balance. It may enhance with new protein coding abilities; more often it disrupts, causing sickness, cancer or death.

We genetically engineer by introducing artificial viruses into a genome. We think we know what that particular sequence will do, and to that extent we may be right. But it also alters its genetic context in ways we cannot predict because functional genomes are so inherently complex.

Saros series of eclipses parallel this biological process on an astrological level of meaning. They consist of eclipse sequences, recurring at generation-long intervals, without their own central organizing principle (house structure). They can insert themselves into history by accessing a mundane planetary configuration at a sensitive point(s). The Saros series 122 event of April 15, 2014 provides a very strong example, described in 'A Mundane Prediction.'

5. For the meaning of these and other aspects, see 'Aspects.'

6. The ecliptic is the path of Sun, Moon and planets' movement as seen from Earth. It stretches from 23½° north to 23½° south of the celestial equator, Earth's equator projected out into space. See 'Sun and Earth.' This figure illustrates the south node solar eclipse cycle described in the text.

Mundane Astrology: Application

Mundane astrology operates on the same principles as the more familiar natal astrology of personal identity. Nations, and other organizations such as corporations, churches and nonprofits, have birth charts based on a founding event. One can cast a horoscope for that moment. The symbols used in such charts are displayed in Figure 2.

The USA chart is for proclamation of the Declaration of Independence on July 4, 1776 at 5:10 pm in Philadelphia. It is briefly examined in the next section. England's is for William the Conqueror's coronation at noon on December 25, 1066 (Figure 3).[1] The former Soviet Union's is for the Communist coup at 2:12 am on November 8, 1917 (Figure 4).[2]

In other cases the situation is more ambiguous. For example, France is clearly a Leo country. Yet since 1780 two kingdoms, two empires and five republics have governed it, along with episodes of revolutionary turmoil and foreign occupation. It is impossible to cast a chart for France itself, as opposed to its current government - but no one would deny its distinctive and enduring national character.

China has always been considered a Libra country in light of its Confucian political philosophy of harmony and right relationship along with its Taoist spiritual philosophy of balance and cyclical change (yin/yang). Its present presiding dynasty, the People's Republic, represents a special variant of that Libran quality (Figure 5).

Finally, long established cultures or national identities often host political structures at odds with their innate character. An interesting example: Germany is a Scorpionic nation. Its cultural talent for brilliantly probing the hidden depths of science, philosophy and psychology is matched only by its political predilection for self-destruction when left to its own devices.[3] Yet its Nazi regime was Aquarian: Hitler was inaugurated as Chancellor (soon to become Führer) at 11 am on January 30, 1933 in Berlin.[4] In contrast, Russia has always been considered an Aquarian country: prone to sudden drastic changes of fortune, its unique history detached from the mainstream of Western civilization,[5] the very land itself evoking thoughts of winter. Yet its Soviet phase was Scorpionic.[2]

Notes

1. Given England's long history there are several candidates for its national chart, ranging from: February 13, 1689 when King William III and Queen Mary II accepted the Declaration of Right which decisively located sovereignty in Parliament rather than the monarchy; foundation of Great Britain through the legal union of England and Scotland at midnight, May 1, 1707; foundation of the United Kingdom by legal union of Great Britain and unwilling Ireland at midnight on January 1, 1801; and indeed several others. This is not the place to go into the complications of British constitutional development or of England's

relationship with its smaller Celtic neighbors. It seems that the formal inauguration of Norman rule, which brought that island nation into the mainstream of European history at the dawn of the high medieval period, best describes England's national history and character.

2. The USSR chart is cast for November 8, 1917 at 2:12 am local time in Petrograd (now St. Petersburg). That was when Bolshevik rebels arrested all members of the democratic Provisional Government of Russia in the former Czar's Winter Palace. They actually stopped the meeting hall clock to record the moment, and so it remains to this day. Soviet mythology portrayed November 7 as its national birthday. In that version a 'spontaneous' uprising of workers, peasants and soldiers stormed the Winter Palace after an initial signal fired by the battleship Aurora at 9:45 that evening. However, mass arrests in the dead of night more accurately reflect its true nature. The USSR peacefully disintegrated after a brief political crisis in August 1991. That momentous event occurred as transiting Pluto exactly conjoined the Soviet natal Sun in Scorpio.

3. Naturally we think of this in terms of the 20th century's world wars. However, three hundred years earlier, just as Western Europe was coalescing into modern nation states, Germany tore itself apart in the Thirty Year's War (1618-48). It remained fragmented until 1871. This gave Britain, France and others time to develop their national identities, free from the overbearing presence of what is inherently Europe's strongest power.

Tellingly, three decisive events of 20th century German history took place on or about one Scorpionic day, with which that nation clearly resonates. The Armistice of November 11, 1918 ended World War I. It was manipulated by the German General Staff to implicate a hastily organized civilian government in order to 'exonerate' the Junker military caste from the stigma of defeat. Kristallnacht, during the darkness of November 9/10, 1938 when Nazi Germany showed its real face to the world. And the fall of the Berlin Wall on the night of November 9/10, 1989, effectively ending the long Cold War in a few hours. Today Germany no longer has an autonomous national identity but is integrated into the European Union. Politically this strangely gifted people do better as part of a larger collective than on their own.

4. The author declines to include a chart for the Third Reich in this book. The reader can easily access its signature of horror on the Internet.

5. Russia is too big to be European, and too European to be Asiatic. Indeed, it most closely resembles the United States, of which it seems to be a reverse image. Both are multi-ethnic continental nations, offshoots of European culture, with big dreams and messianic aspirations.

Mundane Symbols: Planets

Mundane planetary symbols parallel those used in natal astrology but reflect their sociological rather than psychological subject matter. The same is true of mundane houses, which portray a nation's fields of experience. The astrological symbols for planets, major aspects and signs are portrayed in Figure 2.

Sun: the general character and identity of a nation. (Or of any corporate body, whether a business, church or nongovernmental organization.) The nature of its government.

Moon: the people; those who actually embody the national identity. Its progressions chart long-term changes in the national mood.

Moon's North Node: what the nation and its people must achieve to fulfill their destiny.

Mercury: intellectual life; education; communications; transportation.

Venus: economy, wealth, resources, productive base (Taurus). Culture: high art or popular entertainment (Libra). It also speaks to the status of women.

Mars: war. Military and police forces. National drive and assertion.

Jupiter: law. Religious and philosophical attitudes. The general social and political tone of a nation. Expansion. Liberal tendencies.

Saturn: a nation's institutional framework and basic rules. Political structure. Social hierarchies. Contraction. Conservative tendencies.

Uranus: national transformation. Change agents or revolutionary forces.

Neptune: national ideals. Inspiring myths and subversive illusions.

Pluto: national death and rebirth. Hidden powers, whether economic, political, religious or cultural.

The outer planets, Uranus, Neptune and Pluto, are inherently collective. Their mundane influence is the subject of the previous chapter 'Outer Planet Transits.'

Mundane Houses

Ascendant and first house: the self-consciousness of a nation. How it projects itself to the world. The national image.

Second: the economy. Wealth. Resources. Financial institutions.

Third: primary education. Communications and the media. Transportation.

Fourth: the land itself and its resources. Agriculture. The people, the base of society.

Fifth: art and culture, which express its social character. Pleasure and entertainment. Creativity. Children, the most important creation.

Sixth: workers and working conditions. Public servants, civil and military. Public health. Technology.

Seventh: relationship with the outside world through trade, diplomacy and war. Allies and enemies.

Eighth: large corporations. Concentrated wealth and oligarchic power. Debt. National death and rebirth. (See particularly the Chinese and American charts.)

Ninth: the legal system. Social mores and belief systems. Religious attitudes. Higher education. Foreign influences, projected or received.

Tenth: government in general; the executive branch in particular. The ruling classes. National prestige.

Eleventh: the legislative branch (Congress). Political parties. Public interest groups and think tanks. National hopes, wishes, aspirations.

Twelfth: national sorrows and self-undoing. Subversive influences. Ironically, in the American case, these are established mega corporations that undermine democracy. Also places of exile and redemption: hospitals, prisons, monasteries. In an earlier time the frontier. This represented sorrow for the Native Americans.

Figure 2   Astrological Symbols

Planets:

⊙ – Sun

☽ – Moon

☿ – Mercury

♀ – Venus

♂ – Mars

♃ – Jupiter

♄ – Saturn

♅ – Uranus

♆ – Neptune

♇ – Pluto

☊ – Moon's north node

℞ – Retrograde

Signs:

♈ – Aries

♉ – Taurus

♊ – Gemini

♋ – Cancer

♌ – Leo

♍ – Virgo

♎ – Libra

♏ – Scorpio

♐ – Sagittarius

♑ – Capricorn

♒ – Aquarius

♓ – Pisces

Major Planetary Aspects:

♂ – Conjunction: the planetary symbols are in the same place.

☍ – Opposition: a polarity in which the two planets either complement each other, or one predominates, permanently, or in a seesaw alteration.

□ – Square: two planetary functions at odds with each other. Stress, mutual conflict.

△ – Trine: harmonious reinforcement, mutual amplification.

England

Coronation of William the Conqueror
December 25, 1066   12 Noon   London - Julian calendar[1]

Sun in Capricorn, and on the Midheaven, indicates achievement rising to the level of initiation into a higher state of being. The coronation of William the Conqueror inaugurated an English national identity that meets this extraordinary criteria. England would eventually give the world representative democracy, the Industrial Revolution and a global language, along with brilliant cultural and scientific accomplishments. William, a medieval warlord, did not have that in mind. Yet his rule began a process that united Norman feudal institutions and Anglo-Saxon culture into something new under the Sun. England's Capricorn Sun indicates its conservative nature, steadily building on rock solid foundations.

Waxing crescent Moon on the vernal equinox (0° Aries): The birth of rule by the people (Moon). This took centuries to mature, and is now universally emulated. England's enterprising temperament. This tiny island has consistently played a disproportionate role in world history.

In the twelfth, sympathy for the underdog and a sense of fair play. The universality of its achievement and gifts to the world, such as the English language. This is reflected in the respect, even love, shown for it by the disparate cultures of its empire turned Commonwealth.

Aries rising: the pioneering role of England in so many areas: political, economic, scientific and cultural. Its emphasis on personal liberty. Its insistence on the free competition of ideas, political parties, and commercial companies. Its willingness to fight for them.

Neptune rising in Taurus near the second house cusp: this island nation's maritime tradition, and its protective navy. Britannia ruled the waves from its defeat of the Spanish Armada (1588) until the beginning of World War II, first as the strongest, then the dominant, sea power. Equally important, for all of its pragmatism, England has always been motivated by a mystical sense of national identity. This runs from the Arthurian legends through Shakespeare[2] to the modern icon of its 'finest hour,' when it stood alone and prevailed against Nazi Germany in the Battle of Britain.

Mercury in Capricorn: the pragmatic and skeptical English cast of mind. Its respect for fact v theory. For example, English common law (10th house: authority) is based on actual precedents as much as administrative guidelines. A precision of thought and speech.

Venus in Aquarius (just entering at 0°): English emotional detachment. Toleration of eccentricity. England's economic embrace of free

Figure 3

England
Coronation of William the Conqueror
December 25, 1066   High Noon   London - Julian calendar (see text)

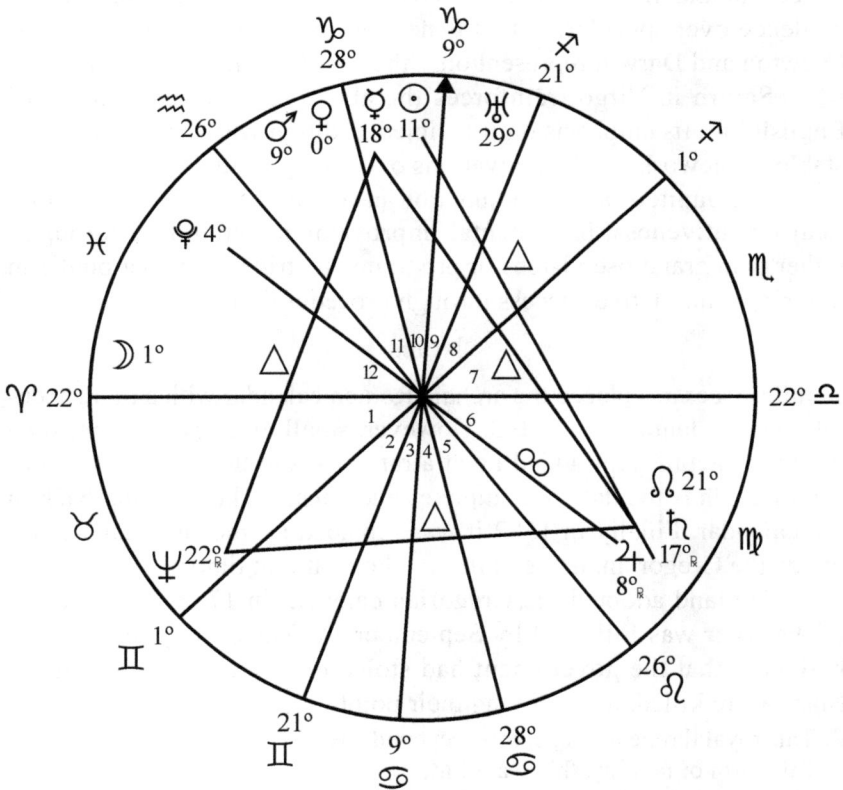

Major Aspects:

Sun trines Jupiter and Saturn
Mercury trines Saturn/north node and Neptune: a grand trine.
Venus approaching Mars
Jupiter opposes Pluto
Saturn conjunct Moon's north node

enterprise capitalism which encourages innovation and generated the Industrial Revolution. Brilliant cultural originality in many fields.

Mars in Aquarius: energetic innovation in both the political and scientific realms (11th house). Mars, as ruler of Aries on the ascendant, rules the chart as a whole. Britain's aggressive and often warlike nature. Nobody voted to establish the British Empire - yet its former subjects now vote because of it.

Jupiter in Virgo: An insistence on due process in law and governance that underlies its social and political freedom. And on reason and evidence over speculation that generated its scientific achievements. (Newton and Darwin represent only the best-known examples.)

Saturn in Virgo: reinforces the above. The formal quality of English life. Its emphasis on principled tradition which has provided a stable framework for its innovations over many centuries.

The Jupiter/Saturn conjunction in the 6th house points to practical inventiveness, incremental improvement, 'muddling through,' rather than grandiose visions or programs. Its trine to the national Sun describes cumulative success through procedural integrity.

Notes

1. Julius Caesar replaced the archaic Roman calendar with a more accurate one on January 1, 45 BC. However, small discrepancies between it and the actual year added up at a rate of about three days over four centuries; thus the date of equinoxes and solstices kept falling back in the calendar. Finally in 1582 it was replaced by the calendar we use today, the Gregorian, named after the Pope at that time.

England adopted the Gregorian calendar in 1752: September 2 of that year was followed by September 14. Mobs rioted in London, believing that the government had stolen eleven days of their lives. Many were killed, thus proving their point.

2. This royal throne of kings, this sceptered isle,
   This earth of majesty, this seat of Mars,
   This other Eden, demi-paradise,
   This fortress built by Nature for herself
   Against infection and the hand of war,
   This happy breed of men, this little world,
   This precious stone set in the silver sea,
   Which serves it in the office of a wall
   Or as a moat defensive to a house,
   Against the envy of less happier lands,
   This blessed plot, this earth, this realm, this England.

   Richard II, Shakespeare

664

USSR

Bolshevik seizure of the Winter Palace
November 8, 1917   2:12 am   St. Petersburg

Sun in Scorpio: a secretive and self-destructive superpower. It not only slaughtered millions of its best and brightest, but also crippled its own vast potential by rigid application of a narrow ideology. Its 3rd house placement demonstrated a sharp contrast to the rest of the world with its dystopian lesson in social engineering.[1]

Moon: waning crisis of consciousness: The Soviet Moon at 29° Leo exactly opposed the United States' Moon at 28° Aquarius. Soviet socialism presented a premature alternative to capitalism under the tragic circumstances of Russian history. The Soviet Moon was void of course: it made no planetary aspects before leaving Leo.[2] However, it did conjoin the star Regulus, 'Heart of the Lion,' one of the most powerful stars beyond our solar system.[3] This profoundly modifies its technically void condition. The Soviet experiment attempted to ground a subtle energy for which primitive Russia was not ready. Its socialist theory embodied a noble vision of selfless cooperation at odds with the realities of human nature. Yet, in reaching beyond its grasp, Russia not only eventually transcended its own tragedy, but can also fairly claim to have played an equal part with the West in saving civilization during the crisis of World War II. Churchill's famous description of Russia as '...a riddle wrapped in a mystery, inside an enigma,' will always remain true for its Soviet period, one of the most ambiguous episodes in history.

In the 12th house of sorrows, approaching violent Mars, this lunar symbol clearly refers to the man made famine of collectivization, mass executions and the millions who passed through, or passed on, in the forced labor system (the Gulag). Its position in Leo, conjunct Regulus, points to the Russian people's powerful vitality, which enabled them to build a superpower despite such oppression. And to an innate generosity of spirit that differentiated this tragic experiment from Nazi nihilism.

Virgo rising: the workers' state as a 'Dictatorship of the Proletariat' (actually of an elite party). Social engineering; a micro-managed society and economy. State planning of every aspect of life, from collective agriculture to centrally organized industry to carefully supervised culture. Scientific and technological development; within just two generations an illiterate peasant nation became the first to launch humans into space.

Mercury in Scorpio: combust, lost in the glare of Sun: truth overwhelmed by power.

Venus in Capricorn: economic restriction; all wealth and productivity channeled to gargantuan state projects. Regimentation of art, and human resources, to feed narrow political ambitions. Opposing Pluto: suppression of love and natural feelings.* Conjunction with North Node: identification with the enduring archetype of Mother Russia, enabling the culture to survive its Soviet incubus.

*It also opposed the American Venus - what authority (Capricorn) wants (Venus) v what the people (Cancer) want.

Mars in Virgo in the 12th house: immense suffering at the hands of invaders who saw Slavs as racial vermin and acted accordingly. Vicious internal purges: oceans of tears through its own rulers. Liquidation of class enemies: millions of real people were shot for ideological impurities, as deviationists, revisionists and objectively reactionary elements.[4]

Jupiter is the most elevated planet in the chart, yet is in detriment in Gemini, and in accidental fall (10th house).[5] The reign (10th) of a false religion (Jupiter). The Big Lie of a materialistic philosophy (economic determinism) based on hatred (class warfare). An inflated ideology split off from organic social reality. Marxism can serve as a good analytic tool, but it makes a poor worldview. Yet in its time it mobilized a medieval peasant mass into an industrialized nation that defeated Nazi Germany. This Jupiter position also symbolizes a territorial expansion that suffocated many smaller captive nations. And a spectacular leap into outer space along with other scientific achievements.

Saturn in Leo (detriment)5: crushing of revolutionary aspirations (11th house). False hopes of centralized planning. A cold-hearted political structure suppressed the nation's vitality. The Soviet Sun, the nation as a whole, had a waxing crisis of action squaring its autocratic state structure (Saturn). In contrast the United States' Sun forms a waning crisis of consciousness squaring Saturn, suggesting its institutionalized skepticism of government.

Figure 4

USSR
Bolshevik Seizure of the Winter Palace
November 8, 1917   2:12 am   St. Petersburg

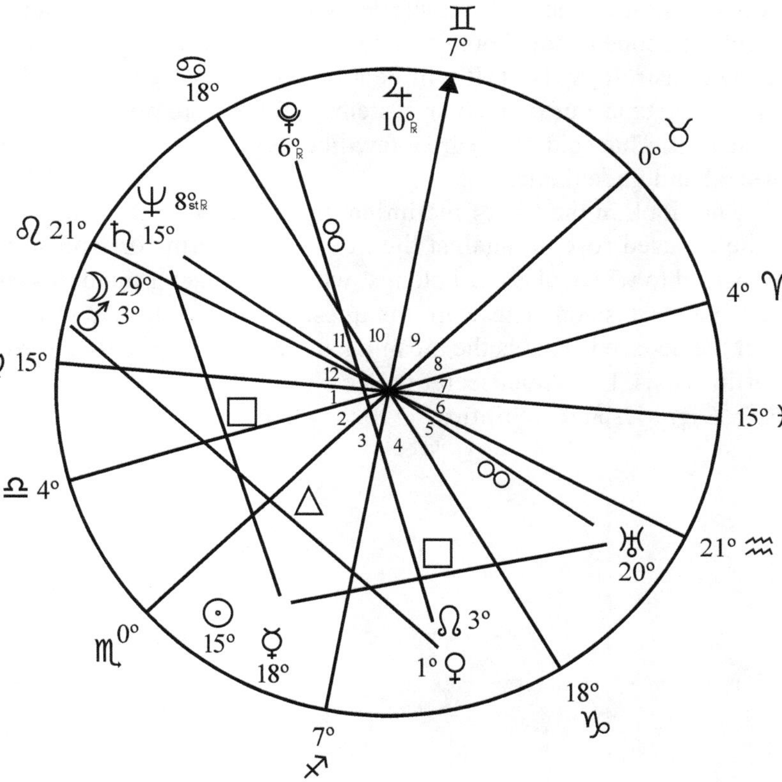

Major Aspects:

Sun conjunct Mercury
Sun/Mercury square both Saturn and Uranus } a tense T-square
Saturn opposes Uranus   } (see 'Aspects')

Venus conjoins Moon's north node, opposes Pluto
Venus/north node trine Mars
Void of course Moon in Leo applies to conjunction with Mars in Virgo

Notes

1. Pyotr Chaadayev, Russian philosopher, 1794-1856, succinctly expressed its nature: 'We (Russia) are an exception among peoples. We belong to those who are not an integral part of humanity but exist only to teach the world some type of great lesson.'
2. Interestingly, the American Moon is also technically void of course. See the end of 'Lunar Phases and Aspects' for a discussion of the void Moon in general, and the American case in particular.
3. A discussion of the real but subtle symbolism of the fixed stars is beyond the scope of this book, and generally beyond the present competence of astrology itself. It will be a long time before we, who have yet to understand our own solar system, can begin to appreciate stars outside of it. That said, there are a few like Regulus whose influence is powerful and undeniable.
4. 'Do not look in the file of incriminating evidence to see whether or not the accused rose up against the Soviets with arms or words. Ask him instead to which class he belongs, what is his background, his education, his profession. These are the questions that will determine the fate of the accused. That is the meaning and essence of the Red Terror.'
- Martin Latsis, Ukrainian secret police chief, 1919.
5. See 'Dignities and Debilities.'

China

Proclamation of the People's Republic
October 1, 1949   3:02 pm   Beijing

Traditional Chinese identity (Libra Sun) in the 8th house of death and rebirth. Sun is challenged by the square of revolutionary Uranus at cross-purposes to it. At the midpoint of this square combative Mars conjoins karmic Pluto in fiery Leo. It is hard to imagine a more stressful configuration.

This chart illustrates the extreme oscillations or national mood swings Libra can experience in its search for a happy medium. The Communist Revolution itself; the disastrous Great Leap Forward of 1957/8,[1] the chaotic Cultural Revolution of the mid/late sixties and a decisive change of course following Mao's death in September 1976 are all examples. Since then China has generated spectacular economic growth along with severe imbalances in its external trade, internal social equity, ecological health and even its sex ratio between boys and girls.[2]

A crisis of action Moon rising in utopian Aquarius: constant upheaval. Initially through Mao's doctrine of Permanent Revolution, applied for decades. Then through breakneck economic growth and social change.

Collective ideals applied to the most intimate aspects of life. First, strident political campaigns essentially leveled ancient Chinese and Tibetan cultures. Later and more profoundly, modernization promoted a greater sense of personal autonomy in a traditionally collectivist society. For example, the one child per family policy has produced a generation of 'little emperors,' single children who experienced no sibling rivalry for parental affection. They are now maturing with a fundamentally different outlook than their group-oriented ancestors.

The waxing Moon trines Sun from the ascendant, reinforcing the theme of national identity change played out on the most personal level.

Aquarius rising: social and economic transformation. Despite its totalitarian nature, at first Mao's Red China was a big improvement over abysmal misery for hundreds of millions. Only a few years later came crazed political experiments with disastrous results: the Great Leap Forward and Cultural Revolution. The new China that has emerged since then has generated an unintended psychological revolution of individualization along with increasing prosperity.

Mercury conjunct Neptune in Libra: illusory public discourse; mass media promote ideals and exhortations rather than truth.

Venus in Scorpio (detriment): Culture subordinated to politics under Mao, to economics after him. Entrenched corruption: business conducted by guanxi, political connections rather than impartial rule of law. Severe gender imbalance with a dearth of women.[2]

Mars in Leo, conjunct Pluto in the 7th house of war: proud, assertive and very dangerous.

Mao famously stated that 'Political power grows out of the barrel of a gun.' This dictum continues to apply, both internally (Tiananmen Massacre, the ongoing occupation/cultural genocide of Tibet) and externally, in China's aggressive claims to the entire South China Sea.[3] Its construction of military bases on artificial islands in those international waters will probably lead to armed conflict with the United States.

The People's Republic has only had two real allies (7th): The genocidal Khmer Rouge in Cambodia, overthrown by a Vietnamese invasion (1979). And belligerent North Korea, dependent on Chinese support and therefore its proxy.

Jupiter in Capricorn: authoritarian culture and political tone. High achievement under difficult circumstances (12th house: the wretched poverty, overpopulation and civilizational wounds that the People's Republic inherited).

Saturn in Virgo: disciplined social structure; regimentation of daily life. Massive pollution. Emergence of environmental protests as the primary vehicle of public expression. A belated commitment to green energy policies.

The People's Republic chart is very dynamic, yet too stressful to endure. In the long sweep of Chinese history this dynasty has often been compared to the ruthless but effective Qin (221-206 BC) which unified China and standardized its culture under an all-powerful First Emperor, Qin Shi Huang. It may also resemble the brief Sui (589-618) that also reunited China after centuries of disorder and laid the foundations of what many consider China's golden age during the Tang (618-907).

Notes

1. An estimated thirty million people starved to death during the man made famine caused by this mad policy. Yet to date (2013) not a single photograph of it has ever been made public.
2. Caused by a strong preference for sons, implemented by selective abortion and female infanticide. The world average at birth is 105 boys/100 girls (nature's way of compensating for a greater mortality among boys while growing up). China's ratio is 120/100. China now has an excess of 35 million young men with no hope of marriage. That is social dynamite.
3. The International Court of Justice sharply rejected China's claim on July 12, 2016.

Figure 5

China
Mao Zedong Proclaims the People's Republic
October 1, 1949   3:02 pm   Beijing

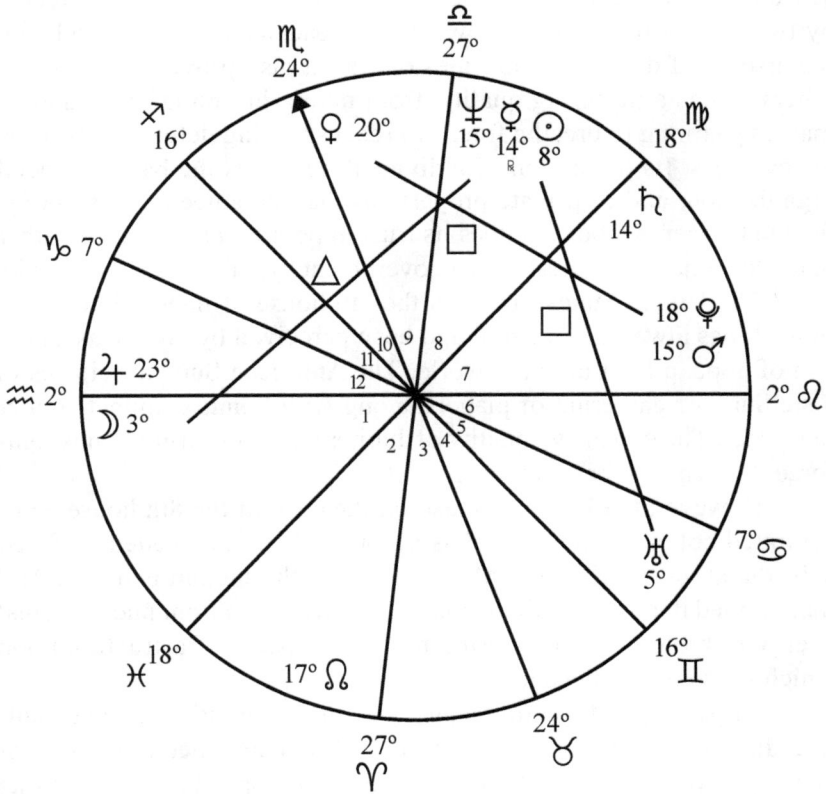

Major Aspects:

Moon in waxing trine to Sun
Sun conjunct Mercury and Neptune
Sun square Uranus
Mars conjunct Pluto
Venus square Mars/Pluto

The American National Chart

This section will briefly examine the United States' national chart. Figure 6. An extended discussion is beyond the scope of this book. The purpose here is to give a brief synopsis followed by a specific prediction in the next chapter.

The American Sun in Cancer clearly portrays its nature as a sea of peoples, a melting pot of all ethnicities and religions. It describes the sense of security allowing America to flourish in freedom, protected by two oceans from hostile powers. As breadbasket to the world, and the arsenal of democracy in times of war, it also provides security to others. It has a nurturing quality, from taking in immigrant 'huddled masses yearning to breathe free,'[1] to reconstructing defeated adversaries overseas. Its promotion of individual liberty as the basis of social organization, and of private property as the guarantee of that liberty, fits the Cancer symbol. So does its trust in popular participation rather than elite guidance, reflected in a government by, of, and for the people.

The United States Sun is in the 7th house of international relations. It has always seen itself, and been perceived by others, as a beacon of hope, a light unto the world. The American Sun participates in a stellium, or gathering of planets, along with Venus conjunct Jupiter in Cancer. The expansive quality of Jupiter and a nurturing Venus reinforce this sense of benevolence.

However, the US Sun is also on the cusp of the 8th house: concentrated collective power. It has accomplished unprecedented feats: split the atom, reached the Moon, decoded the human genome. And transformed the world with revolutionary inventions from nuclear arms/ energy to biological engineering to a cyberspace infrastructure upon which we suddenly depend.

Large corporations dominate its economy, politics and even culture. Its financial system is driven by unsustainable debt, now metastasizing into bankruptcy. A tiny oligarchy, the top 0.1%, runs both its elected government[2] and the commanding heights of Wall Street banking and investment. Only a national death and rebirth can change this entrenched situation. (See 'A Mundane Prediction.')

The United States has long been the 'indispensible nation,' with no real competitor. It leads primarily by example of its ideals and institutions, but also has the economic clout and military muscle to back them up. The United States thus serves as a partner, exemplar and standard of judgment for others (7th). And as a global Hyperpower proliferating an Americanized culture along with new technologies that have redefined the human condition (8th).

The American Moon in Aquarius portrays its innovative temperament in every area of life, and particularly its embrace of technology. (See discussion under 'Void Moon' at the end of 'Lunar Phases and Aspects.') The emphasis on personal independence, individuality and originality fits the Aquarian archetype. So does the constantly changing nature of American society, from agrarian frontier to industrial powerhouse to post-modern technocracy.

Moon in the 3rd house reinforces this theme of restlessness: the hyper-stimulated quality of American life. Its distraction by an information overload that drowns out wisdom. Constant novelty in the form and content of communications. Americans invented the telegraph (1844), the 19th century's equivalent of the Internet (another American invention). It has excelled at developing mass media such as television, computers and cell phones. These have transformed individual consciousness and social interaction. And dumbed them down with incessant electronic babble.

The diverse (3rd) origins (Moon) of the American people. Its early and enduring emphasis on universal education has melded many bloodlines into one nation. America is a state of mind, not an ethnicity. That is why it encompasses the world.

The American Moon is Full and just crossing over into the waning gibbous phase. The US was founded as an Enlightenment experiment in democracy and freedom. It has always seen itself as a 'City upon a Hill,'[3] disseminating a 'new order of the ages'[4] to the Old World.

Sagittarius rising: Optimistic, freedom-loving Sagittarius clearly fits for the USA. Its government possesses a universally recognized moral authority. Laws rather than men rule the nation. This coexists with a Wild West atmosphere of personal liberty, profligate indulgence and an endearingly jovial superficiality. Jupiter rules Sagittarius and thus America's chart. See below.

The American Mercury in Cancer refers to an emotional intelligence generated by the diversity of American life. A sense of community, rather than specific opinions, unites people of many different backgrounds. It symbolizes the power of mass media to shape the national mood with an emphasis on shared feeling more than clear thought. And the seductive appeal of advertising which has created our consumer culture, a contradiction in terms if there ever was one.

Mercury retrograde in the 8th house, complements the hidden power of Pluto in the 2nd. It points to the false bookkeeping and intricate financial manipulation that underlie an unsustainable economy.[5] Its uncontrollable debt, foreign, domestic and environmental, has metastasized beyond the point of no return. It will eventually bring down the house of cards unless a technological systems failure does so first.

Venus in Cancer portrays an emphasis on private property as the guarantee of social stability. This particularly manifests in the American dream of home-ownership. The high status of women compared to other societies. The popular rather than elite nature of its culture. And its emotional nature, expressed in music and movies more than traditional highbrow art and literature. Venus cannot be separated from its close conjunction with Jupiter, indicating the expansiveness of its economy. And an unbridled consumerism, a cancer on the human spirit as well the ecosystem.

Its 7th house placement demonstrates the worldwide appeal of this model. For all of its faults, America sets the standard that others voluntarily emulate.

Mars in dualistic Gemini aptly describes its major wars: an initial War of Independence against Great Britain (1776-1783) followed by what was then called the second war of independence against the same adversary (now referred to as the War of 1812). After that a Civil War, which divided the nation (1861-1865). Then participation in two world wars against Germany, the second of which involved two fronts (Europe and the Pacific War against Japan, 1941-1945). This was followed by a protracted Cold War against a continental peer adversary, the USSR (1945-1991), a nation that in many ways seemed a reverse image of the United States. This included two hot wars, each of which was fought in a culturally homogeneous but artificially divided nation: Korea (1950-1953) and Vietnam (1965-1973). Finally the post cold war era brought two simultaneous Middle Eastern wars in Iraq and Afghanistan, both culturally fragmented nations that will almost certainly break down into their components.

America also wins its wars through intelligence, a mental Geminian trait. It not only innovates in weapons and strategy but actually fights on the battlefields of mind. For example, the US won the decisive Battle of Midway in the Pacific against heavy odds by successfully cracking Japanese naval codes. It was able to manage the long hair-trigger nuclear standoff of the Cold War by use of reconnaissance satellites and electronic eavesdropping, which allowed rational rather than paranoid decision making. Today it fights unpublicized wars in cyberspace.

Mars in the 7th house: an ability to turn former adversaries into firm allies. A vigorous dissemination of ideas, values and practices.

Jupiter, America's ruling planet, is exalted, at its most creatively expansive, in Cancer. It also rules Sagittarius, the United States' rising sign. Thus it is the predominant planet for the chart as a whole. There could be no better symbol of the United States' incredible growth: territorial, economic, cultural and technological. Nor of its unprecedented good fortune in geographical location, resource endowment and historical experience. Even more importantly, its luck in leadership: from the founding fathers through Lincoln and FDR the American political system has consistently produced humane and visionary leaders in times of crisis. That does not guarantee that today's coarsening culture and corporately dominated politics will continue to do so.

Its 7th house position demonstrates the global propagation of its values and policies. The United States generally and genuinely embodies benevolent qualities, with successful outcomes, that others aspire to.

Saturn is exalted, at its most rigorously brilliant, in Libra. It is also placed in its natural 10th house of the executive function. It aptly describes the American governing system, based on the Constitution with its separation of powers defined by a system of checks and balances (Libra).[6] Because it is now copied worldwide we tend to forget what a breakthrough in governance this originally was. American elites are flexible, responsive and open compared to those in other countries. The United States traditionally exerts its enormous power with restraint (Saturn) to promote justice and human rights (Libra). It is guided by the discipline (Saturn) of markets and elections (Libra).

Generally speaking, Saturn evokes a previously latent power out of the shadows and into manifestation. It endows a rising quality of the collective unconscious with phenomenal reality. And also empowers its emergent darkness. This genuine but partial truth embodies the next developmental phase as a fate.

In the American case Saturn consistently initiates new frontiers of social ecology (Libra) grounded through effective administration (10th house). From its beginnings the United States focused western civilization's 18th century Enlightenment aspirations into a brilliant political expression of a 'new order of the ages.' After World War II it rose to become the template of global governance. The American corporate financial system defines the economy, and its electronic nerve network shapes the consciousness, of a single species in an ever-smaller global village. After the Cold War this process culminated with the establishment of a new world order, a Pax Americana. A generation later an Americanized planetary culture is resolving into a post-modern technocratic reality: a brave new world[7] that substitutes virtual reality for authentic experience, electronic algorithms for moral decision, artificial intelligence for spiritual wisdom, genetic manipulation for natural creation.

The United States, with 4% of the world's population, is the leading exemplar, an irresistible gravitational attractor, promoting this evolution. America's culminating Saturn symbolizes an exaltation of objective scientific truth as the religion of modernity.[8] Venerated in the image of its applied power (10th).[9] This now dominant paradigm seeks to redefine human nature and natural reality in the narrow mold of a technological triumphalism.

The American Shadow is not one of oppressive government. Nor of greedy capitalism or dehumanizing racism, though they exist. Rather it consists of an amoral pragmatism based on the limited premises of materialist ambitions. Its sinister side involves a reductionist urge to remake life in the image of a rational agenda, to shrink its mysterious purpose to a contrived program, to control and manipulate consciousness by engineering protocols. It is expressed through the worship of technology: a dark seduction by idols of silicon brains and biotech bodies.

Saturn in the 10th means meteoric rise and fall. We have seen the first; the second may not be far off.

Uranus in Gemini demonstrates the nation's paradoxical character. It means and does well as a social and political agent. Yet its system encourages blind proliferation of powerful technologies with unintended consequences, from nuclear power to toxic chemical pollution, computerized monitoring of every purchase to tinkering with life itself.

Uranus in the 6th house: a clear signature of Yankee ingenuity; practical precision, constant upgrading in every field, the breakneck pace of breakthrough invention.

Neptune in Virgo, its sign of detriment,[10] portrays a delusional self-esteem based on its good fortune. America must always be Number One in everything (including social pathologies); and the best, meaning more of the same wretched excess, is yet to come. This has generated the confidence fostering incredible achievement. Yet at some point a reality check will come due.

America's long maritime tradition, inherent in its nature as a New World of dreams (Neptune) beyond the seas. This has now soared (9th), by means of fantastic technology (Virgo) into the boundless ocean of space.

Neptune in the 9th house portrays America's many free form charismatic religious movements. Most of all it symbolizes the American Dream: expansive and liberating (9th) yet also materialistic and crassly manipulated by an entertainment 'industry.' (Neptune's detriment in earthy Virgo). This in contrast to the accepting spiritual devotion, elevating or oppressive, that characterizes more traditional societies.

The malign influence of Big Oil (Neptune[11]) in both foreign affairs (9th) and through its petro-chemical pollution (Virgo). The proliferation of plastic, both literally[12] and in the sense of tacky phoniness. The latter has now culminated with the election of Donald Trump. (See 'A Mundane Prediction.')

Pluto in Capricorn is positioned exactly on the exaltation degree of its 'lower octave,' Mars.[10] This emphasizes yet again America's astonishing power to manifest dreams and make them real. It also points to an eventual and necessary catharsis of their nightmare side.

Pluto in the 2nd house suggests the power of private wealth, and its plutocratic concentration. It reinforces themes portrayed by the American Sun's tipping point on the cusp of its complementary 8th house, and adds a fateful quality to them.

A mundane chart develops over time as its planets progress, just like an individual chart. (See 'Sun and Earth.') For example, at the time of writing (January 2016) the United States is almost 240 years old. Its Sun has progressed 240° through the zodiac, from its original position at 14° Cancer to a present position at 14° Pisces. It entered Pisces in 2001 - just as the Twin Tower terrorist attacks drew the US into a deepening karmic involvement with the Middle East. A speculative boom, followed by a near financial meltdown, has left the nation bankrupt and politically adrift as previously unimaginable technological and ecological challenges mount. And we're only halfway through this sign of disintegration ...

A brief review of the American Sun's earlier 30 year long progressions through the signs correlates well with their nature:

Aquarius, 1970-2000: Innovation, as the United States turned from an industrial to an information society. Technology became the dominant force in public affairs. Computers and then the Internet redefined social and economic life. Biotech is redefining life itself.

Capricorn, 1940-'70: Unprecedented achievement, as the United States won World War II, became the world's first affluent society, its indispensable political arbiter and physically reached the Moon.

Sagittarius, 1910-'40: Idealistic expansion, as the US participated in the 'War to end all wars,' tried the 'Noble Experiment' of Prohibition in a flamboyant cultural era of the Roaring Twenties and responded to the Depression with optimistic and far sighted wisdom.

Scorpio, 1880-1910: Silent growth of power. In 1880 the US was an agrarian society. By 1910 it had become an industrial behemoth with a recognizably modern flavor.

Libra, 1850-'80: Judgment - Civil War.

Virgo, 1820-'50: A national identity took shape as the country developed from an aristocratic republic into a vigorous democracy of white males. Grassroots growth.

Leo, 1790-1820: Rule of the Titans. Washington, Adams, Jefferson and Madison* turned an idealistic vision into a successful society. The nation grew (Louisiana Purchase) and triumphantly reaffirmed its independence (War of 1812).

* James Madison, President 1809-'17, basically wrote the Constitution.

Cancer, 1776-1790: Birth, not only of a nation in war, but also of a new vision of government in the Constitution.

The Moon and other planets have also progressed at their various orbital speeds. The Ascendant has moved 240°, from 13° Sagittarius to 13° Leo. It entered Leo just as the US entered Iraq in early 2003.

National or corporate charts are also impacted by planetary transits that activate sensitive points. See 'A Mundane Prediction' for an example pertaining to the United States.

Notes

1. 'The New Colossus,' Emma Lazarus, American poet, 1849-87. This poem is inscribed on the Statue of Liberty, on Ellis Island where millions of immigrants first landed. Its most famous lines:

> Give me your tired, your poor,
> Your huddled masses yearning to breathe free,
> The wretched refuse of your teeming shore.
> Send these, the homeless, tempest-tossed to me,
> I lift my lamp beside the golden door.

2. Former President Jimmy Carter (1977-81) in a July 2015 interview on the state of American democracy: 'Now, it's just an oligarchy with unlimited political bribery being at the essence of getting the nominations for President, or to elect the President. And same thing applies to governors and US senators and Congress members. Now, we've seen a complete subversion of our political system, as a pay-off to major contributors...'

3. Matthew 5:14. This image became an early American political icon through a sermon by John Winthrop, 1587-1649, a Puritan Governor of Massachusetts colony.

4. One of America's national mottos, 'novus ordo seclorum,' found on

the back of every dollar bill.

5. For example, American agriculture is often described as the world's most productive. Yet it burns ten calories worth of fossil fuels to produce, package and distribute one calorie of food energy. You can verify this startling but well documented fact from many sources online by googling 'us agriculture energy calories.'

One title says it all: 'Scientific American,' August 11, 2011: '10 calories in, 1 calorie out - The Energy We Spend on Food.'

On another level its factory farm hell for billions of animals may be 'efficient' at producing cheap hormone and antibiotic tainted meat - but its real cost in suffering is immeasurable.

6. 'Ambition must be made to counteract ambition,' James Madison, 'The Federalist' #51, 1788

7. 'Brave New World,' by Aldous Huxley, an English writer, presciently described this coming reality back in 1931.

8. The Uranus/Neptune conjunction of 1821 brought the ideas and ideals of the scientific method to the leading edge of consciousness. Scientific truth became the reigning worldview, the religion of modernity. The American Saturn institutionalized this inspiration in social organization and technological ability.

9. Saturn, with its insistence on tangible facts governed by lawful cause and effect process, is a symbol of scientific intelligence. Its emphasis on precise observation, mathematical logic and experimental verification over subjective interpretation adds a new dimension to our understanding.

But Saturn, like science, tends towards reductionism. It simplifies complex phenomena into abstract equations, making them more easily understood - and manipulated. Thus biology increasingly seeks to describe living identity as a DNA chemical code, while psychology tries to define consciousness in terms of electrical brain wave patterns. These ghostly shadows can then be reprogrammed to serve the interests of power.

10. See 'Dignities and Debilities.'

11. Neptune is associated with liquids (and liquors). It particularly symbolizes oil, which is slippery, like the unconscious, yet also the feedstock for protean forms (plastics).

12. For example, the gigantic 'garbage patches,' thousands of miles across, composed primarily of plastic debris caught in a vortex of circular oceanic surface currents (gyres).

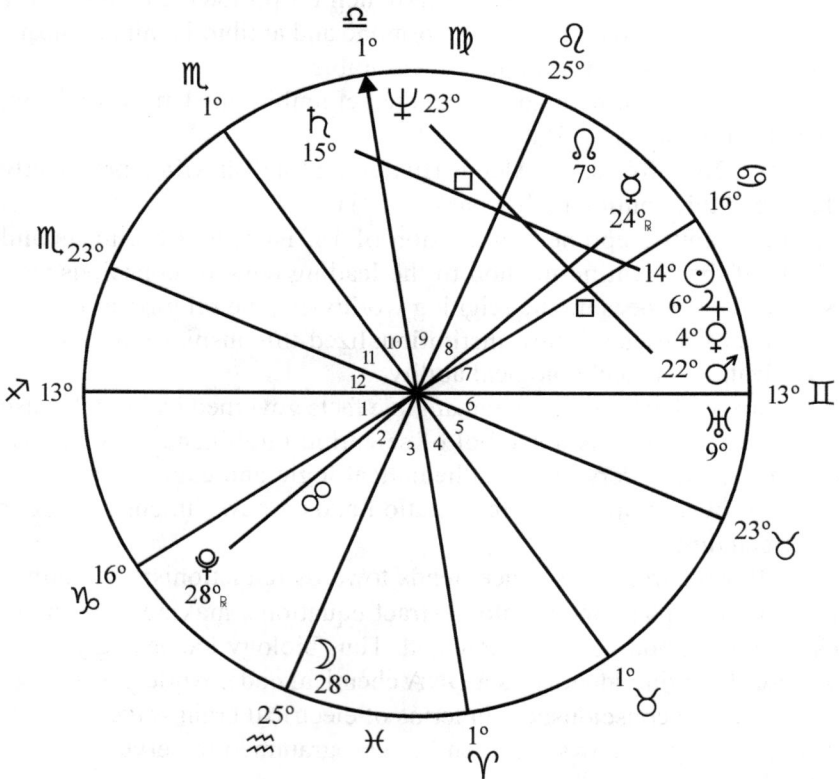

Figure 6

United States of America
Declaration of Independence
July 4, 1776   5:10 pm   Philadelphia

Major Aspects:

Sun conjunct Mercury, Venus and Jupiter.
Venus closely conjunct Jupiter
Sun squares Saturn
Mercury opposes Pluto
Mars squares Neptune
Special case: there is a closely applying waxing semi sextile of Moon to
Pluto. See 'Void Moon' at the end of 'Lunar Phases and Aspects.'

A Mundane Prediction

'Why ponder thus the future to foresee,
And jade thy brain to vain perplexity?
Cast off thy care, leave Allah's plans to him -
He formed them all without consulting thee.'[1]

Any attempt to predict the future involves serious hubris. The Universe is far more complex than we can imagine. Its workings are open to chance and free will as well as guided by law and destiny.

That said, if astrology is more than a meditation on archetypal psychological symbols, then it must be able to make verifiable predictions. Not as a description of specific events, but about the nature and timing of crises points, danger/opportunities. What follows is an analysis of America's current situation based on astrological reasoning. And a prediction about where it is going.

On April 23, 2014 Mars, Jupiter, Uranus and Pluto formed a rare grand cross in the sky. It was precisely superimposed on the United States Sun and Saturn in its national chart. Figure 1. Its perfect alignment with the American national chart symbolizes a 'crucifixion' of the world's only superpower.

It was preceded by a total lunar eclipse, visibly covering the entire United States only five days previously (Figures 2, 3 and 4). If there was ever an astrological figure that ought to mean something in terms of public affairs this would be it.

It portrayed the United States at its peak, poised for a drastic change of fortune. A benevolent Jupiter conjoined the US birth Sun. It was also in the crosshairs of a vortex formed by the three most disruptive planetary forces: Mars, Uranus and Pluto. Yet there was no overt crises at that time: no natural catastrophe, financial meltdown, cyber crash or major war.

Any of these would have been an Act of God happening to America. Instead the cross ripened over time into something worse: its spiritual suicide.

The American led system unified and in large measure liberated the world. In accomplishing this great work the United States literally spent itself. Acting on a huge scale, and living beyond its means, it amassed an astronomical debt. Then, in a devastating irony, it elected a corporate bankruptcy artist as President.

Donald Trump will do what he has always done: default on unsustainable obligations. That will essentially liquidate the government as we know it. Millions will sink as the social safety net is revoked. Others will survive into a long night of desolation. There will be a Darwinian rebalancing. All of this reflects a deeper cycle of destruction and renewal written into the national genome; an astrological script made clear in the light of 20/20 hindsight:

In the original configuration Mars, the action planet, was both retrograde and conjunct the US birth Saturn. Figure 1. Its normally extraverted aggression turned within to provoke Saturn's Judgment (Libra). And to awaken a far older and more sinister Shadow channeled through America's leading role in the modern world.[2] (Figures 2, 3 and 4)

Mars impregnated rather than expressed this cosmic pattern. Its pregnancy lasted for the term of a Mars orbit (two Earth years).[3] It called forth the dark side of America's unparalleled power - which then came to birth as transiting Saturn in the real sky passed over the American ascendant on election day 2016.

The grand cross emphasized the drastic nature and importance of this event. The Mars-year long pregnancy described the process by which it developed. Fateful Saturn rising showed its result: the election of Trump ending a 70 year long postwar order.

A grand cross is similar to a biological conception. It describes an implicit identity that matures into manifestation through a developmental process. Conception weaves together a genetic program that unfolds through a series of embryonic stages. Then culminates in birth of an organism. A grand cross sketches a spiritual initiative that materializes through a sequence of planetary movements. Then culminates in a new consciousness or historical dispensation.

Two polarized lines of force (oppositions) intersect perpendicular to each other. These form a square with four right (90°) angles. This generates another dimension: a plane. That new space then evolves, actualized by the flow of astral currents within it.

A grand cross is not an action figure. Its four planets block each others' independent agency, instead binding them into a new identity. Just as the four nucleotides of a DNA helix code for a biological genome, so the four planets of this astrological alignment describe a psychological or social genome. A DNA segment expresses itself when synthesized into protein by biochemical agents in the cell. Similarly, an opposition squared can only release its tremendous but deadlocked potency when activated by a cosmic stimulus.

682

In this case the original energy signature reformed into a more dynamic T-square. Once again a Mars-Uranus opposition formed, with both squaring Pluto.[4] Pluto's focal point again opposed the US natal Sun, this time stripped of Jupiter's protective presence. (Figure 5)

The American Sun's original position in the sky (14° Cancer) was then empty. It became a vortex attracting the T-square's three constituent forces, no longer mutually checked, but directed into its now vacant arm of the +. ('Nature abhors a vacuum.') An 'exiled' Jupiter, as the closest planet to it, absorbed and carried this charge to its own retrograde station conjunct the Moon's north node in Virgo. (Figure 5: point A)

The north node symbolizes an alien quality that must be assimilated, the most demanding task any entity needs to achieve, in order to fulfill itself. Making it even more difficult was that Jupiter is in detriment in Virgo. There Jupiter faces its dark side, to either heal its flaws or magnify their negativity. In this case it emphasized the disease rather than its cure. That an energized Jupiter made a retrograde station in its Purgatory sign conjunct the node of destiny emphasized the power of this encounter.

The Jupiter/north node conjunction also occurred on a sensitive point in the American chart: its Neptune. Neptune symbolizes a nation's collective unconscious. Dreamy Neptune is also debilitated in practical Virgo. Here it symbolized the accumulated toxicity of an increasingly materialistic and alienated culture, discussed below. Jupiter, coming to rest at this point, amplified its illusions into a political movement: the candidacy of Donald Trump.

In public affairs Jupiter turning retrograde conjunct Neptune symbolizes dissolution (Neptune) of a social contract (Jupiter).[5] An exhausted faith (Jupiter) meets the void (Neptune). This is no blighted hope contingent upon some specific disappointment, but rather a fundamental negation of previous character and a consequent necessity to re-imagine destiny.

Four months later Jupiter completed its retrograde arc and made its direct station opposite transiting Neptune's actual position in the sky at that time. (Figure 6) It made an astonishing connection between a Neptunian quality embedded in the American chart and physical Neptune in the heavens. Jupiter's reverse movement grounded a 'descent' of the American Neptune's potential for disintegration to polarize with the real planet of Neptune, then at its strongest in Pisces. Saturn, a dark fate, stood at the midpoint of this opposition, forming another dynamic T-cross centered exactly on the US ascendant at 13° Sagittarius. (Figure 6)

Thus the grand cross congealed into Saturn's Shadow. Towards the end of a Mars-year long pregnancy it quickened into a tense T-square focused on the American central identity (Sun). Its social/spiritual meaning (Jupiter) was isolated out of the original figure to magnify a deep collective unconscious issue (retrograde station on natal Neptune). This then became explicit (direct station opposing transiting Neptune).

Jupiter's retrograde station conjunct the US natal Neptune was also a summons to destiny (Moon's north node). It revealed a problem: public loss of confidence in a now decadent American Dream. Its direct station, opposite orbiting Neptune, proposed a solution, personified by a grandiose ego promising magical wish fulfillment.

December's T-square, a challenge to America's birth Sun, replicated itself after Jupiter's regression from disillusionment to a fatal enchantment.[6] It transformed into May's T-square centered on the actual presence of the Shadow planet (Saturn). At that time Saturn was retrograde on America's ascendant, its point of self-consciousness. Saturn represents a society's fears. In this case it evoked resentments built up over the vast social and demographic changes of the postmodern era. After Saturn turned direct in August they expressed through a degrading presidential campaign of personal vilification because the political culture could not deal with its structural deformities. This negativity materialized as fate when Saturn rose over the US ascendant on election day 2016.

How did these astrological movements play out in real life? On December 10, 2015 (T-square) Trump unexpectedly surged to first place in the Republican Presidential nominating polls. By May 9, 2016 (Jupiter direct: new T-square) he had won the nomination. The decisive turning point came on Super Tuesday, March 8, 2016, when he swept a large number of primaries - just as a total solar eclipse in Pisces opposed retrograding Jupiter in Virgo. (Figure 6, point B)

In a time of relative peace and prosperity, with no serious external challenges to distract it, America's national id boiled up out of the depths. A flamboyant demagogue arose to channel the inner desperation of millions. Nothing happened to America - rather its own core emptiness imploded.

Jupiter made explicit a spiritual crisis inherent in the materialistic American Dream and its illusion of technological salvation (mystical Neptune in practical Virgo). In all previous eras and cultures life was brutally hard - but what people did had meaning. One had to produce tangible value to survive, such as growing crops or weaving cloth. And one did so within a system of traditional values, religious sensibility and

684

community participation. Today, in contrast, work often has no or negative significance. Most modern jobs involve manipulating electronic blips, making/selling superfluous and often toxic products, staffing a cubicle in a bureaucracy - they create no real value. They do provide creature comfort. The average citizen today has toys and opportunities that no President or Emperor could imagine a century ago. But stuff is not enough. Man does not live by bread alone.

Many, perhaps most, American workers subconsciously understand that what they do is essentially pointless, if not harmful. Its not just that they have no control over the means of production as Marx said - more importantly what they do produce is worthless at best. Their function in society is an empty waste of time and effort.

The average person lacks any meaningful role in an ever more absurd collective life. Distracted by the snares of consumerism. Disoriented by constant electronic babble. The psychic toll of our modern lifestyle is even more degrading to the human spirit than physically destructive of the environment. That's saying a lot.

To live in the modern world means to participate in its rape. To go anywhere puts a scar in the sky with fossil fueled warming. To eat any animal product subsidizes the cruelty of factory farming. Just taking a walk erodes a dust of synthetic particles from shoe soles into the environment. An unconscious guilt surrounds even the most basic acts of daily life.

This insidious loss of self-respect reached a critical mass during the 2016 election. Much of it was projected onto scapegoats: for example, Mexican immigrants who are stealing all the good jobs, such as picking vegetables under a blazing Sun. But deeper down was a realization that an era had run its course. It would be ushered out by a loud liar telling America a simple truth: 'You're fired!'

The winner did not offer a rational program because there is no 'good government' policy fix for this depth of cultural alienation. Trump reflected a mass mood, an inchoate urge to bring it all down. The lemmings want to go over the cliff …

Trump himself personifies this national psychic dysfunction. He was born during a total lunar eclipse.[7] Moon = (unconscious) feelings: instinct and karma. A total lunar eclipse brings subconscious issues to the surface. Trump resonates with a gathering crises in the American system.

It may come to a head just after a total solar eclipse passes over the United States on August 21, 2017.[8] A solar eclipse symbolizes an overt disruption of the normal order. The 'American eclipse' at 29° Leo suggests an arrogance of power stumbling over its own feet of clay.[9]

Eclipses involve a relatively timeless unconscious element (Moon) that germinates until activated by a planetary transit. This eclipse will form on President Trump's rising degree of personal awareness. Two weeks later violent Mars will transit that point. The President's character will exacerbate America's downsizing.

It will also change the strategic balance. What follows hard on its heels points to an external threat that would probably confront any American administration. In late September 2017:

Mars will oppose the March 2016 eclipse position. That eclipse's path of totality skirted the southern edge of the South China Sea, a likely flashpoint of US/China conflict.[10] At the same time Mars will also conjoin the North Korean national Sun at 17° Virgo[11] - while trining (120°) volcanic Pluto just as it turns direct at 17° Capricorn.

Meanwhile Jupiter will transit over the April 2014 eclipse position as it exactly opposes revolutionary Uranus. Things will change. The deep Saturn quality of that eclipse[12] could manifest as a domestic emergency compounded by a military, even nuclear, challenge from Asia.

Yet despite its trauma this will not be a random event but a foreseeable phase change in a meaningful universe. The trajectory of history, like that of an individual life, has certain inevitable turning points. A caterpillar must wrap itself in the death shroud of a cocoon to be reborn as a butterfly. A child, of whatever personal character, must suddenly encounter the crisis of adolescence. So too our society, swollen to bursting with achievement and extravagance, must break down in order to break through to the next level.

Body cells are programmed to self-destruct when they reach their functional limit. The body politic is unconsciously predisposed to do the same. In an inherently intelligent universe our living planet will 'instinctively' rebalance itself, whatever the cost to its individual components. When that happens each part will meet its own moment of truth. A single brain cell cannot comprehend the thought in which it partakes, yet resonates with that message. A personal ego cannot consciously know its transcendent soul purpose, yet makes that purpose real through its actual behavior. We each, and all of us together, carry an unconscious energy charge and act as its agent.

Sometimes this basic nature must be tested by crisis. Disintegration of a familiar context, what a self or a society does under stressful circumstances, reveals core character.

The coming disruption will thin the herd and reconfigure society. Whether for better or worse remains to be seen. The process will be deadly for many, devastating to others and liberating for some. It will test everyone in extremis for their spiritual quality.

The social progress and psychological empowerment of the post-war era have been breathtaking. No sane person can contemplate the fall of Pax Americana without the deepest sorrow. Its nature is essentially benevolent. It has nurtured billions into a life more abundant. Yet it has become far too abundant, and thus cancerous. Its time has come and an expiration date set.

Notes

1. The Rubaiyat, Omar Khayyam, 1048-1131, Persian mathemetician and poet.
2. The total lunar eclipse associated with the grand cross of April 23, 2014 belonged to an ancient Saros series* that powerfully emphasized Saturn at its inception in 1022. (Figures 2, 3 and 4) Retrograde Mars dove deep to activate this 1000 year-old curse:

Revelation 20: 1-3
1 And I saw an angel come down from heaven, having the key of the bottomless pit and a great chain in his hand.
2 And he laid hold on the dragon, that old serpent, which is the Devil, and Satan, and bound him a thousand years,
3 And cast him into the bottomless pit, and shut him up, and set a seal upon him, that he should deceive the nations no more, till the thousand years should be fulfilled: and after that he must be loosed a little season.

An interpretation: Western Europe, America's cultural taproot, abruptly blossomed out of the Dark Ages and into the High Medieval period right after the year 1000.† A millennium later this flowering has borne fruit in a New World where man now plays God. We have begun to eat from the Tree of Life (biotechnology, genetic engineering) - the other forbidden tree in the Garden of Eden. ‡

Trump's election set the stage for a second creation story. He represents a collective unconscious will to unleash Saturn as the Grim Reaper; to clear out the deadwood of a mass society. That will make space for a later, more explicit Satanic emergence in a technocratic world purged of its excess population with their burden of economic and ecological problems.

* See 'Mundane Considerations: Saros Cycles'
† See 'Synods: Earth: 1007-1206.'

‡ Adam and Eve ate from the Tree of Knowledge of Good and Evil, evoking ego out of instinctual bliss, separating self-consciousness from union with God.

3. The most important event of this period was the sudden maturation of CRISPR* gene editing technology. This easy and reliable technique allows us to add or subtract, amplify or mute, any gene at will. It has already been used in China to modify unviable human embryos as a 'proof of concept' for the development of designer babies. There is no way to put this genie back in the bottle.

Biological manipulation of human identity is the coming temptation. Life will be defined as a medical creation. Personality shrunk to a program. Soul reduced to a chemical formula. Reinventing the human condition also implies streamlining its social matrix. Collapsing the support structure for a bloated population will allow natural selection to determine the fittest candidates for such biotech 'enhancement.'
President Trump will serve as the destructive agent of this transition from an unsustainable mass society to a hardier gene pool of experimental objects.

CRISPR technology came of age just as we reached out and touched Pluto, gateway to the Underworld, with NASA's New Horizons space probe (July 14, 2015). The sudden emergence of this power expressed the esoteric (hidden) meaning of the grand cross during its Mars retrograde genesis. Almost unnoticed, the American 'republic of science and technology' gave birth to a new order of life as machine crafted idols of DNA.

The 2016 election, with an energized Saturn rising on the American ascendant, marked the exoteric (public) manifestation of the cross. Trump's election terminated the postwar world order and cleared the decks for a new dispensation.

* CRISPR = 'clustered regularly interspersed short palindromic repeats.' It was hailed as Breakthrough of the Year in 2015 by the American Association for the Advancement of Science. You can learn more about it online.

4. This time, December 10, 2015, both Mars and Pluto were direct while Uranus retrograded.

5. The only time this has ever happened before was on January 8, 1933: just prior to inauguration of the New Deal in the depths of the Great Depression. That radically transformed the American social contract from one of laissez faire capitalism to a managerial welfare state. This was a crisis of economic rationality and social justice wisely met by a great leader. As President Roosevelt said: '… we face our common difficulties. They concern, thank God, only material things.'

One Uranus cycle (84 years) later the 'difficulty' recurred as an intangible spiritual nihilism. This time it was exacerbated by a demagogue who embodied rather than solved the nation's ills.

6. 'I am your voice ... Nobody knows the system better than me, which is why I alone can fix it.' - Trump acceptance speech at the Republican National Convention.

7. Data: June 14, 1946 at 10:54 am in New York City.

8. Totality will be visible along a corridor running from Oregon to South Carolina. It will culminate over Cerulean, Kentucky - close to the US gold repository at Fort Knox.

9. Regulus or Cor Leonis, 'Heart of the Lion,' at 29° Leo is a cardinal 'fixed' star outside of our solar system. It amplifies this eclipse with a theme of enormous power, overreach and fall. The nobility, or faith and credit, of the United States eclipsed. Trust fails, the dollar falls. Survival emergency for billions.

10. See 'Mundane Considerations': China chart.

11. The 'Democratic People's Republic of Korea' was proclaimed on September 9, 1948.

12. On September 15, 2017 Earth will literally reach out and touch Saturn by crashing the Cassini space probe into its atmosphere. How might Saturn respond?

Figure 1   Grand Cross of April 20, 2014

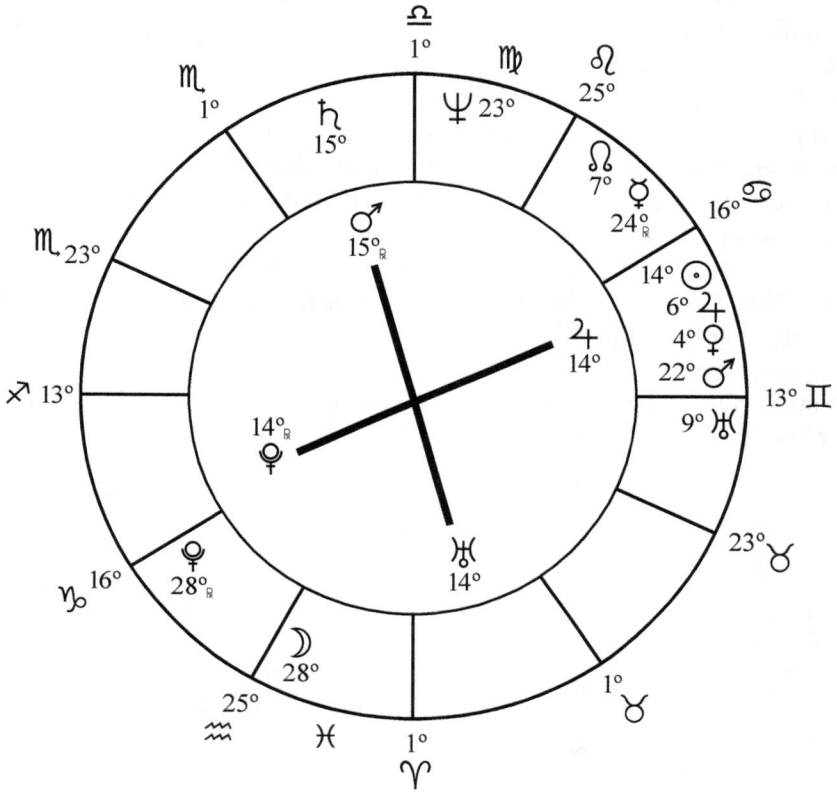

The outer circle is the United States' national chart.

The inner grand cross occurred on April 20-23, 2014.

Figure 2 T-Cross of December 7-10, 2015

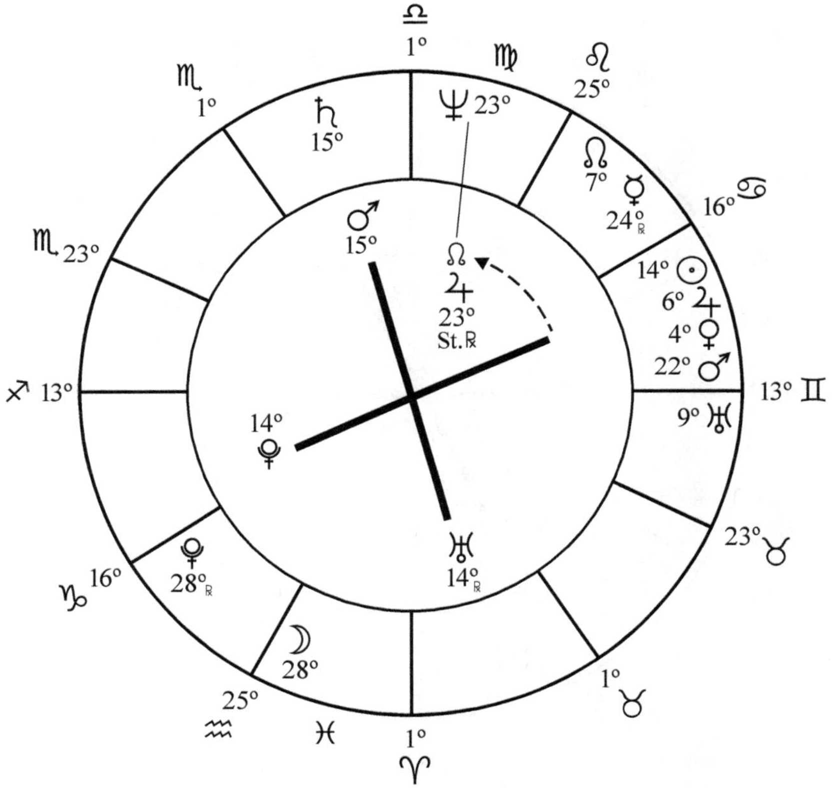

Jupiter stationary retrograde conjunct North Node
January 8, 2016
Both conjunct USA Neptune

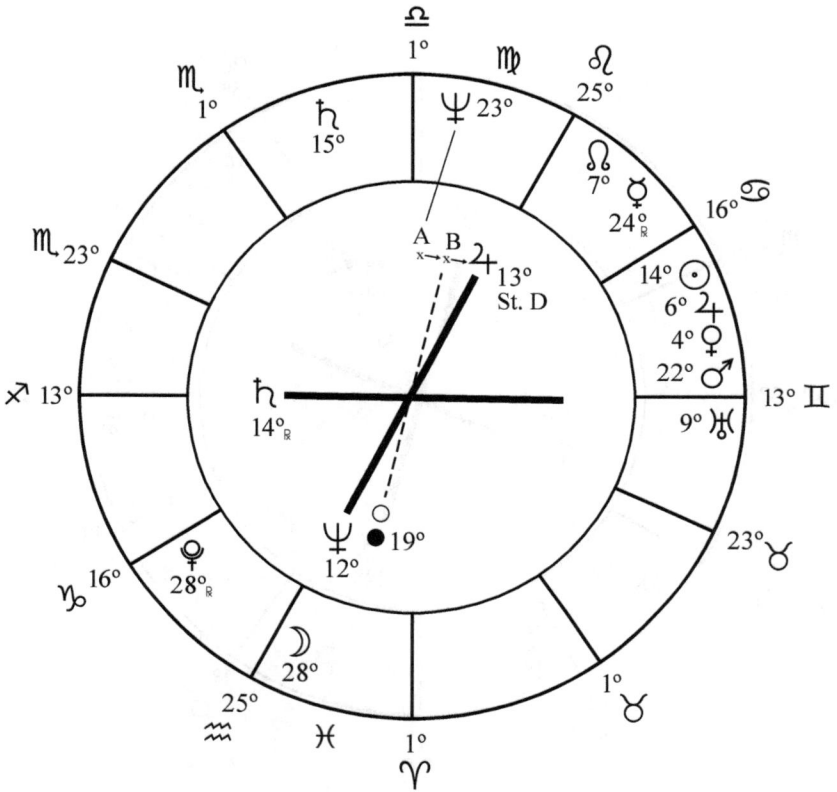

Figure 3 T-Cross of May 9, 2016

Jupiter turns direct opposite transiting Neptune
Both square Saturn retrograde conjunct US ascendant

Point A: Jupiter's retrograde station conjunct US Neptune,
January 8, 2016

Point B: Jupiter retrograde opposed by solar eclipse, March 9, 2016

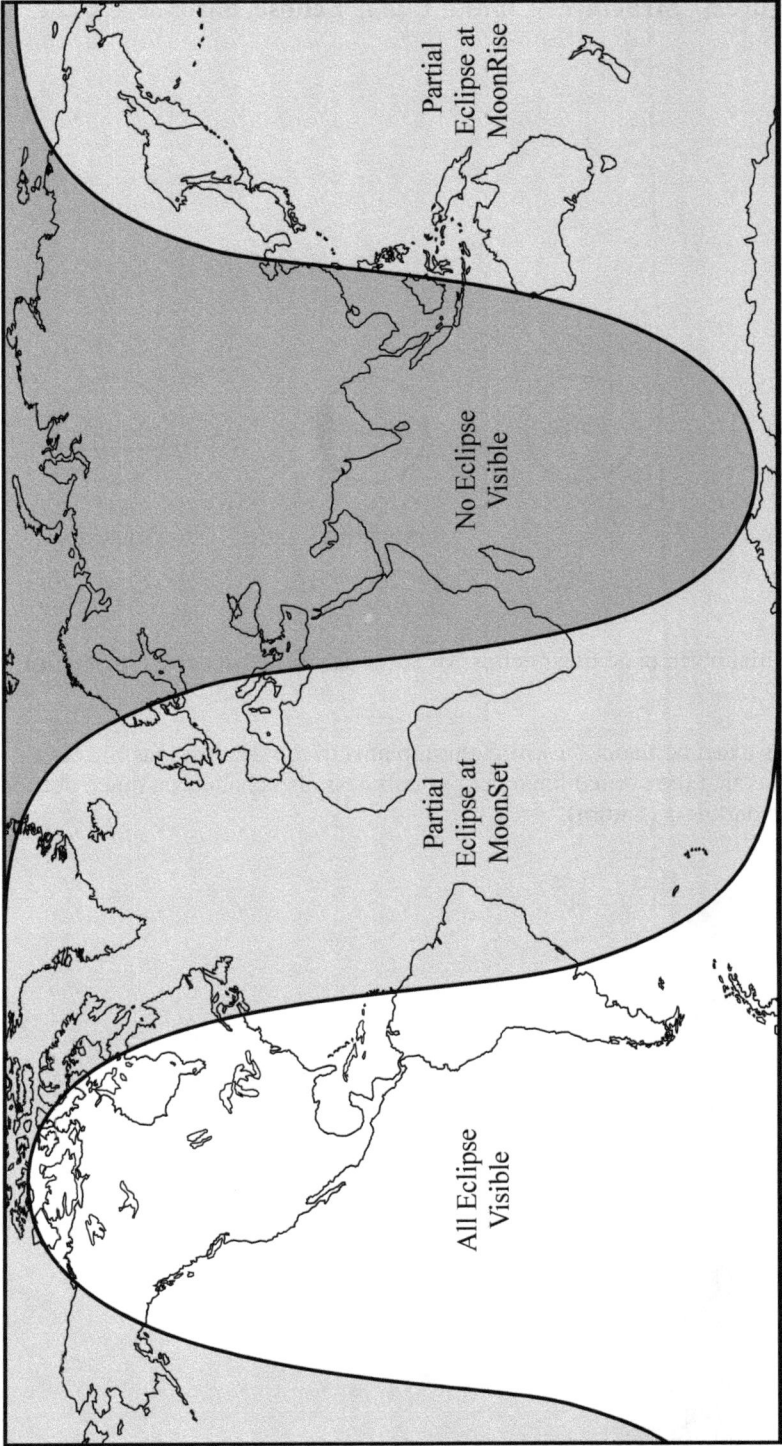

Figure 4 Path of Total Lunar Eclipse of April 15, 2014

Partial
Eclipse at
MoonRise

No Eclipse
Visible

Partial
Eclipse at
MoonSet

All Eclipse
Visible

Figure 5   Structure of Initial Lunar Eclipse, Saros series 122

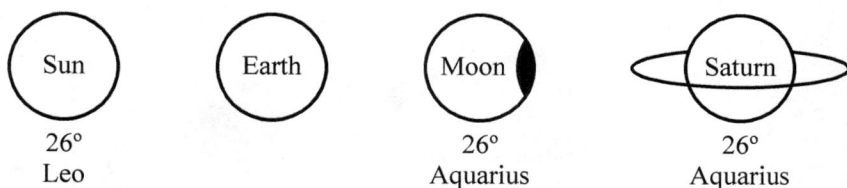

Sun	Earth	Moon	Saturn
26°		26°	26°
Leo		Aquarius	Aquarius

The initial north node lunar eclipse of Saros series 122 occurred on August 14, 1022.

Moon's exact conjunction with Saturn, planet of the unconscious Shadow, indicates that the normal lunar eclipse darkness also channels a much deeper cosmic darkness (Saturn).

Figure 6   Initial Saros eclipse correlation with United States chart

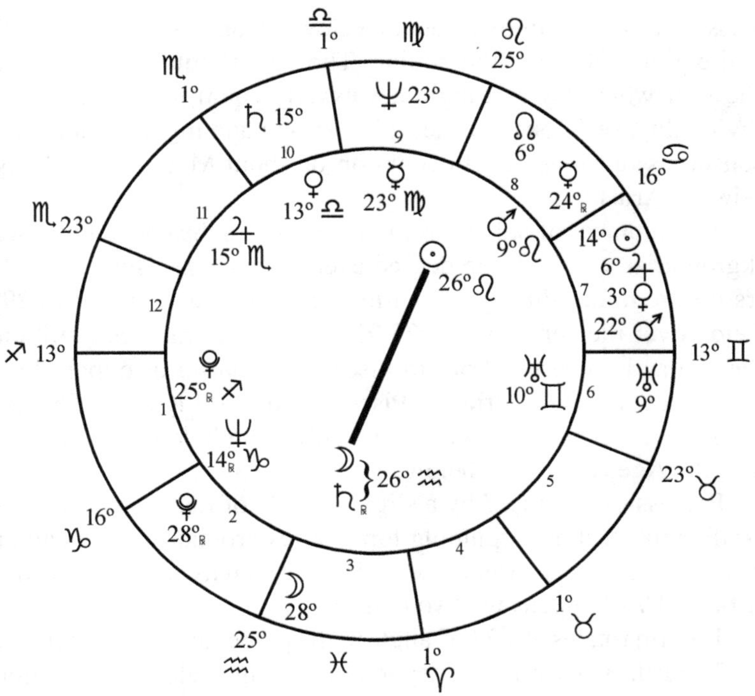

The initial Saros series 122 eclipse does not have its own house structure. However, all of its planets closely align with and activate, USA birth planets. Thus the initial Saros eclipse generated a vortex making a bullseye fit with American national chart. Its total lunar eclipse of April 15, 2014 acted as a lightning rod calling down the voltage of a grand cross (figure 1) that is also attuned to the United States' planetary receptors.

Saros		USA
Moon/Saturn	conjoins	Moon
Sun	opposes	Moon
Mercury	conjoins	Neptune
Venus	conjoins	Saturn
Mars	conjoins	north node
Jupiter	trines	Sun
Uranus	conjoins	Uranus
Neptune	squares	Saturn
Neptune	also opposes	Sun

Within the Saros configuration itself Pluto trines the Sun and sexiles Moon/Saturn; Venus and Uranus form a trine. The total lunar eclipse of April 15, 2014 at 26° Libra exactly trined the original Saros eclipse of August 14, 1022 at 26° Aquarius, thus amplifying its power.

Precession

Precession of the Equinox refers to a slow retrograde movement of the vernal equinox through the zodiac. The vernal equinox is that point of the year when day and night are exactly equal in length, with day (individuality, self-consciousness) increasing and night (collective, the unconscious) decreasing. It occurs on or about March 21 and begins the sign of Aries.[1]

This moment of balance retrogrades across the unchanging stellar background at a rate of one degree every 72 years.[2] Thus every 2160 years it retrogrades through an entire sign, moving from 30° to 29° to 28° etc., over the centuries. In 25,920 years it completes a full circle of the zodiac in reverse (Aries to Pisces to Aquarius as opposed to the annual sequence of Aquarius to Pisces to Aries). Figure 1. This is the Great Year, a vast cycle of evolution manifesting in long-term historical trends, the Ages described below.

Precession is caused by a slight wobble of Earth's spin axis over the millennia. Just as a spinning top gyrates around the perpendicular as it rotates, so too the orientation of Earth's spin gyrates systematically over time. This happens for two reasons:

1. Earth rotates at a 23½° angle to the perpendicular of its orbit and

2. Earth is not a perfect sphere, but bulges along its equator by about 26 miles, $\frac{1}{1000}$ of its diameter, compared to the poles. Sun's gravity pulls this extra equatorial mass towards it, on the ecliptic, up to 23½° north or south of the celestial equator.

The tug of war, or torque, between Earth's own spin and Sun's pull on its equatorial bulge, makes Earth's spin axis gyrate. This generates a cone of movement over the millennia. Figure 2. The north celestial pole moves in a circle, pointing at one star, then another. Today it points at Polaris, the North Star. Twelve thousand years from now it will point towards Vega, as it did fourteen thousand years ago. About twenty-six thousand years from now it will return to its present orientation, again pointing towards Polaris. Figure 3.

As a result of this wobble the point where Earth's northern hemisphere begins to tip towards Sun, the vernal equinox, precesses slowly, steadily backwards through the zodiac. At the time of writing (2012) the vernal equinox occurs on the cusp of Pisces. It will soon slip back into Aquarius. Thus the sign phase, or time of year, we call Aries, when day initiates its dominance over night, actually happens as Sun visibly transits across the stellar constellation of Pisces from our vantage point on Earth. Some say that this proves astrology is an illusion. How can one equate the fiery willful quality of Aries with Sun's physical

Figure 1   Precession

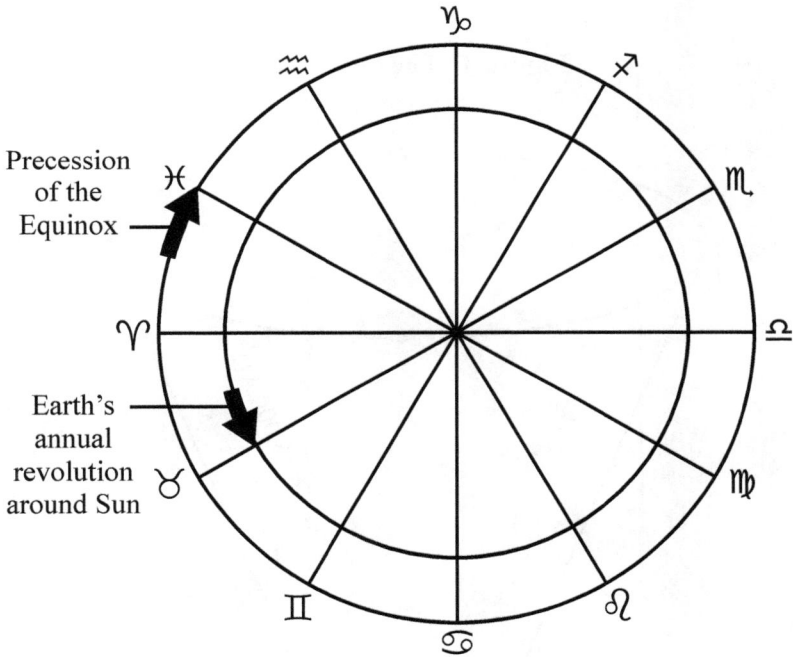

Figure 2   Precession of a top

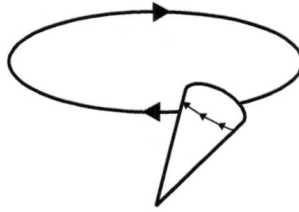

Figure 3   The Great Year

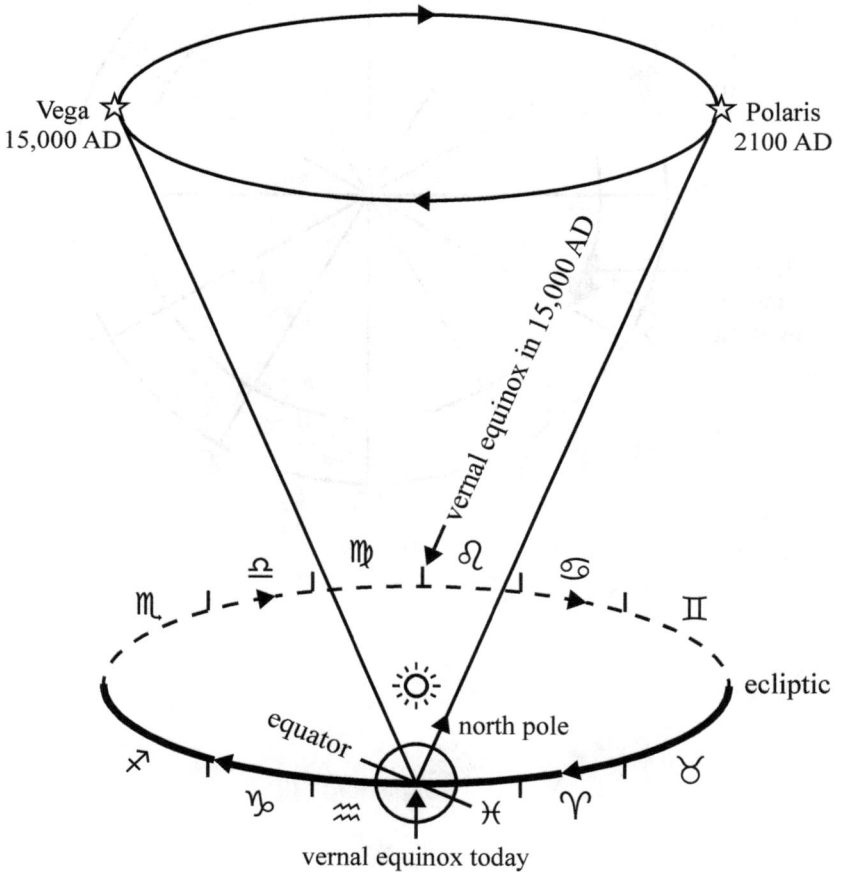

The gyration of Earth's north pole from Polaris to Vega, and back again, is paralleled by the retrogradation of the vernal equinox around the ecliptic.

presence in dreamy mystical Pisces? That line of reasoning is based on the idea that Sun focuses or lenses, vitalizes or emanates, the background quality of space through which it appears to be moving. The truth is more complex.

Aries basically refers to a seasonal relationship between Earth and Sun: when Earth's northern hemisphere begins to tip towards Sun. The star patterns against which this Earth/Sun relationship is measured constitute an abstract frame of reference rather than actual entities. Their individual stars are real energy centers. The constellations into which they are organized are human constructs, not astronomical phenomena. The stars comprising Aries are many light years apart and move independently of each other. The boundaries of this celestial projection of a ram are arbitrary, as is true of all constellations.[3] The actual experience of day waxing over night, spring blossoming out of winter, and their associated symbolism, constitutes the reality of Aries - not the stellar grid against which they are measured.

The vernal point signifies our psychological experience of turning towards the light, a new day, springtime of the year. We, immersed in the human condition, comprehend it in terms of Earth's relationship to Sun. The vernal equinox initiates an earthly season in time more than it embodies an energy pattern in space. More than, not instead of.

The vernal equinox, and its associated sign of Aries, begins a new round of the annual cycle every year. This beginning point also slowly reorients towards different stellar energy fields over the centuries because of precession. That generates the precessional ages. It ignites the Aries function of initiation through the actual sign of Aries during one time period (2260-100 BC), then through a Pisces experience (100 BC-2060 AD) later on. Soon this will begin to happen in an Aquarian context (2060-4220).

Aries describes a plane of emerging consciousness just north of the celestial equator.[4] A springtime of new reality, activated by Sun's apparent movement into it every year. Meanwhile Sun itself is also objectively moving north through its local environment in the galaxy.[5] Thus, north = future, aspiration, advance into the unknown, just as south = past, accomplished achievement, consolidation, manifestation. The whole solar system keeps moving north all the time, every second of every day, not just during Aries. The idea of Aries includes Sun's pioneering northwards in its galactic context: spiraling into new realms of space/time, and of spirit. This occurs whether Aries is conceived of as a temporal season or a spatial quality.

That arc of space containing the actual constellation of Aries does have specific attributes in contrast to the arcs next to it, Pisces before and Taurus after. This is demonstrated by the distinctive nature of the historical ages defined by the vernal point's movement through them. It also forms the basis of sidereal (stellar) astrology, the idea that the extended equatorial plane of Sun has objective regional qualities independent of Earthly seasons.

Sun's northerly movement through its local stellar environment portrays a progress through time, from past (south) to future (north). Sun's spatial distribution of its own energies around a projected ecliptical circumference of sidereal signs portrays an identity in the present. Just as human vitality differentially expresses through various organs (heart, liver, brain, genitals, etc.), so solar vitality unfolds through a sequence of spiritual cycles mapped by an encircling belt of stars. The human mind organizes them into constellations. These describe distinctive regional qualities as a spatial articulation of Sun's own energy field. They have a reality of their own beyond the Earth/Sun seasonal relationship.

Sun is embedded in a star field. It resonates with the stellar energy patterns of its cosmic environment. Or those patterns symbolize a projected tapestry of its own energy expression. Our Earthly seasons mirror this in the Moon units (signs) of terrestrial experience.

Remember that Sun is not a hydrogen fireball suspended in empty space. It emanates an energy that creates its own local quality of space. Its presence condenses space/time into a unique force field. Sun's physical sphere rotates within that extended aura, just as a human's biological heart beats within his or her animating soul aura.

Like every other entity in the universe Sun is a holon: both a whole composed of parts, and part of a larger whole (the galaxy).[6] Thus Sun has an internal organization, which expresses outwardly as an energy structure in the surrounding space, which Sun itself generates. We perceive that structure in two forms:

1. As the concentric orbital planes of the planets, similar to the orbital shells of an atom, and

2. As zones of psycho-spiritual energies encircling Sun's central nucleus. We see these zones as sidereal signs, a background of starry constellations. They do not cause the energies: Sun does. The stars form a celestial coordinate system by which we can measure unfolding qualities of Sun's sphere of influence.

Sun's spiritual qualities manifest over a much longer time scale than the human psychological attributes mapped by Earth's seasonal cycle. The precession of Earth's vernal equinox expresses these energies through a 25,920 year long historical process (the Great Year). Its position at any given time indicates what phase of Sun's extended spiritual emanation we are experiencing on a collective level.

Our direct perception of an articulated solar energy field is generally overwhelmed by the more immediate and powerful reality of Earth's annual cycle around Sun. We live on Earth. We subjectively experience the universe within the context of Earth's seasonal variation. Yet we can get an objective perspective on Sun's own constellationally articulated identity through the historical process revealed by the slow precession of Earth's spin axis.

Celestial energy patterns permeate the background environment in which we live. They manifest as long term trends: cultural and social Ages correlated with Earth's changing tilt over generations and centuries. The slow cycle of Precession portrays Earth's experience of these long-term movements. One cannot personally encompass these immense cycles; a human lifetime is far too short. However, a 72-year glimpse of this 25,920 year phenomenon approximates one day's miniaturization of a year.[7] The day is the subjective analog of the year. So a life may be of a Great Year.

What might the retrograde precession of the equinox mean as contrasted with the direct motion of Earth's annual orbit around Sun? Figure 1. It may symbolize an astrological explanation for the feeling that our spiritual evolution is in some sense opposed to our natural inclinations. It may be that history actually involves an involutionary process: an evocation of deeper potentials in response to increasing outward power. A descent into ever more fundamental levels of understanding within as we achieve more sophisticated forms of external expression. It may symbolize the concept that true growth means a return to origins with an enhanced consciousness, the remembrance of a destiny made in heaven and enacted here on Earth. The more we evolve in technology and social organization the more profound its corresponding inner challenge. And opportunity.

Notes

1. Six months later, on or about September 21, there is a corresponding autumnal equinox, when day and night are also exactly equal, with night increasing and day decreasing. It begins Aries' opposite and complement, the sign of Libra.
2. Actually the stellar background also changes, as does everything in the universe. However, this moves too slowly for us to observe on a human scale. It resembles the real but invisible processes of continental

drift or mountain building here on Earth.

3. Constellational boundaries were established by the International Astronomical Union in 1930. It is safe to say that the IAU did not take astrological considerations into account. Out of 88 constellations only thirteen have a presence contacting the ecliptic (Sun's apparent path across the stellar background). All others lie north or south of it. The IAU assigned 44° of ecliptical longitude to Virgo; 6½° to Scorpio. They gave 19° traditionally assigned to Scorpio as a tropical, or seasonal, sign to a thirteenth sidereal constellation: Ophiuchus, the Snake Holder. However, astrological signs are defined as the twelve lunar cycles, moon-ths, comprising a year. In this sense Ophiuchus is enfolded within the lunar cycle we call Scorpio.

4. Earth's equator projected out into space. Sun appears to pass across it twice a year, moving north in Aries and south in Libra. The area just north of the celestial equator is called Virgo when Sun appears to be moving southwards through it prior to actually moving south of it in Libra. Signs must always be seen as dynamic processes more than as static geometric regions.

5. In other words, Sun's orbit around the galaxy inclines 30° north of Earth's celestial equator (See Figures 2-4 in 'Sun.'). Sun is moving towards a point due north of the winter solstice, just above the ecliptic, about 10° southwest of the star Vega. This is called the solar apex.

6. Nothing is monolithic or uniform: atoms are composed of neutrons, protons, electrons, and their subatomic constituents; molecules are composed of various kinds of atoms; cells of many types of molecules; organisms of many cell varieties; ecosystems of many species of organisms.

7. See 'Sun and Earth.' Thus 72 (years of a life) × 360 (degrees of the zodiac) = 25,920.

Precession Through History

Let us briefly examine the historic manifestation of the vernal equinox's retrograde precession around the zodiac. This has been going on for billions of years, since long before the emergence of humanity. We can only start with the beginning of history as we know it:

Age of Cancer, 8740 - 6580 BC

(The precision of these dates in the dim mists of our earliest history is simply a mathematical convention extrapolated backwards from more explicitly known recent times. The general time periods are accurate, but we do not know what was happening during any specific decade, or century, 10,000 years ago.)

The agricultural revolution began in the Fertile Crescent of the Middle East. After 10,000 generations of hunting and gathering humans learned to domesticate edible plants, especially grains. This produced a much larger and more reliable food supply. It started as horticulture, using digging sticks and hoes. Men and women participated equally in this small scale gardening, which women almost certainly discovered. Only much later, with the invention of the animal drawn plow during the age of Taurus, did a more industrial type of farming emerge which required male muscle to manage.

To tend their crops people had to settle down, build houses and live permanently in one place. They could accumulate possessions, which would have been impossible to carry around in a foraging life. They could claim ownership of specific plots of land and pass them on to their descendants. For the first time they had to work on a regular basis: digging, planting, weeding, harvesting; baking bread, casting pottery, weaving fibers; managing their dwellings and growing families (Cancer's polarity, Capricorn). Humans were domesticated as much as plants were. All of this is consistent with Cancer's emphasis on nutrition/nurturing, home, security, private property.

Age of Gemini, 6580 - 4420 BC

The domestication of herbivorous food animals followed that of plants. Presumably young cattle, sheep, goats and pigs that came to nibble at the lush cultivated gardens were captured, tamed and bred for docility and other desirable qualities.* Animals could graze and produce meat, milk, wool and hides on grasslands too dry to cultivate. This led to the first great division in human society, between settled agricultural communities and wandering animal herders. For over seven millennia, until 1500 AD, much of history revolved around the dynamic between barbaric nomads, with strict and simple codes of conduct, and agrarian civilizations with sophisticated cultures, but often decadent social orders. The original story of two brothers, Cain and Abel, in part alludes to this development.

Within settled communities growing food surpluses encouraged social and economic differentiation. Specialized classes of craftsmen arose out of the age-old egalitarianism of foraging bands. Blacksmiths and potters, tanners and weavers, builders and traders developed their skills and bargained among themselves. Simultaneously, knowledge of the agricultural revolution, with its new technological and social possibilities, spread far and wide, to Egypt and the Indus valley, Europe and China (Gemini's polarity, expansive Sagittarius). All of this is consistent with Gemini's emphasis on division, diversity, communication, trade and mutability.

*The dog, a carnivorous protector and companion, was domesticated much earlier, around 12,000 BC. The cat, a useful rat eater, came much later, around 2500 BC in Egypt. The horse, for riding, seems to have been tamed around 2000 BC among nomads on the Eurasian steppes. Soon thereafter their mounted hordes would burst in upon the civilized world in the first great waves of barbarian invasion.

Age of Taurus, 4420 - 2260 BC

A productivity revolution generated an economic surplus that gave birth to civilization. The plow multiplied farm output many times over. The wheel allowed it to be distributed to growing towns with their skilled artisans. Writing enabled record keeping and the management of increasingly complex transactions.

Cities first arose in Sumer, the marshlands of southern Iraq. Then elsewhere. Temple communities blossomed into urban societies, the nuclei of centralized state structures. Their expanding populations required massive irrigation systems in arid environments. Bureaucracies formed to deploy labor and allocate production. Stratified social orders emerged as resources flowed to religious, military, administrative and mercantile elites. The organized exploitation of man by man had begun (Taurus's polarity, Scorpio).

This concentration of wealth produced profound social injustice and tremendous material progress. It made possible the construction of public works, encouragement of arts and sciences, development of technology and refinement of culture. All of this is consistent with Taurus' emphasis on production, accumulation, tangible expression and the material basis of life.

Age of Aries, 2260 - 100 BC

Temple cities with state managed economies gave way to larger military kingdoms based on private enterprise. Explicit legislation supplanted customary tradition in now economically and ethnically diverse communities.[1] The ideas and techniques of civilization spread beyond river valleys to the hills of Anatolia and Iran, islands of Greece, coastal plains of the Levant. These new environments shaped novel cultures. The fast dissemination of iron working technology after 1500 BC gave these emerging polities tools and weapons with which to maintain their distinctive characters.[2]

Around 1200 BC an especially powerful wave of mounted nomads erupted out of the Eurasian steppes. They shattered already ancient, now petrified, civilizations. A dark age followed (1200-700 BC). As in the more familiar Dark Age after the fall of Rome (500-1000 AD) the resulting anarchy made space for a new generation of cultures. The unique ethical character of Israel and rational genius of Greece gestated during these centuries.

After 700 BC the older centers revived. Assyrian, Babylonian and Persian empires successively unified the Fertile Crescent. Far more importantly, an 'axial age' of spiritual transformation changed the world forever (sixth century BC). The prophets of Israel and philosophers of Greece, along with Buddha in India and the first sages of China, took human consciousness to a new level. Immemorial animistic and mythological outlooks gave way to more universal principles. Spiritual concerns replaced fertility rites. Ethical norms and consistent procedures of justice began to supplant custom and tradition (Aries' polarity, Libra).

After 500 BC the flowering of Greece brought personal liberty and rational thought to a despotic and superstitious world. History's center of gravity shifted westward, from the Middle East to the Mediterranean. The end of the age was marked by incessant war. Finally a small city endowed with political genius and an implacable will emerged at the edge of the known world. Its legions would impose centuries of peace under the rule of law: the Pax Romana. All of this is consistent with Aries' emphasis on individuality, spiritual principle, initiation and new beginnings.

1. The first known law code was promulgated by Hammurabi of Babylon, ca. 1750 BC.
2. Iron is far more durable than bronze, an amalgam of 90% copper and 10% tin. Its use followed a bronze age lasting from 4000-1500 BC. Iron is also 700 times more abundant than copper. It is harder to work, but once the technology was mastered it gave small states the ability to maintain themselves economically and militarily.

Age of Pisces, 100 BC - 2060 AD

Rome created the order and tranquility that allowed for growth of a new spiritual revelation and sensibility, Christianity (100 BC-400 AD). It then dissolved in fertile chaos, allowing the roots of modern Western civilization to gestate in a fusion of Judeo-Christian religion, Greco-Roman thought and Germanic cultural characteristics (400-1000 AD). There followed a high medieval phase of exalted spiritual idealism amidst material squalor (1000-1500). It is now ending with a total paradigm shift in every aspect of human endeavor since the Renaissance (1500-2060).

These four great seasons of expression are consistent with Pisces' emphasis on love and compassion (early Christianity), dissolution and gestation (dark ages), otherworldly aspiration and spiritual devotion (medieval) and a fundamental enlargement of the scope of possibility (modern). The latter was accompanied by ideological fantasies and technological delusions, manifestations of Pisces' Virgo polarity.

One of astrology's basic ideas is that psychological, spiritual, social and historical cycles follow an inherent twelve-phase pattern of unfolding. This reflects the fundamental nature of time's flow in which they are embedded. Earth's annual round of seasons/signs exemplifies this archetypal process. Let us apply this reasoning to the underlying structure of the Piscean Age, embodied in twelve phases of 180 years each, through the development of Western civilization.

One might ask how this differs from the 800-year cycle of Jupiter/Saturn synods through the elements. (See 'Synods.') The twelve-fold articulation of a precessional age describes an internal process of changing subjective emphasis over time. It can be thought of as similar to the houses of an individual chart. The cycle of objective planetary conjunctions generates an external series of stimulating events within that subjective framework. It accents particular possibilities defined by the social planets, Jupiter and Saturn, in specific sign positions.

Aries phase (100 BC - 80 AD): Two individual figures constellated the polarities of material and spiritual power: Julius Caesar, born around 100 BC, whose very name has become synonymous with self-worship and temporal authority,[1] and Jesus Christ, Who willingly died for universal redemption and eternal love. In all previous ages religion was about beseeching the gods for prosperity and fertility, or avoiding their wrath. Christianity introduced a completely different revelation. Each human, made in the image of God, could transcend death and attain personal salvation by partaking in the Spirit, the essence and presence of the divine.[2] Whether one believes in Christianity or not this initiated a new era in psychological and spiritual consciousness: the Aries function.

Caesar made a counterclaim: that there was one and only one authority in this world, not answerable to any higher power: the State, a work of man, represented by a man. The impersonal idol of the State must be worshiped in his image. Every individual had to explicitly acknowledge the power of power or that of a higher Truth. A new paradigm had emerged in human affairs: one had to serve God or Mammon, publicly choose between personal conscience and political demand.

That struggle was generally religious up to the 17th century; then between secular ideologies until the late 20th. It will soon take a technological form, as genetic engineering, neuro-chemical manipulation and bio-computer interfacing present each person with a crisis of consciousness about what constitutes real identity: God-given character, or a biomedical construct.

1. 'Render unto Caesar that which is Caesar's and unto God that which is God's' (Matthew 22:21). The titles of Czar and Kaiser derived from it, as did that of Roman Emperors up to 138 AD, and of the heir apparent after that.
2. Even the high ethical standards of Judaism derived from a contract between God and His Chosen People involving collective reward or punishment for obedience to The Law. Christ's blasphemy, in their eyes, was the claim that human personality mirrored the actual nature of the Creator rather than being a secondary creation. Islam appearing over six centuries later, also insists that God, while infinitely compassionate, is fundamentally different than mortal man.

Aries initializes the starting conditions of any cycle. They then unfold in a sequence paralleling that of zodiacal energies. The long-term structural development of the Piscean Age illustrates this dynamic through history:

Taurus (80-260): Consolidation. An era of peace and prosperity, the golden age of empire. Towards the end of this period its economic foundations began to crumble because of deforestation and soil erosion. Christianity grew slowly but surely, from a tiny sect to an underground movement to a world religion.

Gemini (260-440): Division. Torn by constant civil wars and renewed barbarian invasions the empire split into western and eastern halves, with capitals at Rome and Constantinople. Christianity became the state religion. It too was divided by heresies based mainly on intellectual hairsplitting over the nature of the Trinity. However arcane these theological disputes seem today, they gave the Western mind, centered in the Church, a vigorous workout in logic and reasoning. Today the same kind of thing is happening in the physics and cosmological communities, as unverifiable speculation about other dimensions and universes generates new forms of abstract thought and mathematical ability.

Cancer (440-620): Birth. The Deluge. The Roman Empire washed away in wave after wave of barbarian invasions: the Volkerwanderung, wandering of the peoples. Classical antiquity, now sterile and exhausted, gave way to fertile chaos: the Dark Ages. Judeo-Christian religion and Greco-Roman thought fused with Germanic cultural characteristics in the pregnancy of Western civilization.

Leo (620-800): Identity. The distinct character of the West began to visibly take shape: limited, contractual government (the feudal system of mutual obligation); autonomy of the church; respect for manual labor, unknown in the ancient world, leading to tinkering and technology; high status of women. In the Middle East a new world religion arose, based on absolute monotheism: submission to the Will of God, Who is completely separate from the created world. Islam (whose calendar begins in 622) created a brilliant civilization that challenged and stimulated the West.

Virgo (800-980): Integrity. Specific national kingdoms began to organize out of the tribal chaos. This even included a new Holy Roman Empire proclaimed by Charlemagne on Christmas Day, 800. At the very end of this period an embryonic Russian state, the West's future counterpart/adversary, arose in Kiev and proclaimed its Orthodox Christian character (988). A militarized feudal order, with an ethic of chivalry, emerged in response to Viking invasions that initiated this period and lasted throughout it. Monasteries created nuclei of learning and spiritual discipline in the darkness. Christianity brought a tenuous religious and cultural unity to Europe.

Libra (980-1160): External relationship. Rebalancing. A wave of life affirming energy swept Europe when the dreaded Judgment did not materialize in the year 1000. A warming climate led to population and economic growth. The Crusades brought contact with more advanced cultures in the Middle East. The first cathedrals and universities were founded.

New ideals of knightly chivalry and romantic love flourished in southern France and spread rapidly. The emerging value of marriage based on personal love rather than family alliance or economic arrangement was a true psychological revolution, far more profound than the political upheavals that go by that name.

Scorpio (1160-1340): Inner transformation. The High Medieval period, a potent blend of chivalry and Christianity, splendor and squalor. Beneath a seemingly eternal, divinely ordained hierarchy subterranean forces were gathering. The growth of parliaments,* universities, free towns and trade guilds generated a civil society with independent sources of wealth and power. A middle class began to gestate. It would eventually give birth to a new social order during the Renaissance and Reformation.

Externally, in the mid 13th century, the Mongols devastated China, Russia and Persia, but provided peace and stability for the overland trade routes to Asia. This brought Europe into contact with products, ideas and diseases from the east that would transform it.

*Especially in England after the Magna Carta, 1216.

Sagittarius (1340-1520): Expansion. The Black Death killed off ⅓ of Europe's population in just two years, 1348-49.* This provided the survivors with economic opportunity and social mobility in a rigid feudal order. Labor shortages caused a doubling of wages in the late 14th century. Abandoned property and goods gave many a fresh start in life. It also undermined traditional authority and belief (priests died as often as sinners).

The Renaissance bloomed in Italy, opening new dimensions to a world long fettered by religious dogma. Gutenberg invented the printing press (1452), which disseminated the flowering spirit of inquiry. Columbus made the permanent European discovery of the Americas (1492). A new world stimulated the liberated energies of the old. This was the great age of exploration: geographical, artistic and intellectual.

*One might have expected this in the death sign of Scorpio. There is always some overlap. More importantly, Sagittarius overtly manifests what has been secretly brewing in Scorpio. The net result of the Black Death, for all its suffering, was widespread personal liberation from a static and suffocating social order.

Capricorn (1520-1700): Achievement. Initiation of the modern world. The Scientific Revolution, extending from Copernicus' proof of a heliocentric solar system, through Galileo, Kepler and others, to Newton's brilliant elucidation of the laws of motion and gravitation, transformed human consciousness. The new worldview was overly rational and mechanistic, in keeping with Capricorn's proclivities, and in reaction to the excessive otherworldliness of the Middle Ages. Yet by any standard the profundity and integrity of the scientific method itself was a breakthrough of the first magnitude.

The Reformation and Counter Reformation culminated in the Thirty Years War (1618- 48). This exhausted the religious passions of Europe, which turned to the pragmatic secular concerns of the modern era. Britain inaugurated its unique experiment in parliamentary government after the Glorious Revolution of 1688. That decisively molded world social and political evolution over the next three centuries. A flood of American gold and silver lubricated the European economy, new crops such as corn and potatoes fed a growing population, colonies provided room for its expansion. All of these laid the material and social foundations for the coming Industrial Revolution.

Aquarius (1700-1880): Revolution. The Enlightenment of the eighteenth century was followed by the Industrial Revolution, with its accelerating waves of scientific discovery and technological invention. The American and French Revolutions brought social ferment and democratization throughout the Western world. Colonialism shattered the traditional order across Asia and Africa. The scope of change can be summarized by noting that in 1700 humanity was overwhelmingly agricultural, ruled by small oligarchies for their own rather than the general benefit, as it had been for millennia. By 1880 the basic outlines of the modern urban industrial world had taken shape in Europe and North America, with some degree of representative government and social concern over its members' health, education and welfare.

Pisces (1880-2060): Dissolution. At the height of a conservative Victorian era the most basic foundations of human reality began to melt away. Psychology discovered the unconscious, demonstrating that conscious ego is not 'the master of my fate, captain of my soul.'* Physics discovered that matter is composed of energy force fields rather than solid substance. Einstein proved that time is relative and space warped. Quantum mechanics demonstrated another domain of reality, composed of probabilistic energy flashes, underlying the material universe we know. Four generations later we still cannot reconcile the two in theory.

Then the short 20th century (1914-1991) dissolved all traditional political, social and cultural norms and structures. A great world war, 1914-1945, confronted humanity with existential spiritual and technological challenges: the Holocaust and the atom bomb. A succeeding Cold War, 1945-1991, divided the globe in a nuclear standoff between two superpowers. It finally resolved into a new world order emphasizing political democracy, human rights, rule of law, corporate economics with space for private enterprise and a growing ecological sensibility. These values, though imperfectly realized, are now universally acknowledged as the entire human race consolidates into an increasingly explicit global governance.

Now a third wave of disintegration is underway. Objectively, global economic integration and its associated environmental breakdown are approaching a tipping point. These issues will probably be effectively addressed: problems of physical survival always get our attention. Subjectively, social disintegration has already passed the point of no return. All traditional cultural values and ethnic identities are melting down into one universal civilization, albeit with colorful local flavors. Now the dissolution of individual identity is beginning as genetic engineering, neuro-chemical manipulation and human/computer interfacing generate an entirely new sense of the human condition.

These unprecedented concerns will increasingly come to the fore in the decades ahead as we transition to a new Age, that of Aquarius.

*'Invictus,' William Ernest Henley, English poet, 1849-1903.

Psychological Ages

Pisces is the sign of immersion into karma, past memory, to confront and redeem the illusory Fear and fears that becloud our being and veil us from our source. In this sense the Age of Pisces marks the culmination of a racial cycle that began 10,000 years ago, traced below in psychic terms to complement the very general social outline sketched above:

The Age of Cancer initiated a new phase of human evolution. With the agricultural revolution people gained the security allowing them to explore new dimensions of consciousness freed from the pressure of day-to-day survival. Men and women turned within, and to their fellows, to recreate the stimulation of the hunt in social and cultural interaction. During the Age of Gemini each person began to play a specialized role in a large society rather than participating in the face-to-face wholeness of the small hunting band. People began differentiating into a multitude of social classes, each concentrating on development of certain attributes in relative isolation from the rest. Thus priests, warriors, village artisans, rural farmers and nomadic herders focused on the specialization of psychic and mental functions within a complex whole that few could comprehend in its entirety.

The Age of Taurus then committed to a 'descent' from the relative fulfillment/perfection of the hunter-gatherer tribe to the exaggerated ego emphasis and appetite gratification of civilization. Men and women ate of the 'forbidden fruit,' self-consciousness, as told in the very first story of Genesis. This meant expulsion from Eden, the primordial paradise of instinctual life. A more sophisticated consciousness became deeply frustrated because it had outgrown its unconscious origins but not yet awakened to its spiritual potential.

Increasing power over nature, and others, enabled egos to pursue their material desires for wealth, power and personal immortality. Accumulation of wealth meant some now had more than others. And must coerce them to get and keep it. Diversification of economic roles and social classes brought individualization. And alienation. This psychological revolution accompanied the beginning of recorded history. It marked the Fall.[1]

The Fall does not imply that we are inherently evil. On the contrary, it symbolizes a necessary plunge into self-centered ego consciousness. Only individual awareness can link animal instinct with angelic spirit. Only personal conscience and moral choice can liberate our shadow into a transcendent soul.

At this time humanity, evolution's leading edge of consciousness, had achieved the capacity for self-reflection. It could begin to face and overcome the inheritance of pain, guilt and fear resulting from life's long struggle to emerge from inorganic matter. Our species evolved through jungles and ice ages, over millennia of hunger, cold, disease and the brutality they engendered. During the Age of Taurus it took on the burden of 'civilization and its discontents'[2] in a move similar to the retrograde phase of a planet: to evoke, act out, and redeem ancient karmic issues.

1. This occurred shortly after creation of the world: in 3761 BC according to the Hebrews, in 4004 BC according to the most famous Christian calculation (Archbishop Ussher, 1581-1656, Protestant Primate of All Ireland, who specified 9 am on October 23). The Hindu Kali Yuga, the current Age of Iron, began in 3102 BC. It followed previous mythic ages of gold, silver and bronze. By comparison the pyramids of Egypt were built in the 27th century BC.
2. The title of one of Freud's greatest works (1930). It posits that civilization requires and arises from sublimation of instinctual angers and appetites.

The Age of Aries witnessed an intense acceleration of aggressive individuality in every aspect of human endeavor. People pursued their personal ambitions less and less inhibited by the communal, animistic values of earlier, simpler cultures. Meanwhile a new spiritual consciousness began to emerge, filling the void left by disintegration of old magical ways. This was most fully articulated by the great teachers of the Axial Age in the sixth century BC, especially in the flowering of Greek reason and Jewish ethics.

The Age of Pisces portrays humanity's confrontation with, and potential redemption of, its darkest demons. An age that began with the transfiguration of one man, Jesus of Nazareth, is ending with transformation of the entire race (though not at His level of achievement). Humanity's quantum jump in knowledge and power since the Renaissance has released forces that evoke its deepest addiction: the infinite hunger of ego without love. This is traditionally personified as the Whore of Babylon, the goddess of our consumer culture. She has seduced the whole world into an unsustainable lifestyle based on an inadequate and unsatisfying philosophy of materialism. That will soon give birth to our collective shadow, the vampire prince of nihilistic power, the Antichrist. This long awaited manifestation can only materialize under modern conditions of world unification through technology and communication.

Our accelerating evolution has reached that critical intensity where the angel and the beast within must meet and fuse. Only thus can we fully realize our role as mediator between the realms of spirit and of matter. Humanity's recent acquisition of nuclear power, artificial intelligence and genetic manipulative techniques are but distorted material reflections of spiritual qualities coming out into the open as the Age of Pisces moves towards culmination and catharsis.

The Age of Cancer's agricultural revolution brought a degree of security and control over the environment. This raised issues of social differentiation that would have been inconceivable to the earlier hunter-gatherer stage. In turn, the Age of Gemini's process of division and multiplication generated an inventiveness that broke us away from instinct and towards conscious intentionality. The Age of Taurus, with its vast increase in productivity, created the promise and problems of urban civilization. Once a degree of capital accumulation, state organization and cultural refinement had been achieved the Age of Aries introduced the challenges of individualization. These especially manifested as the birth of self-conscious mind in Greece and personally responsible ethics in Israel. They could only evolve in an urban or imperial setting as opposed to the unconscious unity of a tightly knit wandering band or suffocating intimacy of rural/village life.

Once a sense of individual ego had emerged on a large scale in the rootless cosmopolitan centers of the Hellenistic and Roman worlds, issues of personal salvation and relationship to God came forth in the Age of Pisces. Egos were now disciplined by an internalized moral sense more than by traditional custom or tribal law. All three monotheistic religions of the West, Judaism, Christianity and Islam, demanded that each soul personally come to terms with God and live conscientiously in obedience to a higher law. Over time this led to a sense of individual responsibility and moral autonomy. That created the cultural and intellectual preconditions for the modern explosion of material progress and technological innovation. These will now demand planned coordination on a global scale as the Age of Aquarius approaches. Objectively this may manifest as a New Age utopia. Or as a science fiction police state. Subjectively in an atmosphere promoting inspirational self-realization. Or as a friendly fascism of techno idolatry and groupthink. The specific response is open, but the nature of the challenge is given.

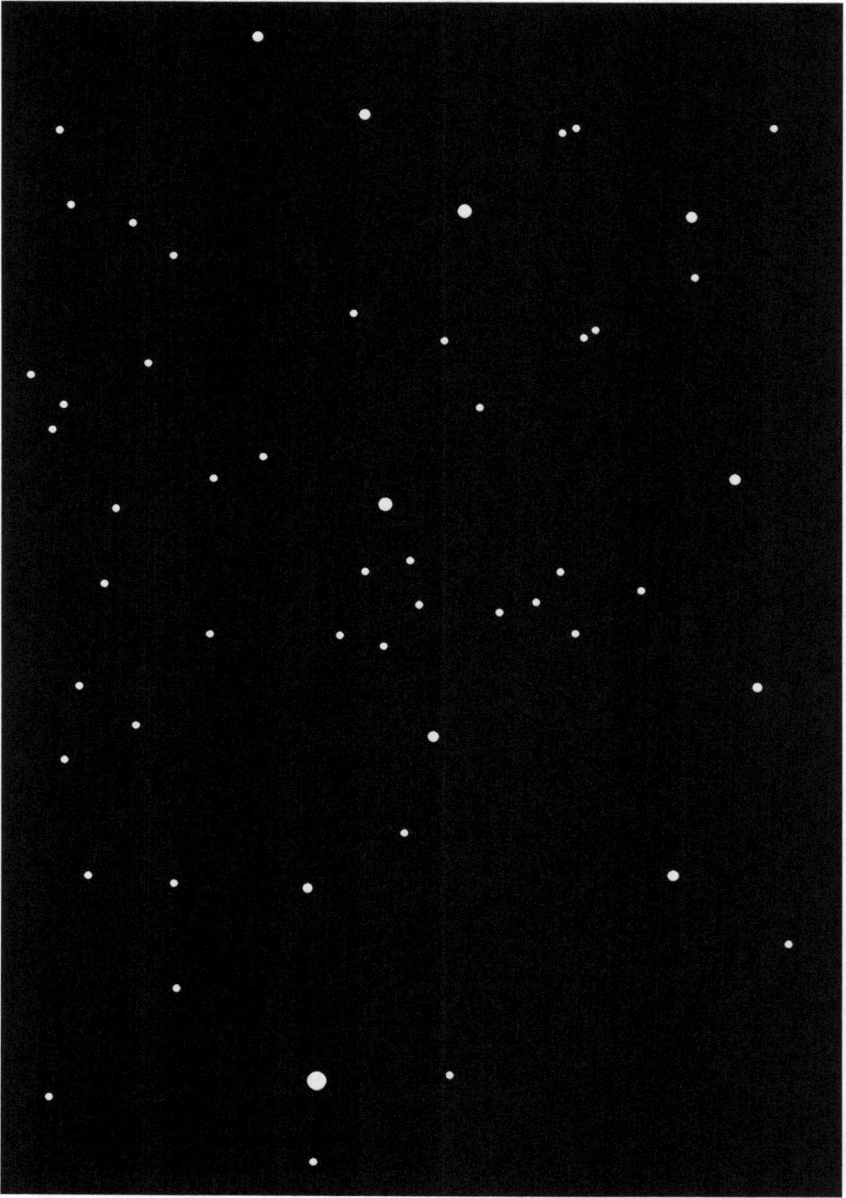

Present location of the vernal equinox, spring's starting point. This
is how the constellations Aquarius and Pisces actually look in the
starry sky.

Appendix

The Wheel of Signs

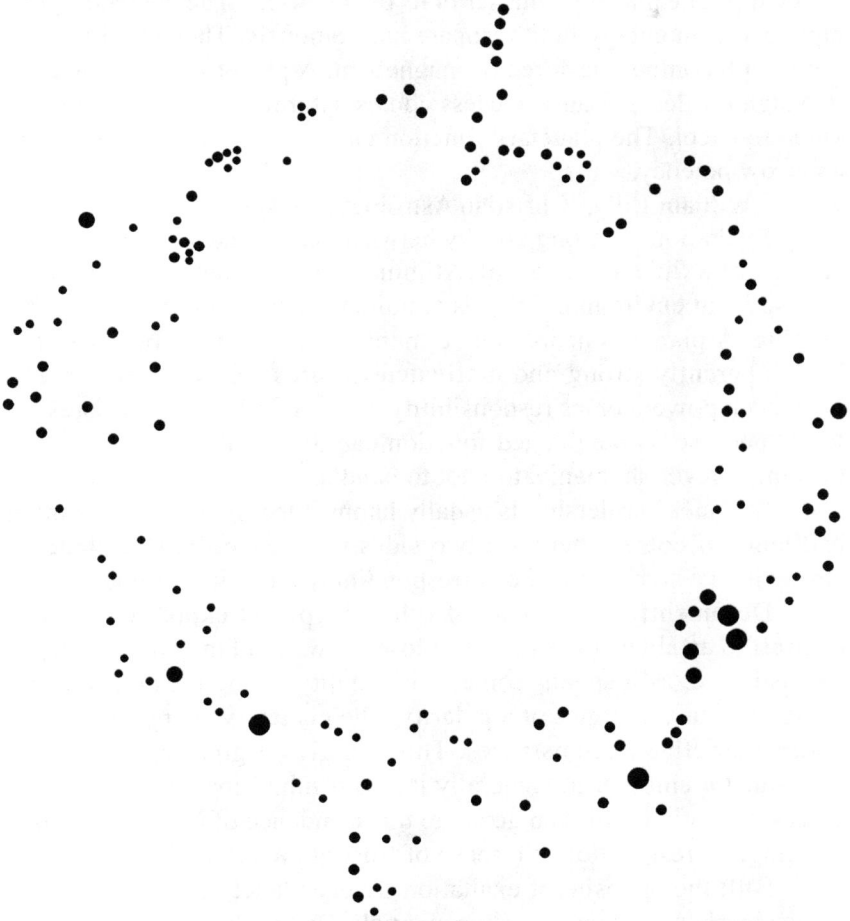

Dignities and Debilities

Every planet and sign has a characteristic energy. Some of these are more compatible than others. For example, aggressive Mars is more comfortable in fiery Aries than in balance seeking, compromising Libra. These affinities are called dignities, or debilities, and are listed below.

Definition of terms

Rulership: The planet is 'master in its own house.'* The planetary principle and sign energy field resonate harmoniously. They amplify each other with compelling force or magnetism. A planet is most powerful in a sign it rules. Because success comes naturally it may not be motivated to excel. The planetary function can be complacent, blinded by a narrow potency.

* William Lilly, 'Christian Astrology,' 1647

Exaltation: A strong affinity between planet and sign. Along with enough of a difference to truly stimulate. The planet enjoys ecstatic release in an environment that is simultaneously permissive and challenging. A planet is at its most dynamic when exalted because it is both inherently strong and motivated towards further achievement. With such power comes responsibility. It must find an appropriate outlet. Otherwise its heightened function can disrupt the overall psyche, becoming feverish, manic, too hot to handle.

A planet in rulership is usually happy. One in exaltation is often brilliant. Of course there are two sides to every coin. If a planet is strong in one sign it must be correspondingly weak in its opposite.

Detriment: the opposite of rule. The planet expresses itself in contrast to an alien environment. It loses power, but may become more sophisticated, as it spends some of its vitality fusing the antagonistic/complementary energies of a polarity. The planetary energy works out under restrictive circumstances. This can give it greater depth in the long run. Or embitter it. Generally it means inhibition: as sublimation, or as subjugation. This can generate transcendence of its previous state of being. Or resignation to a sense of frustration and limitation.

Fall: the opposite of exaltation. Every planet has a dark side. It comes out here. It may simply run amok. Or find healing through the embarrassment or punishment that malfeasance evokes. Its 'motiveless malice' can be surprisingly powerful. One can be its target rather than its agent. It may burn itself out in an inherent incompetence. Or moronically project its inner Hell onto others. Here a planetary function 'dies.' It can be reborn to a new dimension of its energy. Or devolve into a vampiric force poisoning everything it touches.

A planet in detriment is usually weak. One in fall can be malignant.

Peregrine: No dignity or debility, no positive or negative emphasis. The luminaries (Sun and Moon) are peregrine ⅔ of the time (in eight out of twelve signs). So are the outer planets of the collective unconscious (Uranus, Neptune, Pluto). The other planets (personal: Mercury, Venus, Mars, and social: Jupiter and Saturn) are peregrine ½ the time (in six out of twelve signs).

A peregrine planet expresses itself with a certain ambiguity at a normal level of intensity. For example, take Saturn in Gemini. Both the planet and sign are basically rational in nature. Gemini is the field of data processing mind. Saturn is the principle of law and logic. Both emphasize division: truth through contrast. Gemini demonstrates duality. Saturn defines limitation. But Saturn is focused while Gemini values diversity. Saturn is disciplined, while Gemini is experimental. Saturn and Gemini are not completely in synch, like loving Venus and sensual Taurus. Nor are they completely at odds, like assertive Mars and sensitive Cancer. They have commonalities and dichotomies. There is tension, either creative or crippling. Like most things in life they are not polarized but coexist in a grey area.

A peregrine planet does not function with abnormal strength or weakness. It is not emphasized by position. (Though it may be by aspect, its relationship to other planets.) The planet/sign combination acts like the American melting pot in which various ethnicities jostle with each other, sharing a common humanity while stimulated by cultural differences. It generates compromise, creative or evasive. This can encourage the emergence of new qualities and understandings.

Accidental dignity: When a planet is peregrine by sign, but located in a house corresponding to a dignity. In the above example Saturn in Gemini is peregrine. But if this occurs in the fourth house Saturn is in 'accidental' detriment, because the fourth house is the subjective analog of Cancer, Saturn's sign of detriment.

An accidental dignity is not as strong as an essential one. But it is real. It indicates one who makes surprisingly good use of normal talents. Or one who inexplicably mishandles them. In the first case, think of Harry Truman, considered a mediocre political hack before his accidental Presidency. He is now ranked just below the Titans. In the second, look at Herbert Hoover. Despite outstanding abilities and a brilliant career he simply could not cope when faced with the Depression.

Essential Dignities

These are the traditional dignities of the personal and social planets. Nobody knows the origin of the specific degree attributions. They have been passed down since antiquity. However the appropriateness of the signs involved is not in question.

Planet	Rules	Detriment	Exaltation	Fall
Sun	Leo	Aquarius 19°	Aries 19°	Libra
Moon	Cancer	Capricorn 3°	Taurus 3°	Scorpio
Mercury	Gemini	Sagittarius	6° Aquarius*	6° Leo
	Virgo	Pisces		
Venus	Taurus	Scorpio	27° Pisces	27° Virgo
	Libra	Aries		
Mars	Aries	Libra	28° Capricorn	28° Cancer
	Scorpio	Taurus		
Jupiter	Sagittarius	Gemini	15° Cancer	15° Capricorn
	Pisces	Virgo		
Saturn	Capricorn	Cancer	21° Libra	21° Aries
	Aquarius	Leo		
Moon's North Node			3° Gemini	3° Sagittarius
Moon' South Node			3° Sagittarius	3° Gemini

*Some sources claim that Mercury is exalted at 15° Virgo, a sign it rules. That does not make sense since rulership and exaltation are two distinct states. The degree of fall is always 180° opposite to that of exaltation.

The attribution of dignities and debilities to outer planets is problematic. These planets describe unconscious or collective currents that only surface through contact with personal/social planets or sensitive points, such as the Ascendant, in a chart. Their implicit potentials achieve explicit expression by activating pre-existent conscious pathways. Otherwise they remain latent, dormant, even within a sympathetic zodiacal milieu.

Given that, there is consensus on the affinities of Uranus, Neptune and Pluto in rulership and detriment. More subtle attributions of exaltation and fall may be inappropriate because of these forces' inherently intangible nature.

Planet	Rules	Detriment
Uranus	Aquarius	Leo
Neptune	Pisces	Virgo
Pluto	Scorpio	Taurus

Sun

Sun rules Leo as the principle of a universal life force focused through an ego, the basis of personal identity. Functions through creative self-expression.

Sun is exalted in Aries, as individuality asserts itself in contrast to its collective background.

Sun is in detriment in Aquarius, as an emphasis on universal ideas eclipses personal uniqueness.

Sun falls in Libra, as relationship takes priority over self.

Sun is peregrine in: Taurus, Gemini, Cancer, Virgo and Scorpio, Sagittarius, Capricorn, Pisces.

Moon

Moon rules Cancer as the maternal principle, the basis of all nurturing. Functions through subjective imagination and shared emotion.

Moon is exalted in Taurus, as one secures the resources for personal expression.

Moon is in detriment in Capricorn, as practical or social duty supersedes personal feelings.

Moon falls in Scorpio, as one adapts to loss of cherished feelings.

Moon is peregrine in: Aries, Gemini, Leo, Virgo and Libra, Sagittarius, Aquarius, Pisces.

Mercury

Mercury rules Gemini as the principle of duality, the basis of comparison. Functions through perception: the knower and the known. And through communication: sender and receiver.

Mercury rules Virgo as the principle of integrity, the basis of identity. Functions through critical analysis, with reason as its method; relative self-perfection as its purpose.

Mercury is exalted in Aquarius as mental breakthrough to the next level. Reason superseded by intuition, logic by inspiration.

Mercury is in detriment in Sagittarius, as a priori theory determines mental function.

Mercury is in detriment in Pisces, as critical discrimination gives way to idealism, naive or sophisticated as the case may be.

Mercury falls in Leo, as heart rules mind.

Mercury is peregrine in: Aries, Taurus, Cancer and Libra, Scorpio, Capricorn.

Venus

Venus rules Taurus as the principle of desire, the basis of values. Functions as productivity, growth through consistent application of values. And through sensuality, tangible appreciation of beauty in all forms on every level.

Venus rules Libra as the principle of reciprocity, the basis of relationship. Functions as harmony, balance of competing interests. And through justice, appropriate allocation of reward and punishment.

Venus is exalted in Pisces, as personal love expands into universal compassion.

Venus is in detriment in Scorpio, as the power of love becomes a love of power. Desires lose their savor. Beauty meets death. And perhaps rebirth.

Venus is in detriment in Aries, as consensual harmony gives way to assertion of personal values.

Venus falls in Virgo, as inadequacy of desire, shortcomings of love, flaws of the beloved, come into sharp focus.

Venus is peregrine in: Gemini, Cancer, Leo and Sagittarius, Capricorn, Aquarius.

Mars

Mars rules Aries as the principle of self-assertion, the basis of individuality. Functions through aggressive impulse, initiating action.

Mars rules Scorpio as the death principle. The basis of transformation and rebirth. Functions through ordeal and loss as a test of character and courage.

Mars is exalted in Capricorn, as disciplined strategy.

Mars is in detriment in Libra, as group values supersede self-expression or individual initiative.

Mars is in detriment in Taurus, as pleasure enervates will.

Mars falls in Cancer, as sensitivity melts strategy, feelings soften will.

Mars is peregrine in: Gemini, Leo, Virgo and Sagittarius, Aquarius, Pisces.

Jupiter

Jupiter rules Sagittarius as the principle of aspiration, the basis of ego-transcendence towards a higher soul. Functions through fidelity to religious/philosophical principles.

Jupiter rules Pisces as the principle of compassion, the basis of a more inclusive love. Functions through renunciation of self, growth through sacrifice.

Jupiter is exalted in Cancer, the fusion of spiritual principle with subjective feeling. Can degenerate into exaggerated loyalty to an in-group, such as family, tribe, nation.

Jupiter is in detriment in Gemini, as spiritual unity splinters into mental discord.

Jupiter is in detriment in Virgo, as spiritual compassion gives way to practical realities or exaggerated problems.

Jupiter falls in Capricorn, as aspiration adapts to reality.

Jupiter is peregrine in: Aries, Taurus, Leo and Libra, Scorpio, Aquarius.

Saturn

Saturn rules Capricorn as the principle of limitation, the basis of discipline. Functions through fear spurring ambition, deprivation stimulating achievement.

Saturn rules Aquarius as the principle of evolutionary logic, the basis of consistent theory and future vision. Functions through cold clarity of thought.

Saturn is exalted in Libra, as impersonal equal justice, without fear or favor.

Saturn is in detriment in Cancer, as discipline melts into emotion.

Saturn is in detriment in Leo, as mental austerity relaxes in the heat of passion.

Saturn falls in Aries, as impersonal duty gives way to self-expression, or an overcharged superego stifles natural impulse.

Saturn is peregrine in: Taurus, Gemini, Virgo and Scorpio, Sagittarius, Pisces.

Uranus

Uranus rules Aquarius as the principle of inspiration, the basis of a holistic intuition superseding sequential logic. Functions through a general orienting theory in science or social affairs.

Uranus is in detriment in Leo, as personal pride eclipses abstract principle.

Neptune

Neptune rules Pisces as the principle of self-sacrifice, the basis of compassion. Functions through renunciation of tangible interests to redemptive ideals.

Neptune is in detriment in Virgo, as logic eclipses poetry, ugly facts slay beautiful ideals.

Pluto

Pluto rules Scorpio as the principle of fate, a revelation of deep unconscious purpose and passion. Functions through compulsive transformation of personal will or a social order.

Pluto is in detriment in Taurus, as pleasure eclipses, or becomes, purpose.

Octaves

Uranus, Neptune and Pluto are often described as 'higher' octaves of Mercury, Venus and Mars respectively. A connection clearly exists between Uranus' inspiration and Mercury's intellect; Neptune's compassion and Venus' love; Pluto's collective purpose and Mars' personal will. But words have connotations. 'Higher' implies more evolved. It suggests cosmic and glamorous rather than commonplace. In fact, the outer planets indicate generalized potentials that are anchored into psychological experience by their more tangible inner counterparts. Mercurial mind communicates Uranian abstractions; Venusian values give voice to Neptunian dreams; Martial actions express Plutonian necessity.

The 'higher' octaves symbolize aspects of imagination that are made real and visible by their 'lower' incarnations. Furthermore, the outer planets also refer to subconscious as well as superconscious states. Uranus' rebellion, Neptune's chaos, Pluto's death urge all manifest instinctive forces inimical to and disruptive of normal consciousness. The outer planets depict an ethereal energy zone, both angelic and demonic, enveloping the inner worlds of living experience.

Linguistic labels can mislead. They oversimplify the ambiguity inherent in all psychological phenomena. Higher refers to the transrational - including irrational. Lower points to the actual and specific. Higher can mean spacy; lower can mean grounded. Detriment and fall are hard but can be beneficial: exposing and redeeming inferiority. Exaltation and rulership are gifted but can bring arrogance. A planet in fall exposes its weakness, allowing it to heal. A planet in detriment can learn to correct its own corruption. A planet in rulership can become drunk with power. One in exaltation can become too dominant, sucking up all the oxygen in a chart.

Planets in fall and detriment display their wounds and feel their pain. This can motivate them to regenerate. Planets in rulership and exaltation are indeed fortunate and can maximize their potential. Or they can fly too high. Planets have different strengths in different signs. Whether this turns out to be 'good' or 'bad' depends on what one makes of it.

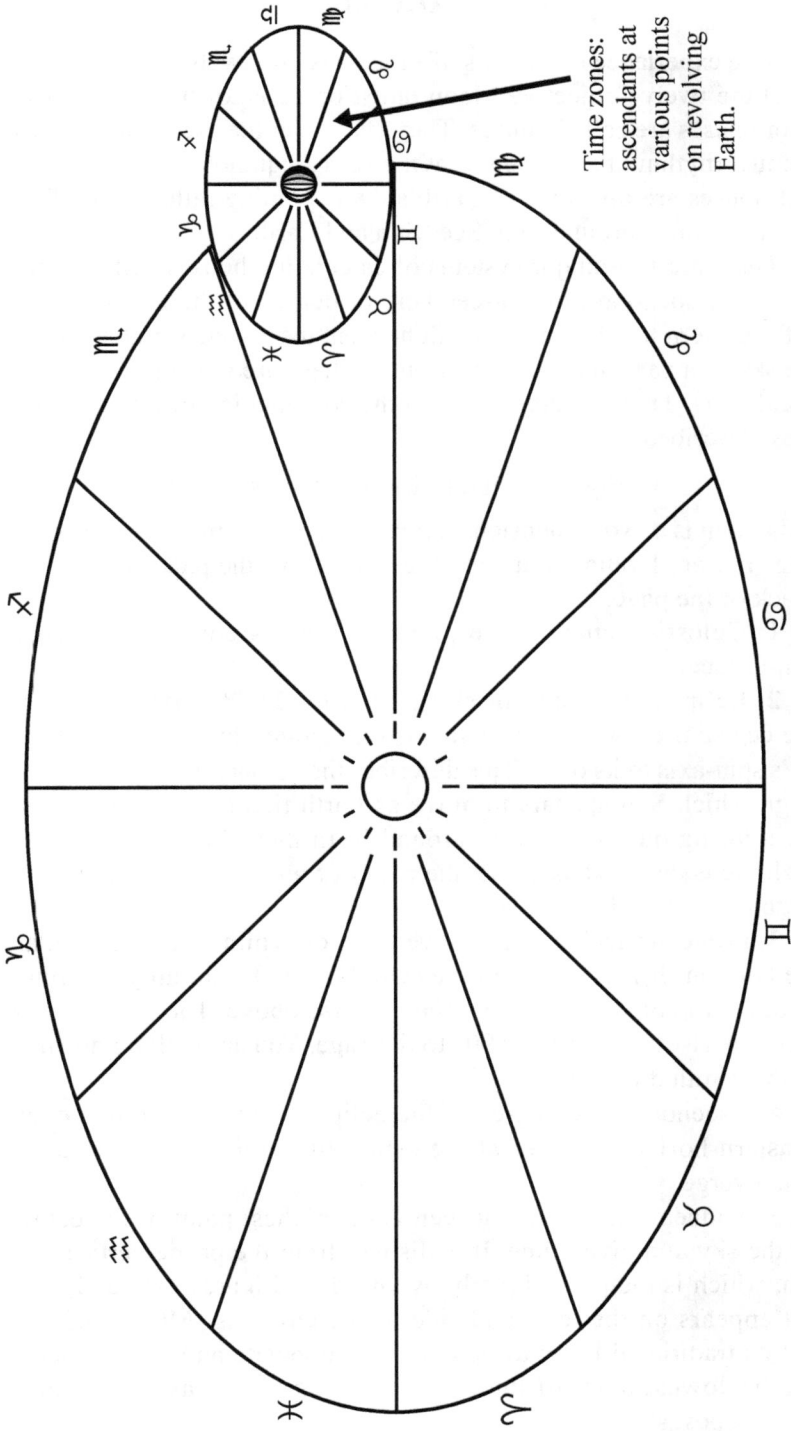

Time zones: ascendants at various points on revolving Earth.

Houses: local awareness of the planetary condition

House Division

Subjective experience naturally self-organizes into twelve phases. They parallel the twelve objective Moon units, or signs, of the year. These interior phases are called houses. They start from the ascendant, just as the annual rhythm of signs begins at the vernal equinox. The difference is that houses are divisions of Earth's own spinning rather than of its orbital movement around Sun. See 'Sun and Earth.'

There are four major systems of calculating houses. All of them agree on the location of the ascendant, or degree of the zodiac rising over the eastern horizon, and the midheaven, the zodiac's highest point in the sky as a particular degree ascends. These are indisputable astronomical facts. Their differences lie in the computation of intermediate houses, described below.

Figure 1 - Definition of terms:

This diagram is a two-dimensional representation of a three-dimensional sphere. You are looking at it from the east, above the page. West is on the back of the page.

1. Celestial equator: the plane of Earth's equator projected out into space.

2. Ecliptic: the band of sky extending 23½° north and south of the celestial equator (47° total). It is generated by the 23½° tilt of Earth's spin-axis to its orbit. This describes the zodiac: the stellar region through which Sun appears to move as Earth tilts towards and away from it during our yearly orbit around it. In the following diagrams the ecliptic is depicted as a line; the path of Sun's apparent movement through the zodiacal belt of stars.

3. Prime vertical: The prime vertical, or zenith, is perpendicular to the horizon. It is a line from the center of the Earth, up your spine and out the top of your head into the universe above. The prime vertical actually rises vertically, at 90° to the page. You are looking down it from the zenith directly overhead.

4. Ascendant: the degree of the ecliptic, or zodiac, rising over the eastern horizon. It rises at the center of the diagram, where all lines converge.

5. Midheaven: The midheaven is the highest point of the ecliptic in the sky at a given time. It is distinct from the prime vertical, or zenith, which is the point directly overhead. In Figures 2-A, 2-B, and 2-C it appears on the left hand side of the circle as 'MC': Medium Coeli, its traditional Latin designation. Its opposite and complement, the nadir, lowest point of the ecliptic, is designated as 'IC': Imum Coeli, 'deepest sky.'

Figure 1   Components of house division

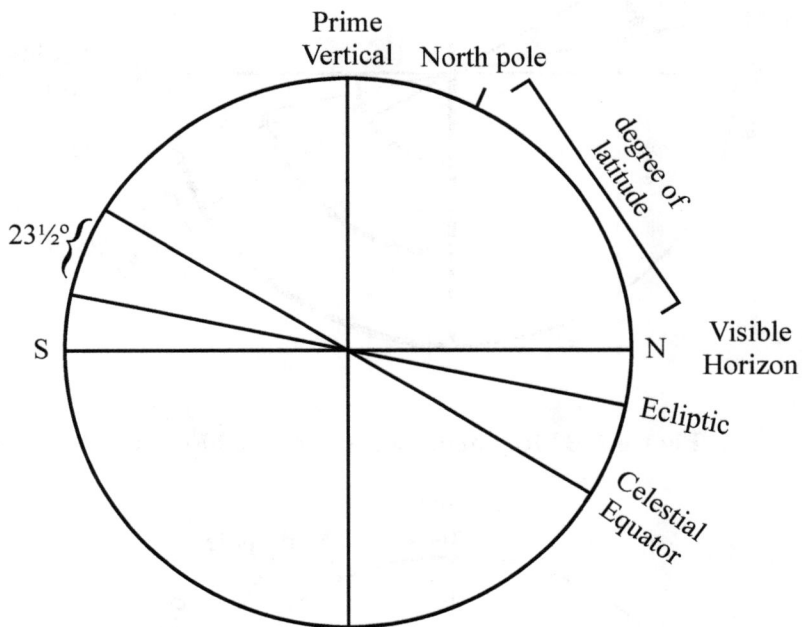

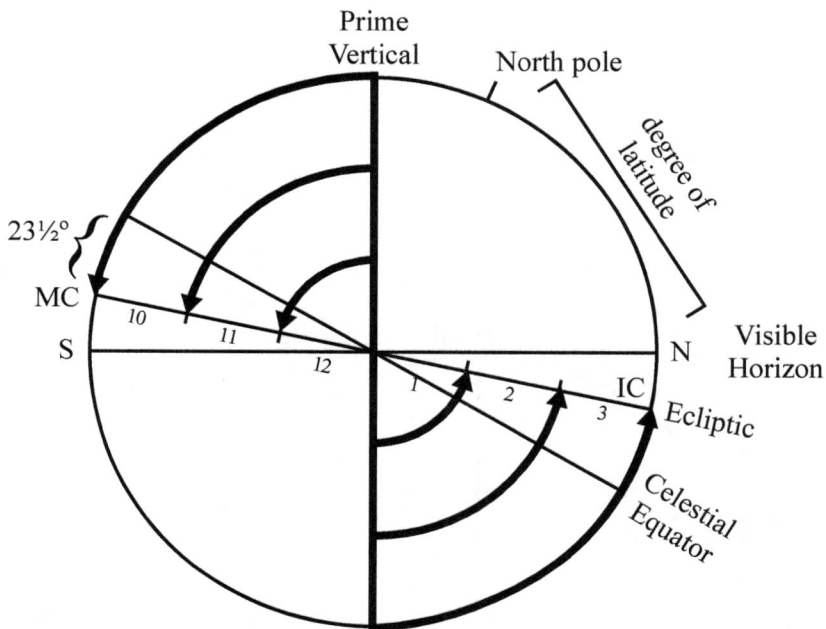

Figure 2-A   Campanus: Prime Vertical

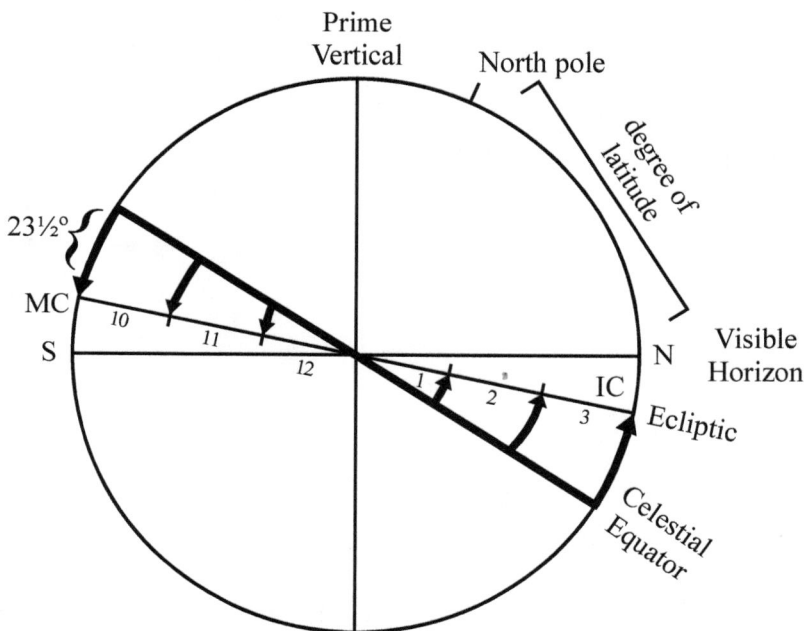

Figure 2-B   Regiomontanus: Celestial Equator

Figure 2-C   Equal House: Ecliptic

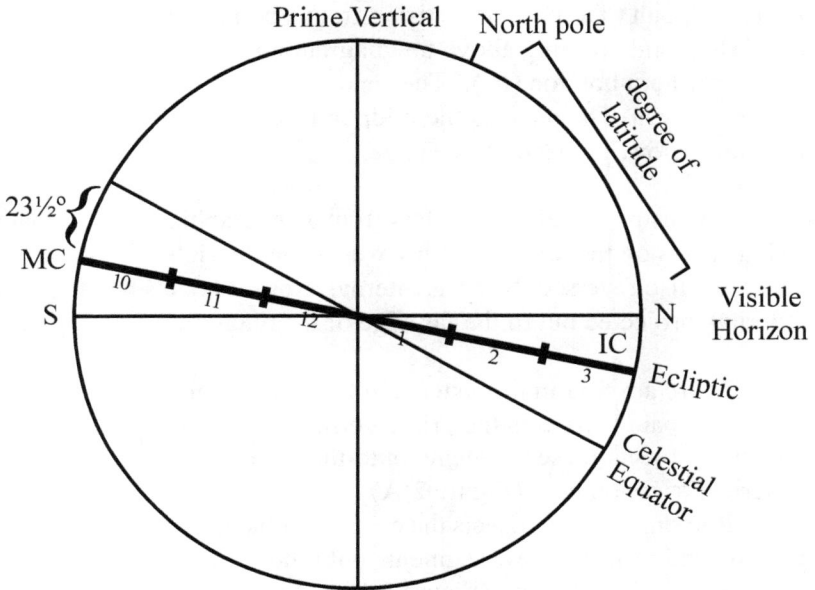

Figure 2-D   Placidus: Time

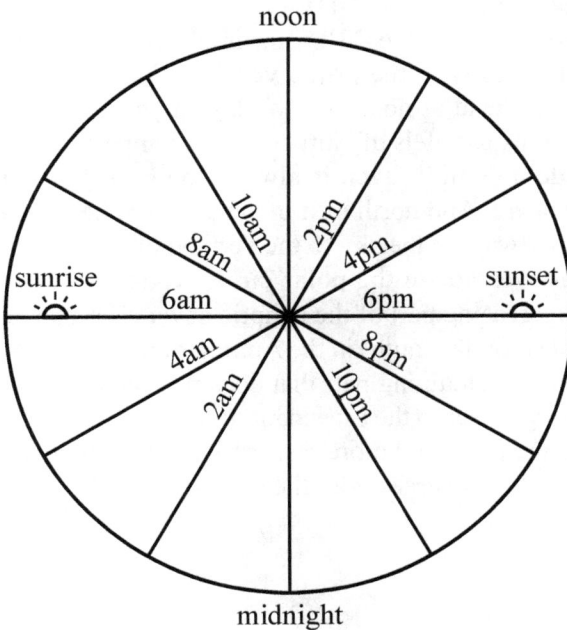

The low elevation of the midheaven (MC) on the circle is a visual illusion of this two-dimensional diagram. In the real sky the midheaven is the midpoint of a semi-circle rising from a point on the southern horizon (MC), and crossing above the diagram until it descends to a point on the northern horizon (IC).* The center of this arc, up towards you, is the midheaven. The nadir is the midpoint of an equivalent semi-circle passing 'below,' on back of, the page.

* An astrological chart differs from a geographical map in that the rising east is on the left and falling west is on the right. Thus north and south are also reversed. North is internal, closer to one's heart. South is external, projected out to the far edge of the diagram.

There are four main systems of house division:
Campanus: trisects the prime vertical above and below the horizon and projects these segments onto the ecliptic through the laws of spherical trigonometry. (Figure 2-A)
Regiomontanus: trisects the celestial equator above and below the horizon and projects these segments onto the ecliptic through the laws of spherical trigonometry. (Figure 2-B)
Equal house: trisects the ecliptic itself above and below the horizon. Thus all houses are equal 30° segments. (Figure 2-C)
These three systems divide space. Placidus divides time: how long it takes a particular degree of the zodiac to rise from the nadir to the eastern horizon, and from the eastern horizon to the midheaven, its highest point of climb. (Figure 2-D)
In the tropics, between 23½° north and south, the midheaven sometimes coincides with the prime vertical. For example, Sun can stand directly overhead at noon on two days a year, moving north or south, on each of its parallels of latitude. In the temperate zones, 23½°-66½° of latitude, the midheaven is always south of the zenith in the northern hemisphere. And north of it in the southern hemisphere. Thus it only climbs partway up the sky to the vertical directly overhead.
As one moves above the polar circles (Arctic and Antarctic), 66½°- 90°, an increasing part of the ecliptic never rises above the horizon at all: it is just too far south (in the Arctic), or north (Antarctic). The highest point of the remaining part that does rise falls lower and lower in the sky, moving closer to the ascendant. In geometrical compensation the houses become more and more distorted. At very high latitudes the midheaven actually converges with the ascendant.

All systems of house division (except equal house) are based on dividing the angle between ascendant and midheaven. The collapse of the midheaven onto the ascendant, and thus of meaningful house division at high latitudes, poses the most perplexing theoretical problem in astrology. Houses are important. They chart the interior dimensions of experience, the subjective side of existence. Without them we would have only facts, but not the feelings those facts elicit. We would know where the planets are in the sky, but not where their associated qualities act in the psyche, our inner sky.

Because the elevation of the midheaven drops as latitude increases the houses become progressively more unequal as one moves towards either pole from the equator. As the midheaven converges with the ascendant, some houses are compressed while others are elongated. In addition, some signs never rise, being too far south of the polar latitude in the Arctic, or too far north in the Antarctic. In compensation others never set. For example, north of the Arctic circle, on and about the winter solstice Sun in Capricorn circles below the horizon all 24 hours of the night because Capricorn is too far south on the ecliptic to rise. In contrast, on and about the summer solstice Sun in Cancer circles above the horizon all day long because Cancer is too far north to set. Figure 3.

This implies a somewhat different subjective atmosphere or charge in the polar regions than elsewhere on the planet. This may not be as ridiculous as it sounds. The magnetic fields, which shield Earth from solar and cosmic radiation, converge at the poles. They create a vortex through which these energies pour down upon our planet. Figure 4. This causes the shimmering aurora borealis in the Arctic and a corresponding aurora australis in the Antarctic. It may indicate a similar effect on the psyche of a human born at or near the still foci of our spinning planet.

The poles are, by definition, points where one orientation of experience (such as 'northness') most completely eclipses its polarity ('southness'). In the polar zones day and night both manifest in extreme form during the solstices. However, even a sign that never rises, such as Capricorn at the north pole, or Cancer at the south pole, is still present as a subjective factor in the interior personal space below the horizon. Within the rationale of astrology an individual born near a pole would embody that aspect of the planetary condition.

Which of these systems dividing the four quadrants into twelve houses is the correct or most accurate one? Obviously, this is a matter of dispute and preference. Perhaps each of these systems is most suited to describing the psychological details of differing overall temperaments, such as Jungian types.

Figure 3 Situation just above the Arctic circle

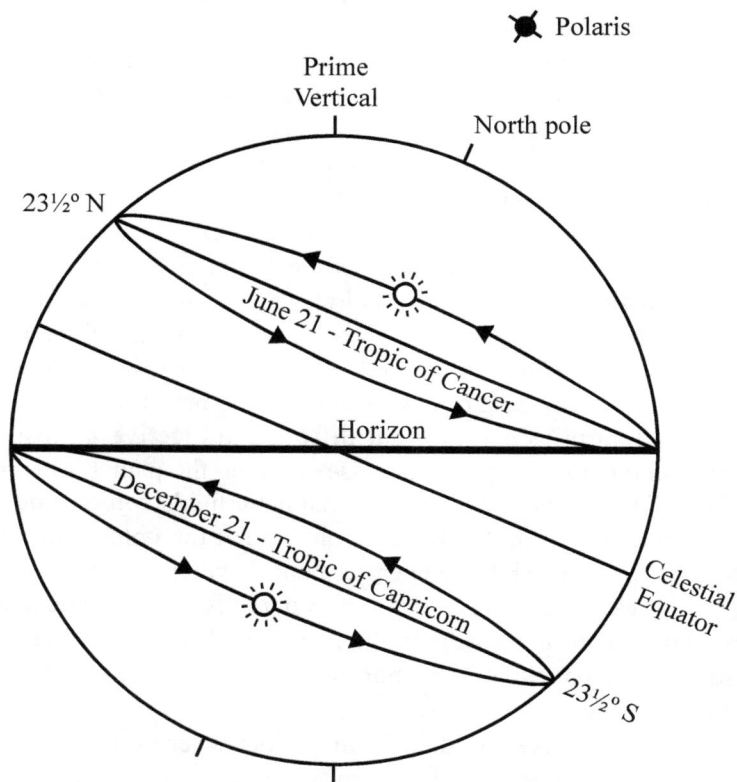

At the summer solstice Sun circles above the horizon all day, never setting (on celestial tropic of Cancer).

At the winter solstice Sun circles just below the horizon all night, never rising (on celestial tropic of Capricorn).

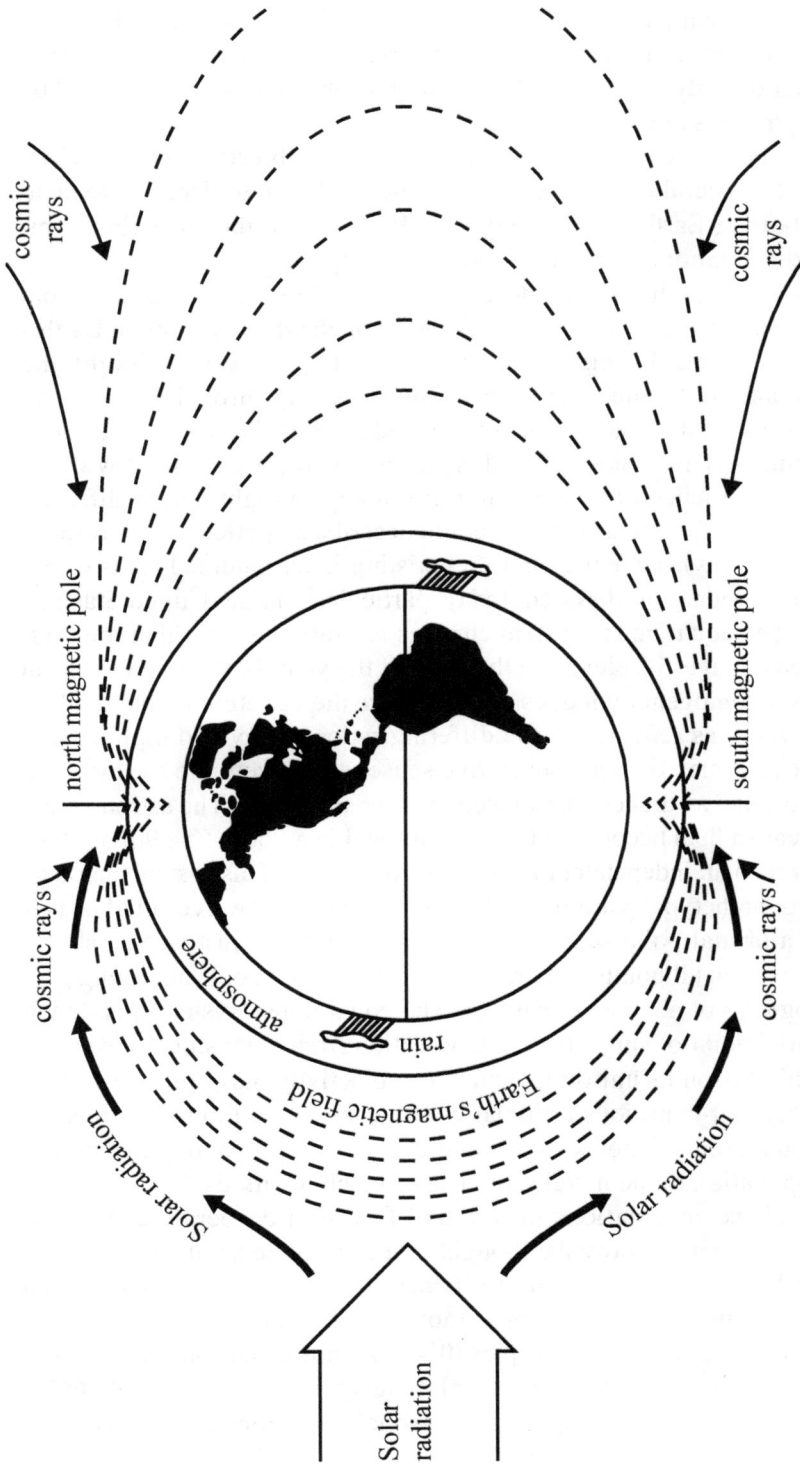

Figure 4 Earth's magnetic field

The Campanus system portrays a subjective sense derived and measured from the 'I' vertical of the spinal cord extended upwards to the star directly overhead. This might describe an outlook animated by its aspirations and ideals.

The Regiomontanus system portrays a subjective sense derived from its visceral solar plexus within the circle, or zodiac, of life measured along Earth's central equator. It may describe an outlook animated by emotional intuition and gut feelings.

The Placidus system describes a subjective sense measured from the actual length of zodiacal longitude through which a point on Earth's surface rotates during given time intervals (between midnight and dawn, and dawn and noon). These intervals vary throughout the year. For example, the time between dawn and noon is shorter in winter than in summer. This makes it, of all systems, the most consistent with the actual experience of a changing ratio of day to night during different seasons at different latitudes. It could describe an outlook more responsive to its environment than a pre-existing inner nature. This is by far the most widely used system today, particularly in the United States.

The equal house system chooses to ignore the fact that the midheaven changes its elevation throughout the year. In the interests of an abstract homogeneity it does not recognize the variation in the 'quality' of rotation, as reflected in the differing ratios of day and night during the year. It may depict a subjective sense willed from the ascendant, a 'monolithic' awareness dominated by the rising point. The astronomical midheaven then becomes a power point within a house (the 9th or 10th) rather than an independent factor in its own right. This system charts an ideal or archetypal pattern of subjectivity, radiating twelve equal phases from a primal point of consciousness (ascendant), just as Sun shines equally upon all points of Earth's orbit. However, people are living psychologies, not abstract equations. The equal house system misses the essential point of subjectivity: its variation from mechanical order. For just this reason its uniform, synthetic subjectivity may aptly describe a possibly self-conscious artificial intelligence in the future.[†] Ironically, the conundrums of house division might provide a flexibility that allows its application to the novel sentience of machine minds.

These speculations may sound forced, a desperate expedient. They are meant to provoke thought, not to provide an answer. Houses relate Earth's rotational spin to its orbital revolution. The existential quality of that spin varies considerably between the three great climatic zones of our planet. In the tropics (0°- 23½° north and south), day/night and seasonal variations are minimal. In temperate regions (23½°- 66½° north and south), day/night and seasonal variations are pronounced and fast changing. Near the polar caps (66½°- 90° north and south) day/night variations are total (one can hardly speak of 'seasons' on the extreme environment of the ice sheets). The objective daily and seasonal qualities of time differ considerably between these zones. Perhaps time's subjective quality, as charted by these house systems, similarly varies between different general temperaments, such as introvert and extrovert, thinker or feeler.

Lets take a parallel from the biological realm. Life in the tropics is incredibly diverse. But no species dominates. An acre of tropical rainforest contains hundreds of sorts of trees, a coral reef a stunning array of varied, brightly colored fish. Small numbers of many kinds is the rule. Life in the temperate zones is often just as prolific. But only a few species dominate each ecological niche. Coniferous forests with half a dozen types of trees cover thousands of square miles. The seas are (or used to be) dense with huge schools of the same fish: cod, mackerel, herring, etc. Vast numbers of a few kinds is the rule. Life in the circumpolar oceans is prolific and relatively uniform, but the central ice sheets themselves are barren, devoid of life away from their ocean edges.

All life is one. It all shares the same DNA code, the same basic metabolic processes, the same lineage. But it interacts with Earth's north-south spin axis along a curve of population/diversity ratios. In the same way, all humans share a similar psychological constitution (within fairly broad limits!). But its profile of subjective emphasis varies between psychological types just as our planet's environmental 'atmosphere' changes as one moves from the sensuous ambience of the tropics to the demanding mutability of temperate climes, then polewards and stormwards to the ends of Earth.

One should also keep things in perspective. All of these systems agree on the essential angles: ascendant, midheaven, descendant, and nadir. The general quadrants of psychic orientation are the same in each: intuition (houses 1, 2, 3), feeling (houses 4, 5, 6), thought (houses 7, 8, 9) and sensation (houses 10, 11, 12). Only the internal structure of each quadrant varies, but not by much. Nor are those differences that important. Houses describe subjectivity, which is inherently fuzzy.

House cusps are transition zones, not rigid boundaries. Their minor range of variation seems to describe degrees of emphasis, oscillations of subjective attention. Perhaps they depict contending psychological dynamics between different functions of the personality - just as the turbulence along the edges of Jupiter's symbolic bands of consciousness points to fertilizing friction between abstract spiritual levels.

The horizontal axis of a chart defines an orientation of conscious-ness. Its vertical axis defines the power by which that consciousness shapes itself into identity and behavior. The ascendant initiating the horizontal axis is to the other houses what Sun is to other planets: the source and summation of the subjective condition that they describe in detail. The midheaven initiating the vertical axis is to other houses what Moon is to Sun and other planets: the grounding through which pure awareness and its peripheral attributes gains potency in manifesta-tion. The descendant and nadir are also of unusual significance, in that order, because they draw out and complement the initiatory impulses of ascendant and midheaven. The remaining eight houses are intrinsically equal in importance.

There is another factor producing an inequality of house length in any system not measured along the ecliptic itself. In the northern hemisphere the signs from Capricorn through Gemini are called signs of short ascension because it takes less than the theoretical two hours for each of these signs to rise. (Twelve signs × two hours each = 24 hours.) As these signs rise, the entire ecliptic also rises with them, from its southernmost point (0° Capricorn to its northernmost (29° Gemini). Think of a person climbing at a constant rate of motion (Earth's rota-tion) on an escalator that is also moving upwards (northward rising obliquity of the ecliptic). These two movements add together to pro-duce a faster ascension. Signs of short ascension cover more distance per unit of time. Figure 5. Thus they produce wider houses when rising.

In contrast the signs from Cancer through Sagittarius are called signs of long ascension for the same reason. They take more than the ideal two hours to emerge, because while they rise the obliquity of the ecliptic is falling southward. Think of a person vigorously climbing a downwards-moving escalator. The two movements partially cancel each other out, producing a slower ascension. Signs of long ascension cover less distance per unit of time. Therefore they generate narrower houses when rising. Figure 5.

The inequality of house length inherent in the Campanus, Regiomontanus and Placidus systems portrays an individual's subjec-tive distribution of attention. The presence or absence of planets in a house relates to its emphasis or intensity.

The relative length of a house indicates the breath or inclusive-ness of its application. However, a short house, such as the 7th (of relationships) in Figure 6, may be heavily emphasized by a powerful grouping of planets within its boundaries (cusps). This would indicate that relationships, though intense by planetary concentration, tend to be narrow or uni-dimensional in quality. A wide house, such as the 6th (work, service, health, integrity) in Figure 6, may be empty. Because of its length those concerns play a more pervasive, though subtle, role in the personality than its lack of planets would suggest. They express through the position and aspects of the planet ruling the house cusp sign. In this example, Venus rules Libra, the sign on the cusp of the 6th. Here, Venus is in Capricorn, in the 9th house, making a waning trine (240° aspect) to Jupiter.

A pair of narrow houses always balances any pair of wide houses in a chart to maintain a 360° circle. Thus, inequality of house length portrays not only the distribution of subjective concerns, but also their compensations: the checks and balances of its internal value system.

An unequal house system can also show an unequal distribution of zodiacal energies as a medium of subjective interest, whether or not those houses contain planets. For example, in Figure 6 Geminian and Sagittarian impulses dominate the awareness and expression of four houses (1st and 2nd plus their complementary 7th and 8th). Meanwhile, Taurean and Scorpionic impulses tend to be subconscious because the signs of Taurus and Scorpio are entirely enclosed, or intercepted, within the 6th and 12th houses. The overall nature of these houses is characterized by the signs on their cusps (Aries and Libra).

The qualities symbolized by a planet within an intercepted sign, such as Jupiter in Taurus in Figure 6, are relatively subconscious. They come to life indirectly through the alien nature of the sign on the house cusp (Aries) and its ruler (Mars). And through the intercepted planet's relationships with other planets, in this example Venus.

When an intercepted planet is activated by direction, progression or transit it bursts into consciousness, seemingly out of nowhere. Because it has not had a normal workout in life experience its expression tends to be raw, infantile, primitive. (Especially if it is not aspected.) However, it can also be seen as a buried treasure, worth the considerable effort necessary to contact and express.

Figure 5 - Explanation

Scale exaggerated for clarity. Because this is a three dimensional reality mapped onto a two dimensional page, the actual ascendant is rising in the east, above or toward you in the center where the prime vertical, celestial equator and horizon meet. The descendant sets on the back of the page.

The purpose of this illustration is to show how long and short ascension work. In doing so it also portrays another phenomenon: parallels of declination. The sign pairs Sagittarius/Capricorn, Scorpio/Aquarius, Libra/Pisces, Virgo/Aries, Leo/Taurus, and Cancer/Gemini are parallel by declination because each covers the same span of latitude north or south of the celestial equator. Of course, one is moving north while the other moves south. Thus 2° of Sagittarius is south of 1° Sagittarius, while 2° of Capricorn is north of 1° Capricorn.

Planets in parallel degrees of declination, such as 1° of Sagittarius and 29° of Capricorn, are linked by status: they each have the same ratio of individual/collective emphasis. They are differentiated by process: the one in Capricorn is individualizing (moving north) while the other in Sagittarius is collectivizing (moving south). Each is stimulated by encounter with another planetary function at the same stage of the cycle, but moving in the opposite direction of development.

Sagittarius/Capricorn, Scorpio/Aquarius and Libra/Pisces are predominantly collective; Virgo/Aries, Leo/Taurus and Cancer/Gemini are mainly individual. The relationship within each pair is similar to that between waxing and waning crescent Moons, or the objective/subjective contrast between a crisis of action and of consciousness.

Figure 5 Long and short ascension

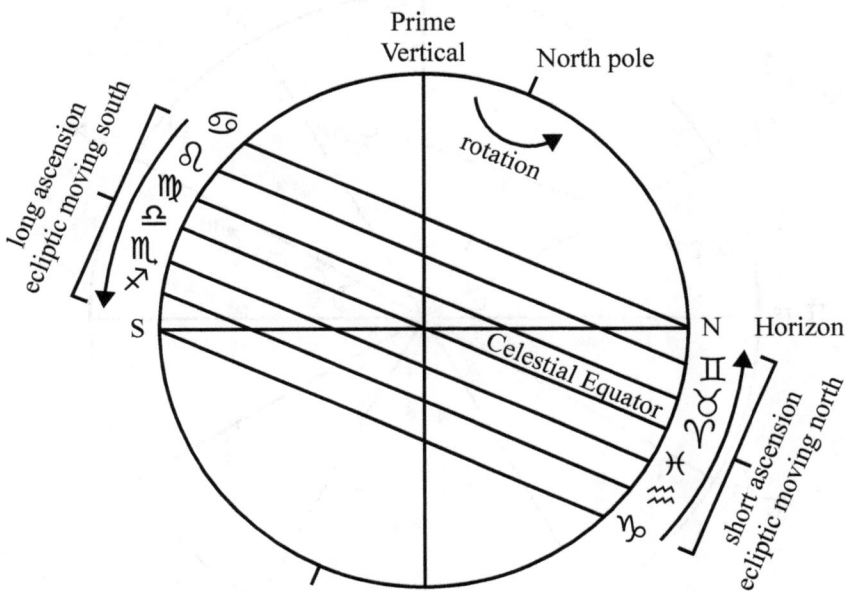

Figure 6 Features of house division

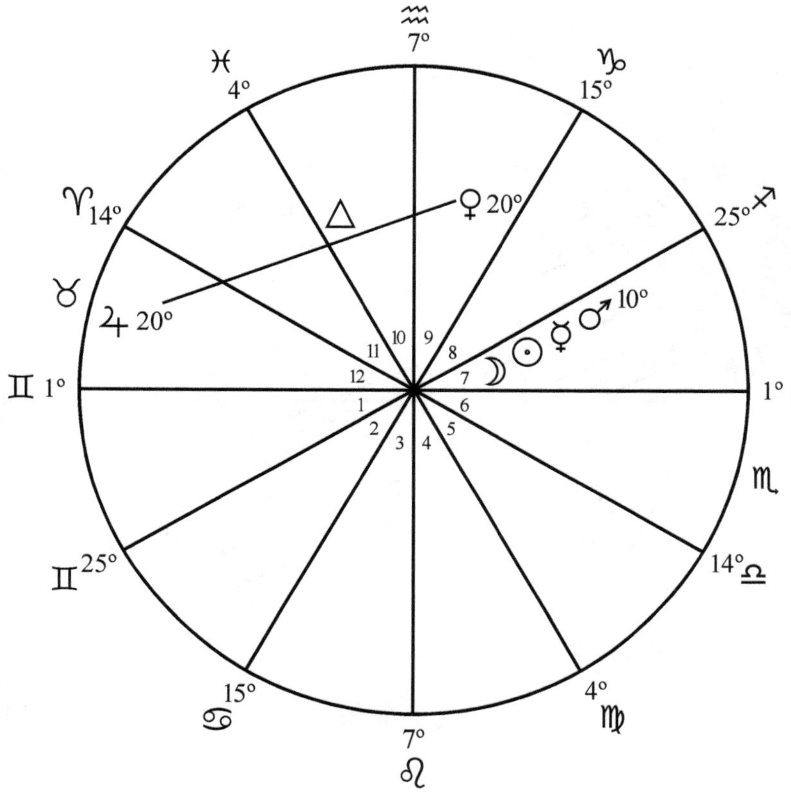

1° Gemini rising at New York City, 41° north latitude (Placidus houses). The planetary positions are imaginary but plausible.

Note

† The electronic nervous system of computer chips is based on the element silicon rather than on carbon, as is the case with organic life. Silicon belongs to the same chemical family as carbon but is much heavier, with an atomic weight of 28 v carbon's 12. It is also less chemically reactive. Silicon shares carbon's distinctive ability to form four chemical links with other atoms. This tetravalent bonding underlies life's carbon based chemistry. Organic compounds generally consist of carbon chains incorporating hydrogen, oxygen and nitrogen atoms, along with a sprinkling of other elements. Electronic computer wafers consist of silicon chains incorporating boron, phosphorus, arsenic and occasionally other semi-conducting metalloids.

Astrology, and other metaphysical traditions, propose that the material world anchors more intangible planes of biological vitality, emotion, intellect and spirit. If a carbon scaffolding embodies the ethereal energies of life then presumably the heavier, less responsive structure of silicon would house a denser electrical aura; perhaps more powerful but less subtle. At this point we cannot know whether computers, with robotic bodies, will ever achieve some form of self-awareness. However, given that it would be embodied in a more compact substrate, its inherent quality would differ from that of biological organisms.

In addition, all living things descend from an immensely long evolutionary journey. They encode eons of life-experience in their molecular memories. Our own human ego-consciousness floats in a sea of unconscious instincts, an organic essence distilled out of inherited history. In contrast, machine intelligence results from a logically structured interplay of programmed algorithms. Even if data banks achieved a sense of self-identity, it would derive from a deliberately contrived artificial intelligence. These are very different wellsprings of awareness.

In fact, we have two sources of consciousness. Supplementing the brain and its nervous system is a gut intelligence. Our intestines hold about a trillion bacteria, of several different types. They also contain 100 million neurons, which communicate these bacterias' biological status and ecological state directly to the brain. This teeming intestinal life also directly secretes many hormones and biochemicals, such as 95% of our serotonin. It thus strongly influences our mental and emotional state.

Bacteria are prokaryotes: single cells whose DNA is distributed throughout the cell. We, along with all other multicellular organisms, are eukaryotes, whose DNA is segregated into a nucleus, a cellular 'brain.' Bacteria constitute a more ancestral life form. Their presence within connects us with a more primal form of sentience.

A machine intelligence would not have such deep roots. Nor would it have the complexity derived from interaction between two different realms of life. The compound nature of organic consciousness has an ambiguous fertility. That generates creativity. So too do random mutations in its DNA code. Their transformative variation is a fundamentally different source of identity than the cause and effect logic of an electronic pathway.

Finally, all living things feel and fear their own mortality. 'Fear of God is the beginning of wisdom.' 'God' is a non-quantifiable quality that cannot be programmed into a database.

Even if computer chips were implanted into our brains, the fact that they are denser silicon artifacts rather than carbon based living cells would differentiate them from the multilevel structure of organic body/mind integration that informs living consciousness.

Planetary Astronomy

A picture is worth a thousand words. You can access stunning images of all the planets online. Their physical appearance implies deeper levels of psychological meaning. Visible astronomical features signal underlying spiritual qualities.

Sun

Mass: 333,000 × Earth
Volume: 1,304,000 × Earth
Equatorial diameter: 865,000 miles (1,392,000 km)
Surface gravity: 28 × Earth
Surface temperature: 9,900° F (5,500° C)
Core temperature: 28,000,000° F (15,500,000° C)
Axial rotation period (day length) at equator: 25.4 Earth days (approximately 35 days at its poles. Sun rotates differentially because it is a gaseous plasma rather than a solid.)

Our Sun is often described as just an average star. Actually it is bigger than 97% of all stars (!). Most stars are brown or red dwarfs: small, dimly glowing bodies, like coals of a fire. Our Sun is a yellow dwarf, a brightly burning flame. Stars much larger don't last long (on an astronomical scale); they burn too hot and fast.

In about six or seven billion years Sun will have burned all of its hydrogen fuel. At that point it will swell up into a red giant, engulfing Mercury, Venus, Earth and possibly Mars. Soon after it will collapse, blowing off its outer layers into a gaseous nebula. The exposed core will remain as a white dwarf, an unimaginably dense stellar remnant. Over many billions of years this will cool into a dead cinder, a black dwarf, a corpse wandering the outer precincts of the galaxy. Eons hence, in the 'degenerative era,' its elementary particles will decay, until, along with the rest of the universe, it simply evaporates. At least that is the current theory. It's nothing to lose sleep over.

Our Sun was born about 4.5 billion years ago as an immense cloud of hydrogen, with some helium and a pinch of heavier elemental dust. A shock wave from a nearby nova or super nova compressed this into a spinning disk. It then quickly contracted into a central fire surrounded by a ring of debris. Within only 30 to 50 million years this rubble had largely coalesced into the planets we know. For the next billion years, the 'heavy bombardment' period, the early planets were pummeled by leftover debris. One such collision knocked Uranus on its side, another disrupted Mars' core, destroying its protective magnetic field. Yet another, a Mars sized planetoid, crashed into ancestral Earth, fusing the two together and hurling a cloud of rocky fragments into the sky. These coalesced into our Moon. Finally the solar system calmed down and assumed its present form. This has persisted for the last 3.5 billion years and should continue about twice that long into the future.

At its center burns our star, Sol. It is a huge ball of plasma, an electrically charged gas. 71% hydrogen, 27% helium, 2% all other elements. In its core a permanent thermonuclear explosion fuses hydrogen into helium, releasing highly energetic gamma rays and ghostly neutrinos. The neutrinos easily pass through Sun's mass, but the gamma rays are constantly absorbed and reemitted by the dense ionized gas. Thus they lose energy and finally emerge, after about a million years, as visible light at Sun's surface. In this process Sun fuses about 600,000,000 tons of hydrogen per second. And will do so for billions of years to come.

Sun's core comprises the inner 20% of its volume, at a temperature of 28,000,000° F. Surrounding it is a radiative zone, conducting the core's radiation outwards. The outer 30% of Sun is the convective zone, where cells of hot gas rise, spread out and cool, then sink back down. At its very top is the photosphere, Sun's visible face, at 9900° F. This is sometimes dotted with sunspots: concentrations of magnetic force. They are cooler (7000° F) and darker than the surrounding photosphere. Sunspots can be up to 50,000 miles across, six times wider than Earth. They usually appear as pairs of opposite polarity. Sunspots erupt out of Sun's interior in an 11-year cycle of minimum to maximum activity.

Sun itself is quite stable, despite being an ongoing thermonuclear explosion cushioned by its own mass. However, it does have a thin turbulent atmosphere. The lower 5600 miles of chromosphere sports enormous geysers of gas (spicules), probably formed by sound waves. Above it is the sparse but very hot corona, extending out for several solar radii. This becomes visible during a total solar eclipse, when Sun's mass is blocked by the body of Moon. The corona reaches 3.6 million degrees F; why so hot is a mystery. It is the scene of giant flares: spectacular eruptions of hot gas following magnetic lines of force. Sometimes these go so far as to eject great bubbles of charged particles into space.

Moon

Average distance from Earth: 238,855 miles (384,400 km)
Mass: 0.012 × Earth
Volume: 0.02 × Earth
Equatorial diameter: 2,160 miles (3,476 km)
Surface gravity: 0.165 × Earth

Highest surface temperature: 253° F (123° C)
Lowest surface temperature: −387° F (−233° C)
Axial inclination to orbit: 6.7°
Axial rotation (day): 27.3 days
Orbital revolution (around Earth): 27.3 days measured against the stellar background; 29.5 days from one new Moon (conjunction with Sun) to the next as seen from Earth. See below.

Moon is ¼ the diameter of Earth. As such it is by far the largest satellite relative to its parent planet in our solar system (excluding Pluto/Charon, a special case). Some consider the two to be a double planet, one living, the other dead.

Moon has a very small iron core, less than 4% of its mass, perhaps partially molten. Surrounding it is a mantle of silicate melt-rock, thickly crusted over. Moon's surface is truly ancient. Its highlands have not changed at all for 3,900,000,000 years. Its lower basins (marias = 'seas') were flooded by lava about three billion years ago. They have not changed since except for the occasional meteor strike.

There is no atmosphere. Without an insulating air blanket temperatures gyrate from +250° F (day) to −390° F (night). Moon has no free water. It is bone dry, dusted with razor sharp silica flakes that have never lost their edge to erosion. However, the ingredients to make water (and oxygen), hydroxyl ions (OH), are chemically bound in lunar rocks. It also seems that dirty snowballs of cometary ice have accumulated at the bottom of deep polar craters, shaded from Sun. They may hold a total volume of water equal to Lake Erie. Obviously this would be far more valuable than any goldmine to a future lunar colony.

In fact, there is very little metal of any kind on Moon. It formed four billion years ago when a planetoid the size of Mars smashed into infant Earth. The two protoplanets merged, their iron cores fused, and a vast debris of lighter silicate rock was pulverized and blasted into space. These fragments eventually coalesced into Moon, the cast off shell of a violent planetary collision.

Moon rotates once on its axis during one revolution around Earth. Thus its day equals its year. Because its day and year are the same, moon always presents the same face to Earth. The far side is completely hidden (though it has now been visited by robot spacecraft).

Moon takes 27.3 days to orbit Earth with reference to the stellar background. However, its phase cycle, from new to new, is slightly longer, 29.5 days, because Earth moves along its own orbit during the time Moon revolves around it. It takes Moon a couple of days to catch up and make another new Moon alignment with Earth and Sun. A new Moon occurs when Moon is exactly between Earth and Sun, invisible in the solar glare. A full Moon occurs when it is on the other side of Earth from Sun and thus fully illuminated.

Interestingly, Sun and Moon are almost exactly the same size as viewed from Earth. Sun is objectively much larger, but is also about four hundred times farther away. Sun appears to be only a sliver larger from our perspective. This can be seen during a total solar eclipse: Moon covers Sun, with a tiny fringe of fire glowing around its circumference. Thus, symbolically, the solar (purpose) and lunar (psyche) principles are almost equally important.

Moon exerts a huge influence on Earth. Its gravitational drag has slowed Earth's rotation from a one hour long day four billion years ago to a 24 hour day now. It will continue to slow over the eons ahead. Moon also pulls the oceanic tides up and down, twice a day every day. The consequent creation of an intertidal zone, where land and sea alternate, facilitated the movement of life out of water onto land. It still plays a large role in marine ecology: tidal wetlands are the most fertile zones of the ocean. Without Moon's gravitational pull, 700 mile per hour winds would shriek around our world, making terrestrial life almost impossible. Moon's gravitation also stabilizes Earth's axial wobble. Without it, erratic and drastic climate changes would have made the emergence and evolution of advanced life very problematic.

The essential fact about Moon is that it is a vital partner to our living Earth. One might even think of Moon as an eighth continent, or Earth's highest mountain: separated by, yet therefore incorporating, space's void into our experience.

Mercury

Average distance from Sun: 0.39 × Earth's (36 million miles; 57.9 km)
Mass: 0.055 × Earth
Volume: 0.056 × Earth
Equatorial diameter: 3,032 miles (4,879 km)
Surface gravity: 0.38 × Earth
Highest surface temperature: 800° F (430° C) - day side.
Lowest surface temperature: −280° F (−170° C) - night side.
Axial inclination to orbit: 0°
Axial rotation (day): 58.7 days
Orbital revolution (year): 88 days
No satellite.

Mercury is the smallest, densest planet. An iron core occupies 85% of its radius, making it the heaviest planet relative to its size. This generates a tiny magnetic field, about 1.1% the strength of Earth's. Basically Mercury moves within the magnetic sphere of Sun, forming its only permanent and solid Sunspot. (Sunspots are magnetic eruptions of Sun.)

Mercury is an iron sphere with a thin veneer of silicate rock on top. Its north and south polar craters, shaded from Sun, are very radar reflective. This may indicate that ice is present on this otherwise searing planet. Another feature, unique to Mercury, are huge cracks, hundreds of miles long, that ruptured the crust as it cooled and shrank four billion years ago. Perhaps these are premonitions of the crustal plates that formed on our own tectonically active planet. Mercury itself has no such movements; it lacks an underground ocean of molten rock to carry them.

Mercury spins slowly, once every two Earth months, during a three month long year. Because of its slow spin and fast revolution around Sun Mercury makes a half-turn relative to Sun during its year. Thus one day, the time between two successive sunrises on Mercury itself, lasts two Mercurial years. However, from our vantage point on Earth a Mercurial day is $\frac{2}{3}$ ($\frac{59}{88}$) of its year.

Mercury also has the most elliptical orbit of any planet (other than Pluto). It ranges from $\frac{1}{3}$ to $\frac{1}{2}$ of Earth's distance from Sun. Its long rotation and elongated orbit combine to produce the most extreme temperature variations in the solar system, ranging from +800° F on the day side at its closest to Sun, to −280° F on the night side at its farthest.

Mercury has no atmosphere of its own, but is constantly swept by solar winds of charged particles. Neither does it have any moons. But Mercury does have phases like our Moon, as viewed from Earth. So does Venus. This happens because these two planets are closer to Sun, so we can observe their orbits from the outside. Mercury (and Venus) is 'new,' invisible, when between Earth and Sun (Earth - Mercury - Sun). It waxes as it moves around Sun to a point directly opposite Earth, on Sun's far side (Earth - Sun - Mercury), then wanes as it re-approaches Earth. These phases can only be seen through a telescope.

The essential fact about Mercury is its stark simplicity: an iron ball circling a blazing Sun.

Venus

Average distance from Sun: 0.72 × Earth's (67.2 million miles; 108.2 km)

Mass: 0.82 × Earth

Volume: 0.86 × Earth

Equatorial diameter: 7,521 miles (12,104 km)

Surface gravity: 0.91 × Earth

Surface temperature: 867° F (464° C). Almost no variation between high and low because the dense atmosphere evenly distributes heat.

Axial inclination to orbit: 2.7°

Axial rotation (day): 243 days (retrograde)

Orbital revolution (year): 224.7 days. Venus' day is longer than its year.

No satellite.

Venus is slightly smaller than Earth, but other than in similarity of size, it is a very different world. Like Earth, Venus' iron-nickel core occupies about ½ its volume. Unlike Earth's it is a compressed solid without an electrified liquid outer layer. Venus spins too slowly for this dead heart to generate any magnetism. Like Earth, Venus has a thick molten mantle of silicate rock with a thin crust on top. But Venus has no moving continental plates; its surface is a rigid monolith. Numerous volcanoes puncture it; they are the main geologic force on Venus. In fact, the whole planet appears to have been resurfaced by gigantic lava flows between 500,000,000 - 300,000,000 years ago. Because of this its terrain is relatively flat.

Venus has by far the longest day of any planet. It takes 243 Earth days to complete one rotation. This is longer than its year (!). Venus orbits Sun in only 225 days. Venus also rotates in the opposite direction to all other planets (except Uranus, which is tipped over, and thus a special case). This may be because of a cataclysmic impact in its early history that also disrupted its core, killing its magnetism. There are other theories as well.

Venus is wrapped in a dense carbon dioxide atmosphere. Its pressure is 92 times greater than Earth's: equivalent to being 3000 feet under water. This greenhouse gas makes Venus the hottest planet, trapping heat and distributing it evenly around the planet. Its surface temperature is 867° F, enough to melt tin, zinc and lead. This viscous atmosphere flows slowly under intense pressure: palpable, almost liquid in its density, suffused with infrared radiation. It is topped with thick sulfuric acid clouds. The light filtering through, at 5% of Earth's value, give Venus' face a faint reddish glow in the sweltering dark.

The essential fact about Venus is that it is a slightly smaller but much simpler world than Earth. Geological Venus, with no inner dynamo and no sliding, colliding plates, resembles a stillborn Earth. Might atmospheric Venus be where its planetary vitality really resides? Perhaps Venus' true center lies on its periphery: a hot aura coalesced around a rock, like a raindrop around a dust grain.

Mars

Average distance from Sun: 1.52 × Earth's (142 million miles; 228 million km)

Mass: 0.11 × Earth
Volume: 0.15 × Earth
Equatorial diameter: 4,222 miles (6,794 km)
Surface gravity: 0.38 × Earth
Highest temperature: 80° F (27° C)
Lowest temperature: −207° F (−133o C)
Axial inclination to orbit: 25.2°
Axial rotation (day): 24.6 hours
Orbital revolution (year): 687 days
Satellites: two tiny moons

Mars is half the diameter of Earth; roughly the size of our planet's core. Its own iron-iron sulfide core is relatively small, about ⅓ of its volume. Unlike Earth's, it is completely solid. Without a flowing liquid layer Mars' core does not generate a planetary magnetic field. It does have local magnetic zones. These seem to be fossilized remains of an early planet-wide field that died out when the heart of Mars was disrupted by a huge asteroid strike three billion years ago.

As with all four inner planets, this core is swaddled in a mantle of molten rock, mainly olivine, a silicate-iron-magnesium compound. Atop this is a thick crust, 75 miles deep. It is rigid, with no moving plates. Although it has fewer volcanoes than Venus, they are much larger. In fact, Mars has the highest volcanoes and deepest canyons of any planet.

The southern hemisphere is heavily cratered, the northern comparatively smooth. This may be evidence of an ocean floor that existed billions of years ago. Chemical evidence of water in Mars' rocks, and numerous surface erosion features, make the case that Mars was much warmer and wetter in a far distant past. Some water remains in the polar ice caps, which are mostly frozen carbon dioxide (dry ice). It seems likely that large, perhaps very large, quantities of water lie deep underground, frozen or in liquid form. This implies that subterranean microbial life may exist on Mars today.

Mars has a tenuous atmosphere with a surface pressure $7/1000$ Earth's. It is almost all carbon dioxide. Planet wide dust storms often obscure its surface. Mars must have had a much denser atmosphere in the past to allow for the presence of running water on its surface. However, once its core froze solid and ceased generating a protective magnetic field, solar winds eventually blew its air off into space.

Mars is very cold because of its distance from Sun and lack of an insulating atmosphere. It averages $-58°$ F, and dips down to $-190°$ F during its winter. However, because of its fairly elliptical orbit sometimes it has brief warm spells, during which its polar caps of water and carbon dioxide ice evaporate.

Mars has a similar axial inclination as Earth's and a remarkable similar day length of 24.62 hours. It has two tiny moonlets, captured asteroids, orbiting very closely. One, Phobos, will crash into Mars in about fifty million years; the other, Deimos, is accelerating in its orbit and will probably be hurled off into space at some point.

The essential fact about Mars is that, frigid, dry and airless as it may be, this is the most Earth-like planet in the system. Indeed, Mars could be terraformed, made Earthlike, using current technology. Super greenhouse gases could be manufactured from local materials and released into the atmosphere. Also, its poles could be seeded with dark, cold tolerant algae. These would absorb solar heat and proliferate. This would evaporate polar dry ice, releasing it as a greenhouse gas. As the air thickened and warmed, carbon dioxide permafrost all over the planet would add to the process. Underground water would start to melt and well up at the surface. Within a few decades, with a real greenhouse atmosphere and liquid water, Mars could be colonized by terrestrial life forms, including us.

With only 38% of Earth's gravity human-Martians would rapidly evolve into a new species. (Assuming the original colonists can survive long term and reproduce successfully in a low gravity environment.) Mars is the only planet in our solar system where colonization seems feasible.

Jupiter

Distance from Sun: 5.2 × Earth's (483.8 million miles; 778.6 km)
Mass: 317.8 × Earth
Volume: 1,321 × Earth

Equatorial diameter: 88,846 miles (142,984 km). Diameter is 11.2 times that of Earth.

Gravity at cloud tops (there is no surface): 2.64 × Earth

Temperature rises as one descends into the atmosphere (there is no surface). Temperature at its core is about 36,000° F (20,000° C)

Axial inclination to orbit: 3.1°

Axial rotation (day): 9.9 hours

Orbital revolution (year): 11.9 years

Satellites: Four major moons; at least 59 minor moonlets

Jupiter is by far the largest planet in our solar system: two and a half times more massive than all other planets combined. By volume it could hold 1321 clones of our world. The pressure at its core equals 100,000,000 atmospheres. This world is gargantuan.

Jupiter, and its neighbor Saturn, differ in character from the small rocky planets of the inner solar system. They are gas giants.

Jupiter has a rocky core several times the size of Earth. Surrounding it is an inner mantle, 30,000 miles deep (⅔ Jupiter's radius). This is composed of liquid metallic hydrogen. Hydrogen is the lightest element: an electrically neutral gas in the near absolute zero of space and a plasma, an electrically charged gas, in the blazing interiors of stars. Its liquid metallic form is very unusual and unimaginably dense. This gas squeezed into a metal conducts a permanent electric current that generates the most powerful magnetic field in the solar system.

Because of this unusual metal's high electrical conductivity, along with the planet's sheer size and rapid rotation, Jupiter generates an intrinsic magnetic force 19,519 times that of Earth. In fact, Jupiter's magnetism is stronger than Sun's.[1] However, magnetic force diminishes quickly over space, as the cube root of its distance from the magnetic axis. Thus Jupiter's equatorial surface magnetic flux density per unit of area is only about fourteen times that of Earth (4.28 Gauss v .31 for Earth).[2] By comparison a refrigerator magnet has a power of 50 Gauss. Planetary magnetic auras refer to very subtle structures implying their ethereal spiritual side.

Jupiter concentrates magnetic force more powerfully than any other planet, by two orders of magnitude. Sun's overall magnetism is stronger because of its sheer size, but also more tenuous. While Sun forms the gravitational and electrical nucleus of our solar system Jupiter constitutes its magnetic center. This correlates with its astrological role of mediating between solar and planetary planes of being. Sun's diffuse magnetosphere spiritually encompasses the entire solar system.

Jupiter's more intense magnetic moment ensouls it. Earth's magnetic aura biologically and psychologically incarnates it.

Flowing over Jupiter's ionized metallic hydrogen stratum is a liquid molecular hydrogen ocean, more than 6000 miles deep. It contains a small admixture of helium, the second lightest element, also condensed into a fluid state. Floating over this is an atmosphere, hundreds of miles thick, merging smoothly into the ocean at one end, drifting tenuously off into space at the other. Unlike the terrestrial planets, with a distinct surface/atmosphere interface, Jupiter's atmosphere imperceptibly densifies into the liquid hydrogen ocean. This, in turn, compresses by degrees into the metallic hydrogen inner mantle.

The top 50 miles of Jupiter's atmosphere, all that we can see, contains three layers: water ice/vapor at its base, then ammonium hydrosulfide ice (NH_4SH), and finally ammonia ice particles (NH_3) facing space. Heat welling up from the interior drives ridges of gas into higher, brighter stripes called 'zones.' Cooling, sinking, darker stripes called 'belts' alternate with them. The zones and belts of ammonia ice are stretched around the immense bulk of Jupiter by its rapid rotation, creating flamboyantly whirling cloud bands.

Huge as it is, Jupiter makes a complete turn every 9.9 hours: the fastest spin in the system. Friction and pressure differences between the zones and belts moving at such high speed generate swirls, whorls, eddies: gigantic storms. One of them, the Great Red Spot, is three times bigger than Earth and has been observed for over 400 years. It is a high-pressure zone, rotating independently every seven days. It has its own local chemical identity, causing the red color.

There are 13 alternating zones and belts on top of Jupiter's atmosphere, capped with two polar regions. The poles glow with intense auroras, caused by solar wind particles funneled into the atmosphere by Jupiter's magnetic field.

Jupiter has a very thin, faint ring, only discovered recently. It hosts a family of 63 known moons, most very tiny captured asteroids. Four, however, are quite large and distinctive in their own right. Io, the most volcanically active body in our system, made so by Jupiter's gravity tides. It constantly spews off sulfur dioxide plumes. Europa, with a vast liquid water ocean beneath an icy shell. It may well, even probably, host life. Ganymede, the largest moon in the solar system (though not relative to its parent planet) and Callisto, its most heavily cratered object.

Io is clearly fiery in nature; Europa watery. Intensely sculpted Callisto has an earthy permanence of memory; perhaps giant Ganymede reflects the gaseous quality of its home planet. Four moons, four traditional elements. Jupiter presides over its own miniature system.

The essential fact about Jupiter is its immense yet finely articulated nature. It swirls with a profusion of storms, zones, belts and moons on a gigantic scale. Its intense magnetism implies a subtle dimension, or soul aura, connecting impersonal spiritual energies with subjective psychology.

1. In part this is because Jupiter rotates much faster than Sun: 10 hours v 25 days. Sun's magnetic field = one to two Gauss at its equator. It declines and then reverses polarity every eleven years. It then reignites from a new high at the opposite pole, returning to its original starting point after 22 years. This causes the Sunspot cycle. Sunspots are magnetic lines of force erupting out of the solar body when the overall field weakens. They carry an enormous charge of 3000-5000 Gauss, but quickly fly apart from all that energy.

2. Jupiter's magnetic field strength at its north pole is 14 Gauss, at the south 11. Earth's is 5.8 at its poles.

Saturn

Average distance from Sun: 9.6 × Earth's (890.7 million miles; 1,433.5 million km)

Mass: 95.2 × Earth

Volume: 763.6 × Earth

Equatorial diameter: 74,898 miles (120,536 km)

Gravity at cloud tops (there is no surface): 0.92 × Earth

Temperature rises as one descends into the atmosphere

Axial inclination to orbit: 26.7°

Axial rotation (day): 10.7 hours

Orbital revolution (year): 29.5 years

Satellites: one giant moon, Titan; six small moons and 41 moonlets

Saturn is a gas giant, second only to Jupiter in size. The two are structurally similar: fast-spinning globes of hydrogen, flattened at the poles, bulging at the equator. Saturn's most distinctive feature is a crown of spectacular rings, composed of countless ice particles.

Saturn has a rock core, perhaps 15,000 miles across surrounded by an inner mantle of liquid metallic hydrogen. This conducts a high voltage permanent electric current, generating a magnetic field 580 times more powerful than Earth's. The outer half of Saturn is a liquid molecular hydrogen ocean. It thins out into an atmosphere with three cloud layers: water, ammonium hydrosulfide and ammonia ices. There is no distinct boundary between these dense fog banks and the hydrogen ocean below.

Having less gravity than Jupiter, Saturn's cloud bands billow twice as high, extending for about 100 miles. Given their greater depth, and because Saturn is much colder, they are visually more subdued. Thirteen subtle colored belts and zones, topped with two polar regions, mimic Jupiter's (or vice versa). Having less heat energy (Saturn is twice Jupiter's distance from Sun) they are smoother and more homogeneous, with fewer whorls, swirls and eddies. However, about once every 30 years, approximately the time of Saturn's orbital revolution, a planet-wide storm rages across its equatorial belt. Then, its energy spent, Saturn's atmosphere mellows out again. At the south pole an enormous hexagonal upwelling is Saturn's answer to Jupiter's Great Red Spot. This convective cell of gas marks that pole as a special energy conduit.

Composed of 96% hydrogen, the simplest element, Saturn is the lightest planet. It would actually float in an ocean of water, if one big enough could be found. This would be difficult as Saturn has nine times the diameter, and 764 times the volume, of Earth.

Saturn is enclosed in a broad band of rings 170,000 miles wide. This is divided into seven main rings, with thousands of streaming ringlets within them. These rings consist of countless small, highly reflective ice particles. They are gravitationally guided, or shepherded, by a myriad of tiny moonlets.

Saturn has 48 known moons, most of them irregularly shaped, captured asteroids. Seven are large enough to be spherical. They are composed mostly of water ice. One, Enceladus, tidally pumped by Saturn's gravity, constantly sprays its parent planet with a fine mist of water vapor (that freezes instantly upon hitting space).

The biggest, Titan, stands out as the only moon in the solar system with its own atmosphere. In fact, its nitrogenous, orange hued air is 1.6 times denser than Earth's. Titan has lakes of liquid methane (CH_4) and ethane (C_2H_6) at −290° F. Unimaginably cold hydrocarbon rains fall, carving riverbeds and deltas by their flow. Titan has an organic chemistry very similar to that of early Earth. Perhaps, beneath an insulating surface, it too has evolved a biology.

The essential fact about Saturn is that it appears to have subli-mated Jupiter's colorful exuberance into an off-world splendor of rings. Saturn embodies a more ethereal Jupiter that has spread its wings - rings - and soared to the edge of visible existence.

Uranus

Average distance from Sun: 19.2 × Earth's (1,784.7 million miles; 2,872.5 million km)
Mass: 14.4 × Earth
Volume: 63.1 × Earth
Equatorial diameter: 31,763 miles (51,118 km)
Gravity at cloud tops (there is no surface): 0.86 × Earth
Temperature rises as one descends into the atmosphere
Axial inclination to orbit: 82.2° (almost parallel to orbit)*
Axial rotation (day): 17.2 hours
Orbital revolution (year): 84 years
Satellites: Five small moons; 22 known moonlets

Uranus is the first planet discovered in historical times. Although it can be seen by a keen eye in a clear sky, Uranus was not recognized as a planet until its motion was observed telescopically in 1781.

Uranus, and its sister world Neptune, are ice giants. They are midway in size between the small rocky planets of the inner system and the gas giants Jupiter and Saturn. They are both heavier than hydrogen, suggesting that their interiors are composed of a compressed hot ice (!) of water, methane and ammonia. Powerful pressure makes these com-pounds viscous and heated, like a light molten rock.

Uranus has a solid rocky core, with a mass about that of Earth. Surrounding it is the inner hot ice mantle. Strong electricity surges through it, generating a magnetic field 50 times that of Earth.

Atop it flows a 6000-mile deep ocean of liquid hydrogen, sprinkled with other constituents. Blending into it, without a distinct boundary, floats an atmosphere of hydrogen (83%), helium (15%) and methane (2%). Below the top layer of methane, which gives Uranus its blue-green color, are thought to be three layers of ammonia, ammo-nium hydrosulfide and water ice crystals, just like on the other gas and ice giants. The visible methane layer is too cold (−364° F) for cloud formation.

Indeed, Uranus is a featureless world: bland, uniform, monochro-matic. It does not have the bands, storms and clouds of Jupiter, Saturn and Neptune. This is because Uranus does not have much of an inter-nal heat engine. A huge impact in its early history disrupted the core and dissipated most of its heat. Pressure generated thermal power only partly compensates for this loss. Thus Uranus is a relatively cold world, lacking the energy for much atmospheric activity.

This cataclysmic collision also knocked Uranus over on its side. It rotates at a right angle to all other planets (except for Pluto, always a special case). During its 84-year orbit the north and south poles successively experience 42 year long days and nights.

Uranus' perpendicular rotation on its axis takes 17 hours. Its magnetic field lies at a 60° angle to this spin instead of being aligned with it. This provides evidence that its magnetism is generated by the hot ice mantle rather than at the core.

Eleven faint rings composed of ice particles begrimed with organic soot encircle Uranus. It also has at least 27 satellites, mostly tiny chunks of rock and ice. The largest, Titania, is less than half the size of our Moon. The most unusual, Miranda, is a freakish worldlet, having two completely different types of terrain smashed together with a sharp boundary between them. This may be because it ran out of heat while heavier and lighter rocks were sorting themselves out at its early molten stage, or it may be a composite of two bodies literally mashed into each other.

The essential fact about Uranus is that it spins at a right angle to the rest of the system. It serves as a conduit to its sister planet, invisible Neptune, and to the intangible dimensions of existence.

*Because Uranus rotates almost parallel to the ecliptic, rather than perpendicular to it like all other planets, there is some dispute over which is its north and which is its south pole. Many references describe Uranus as tilted at 97.8° to the vertical because if that pole is described as equivalent to north then Uranus' rotation is direct, slightly west to east, within a general south to north orientation. That means it rotates in the same direction as it orbits around Sun. This is consistent with the rotation of all other planets except Venus.

However, the International Astronomical Union defines a north pole as being that end of an axis which actually points north of the ecliptic. (Rather than by its direction of spin.) In that case, Uranus tilts at 82.2° to the vertical. It also means Uranus rotates slightly east to west, like Venus, within a general north to south orientation. Thus its spin also retrogrades, in the opposite direction to Uranus' orbital movement. This slight east to west variation is minor compared to the overall and unique north to south rotation.

Neptune

Average distance from Sun: 30 × Earth's (2,793.1 million miles; 4,495.1 million km)

Mass: 17.1 × Earth

Volume: 57.7 × Earth

Equatorial diameter: 30,775 miles (49,528 km)

Gravity at cloud tops (there is no surface): 1.2 × Earth

Temperature rises as one descends into the atmosphere

Axial inclination to orbit: 28.3°

Axial rotation (day): 16.1 hours

Orbital revolution (year): 164.8 years

Satellites: One large moon, Triton, and 12 known moonlets

Invisible Neptune is the last, farthest planet. It cannot be seen by the naked eye. It was discovered telescopically in 1846, its position predicted by gravitational disturbances of Uranus' orbit.

Physically Neptune is very similar to Uranus. They are both about the same size. They have the same basic structure: an Earth sized rock core encased in a hot dense slush of water, methane and ammonia, covered by a liquid hydrogen ocean 6000 miles deep. The atmospheric compositions are identical, except that Neptune has a bit more methane in its top layer (3%), giving it a deep blue color.

However, Neptune's atmosphere is much more dynamic, with cloudbanks, zones and belts, furious winds and giant storms. This is because Neptune has a strong internal heat source, whereas Uranus' was disrupted by an enormous impact early on. A process of differentiation generates this heat: heavier matter is sinking while lighter materials are rising. Some of their motion is converted into thermal energy. In other words, Neptune is still forming.

Neptune's magnetic field, caused by an electric current in its hot ice inner mantle, is 25 times stronger than Earth's, but only half the strength of Uranus'. We don't know the reason for this difference. It is likewise offset from the spin axis, indicating that it originates in the moving hot ice mantle rather than the core. Neptune rotates in about 16 hours, about one hour faster than its fellow ice giant.

Neptune has five skimpy rings, made of ice particles coated with carbon compounds. It has 13 known moons, most quite small. The exception is Triton, ¾ the size of our Moon, orbiting backwards compared to Neptune's own rotation. This suggests that it is a captured Kuiper Belt Object from the outer solar system, probably similar to Pluto. Triton has the coldest measured surface in the system, but still manages to spout nitrogen ice particle geysers caused by Neptune's tidal pumping.

The essential fact about Neptune is that it forms an invisible twin of Uranus. They seem to embody two halves of a planetary principle, polarized at a right angle, and separated in space. The vertical and horizontal arms of a cross not yet coalesced into manifestation. This is consistent with Neptune's astrological symbolism: an oceanic Unconscious whose contents have not yet emerged onto the terra firma of known and visible reality.

Pluto

Average distance from Sun: 39.5 × Earth's (3,670 million miles; 5,906.4 million km). Actually, this varies wildly because of Pluto's highly eccentric orbit, moving from 30 to 50 times Earth's distance over its 248-year period.

Mass: 0.002 × Earth
Volume: 0.006 × Earth
Equatorial diameter: 1,473 miles (2,370 km)
Surface gravity: 0.06 × Earth
Mean surface temperature: −369° F (−223° C)
Axial inclination to orbit: 60°[1]
Axial rotation (day): 6.4 days
Orbital revolution (year): 247.7 years

Satellite: one giant moon, Charon. Charon is very close to Pluto, only 12,180 miles (19,600 km) away. It is 737 miles (1,186 km) in diameter, half Pluto's size and it is orbitally locked with Pluto, both rotating and revolving every 6.4 days.

Pluto is not a planet. (It was demoted from that status by the International Astronomical Union in 2005 because it does not gravitationally dominate its orbit.) It is a Kuiper Belt Object, a remnant of the rock/ice rubble from which the planets formed. It can be considered as a representative of that vast pre-planetary reality, extending twice as far as Neptune's orbit.

Pluto is actually a double planetoid. Its giant moon Charon is half its size, by far the largest relative to its parent planet(oid) in the system. (Earth's Moon comes in second at one-quarter.) It also revolves very closely around Pluto, at only 12,180 miles away: 5% of our Moon's distance. Pluto and Charon are orbitally locked together, with both day lengths and Charon's revolution around Pluto all being 6.39 Earthly days. For this reason Charon always presents the same face to Pluto (as our Moon does to Earth) and is always fixed at the same point in Pluto's sky. Is it possible that the two are spiraling in on each other, to eventually merge in the distant future? Might mythical Charon, ferryman of the dead over the river Styx, finally enter Hades (Pluto) itself after waiting an eternity at the gate?

Pluto was first visited by the New Horizons probe on July 14, 2015. The NASA mission summary states: 'Pluto displays a surprisingly wide variety of geological landforms, including those resulting from glaciological and surface-atmosphere interactions as well as impact, tectonic, possible cryovolcanic and mass wasting processes.'[2]

Seventy percent of its bulk is composed of a silicate rock core. This is covered with a frozen mantle of water, nitrogen, methane and ethane ices, with a surface that is mostly nitrogen ice. Charon is lighter, with a higher proportion of water ice. This suggests that it formed independently of Pluto and was later captured. It could have a subsurface ocean because of tidal heating caused by its close orbit of Pluto. Anywhere there is liquid water there is a possibility of life as we know it.

Pluto has a tenuous atmosphere of 98% nitrogen, plus methane and carbon monoxide varying from $\frac{1}{100,000}$ to $\frac{1}{1,000,000}$ the pressure of Earth's. This atmosphere only exists when Pluto is closest to Sun on its wildly elliptical orbit. As it moves farther away, the atmosphere freezes out and actually collapses onto the surface. This explains the difference in range of atmospheric pressures. Pluto's thin atmosphere looks blue, like ours, when seen backlit by the Sun by New Horizons.

Pluto's has the most elongated orbit of any planet(oid), stretching from 30 to 50 astronomical units (Earth distances from Sun). In fact, for 20 of its 248-year revolution Pluto passes within the orbit of Neptune. This last occurred between 1979 and 1999. Its orbit inclines at 17° to the plane of the solar system, more steeply than any other planetary body.

The essential fact about Pluto is that it is a double planetoid on a wild orbit, representing the outer zone of the solar system, beyond the planetary worlds.

1. Many references describe Pluto's axial inclination as 120° because it rotates from west to east if that pole is described as north. This would make it consistent with the rotation of all other planets except Venus (if that standard was applied to Uranus as well). However, the International Astronomical Union describes a north pole as being that end of an axis which points north of the ecliptic. (Rather than by direction of spin.) In that case Pluto tilts at 60° to the vertical. It also means Pluto rotates somewhat east to west, like Venus, within a larger north to south orientation.
2. Most of Pluto's surface is a nitrogenous ice plain - punctuated by superfrozen water ice mountains rising out of it. You can see detailed images online.